FIFTH EDITION

LEGAL ASPECTS OF HEALTH CARE ADMINISTRATION

George D. Pozgar, MBA

Instructor, Graduate Program in Health Care Administration
New School for Social Research
New York, New York
Instructor, Undergraduate Program in Health Care Administration
St. Joseph's College
Patchogue, New York
President
GP Management Consulting Int'l.
East Northport, New York

and

Legal and Editorial Review:

Nina Santucci Pozgar, Esq.

Bureau Chief, White Collar Crime
Suffolk County District Attorney's Office
Hauppauge, New York

AN ASPEN PUBLICATION®
Aspen Publishers, Inc.
Gaithersburg, Maryland
1993

This publication is designed to provide accurate and authoritative information in regard to the Subject Matter covered. It is sold with the understanding that the publisher is not engaged in rendering legal, accounting, or other professional service. If legal advice or other expert assistance is required, the service of a competent professional person should be sought. *(From a Declaration of Principles jointly adopted by a Committee of the American Bar Association and a Committee of Publishers and Associations.)*

Library of Congress Cataloging-in-Publication Data

Pozgar, George D.
Legal aspects of health care administration/
George D. Pozgar; and legal and editorial review, Nina Santucci Pozgar. — 5th ed.
p. cm.

Includes bibliographical references and indexes.
ISBN 0-8342-0360-X
1. Medical laws and legislation—United States. 2. Medical personnel—Malpractice—United States. I. Pozgar, Nina S. II. Title.
[DNLM: 1. Delivery of Health Care—United States. 2. Legislation, Medical—United States. 3. Malpractice. W 32.5 AA1 P893L]
KF3821.P69 1993
344.73'041—dc20
[347.30441]
DNLM/DLC
for Library of Congress
92-48247
CIP

Aspen Publishers, Inc. grants permission for photocopying for limited personal or internal use. This consent does not extend to other kinds of copying, such as copying for general distribution, for advertising or promotional purposes, for creating new collective works, or for resale. For information, address Aspen Publishers, Inc., Permissions Department, 200 Orchard Ridge Drive, Suite 200, Gaithersburg, Maryland 20878.

Editorial Resources: Barbara Priest
Marita Menaker

Library of Congress Catalog Card Number: 92-48247
ISBN: 0-8342-0360-X

Printed in the United States of America

2 3 4 5

Table of Contents

Preface

As with previous editions, the basic purpose of the fifth edition of *Legal Aspects of Health Care Administration* is to arm the health care professional with a working knowledge of health law. The fifth edition contains an extensive update of those chapters contained in the fourth edition. Rather than frustrate the reader with confusing legal jargon, this text provides information and explanations written in commonly understood terminology. This approach will aid in demystifying the law as it applies to health care.

Further, this edition provides the reader with the necessary background on a wide variety of health care topics, enabling professionals to deal with the common legal and practical problems facing the health care industry. Because the law is in a constant state of flux, health care professionals must possess a basic knowledge of the law as it applies to their areas of responsibility. This book answers this need and serves both as a text for the classroom and as a reference for the practicing professional. As such, it should be included in the management curriculum of health care administration programs.

The outcomes in the cases presented in this text are generally governed both by the applicable statutes and by common law principles. As with any review of the law, it must be remembered that state statutes and court decisions in one state are not binding in any other state.

Acknowledgments

The author especially acknowledges Aspen Publishers, Inc., whose guidance and assistance was so important in making this publication a reality. Many thanks to Aspen for permitting use of special adaptations from its publication *Long-Term Care and the Law: A Legal Guide for Health Care Professionals*.

Special thanks to Touro College–Jacob D. Fuchsberg Law Center, and Daniel P. Jordan, Jr., Head Law Librarian and Assistant Professor of Law, for use of the college's library facilities.

Many thanks to those I have instructed in the legal aspects of health care administration from the New School for Social Research, Molloy College, Long Island University–C.W. Post College, Saint Francis College, and Saint Joseph's College, as well as those whom I have instructed through the years at various seminars, for their inspiration. Many thanks to you all.

The author also wishes to acknowledge Nicholas Fortuna, Esq., for his review and editorial comments on labor law; Mrs. Ruth Glick, Director of the Medical Library at Huntington Hospital; and the staffs at the Huntington Library and the Library of Congress for their guidance in locating research materials.

Chapter 1

Introduction to Law

Laws are the very bulwarks of liberty; they define every man's rights, and defend the individual liberties of all men.

J.G. Holland (1819–1881)

OUTLINE

Public Health Service
Health Care Financing Administration
Social Security Administration
Family Support Administration
Office of Human Development Services
Administration on Aging
Federal Council on Aging
National Institute on Aging
Department of Justice
Department of Labor
National Labor Relations Board

This chapter provides health care professionals with some elementary information regarding the law, the functioning of the legal system, and the roles of the different branches of government in creating, administering, and enforcing the law in the United States.

Supreme Court Justice Oliver Wendell Holmes said that the law is a magic mirror in which we see reflected not only our own lives but also the lives of those who went before us. Thus a history of American law is a history of the United States and the internal stresses of its society.[1] "The government of the United States has been emphatically termed a government of laws, and not of men. It will certainly cease to deserve this high appellation, if the laws furnish no remedy for the violation of a vested right." *Marbury v. Madison,* 5 U.S. (1 Cranch) 137, 163 (1803).

Most definitions of law describe it as a system of principles and processes by which people in a society deal with their disputes and problems, seeking to solve or settle them without resorting to force. Simply stated, laws are general rules of conduct that are enforced by government, which imposes penalties when prescribed laws are violated.

Laws govern the relationships between private individuals and organizations and between both of these parties and government. *Private law* deals with the relationships between private parties; *public law* deals with the relationships between private parties and government. Laws regulate the activities of individuals in international situations as well as in federal, state, local, and municipal settings.

One important segment of public law is criminal law, which prohibits conduct deemed injurious to public order and provides for punishment of those found to have engaged in such conduct. Public law also consists of countless regulations designed to advance societal objectives by requiring private individuals and organizations to adopt specified courses of action in their activities and undertakings. The thrust of most public law is to attain what society deems valid public goals.

Private law is concerned with the recognition and enforcement of the rights and duties of private individuals and organizations. Tort and contract actions are two basic types of private law. In a *tort* action, one party asserts that the wrongful conduct of another has caused harm, and the injured party seeks compensation for the harm suffered. Generally, a *contract* action involves a claim by one party that another party has breached an agreement by failing to fulfill an obligation. Either remuneration or specific performance of the obligation may be sought as a remedy.

SOURCES OF LAW

The basic sources of law are common law, which is derived from judicial decisions; statutory law, which emanates from the federal and state legislatures; administrative law, prescribed by administrative agencies; and constitutional law. In those instances in which the written laws are either silent, vague, or contradictory to other laws, the judicial system often is called on to resolve those disputes until such time as appropriate legislative action can be taken to clear up a particular legal issue.

Common Law

The term *common law* is applied to the body of principles that has evolved and continues to evolve and expand from judicial decisions that arise during the trial of actual court cases. Many of the legal principles and rules applied today by courts in the United States have their origins in English common law.

Because it is impossible to have a law that covers every potential human event that might occur in society, the judicial system is thus doubly necessary. It not only serves as a mechanism for reviewing legal disputes that arise in the written law, but it is also an effective review mechanism for those issues on which the written law is silent or in instances of a mixture of issues involving both written law and common-law decisions. For example, in the *Cruzan* case, discussed in Chapter 15, the issue decided by the U.S. Supreme Court revolved around the consideration of existing statutory law and prior judicial decisions.

Common Law in England

Law reflects to a large degree the civilization of those that live under it. Its progress and development are mirrors not merely of material prosperity but of the method of thought and of the outlook of the age.[2]

The common law of England is much like its language. It is as varied as the nations that have peopled its land in different parts and different periods. Some of it is derived from the Britons, the Romans, the Saxons, the Danes, and the Normans.

> To recount what innovations were made by the succession of these different nations, or estimate what proportion of the customs of each go to the composing of our body of common law, would be impossible at this distance of time. As to a great part of this period, we have no monuments of antiquity to guide us in our inquiry; and the lights which gleam upon the other part afford but dim prospect. Our conjectures can only be assisted by the history of the revolutions effected by these several nations.[3]

The Romans governed the island, as a province, since the time of Claudius, A.D. 43, and they did not leave until A.D. 448. It was a time of peace and cultivation of the arts. Roman laws were administered as laws of the country. When the Romans left Britain to attend to their own domestic safety, the Picts and the Scots broke in on the inhabitants of the south. Unable to oppose the attack, these southern inhabitants appealed to the Saxons for assistance. The Saxons came from German lands and drove the northern invaders back inside their own borders.[4] The Saxons contended with the Danish raiders from the eighth to the eleventh centuries.

The law, before the Norman Conquest in A.D. 1066, was dispensed primarily on tradition and local customs and, for the most part, dealt with violent crimes. The kings during this period were concerned more with enforcing customary law than with amending it. The courts mainly consisted of open-air meetings where no records were maintained. "For the Anglo-Saxons justice was a local matter, administered chiefly in the shire courts, and was largely dependent upon local customs, preserved in the memory of those persons who declared the law in the court."[5] The Saxons turned against the Britons and forced great numbers of them into the mountains of Wales, dividing the remainder of the dominion into seven independent kingdoms.[6]

> The circumstances of this revolution are related to be of a kind differing from most others. The Saxons are described as a rude and bloody race; who beyond any other tribe of northern people, set themselves to exterminate the original inhabitants, and destroy every monument and remains of their establishment. In so general a ruin, it cannot be imagined that the customs of the native Britons, or the laws ingrafted upon them by the Romans, could meet with any favour.[7]

The kingdoms were, for a time, independent of one another and a variety of laws grew among the Saxons themselves. During the reign of Alfred, the Danes, who had long harassed the kingdom, were settled by treaty in Northumberland. The Danes were considered in some measure to be part of the nation. They enjoyed their own laws within their district. When their own kings sat on the English throne, their laws pervaded, in some degree, all parts of the country. Toward the latter part of the Saxon times, the kingdom was governed by several different laws and local customs.[8]

> The most general of these were the three following: the Mercian Law, the West-Saxon Law, and the Danish Law. If any of the British or Roman customs still subsisted, they were sunk into, and lost in one of these laws; which governed the whole kingdom and have since received the general appellation of The Common Law.[9]

The Normans, after their conquest in A.D. 1066, had little regard for Anglo-Saxon laws. They considered themselves apart from such laws.

> It is obviously impossible to attempt an adequate picture of Anglo-Saxon life. It was a wild time. Men lived in terror of the vast forests, where it was easy to be lost and succumb to starvation, of their fellow man who would plunder and slay, and above all of the Unknown, whose inscrutable ways seemed constantly to be bringing famine and disaster. The uncertainties of modern life pale into insignificance when regarded from the standpoint of these men. It is natural, there-fore, that their law should reflect their reaction against the environ-ment. It was conservative and harsh. Violence, robbery and death formed its background.[10]

Land disputes involved the Saxons who held the land before the conquest and the Normans who dispossessed them. Evidence in such disputes was often the result of oral testimony from neighboring landowners.

> The principal change introduced by the Norman Conquest, so far as the central jurisdiction was concerned, was that the King's court now became, for the first time, the court in which disputes relating to land-tenure among the King's tenants-in-chief were regularly decided . . . there is no hint of any professional judiciary at this period. The trials were held locally in the presence of the county court or several county courts by the King's representatives, sent out from Curia Regis (the King's Court) and the tenants-in-chief. The presiding officer was often a cleric.[11]

After the Norman Conquest, in A.D. 1066 a system of national law began to develop based on custom, foreign literature, and the rule of strong kings. The first royal court was established in A.D. 1178. This court, enlisting the aid of a jury, heard the complaints of the kingdom's subjects. Because there were few written laws, a body of principles evolved from these court decisions, which became known as "common law." These decisions were used by judges in deciding subsequent cases. As Parliament's power to legislate grew, the initiative for developing new laws passed from the king to Parliament.

Malpractice in England. Although malpractice is not nearly the problem in England as in the United States, it is no stranger to English common law. "The first recorded case of medical malpractice in English common law was noted in 1329. By 1518 when the College of Physicians of London was incorporated, malpractice litigation was common enough for the charter to include disciplinary provisions for malpractice."[12]

Common Law in the United States

During the colonial period, English common law began to be applied in the colonies. According to John Dickinson in his *Letters from a Farmer* in Pennsylvania in 1768,

> The common law of England is generally received. . . ; but our courts EXERCISE A SOVEREIGN AUTHORITY, in determining what parts of the common and statute law ought to be extended: For it must be admitted, that the difference of circumstances necessarily require us, in some cases to REJECT the determination of both. . . . Some of the English rules are adopted, others rejected.[13]

Joseph Story, in an 1829 U.S. Supreme Court decision, wrote, "The common law of England is not to be taken in all respects to be that of America. Our ancestors brought with them its general principles, and claimed it as their birthright but they brought with them and adopted only that portion which was applicable to their situation."[14]

> The size of the country and the abundance of its natural resources made impossible the importation of the common law exactly as it had been developed in England. Measured by English standards, America had superabundant land, timber, and mineral wealth. American law had to serve the primary need of the new society—to master the vast land areas of the American continent. The decisive facts upon which the law had to be based were the seemingly limitless expanses of land and the wealth and variety of natural resources.[15]

After the Revolution, each state, with the exception of Louisiana, adopted all or part of the existing English common law and added to it as needed. Louisiana civil law is based to a great extent on the French and Spanish laws and, especially, on the Code of Napoleon. As a result, there is no national system of common law in the United States, and common law on specific subjects may differ from state to state.

> Case law—court decisions—did not easily pass from colony to colony. There were no printed reports to make transfer easy, though in the 18th century some manuscript materials did circulate among lawyers. These could hardly have been very influential. No doubt custom and case law slowly seeped from colony to colony. Travelers and word of mouth spread knowledge of living law. It is hard to say how much; thus it is hard to tell to what degree there was a common legal structure.[16] Judicial review started to become part of the living law during the decade before the adoption of the federal Constitution. During that time American courts first began to assert the power to rule on the constitutionality of legislative acts and to hold unconstitutional statutes void.[17]

Cases are tried on common-law principles unless a statute governs. Even though statutory law has affirmed many of the legal rules and principles initially established by the courts, new issues continue to arise, especially in private-law disputes, which require decision making according to common-law principles. Common-law actions are initiated mainly to recover money damages and/or possession of real or personal property.

When a common-law principle has been enunciated by a higher state court, that principle must be followed by the lower courts within the state where the decision was rendered. A decision in a case that sets forth a new legal principle establishes a *precedent*. Trial courts or those on equal footing are not bound by the decisions of other trial courts. Also, a principle established in one state does not set precedent for another state. Rather, the rulings in one jurisdiction may be used by the courts of other jurisdictions as guides to the legal analysis of a particular legal problem. Decisions found to be reasonable will be followed.

The position of a court or agency, relative to other courts and agencies, determines the place assigned to its decision in the hierarchy of decisional law. The decisions of the U.S. Supreme Court are highest in the hierarchy of decisional law with respect to federal legal questions. Because of the parties or the legal question involved, most legal controversies do not fall within the scope of the Supreme Court's decision-making responsibilities. On questions of purely state concern—such as the interpretation of a state statute that raises no issues under the U.S. Constitution or federal law—the highest court in the state has the final word on proper interpretation.

Res Judicata. In common law, the term *res judicata*—meaning the thing is decided—refers to that which has been acted on or decided by the courts. According to *Black's Law Dictionary*, it "designates a point or question or subject-matter which was in controversy or dispute and has been authoritatively and finally settled by the decision of a court; that issuable fact once legally determined is conclusive as between the parties in same or subsequent proceeding."

Stare Decisis. The common-law principle *stare decisis* ("let the decision stand") provides that when a decision is rendered in a lawsuit involving a particular set of facts, another lawsuit involving an identical or substantially similar situation is to be resolved in the same manner as the first lawsuit. The resolution of later lawsuits will be arrived at by applying the rules and principles of preceding cases. In this manner, courts arrive at comparable rulings. Sometimes slight factual differences may provide a basis for recognizing distinctions between the precedent and the current case. In some cases, even when such differences are absent, a court may conclude that a particular common-law rule is no longer in accord with the needs of society and may depart from precedent. It should be understood that principles of law are subject to change, whether they originate in statutory or in common law. Common-law principles may be modified, overturned, abrogated, or created by new court decisions in a continuing process of growth and development to reflect changes in social attitudes, public needs, judicial prejudices, or contemporary political thinking.

Malpractice in the United States. The first common-law case in the United States in which physicians were held legally responsible for a negligence-related action occurred as early as 1794. Since that time, physicians have experienced recurring periods of substantial increases in the number of malpractice cases. The first such increase occurred in the 15 years before the Civil War.[18] Increases in malpractice cases and concern about them occurred at the beginning of this century and also in the years before World War II.

> In 1941, The Journal of the American Medical Association published studies showing that 1,296 malpractices had occurred between 1900 and 1940, with more than 500 between 1930 and 1940. The explanations for these increases in malpractice cases are similar to opinions expressed about the current malpractice situation: increased patient expectations, improvements in diagnostic procedures, and erosion of the patient–physician relationship, particularly in large urban centers.[19]

The Harvard Medical Malpractice Study, commissioned by New York State to determine the rate of medical injury in New York hospitals, revealed that 3.7 percent of patients entering New York hospitals in 1984 were injured by the care provided, "but only a tenth of those who were treated negligently filed malpractice suits."[20] The research group conducting the study suggested that "only one claim makes its way into the tort system for every eight cases of injury caused by medical negligence."[21] The study, which cost $3.1 million and ran 1,200 pages, was funded primarily by New York State with a grant from the Robert Wood Johnson Foundation. The study involved four years of research and included the review of more than 30,000 medical records.[22]

Statutory Law

Statutory law is written law emanating from a legislative body. Although a statute can abolish any rule of common law, it can do so only by express words. The principles and rules of statutory law are set in hierarchical order. The Constitution of the United States adopted at the Constitutional Convention in Philadelphia in 1787 at Independence Hall and ratified by the states, with its duly ratified amendments, is highest in the hierarchy of enacted law. Article VI of the Constitution declares

> This Constitution, and the Laws of the United States which shall be made in Pursuance thereof; and all Treaties made, or which shall be made, under the Authority of the United States, shall be the supreme Law of the Land; and the Judges in every State shall be bound thereby, any Thing in the Constitution or Laws of any State to the Contrary notwithstanding.

The clear import of these words is that the U.S. Constitution, federal law, and federal treaties take precedence over the constitutions and laws of states and local jurisdictions.

Statutory law may be amended, repealed, or expanded by action of the legislature. States and local jurisdictions may enact and enforce laws that do not conflict with federal law. Statutory laws may be declared void by a court for several reasons. For example, a statute may be found unconstitutional because it does not comply with a state or federal constitution, because it is vague or ambiguous, or, in the case of a state law, because it is in conflict with a federal law.

In many cases involving statutory law, the court is called on to interpret how a statute applies to a given set of facts. For example, a statute may state merely that no person may discriminate against another person because of race, creed, color, or sex. A court then may be called on to decide whether certain actions by a person are discriminatory and therefore violate the law.

Administrative Law

Administrative law is the extensive body of public law issued by administrative agencies to administer the enacted laws of the federal and state governments. It is the branch of law that controls the administrative operations of government. Congress and state legislative bodies realistically cannot oversee their many laws; therefore, they delegate implementation and administration of the law to an appropriate administrative agency.

The Administrative Procedures Act[23] describes the different procedures under which federal administrative agencies must operate.[24] The act prescribes the procedural responsibilities and authority of administrative agencies and provides for legal remedies for those wronged by agency actions. The regulatory power exercised by administrative agencies includes power to license, power of rate-setting (e.g., Health Care Financing Administration), and power over business practices (e.g., National Labor Relations Board).

Rules and Regulations

Administrative agencies have both legislative and judicial functions. They have the authority to formulate rules and regulations considered necessary to carry out the intent of legislative enactments.

> [A] "rule" means the whole or a part of an agency statement of general or particular applicability and future effect designed to implement, interpret, or prescribe law or policy or describing the organization, procedure, or practice requirements of an agency and includes the approval or prescription for the future of rates, wages, corporate or financial structures or reorganizations thereof, prices, facilities, appliances, services or allowances therefor or of valuations, costs, or accounting, or practices bearing on any of the foregoing. . . .[25]

Agencies have the authority to prescribe generally what shall or shall not be done in a given situation, as well as the power to administer and enforce their rules and regulations.

Rules and regulations established by an administrative agency must be administered within the scope of authority delegated to it by Congress. Although an agency must comply with its own regulations [*Lipp v. United States*, 181 Ct. Cl. 355 (1967)], they must be consistent with the statute under which they are promulgated. An agency's interpretation of a statute cannot supersede the language chosen by Congress. An executive regulation that defines some general statutory term in a too restrictive or unrealistic manner is invalid. *Tasker v. United States*, 178 Ct. Cl. 56 (1976). Agency regulations and administrative decisions are subject to review by the courts when questions arise as to whether an agency has overstepped its bounds in its interpretation of the law.

§702: Right To Review

A person suffering legal wrong because of agency action, or adversely affected or aggrieved by agency action within the meaning of a relevant statute, is entitled to judicial review thereof. An action in a court of the United States seeking relief other than money damages and stating a claim that an agency or an officer or employee thereof acted or failed to act in an official capacity or under color of legal authority shall not be dismissed nor relief therein be denied on the grounds that it is against the United States or that the United States is an indispensable party. The United States may be named as a defendant in any action, and a judgment or decree may be entered against the United States: Provided, That any mandatory or injunctive decree shall specify the Federal officer or officers (by name or by title), and their successors in office, personally responsible for compliance. Nothing herein (1) affects other limitations on judicial review or the power or the duty of the court to dismiss any action or deny relief on any other appropriate legal or equitable ground; or (2) confers authority to grant relief if any other statute that grants consent to suit expressly or impliedly forbids the relief which is sought.[26]

§703: Form and Venue of Proceeding

The form of proceeding for judicial review is the special statutory review proceeding relevant to the subject matter in a court specified by statute or, in the absence or inadequacy therof, any applicable form of legal action. . . . If no special statutory review proceeding is applicable, the action for judicial review, may be brought against the United States, the agency by its official title, or the appropriate officer.[27]

§704: Actions Reviewable

Agency action made reviewable by statute and final agency action for which there is no other adequate remedy in a court are subject to judicial review. A preliminary, procedural, or intermediate agency action or ruling not directly reviewable is subject to review on the review of the final agency action. Except as otherwise expressly required by statute, agency action otherwise final is final for the purposes of this section. . . .[28]

§705: Relief Pending Review

When an agency finds that justice so requires, it may postpone the effective date of action taken by it, pending judicial review. On such conditions as may be required and to the extent necessary to prevent irreparable injury, the reviewing court, including the court to which a case may be taken on appeal from or on application for certiorari or other writ to a reviewing court, may issue all necessary and appropriate process to postpone the effective date of an agency action or to preserve status or rights pending conclusion of the review proceedings.[29]

§706: Scope of Review

To the extent necessary . . . the reviewing court shall decide all relevant questions of law, interpret constitutional and statutory provisions, and determine the meaning or applicability of the terms of an agency action. The reviewing court shall—

(1) compel agency action unlawfully withheld or unreasonably delayed; and
(2) hold unlawful and set aside agency action, findings, and conclusions found to be—
   (A) arbitrary, capricious, an abuse of discretion, or otherwise not in accordance with law;
   (B) contrary to constitutional right, power, privilege, or immunity;
   (C) in excess of statutory jurisdiction, authority, or limitations, or short of statutory right;
   (D) without observance of procedure required by law;
   (E) unsupported by substantial evidence . . . or otherwise reviewed on the record of an agency hearing provided by statute; or
   (F) unwarranted by the facts to the extent that the facts are subject to trial de novo by the reviewing court.

In making the foregoing determinations, the court shall review the whole record or those parts of it cited by a party, and due account shall be taken of the rule of prejudicial error.[30]

Recourse to an administrative agency for resolution of a dispute may be a prerequisite to review of the dispute by a court. Administrative procedures should be allowed to run their full course before recourse is had to the courts. The Washington Court of Appeals in *Valley View Convalescent Home v.*

Department of Social Services, 599 P.2d 1313 (Wash. Ct. App. 1979), held that the department, in revoking the appellant's license and certification, had failed to follow proper statutory procedure, where the notices of revocation and decertification accompanied the department's statements of deficiencies, and both notices imposed revocation with no time period for correction. The "Department of Social and Health Services is bound by federal statutes and the rules and regulations promulgated thereunder when the Department accepts federal funds for medical assistance. Social Securities Act, Sec. 1902, 42 U.S.C.A. Sec. 1396a." *Id.* at 1314. The Commonwealth Court held in *Fair Rest Home v. Commonwealth, Department of Health,* 401 A.2d 872 (Pa. Commw. Ct. 1979), that the Department of Health was required to hold a hearing before it ordered revocation of the rest home's license to operate a nursing home. "The Department lapses when in a revocation proceeding it does not give careful consideration to its statutorily mandated responsibility to hear testimony." *Id.* at 873.

Regulations and decisions of administrative agencies that are reviewed by the courts may be upheld, modified, overturned, or reversed and remanded for further proceedings. The owner and operator of a licensed residential care facility brought an action challenging regulations, promulgated by the Department of Human Services through its Office of Long Term Care, governing administration of medicines in residential care facilities. *Department of Human Services v. Berry,* 764 S.W.2d 437 (Ark. 1989). The regulations challenged by the owner state

> 3. Under no circumstances shall an operator or employee or anyone solicited by an operator or employee be permitted to administer any oral medications, injectable medications, eye drops, ear drops or topical ointments (both prescription and non-prescription drugs).
> 4. In addition, any owner and/or operator of a Residential Care Facility who is a licensed nurse who administers any medication to a resident will be in violation of operating an unlicensed nursing home.

Id. at 439.

The circuit court held that the regulations were invalid and the Department of Human Services appealed. The supreme court, reversing the circuit court's decision, held that the regulations were reasonable in light of the distinctions between residential care facilities and nursing homes.

> In reviewing the adoption of regulations by an agency under its informal rule making procedures, a court is limited to considering whether the administrative action was arbitrary, capricious, an abuse of discretion or otherwise not in accordance with the law.
> • • • •
> A court will not attempt to substitute its judgment for that of the administrative agency.

. . . .

A rule is not invalid simply because it may work a hardship, create inconveniences, or because an evil intended to be regulated does not exist in a particular case.

Id. at 438.

Although the appellee was not victorious in this particular case, many instances are discussed in the text in which those who challenge the decisions of administrative agencies have been successful.

Administrative law is particularly important to those in the health care industry. Health care facilities are inundated with a proliferation of administrative rules and regulations affecting every aspect of their operations.

The Administrative Procedures Act provides that each agency must make available to the public, by publication in the *Federal Register,* the following information:

§552: Public Information Agency Rules, Opinions, Orders, Records, and Proceedings

(A) descriptions of its central and field organization and the established places at which, the employees . . . from whom and the methods whereby, the public may obtain information, make submittals or requests, or obtain decisions;

(B) statements of the general course and method by which its functions are channeled and determined, including the nature and requirements of all formal and informal procedures available;

(C) rules of procedure, descriptions of forms available or the places at which forms may be obtained, and instructions as to the scope and contents of all papers, reports, or examinations;

(D) substantive rules of general applicability adopted as authorized by law, and statements of general policy or interpretations of general applicability formulated and adopted by the agency; and

(E) each amendment, revision, or repeal of the foregoing.[31]

Besides the many federal agencies regulating health care, each state has its own system of administrative law. Health care facilities, both public and private, which fail to comply with state law, as with federal law, can be subject to civil penalties.

The following case illustrates how different laws within a state may be in conflict, one with the other. The Supreme Court of California in *Kizer v. County of San Mateo,* 806 P.2d 1353 (Cal. 1991), granted review to determine whether California Government Code section 818 of the Tort Claims Act prevents the state from imposing civil penalties pursuant to the state's Long-Term Care, Health, Safety and Securities Act. Section 818.2 of the Government Code provides that "[a] public entity is not liable for an injury caused by adopting or failing to adopt an enactment or by failing to enforce any law." Under the state's Long-Term Care, Health, Safety and Securities Act, a licensed health care facility is required to comply with statutory requirements. The act authorizes the California Department of Health Services to inspect health care facilities for compliance with statutes and regulations on patient care and to issue citations and penalties to facilities that do not comply with provisions of the act. The court held that the Tort Claims Act prohibiting assessment of punitive damages against a public entity does not prevent the state from imposing statutory civil penalties on a state-licensed, county-operated, long-term health care facility.

As with health care providers, state agencies that fail to comply with federal regulations can be subject to statutory penalties. Evidence supported a statutory penalty of $89,429 against the Colorado Department of Social Services for failing to conduct required inspections to review the care received by Medicaid patients in *Colorado Department of Social Services v. Department of Health and Human Services,* 928 F.2d 961 (10th Cir. 1991). Congress had subjected the states to penalties for failure to perform inspections pursuant to 42 U.S.C.A. sections 1396a(a)(26, 31), 1396 b(g)(1). To receive Medicaid funds, a state must submit quarterly reports demonstrating that the state has an effective program of medical review of the care of patients in skilled nursing facilities and in intermediate care facilities. The state's "failure to review even a single patient constitutes a failure to inspect that facility." *Id.* at 965. The state agency's admitted failure to review the care of three Medicaid recipients at a health care facility represented failure to inspect the facility, making the assessment of a statutory penalty against the state proper. *Id.* at 965.

GOVERNMENT ORGANIZATION

The three branches of the federal government are legislative, executive, and judicial (Fig 1-1). Figure 1-2 illustrates a typical example of a state government organization. A vital concept in the constitutional framework of government on both federal and state levels is the separation of powers. Essentially, this principle provides that no one branch of government is clearly dominant over the other two; however, in the exercise of its functions, each may affect and limit the activities, functions, and powers of the others.

Legislative Branch

On the federal level, legislative powers are vested in the Congress of the United States, which consists of a Senate and a House of Representatives. The

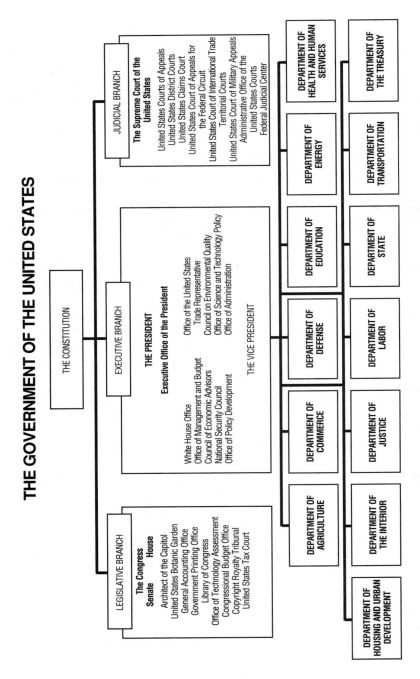

Figure 1-1 The Government of the United States

function of the legislative branch is to enact laws that may amend or repeal existing legislation and to create new legislation. It is the legislature's responsibility to determine the nature and extent of the need for new laws and for changes in existing laws. The work of preparing and considering federal legislation is carried out, for the most part, by committees of both houses of Congress. There are 16 standing committees in the Senate and 22 in the House of Representatives. "The membership of the standing committees of each house is chosen by a vote of the entire body; members of other committees are appointed under the provisions of the measure establishing them."[32]

Legislative proposals are assigned or referred to an appropriate committee for study. The committees conduct investigations and hold hearings where interested persons may present their views regarding proposed legislation. These proceedings provide additional information to assist committee members in their consideration of proposed bills. A bill may be reported out of a committee in its original form, favorably or unfavorably; it may be reported out with recommended amendments; or the bill might be allowed to lie in the committee without action. Some bills eventually reach the full legislative body, where, after consideration and debate, they may be approved or rejected.

The U.S. Congress and all state legislatures are bicameral (consisting of two houses), except for the Nebraska legislature, which is unicameral. Both houses in a bicameral legislature must pass identical versions of a legislative proposal before the legislation can be brought to the chief executive.

Executive Branch

The primary function of the executive branch of government on the federal and state level is to enforce and administer the law. The chief executive, either the President of the United States or the governor of a state, also has a role in the creation of law through the power to approve or veto legislative proposals.

The U.S. Constitution provides that "the executive Power shall be vested in a President of the United States of America. He shall hold his Office during the Term of four years, . . . together with the Vice President, chosen for the same term." The President serves as the administrative head of the executive branch of the federal government, which includes 13 executive departments (see Fig 1-1), as well as a great variety of agencies, both temporary and permanent.

> The Cabinet, a creation of custom and tradition dating back to George Washington's administration, functions at the pleasure of the President. The Cabinet is composed of the 13 executive departments. Its purpose is to advise the President upon any subject on which he requests information (pursuant to Article II, section 2 of the Constitution).[33]

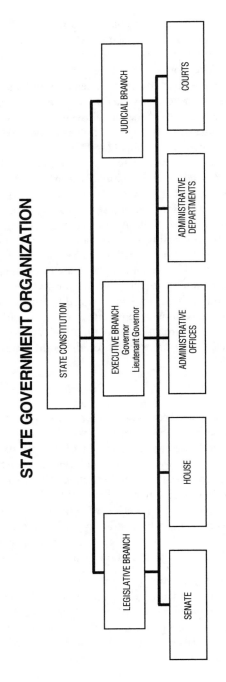

Figure 1-2 State Government Organization

Each department is responsible for a different area of public affairs, and each enforces the law within its area of responsibility. For example, the Department of Health and Human Services administers much of the federal health law enacted by Congress. Most states also are organized on a departmental basis. These departments administer and enforce state law concerning public affairs.

On a state level, the governor serves as the chief executive officer. The responsibilities of a state governor are provided for in the state's constitution. The Massachusetts State Constitution, for example, describes the responsibilities of the governor as including

- presenting an annual budget to the state legislature
- recommending new legislation
- vetoing legislation
- appointing and removing department heads
- appointing judicial officers
- acting as Commander-in-Chief of the state's military forces (the Massachusetts National Guard)[34]

Judicial Branch

> As I have said in the past, when government bureaus and agencies go awry, which are adjuncts of the legislative or executive branches, the people flee to the third branch, their courts, for solace and justice.[35]
>
> Justice J. Henderson, Supreme Court of South Dakota

The function of the judicial branch of government is adjudication—resolving disputes in accordance with law. As a practical matter, most disputes or controversies that are covered by legal principles or rules are resolved without resort to the courts.

Alexis de Tocqueville, a foreign observer commenting on the primordial place of the law and the legal profession, stated, "Scarcely any political question arises in the United States that is not resolved, sooner or later, into a judicial question."[36]

> It is emphatically the province and duty of the judicial branch to say what the law is. Those who apply the rule to particular cases, must of necessity expound and interpret that rule. If two laws conflict with each other, the courts must decide on the operation of each.
>
> So if a law be in opposition to the constitution; if both the law and the constitution apply to a particular case, so that the court must either

decide that case conformably to the law, disregarding the constitution; or conformably to the constitution, disregarding the law; the court must determine which of these conflicting rules govern the case. This is the very essence of judicial duty.

• • • •

. . . , it is apparent, that the framers of the constitution contemplated that instrument, as a rule for the government of courts, as well as of the legislature.

Why otherwise does it direct the judges to take such an oath to support it?

Marbury v. Madison, 5 U.S. (1 Cranch) 137, 177–180 (1803).

The decision as to which court has jurisdiction—the legal right to hear and rule on a particular case—is determined by such matters as the locality in which each party to a lawsuit resides and the issues of a lawsuit. Each state in the United States provides its own court system, which is created by the state's constitution and/or statutes. The oldest court in the United States, established in 1692, is the Supreme Judicial Court of Massachusetts.[37] Most of the nation's judicial business is reviewed and acted on in state courts. Each state maintains a level of trial courts that have original jurisdiction. This jurisdiction may exclude cases in which the monetary value of the claim is less than a specified minimum and cases involving probate matters (i.e., wills and estates) and workers' compensation. Different states have designated different names for trial courts (e.g., superior, district, circuit, or supreme courts). Also on the trial court level are minor courts such as city, small claims, and justice of the peace courts. States such as Massachusetts have consolidated their minor courts into a statewide court system.

There is at least one appellate court in each state. Many states have an intermediate appellate court between the trial courts and the court of last resort. Where this intermediate court is present, there is a provision for appeal to it, with further review in all but select cases. Because of this format, the highest appellate tribunal is seen as the final arbiter in cases that possess importance in themselves or for the particular state's system of jurisprudence. (Fig 1-3 depicts a typical state court system.)

The trial court of the federal system is the U.S. district court. There are 89 district courts in the 50 states (the larger states having more than one district court) and one in the District of Columbia. The Commonwealth of Puerto Rico also has a district court with jurisdiction corresponding to that of district courts in the different states. Generally, only one judge is required to sit and decide a case, although certain cases require up to three judges. The federal district

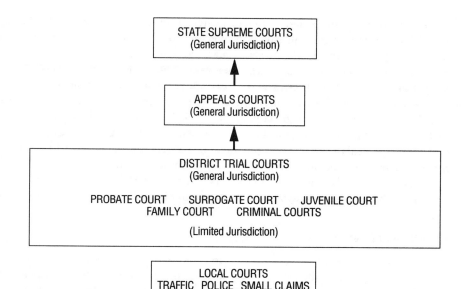

Figure 1-3 State Court System

courts hear civil, criminal, admiralty, and bankruptcy cases. The Bankruptcy Amendments and Federal Judgeship Act of 1984 (28 U.S.C. §151) provided that the bankruptcy judges for each judicial district shall constitute a unit of the district court to be known as the bankruptcy court.[38]

The U.S. courts of appeals (formerly called circuit courts of appeals) are appellate courts for the 11 judicial circuits. Their main purpose is to review cases tried in federal district courts within their respective circuits, but they also possess jurisdiction to review orders of designated administrative agencies and to issue original writs in appropriate cases. The courts of appeals are intermediate appellate courts created to relieve the U.S. Supreme Court of having to consider all appeals in cases originally decided by the federal trial courts.

The Supreme Court, the nation's highest court, is the only federal court created directly by the Constitution.

> The Judicial Power of the United States, shall be vested in one supreme Court, and in such inferior Courts as the Congress may from time to time ordain and establish. The Judges, both of the supreme and inferior Courts, shall hold their offices during good Behaviour, and shall, at stated Times, receive for their Services, a Compensation, which shall not be diminished during their Continuance in Office.[39]

Eight associate justices and one chief justice sit on the Supreme Court. The Court has limited original jurisdiction over the lower federal courts and the highest state courts. In a few situations, an appeal will go directly from a federal or state court to the Supreme Court, but in most cases today, review must be sought through the discretionary *writ of certiorari,* an appeal petition. In addition to the aforementioned courts, there are special federal courts that have jurisdiction over particular subject matters. The U.S. Court of Claims has jurisdiction over certain claims against the government. The U.S. Court of Customs and Patent Appeals has appellate jurisdiction over certain customs and patent matters. The U.S. Customs Court reviews certain administrative decisions by customs officials. Also, there are a U.S. Tax Court and a U.S. Court of Military Appeals. (The federal court system is illustrated in Fig 1-4.)

Separation of Powers

The concept of separation of powers—in effect, a system of *checks and balances*—is illustrated in the relationships among the branches of government in regard to legislation. On the federal level, when a bill creating a statute is enact-

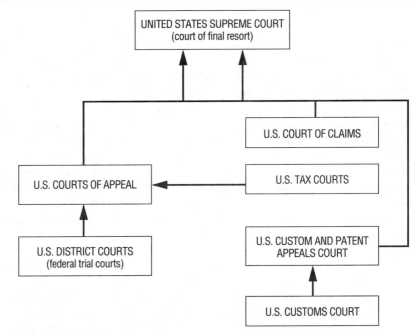

Figure 1-4 Federal Court System

ed by Congress and signed by the President, it becomes law. If the President vetoes a bill, it takes a two-thirds vote of each house of Congress to override the veto. The President also can prevent a bill from becoming law by avoiding any action while Congress is in session. This procedure, known as a *pocket veto*, temporarily can stop a bill from becoming law and permanently may prevent it from becoming law if later sessions of Congress do not act favorably on it.

A bill that has become law may be declared invalid by the Supreme Court if the Court decides that the law is in violation of the Constitution. "It is not entirely unworthy of observation, that in declaring what shall be the Supreme law of the land, the constitution itself is first mentioned; and not the laws of the United States generally, but those only made in pursuance to the constitution, have that rank." *Marbury v. Madison* at 180.

Even though a Supreme Court decision is final regarding a specific controversy, Congress and the President may generate new, constitutionally sound legislation to replace a law that has been declared unconstitutional. The procedures for amending the Constitution are complex and often time consuming, but they can serve as a way to offset or override a Supreme Court decision.

ADMINISTRATIVE DEPARTMENTS AND AGENCIES

The following sections review many of the federal administrative agencies and departments that affect the health care industry. Besides the federal-level departments and agencies described below, many departments and agencies on the state and local levels also address many of those matters addressed on the federal level (public health, finance, education, welfare, labor, housing, and other needs and concerns of state residents).

Department of Health and Human Services (DHHS)

The Department of Health and Human Services (DHHS) (Fig 1-5), a cabinet-level department of the executive branch of the federal government, is concerned with people and is most involved with the nation's human concerns. The secretary of DHHS, serving as the Department's administrative head, advises the President with regard to health, welfare, and income security plans, policies, and programs. Within the DHHS are five operating divisions: the Social Security Administration, the Health Care Financing Administration, the Office of Human Development Services, the Public Health Service, and the Family Support Administration. The DHHS is responsible for developing and implementing appropriate administrative regulations for carrying out national health and human services policy objectives. The DHHS is the main source of regulations affecting the health care industry.

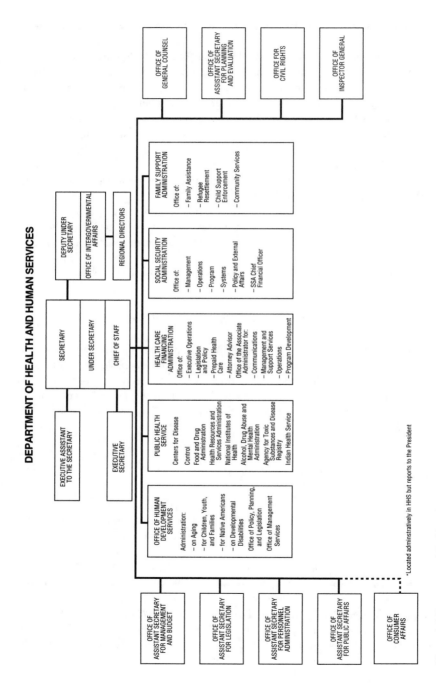

Figure 1-5 Department of Health and Human Services

The DHHS is responsible for many of the programs designed to meet the needs of senior citizens, including Social Security benefits (e.g., retirement, survivors, and disability), Supplemental Security Income (which assures a minimum monthly income to needy persons and is administered by local Social Security offices), Medicare, Medicaid, and programs under the Older Americans Act (e.g., in-home services such as home health and home delivered meals, and community services such as adult day care, transportation, and ombudsman services in long-term care facilities).

Public Health Service

The mission of the Public Health Service (PHS) is to promote the protection of the nation's physical and mental health. The PHS accomplishes its mission by coordinating with the states setting and implementing national health policy and pursuing effective intergovernmental relations; generating and upholding cooperative international health-related agreements, policies, and programs; conducting medical and biomedical research; sponsoring and administering programs for the development of health resources, the prevention and control of diseases, and alcohol and drug abuse; providing resources and expertise to the states and other public and private institutions in the planning, direction, and delivery of physical and mental health care services; and enforcing laws to ensure the safety of drugs and protection against impure and unsafe foods, cosmetics, medical devices, and radiation-producing projects.[40]

Within the PHS are smaller agencies responsible for carrying out the purpose of the division and DHHS, such as the National Institutes of Health (NIH) and the Food and Drug Administration (FDA).

The NIH is the principal federal biomedical research agency. It is responsible for conducting, supporting, and promoting biomedical research.

The FDA supervises and controls the introduction of drugs, foods, cosmetics, and medical devices into the marketplace and protects society from impure and/or hazardous items. Virtually every consumer product in a supermarket or a drugstore is regulated by the FDA. The FDA engages in the following activities:

- inspects plants where foods, drugs, cosmetics, or other products are made or stored to make sure good practices are being observed
- reviews and approves new drug applications and food additive petitions before new drugs or new food additives can be used
- approves every batch of insulin and antibiotics and most color additives before they can be used
- sets standards for consumer products, such as foods that are made according to set recipe, and tests products to ensure that they meet government standards

- conducts reviews of all prescription and nonprescription medicines, biologic drugs, and veterinary drugs now on the market to make sure they are safe, effective, and properly labeled
- develops regulations for proper labeling (e.g., the FDA developed new regulations requiring cosmetic ingredient labeling and nutrition labeling on many foods)
- works with the industries it regulates to help them develop better quality-control procedures
- tests drugs regularly after approval to ascertain whether they meet standards of potency, purity, and quality
- issues public warnings when hazardous products have been identified[41]

Health Care Financing Administration

The Health Care Financing Administration (HCFA) is responsible for administering Medicare and Medicaid programs. The HCFA is also responsible for the related medical care quality assurance provisions of Medicare and Medicaid. Under the Medicare program, the HCFA develops and implements policies and procedures and provides guidance related to program recipients, including nursing facilities, hospitals, physicians, and the contractors who process claims such as Blue Cross and Blue Shield. Under the Medicaid program, the HCFA provides grants to the states for medical care services for those who are unable to pay. The HCFA is also responsible for working with the states under the Medicaid program to develop approaches toward meeting the needs of the indigent.[42]

Social Security Administration

The Social Security Administration oversees the nation's social insurance program. Social Security provides retirement income to most citizens older than age 65 years. (Persons aged 62 years may qualify under certain conditions.) The program is funded by contributions from both employers and employees. The funds are pooled into special trusts. When the earnings of an employee are reduced or discontinued because of death or disability, Social Security benefits are paid to assist the employee and his or her family.

Family Support Administration

The Family Support Administration (FSA) serves as adviser to the secretary of DHHS for children and families; provides leadership and direction to family support programs; recommends actions that improve the coordination of family support programs with other DHHS programs, federal agencies, state and local governments, and private sector organizations; directs and coordinates programs with the secretary of labor for employment and training; manages and provides leadership and planning and develops FSA programs; and supervises the use of research and evaluation funds and controls equal employment opportunity programs for FSA.[43]

Office of Human Development Services

The Office of Human Development Services (OHDS) provides leadership and direction to programs for the aging; children, youth, and families; Native Americans; those living in rural areas; and handicapped persons. The OHDS is responsible for the management and provision of leadership in planning and developing OHDS programs; supervision of research; control of equal employment opportunity and civil rights policies and programs for the OHDS; directing public affairs, regional operations, and correspondence and assignment tracking activities; and recommendations for program improvements.[44]

Administration on Aging

The Administration on Aging (AoA), established by Congress on October 1, 1965, is the only federal agency devoted exclusively to the concerns and potential of this country's older population.[45] The AoA is located within the DHHS. The commissioner of the AoA is appointed by the President with the advice and consent of the Senate. The primary goals of the AoA, as envisioned by the act, are

- to create and support a national network of state agencies on aging and area agencies on aging covering the entire nation and its territories
- to develop and oversee responsive systems of services and opportunities to meet the social and human service needs of the elderly in each and every community of this nation
- to serve as a visible advocate on behalf of the elderly within the DHHS and with other federal agencies, national organizations, and programs affecting older people[46]

The AoA comprises ten regional offices that assist the states in developing responsive community-based systems of comprehensive and coordinated services throughout the nation. The AoA allocates funds to the states and territorial units based on the 60+ years population in each area. The different states and territorial units then make grants to the 670 area agencies on aging. The AoA also works with many other national, professional, and voluntary organizations concerned with long-term care, elder abuse, transportation, caregiver support, etc.

Federal Council on Aging

The Federal Council on Aging (FCoA), composed of 15 members, is responsible for advising and assisting the President on matters relating to the special needs of older Americans. Funds appropriated for the council are included in the overall appropriations of the DHHS. The council

- reviews and evaluates, on a continuing basis, federal policies regarding the aging and programs and other activities affecting the aging conducted or assisted by all federal departments and agencies for the purpose of appraising their value and their impact on the lives of older Americans
- serves as a spokesperson on behalf of older Americans by making recommendations to the President, to the secretary, to the commissioner, and to the Congress with respect to federal policies regarding the aging and federally conducted or assisted programs and other activities relating to or affecting them
- informs the public about the problems and needs of the aging by collecting and disseminating information, conducting or commissioning studies and publishing the results thereof, and by issuing publications and reports
- provides for public forums for discussing and publicizing the problems and needs of the aging and obtaining information relating thereto, by conducting public hearings, and by conducting or sponsoring conferences, workshops, and other such meetings[47]

The council is required by law to prepare an annual report for the President regarding FCoA activities, public meetings, and recommendations. Copies of the FCoA annual report are distributed to members of Congress, governmental and private agencies, institutions of higher education, and others interested in FCoA activities.

Recommendations by the FCoA can have an effect on all federal departments. For example, because of increasing labor shortages, the FCoA in its 1988 Annual Report to the President communicated,

> One of the key factors to solving a share of these shortages could be a quality of life for older Americans that included an extended worklife, aided by such programs as ABLE (Ability Based on Long Experience) which coordinates employer and senior employee needs, and the Council feels that tax changes favoring older workers should be considered.
>
> To this end the FCoA sees the Department of Labor playing a larger and more influential role in legislative and administrative decisions affecting older Americans.[48]

National Institute on Aging

The National Institute on Aging (NIA) is one of 13 institutes of the NIH. The NIA is responsible for the "conduct and support of biomedical, social, and behavioral research and training related to the aging process and the diseases and other special problems and needs of the aged."[49] The NIA engages in collaborative activities with other NIH institutes and federal agencies. Research is conducted through interventions and other clinical trials, where appropriate.[50] The priorities of the NIA are as follows:

- Alzheimer's disease and related dementias
- understanding aging
- frailty, disability, and rehabilitation
- health and effective functioning
- long-term care for older people
- special older populations
- training and career development
- international activities (e.g., cross-cultural and cross-national comparative studies involving diverse populations)[51]

Department of Justice

The Department of Justice is responsible for enforcing the laws of the United States. The attorney general is the administrative head of the department, which consists of various offices, divisions (e.g., the Antitrust, Civil, Criminal, Civil Rights, and Tax Divisions), bureaus (e.g., the Federal Bureau of Investigation and the Drug Enforcement Administration), and boards (e.g., the Executive Office for Immigration Review).

Department of Labor

The Department of Labor is the ninth executive department of the executive branch of government. The secretary of labor advises the President on labor policies and issues. The functions of the Department of Labor are to

> foster, promote, and develop the welfare of wage earners of the United States, to improve working conditions, and to advance opportunities for profitable employment. In carrying out this mission, the department administers a variety of federal labor laws guaranteeing workers' rights to safe and healthful working conditions, a minimum hourly wage and overtime pay, freedom from employment discrimination, unemployment insurance, and workers' compensation. The department also protects workers' pension rights; provides for job training programs; helps

workers find jobs; works to strengthen free collective bargaining; and keeps track of changes in employment prices and other national economic measurements. As the department seeks to assist all Americans who need and want to work, special efforts are made to meet the unique job market problems of older workers, youths, minority group members, women, the handicapped, and other groups.[52]

Within the Department of Labor are various agencies responsible for carrying out the purpose of the department (e.g., Occupational Safety and Health Administration).

National Labor Relations Board

The National Labor Relations Board (NLRB) is an agency, independent of the Department of Labor, responsible for preventing and remedying unfair labor practices by employers and labor organizations or their agents and conducting secret ballot elections among employees in appropriate collective bargaining units to determine whether they desire to be represented by a labor organization. The NLRB conducts secret ballot elections among employees who have been covered by a union-shop agreement to determine whether they wish to revoke their union's authority.

The general counsel of the NLRB has final authority to investigate charges of unfair labor practices, issue complaints, and prosecute such complaints before the NLRB. There are 33 regional directors, under the direction of the general counsel, who are responsible for processing representation, unfair labor practice, and jurisdictional dispute cases.[53]

NOTES

1. B. SCHWARTZ, THE LAW IN AMERICA 15 (1974).

2. A.K.R. KIRALFY, POTTER'S HISTORICAL INTRODUCTION TO ENGLISH LAW 9 (1962).

3. J. REEVES, HISTORY OF THE ENGLISH LAW 2 (1814).

4. *Id.*

5. G.W. KEETON, ENGLISH LAW 70 (1974).

6. *Id.* at 3.

7. *Id.*

8. *Id.*

9. *Id.*

10. KIRALFY, *supra* note 2, at 9–10.

11. KEETON, *supra* note 5, at 70.

12. U.S. DEPARTMENT OF HEALTH AND HUMAN SERVICES, TASK FORCE ON MEDICAL LIABILITY AND MALPRACTICE 3 (1987) [hereinafter TASK FORCE].

13. SCHWARTZ, *supra* note 1, at 29.

14. *Id.*

15. *Id.* at 30, 31.

16. L. FRIEDMAN, A HISTORY OF AMERICAN LAW 92 (1985).

17. SCHWARTZ, *supra* note 1, at 51.

18. TASK FORCE, *supra* note 12, at 3.

19. *Id.*

20. Zinman, *Study Finds Hospitals 'Harm' Some,* 50 NEWSDAY 17 (1990).

21. The Robert Wood Johnson Foundation, *The Tort System for Medical Malpractice: How Well Does It Work, What Are the Alternatives?,* ABRIDGE, Spring 1991, at 2.

22. The Robert Wood Johnson Foundation, *Negligent Medical Care: What Is It, Where Is It, and How Widespread Is It?,* ABRIDGE, Spring 1991, at 6.

23. 5 U.S.C.A. §500 *et. seq.* (West 1977).

24. An "agency means each authority of the Government of the United States, . . . but does not include—(A) the Congress; the courts of the United States; . . . . " 5 U.S.C.A. §551 (West 1977).

25. 5 U.S.C.S. §551 (Law. Co-op. 1989) at 69.

26. 5 U.S.C.S. §702 (Law. Co-op. 1989) at 282, 283.

27. 5 U.S.C.S. §703 (Law. Co-op. 1989) at 350.

28. 5 U.S.C.S. §704 (Law. Co-op. 1989) at 367.

29. 5 U.S.C.S. §705 (Law. Co-op. 1989) at 418.

30. 5 U.S.C.S. §706 (Law. Co-op. 1989) at 430.

31. 5 U.S.C.S. §552 (Law. Co-op. 1989) at 100.

32. OFFICE OF THE FEDERAL REGISTER, NATIONAL ARCHIVES AND RECORDS ADMINISTRATION, THE UNITED STATES GOVERNMENT MANUAL 1988/89 at 29 (1988).

33. *Id.* at 13.

34. D. LEVITAN, YOUR MASSACHUSETTS GOVERNMENT 14 (10th ed. 1984).

35. Heritage of Yankton, Inc. v. S.D. Dept. of Health, 432 N.W.2d 68, 77 (S.D. 1988).

36. SCHWARTZ, *supra* note 1, at 15.

37. LEVITAN, *supra* note 34, at 32.

38. THE UNITED STATES GOVERNMENT MANUAL, *supra* note 32, at 71–72.

39. U.S. CONST. art. III, §1.

40. THE UNITED STATES GOVERNMENT MANUAL, *supra,* at 296.

41. UNITED STATES FOOD AND DRUG ADMINISTRATION, WE WANT YOU TO KNOW ABOUT TODAY'S FDA (1974).

42. *Id.* at 307–308.

43. THE UNITED STATES GOVERNMENT MANUAL, *supra* note 32, at 309–310.

44. *Id.* at 293–294.

45. Department of Health and Human Services, The Administration on Aging, *Fact Sheet,* March 1988, at 1.

46. *Id.*

47. Federal Council on the Aging, Annual Report to the President 1989, 1–2; *see also,* 42 U.S.C.A. §3015(d) (1992).

48. Federal Council on the Aging, Annual Report to the President 1988, at 17.

49. National Institute on Aging, National Institutes of Health, *Fact Sheet*, June 1990, at 1.

50. *Id.*

51. *Id.*

52. THE UNITED STATES GOVERNMENT MANUAL, *supra,* at 400.

53. *Id.* at 631.

Chapter 2
Tort Law

Every instance of a man's suffering the penalty of the law, is an instance of the failure of that penalty in effecting its purpose, which is to deter from transgression.

Whately

OUTLINE

    Fraud
    Invasion of Privacy
    Intentional Infliction of Mental Distress
  • Products Liability
    Negligence
    Breach of Warranty
      Express Warranty
      Implied Warranty
    Strict Liability
    Products Liability Defenses
  • Conclusion

A tort is a civil wrong, other than a breach of contract, committed against a person or property (real or personal) for which a court provides a remedy in the form of an action for damages. The basic purposes of tort law are

  • preservation of peace between individuals by providing a substitute for vengeance
  • culpability—to find fault for wrongdoing
  • deterrence—to discourage the wrongdoer (tort-feasor) from committing future torts
  • compensation—to indemnify the injured person(s) of wrongdoing

The conclusion reached by the Harvard Medical Practice Study commissioned after a review of some 30,000 medical records was that

> between 2,967 and 3,888 malpractice claims are filed by patients each
> year in the state. Comparing these figures with their estimate for the
> number of medical injuries caused by negligence during the same
> period (27,179), the research group suggested that only one claim
> makes its way into the tort system for every eight cases of injury
> caused by medical negligence.
>
> • • • •
>
> Moreover, because prior research has shown that only about 50 per-
> cent of claimants ever receive compensation, the study team estimates
> that 16 times as many people actually suffer injuries due to negligence
> as receive compensation through the tort system.
>
> • • • •
>
> Martin Hatlie of the American Medical Association . . . believes, "the
> message the tort system is sending to doctors is not so much deter-

rence, in terms of practicing good medicine, but more just 'drive defensively,' because any patient you may see may be a litigant."[1]

Because an adverse medical outcome generally results in some financial damage, the effect of finding fault by the court is to determine who shall bear the cost of an unfavorable outcome—the provider or the recipient of health care. To avoid cost, the plaintiff must prove the negligence of the provider. Conversely, the provider fights to avoid fault determination. Underlying this adversarial proceeding is the assumption that if the provider is forced to bear the cost, it will discourage further acts of negligence by the provider and by other similarly situated providers of health care. However, "professional liability insurance insulates the individual physician's wallet from the actual cost of claims."[2] Assessing monetary damages for the purpose of deterrence "works only if tort-feasors are required to bear the full cost of injury causing behavior. Such a cost necessarily recognizes the value of life itself."[3]

The three basic categories of tort law are negligent torts, intentional torts, and torts in which liability is assessed irrespective of fault (e.g., against manufacturers of defective products). Although most incidents that raise issues of liability concern harm allegedly resulting from negligence, a person also may be liable for intentional wrongs. Intentional tortious conduct (conduct implying civil wrong) that may arise in the context of patient care includes assault, battery, false imprisonment, invasion of privacy, and infliction of mental distress. Liability, irrespective of fault, may be imposed in certain situations in which the activity, regardless of intentions or negligence, is so dangerous to others that public policy demands absolute responsibility on the part of the tort-feasor.

There are two main differences between intentional and negligent wrongs. The first is intent, which is present in intentional but not in negligent wrongs. For a tort to be considered intentional, not only must the act be committed intentionally, but also the wrongdoer must realize to a substantial certainty that harm would result. The second difference is less obvious. An intentional wrong always involves a willful act that violates another's interests; a negligent wrong may not involve committing an act at all. In certain situations involving negligence, a person may be held liable for not acting in the way that a reasonably prudent person would have acted.

NEGLIGENCE

Negligence is a tort—a civil or personal wrong distinguished from criminal conduct. It is the unintentional omission or commission of an act that a reasonably prudent person would or would not do under given circumstances. It is a form of conduct caused by heedlessness or carelessness that constitutes a departure from the standard of care generally imposed on reasonable members of society. Negligence can occur

- where one has considered the consequences of an act and has exercised the best possible judgment
- where one fails to guard against a risk that should be appreciated
- where one engages in certain behavior expected to involve unreasonable danger to others

Forms of Negligence

The basic forms of negligence are

- *malfeasance*—execution of an unlawful or improper act (e.g., administering contraindicated medication)
- *misfeasance*—improper performance of an act, resulting in injury to another (e.g., bathing a patient in scalding hot water)
- *nonfeasance*—failure to act, when there is a duty to act, as a reasonably prudent person would in similar circumstances (e.g., failing to order diagnostic tests or prescribe medications that should have been ordered or prescribed under the circumstances)
- *malpractice*—negligence or carelessness of a professional person (e.g., a nurse, pharmacist, physician, accountant)
- *criminal negligence*—reckless disregard for the safety of another (i.e., willful indifference to an injury that could follow an act)

Degrees of Negligence

There are basically two degrees of negligence:

- *ordinary negligence*—failure to do what a reasonably prudent person would do, or the doing of that which a reasonably prudent person would not do, under the circumstances of the act or omission in question
- *gross negligence*—intentional or wanton omission of care that would be proper to provide or the doing of that which would be improper to do

Elements of Negligence

The four elements that must be present for a plaintiff to recover damages caused by negligence are

- duty to care   *or standard of care*
- breach of that duty
- actual injury
- causation/proximate cause

All four elements must be present for a plaintiff to recover for damages suffered as a result of a negligent act. When the four elements of negligence are proved, the plaintiff is said to have presented a *prima facie* case of negligence, which will enable the plaintiff to prevail.

The burden of proof in a negligence case is not as great as the "beyond a reasonable doubt" standard borne by a prosecutor in a criminal case. Therefore, if a plaintiff supports his or her negligence claim with evidence sufficient to outweigh the evidence presented by the defendant, the defendant will be found liable for the negligent act he or she committed. The defendant then will be ordered by the court, in accordance with the verdict rendered by the jury or by the court itself, to compensate the plaintiff monetarily for the harm the plaintiff suffered. The purpose of compensatory damages is to put the injured party in the same financial situation he or she was in before he or she suffered any harm. Besides compensatory damages, in some cases punitive damages could be awarded by the court to the plaintiff, for pain and suffering caused by conduct of the defendant that would be considered egregious.

Duty To Use Due Care

The first requirement in establishing negligence is for the plaintiff to prove the existence of a legal relationship between him- or herself and the defendant. *Duty* is defined as a legal obligation of care, performance, or observance imposed on one to safeguard the rights of others. This duty may arise from a special relationship such as that between a physician and a patient. The existence of this relationship implies that a physician–patient relationship was in effect at the time an alleged injury occurred. The duty to care can arise from a simple telephone conversation. It can arise out of a physician's voluntary act of assuming the care of a patient. Duty also can be established by statute or contract between the plaintiff and defendant. For example:

> [A]fter showing it has provided reasonable care for the safety and well-being of its patient under the circumstances presented, a nursing

home is not liable for injury caused by an untoward event unless it has breached a contractual agreement to furnish special care beyond that usually furnished which relates to the injury giving rise to the cause sued on.[4]

The duty owed to a patient in *O'Neill v. Montefiore Hospital,* 11 A.D.2d 132, 202 N.Y.S.2d 436 (1960), was clear. The plaintiff sought recovery against the hospital for failure to render necessary emergency treatment and against a physician for his failure and refusal to treat her spouse. The deceased, Mr. O'Neill, who was experiencing pains in his chest and arms, had walked with his wife to the hospital at 5 A.M. He claimed that he was a member of the Hospital Insurance Plan (HIP). The emergency department nurse stated that the hospital had no connection with HIP and did not take care of HIP patients. After reflecting a few moments, the nurse indicated that she would try to get an HIP physician for Mr. O'Neill. The nurse called Dr. Graig, an HIP physician, and explained the patient's symptoms. She then handed the phone to Mr. O'Neill, who said, "Well, I could be dead by 8 o'clock." He concluded his phone conversation and spoke to the nurse, indicating that he had been told to go home and come back when the HIP was open. Mrs. O'Neill asked that her husband be seen by a physician. The nurse again requested that they return at 8 o'clock. Mr. O'Neill again commented that he could be dead by 8 o'clock. He then left with his wife to return home, pausing occasionally to catch his breath. On arriving at home, Mr. O'Neill began to undress with the assistance of his wife, and he suddenly fell to the floor and died. Dr. Graig claimed that he offered to come to the emergency department, but that Mr. O'Neill said he would wait and see another HIP physician at 8 o'clock that morning. The supreme court, Bronx County, entered a judgment dismissing the complaint, and the plaintiff appealed. The supreme court, appellate division, held that a physician who undertakes to examine or treat a patient and then abandons him or her may be held liable for malpractice. The proof of the record in this case indicated that the physician undertook to diagnose the ailments of the deceased, by telephone, thus establishing at least the first element of negligence—duty of care. The finding of the trial court was reversed, and a new trial was ordered.

The surviving parents in *Hastings v. Baton Rouge Hospital,* 498 So.2d 713 (La. Ct. App. 1986), brought a medical malpractice action against the hospital; the emergency department physician, Dr. Gerdes; and the thoracic surgeon on call, Dr. McCool, for the wrongful death of their 19-year-old son who had been brought to the emergency department at 11:56 P.M. as a result of two stab wounds and weak vital signs. Dr. Gerdes decided that a thoracotomy had to be performed. He was not qualified to perform the surgery and called Dr. McCool, who was on call that evening for thoracic surgery. Dr. Gerdes described the patient's condition, indicating that he had been stabbed in one of his major blood vessels. At trial, Dr. McCool claimed that he did not recall Dr. Gerdes' saying that a major blood vessel could be involved. Dr. McCool asked Dr. Gerdes to transfer the patient to the Earl K. Long Hospital. Dr. Gerdes said, "I can't transfer this patient." Dr. McCool replied, "No. Transfer him." Nurse Kelly was not comfortable with the decision to transfer the patient and offered to accompany him in the ambulance. Dr. Gerdes re-examined the patient, who exhibited marginal vital signs, was restless, and was draining blood from his chest. The ambulance service was called at 1:03 A.M., and by 1:30 A.M. the patient had been placed in the ambulance for transfer. The patient began to fight wildly, the chest tube came out, and the bleeding increased. The patient virtually bled to death. An attempt to revive him from a cardiac arrest was futile, and the patient died after having been moved back to the emergency department. The duty of care in this case cannot be reasonably disputed. Louisiana statute imposes a duty on hospitals licensed in Louisiana to make emergency services available to all persons residing in the state regardless of insurance coverage or economic status. The hospital's own bylaws provided that no patient should be transferred without due consideration for his or her condition and the facilities existing for his or her care. The Nineteenth Judicial District Court directed a verdict for the defendants, and the plaintiffs appealed. The court of appeals affirmed the district court's decision. On further appeal, the supreme court held that the evidence presented to the jury questions whether the defendants were negligent in their treatment of the victim. The findings of the lower courts were reversed, and the case was remanded for trial.

Some duties are created by statute, as when a statute specifies a particular standard that must be met. Many standards are created by administrative agencies under the provisions of a statute. In general, the violation of a statute or regulation is evidence of negligence.

Duties can be created by an institution through its internal rules and regulations. The courts hold that such internal rules are indicative of the organization's knowledge of the proper procedure to follow and, hence, create a duty. Thus, if an employee of an institution fails to follow an operating rule of that institution and, as a result, another person is injured, the employee who violated the rule would also be considered negligent.

A duty of care also may be created by a contract. Where there is a contractual duty of care and an injury occurs, patients have a choice of theories on which lawsuits may be pursued—breach of contract or, alternatively, tort. In some jurisdictions, the statute of limitations for breach of contract is longer than for negligence actions. In such cases, the existence of a contractual duty of care may extend the liability of a health care facility for several years.

Standard of Care

When injury has been suffered by a patient, the patient must show that the defendant failed to meet the prevailing standard of care for the defendant to be held liable for negligence. That an injury is suffered, without proof that the defendant deviated from the practice of competent members of his or her profession, is not sufficient for imposing liability.

Duty requires that all health care workers conform to a specific standard of care to protect others. A nurse, for example, who assumes the care of a patient has the duty to exercise in the care and treatment of the patient that degree of skill, care, and knowledge ordinarily possessed and exercised by other nurses. A nurse must be reasonable in the exercise of professional judgment as to the care he or she renders; however, reasonable judgment must not represent a departure from the requirements of accepted nursing practice.

> Persons who are known to have mental or physical disabilities, or who are young and inexperienced, are entitled to a degree of care exercised by others proportioned to their incapacity to protect themselves. They are not to be accorded the same treatment as persons of mature years and of sound mentality. No general rule can be articulated, for the standard of care in situations involving victims having these characteristics requires that a determination of what constitutes "reasonable care" be made in each individual case, taking into consideration the victim's known mental and physical condition. Generally the greater the disability, the greater is the degree of care required. The rationale for this principle of law is that natural justice requires that greater consideration and care are due to persons known to be unable to care of themselves than to those who are fully able to do so.[5]

Duty is often difficult to establish. However, "firmly rooted in the common law lies the concept that although one individual need do nothing to rescue another from peril not of that individual's own making, nevertheless, a person who undertakes to do an act must do it with reasonable care."[6] Once a duty of care has been established, the standard that the person owing the duty must meet to avoid potential liability must be determined.[7]

The standard of care describes what conduct is expected of an individual in a given situation. The general standard of care that must be exercised is that which a reasonably prudent person would do acting under the same or similar circumstances.

> [T]he standard of conduct of a reasonable person may be: (a) established by a legislative enactment or administrative regulation which so provides, (b) adopted by the court from a legislative enactment or an administrative regulation which does not so provide, or (c) established by judicial decision, or, (d) applied to the facts of the case by the trial judge or jury, if there is no such enactment, regulation or decision.[8]

The "reasonably prudent person" concept describes a nonexistent, hypothetical person who is set up as the community ideal of what would be considered reasonable behavior. It is a measuring stick representing the conduct of the average person in the community, under the circumstances facing the defendant at the time of the alleged negligence. The reasonableness of conduct is judged in light of the circumstances apparent at the time of injury and by reference to different characteristics of the actor (e.g., age, sex, physical condition, education, knowledge, training, mental capacity). The actual performance of an individual in a given situation will be measured against what a reasonably prudent person would or would not have done. Deviation from the standard of care will constitute negligence if there is a resulting injury.

In determining how a reasonably prudent person should perform in a particular situation, courts may use the services of an expert witness to testify regarding the professional standard of care required in the same or similar communities.

Expert testimony is necessary because the jury is not trained or qualified to determine what the reasonably prudent professional's standard of care would be under similar circumstances. Essentially, the expert testifies to aid the judge and the jury by providing a measure for properly assessing the actual conduct required of the professional.

> Expert testimony is required to establish the specific standard of care for professionals, and to assist in the determination of a professional's conformity to the relevant standard, even in bench trials, except where the matter under investigation is so simple, and the lack of skill so obvious, as to be within the range of the ordinary experience and comprehension of even nonprofessional persons.[9]

The courts have been moving away from reliance on a community standard and have applied an "industry" or "national" standard. This trend has developed as a result of a more reasonable belief that the standard of care should not vary with the locale where an individual receives care. The conduct of health professionals and health care facilities will be increasingly compared with what is considered reasonable in the industry in view of current professional practice. It would be unreasonable for any one health care facility and/or health professional to set the standard simply because there is no local basis for comparison.

> [I]n regard to health care professionals, geographical proximity rules are increasingly giving way to a national standard, with the standard in the professional's general locality becoming simply a factor in determining whether the professional has exercised that degree of care expected of the average practitioner in the class to which he/she belongs.[10]

The ever-evolving advances in medicine, mass communications, availability of medical specialists, the development of continuing education programs, and the broadening scope of governmental regulations continue to raise the standard of care required of health professionals, nursing facilities, and hospitals.

The courts have been increasingly adopting the view that the practice of medicine should be national in scope. In *Dickinson v. Mailliard,* 175 N.W.2d 588 (Iowa 1970), the court stated

> Hospitals must now be licensed and accredited. They are subject to statutory regulation. In order to obtain approval they must meet certain standard requirements. . . . It is no longer justifiable, if indeed it ever was, to limit a hospital's liability to that degree of care which is customarily practiced in its own community. . . . [M]any communities have only one hospital. Adherence to such a rule, then, means the hospital whose conduct is assailed, is to be measured only by standards which it has set for itself.

Id. at 596.

The Court of Appeals of Maryland, in *Shilkret v. Annapolis Emergency Hospital Association,* 349 A.2d 245 (1975), stated

> [A] hospital is required to use that degree of care and skill which is expected of a reasonably competent hospital in the same or similar circumstances. As in cases brought against physicians, advances in the profession, availability of special facilities and specialists, together with all other relevant considerations, are to be taken into account.

Id.

Evidence of the standard of care applicable to professional activities may be found in several documents such as the regulations of governmental agencies and the standards established by such private organizations as the Joint Commission on Accreditation of Healthcare Organizations. The personnel of a health care facility, subject to such regulations or standards, are responsible for meeting the standards of care prescribed. A professional's failure to do so provides a basis for finding the professional and the facility liable for negligence.

Although the courts tend to favor a broader standard of care, the community standard can be extremely important in any given situation.

> Assume for a moment that the question is whether a doctor in a remote area of Alaska has placed patients at an unnecessarily high risk by receiving telephone inquiries from nurses in Eskimo villages

at even more remote areas and attempting to prescribe by phone. Clearly, such conduct would violate the standard of care in San Francisco, and in San Francisco, would place his patients in an "unnecessarily" high risk situation. For the doctor in Alaska, on the other hand, this method of consultation may be the only possible one, and thus not at all unnecessary or a gross and flagrant violation.[11]

The standard of care required of physicians was established for the first time in Michigan by statute.[12] The Michigan medical malpractice law holds general practitioners accountable for medical treatment that meets the recognized standard of care in the community in which they practice. In effect, the law also holds medical specialists accountable to the recognized standard of care within their specialty.

To prove a *prima facie* case of malpractice, the patient must produce expert testimony to establish the recognized standard of care attributable to physicians under like circumstances and that the physician whose conduct is being challenged departed from the requisite standard when he or she treated the patient. *Strain v. Ferroni,* 405 Pa. Super. 349, 592 A.2d 698 (1991). Generally, most states hold professionals and people with special skills (e.g., physicians, nurses, and dentists) to a standard of care that is reasonable in the light of their special abilities and knowledge.

The parents in *Wickliffe v. Sunrise Hospital,* 706 P.2d 1383 (Nev. 1985), sued the hospital for the wrongful death of their teenage daughter who suffered respiratory arrest while recovering from surgery. The Supreme Court of Nevada held that the level of care to which the hospital must conform is a nationwide standard. The hospital's level of care is no longer subject to narrow geographic limitations under the so-called locality rule; rather, the hospital must meet a nationwide standard.

Further, the Georgia Court of Appeals in *Hodges v. Effingham,* 182 Ga. App. 173, 355 S.E.2d 104 (1987), held that application of the locality rule, rather than a general standard of nursing care, was erroneous in an action against the hospital. The alleged failure of nurses to take an accurate medical history of the patient's serious condition and convey the information to the physician drew into question the professional judgment of the nurses, not the hospital's services or facilities. The jury should have been instructed as to the general standard of nursing required.

For liability to be established, based on a defendant's failure to follow the standard of care outlined by statute, the following elements must be present: (1) The defendant must have been within the specified class of persons outlined in the statute, (2) the plaintiff must have been injured in a way that the statute was designed to prevent, and (3) the plaintiff must show that the injury would not have occurred if the statute had not been violated.

There are no degrees of care in fixing responsibility for negligence, but the standard is always that care which a prudent person should use under like circumstances. The duty to exercise reasonable care is a standard designed to protect a society's members from unreasonable exposure to potentially injurious hazards; negligence is conduct that falls short of the reasonable care standard. Perfection of conduct is humanly impossible, however, and the law does not exact an unreasonable amount of care from anyone.[13]

Breach of Duty

Once the duty to care has been established, the plaintiff must show that the defendant breached that duty by failing to comply with the accepted standard of care required. Breach of duty is the failure to conform to or the departure from a required duty of care owed to a person. The obligation to perform according to a standard of care may encompass either doing or refraining from doing a particular act. Evidence of a breach of duty can be offered through direct testimony, circumstantial evidence, *res ipsa loquitur*, etc. The test of breach of duty relies on the reasonably prudent person doctrine: Did the defendant act reasonably under the circumstances?

A review of the *Hastings* case discussed above indicates a severe breach of duty where hospital regulations provide that when a physician cannot be reached or refuses a call, the chief of service is to be notified so that another physician can be obtained. This was not done. It is not necessary to prove that a patient would survive if proper treatment had been administered but only that the patient would have had a chance of survival. As a result of Dr. Gerdes' failure to obtain another physician and Dr. McCool's failure to perform the necessary surgery, the patient had no chance of survival.

Injury/Actual Damages

A defendant may be negligent and still not incur liability if no injury or actual damages result to the plaintiff. The presence of damages is essential for a malpractice case because the purpose of legal redress is to obtain some compensation for damages suffered. The term *injury* includes more than physical harm. Without harm or injury, there is no liability. Injury is not limited to physical harm but includes loss of income or reputation and compensation for pain and suffering.

The occurrence of an injury, standing alone, does not establish negligence for which the law imposes liability, since the injury may be the result of an unavoidable accident, or an act of God, or some cause so remote to the person sought to be held liable for negligence that he cannot be charged with responsibility for the injury. As it has been said, rules of law and parameters for conduct cannot be premised on mere possibility.[14]

Proximate Cause/Causation

There must be a reasonable, close, and causal connection or relationship between the defendant's negligent conduct and the resulting damages suffered by the plaintiff. The defendant's negligence must be a substantial factor causing the injury. *Proximate cause* is a term referring to the relationship between a breached duty and the injury. The breach of duty must be the proximate cause of the resulting injury. The mere departure from a proper and recognized procedure is not sufficient to enable a patient to recover damages unless the plaintiff can show that the departure was unreasonable and the proximate cause of the patient's injuries.

Causation in the *Hastings* case was well established. In the ordinary course of events, a man or woman does not bleed to death in a hospital emergency department over a two-and-one-half-hour period without some surgical intervention to save his or her life.

In *Northern Trust Co. v. Louis A. Weiss Memorial Hospital,* 493 N.E.2d 6 (Ill. App. Ct. 1986), causation was established by expert testimony that the delay in notification of the attending physicians of a newborn's condition had increased the likelihood of permanent damage and that adequate medical treatment had not been instituted after respiratory distress was detected. The record supported a judgment awarding $1.5 million in damages for negligent postnatal care. In *Gooden v. Tips,* 651 S.W.2d 364 (Tex. Ct. App. 1983), the plaintiff's petition alleged that the physician was negligent in failing to warn his patient not to drive an automobile while under the influence of the drug Quaalude and that this was a proximate cause of the personal injuries sustained by one plaintiff when struck by a car driven by the patient. The court of appeals held this was sufficient to state a cause of action against the physician. The decision of the district court, granting judgment for the physician, was reversed, and the case was remanded for determination.

> The primary wrong upon which a cause of action for negligence is based consists in the breach of a duty on the part of one person to protect another against injury, the proximate result of which is an injury to the person to whom the duty is owed. These elements of duty, breach, and injury are essentials of actionable negligence, and in fact most judicial definitions of the term 'negligence' or 'actionable negligence' are couched in those terms. In the absence of any one of them, no cause of action for negligence will lie.[15]

Foreseeability. Foreseeability is the reasonable anticipation that harm or injury is likely to result from an act or an omission to act. The test for foreseeability is whether anyone of ordinary prudence and intelligence should have anticipated the danger to others caused by his or her negligence. *Clark v. Wagoner*, 452 S.W.2d 437, 440 (Tex. 1970). "The test is not what the wrongdoer believed would occur; it is whether he ought reasonably to have foreseen that the event in question, or some similar event would occur." *Id.* at 440.

If the action of a defendant meets or surpasses the recognized standard of care and injury results, there has been no negligence or carelessness—just an unavoidable accident. There is no expectation that the actor can guard against events that cannot reasonably be foreseen or that are so unlikely to occur that they would be disregarded. For example, in *Haynes v. Hoffman,* 164 Ga. App. 236, 238(3), 296 S.E.2d 216 (1982), the plaintiff had brought a medical malpractice action against the defendant physician for his alleged negligence in prescribing a medication to which the plaintiff suffered an allergic reaction. The trial court returned a verdict in favor of the defendant, and the plaintiff appealed. The evidence at trial had revealed that the plaintiff had not disclosed her history of allergies to the physician. The physician testified that, at the time of the physical examination of the plaintiff, she denied having any allergies. The physician testified that he would not have prescribed the drug had he known the plaintiff's complete history. By failing to disclose her allergies to the physician, the plaintiff was contributorily negligent. "Foreseeability" involves guarding against that which is probable and likely to happen, not against that which is only remotely and slightly possible.

If a defendant's actions fail to meet the standard of care, there has been negligence, and the jury must make two determinations. First, was it foreseeable that harm would occur from the failure to meet the standard of care? Second, was the carelessness or negligence the proximate or immediate cause of the harm or injury to the plaintiff? "The broad test of negligence is what a reasonably prudent person would foresee and would do in the light of this foresight under the circumstances."[16]

The question of foreseeability was an issue in *Ferguson v. Dr. McCarthy's Rest Home,* 335 Mass. 733, 142 N.E.2d 337 (1957). The plaintiff, a resident in the defendant's nursing facility, suffered from paralysis of the left side but was able to roll toward the left side in bed. The defendant had knowledge of this ability. A radiator, which was approximately the same height as the bed, was next to the plaintiff's bed on the left side. During the night, the plaintiff's left foot came in contact with the radiator and she suffered third-degree burns. She had been placed too close to the left side of the bed in an effort to prevent her from rolling out of the bed, which had not been equipped properly with bed rails. The court held that this type of accident was "foreseeable" with respect to a person in the plaintiff's condition, particularly because the defendant had knowledge of the plaintiff's condition. The defendant should have shielded the radiator or not placed the plaintiff next to it.

Summary Case

All the elements necessary to establish negligence were well established in *Niles v. City of San Rafael,* 42 Cal. App. 3d 230, 116 Cal. Rptr. 733 (1974). On June 26, 1973, at approximately 3:30 P.M., a young boy got into an argument with another boy on the ball field and was hit on the right side of his head. He rode home on his bicycle and waited for his father who was to pick him up for the weekend. At approximately 5:00 P.M., his father arrived to pick him up. By the time they arrived in San Francisco, the son appeared to be in a great deal of pain. His father then decided to take him to Mount Zion Hospital, which was a short distance away. He arrived at the hospital emergency department at approximately 5:45 P.M. On admission to the emergency department, the boy was taken to a treatment room by a registered nurse. The nurse obtained a history of the injury and took the patient's pulse and blood pressure. During his stay in the emergency department, the young boy was irritable, vomited several times, and complained that his head hurt. An intern who had seen the patient wrote "pale, diaphoretic, and groggy" on the patient's chart. Skull x-rays were ordered and found to be negative except for soft tissue swelling that was not noted until later. The intern then decided to admit the patient. A second-year resident was called, and he agreed with the intern's decision. The intern was called later by an admitting clerk who indicated that the patient had to be admitted by a private attending physician. The resident went as far as to write "admit" on the chart and later crossed it out. A pediatrician who was in the emergency department at the time was asked to look at the patient. The pediatrician was also the paid director of the Mount Zion Pediatric Out-Patient Clinic. The pediatrician asked the patient a few questions and then decided to send him home. The physician could not recall what instructions he gave the patient's father, but he did give the father his business card. The pediatrician could not recall giving the father a copy of *Head Injury Instructions*, an information sheet that had been prepared for distribution to patients with head injuries. The sheet explained that an individual should be returned to the emergency department should any of the following signs appear:

- a large, soft lump on the head
- unusual drowsiness (cannot be awakened)
- forceful or repeated vomiting
- a fit or convulsion (jerking or spells)

- clumsy walking
- bad headache
- one pupil larger than the other

The patient was taken back to his father's apartment at about 7:00 P.M. A psychiatrist friend dropped by at approximately 8:45 P.M. He examined the patient and noted that one pupil was larger than the other. Because the pediatrician could not be reached, the patient was taken back to the emergency department. A physician on duty noted an epidural hematoma during his examination and ordered that a neurosurgeon be called.

Today, the patient can move only his eyes and neck. A lawsuit against Mount Zion and the pediatrician for $5 million was instituted. The city of San Rafael and the public school district also were included in the lawsuit as defendants. Expert testimony by two neurosurgeons during the trial indicated that the patient's chances of recovery would have been very good if he had been admitted promptly. This testimony placed the proximate cause of the injury with the hospital. The final judgment was $4 million against the medical defendants, $2.5 million for compensatory damages, and another $1.5 million for pain and suffering. The pediatrician's insurance carrier paid $100,000, and the hospital's insurance carrier paid the balance. The school district was liable for $25,000.

Case Lessons

Each case presented in this text illustrates real-life experiences of plaintiffs and defendants. It is anticipated that the reader will learn from these experiences and apply them to real-life situations. The many lessons in this particular case include

- A physician must conduct a thorough and responsible examination and order the appropriate tests for each patient
- A hospital must ensure that adequate patient care is rendered in the facility
- A patient's vital signs should be monitored closely and documented in the medical record
- Corrective measures must be taken when a patient's medical condition signals a medical problem
- A complete review of a patient's medical record must be accomplished before discharging a patient from the hospital. Review of the record must include review of test results, nurses' notes, residents' and interns' notes, and the notes of any other physician or consultant who may have attended the patient
- An erroneous diagnosis leading to the premature dismissal of a case can result in liability for both the hospital and physician

INTENTIONAL TORTS

Assault and Battery

It has long been recognized by law that a person possesses a right to be free from aggression and the threat of actual aggression against one's person. The right to expect others to respect the integrity of one's body has roots in both common and statutory law. The distinguishing feature between assault and battery is that assault effectuates an infringement on the mental security or tranquility of another whereas battery constitutes a violation of another's physical integrity.

Assault

An assault is the deliberate threat, coupled with the apparent present ability, to do physical harm to another. No actual contact is necessary. It is the deliberate threat or attempt to injure another or the attempt by one to make bodily contact with another without his or her consent. To commit the tort of assault, two conditions must exist. First, the person attempting to touch another unlawfully must possess the apparent present ability to commit the battery; and second, the person threatened must be aware of or have actual knowledge of an immediate threat of a battery and must fear it.

Battery

A battery is an intentional touching of another's person, in a socially impermissible manner, without that person's consent. It is intentional conduct that violates the physical security of another. An act that otherwise would be considered to be an assault may be permissible if proper consent has been given or if it is in defense of oneself or of a third party. The receiver of the battery does not have to be aware that a battery has been committed (e.g., a patient who is unconscious and has surgery performed on him or her without his or her consent, either expressed or implied, is the object of a battery). The unwanted touching may give rise to a cause of action for any injuries brought about by the touching.

The law provides a remedy to the individual if consent to a touching has not been obtained or if the act goes beyond the consent given. Therefore, the injured person may initiate a lawsuit against the wrongdoer for damages suffered. Punitive damages in *Peete v. Blackwell,* 504 So.2d 22 (Ala. 1986), in the amount of $10,000 were awarded to a nurse in her action against a physician for assault and battery. Evidence showed that the physician struck the assisting nurse on the arm and cursed at her when the physician ordered her to turn on the suction. Although there were no injuries, $1 in compensatory damages and $10,000 in punitive damages were awarded by the jury.

In the health context, the principle of law concerning battery and the requirement of consent to medical and surgical procedures is critically important. Liability for acts of battery is most common in situations involving lack of or improper consent to medical procedures. Liability of hospitals and health care professionals for acts of battery is most common in situations involving lack of or improper patient consent to medical and surgical procedures. It is inevitable that a patient in a hospital will be touched by many persons for many reasons. Procedures ranging from bathing to surgery involve some touching of a patient. Therefore, medical and surgical procedures must be authorized by the patient. If they are not authorized, the person performing the procedure could be subject to an action for battery.

It is of no legal importance that a procedure constituting a battery has improved a patient's health. If the patient did not consent to the touching, the patient may be entitled to such damages as can be proved to have resulted from commission of the battery. The Supreme Court of New Jersey in *Perna v. Pirozzi,* 457 A.2d 431 (N.J. 1983), held that a patient who consents to surgery by one surgeon but who is actually operated on by another has an action for medical malpractice or battery. Proof of unauthorized invasion of the plaintiff's person, even if harmless, entitles him or her to nominal damages.

Not only must individual staff members be aware of potential assault and battery hazards by fellow employees, as well as themselves, but they also must be alert to potential problems between patients (e.g., problems caused by smoking, racial or religious bias, and emotional conflicts). A health care facility has a particular duty to supervise especially closely those patients whose mental condition makes it probable that they will injure themselves or others.

False Imprisonment

False imprisonment is the unlawful restraint of an individual's personal liberty or the unlawful restraining or confining of an individual. The personal right to move freely and without hindrance is basic to our legal system. Any intentional infringement on this right may constitute false imprisonment. Actual physical force is not necessary to constitute false imprisonment. All that is necessary is that an individual who is physically "confined" to a given area experience a reasonable fear that force, which may be implied by words, threats, or gestures, will be used to detain the individual or to intimidate him or her without legal justification. Excessive force used to restrain a patient may produce liability for both false imprisonment and battery.

In certain cases, preventing a patient from leaving a health care facility may constitute false imprisonment. For example, detaining a patient until the bills are paid would qualify as false imprisonment.

A patient's insistence on leaving should be noted on the medical record. The patient also should be informed of the possible harm in leaving against medical advice. If a patient ultimately decides to leave against medical advice, he or she should be requested to sign a discharge against advice and release form.

A patient does not actually have to be constrained to be falsely imprisoned. A threat of restraint that a patient may reasonably expect to be carried out may be enough to constitute false imprisonment. To recover for damages, a plaintiff must be aware of the confinement and have no reasonable means of escape. Availability of a reasonable means of escape may bar recovery. To lock a door when another is reasonably available to pass through is not imprisonment. However, if the only other door provides a way of escape that is dangerous, the law may consider it an unreasonable way of escape, and therefore, false imprisonment may be a cause of action. Whether false imprisonment has taken place will be a matter for the courts to decide. No actual damage need be shown for liability to be imposed.

Where legal justification is absent and an arrest or imprisonment is false, the person denied free movement will be permitted to seek a remedy at law for any injury. There are occasions and circumstances when a person must be confined, such as persons who may present a danger to themselves or others. In this example, the right to move about freely has been violated, but the infringement occurs for reasons justifiable under the law.

The plaintiff in *Celestine v. United States,* 841 F.2d 851 (8th Cir. 1988), brought an action alleging battery and false imprisonment because security guards had placed him in restraints. The plaintiff-appellant sought psychiatric care at a Veterans Administration (VA) hospital and became physically violent while waiting to be seen by a physician. The VA security guards found it necessary to place the individual in restraints until he could be examined by a psychiatrist. The U.S. Court of Appeals for the Eighth Circuit held that the record supported a finding that the hospital was justified in placing the patient under restraint. Under Missouri law, no false imprisonment or battery occurred in view of the common-law principle that a person believed to be mentally ill could be restrained lawfully if such was considered necessary to prevent immediate injury to that person or others.

Protocols should be instituted for handling patients diagnosed as having contracted a highly contagious disease. Detaining such patients, without statutory protection, constitutes false imprisonment. State health codes generally provide guidelines for caring for such patients. For example, title 10, part 2, section 29, of the New York State Sanitary Code states, "Whenever a case of a highly communicable disease . . . comes to the attention of the city, county, or district health officer, he shall isolate such patients as in his judgment he deems necessary." In addition, statutes in many states allow mentally ill and intoxicated individuals to be detained by a hospital if they are found to be dangerous to themselves or others. Those who are mentally ill, however, can be restrained only to the degree necessary to prevent them from harming themselves or others. If a mentally ill patient cannot be released, procedures should be followed to provide commitment to an appropriate institution for the patient's care.

The patient in *Davis v. Charter by the Sea,* 358 S.E.2d 865 (Ga. Ct. App. 1987), was found not to be entitled to a directed verdict on a false-imprisonment claim arising from her overnight, involuntary detention at a hospital. Evidence that the patient was highly intoxicated, confused, incoherent, and experiencing a low diastolic blood pressure raised a jury question as to the existence of a medical emergency that authorized her detention.

Restraints

Restraints generally are used to control behavior when patients are disoriented or may cause harm to themselves (e.g., from falling, contaminating wounds, or pulling out hypodermics) or to others. The use of restraints raises many questions of a patient's rights in the areas of autonomy, freedom of movement, and the accompanying health problems that can result from continued immobility. In general, a patient has a right to be free from any physical restraints imposed or psychoactive drugs administered for purposes of discipline or convenience and that are not required to treat a patient's medical symptoms.

Patient care plans should indicate an effort to find alternative treatments to the use of restraints. If there is no alternative, there should be documentation in the patient's medical record of no alternative to the use of restraints. Documentation should include

- the need for restraints
- consents for the application of restraints
- patient monitoring
- reappraisals of the continuing need for restraints on the patient's medical record

Defamation of Character

Defamation of character consists of oral or written communication to someone other than the person defamed that tends to hold that person's reputation up to scorn and ridicule in the eyes of a substantial number of respectable people in the community. Libel results from the written word, and slander is from the spoken word. Libel can be presented in signs, photographs, letters, cartoons, etc. To be an actionable wrong, defamation must be communicated to a third person. Defamatory statements communicated only to the injured party are not grounds for an action.

Defamation "on its face" is actionable without proof of special damages. In certain cases, a court will presume that the words caused injury to the person's reputation. There are four generally recognized exceptions where no proof of actual harm to reputation is required to recover damages: (1) accusing someone of a crime; (2) accusing someone of having a loathsome disease; (3) using words that affect a person's profession or business; and (4) calling a woman unchaste. Professionals are legally protected against libel when complying with a law that requires the reporting of venereal or other diseases, which could be considered loathsome.

Libel

A statement in a hospital newsletter regarding the discharge of a nursing supervisor constituted libel *per se* in *Kraus v. Brandsletter,* 562 N.Y.S.2d 127 (App. Div. 1990), in which the newsletter indicated that the hospital's medical board had discharged the nursing supervisor after a unanimous vote of no confidence. Couching the board's determination in terms of a vote gave the impression that the board's determination had been based on facts that justified the board's opinion. The statement tended to injure the nurse's reputation as a professional in that it did not refer to specifics of her performance but rather referred to her abilities as a professional in general. The reasonable interpretation of the statement in the newsletter was that the supervisor was incompetent in her professional capacity, thus giving rise to a cause of action for libel *per se*. An alleged statement that the physician said, "You nurses will receive your Christmas bonus early, your boss is going to get fired" (*Id.* at 129) was not slander *per se* in that it did not injure the nurse in her professional capacity. In addition, the statement that she was going to be fired was true.

A defendant nurse who was employed by a VA hospital was directed by her superior to submit a Report of Contact concerning a disagreement with the plaintiff nurse, who also was employed by the VA hospital. The defendant nurse was found to have been acting within the parameter of her duties in submitting such a report. The court held that the report could not be the basis for a cause of action in libel. Statements made by a federal officer in the course of disciplinary proceedings, evaluations, complaints, and related investigations that the official was under a duty to complete are within the scope of the official's duties. Therefore, such statements cannot be the basis for a cause of action in libel. *Malone v. Longo,* 463 F. Supp. 139 (E.D. N.Y. 1979).

A libel suit was brought against the Miami Herald Publishing Company more than two years after its publication of an editorial cartoon depicting a nursing facility in a distasteful manner. *Keller v. Miami Herald Publishing Co.,* 778 F.2d 711 (11th Cir. 1985). The cartoon was described in the following manner:

> On October 29, 1980, The Herald published an editorial cartoon which depicted three men in a dilapidated room. On the back wall was written "Krest View Nursing Home," and on the side wall there was a board which read "Closed by Order of the State of Florida." The room itself was in a state of total disrepair. There were holes in the floor and ceiling, leaking water pipes, and exposed wiring. The men in the room were dressed in outfits resembling those commonly appearing in caricatures of gangsters. Each man carried a sack with a dollar sign on it. One of the men was larger than the other two and was more in the forefront of the picture. One of the others addressed him. The caption read: "Don't Worry, Boss, We Can Always Reopen It As a Haunted House for the Kiddies."

Id. at 713.

The court held that the newspaper's editorial cartoon depicting persons resembling gangsters in a dilapidated building, identified as a particular nursing facility that had been closed by state order, was an expression of pure opinion and thus was protected by the First Amendment against the libel suit alleging that the cartoon defamed the owner of the facility.

The court in *Wisconsin Association of Nursing Homes,* 285 N.W.2d 891 (Wis. Ct. App. 1979), would not compel the newspapers to accept and print an advertisement in the exact form submitted by the Wisconsin Association of Nursing Homes and various individual homes.

> Plaintiffs allege in their complaint that the defendants published a series of "investigative reports" in the Milwaukee Journal which dealt with the quality of care and services in several nursing homes. Plaintiffs further characterized the conclusions of the article as being false and erroneous. As a result, the plaintiffs prepared a full page advertisement which purported to respond to, and refute the allegations set out in the above mentioned "reports." The defendant newspaper refused to publish the advertisement in the form presented, and referred the question of possibly libelous matter to the attention of plaintiffs' attorneys.

Id. at 893.

The court held that it was within the newspaper's journalistic discretion to reject the advertisement on the ground that it contained possibly libelous material. "[T]he clear weight of authority has not sanctioned any enforceable right of access to the press. In sum, a court can no more dictate what a privately owned newspaper can print than what it cannot print." *Id.* at 894.

Unlike broadcasting, the publication of a newspaper is not a government conferred privilege. As we have said, the press and the government have had a history of disassociation.

We can find nothing in the United States Constitution, any federal statute, or any controlling precedent that allows us to compel a private newspaper to publish advertisement without editorial control merely because such advertisements are not legally obscene or unlawful.[17]

The appellee in *Stevens v. Morris Communications Corp.,* 317 S.E.2d 652 (Ga. Ct. App. 1984), alleged that a newspaper article, which identified her as a representative of a convalescent center at a city council meeting, had defamed her by implying her responsibility for the convalescent center's problems of maintenance and disrepair. The court held that the appellee was not defamed by the article. Using the reasonable person test, the court found that it was highly unlikely that a reasonable person could have read the newspaper article as being defamatory.

Slander

There are few slander lawsuits because of the difficulty in proving defamation, the small awards, and the high legal fees.

The Georgia case of *Barry v. Baugh,* 111 Ga. App. 813, 143 S.E.2d 489 (1965), involved a nurse who brought a defamation action, charging that a physician had slandered her in the course of a consultation concerning the commitment of her husband to a mental institution. The nurse requested damages for mental pain, shock, fright, humiliation, and embarrassment. The nurse alleged that if the physician's statement were made known to the public, her job and reputation would be affected adversely. The court held that the physician's statement concerning the nurse did not constitute slander because the physician was not referring to the nurse in a professional capacity.

With slander, the person bringing suit generally must prove special damages; however, when any allegedly defamatory words refer to a person in a professional capacity, the professional need not show that the words caused damage. It is presumed that any slanderous reference to someone's professional capacity is damaging; the plaintiff therefore has no need to prove damages. In this case, however, because the court held that the physician's statement did not refer to the nurse in her professional capacity, the plaintiff had to demonstrate damages in order to recover. The plaintiff was unable to show damages.

Professionals who are called incompetent in front of others have a right to sue to defend their reputation. However, it is difficult to prove that an individual comment was injurious. If the person making an injurious comment cannot prove the comment is true, that person can be held liable for damages.

Therefore, health professionals should avoid making disparaging remarks about other health professionals.

An administrator's statements made to a physician's supervisor regarding the physician's alleged professional misconduct is not grounds for a defamation action so long as the statements are made in good faith. A hospital administrator has a duty to report complaints about alleged professional misconduct of physicians working in the hospital. The administrator has qualified privilege to report such complaints to the physician's supervisor and other hospital officials as necessary. *Miller-Douglas v. Keller,* 579 So.2d 491 (La. Ct. App. 4th Cir. 1991).

Defenses to a Defamation Action

Essentially, the two defenses to a defamation action are *truth* and *privilege.* When a person has said something that is damaging to another person's reputation, the person making the statement will not be liable for defamation if it can be shown that the statement was true. A privileged communication is one that might be defamatory under different circumstances but is not defamatory under the circumstances in which it was made because of a higher duty with which the person making the communication is charged. For example, many states have statutes providing immunity to doctors and health care institutions in connection with peer review proceedings. The person making the communication must do so in good faith, on the proper occasion, in the proper manner, and to persons who have a legitimate reason to receive the information.

There are two types of privilege that may provide a defense to an action for defamation. "Absolute privilege" attaches to statements made during judicial and legislative proceedings as well as to confidential communications between spouses. "Qualified privilege," however, which attaches to statements such as those made as a result of a legal or moral duty to speak in the interests of third persons, may provide a successful defense only when such statements are made in the absence of malice. If it can be shown that a statement was made as a result of some hatred, ill will, or spite on the part of the speaker, the law will not permit that speaker to hide behind the shield of privilege and avoid liability for defamation.

The defense of privilege is illustrated in the case of *Judge v. Rockford Memorial Hospital,* 17 Ill. App. 2d 365, 150 N.E.2d 202 (1958). There, a nurse brought an action for libel based on a letter written to a nurses' professional registry by the director of nurses at the hospital to which the nurse had been assigned by the registry. In the letter, the director of nurses stated that the hospital did not wish to have the nurse's services available to them because of certain losses of narcotics during times when this particular nurse was on duty. The court refused the nurse recovery. Because the director of nurses had a legal duty to make the communication in the interests of society, the director's letter constituted a privileged communication. Therefore, the court held that the letter did not constitute libel because it was privileged.

Public figures have more difficulty in pursuing defamation litigation than the average individual. One who occupies a position of considerable public responsibility is considered a public figure for the purposes of the law of defamation and is generally more vulnerable to public scrutiny. Legal action against a defendant generally will be denied in the absence of any showing of actual malice in connection with alleged defamatory references to a plaintiff. "Actual" malice applies only in cases involving public figures and encompasses knowledge of falsity or recklessness as to truth.

The chairman of a publicly owned and operated county hospital in *Drew v. KATV Television,* 293 Ark. 555, 739 S.W.2d 680 (1987), brought a suit against a television station for defamation on two separate occasions. It had been reported during one news broadcast that the board chairman had been charged with a felony when, in fact, he had been charged with two misdemeanor counts of solicitation to tamper with evidence. These charges were dismissed at trial. The second news report implied that he was involved in a drug investigation being conducted at the hospital where he served as chairman of the board. The plaintiff occupied a position of considerable public responsibility, and he was considered a public figure for the purposes of the law of defamation. The circuit court dismissed the case on the defendant's motion for summary judgment, and the plaintiff appealed. The Supreme Court of Arkansas held that summary dismissal of the plaintiff's action against the television station was properly ordered by the trial court in the absence of any showing of malice in connection with the allegedly defamatory references to the plaintiff during the news broadcasts.

Fraud

Fraud is defined as the willful and intentional misrepresentation that could cause harm or loss to a person or property. A health care professional who knows he or she has no foundation for believing a statement to be true and makes it anyway to the detriment of the patient can be held liable for fraud.

Invasion of Privacy

The right to privacy is implied in the Constitution, according to the Supreme Court. The right of privacy is recognized by the law as the right to be left alone—the right to be free from unwarranted publicity and exposure to public view, as well as the right to live one's life without having one's name, picture, or private affairs made public against one's will. Health care facilities and professionals may become liable for invasion of privacy if, for example, they divulge information from a patient's medical record to improper sources or if they commit unwarranted intrusions into a patient's personal affairs.

Patients have a right to personal privacy and a right to the confidentiality of their personal and clinical records. Invasion of privacy is a wrong that invades the right of a person to personal privacy. Absolute privacy has to be tempered with reality in the medical or nursing care of any patient, and this fact is recognized by the courts.

Disregard for a patient's right to privacy is legally actionable, particularly when patients are unable to protect themselves adequately because of unconsciousness or immobility. Unfortunately, familiarity with a health facility's environment tends to diminish the conscious concern that facility personnel should have for the protection of the privacy of patients. The plaintiff, a former hospital employee in *Vernuil v. Poirier,* 589 So.2d 1202 (La. Ct. App. 4th Cir. 1991), was awarded $15,000 in a legal action against her supervisor and hospital for invasion of privacy. The plaintiff claimed that while she was a patient and in the postoperative recovery room, her supervisor lifted her sheet in an attempt to view her abdominal incision. The court of appeals held that evidence sustained a finding of invasion of privacy. Because the supervisor's conduct occurred during the time and place of his employment, the hospital was jointly liable for damages. "Ensuring a patient's well being from all others, including staff, while the patient is helpless under the effects of anesthesia is part of its normal business." *Id.* at 1204.

The liberty extended to the publication of personal matters, names, or photographs varies. Many public figures will not be heard to complain if their lives are given publicity, and ordinary citizens who voluntarily adopt a newsworthy course of conduct have no grounds for complaint if the activity is reported along with their names and pictures. Generally, the subject of a newsworthy occurrence cannot complain if his or her identity is exposed and exploited by unwarranted publication.

The news media should be accommodated within the limitations placed on such communications by the administration of the hospital and applicable statutes and/or regulations pertaining to the release of information. In any event, a patient's right of privacy must be protected. Public relations officers and other health care professionals should restrict their interviews and news releases to avoid any injury to the reputation of a patient.

The press should not be given detailed statements about the physical condition of a patient. Health care professionals are in no position to make any comments concerning the occurrence that led to a patient's hospitalization. Comments concerning a patient's physical condition should come from the physician. Because such matters do involve protected information, disclosure should be with the patient's permission.

Intentional Infliction of Mental Distress

The intentional or reckless infliction of mental distress is characterized by conduct that is so outrageous that it goes beyond the bounds tolerated by a decent society. It is a civil wrong for which a tort-feasor can be held liable for damages. Mental distress includes mental suffering resulting from painful emotions such as grief, public humiliation, despair, shame, and wounded pride. Liability for the wrongful infliction of mental distress may be based on either intentional or negligent misconduct. A plaintiff may recover damages if he or she can show that the defendant intended to inflict mental distress, and knew or should have known that his or her actions would give rise to it. Recovery generally is permitted even in the absence of physical harm.

The circuit court in *Johnson v. Women's Hospital,* 527 S.W.2d 133 (Tenn. Ct. App. 1975), found that the intentional infliction of emotional distress was committed by a physician and hospital through certain of its employees. The mother of a premature infant who died shortly after birth had gone to her physician for a six-week check-up. She noticed a report in her medical chart that stated that the child was past the fifth lunar month in development and that hospital rules and state law prohibited disposal of it as a surgical specimen. The mother had understood that the body had been disposed of by common traditions of human dignity. On questioning her physician, he requested that his nurse take her to the hospital. At the hospital, she was taken by a hospital employee to a freezer, which was opened, and she was handed the jar containing her premature infant. The circuit court entered a judgment in favor of the plaintiffs, and the defendants appealed. The court of appeals held that the jury could properly find that the hospital agreed to handle the infant's body properly and failed to do so. The jury could properly find that the hospital's conduct in displaying the infant was outrageous. There was no proof that the physician or his nurse was guilty of outrageous conduct. The award of compensatory damages in the amount of $100,000 was not so excessive as to shock the conscience of the court.

An action, in *Greer v. Medders,* 336 S.E.2d 329 (1985), was brought by a patient and his wife against a physician for the intentional infliction of emotional distress. The superior court entered summary judgment for the physician, and the plaintiff appealed. The defendant physician was covering for the attending physician who was on vacation. The patient, Mr. Greer, was in the hospital and had not seen the covering physician for several days, so he called the physician's office to complain. The physician later entered the patient's room, in an agitated manner, and became verbally abusive in the presence of Mrs. Greer and a nurse. He said to the patient, "Let me tell you one damn thing, don't nobody call over to my office raising hell with my secretary . . . I don't have to be here every damn day checking on you because I check with physical therapy . . . I don't have to be your damn doctor." *Id.* at 329. When the physician left the room, Mrs. Greer began to cry, and Mr. Greer experienced episodes of uncontrollable shaking for which he had psychiatric treatment. The Court of Appeals of Georgia held that the physician's abusive language willfully caused emotional upset and precluded summary judgment for the defendant.

PRODUCTS LIABILITY

Products liability is the liability of a manufacturer, seller, or supplier of chattels to a buyer or other third party for injuries sustained because of a defect in a product. An injured party may proceed with a lawsuit against a seller, manufacturer, or supplier on three legal theories: negligence, breach of warranty (express or implied), and strict liability.

Negligence

Negligence, as applied to products liability, requires the plaintiff to establish duty, breach, injury, and causation. The manufacturer of a product is not liable for injuries suffered by a patient if they are the result of negligent use by the user. Product users must conform to the safety standards provided by the manufacturers of supplies and equipment. Failure to follow proper safety instructions can prevent recovery in a negligence suit if injury results from improper use.

Manufacturers are liable for injuries that result from the unsafe design of their products. To reduce the risks of liability, they generally provide detailed safety instructions to the users of their products. It can be assumed that failure to provide such instructions could be considered negligence on the part of the manufacturer.

An action in *Airco v. Simmons National Bank, Guardian, et al.,* 638 S.W.2d 660 (Ark. 1982), was brought against a physician partnership that provided anesthesia services to the hospital and Airco, Inc., the manufacturer of an artificial breathing machine used in the administration of anesthesia. It was alleged that the patient suffered irreversible brain damage because of the negligent use of the equipment and its unsafe design. The machine had been marketed despite prior reports that there was a foreseeable danger of human error brought about by the presence of several identical black hoses and the necessity of connecting them correctly to three ports of identical size that had been placed too close together and lacked adequate labels and warnings. The jury awarded $1,070,000 in compensatory damages against the physician partnership and Airco, Inc. Punitive damages in the amount of $3 million were awarded against Airco, Inc. On appeal of the punitive damages award, the Supreme Court of Arkansas held that the evidence for punitive damages was sufficient for the jury. The manufacturer had acted in a persistent reckless disregard of the foreseeable dangers in the machine by continuing to sell it with the known hazardous design.

Negligence, as well as breach of warranty and strict liability, was not established in the well-publicized case of the 1980s involving a woman who had died from the ingestion of Tylenol capsules tainted with potassium cyanide. The decedent's estate in *Elsroth v. Johnson & Johnson,* 700 F. Supp. 151 (S.D.N.Y. 1988), sued the manufacturer and the retail grocery store, which sold the over-the-counter drug. The defendants moved for a summary judgment. The U.S. district court held that the retailer did not have a "duty" to protect the decedent from acts of tampering by an unknown third party. The manufacturer was not liable under an inadequate warning theory. Manufacturers are under a duty to warn of the dangers that may be associated with the normal and lawful use of their products. They, however, need not warn that their products may be susceptible to criminal misuse.

The negligent use of a Bovie plate led to liability in *Monk v. Doctors Hospital,* 403 F.2d 580 (D.C. Cir. 1968). The patient was admitted to the hospital for abdominal surgery. Before surgery the patient asked the surgeon also to remove three moles from the right arm and one from the right leg. The surgeon instructed a hospital nurse to prepare a Bovie machine but was not present while the machine was set up. The nurse placed the contact plate of the Bovie machine under the patient's right calf in a negligent manner, and the patient suffered burns. The patient introduced instruction manuals, issued by the manufacturer, supporting a claim that the plate was placed improperly. These manuals had been available to the hospital. The trial court directed a verdict in favor of the hospital and the physician. The appellate court found that there was sufficient evidence from which the jury could conclude that the Bovie plate was applied in a negligent manner. There also was sufficient evidence, including the manufacturer's manual and expert testimony, from which the jury could find that the physician was independently negligent.

This case demonstrates the necessity for a hospital to require conformity to the safety standards provided by the manufacturers of hospital supplies and equipment. As evidenced in the above case, such failure can cause a hospital and its staff to be held liable for negligence. This case also should alert manufacturers of the necessity to provide appropriate safety instructions to the users of their products. It can be assumed that failure to provide such instructions could be considered negligence on the part of the supplier.

Failure of a physician to warn his or her patient of the potential side effects of a particular drug, of which the physician is aware, will result in liability on the part of the physician, not the drug manufacturer, for injuries suffered by the patient. The drug manufacturer's failure to warn was not the proximate cause of the patient's injury in *Garside v. Osco Drug,* 764 F. Supp. 208 (D. Mass. 1991). It was the physician who had the duty to pass on the information and failed to do so. The physician's failure to pass on the information was an intervening superseding cause.

Breach of Warranty

To recover under a cause of action based on a breach of warranty theory, the plaintiff must establish first whether there was an express or implied warranty.

Express Warranty

An express warranty includes specific promises or affirmations made by the seller to the buyer, such as that expressed in *Crocker v. Winthrop Laboratories,* 514 S.W.2d 429 (Tex. 1974). The patient, Mr. Crocker, had been admitted to the hospital for a hernia operation. His physician prescribed both Demerol and Talwin for pain. After discharge from the hospital, Mr. Crocker developed an addiction to Talwin and was able to obtain prescriptions from several physicians to support his habit. He was eventually admitted to the hospital for detoxification. After six days, Mr. Crocker walked out of the hospital and went home. He became agitated and abusive, threatening his wife, and she eventually called a physician at his request. The physician went to Mr. Crocker's home and gave him an injection of Demerol. Mr. Crocker retired to bed and died. Action was brought against the drug company for the suffering and subsequent wrongful death that occurred as the proximate result of the decedent's addiction to Talwin. The district court rendered a judgment for the plaintiff, and the court of appeals reversed. On further appeal, the Supreme Court of Texas held that when a drug company positively and specifically represents its product to be free and safe from all dangers of addiction and when the treating physician relies on such representation, the drug company is liable when the representation proves to be false and injury results.

A blow to the cigarette industry occurred recently when the U.S. Supreme Court in *Cipollone v. Liggett Group, Inc., et. al.,* 1992 WL 138529 (U.S.), held that the 1965 Federal Cigarette Labeling and Advertising Act

> did not pre-empt state law damages actions; the 1969 Act pre-empts petitioner's claims based on a failure to warn and the neutralization of

federally mandated warnings to the extent that those claims rely on omissions or inclusions in respondeats' advertising or promotions; the 1969 Act does not pre-empt petitioner's claim based on express warranty, intentional fraud and misrepresentation, or conspiracy.

Id. at 15.

Implied Warranty

Implied warranties are in effect when the law implies that one exists by operation of law as a matter of "public policy" for the protection of the public. *Jacob E. Decker & Sons v. Capps,* 139 Tex. 609, 164 S.W.2d 828 (1942). This case involved the question of the liability of a manufacturer of food products to the consumer for damages sustained by ingestion of contaminated sausage. One member of the family died, and others became seriously ill as a result of eating the contaminated food. The jury found that the sausage had been contaminated before it was packaged by the defendant and that it was unfit for human consumption. The Supreme Court of Texas decided that the defendant was liable for the injuries sustained by the consumers of the contaminated food under an implied warranty. Liability in such a case is based neither on negligence nor on a breach of the usual implied contractual warranty. It is based on the broad principle of the public policy to protect human health and life.

The patient in *Perlmutter v. Beth David Hospital,* 308 N.Y. 100, 123 N.E.2d 793 (1955), contracted serum hepatitis from a blood transfusion and relied on an implied sales warranty as the basis of her suit. The court denied recovery, pointing out that even though a separate charge of $60 was made for the blood, the charge was incidental to the primary contract with the hospital for services. Because there was no claim of negligence, the pronouncement of the court that blood provided by the hospital was a service, rather than a sale, barred recovery by the patient. The rationale of this case did not extend to relieve commercial blood banks from liability on the basis of strict liability warranty theories. Action could have been instituted against the hospital if it had been shown that the hospital was negligent in handling the blood.

Strict Liability

Strict liability refers to liability without fault. Neither care nor negligence nor ignorance will save the defendant from liability. Strict liability makes possible an award of damages without any proof of negligence on the part of the manufacturer. The plaintiff needs only to show that he or she suffered injury while using the manufacturer's product in the prescribed way.

The following elements must all be present for a plaintiff to proceed with a case on the basis of strict liability:

- The product must have been manufactured by the defendant
- The product must have been defective at the time it left the hands of the manufacturer or seller. A defect in a product normally consists of a manufacturing defect, a design defect in the product, and/or an absence or inadequacy of warnings for the use of the product
- The plaintiff must have been injured by a specific product
- The defective product must have been the proximate cause of injury to the plaintiff

A blood bank in *Weber v. Charity Hospital of Louisiana at New Orleans,* 487 So.2d 148 (La. Ct. App. 1986), was held strictly liable to a hospital patient who developed hepatitis from a transfusion of defective blood during surgery. Evidence established that the blood bank collected, processed, and sold the blood to the hospital. Although the hospital administered the blood, absent any negligence in its handling or administration it was not liable for the patient's injury. Many states have enacted statutes to exempt blood from the product category and thus remove blood products from the theory of strict liability.

In *Mulligan v. Lederle Laboratories,* 786 F.2d 859 (8th Cir. 1986), the plaintiff, a medical laboratory technician, brought an action against the drug manufacturer as the result of the side effects of the drug Varidase. The plaintiff developed several chronic health problems including mouth sores, microscopic hematuria, and red cell cast, indicating kidney disease. The U.S. District Court for the Eastern District of Arkansas awarded $50,000 in compensatory damages and $100,000 in punitive damages for failure of the drug manufacturer to warn of the side effects of the drug Varidase. On appeal by the manufacturer, the court of appeals held that the products liability action was not barred by a three-year statute of limitations contained in an Arkansas products liability act and that the evidence was sufficient to award punitive damages. Evidence presented at trial indicated that several side effects were associated with the drug.

Strict liability may be imposed on the manufacturer of a device that causes injury to a plaintiff, even though he or she was not the purchaser of the device, if the product was defective and that defect was the actual and proximate cause of his or her injury or damages. A case in point is *Kimberly Gerringer v. Gordon A. Runnells,* (Cal., Sacramento City Super. Ct. Nov. 13, 1973), in which a seven-year-old child suffered permanent brain damage as a result of convulsions caused by the leaking of an intravascular dose of a local anesthetic, Xylocaine, beyond the cuff (a medical device, similar to a blood pressure cuff, used to control the flow of blood). This leaking was allegedly a hazard of the procedure about which the manufacturer failed to notify the medical public. Damages awarded against the manufacturer of the automatic cuff amounted to $30,000.

Liability also may be based on the concept of *res ipsa loquitur* ("the thing speaks for itself") by showing all the following:

- The product did not perform in the way intended
- The product was not tampered with by the buyer or third persons
- The defect existed at the time it left the defendant manufacturer

Products Liability Defenses

Defenses against recovery in a products liability case include

- *contributory negligence* (e.g., use of a product in a way that it was not intended to be used)
- *assumption of the risk* (e.g., voluntary exposure to such risks as radiation treatments and chemotherapy treatments)
- *intervening cause* (e.g., an intravenous solution contaminated by the negligence of the product user, rather than that of the manufacturer)
- *disclaimers* (e.g., manufacturers' inserts and warnings regarding usage and contraindications of their products)

CONCLUSION

Successful products liability cases tend to have a negative impact on the development and use of new drugs. In addition, manufacturers tend to remove older technologies from the marketplace to decrease their exposure to liability and potential financial risks.

On the positive side, the slipshod manufacture of products is discouraged. This is increasingly evident in the sale of food products where consumers are demanding full disclosure of the contents of packaged products.

NOTES

1. The Robert Wood Johnson Research Foundation, *The Tort System for Medical Malpractice: How Well Does It Work, What Are the Alternatives?*, ABRIDGE, Spring 1991, at 2.

2. *Id.*

3. Turner W. Branch, *The Rise of Hedonic Damages and the Fall of Punitive Damages*, TRIAL DIPL. J., March/April, 1992, at 95.

4. Murphy v. Allstate Ins. Co., 295 So.2d 29, 34–35 (La. Ct. App. 1974).

5. 57A Am. Jur. 2d §199 (1989).

6. 57A Am. Jur. 2d §208 (1989).

7. 57A Am. Jur. 2d §143 (1989).

8. 57A Am. Jur. 2d §148 (1989).

9. 57A Am. Jur. 2d §193 (1989).

10. *Id.*

11. Greene v. Bowen, 639 F. Supp. 544, 561 (E.D. Cal. 1986).

12. HOSP. WEEK, January 6, 1978, at 1.

13. 57A Am. Jur. 2d §26 (1989).

14. 57A Am. Jur. 2d §78 (1989).

15. 57A Am. Jur. 2d §80 (1989).

16. 57A Am. Jur. 2d §134 (1989).

17. Associates & Aldrich Co. v. Times Mirror Co., 440 F.2d 133, 136 (9th Cir. 1971).

Chapter **3**

Criminal Aspects of Health Care

Laws are made to restrain and punish the wicked; the wise and good do not need them as a guide, but only as a shield against rapine and oppression; they can live civily and orderly, though there were no law in the world.

John Milton (1608–1674)

OUTLINE

Criminal law is society's expression of the limits of acceptable human and institutional behavior. A crime is any social harm defined and made punishable by law.[1] The objectives of criminal law are to maintain public order and safety, protect the individual, use punishment as a deterrent to crime, and rehabilitate the criminal for return to society.

Crimes generally are classified as misdemeanors or felonies. The difference between a misdemeanor and a felony revolves around the severity of the crime. A *misdemeanor* is an offense punishable by less than one year in jail and/or a fine (e.g., petty larceny and driving while intoxicated). A *felony* is a much more serious crime, generally punishable by imprisonment in a state or federal penitentiary for more than one year (e.g., rape, murder).

Peculiar to hospitals, nursing facilities, and psychiatric institutions is that patients are helpless and at the mercy of others. Health care facilities are far too often places where the morally weak and mentally deficient prey on the physically and sometimes mentally helpless. The very institutions designed to make you well and feel safe can provide the setting for criminal conduct.

This chapter presents the procedural aspects of criminal law, as well as several criminal cases that have occurred in the health care industry. The cases reviewed are by no means exhaustive for a particular health care institution or profession. The purpose of this chapter is to provide students and health care professionals with an elementary review of the criminal law as it applies to health care.

ARREST

Prosecutions for crimes generally begin with the arrest of a defendant by a police officer or with the filing of a formal action in a court of law and the issuance of an arrest warrant or summons. On arrest, the defendant is taken to the appropriate law enforcement agency for processing, which includes paperwork and finger printing. Accusatory statements, such as misdemeanor complaints and felony complaints, also are prepared by the police. Detectives are assigned to cases when necessary to gather evidence, interview persons suspected of committing a crime and witnesses to a crime, and assist in preparing a case for possible trial. After processing has been completed, a person is either detained or released on bond.

A felony complaint commences a criminal proceeding; however, an individual may be tried for a felony after indictment by a grand jury unless the defendant waives presentment to the grand jury and pleads guilty by way of a superior court information. Felony cases are presented to a grand jury by a district attorney or an assistant district attorney. The grand jury is presented with the prosecution's evidence and then charged that they may indict the target if they find reasonable cause to believe from the evidence presented to them that all the elements of a particular crime are present. The grand jury may request that witnesses be subpoenaed to testify. A defendant may choose to testify and offer information if he or she wishes. Actions of a grand jury are handed up to a judge, after which the defendant will be notified to appear to be arraigned for the crimes charged in the indictment.

ARRAIGNMENT

The arraignment is a formal reading of the accusatory instrument and includes the setting of bail. The accused should appear with counsel or have counsel appointed by the court if he or she cannot afford his or her own. After the charges are read, the defendant pleads guilty or not guilty. A not guilty plea is normally offered on a felony. On a plea of not guilty, arrangements are made by the defense attorney and the prosecutor regarding bail. After arraignment of the defendant, the judge will set a date for the defendant to return to court.

Between the time of arraignment and the next court date, the defense attorney and the prosecutor confer about the charges and evidence in the possession of the prosecutor. At that time, the defense will offer any mitigating circumstances it believes will cause the prosecutor to lessen or drop the charges.

CONFERENCE

Both felony and misdemeanor cases are taken to conference, and plea bargaining commences with the goal of an agreed-on disposition. If no disposition can be reached, the case is adjourned, motions are made, and further plea bargaining takes place. Generally after several adjournments, a case is assigned to a trial court.

THE PROSECUTOR

The role of the prosecutor in the criminal justice system is well defined in *Berger v. United States,* 295 U.S. 88 (1935).

> The United States Attorney is the representative not of an ordinary party to a controversy, but of a sovereignty whose obligation to govern impartially is compelling as its obligation to govern at all; and whose interest, therefore, in a criminal prosecution is not that it shall win a case, but that justice will be done. As such, he is in a peculiar and very definite sense the servant of the law, the twofold aim of which is that guilt shall not escape or innocence suffer.

The potential of the prosecutor's office is not always fully realized in many jurisdictions. In many cities the combination of the prosecutor's staggering caseload and small staff of assistants prevents sufficient attention being given to each case.[2]

THE DEFENSE ATTORNEY

The defense attorney generally sits in the proverbial hot seat, being perceived as the "bad guy." Although everyone seems to understand the attorney's function in protecting the rights of those represented, the defense attorney is often not very popular.

> There is a substantial difference in the problem of representing the "run-of-the-mill" criminal defendant and one whose alleged crimes

have aroused great public outcry. The difficulties in providing representation for the ordinary criminal defendant are simple compared with the difficulties of obtaining counsel for one who is charged with a crime which by its nature or circumstances incites strong public condemnation.[3]

THE CRIMINAL TRIAL

The processes of a criminal trial are similar to that of a civil trial and include jury selection, opening statements, presentation of witnesses and other evidence, summations, instructions to the jury by the judge, jury deliberations, verdict, and opportunity for appeal to a higher court. A criminal trial generally is conducted in the following manner:

- Jurors are selected
- Jury is sworn
- Prosecutor (representing the people) opens
- Defense attorney opens (optional)
- Prosecutor calls witnesses
- Defense attorney cross-examines
- Defense attorney calls witnesses
- Prosecutor cross-examines
- Defense attorney sums up
- Prosecutor sums up
- Judge charges the jury by explaining the legal aspects of the case
- Jury deliberates and returns a verdict
- Appeals go to a higher court

Many areas of criminal law can have an impact on health care employees. The following paragraphs discuss some of the more common areas where health care employees have been confronted with criminal charges.

DRUGS

Drug abuse has been described as the number one problem facing the United States today. It is no surprise that health care facilities and health professionals are affected by the theft of drugs, drug abuse, and the illegal sale of drugs.

There appears to be no end to the stream of cases entering the nation's court-rooms.

The ophthalmologist in *Bouquett v. St. Elizabeth's Corp.,* 538 N.E.2d 113 (Ohio 1989), brought an action to challenge suspension of his medical staff privileges after a felony conviction in a federal court for conspiracy to distribute Dilaudid. He later was sentenced to five years of incarceration. The court of common pleas upheld the hospital's summary suspension, and the court of appeals upheld in part and remanded in part. On further appeal, the supreme court held that the conviction of the ophthalmologist justified summary suspension of his staff privileges pursuant to a hospital bylaw permitting summary suspension in the best interest of patient care in the hospital. Hospital boards of trustees of private hospitals have broad discretion in determining who shall be granted medical staff privileges. Unless a hospital has been arbitrary and capricious or has abused its discretion, the courts generally will not interfere with a hospital's decision to suspend physicians convicted on drug-related felony charges. Summary suspension of a physician extends beyond technical skills and medical competence. It encompasses the perceived integrity of a physician, which becomes suspect after conviction of a felony.

The pharmacists in *Brown v. Idaho State Board of Pharmacy,* 746 P.2d 1006 (Idaho Ct. App. 1987), had admitted to using marijuana approximately twice a week. During a hearing by the Idaho State Board of Pharmacy, the hearing officer admitted into evidence a copy of a judgment of a conviction on Brown's plea of guilty to a criminal charge of possession of drug paraphernalia. Brown's license was suspended by the Idaho State Board of Pharmacy. On appeal, the Court of Appeals of Idaho held that revocation of his license was supported by evidence that he engaged in the illegal use of marijuana and that he also had participated in the sale and delivery of a misbranded drug.

CHILD ABUSE

Child abuse statutes provide protection from civil suits for those making or participating in a good-faith report of suspected child abuse. Most states also provide immunity from criminal liability. The New York State Social Services Law provides that "[a]ny person, official, or institution participating in good faith in the making of a report, the taking of photographs, or the removal or keeping of a child pursuant to this title shall have immunity from any liability, civil or criminal, that might otherwise result by reason of such actions."[4] Even in states that do not provide immunity, it is unlikely that anyone making a good faith report of suspected child abuse would be subject to criminal liability. State laws generally specify what persons (e.g., physicians, nurses, and social workers) are required to report suspected child abuse that comes before them in their official capacity. In some states, failure to report a case of suspected child abuse carries criminal penalties, as well as civil liability for the damages resulting from such failure.[5]

The pediatrician in *Satler v. Larsen,* 520 N.Y.S.2d 378 (App. Div. 1987), had reported the possibility of child abuse to the Bureau of Child Welfare. The report of suspected child abuse was held not actionable in the absence of a persuasive showing that the report was made in bad faith. Summary dismissal was appropriate with respect to defamation claims brought against the pediatrician for reporting suspected child abuse. The four-month-old infant had been brought to the physician's office in a comatose state with a bilateral subdural hematoma. This occurred one day after the child had been discharged from the hospital.

The psychologist in *E.S. by D.S. v. Seitz,* 413 N.W.2d 670 (Wis. Ct. App. 1987), was immune from liability in a suit charging her with negligence in formulating and reporting her professional opinion to a social worker that a father had sexually abused his three-year-old daughter. It was undisputed that the psychologist had made the report in compliance with the Wisconsin statute, after having examined the child in the course of her professional duties as a mental health professional.

The Minnesota Board of Psychology in *In re Schroeder,* 415 N.W.2d 436 (Minn. Ct. App. 1987), was found to have acted properly when it placed the license of a psychologist on conditional status. The psychologist had failed to report incidents of the sexual abuse of a child. The court held that there was no merit to the psychologist's contentions that the child abuse reporting laws were not clear and that they did not apply to one patient who was a grandfather and who had been charged with the child's care at the time of the incident in question. The psychologist had argued that he was not required to report past abuse that was not ongoing, that a report made five weeks after the incident was not untimely, and that the reporting laws were not constitutional in that the laws violated the privacy rights of clients and the privilege against self-incrimination.

The criminal and civil risks for health professionals lie not in reporting in good faith suspected incidents of child abuse, but in failing to report such incidents. Article 6, title 6, section 420 of the New York State Social Services Law provides for the following civil and criminal penalties for failure to report suspected child abuse incidents:

1. Any person, official or institution required by this title to report a case of suspected child abuse or maltreatment who willfully fails to do so shall be guilty of a class A misdemeanor.
2. Any person, official or institution required by this title to report a case of suspected child abuse or maltreatment who knowingly and willfully fails to do so shall be civilly liable for the damages proximately caused by such failure.

CRIMINAL NEGLIGENCE

Criminal negligence is the reckless disregard for the safety of others. It is the willful indifference to an injury that could follow an act.

The defendants in *State v. Brenner,* 486 So.2d 101 (La. 1986), were charged with cruelty to the infirm. The defendants brought a challenge stating that the criminal statutes under which they were charged were constitutionally vague. According to the court, Section 14.12 of Louisiana Revised Statutes defines criminal negligence as follows:

> Criminal negligence exists when, although neither specific nor general criminal intent is present, there is such disregard of the interest of others that the offender's conduct amounts to a gross deviation below the standard of care expected to be maintained by a reasonably careful man under like circumstances.

Id. at 103.

Criminal negligence requires

> a gross deviation below the standard of care expected to be maintained by a reasonably careful man under like circumstances. . . . It calls for substantially more than the ordinary lack of care which may be the basis of tort liability, and furnishes a more explicit statement of that lack of care which has been variously characterized in criminal statutes as "gross negligence" and "recklessness."

Id.

In the bill of particulars, the state alleged that the administrator of the nursing facility neglected and/or mistreated residents by failing to assure that the nursing facility was maintained in a sanitary manner; necessary health services were performed; the staff was properly trained; there were adequate medical supplies and sufficient staff; records were maintained properly; and the residents were adequately fed, watered, and cared for. There were allegations that the director of nursing neglected and/or mistreated the residents and also failed to properly train the staff at the nursing facility in correct nursing procedures. The controller was alleged to have failed to purchase adequate medical supplies for proper treatment. The admissions director allegedly failed to exercise proper judgment regarding admissions procedures, and the physical therapist allegedly failed to provide adequate physical therapy services. The defendants asserted that the term *neglect* was unconstitutionally vague. The Supreme Court of Louisiana, on appeal by the defendants from two lower courts, held that the phrases "intentional or criminally negligent mistreatment or neglect" and "unjustifiable pain and suffering" were not vague and that they were sufficiently clear in meaning to afford a person of ordinary understanding fair notice of the conduct that was prohibited. *Id.* at 101, 104.

FALSIFICATION OF RECORDS

Falsification of medical and/or business records is grounds for criminal indictment. Civil liability for damages suffered as a result of falsification of records is available to those damaged by such actions.

Two of the defendants, orthopedic surgeons, Drs. Lipton and Massoff, in *People v. Smithtown General Hospital,* 93 Misc. 736, 402 N.Y.S.2d 318 (Sup. Ct. 1978), on the morning of July 3, 1975, performed an orthopedic procedure on a patient. The prosthesis used during surgery was supplied by a general sales manager, Mr. MacKay, who was present in the operating room during most of the operation, which began at 8:00 A.M. and ended at 11:30 A.M. After completion of the operation, an x-ray of the patient revealed that the "head of the femur popped out of the acetabulum." At the request of Dr. Lipton, the salesman was located at a golf course and requested to return to the hospital. On arriving back in the operating room, he found Dr. Massoff reopening the hip. Dr. Massoff attempted to remove the prosthesis. Mr. MacKay offered his assistance and was successful in removing the prosthesis. Dr. Massoff then left and returned to his office. With the consent of Dr. Lipton, Mr. MacKay removed the cement from the bone shaft and reinserted the prosthesis. An indictment charged Dr. Lipton with the intent to defraud and to conceal crimes of "Unauthorized Practice of Medicine and Assault," for omitting to make a true entry in his operative report in that he did not indicate that a nonphysician assisted in the patient's surgery. A similar indictment was returned against a supervising nurse and the hospital for failure to make a true entry in the operating room register. Section 175.00 of the Penal Law of the State of New York defines a business record as "any writing or article, including computer data or a computer program, kept or maintained by an enterprise for the purpose of evidencing or reflecting its condition or activity." In each indictment, it was charged that the defendants were in violation of a duty imposed on them by law or by the nature of their positions.

Section 175.05 of the Penal Law of the State of New York provides that

> [a] person is guilty of falsifying business records in the second degree when, with the intent to defraud, he:
>
> • • • •
>
> 3. Omits to make a true entry in the business records of an enterprise in violation of a duty to do so which he knows to be imposed upon him by law or by the nature of his position; or

4. Prevents the making of a true entry or causes the omission thereof in the business records of an enterprise.

Section 175.10 of the Penal Law of the State of New York provides that "a person is guilty of falsifying business records in the first degree when he commits the crime of falsifying business records in the second degree, and when his intent to defraud includes the intent to commit another crime or to aid or conceal the commission thereof."

The supreme court held that the salesman could be found guilty of unlawfully engaging in the practice of medicine without the prior informed consent of a patient under circumstances that did not constitute an emergency. Dr. Lipton should have sought the assistance of another surgeon before turning a surgical case over to a layman. A motion to dismiss the indictments against the physicians and nurse charged with falsifying business records in the first degree was denied. A motion to dismiss the indictments for assault in the second degree was granted.

FRAUD

The cover story of the February 24, 1992, issue of *U.S. News and World Report* states that up to $80 billion is stolen each year from taxpayers and insurers through white collar crimes. "The thing that spooks insurers and federal regulators these days is that the scams are growing dramatically bigger, bolder and more sophisticated."[6]

Office of Inspector General

The Office of Inspector General (OIG) was established at the Department of Health and Human Services (DHHS) by Congress in 1976 to identify and eliminate fraud, abuse, and waste in DHHS programs and to promote efficiency and economy in departmental operations. It carries out this mission through a nationwide network of audits, investigations, and inspections. To help reduce fraud in the Medicare and Medicaid programs, the OIG investigates violations of the Medicare and Medicaid antikickback statute, 42 U.S.C. §1320a–7b(b). Violators are subject to criminal penalties or exclusion from participation in the Medicare and Medicaid programs.[7] This statute is very broad, and among other things, it penalizes anyone who knowingly and willfully solicits, receives, offers, or pays anything of value as an inducement in return for

1. referring an individual to a person for the furnishing or arranging for the furnishing of any item or service payable under the Medicare or Medicaid program, or

2. purchasing, leasing, or ordering or arranging for or recommending purchasing, leasing, or ordering any good, facility, service, or item payable under the Medicare or Medicaid program.[8]

The following are examples of questionable features, identified by the inspector general, that separately or taken together could be construed as a business arrangement that violates the antikickback statute:

- Investors are chosen because they are in a position to make referrals
- Physicians who are expected to make many referrals may be offered a greater investment opportunity in the joint venture than are those anticipated to make fewer referrals
- Physician investors may be actively encouraged to make referrals to the joint venture and may be encouraged to divest their ownership interest if they fail to sustain an "acceptable" level of referrals
- The joint venture tracks its source of referrals and distributes this information to investors
- Investors may be required to divest their ownership interest if they cease to practice in the service area—for example, if they move, become disabled, or retire
- Investment interests may be nontransferable.[9]

There is a price to be paid by those who dare to make a fast dollar through fraudulent activities. The following cases describe several areas in which health professionals have been involved in criminal fraud.

Joint Ventures

The heavy dependence on government funding and related programs (e.g., Medicare and Medicaid) and the continuous shrinkage occurring in such revenues have forced some health care providers to seek alternative sources of revenue. Competition has contributed to the need to seek alternative revenue sources. The traditional corporate structures for health care facilities no longer may be appropriate to accommodate both normal long-term care activities and those additional activities that may need to be undertaken to provide alternative sources of revenue.

The OIG has become aware of a proliferation of arrangements known as "joint ventures" between those in a position to refer business and those providing items or services for which Medicare or Medicaid pays. Joint venture arrangements have involved such services as diagnostic testing and such items as durable medical equipment.[10]

Department of Justice—Fraud Section

The Fraud Section of the Department of Justice directs and coordinates the federal effort against fraud and white collar crime, focusing primarily on frauds against government programs and procurement, transnational and multi-district fraud, the securities and commodity exchanges, banking practices, and consumer victimization. It prosecutes fraud cases of national significance or great complexity.[11] The emphasis on the detection and investigation of fraud is slowly increasing.

> The focus at the FBI and among U.S. attorneys during the 1980s was on violent crime, the drug crisis and the savings and loan scandal. Health-care cases were boring and difficult to prove.
> Those problems still exist. But a sense of alarm is slowly starting to yield more resources for battling health-care fraud. The FBI has tripled its commitment over the past three years, to 95 agents, and early this month Attorney General William Barr announced that 50 more agents would be transferred from counterintelligence duties to health-fraud probes. The number of states with special Medicaid fraud units has grown from 31 in 1984 to 42 today.[12]

> A conviction of a crime based on Medicare or Medicaid fraud in connection with nursing home operations has been held to be a conviction of an industry-related felony within the meaning of a statute providing for the revocation of a nursing home operating certificate on the holder's conviction of an industry-related felony.[13]

The following cases describe several areas in which health professionals have been involved in criminal fraud.

Health Care Frauds

Anesthesiologists—False Claims

The anesthesiologist partnership in *Anesthesiologists Affiliated v. Sullivan,* 941 F.2d 678 (8th Cir., 1991), had been submitting claims for certified nurse anesthetists who were not employees of the partnership.

Home Care Fraud

Home care fraud is a fertile area for scam artists, and it is often hard to detect. "It involves charging insurers for more services than patients got, billing for more hours of care than were provided, falsifying records and charging higher nurses' rates for care given by aides."[14]

Physician and Office Manager

A physician and his office manager in *United States v. Larm,* 824 F.2d 780 (9th Cir. 1987), were convicted of charges that they violated 42 U.S.C. §139h (a)1 by submitting false Medicaid claims for medical services they never rendered to patients. Claims sometimes were submitted even when patients administered allergy injections themselves. In addition, more expensive serums sometimes were billed for rather than those actually given.

Physician—Services Not Rendered

The physician in *State v. Cargille,* 507 So.2d 1254 (La. Ct. App. 1987), was found to have submitted false information for the purpose of obtaining greater compensation than was otherwise permitted under the Medicaid program. Sufficient evidence had been presented to sustain a conviction of Medicaid fraud. The physician had argued that he felt justified for multiple billings for single office visits because of the actual amount of time that he saw a patient. He believed that his method of reimbursement was more equitable than Medicaid.

Pharmacist—False Drug Claims

The pharmacist in *State v. Heath,* 513 So.2d 493 (La. Ct. App. 1987), was convicted on three counts of Medicaid fraud in which the pharmacist had submitted claims for reimbursement on brand name medications rather than on the less expensive generic drugs that were actually dispensed. A licensed pharmacist and former employee of the defendant had contacted the Medicaid Fraud Unit of the Louisiana Attorney General's office and reported the defendant's conduct in substituting generic drugs for brand name drugs. As a result of the complaint, a "call out" was conducted by the Medicaid Fraud Unit.

> In a recipient call out, the Medicaid Fraud Unit sends letters to Medicaid recipients in the general area of the pharmacy involved and asks them to bring all their prescription drugs to the welfare office on a specific date. The call out revealed that some of the prescription vials issued by the aforesaid pharmacies contained generic drugs while the labels indicated that they should contain brand name drugs.

Id. at 495.

The court of appeals in *State v. Beatty,* 308 S.E.2d 65 (N.C. Ct. App. 1983), upheld the superior court's finding that the evidence submitted against a defendant pharmacist was sufficient to sustain a conviction for Medicaid fraud. The state was billed for medications that had never been dispensed, for more medications than some patients received, and in some instances for the more expensive trade name drugs when cheaper generic drugs had been dispensed.

Falsification of Records by Nursing Home Stockholder

The principal stockholder of a nursing home corporation in *Chapman v. United States, Department of Health and Human Services,* 821 F.2d 523 (10th Cir. 1987), was convicted of making 19 false line-item cost entries in reports to the Kansas Medicaid agency. The U.S. court of appeals found that the DHHS did not act unreasonably when it imposed a $2,000 penalty for each of the 19 false Medicaid claims and proposed an additional settlement of $118,136 even though the state had already recovered the $21,115 in excessive reimbursement by setoff. The court found that "the penalty reflects a fair amount of leniency on the part of the Inspector General and the ALJ." *Id.* at 530.

> On the aggravating side of the balance, the record shows that Chapman acted deliberately to submit false data to the Kansas Medicaid agency so that nursing homes owned by him would be reimbursed for goods and services they did not provide. Further, when an audit was scheduled that threatened to reveal the false claims, Chapman had false invoices prepared and checks issued, but not signed, in an effort to cover up the discrepancies that the state audit would reveal.

Id. at 529.

Kickback Arrangements

Kickbacks are criminal acts punishable under federal and state laws. The Social Security Amendments of 1972[15] and expanded in 1977[16] describe prohibited practices that constitute kickbacks. The Medicare Fraud and Abuse Anti-Kickback Law[17] provides whoever knowingly and willfully solicits or receives a kickback, bribe, or rebate "shall be guilty of a felony and upon conviction thereof, shall be fined not more than $25,000 or imprisoned for not more than five years or both."[18]

> Health care provides many opportunities for kickbacks for steering business to suppliers, pharmacies or laboratories. A medical-equip-

ment supplier might pay off a hospital to get a monopoly on its business, or slip cash to a doctor in return for patient referrals; a pharmacy may pay 'incentives' for a nursing home to steer patients its way; labs may reward doctors for a stream of patient referrals."[19]

Kickback arrangements with suppliers generally occur under one of the following three arrangements:

First, arrangements could be made for inflated billings, in which cases invoices exceeded the actual price of the goods purchased. The operator could then receive a cash kickback and proceed to submit the inflated bills in his Medicaid cost reports. Second, arrangements could be made with a supplier for phony billings; that is, the operator could pay bills for nonexistent goods or services and then receive an under-the-table cash kickback. Finally, phony items could be submitted along with regular invoices, with the same method of sharing the spoils.[20]

Referral Fees

An osteopathic physician, board-certified in cardiology, was president of Cardio-Med, Inc., an organization that he formed. The company provides physicians with diagnostic services, one of which was Holter monitoring, a method of recording a patient's cardiac activity on tape, generally for a period of 24 hours. Cardio-Med billed Medicare for the monitoring service and, when payment was received, forwarded a portion to the referring physician. The government charged that the referral fee exceeded that permitted by Medicare and that there was evidence physicians received "interpretation fees" even though the defendant actually evaluated the monitoring data. After a trial by jury, the physician was convicted on 20 of 23 counts in an indictment charging mail fraud, Medicare fraud, and false statement. On appeal in *United States v. Greber,* 760 F.2d 68 (3d Cir. 1985), the physician contended that the evidence was insufficient to support the guilty verdict. The court of appeals held that to the extent that payments made to a physician were made to induce referrals by that physician of Medicare patients to use payor laboratory services, Medicare fraud was established even if the payments also were intended to compensate the physician for professional services in connection with tests performed by the laboratory. Even if only "one" purpose of the payment was to induce future referrals, the Medicare statute had been violated.

Laboratory Kickback

The owner of Tech Diagnostic Medical Lab agreed to kick back 50 percent of the Medicare payments received by Tech-Lab as a consequence of referrals from Total Health Care, a medical service company. Under the scheme, Total Health Care collected blood and urine samples from medical offices and clinics in southern California and sent them to Tech-Lab for testing. Tech-Lab billed Total Health Care, which in turn billed the private insurance carrier or the government-funded insurance programs Medi-Cal and Medicare for reimbursement. Tech-Lab then kicked back half of its receipts to Total Health Care. The owners of Tech-Lab and Total Health Care arranged an identical scheme with a community medical clinic; Kats, the appellant, subsequently purchased a 25 percent interest in the clinic and began collecting payments under the scheme. Kats was convicted of conspiracy to commit Medicare fraud and of receipt of kickbacks in exchange for referral of Medicare patients. He appealed the decision, and the court of appeals in *United States v. Kats,* 871 F.2d 105 (9th Cir. 1989), affirmed the charges against him.

Cash Rebates

Revocation of a physician's license in *In re Alaimo v. Ambach,* 457 N.Y.S.2d 955 (App. Div. 1982), was not considered to be an excessive sanction for his conviction of perjury when he denied that he was receiving kickbacks from suppliers to his three nursing homes. The physician had denied falsely under oath to a grand jury that he had received cash rebates from vendors, when in fact he had received approximately $800 from a pharmacist between December 15, 1974, and January 15, 1975. *Id.* at 956.

Architectural Contract Kickback

Three members of a county council, which served as the governing body of a county hospital, were convicted by a jury of soliciting and receiving a $6,000 kickback from architects. The architects had testified that the appellants and others sought a 1 percent kickback on the hospital project, financed by federal funds, in return for being awarded the architectural contract. The $6,000 was delivered by Mr. Galloway, of the architectural firm of Galloway and Guthrey, to appellant Campbell at the Knoxville airport. The FBI had been informed by the architects, and an investigation was conducted. After the investigation, indictments, and trial by jury, the defendants were each sentenced to one year in prison. On appeal, the U.S. Court of Appeals for the Sixth Circuit, in *United States v. Thompson,* 366 F.2d 167 (6th Cir. 1966), held that the receipt of a kickback constituted an overt act in furtherance of a conspiracy to obstruct lawful government function and was a violation of the general conspiracy statute and a crime against the United States. "To conspire to defraud the United States means primarily to cheat the government out of property or money, but it also means to interfere with or obstruct one of its lawful governmental functions by deceit, craft or trickery, or at least by means that are dishonest." *Hammerschmidt v. United States,* 265 U.S. 182, 188 (1924). Proof that part of the architects' fee was reimbursed with federal funds was not necessary for a conviction. The criminal convictions were affirmed.

Ambulance Service Kickback

A city official was convicted in a federal district court for conspiring to commit Medicare fraud. Some defendants also were convicted of making illegal payments. Bay State Ambulance and Hospital Rental Service, Inc., a privately owned ambulance company, had given cash and two automobiles to an official of a city-owned hospital. The gifts were given as an inducement to the city official for his recommendation that Bay State be awarded the Quincy City Hospital ambulance service contract, for which Bay State received some Medicare funds as reimbursement. The defendants appealed, and the U.S. Court of Appeals for the First Circuit held that the evidence was sufficient to sustain a conviction. *United States v. Bay State Ambulance & Hospital Rental Services,* 874 F.2d 20 (1st Cir. 1989).

Nursing Home Fraud

A two-year probe of proprietary nursing homes in New York City completed in 1960 by Louis I. Kaplan, Commissioner of Investigations, painted a gloomy picture of the industry. The report that resulted from the probe included the following observations:

- Many operators were attracted by the opportunity to make substantial returns on capital investments and were neither socially motivated nor professionally equipped for the undertaking.
- Public regulation, because of the profit incentive, had to become more vigorous if the public interest was to be served.

• • • •

- Nursing home operators had committed crimes by filing false reports and false instruments. Many freely admitted to Kaplan's investigators that they had committed such crimes. "Just about everyone admitted to filing false documents," said one of the investigators.[21]

Although no prosecution resulted from the investigation, it did influence changes in the city's nursing home code that later served as a model for changes in the state's nursing home code. Passage of article 28 in New York State, as well as Medicare and Medicaid regulations in 1965, increased scrutiny of the nursing home industry. In 1975, the governor of New York State appointed a special prosecutor to investigate nursing homes and vendors to the industry.[22] "The activities of the OSP (Office of the Special Prosecutor) quickly attracted federal attention. Section 17 of the Medicare-Medicaid Fraud and Abuse Bill of 1977 uses it as a model for developing legislation to encourage other states to create long-term fraud control units."[23] The Health Care Financing Administration (HCFA) was established by the secretary of DHHS on March 8, 1977. The HCFA places under one administration the oversight of the Medicare and Medicaid programs and related federal medical care quality control staffs. Medicare and Medicaid are the main programs directed by HCFA.[24]

Fraud Against Physicians

The detection, investigation, and prosecution of financial crimes against physicians is not an uncommon occurrence. They involve such areas as computer billing crime, bookkeeper/office manager theft, insurance fraud, cash larceny, checkbook scam, and patient record tampering.

Physicians should be aware of how to analyze larcenous transactions, identify embezzled funds, and recognize the criminal employee.

MURDER

The tragedy of murder in institutions that are dedicated to the healing of the sick has been an all too frequent occurrence. A recent case involved Richard Angelo, a registered nurse on the cardiac/intensive care unit at a Long Island, New York, hospital, who was found guilty of second-degree murder on December 14, 1989, for injecting two patients with the drug Pavulon. Further, he was found guilty of the lesser charges of manslaughter and criminally negligent homicide in the deaths of two other patients. Mr. Angelo had committed the murders in a bizarre scheme to revive the patients and be thought of as a hero. The attorney for the estate of one of the alleged victims had filed a wrongful death suit against Mr. Angelo and the hospital a day before the verdict was rendered by the jury.[25]

In another case, *Hargrave v. Landon,* 584 F. Supp. 302 (E.D. Va. 1984), a nurses's aide was convicted of murder in the first degree when he was found to have injected an elderly patient with a fatal dose of the drug Lidocaine. He was sentenced to life imprisonment by the circuit court. The nurse's aide appealed the judgment of the circuit court, alleging that his due process rights were violated during the trial, in that

1. The trial court failed to grant his motion for change of venue.
2. Because of a "carnival atmosphere" surrounding the trial, the trial court should have, but did not, sequester the jury *sua sponte*.
3. The trial court improperly admitted evidence of other crimes.
4. The evidence was insufficient as a matter of law to sustain the conviction.

Id. at 305.

The U.S. district court held that the nurse's aide failed to establish that he was denied an impartial jury because of adverse pretrial publicity, especially because the tenor of newspaper articles before his trial were primarily informative and factual and that the articles treated the story objectively. The evidence was found to have been sufficient to support petitioner's conviction for murder.

As pointed out in the following case, indictments for murder by health professionals are not limited to the hospital setting. A licensed dentist and oral surgeon, in *People v. Protopappas,* 201 Cal. App. 3d 152, 246 Cal. Rptr. 915 (1988), were convicted in the superior court of second-degree murder for the deaths of three patients, who died after receiving general anesthesia. The record revealed that the three patients received massive doses of drugs, which resulted in their deaths. The dosages had not been tailored to the patients' individual conditions. The dentist had improperly instructed surrogate dentists, who were neither licensed nor qualified to administer general anesthesia, to administer preset dosages for extended time with little or no personal supervision, and the dentist had been habitually slow in reacting to resulting overdoses. In one of the cases, the patient's general physician informed the defendant that the 24-year-old, 88-pound patient suffered from lupus, total kidney failure, high blood pressure, anemia, heart murmur, and chronic seizure disorder and should not be placed under anesthesia even for a short time. The defendant consciously elected to ignore that medical opinion. On appeal, the court of appeals found that there was sufficient evidence of implied malice to support the jury's findings that the dentist and oral surgeon were guilty of second-degree murder.

This is more than gross negligence. These are the acts of a person who knows that his conduct endangers the life of another and who acts with conscious disregard for life. . . . Many murders are committed to satisfy a feeling of a hatred or grudge, it is true, but this crime may be perpetrated without the slightest trace of personal ill-will.

Id. at 927.

To illustrate this point, Professors Perkins and Boyce supplied a number of examples, including the mother who kills an illegitimate infant out of shame even though she may be filled with maternal love, a mercy killing carried out at the victim's own request, and the shooting of a person with the intent to wound, but not to kill, without justification or provocation. *Id.* at 927, 928. The conduct of the defendant

> is not meaningfully distinguishable from any of the acts described above. No reasonable person, much less a dentist trained in the use of anesthesia, could have failed to appreciate the risk of death posed by the procedures he utilized. It is not a question of whether a fatality would occur, only a question of when; and ultimately there were three of them.

Id. at 928.

As the following case points out, not every charge of suspected murder ends in a conviction; however, there is a heavy price to be paid in the mental anguish suffered by those charged with the crime. Two government nurses in *United States v. Narciso,* 446 F. Supp. 252 (E.D. Mich. 1977), were indicted for and convicted of certain offenses arising out of multiple cardiopulmonary arrests in a two-month period at Ann Arbor Veterans Administration Hospital. During the months of July and August of 1975, 35 patients had suffered 51 cardiac arrests. After an intensive investigation, the defendants were charged in June 1976 with five counts of murder by injecting a powerful muscle relaxant, Pavulon, into the patients' intravenous apparatus. The government presented 89 witnesses over a nearly three-month period. The massive set of proofs was entirely circumstantial in nature. The government had sought to show through many witnesses that certain breathing failures were criminal in nature, that the defendants had the opportunity to commit these crimes, that they were present during a critical period, that the drug had to have been injected to produce the observed effect, and that this presence during the critical period was exclusive. There was no direct proof of guilt on any count. No witnesses testified that the defendants had Pavulon in their possession, nor was there any testimony that the defendants injected anything into the patients. The district court granted the defendants' motion for a new trial in the interests of justice and judicial conscience. The defendants were eventually found not guilty of the murders of which they were accused.

Although there may be a duty to provide life-sustaining machinery in the immediate aftermath of cardiopulmonary arrest, there is no duty to continue its use once it has become futile and ineffective to do so in the opinion of qualified medical personnel. Two physicians in *Barber v. Superior Court,* 147 Cal.

App. 3d 1006, 195 Cal. Rptr. 484 (1983), were charged with the crimes of murder and conspiracy to commit murder. The charges were based on their acceding to requests of the patient's family to discontinue life-support equipment and intravenous tubes. The patient had suffered a cardiopulmonary arrest in the recovery room after surgery. A team of physicians and nurses revived the patient and placed him on life-support equipment. The patient had suffered severe brain damage, which placed him in a comatose and vegetative state from which, according to tests and examinations by other specialists, he was unlikely to recover. The patient, on the written request of the family, was taken off life-support equipment. The family, his wife and eight children, made the decision together after consultation with the physicians. Evidence had been presented that the patient, before his incapacitation, had expressed to his wife that he would not want to be kept alive by a machine or "become another Karen Ann Quinlan." There was no evidence indicating that the family was motivated in their decision by anything other than love and concern for the dignity of their loved one. The patient continued to breathe on his own. Showing no signs of improvement, the physicians again discussed the patient's poor prognosis with the family. The intravenous lines were removed, and the patient died sometime thereafter.

A complaint then was filed against the two physicians. The magistrate who heard the evidence determined that the physicians did not kill the deceased because their conduct was not the proximate cause of the patient's death. On motion of the people, the superior court determined as a matter of law that the evidence required the magistrate to hold the physicians to answer and ordered the complaint reinstated. The physicians then filed a writ of prohibition with the court of appeal. The court of appeals held that the physicians' omission to continue treatment, although intentional and with knowledge that the patient would die, was not an unlawful failure to perform a legal duty. The evidence amply supported the magistrate's decision. The superior court erred in determining that as a matter of law, the evidence required the magistrate to hold the physicians to answer. The pre-emptory writ of prohibition to restrain the Superior Court of Los Angeles from taking any further action in this matter, other than to vacate its order reinstating the complaint and to enter a new and different order denying the People's motion, was granted.

PATIENT AND RESIDENT ABUSE

Patient abuse is the mistreatment or neglect of individuals who are under the care of a health care facility. Abuse is not limited to an institutional setting and may occur in an individual's home, as well as an institution. Abuse can take many forms. It can be physical, psychological, medical, financial, etc. It is not always easy to identify, because injuries often can be attributed to other causes. Elderly patients present particular problems because of their advanced age and failing health.

According to a report by the Chairman of the Subcommittee on Health and Long-Term Care, approximately 1.5 million older Americans are victims of abuse each year. "About 5 percent or 1 out of 20 older Americans may be victims of abuse from moderate to severe. It is estimated that 1.5 million older Americans are victims of abuse each year."[26]

Case Reviews

The following cases of abuse are indicative of the magnitude of the problem.

Abuse and Revocation of License

The operator of a nursing facility appealed an order by the Department of Public Welfare revoking his license because of resident abuse in *Nepa v. Commonwealth Department of Public Welfare*, 551 A.2d 354 (Pa. Commw. Ct. 1988). Substantial evidence supported the department's finding. Three former employees testified that the nursing facility operator had abused residents in the following incidents:

- He unbuckled the belt of one of the residents, causing his pants to drop, and then grabbed a second resident, forcing them to kiss. (Petitioner's excuse for this behavior was to shame the resident because of his masturbating in public.)
- On two occasions he forced a resident to remove toilet paper from a commode after she had urinated and defecated in it. (Denying that there was fecal matter in the commode, petitioner's excuse was that this was his way of trying to stop the resident from filling the commode with toilet paper.)
- He verbally abused a resident who was experiencing difficulty in breathing and accused him of being a fake as he attempted to feed him liquids.

Id. at 355.

The nursing facility operator claimed that the findings of fact were not based on substantial evidence and that even if they were the incidents did not amount to abuse under the code. He attempted to discredit the witnesses with allegations from a resident and another employee that one of the former employees jumped into bed with a resident, and that another had taken a picture of a male resident while in the shower and had placed a baby bottle and humiliating sign around the neck of another resident. The court was not impressed. Although these incidents, if true, were reprehensible, they were collateral matters that had no bearing on the witnesses' reputation for truthfulness and therefore could not be used for impeachment purposes. *Id.* at 356, 357. The court held that there was substantial evidence supporting the department's decision and that the activities committed by the operator were sufficient to support revocation of his license.

> We believe Petitioner's treatment of these residents as found by the hearing examiner to be truly disturbing. These residents were elderly and/or mentally incapacitated and wholly dependent on Petitioner while residing in his home. As residents, they are entitled to maintain their dignity and be cared for with respect, concern, and passion.

> Petitioner testified that he did not have adequate training to deal with the patients he received who suffered from mental problems. Petitioner's lack of training in this area is absolutely no excuse for the reprehensible manner in which he treated various residents. Accordingly, DPW's order revoking Petitioner's license to operate a personal care home is affirmed.

Id. at 357.

Abusive Search

The nurse in *People v. Coe,* 501 N.Y.S.2d 997 (Sup. Ct. 1986), was charged with a willful violation of the Public Health Law in connection with an allegedly abusive search of an 86-year-old resident at a geriatric center and with the falsification of business records in the first degree. The resident, Mr. Gersh, had heart disease and difficulty in expressing himself verbally. Another resident claimed that two $5 bills were missing. Nurse Coe assumed that it was Mr. Gersh because he had been known to take things in the past. The nurse proceeded to search Mr. Gersh, who resisted. A security guard was summoned, and another search was undertaken. When Mr. Gersh again resisted, the security guard slammed a chair down in front of him and pinned his arms while the defendant nurse searched his pockets, failing to retrieve the two $5 bills. Five minutes later, Mr. Gersh collapsed in a chair gasping for air. Nurse Coe administered CPR but was unsuccessful, and he died.

Nurse Coe was charged with violation of section 175.10 of the Penal Law for falsifying records, because of the defendant's "omission" of the facts relating to the search of Mr. Gersh. These facts were considered relevant and should have been included in the nurse's notes to make the note regarding this incident more accurate. "The first sentence states, 'Observed resident was extremely confused and talks incoherently. Suddenly became unresponsive. . . .' This statement is simply false. It could only be true if some reference to the search and the loud noise was included." *Id.* at 1001. A motion was made to dismiss the indictment at the end of the trial.

The court held that the search became an act of physical abuse and mistreatment, the evidence was sufficient to warrant a finding of guilt on both charges, and the fact that searches took place frequently did not excuse an otherwise illegal procedure.

> It may well be that this incident reached the attention of the criminal justice system only because, in the end, a man had died. In those instances which are equally violative of residents' rights and equally contrary to standards of common decency but which do not result in visible harm to a patient, the acts are nevertheless illegal and subject to prosecution. A criminal act is not legitimized by the fact that others have, with impunity, engaged in that act.

Id. at 1001.

Physical Abuse

The revocation of a personal care home license was found to be proper in *Miller Home, Inc. v. Commonwealth, Department of Public Welfare,* 556 A.2d 1 (Pa. Commw. Ct. 1989), because of repeated medication violations and resident abuse. Evidence was presented that the son of the personal care home's manager was hired as a staff member after having acted as a substitute, even though he had had physical altercations with residents of the home. On one occasion, the manager's son had punched a female resident, resulting in her hospitalization for broken bones around the eye, and on other prior occasions, he had been involved in less physical altercations that required police intervention on two occasions. *Id.* at 2.

In *Brinson v. Axelrod,* 499 N.Y.S.2d 24 (App. Div. 1986), the court found that the record contained substantial evidence supporting a finding that a nurse's aide had abused an elderly resident by causing injuries to his face and hand. A $450 penalty imposed on the nurse's aide was found to be reasonable.

A nursing facility orderly challenged a determination by the commissioner of the State Department of Health finding him guilty of resident abuse in *Reid v. Axelrod,* 559 N.Y.S.2d 417 (App. Div. 1990). The orderly maintained that the resident struck him with his cane and that he merely pushed the cane away to avoid being struck a second time. A co-employee testified that the orderly struck the resident in the chest after being hit with the cane. The court held that the determination was supported by substantial evidence and that the three-year delay in conducting the hearing did not warrant dismissal of the petition charging the orderly with resident abuse. Public policy requires that residents must be protected from abusive health care workers.

The resident in *Stiffelman v. Abrams,* 655 S.W.2d 522 (Mo. 1983), died from

> 'blows, kicks, kneeings, or bodily throwings intentionally, viciously, and murderously dealt him from among the facility's staff over a period of approximately two to three weeks prior to his death'; that the 'beatings were repeated and were received by the decedent at ninety years of age and in a frail, defenseless, and dependent condition'; that the beatings so administered to the decedent were 'physically and mentally tortuous; that he was caused by them to live out his final days in agony and terror; and that his physical injuries included thirteen fractures to his ribs, subpleural hemorrhaging, and marked lesions to his chest, flanks, abdomen, legs, arms, and hands; that during and following the period of the beatings the decedent lay at the facility for days unattended and unaided as to the deterioration and grave suffering he was undergoing.'

Id. at 526.

   The executors of the estate had brought suit against the operator and individual and corporate owners of the facility for damages for personal injuries resulting in the death of the resident. The executors were requesting under count I, $1.5 million in survival damages because of the physical and mental pain and suffering of the decedent, as well as $3 million for punitive damages, and under count II, $1,504,084.84 in contractual breaches of the resident's admission contract with the facility. The executors claimed that certain standards of care and personal rights contained in the contract were violated. *Id.* at 526, 527. The trial court sustained the nursing facility's motion for dismissal of the case on the grounds that the plaintiffs failed to state a claim on which relief could be granted. On appeal, the judgment of the trial court was reversed with respect to count I and the dismissal of count II was sustained. The case was remanded, requiring the executors to proceed under appropriate statutory authority and not under contract.

Forcible Administration of Medications

   The medical employee *In re Axelrod,* 560 N.Y.S.2d 573 (App. Div. 1990), sought review of a determination by the commissioner of health that she was guilty of resident abuse. Evidence showed that the employee, after a resident refused medication, "held the patient's chin and poured the medication down her throat." *Id.* There was no indication or convincing evidence that an emergency existed that would have required the forced administration of the medication. The court held that substantial evidence supported the commissioner's finding that the employee had been guilty of resident abuse.

> The Commissioner properly found that the notation in the record that 'staff are asked to, please, make every effort to make sure that she [the patient] takes them [her medication]' does not authorize the forcible administration of medication. This is particularly so when the notation was not made by a medical doctor authorized to prescribe medication and when the written policy of the facility, was that the head nurse was to be notified if a patient refused medication.

Id. at 573, 574.

Intimidation of Abusive Resident

A difficult and abusive 80-year-old resident of a veterans home in *Beasley v. State Personnel Board,* 178 Cal. Rptr. 564 (Ct. App. 1981), slapped the face of an aide who was assisting him. The resident, referring to his inability to have sex, said that he might as well have it cut off. The aide responded by indicating that if he did not behave she might accommodate him. A nursing supervisor who passed by at that moment noted that a nursing assistant and a hospital aide who were standing nearby laughed and did nothing to intervene. The aide was fired and the other two employees were suspended for ten days. "After the State Board upheld the overkill, the three employees went by mandate to the superior court where Beasley's dismissal was ruled too severe . . . ." *Id.* at 565. The trial court found that action against the nursing assistant and hospital aide, although harsh, was within discretion. On appeal, the court held that the aide's comments did not constitute misconduct and the Veterans Home nursing assistant and hospital aide did not commit actionable conduct by "sort of laughing." When this incident was viewed "in its context and in light of the whole record," it did not support the state personnel board's finding that the aide's attitude toward patients was poor. *Id.* at 566.

Allegations of Abuse Not Supported by the Evidence

Complaints of resident abuse cannot always be substantiated as was the case in *Mullen v. Axelrod,* 549 N.E.2d 144 (N.Y. 1989). The petitioner, Mr. Mullen, alleged that he was near death as a result of the abuse, mistreatment, and neglect he suffered in the nursing facility. Mr. Mullen claimed that the facility failed to care properly for an ankle injury he sustained. The petitioner developed gangrene, which eventually resulted in amputation of his leg. He filed a complaint with the State Department of Health alleging abuse, mistreatment, and neglect. After investigation, the Department of Health informed the petitioner of its determination that there was "insufficient credible evidence to sustain a violation of the Public Health Law." *Id.* at 145.

Improper Care and a Plea of Nolo Contendere

A nursing facility had been charged with engaging in conduct wantonly endangering a resident by failing to provide necessary and proper care in *Commonwealth v. Hillhaven Corp.,* 687 S.W.2d 545 (Ky. Ct. App. 1984). At a pretrial hearing, the facility asked to have a plea of *"nolo contendere"* accepted and acknowledged, and agreed to pay a maximum fine of $10,000. The court accepted the plea and the commonwealth appealed. Examples of the facility's poor care to the resident included "the failure to provide adequate skin care, nutrition, sanitary care, laboratory work, and medications." *Id.* at 546. The court of appeals held that Kentucky courts have no inherent discretionary power to accept a plea of *nolo contendere* and that all pleas in such matters must be either "guilty" or "not guilty."

PETTY THEFT

Health care facilities must be alert to the potential ongoing threat of theft by unscrupulous employees, physicians, patients, visitors, and trespassers. The theft of supplies and equipment is substantial and costs health care facilities millions of dollars each year.

The physician in *Eufemio v. University of New York,* 516 N.Y.S.2d 129 (App. Div. 1987), was convicted in Maryland for the crime of petty theft, which arose out of financial irregularities at a nursing home that was owned by the physician. The physician moved to New York before the Maryland Commission of Medical Discipline could impose a penalty on him because of his conviction. The commissioner of education's determination that the physician's license to practice medicine should be suspended for three years was upheld by a New York court. The commissioner's determination was subject to confirmation notwithstanding the physician's assertion that the sanctions were too harsh.

Criminal charges of theft were imposed because of misapplication of property in *State v. Pleasant Hill Health Facility,* 496 A.2d 306 (Me. 1985). The facility had commingled the residents' personal funds (Social Security checks and personal allowances) in a corporate account. There were times that the residents' funds remained in the corporate account for three to six months before being transferred to the residents' accounts, during which time the combined funds were used to pay corporate expenses. The facility had described their relationship with the residents as debtor–creditor and not a trust relationship. The facility claimed that the funds were always available to residents, and they were never denied a request for their funds. The Supreme Judicial Court of Maine held that the facility's handling of the residents' funds was not a debtor–creditor relationship but a trust relationship. "Pleasant Hill's commingling of patients' personal need funds with corporate funds and use of the combined funds to pay corporate expenses constituted dealing with the money as its own and a violation of the corporation's trust agreement." *Id.* at 308. The facility argued that it ultimately transferred all the residents' personal funds from a transfer account to the residents' accounts. The court concluded that violation occurred at the moment the residents' personal funds were deposited without segregating them from the corporation's own funds. *Id.* at 308.

TRESPASS AND CRIMINAL MISCHIEF

An abortion clinic, Northeast Women's Center, Inc., brought an action against antiabortion demonstrators who allegedly disrupted its operations by harassing its patients and employees and by trespassing on the clinic's property. The defendants, who were found guilty of trespass, were liable for injury to the clinic's business and property. The district court found the defendants liable under the Racketeer Influenced and Corrupt Organizations Act and assessed $887 in damages, which was trebled by the court to $2,661.

The First Amendment rights of a Catholic priest in *Markley v. State,* 507 So.2d 1043 (Ala. Crim. App. 1987), were found not to have been violated when the circuit court placed him on conditional probation and prohibited his antiabortion protest activities during his period of probation, after his conviction on charges of burglary in the second degree and criminal mischief in the first degree. The charges stemmed from antiabortion demonstrations, which took place at a medical clinic specializing in pregnancy testing, counseling, and abortions. The court of criminal appeals held that limitation of protest activities as a term of probation did not violate the priest's First Amendment rights.

CONCLUSION

It is a sad commentary on today's society that criminal activity takes place in health care facilities around the country. Health care providers must be vigilant in seeking out and putting safeguards in place to ensure the health and safety of their patients and caregivers.

NOTES

1. R.M. PERKINS, CRIMINAL LAW AND PROCEDURE 2 (1972).

2. J. KAPLAN, CRIMINAL JUSTICE: INTRODUCTORY CASES AND MATERIALS 228 (1973).

3. *Id.* at 259.

4. New York State Social Services Law, art. 6, tit. 6, §419.

5. *Id.* at §402.

6. *Health Care Fraud,* U.S. NEWS & WORLD REP., February 24, 1992, at 34.

7. OFFICE OF THE FEDERAL REGISTER, NATIONAL ARCHIVES AND RECORDS ADMINISTRATION, THE UNITED STATES GOVERNMENT MANUAL 1988/89, at 307 (1988).

8. OFFICE OF INSPECTOR GENERAL, DEPARTMENT OF HEALTH AND HUMAN SERVICES, SPECIAL FRAUD ALERT, JOINT VENTURE ARRANGEMENTS 1(1) (May 1989).

9. *Id.* at 2(2).

10. *Id.*

11. THE UNITED STATES GOVERNMENT MANUAL, *supra* note 7, at 375.

12. *Health Care Fraud, supra* note 6, at 43.

13. 53 A.L.R. 4th 689 (1987).

14. *Health Care Fraud, supra* note 6, at 42.

15. 1972 U.S. CODE CONG. & AD. NEWS 5093.

16. 1977 U.S. CODE CONG. & AD. NEWS 3056.

17. Social Security Act, §1128B(b).

18. 42 U.S.C. §1396h(b)(1)(1977).

19. *Health Care Fraud, supra* note 6, at 41.

20. D.B. SMITH, LONG-TERM CARE IN TRANSITION, 91–92 (1981).

21. *Id.* at 102.

22. *Id.* at 92–97.

23. *Id.* at 97.

24. THE UNITED STATES GOVERNMENT MANUAL, *supra* note 7.

25. Colwell, *The Verdict of Angelo,* 50 NEWSDAY 3 (1989).

26. SENATE SUBCOMMITTEE ON HEALTH AND LONG-TERM CARE, ELDER ABUSE: A DECADE OF SHAME AND INACTION, Comm. Pub. No. 752 (1990) at x–xiv.

Chapter 4
Civil Procedure and Trial Practice

OUTLINE

Judicial Notice Rule

Medical Books

Examination of Witnesses

   Hearsay Evidence

   Hypnotically Induced Testimony

   Expert Witness

• Defenses Against Recovery

Assumption of the Risk

Borrowed Servant and Captain of the Ship Doctrines

Comparative Negligence

Contributory Negligence

Doctrine of Charitable Immunity

Good Samaritan Laws

Ignorance of Fact and Unintentional Wrongs

Independent Contractor

Intervening Cause

Statute of Limitations

Sovereign Immunity

• Closing Statements

• Judge's Charge to the Jury

• Jury Deliberation and Determination

• Damages

Plaintiff's Schedule of Damages

   Personal Injuries of Plaintiff

   Punitive Damages

   Surviving Spouse and Children

   Emotional Distress

   Excessive Damages

Joint and Several Liability

• Appeals

• Execution of Judgments

For many students and health care practitioners, this book will be their only formal introduction to the legal aspects of health care administration. This chapter in particular is valuable to both students and health care professionals in understanding the law and its application in the courtroom. Although many of the procedures leading up to and followed during a trial are discussed in this chapter, civil procedure and trial practice are governed by each state's statutory requirements. Cases on a federal level are governed by federal statutory requirements.

PLEADINGS

The pleadings of a case (e.g., summons and complaint), which include all the allegations of each party to a lawsuit, are filed with the court. The pleadings may raise questions of both law and fact. If only questions of law are involved, the judge will decide the case on the pleadings alone. If questions of fact are involved, the purpose of a trial is to determine those facts.

Summons and Complaint

The parties to a controversy are the "plaintiff" and the "defendant." The plaintiff is the person who institutes an action by filing a complaint; the defendant is the person against whom a suit is brought. Many cases have multiple plaintiffs and defendants. An action is commenced by filing an order with a court clerk to issue a writ or "summons."

Although the procedures for beginning an action vary according to jurisdiction, there are procedural common denominators. All jurisdictions require service of process on the defendant (usually through a summons) and a return to the court of that process by the person who served it. Where a summons is not required to be issued directly by a court, an attorney, as an officer of the court, may prepare and cause a summons to be served without direct notice to or approval of a court. Notice to a court occurs when an attorney files a summons and complaint in a court, thereby indicating to the court that an action has been commenced.

The first pleading filed with the court in a negligence action is the "complaint." The complaint identifies the parties to a suit, states a cause of action, and includes a demand for damages. It is filed by the plaintiff and is the first statement of a case by the plaintiff against the defendant. In some jurisdictions, a complaint must accompany a summons (an announcement to the defendant that a case has been commenced). The essential elements contained in a complaint are (1) a short statement of the grounds on which the court's jurisdiction depends (the court's authority to hear the case); (2) a statement of the claim demonstrating that the pleader is entitled to relief; and (3) a demand for judgment for the relief to which the plaintiff deems him- or herself entitled. All these elements apply to any counterclaim, cross-claim, or third-party claim.

The complaint can be served on the defendant either with the summons or within a prescribed time after the summons has been served. Specific formali-

100 LEGAL ASPECTS OF HEALTH CARE ADMINISTRATION

ties must be observed in the service of a summons so that appropriate jurisdiction over a defendant is obtained. Such formalities dictate the manner in which a summons is to be delivered, the time period within which service must be effected, and the geographic limitations within which service must be made. For example, a summons to commence an action in a local municipal court generally would require service within the particular municipality in order for the court to obtain jurisdiction. Where such service is not possible, the action may have to be brought in a different court.

In the preliminary motions, the defendant cites possible errors that would defeat the plaintiff's case. For example, the defendant may object that a summons or a complaint was served improperly, that the action was brought in the wrong county, or that there was something technically incorrect about the complaint. The court then may permit the plaintiff to file a new or amended complaint. However, in some instances, the defects in the plaintiff's case may be so significant that the case is dismissed.

Demurrer

On receiving a copy of the plaintiff's complaint, the defendant can file preliminary objections before answering the complaint. A *demurrer* is a formal objection by one of the parties to a lawsuit that the evidence presented by the other party is insufficient to sustain an issue or case.

Answer

After service of a complaint, a response is required from the defendant in a document called the "answer." In the answer, the defendant responds to each of the allegations contained in the complaint by stating his or her defenses and by admitting to or denying each of the plaintiff's allegations. If the defendant fails to answer the complaint within the prescribed time, the plaintiff can seek judgment by default against the defendant. However, in certain instances a default judgment will be vacated if the defendant can demonstrate an acceptable excuse for failing to answer. Even if a plaintiff has been granted judgment by default, he or she could be required to present the basis for damages at a hearing before a court. A defaulting defendant may be entitled to oppose the evidence presented by the plaintiff at such a hearing, at least to the extent of the damages claimed.

Personal appearance of the defendant to respond to a complaint is not necessary. The defendant's attorney, to prevent default, responds to the complaint with an answer. The defense attorney attempts to show through evidence that the defendant is not responsible for the negligent act. The answer generally consists of a denial of the charges made and specifies a defense or argument justifying the position taken. The defense may show that the claim is unfounded for such reasons as the following: (1) the period within which a suit must be instituted has run out, (2) there is contributory negligence on the part of the plaintiff, (3) any obligation has been paid, (4) a general release was presented to the defendant, or (5) the contract was illegal and therefore canceled by mutual agreement. The original answer to the complaint is filed with the court having jurisdiction over the case, and a copy of the answer is forwarded to the plaintiff's attorney.

Counterclaim

In some cases the defendant may have a claim against the plaintiff and therefore may file a counterclaim. For example, the plaintiff may have sued a hospital for personal injuries and property damage caused by the negligent operation of a hospital's ambulance. The hospital may file a counterclaim on the ground that its driver was careful and that it was the plaintiff who was negligent and is liable to the hospital for damage to the ambulance.

Bill of Particulars

Because a complaint may provide very little information regarding the claim, the defense attorney may request a bill of particulars, which limits the scope and generality of the pleadings. This document requests more specific and detailed information than is provided in the complaint. If a counterclaim has been filed, the plaintiff's attorney may request a bill of particulars from the defense attorney. More specifically, a bill of particulars for a malpractice suit may request the following from the plaintiff's attorney:

- Specify the date and time of day when the alleged malpractice occurred. Does the malpractice claim include
  1. misdiagnosis or failure to diagnose correctly
  2. failure to perform a test or diagnostic procedure
  3. failure to medicate, treat, or operate
  4. a contraindicated test given or a contraindicated test or surgical procedure performed
  5. administration of a medicine or treatment or performance of a test or surgical procedure in a manner contrary to accepted standards of medical practice

- Specify where the alleged malpractice occurred
- Specify how the occurrence of the malpractice is claimed
- Specify all the commissions and/or omissions constituting the malpractice claimed
- List all injuries claimed to have been caused by the defendant's alleged malpractice
- List any witnesses to the alleged malpractice
- State the length of time the plaintiff was confined to bed
- State the weekly earnings of the plaintiff
- State the name and address of the employer

A death action rider also may be attached if the malpractice allegedly caused death. The rider may request such information as the length of time the decedent experienced pain; the date, time, and place of death; and a statement setting forth the cause of death.

DISCOVERY AND EXAMINATION BEFORE TRIAL

Discovery is the process of investigating the facts of a case before trial. The objectives of discovery are to (1) obtain evidence that might not be obtainable at the time of trial; (2) isolate and narrow the issues for trial; (3) gather knowledge of the existence of additional evidence that may be admissible at trial; and (4) obtain leads to enable the discovering party to gather further evidence. The discovery process is available to promote more just trials by preventing unfair surprise. "Discovery rules were to prevent trial by ambush. To deny a party the right to know absolutely at some meaningful time before trial the names and addresses of all witnesses the opposing side proposes to call in its case-in-chief is an insult to this principle."[1]

Discovery may be obtained on any matter that is not privileged and that is relevant to the subject matter involved in the pending action. The parties to a lawsuit have the right to discovery and to examine witnesses before trial. Examination before trial (EBT) is one of several discovery techniques used to enable the parties of a lawsuit to learn more regarding the nature and substance of each other's case. An EBT consists of oral testimony under oath and includes cross-examination. A deposition, taken at an EBT, is the testimony of a witness that has been recorded in a written form. Testimony given at a deposition becomes part of the permanent record of the case. Each question and answer is transcribed by a court stenographer and may be used at the subsequent trial. Truthfulness and consistency are important because answers that differ from those given at trial will be used to erode the credibility of the witness.

Either party may obtain a court order permitting the examination and copying of books and records, such as medical records, as well as the inspection of buildings and equipment. A court order also may be obtained allowing the physical or mental examination of a party when the party's condition is important to the case.

In certain instances, it may be desirable to record a witness's testimony outside the court before the time of trial. In such a case, one party, after giving proper notice to the opposing party and to the prospective missing witness, may require a witness to appear before a person authorized to administer oaths in order to answer questions and submit to cross-examination. The testimony is recorded and filed with the court and is entered in evidence as the testimony of the missing witness. This procedure may be used when a witness is aged or infirm or too ill to testify at the time of trial.

Preparation of Witnesses

The manner in which a witness handles questioning at a deposition or trial is often as important as the facts of the case. Each witness should be well prepared before testifying. Preparation should include a review of all pertinent records. The following are some helpful guidelines for a witness undergoing examination in a trial or a court hearing:

- Review those records (e.g., medical records and other business records) on which you might be questioned
- Do not be antagonistic in answering the questions. The jury already may be somewhat sympathetic toward a particular party to the lawsuit; your antagonism may serve only to reinforce such an impression
- Be organized in your thinking and recollection of the facts regarding the incident
- Answer only the questions asked
- Explain your testimony in simple, succinct terminology
- Do not overdramatize the facts you are relating
- Do not allow yourself to become overpowered by the cross-examiner
- Be polite, sincere, and courteous at all times
- Dress appropriately, and be neatly groomed
- Pay close attention to any objections your attorney may have as to the line of questioning being conducted by the opposing counsel
- Be sure to have reviewed any oral deposition that you may have participated in during EBT

- Be straightforward with the examiner. Any answers designed to cover up or cloud an issue or fact will, if discovered, serve only to discredit any previous testimony you may have given
- Do not show any visible signs of displeasure regarding any testimony with which you are in disagreement
- Be sure to have questions that you did not hear repeated and questions that you did not understand rephrased
- If you are not sure of an answer, indicate that you are not sure or that you just do not know the answer

MOTIONS

The procedural steps that occur before trial are specifically classified as pretrial proceedings. After the pleadings have been completed, many states permit either party to move for a judgment on the pleadings. When this motion is made, the court will examine the entire case and decide whether to enter judgment according to the merits of the case as indicated in the pleadings. In some states, the moving party is permitted to introduce sworn statements showing that a claim or defense is false or a sham. This procedure cannot be used when there is substantial dispute concerning the facts presented by the affidavits.

In many states, a pretrial conference will be ordered at the judge's initiative or on the request of one of the parties to the lawsuit. The pretrial conference is an informal discussion during which the judge and the attorneys eliminate matters not in dispute, agree on the issues, and settle procedural matters relating to the trial. Although the purpose of the pretrial conference is not to compel the parties to settle the case, it often happens that cases are settled at this point.

Dismissal

A defendant may make a motion to dismiss a case, alleging that the plaintiff's complaint, even if believed, does not set forth a claim or cause of action recognized by law. A motion to dismiss can be made before, during, or after a trial. Motions made before a trial may be made on the basis that the court lacks jurisdiction, that the case is barred by the statute of limitations, that another case is pending involving the same issues, and other similar matters. A motion during trial may be made after the plaintiff has presented his or her case on the grounds that the court has heard the plaintiff's case and the defendant is entitled to a favorable judgment as a matter of law. In the case of a motion made by the defendant at the close of the plaintiff's case, the defendant normally will claim that the plaintiff has failed to present a *prima facie* case (i.e., that the plaintiff has failed to establish the minimum elements necessary to justify a verdict even if no contrary evidence is presented by the defendant). After the trial has been completed, either party may move for a directed verdict on the grounds that he or she is entitled to such verdict as a matter of law.

A plaintiff has the right to appeal a lower court's decision to an appellate court if a defendant's motion for dismissal is granted. If the court rules against the defendant's motion for dismissal, as well as any other preliminary objections and motions the defendant may have made, the defendant then will be required to file an answer to the plaintiff's complaint.

Summary Judgment

Either party to a suit may believe that there are no triable issues of fact and only issues of law to be decided. In such event, either party may make a motion for summary judgment. This motion asks the court to rule that there are no facts in dispute and that the rights of the parties can be determined as a matter of law, on the basis of submitted documents, without the need for a trial. Although the courts are reluctant to look favorably on motions for summary judgments, they will grant them if the circumstances of a particular case warrant it.

> A motion for summary judgment is a means for the efficient disposition of a cause of action where there is no genuine issue of material fact and the moving party is entitled to judgment as a matter of law.
>
> • • • •
>
> Of course courts should exercise caution in deciding issues involving policy considerations.
>
> • • • •
>
> However, excessive caution would undercut the purpose of a motion for summary judgment, which provides a means for piercing the allegations of the pleadings to determine whether there are issues requiring disposition at trial.
>
> • • • •
>
> If after drawing all inferences of doubt against the movant, a court finds that there is no genuine basis of material fact, it should enter summary judgment.[2]

NOTICE OF TRIAL

The examination before a trial may reveal sufficient facts that would discourage the plaintiff from continuing the case, or it may encourage one or both parties to settle out of court. Once a decision to go forward is reached, the case is placed on the court calendar. Postponement of the trial may be secured with the consent of both parties and the consent of the court. A case may not be postponed indefinitely without being dismissed by the court. Where one party is ready to proceed and another party seeks a postponement, a valid excuse must be shown. An example of a valid excuse is that the attorney for the party seeking the postponement is engaged in another case. Should a defendant fail to appear at trial, the judge can pass judgment against the defendant by default. A case also can be dismissed if the plaintiff fails to appear at trial.

MEMORANDUM OF LAW

A memorandum of law (or trial brief) is prepared for the court by each attorney. It presents the nature of the case, cites case decisions to substantiate arguments, and aids the court regarding points of law. Trial briefs are prepared by both the plaintiff's and the defendant's attorneys. A trial brief is not required, but it is a recommended strategy. It provides the court with a basic understanding of the position of the party submitting the brief before the commencement of the trial. It also focuses the court's attention on specific legal points that may influence the court in ruling on objections and on the admissibility of evidence in the course of the trial.

THE COURT

A case is heard in the court that has jurisdiction over the subject of controversy. The judge decides questions of law and is responsible for ensuring that a trial is conducted properly in an impartial atmosphere and is fair to both parties of a lawsuit. He or she determines what constitutes the general standard of conduct required for the exercise of due care. The judge informs the jury of what the defendant's conduct should have been, thereby making a determination of the existence of a legal duty.

The judge plays the dominant role in a trial. He or she decides whether evidence is admissible, charges the jury (defines the jurors' responsibility in relation to existing law), and may take a case away from the jury (by directed verdict or judgment notwithstanding the verdict) when he or she believes that there are no issues for the jury to consider or that the jury has erred in its decision. This right on the part of the judge with respect to the role of the jury narrows the jury's responsibility with regard to the facts of the case. The judge maintains order throughout the suit, determines issues of procedure, and is generally responsible for the conduct of the trial.

THE JURY

The right to a trial by jury is a constitutional right in certain cases. Not all cases entitle the parties to a jury trial as a matter of right. For example, in many jurisdictions, a case in equity (a case seeking a specific course of conduct rather than monetary damages) may not entitle the parties to a trial by a jury. An example of an equity case would be one that seeks a declaration as to the title to real property.

An individual may waive the right to a jury trial. If this right is waived, the judge acts as "judge and jury" and becomes the trier of facts as well as issues of law.

Members of the jury are selected from a jury list. They are summoned to court by a paper known as the jury process. Impartiality is a prerequisite of all jurors. The number of jurors who sit at trial is 12 in common law. If there are fewer than 12, the number must be established by statute. Physicians, pharmacists, nurses, and lawyers generally are excused from sitting on a jury.

Counsel for both parties of a lawsuit question each prospective jury member for impartiality, bias, and prejudicial thinking. This process is referred to as the "*voir dire*," the examination of jurors. Once members of the jury are selected, they are sworn in to try the case.

The jury makes a determination of the facts that have occurred, evaluating whether the plaintiff's damages were caused by the defendant's negligence and whether the defendant exercised due care. The jury makes a determination of the particular standard of conduct required in all cases in which the judgment of reasonable people might differ. The jury must pay close attention to the evidence presented by both sides to a suit in order to render a fair and impartial verdict. Jurors who fall asleep during the trial can be replaced with an alternate juror, as was the case in *Richbow v. District of Columbia,* 600 A.2d 1063 (D.C. 1991).

Although the verdict must be based on the theory of wrongdoing, it is not always easy for a jury to determine which side is telling the truth and which is masking the truth with rhetoric. A New York City jury in *Melis v. Kutin, Harper, & St. Vincent's Medical Center,* awarded $26 million to a boy injured in surgery. What was it that so disturbed the jury that caused it to grant such a huge award? According to an article written by an alternate juror, who had invited the jurors to his home three weeks after the trial,

> The defense lawyers were on their feet objecting—they didn't want the jury to see Stephen. But that just raised a question for us: If his injuries were as slight as the defense had been insisting, why the resistance? The judge agreed that it was proper for Stephen to appear at his own trial, and the rear doors to the courtroom were opened.
>
> • • • •
>
> Most of the jurors had begun to cry. But we were also angry. The defense lawyers it seemed, had been trying to put one over on us,

claiming that Stephen was a normal teenage boy with a few minor handicaps.

• • • •

For seven weeks, the jury had sat in that courtroom listening to the defense lawyers belittle Stephen's problems. We saw the doctors refuse to acknowledge Stephen's handicaps or to accept responsibility for them. To the jury at least, it seemed that the doctors had made mistakes, refused to admit them, and then tried to cover them up.[3]

The jury also determines the extent of damages, if any, and the degree to which the plaintiff's conduct may have contributed to his or her injury, thereby mitigating the responsibility of the defendant (contributory negligence).

SUBPOENAS

A subpoena is a legal order requiring the appearance of a person or documents before a court or administrative body. Subpoenas may be issued by attorneys, judges, and certain law enforcement and administrative officials, depending on the jurisdiction. Subpoenas generally include a reference number; names of plaintiff and defendant; date, time, and place to appear; name, address, and telephone number of opposing attorney; and documents requested if a subpoena is for records.

Some jurisdictions require the service of a subpoena at a specified time in advance of the requested appearance (e.g., 24 hours). In other jurisdictions, no such time limitation exists. A subpoena can be served by a court clerk, sheriff, attorney, process server, or other person as provided by state statute.

A *subpoena ad testificandum* orders the appearance of a person at a trial or other investigative proceeding to give testimony. Witnesses have a duty to appear and may suffer a penalty for contempt of court should they fail to appear. They may not deny knowledge of a subpoena if they simply refused to accept it. A "bench warrant," ordering the appearance of a witness in court, may be issued by the court if a witness fails to answer a subpoena. Failure to appear may be excused if extenuating circumstances exist. Witnesses are paid nominal fees for time and travel whether they testify or not. Payment can be requested in advance. A subpoena must allow a reasonable amount of time for travel.

A subpoena for records, known as a *subpoena duces tecum*, is a written command to bring records, documents, or other evidence described in the subpoena to a trial or other investigative proceeding. The subpoena is served on one able to produce such records. Disobedience in answering a *subpoena duces tecum* is considered contempt of court and carries a penalty of a fine or imprisonment.

OPENING STATEMENTS

During the opening statement, the plaintiff's attorney attempts to prove the wrongdoing of the defendant by presenting credible evidence favorable to his or her client. The opening statement by the plaintiff's attorney provides in capsule form the facts of the case, what he or she intends to prove by means of a summary of the evidence to be presented, and a description of the damages to his or her client.

Opening statements can leave lasting impressions on jury members. They are prepared so that each jury member can sympathize with the plaintiff and relate to the injustice and see it happening to themselves. The opening statement must be concise and to the point.

> Jurors typically do not decide the case on the basis of the opening statements. But pulling for one side or another—even just slightly— gives them a point of view. From then on, they tend to look at everything that happens from the vantage point of the side they favor.[4]

In some jurisdictions, a list of witnesses, containing what the lawyers hope to obtain from each witness's testimony, is given to the judge and to the opposition before commencement of the trial. Included on this list are the names, addresses, and occupations of each witness. The order of the names indicates the order in which each witness will be called to the stand. "The most powerful call is not to do right, but to undo wrong. It is not justice that motivates judges and juries—it is injustice, and the power to right a wrong."[5]

The defense attorney makes his or her opening statement indicating the position of the defendant and the points of the plaintiff's case he or she intends to refute. The defense attorney explains the facts as they apply to the case for the defendant.

BURDEN OF PROOF

The party seeking compensation for injuries suffered because of the negligence of another must prove that there actually was such negligence. The burden of proof in a civil lawsuit is the obligation of the plaintiff to persuade the jury regarding the truth of his or her case.

A "preponderance of the credible evidence" must be presented in order for a plaintiff to recover. "Credible evidence" is evidence that in the light of reason and common sense is worthy of belief. A "preponderance of credible evidence" requires that the prevailing side of the case carry more weight than the evidence on the opposing side. If one would envision the "scales of justice," with the evidence presented by the plaintiff on one scale and that presented by the defendant on the opposite scale, the side tipping the scale in their favor will win the suit. If the evidence is evenly balanced between the plaintiff and the defendant, the required burden of proof will not have been met and the plaintiff will not prevail.

The burden of proof in a criminal case requires that the evidence presented against the defendant must be "beyond a reasonable doubt." Note the terminology—"reasonable" doubt—not "all" doubt. In the civil suit, the evidence presented need only tip the scales of justice.

The burden of proof requires that the plaintiff's attorney show that the defendant violated a legal duty by not following an acceptable standard of care and that the plaintiff suffered injury because of the defendant's breach. If the evidence presented does not support the allegations made, the case is dismissed. Where a plaintiff, who has the burden of proof, fails to sustain such burden, the case may be dismissed despite the failure of the defendant to present any evidence to the contrary on his or her behalf. The burden of proof in some states shifts from the plaintiff to the defendant when it is obvious that the injury would not have occurred unless there was negligence.

The burden of proving negligence requires that the plaintiff show by evidence that outweighs the evidence offered by the opposing party that each and every component of negligence is present. This rule is well illustrated in the following case, in which the plaintiff failed to prove an element of an important negligence action—the standard of care to be imposed on the facility. In *Montgomery v. American Nursing Centers,* 349 N.E.2d 516 (Ill. App. Ct. 1976), a resident fell and injured herself in a nursing facility while recuperating from a fractured hip. An incident report prepared by the home indicated that the woman thereafter complained of knee and hip pain. The attending physician, not having read the report, treated her knee but not her hip, because she complained of no such pain during the examination. Two weeks later during a follow-up examination, the physician observed symptoms of a possible hip injury and ordered x-rays, which disclosed a hip fracture. The resident sued the nursing facility for negligence and the physician for malpractice. In her complaint, the resident alleged that the nursing facility had been negligent in failing to supervise her adequately and in failing to report her condition fully to the attending physician. The trial court entered judgment against the nursing facility and a directed verdict for the physician. The resident appealed.

The appeals court noted that residents generally have the burden of proving, through the use of expert testimony, the proper standard of care that is to be imposed on physicians and health care facilities in medical malpractice cases. The appeals court noted an absence of expert testimony as to the proper standard of care required. Because the resident failed to satisfy the burden of proof, the appeals court upheld the trial court's verdict for the physician.

The burden of proof in a criminal case lies with the prosecution. Proof of guilt "beyond a reasonable doubt" is required to convict a criminal defendant—a higher standard than that used in a civil case (which is a fair preponderance of the credible evidence presented).

Violation of a Statute

Violation of a statute may constitute direct evidence of negligence, or it simply may voice a duty that is owed to a particular class of persons who are protected by the statute, ordinance, or regulation. For example, a regulation that specifies a certain nurse–patient ratio requires compliance by health care facilities covered under the statute. The same regulation is an expression of the duty imposed on the facility to provide adequate nursing services to patients. The patients are, therefore, a class of persons identified within the regulation who are to have the benefits of the protection to be gained by having a predetermined minimum standard nurse–patient ratio. Such ratios were taken into account in *Nichols v. Greenacres Rest Home,* 245 So.2d 544, 545 (La. Ct. App. 1971), where it was shown that the nursing facility was in full compliance with all the requirements for the minimum standards for nursing facilities in Louisiana. The rest home had 64 residents, with a total of 19 employees providing 150 hours of nursing care for each 24-hour period. According to applicable standards, only 128 hours of nursing care actually were necessary for compliance.

Violation of Internal Policy and Procedures

Internal policy and procedures or rules of conduct of a health care facility are set for the day-to-day operation of the institution. A violation of a facility's policy and procedures can give rise to evidence for negligence.

Res Ipsa Loquitur

Res ipsa loquitur ("the thing speaks for itself" or "circumstances speak for themselves") is the legal doctrine that shifts the burden of proof from the plaintiff to the defendant. It is an evidentiary device that allows the plaintiff to make a case legally adequate to go to the jury on the basis of well-defined circumstantial evidence. This does not mean that the plaintiff has proven fully the defendant's negligence. It merely shifts the burden of going forward to the defendant—who must argue to dismiss the circumstantial evidence presented as "speaking for itself."

An inference of negligence is permitted from the mere occurrence of an injury when the defendant owed a duty and possessed the sole power of preventing the injury by exercise of reasonable care. For example, the presence of severe burns on a patient's body after being bathed by an employee raises the question of negligence without the need for expert testimony. Negligence is considered so obvious that expert testimony is not necessary. It lies within a layman's realm of knowledge that people generally do not suffer burns from a bath. That alone is sufficient to require a defendant to come forward with a rebuttal. The three elements necessary to shift the burden of proof under the doctrine of *res ipsa loquitur* are as follows:

1. The event would not normally have occurred in the absence of negligence
2. The defendant must have had exclusive control over the instrumentality that caused the injury
3. The plaintiff must not have contributed to the injury

Negligence commonly can be inferred where individuals suffer burns from hot water bottles, heat lamps, steam vaporizers, chemicals, and bedside lamps and where physicians fail to order x-rays to diagnose possible fractures.

An action was brought against the nursing facility in *Franklin v. Collins Chapel Correctional Hospital,* 696 S.W.2d 16 (Tenn. Ct. App. 1985), to recover damages for the wrongful death of an 82-year-old resident. The resident was admitted to the nursing facility with senility, high blood pressure, and incontinence. Extensive thermal burns were discovered soon after the resident was bathed by an attendant. The complaint sought to invoke the doctrine of *res ipsa loquitur* because the injuries suffered by the resident do not occur in a nursing facility in the absence of negligence, and the deceased was in the defendant's "sole care, custody and control." *Id.* at 18. The plaintiffs alleged, among other things, that

• The decedent was placed in scalding hot water sufficient to cause second- and third-degree burns
• The resident was in the care, custody, and control of the defendants
• The defendants failed to secure prompt medical treatment for the resident
• The defendant failed to maintain proper water temperatures
• The defendant failed to discover the burns within a reasonable time after they had been sustained by the resident
• The defendant failed to exercise reasonable and ordinary care under the circumstances

The trial court entered a judgment for the nursing facility pursuant to a jury verdict, and the administrators of the estate appealed. The appeals court held that proof that the nursing facility had exclusive control over the bath wherein burns were allegedly suffered and that the burns normally would not occur absent negligence entitled the administrators to a jury instruction on the doctrine of *res ipsa loquitur*. The case was reversed and remanded for a new trial.

The patient in *Mack v. Lydia E. Hall Hospital,* 503 N.Y.S.2d 131 (App. Div. 1986), was properly permitted to invoke the doctrine of *res ipsa loquitur* in her suit to recover damages for a third-degree burn by an electrocoagulator on the side of her left thigh during surgery. The prerequisites for application of the doctrine were satisfied by evidence that the injury was unusual, the surgeon had exclusive control over the electrocoagulator, and the patient could not have contributed to the injury. The plaintiff's award of $75,000 was not considered excessive.

A major problem with the doctrine of *res ipsa loquitur* is abuse. To permit an inference of negligence under the doctrine of *res ipsa loquitur* solely because an uncommon complication develops would place too heavy a burden on the medical profession and might result in an undesirable limitation on the use of operations or new procedures involving inherent risks of injury despite due care. Abuse can occur when *res ipsa loquitur* is applied to cases in which the facts show no more than a mistake in diagnosis (e.g., surgery for presumed appendicitis) or an adverse result of a medical procedure known to produce some poor results even when all precautions have been taken.

The general rule for all cases of circumstantial evidence, both ordinary negligence cases and *res ipsa loquitur* cases, is that, to make out his or her case, the plaintiff does not have to eliminate all other possible causes or inferences than that of the defendant's negligence, and it is enough for him or her if the evidence makes such negligence more probable than any other cause.[6]

In *Myers v. Hospital Association of City of Schenectady,* 356 N.Y.S.2d 720 (App. Div. 1974), a patient's body was found lying on the ground five floors below the window of his room. The window was not locked when the body was found. The patient had been given a drug the night before that was capable of causing drowsiness. The court found these facts, which were entered into evidence, insufficient to invoke *res ipsa loquitur*. There was not a sufficient, causal relationship between the patient's death and the unlocked window.

EVIDENCE

Evidence consists of the facts proved or disproved during a lawsuit. The law of evidence is a body of rules under which facts are proved. The rules of evidence govern the admission of items of proof in a lawsuit. A fact can be proven by either circumstantial or direct evidence. Evidence must be competent, relevant, and material to be admitted at trial.

Direct Evidence

Direct evidence is proof offered through direct testimony. It is the jury's function to receive testimony presented by witnesses and to draw conclusions in the determination of facts.

Demonstrative Evidence

Demonstrative or "real" evidence is evidence furnished by things themselves. It is considered the most trustworthy and preferred type of evidence. It consists of tangible objects to which testimony refers (e.g., medical instruments and broken infusion needles) that can be requested by a jury. Demonstrative evidence is admissible in court if it is relevant, has probative value, and serves the interest of justice. It is not admissible if it is intended to prejudice, mislead, confuse, offend, inflame, or arouse the sympathy or passion of the jury or to be indecent. Other forms of demonstrative evidence include photographs, motion pictures, x-ray films, drawings, human bodies as exhibits, pathology slides, fetal monitoring strips, infection committee reports, medical staff bylaws, rules and regulations, nursing manuals, policy and procedure manuals, census data, and staffing patterns. The plaintiff's attorney uses all pertinent evidence to reconstruct chronologically the care and treatment rendered.

When presenting photographs as a form of evidence, the photographer or a reliable witness who is familiar with the object photographed must state that the picture is an accurate representation and a fair likeness of the object portrayed. The photograph must not exaggerate a client's physical condition or show coloring of injuries that is prejudicial. Photographs can be valuable legal evidence when they illustrate graphically the nature and extent of a medical injury. Motion pictures are also valuable evidence. They are helpful in re-enacting a crime. The same principles that apply to photographs apply to motion pictures. Motion pictures must not be fraudulently portrayed by destroying continuity (by either cutting or rearranging). Videotape, a modern form of recording events, is admissible in court, assuming appropriate authentication of the matter being taped, the time of the taping, and the manner in which such taping took place.

X-ray films are considered pictures of the interior of the object portrayed and are admitted under the same requirements as photographs and motion pictures. The attorney must show competent evidence that the x-rays taken are the object or body part under consideration—that the x-ray was made in a recognized manner, taken by a competent technician, and interpreted by a competent physician trained to read x-rays. The value of x-rays is that they illustrate fractures, foreign objects, etc.

The plaintiff's injuries are admissible as an exhibit if the physical condition of the body is material. The human body is considered the best evidence of the nature and extent of the plaintiff's injury. If there is no controversy about either the nature or the extent of the injury, such evidence can be considered prejudicial material to which the defendant's attorney should object.

Demonstrations are permitted in some instances to illustrate the extent of injuries. The resident in *Hendricks v. Sanford,* 337 P.2d 974 (Or. 1959), had developed serious bed sores on her back. The defendant objected to the offer of the plaintiff to display her back to the jury. The court found that the plaintiff's injuries, which had healed, were completely relevant as evidence. Even though the injuries had healed and a skin graft had been performed, a declivity of about three-and-one-half inches in diameter and about the depth of a shallow ashtray was still discernible on the plaintiff's back. *Id.* at 976.

> Where an issue as to personal injuries is involved, an injured person may be permitted to exhibit to the jury the wound or injury, or the member or portion of his body upon which such wound or injury was inflicted, and if relevant, the exhibition is allowable in the discretion of the court where there is no reason to expect that the sympathy of the jury will be excited.

Id. at 975.

Documentary Evidence

Documentary evidence is written evidence capable of making a truthful statement (e.g., drug manufacturer inserts, autopsy reports, birth certificates, and medical records). Documentary evidence must satisfy the jury as to authenticity. Proof of authenticity is not necessary if genuineness is accepted by the opposing party. In some instances, concerning wills, for example, witnesses are necessary. In the case of documentation, the original of a document must be produced unless it can be demonstrated that the original has been lost or destroyed, in which case a properly authenticated copy may be substituted.

A sampling of preliminary questions that a witness might be asked on entering a medical record into evidence include the following:

- Please state your name.
- Where are you employed?
- What is your position?
- What is your official title?
- Did you receive a *subpoena duces tecum* for certain records?
- Did you bring those records with you?
- Can you identify these records?

- Did you retrieve the records yourself?
- Are these the complete records?
- Are these the original records or copies of the originals?
- How were these records prepared?
- Are these records maintained under your care, custody, and control?
- Were these records made in the regular course of business?
- Was the record made at the time the act, condition, or event occurred or transpired?
- Is this record regularly kept or maintained?

A manufacturer's drug insert or manual describing the use of equipment is admissible. In *Mueller v. Mueller,* 221 N.W.2d 39 (S.D. 1974), a physician was sued by a patient who charged that as a result of the administration of cortisone over an extended period, she had suffered needlessly a deterioration of bone structure and ultimately a collapsed hip. The jury decided that the physician's prolonged use of cortisone was negligent, and the physician appealed. The appeals court held that the manufacturer's recommendations are not only admissible but also essential in determining a physician's possible lack of proper care.

In another case, *Mulligan v. Lederle Laboratories,* 786 F.2d 859 (8th Cir. 1986), the plaintiff, a medical laboratory technician, brought an action against the drug manufacturer as the result of the side effects of the drug Varidase. The plaintiff developed several chronic health problems including mouth sores, microscopic hematuria, and red cell cast, indicating kidney disease. The trial court awarded $50,000 in compensatory damages and $100,000 in punitive damages for the drug manufacturer's failure to warn of the side effects of the drug Varidase. On appeal by the manufacturer, the appeals court held that the products liability action was not barred by a three-year statute of limitations contained in an Arkansas products liability act and that the evidence was sufficient to award punitive damages. Evidence presented at trial indicated that several side effects were associated with the drug.

Judicial Notice Rule

The judicial notice rule prescribes that well-known facts (e.g., that fractures need prompt attention and that two x-rays of the same patient may show different results) need not be proven, but rather, they are recognized by the court as *fact.* If a fact can be disputed, the rule does not apply.

The plaintiff in *Arthur v. St. Peter's Hospital,* 169 N.J. Super. 575, 405 A.2d 443 (1979), sought treatment in the emergency department of St. Peter's

Hospital after an injury to his left wrist. After being examined, he was sent to the radiology department for x-rays of his wrist. He later was released after being advised that there were no fractures. The plaintiff suffered continued swelling and pain. As a result, he decided to seek care from another physician, who subsequently diagnosed a fracture of the navicular bone. The plaintiff sued, and the hospital motioned for summary judgment, stating that the physicians were independent contractors and not employees of the hospital.

Copies of the emergency department record, x-ray report, and billing record contained the logo of the hospital. There was nothing on the records to identify the physicians as being independent contractors. The court took *judicial notice* that generally people who seek medical help through the emergency departments of hospitals are unaware of the status of the different professionals working there. Unless the patient had been in some manner put on notice that those physicians with whom he might come into contact during the course of his treatment were independent contractors, it would be natural to assume that they were employees of the hospital.

Evidence indicating the propensity of a defendant to commit a negligent act is admissible evidence. The Supreme Court of Suffolk County, Special Term, in *Cotgreave v. Public Administration,* 443 N.Y.S.2d 971 (Sup. Ct. 1981), held that medical malpractice plaintiffs would be allowed to introduce evidence of prior operations on persons other than the patient by the defendant physician, who allegedly intentionally performed unnecessary surgery on the patient. The court had been informed of other cases pending against the surgeon in which allegations were made as to the lack of indications for surgery.

Medical Books

Medical books are considered hearsay because the authors are not generally available for cross-examination. Although medical books are not admissible as evidence, a physician may testify as how he or she formed an opinion and what part textbooks played in forming that opinion. During cross-examination, medical experts may be asked to comment on statements from medical books that contradict their testimony.

Examination of Witnesses

After conclusion of the opening statements, the judge calls for the plaintiff's witnesses. An officer of the court administers an oath to each witness, and direct examination begins. Information must be obtained from each witness in the form of questions by the attorney, not by the attorney's recitation of the story to the witness. On cross-examination by the defense, an attempt will be made to challenge or discredit the plaintiff's witness. Redirect examination by the plaintiff's attorney can follow the cross-examination, if so desired. The plaintiff's attorney may at this time wish to have his or her witness review an important point the jury may have forgotten during cross-examination. The plaintiff's attorney may ask the same witness more questions in an effort to overcome the effect of the cross-examination. Re-cross-examination by the defense may take place if necessary for the defense of the defendant.

A sampling of preliminary questions that a physician might expect to be asked on a personal injury case, for example, may take the following form:

- Name, residence, prior residences?
- Where did you attend medical school?
- Are you licensed in this state?
- Where did you serve your internship?
- Where did you serve your residency?
- Is your practice general or special?
- Are you board-certified in one or more specialties?
- How does a physician obtain board certification?
- Are you presently practicing medicine?
- How long have you been in practice?
- During your_____years of practice, have you had occasion to treat many personal injury cases?
- On or about_____, did you have occasion to see_____on a professional basis?
- Where? Describe his/her condition at the time.
- What, if anything, did you do on that occasion?
- Have you been the attending physician since that date?
- Describe the nature of the examination that you made on_____and from time to time since then.
- Did you see him/her daily, several times a day at first, when he/she was in the nursing facility?
- Did you continue to see him/her? How often?
- What, generally, did your treatment consist of?
- From your examination and treatment of_____, did you determine what injuries were sustained?
- As a result of your examination, did you find it necessary to seek consultation from another physician or specialist?

• Did there come a time when you found it necessary to transfer the resident to another facility?

The credibility of a witness may be impeached if prior statements are inconsistent with later statements and if there is bias in favor of a party or prejudice against a party to a lawsuit. Either attorney to a lawsuit may ask the judge for permission to recall a witness.

After all the witnesses of the plaintiff have taken the stand, the defense may call its witnesses and the process of direct, cross, redirect, and re-cross-examination is repeated until the defense rests.

Hearsay Evidence

Hearsay evidence is based on what another has said or done and is not the result of the personal knowledge of the witness. Hearsay consists of written or oral statements. Where a witness testifies to the utterance of a statement made outside court and the statement is offered in court for the truth of the facts that are contained in the statement, this is hearsay and therefore objectionable.

If a statement is offered not as proof of the facts asserted in the statement but rather only to show that the statement was made, the statement can come into evidence. For example, if it is relevant that a conversation took place, the testimony relating to the conversation may be entered as evidence. The purpose of that testimony would be to establish that a conversation took place and not to prove what was said during the course of the conversation. If testimony is based on personal knowledge, it would be admissible as evidence. *Keyes v. Tallahassee Memorial Regional Medical Center,* 579 So.2d 201 (Fla. Ct. App. 1991).

Because of the ability to challenge hearsay evidence successfully, which rests on the credibility of the witness as well as on the competency and veracity of other persons not before the court, it is admitted as evidence in a trial only under very strict rules. The U.S. district court in *Northeast Women's Center v. McMonagle,* 689 F. Supp. 465 (E.D. Pa. 1988), in a civil action alleging Racketeer Influenced and Corrupt Organization Act (RICO) violations and trespass arising from protests at an abortion clinic, found the trial court to have properly excluded testimony of one of the witnesses. The substance of the proposed testimony was based on double hearsay and not the competent testimony of the witness. A police officer's testimony that he had overheard a drug dealer tell the informant, who was wearing a concealed transmitter, that he could obtain proof for the informant from a pharmacist friend was properly admitted in a disciplinary proceeding. *Brown v. Idaho State Board of Pharmacy,* 746 P.2d 1006 (Idaho Ct. App. 1987). The testimony was presented before the Idaho State Board of Pharmacy for proving a dealer's state of mind and explaining his subsequent visit to the pharmacy. The testimony was not subject to hearsay objection.

Many exceptions to the hearsay rule allow testimony that ordinarily would not be admitted. Included in the list of exceptions are admissions made by one of the parties to the action, threats made by a victim, dying declarations, statements to refresh a witness's recollection if he or she is unable to remember the facts he or she once knew, business records, medical records, and other official records (e.g., certified copies of birth and death records). "Where hearsay evidence is admitted without objection, its probative value is for the jury to determine."[7] The above list of exceptions to hearsay evidence is by no means all-inclusive, and therefore, state statutes should be consulted.

Hypnotically Induced Testimony

Hypnotically induced testimony is admissible as evidence. Hypnotically induced testimony was admissible in *Tardi v. Henry,* 571 N.E.2d 1020 (Ill. App. Ct. 1991), in which the patient claimed that a neurosurgeon sexually assaulted her. Although it was unclear as to what portion of the plaintiff's testimony was hypnotically induced, the evidence overwhelmingly favored the neurosurgeon and could not support a verdict.

Expert Witness

Certain types of litigation require witnesses with specialized knowledge to aid a jury in fact-finding. The expert witness assists the jury when the issues to be resolved in the case are outside the experience of the average juror. Expert testimony, as well as scientific data, is used to assist in establishing the standard of care required in any given situation. Expert witnesses may be used to assist a plaintiff in proving the wrongful act of a defendant or to assist a defendant in refuting such evidence. In addition, expert testimony may be used to show the extent of the plaintiff's damages or to show the lack of such damages.

It is the jury's function to receive testimony presented by witnesses and to draw conclusions in the determination of facts. The law recognizes that a jury is composed of ordinary men and women and that some fact-finding will involve subjects beyond their knowledge. When a jury cannot otherwise obtain sufficient facts from which to draw conclusions, an expert witness who has special knowledge, skill, experience, or training can be called on to submit an opinion. Laymen are quite able to render opinions about a great variety of general subjects, but for technical questions, the opinion of an expert is necessary. At the time of testifying, each expert's training, experience, and special qualifications will be explained to the jury. The experts will be asked to give an opinion concerning hypothetical questions based on the facts of the case. Should the testimony of two experts conflict, the jury will determine which expert opinion to accept.

The Supreme Court of Iowa in *Kastler v. Iowa Methodist Hospital,* 193 N.W.2d 98 (Iowa 1971), held that injuries sustained by the patient from a fall in a shower afforded by the hospital were the result of routine and not professional care. The patient was not required to introduce expert testimony on her behalf.

Expert testimony was not required in *Powell v. Mullins,* 479 So.2d 1119 (Ala. 1985), in which a surgical lap sponge was left in the abdomen of a patient during the performance of a cesarean section. The trial court committed reversible error in directing a verdict in the physician's favor because of the patient's failure to present an expert witness. Testimony of an expert witness generally is not required where an understanding of the physician's alleged lack of skill or due care requires only common knowledge or experience. The evidence in this case demonstrated that no intrasurgical x-rays were taken although the patient was high risk because of her smoking, obesity, and diabetes. The Supreme Court of Alabama held that it was the physician's responsibility to remove all sponges from inside the patient before closing the incision.

DEFENSES AGAINST RECOVERY

Once a plaintiff's case has been established, the defendant may put forward a defense against the claim for damages. The defendant's case is presented to discredit the plaintiff's cause of action and prevent recovery of damages.

This section deals with the defenses available to defendants in a negligence suit. These are principles of law that may relieve a defendant from liability.

Assumption of the Risk

"Assumption of the risk" is knowing that a danger exists and voluntarily accepting the risk by taking a chance in exposing oneself to it, knowing that harm might occur. Assumption of the risk may be "implicitly assumed," as in alcohol consumption, or "expressly assumed," as in relation to warnings found on cigarette packaging.

This defense provides that the plaintiff expressly has given consent in advance, relieving the defendant of an obligation of conduct toward the plaintiff and taking the chances of injury from a known risk arising from the defendant's conduct. For example, one who agrees to care for a patient with a communicable disease and then contracts the disease would not be entitled to recover from the patient for damages suffered. In taking the job, the individual agreed to assume the risk of infection, thereby releasing the patient from all legal obligations.

The following two requirements must be established in order for a defendant to be successful in an assumption of the risk defense: (1) The plaintiff must know and understand the risk that is being incurred; and (2) the choice to incur the risk must be free and voluntary.

Borrowed Servant and Captain of the Ship Doctrines

The borrowed servant doctrine is a special application of the doctrine of *respondeat superior* and applies when an employer lends an employee to another for a particular employment. Although an employee remains the servant of the employer, under the borrowed servant doctrine the employer is not liable for injury negligently caused by the servant while in the special service of another. The borrowed servant rule provides that in certain situations a nurse employed by a hospital may be considered the employee of the physician. In these situations, the physician is the special or temporary employer and is liable for the negligence of the nurse. To determine whether a physician is liable for the negligence of a nurse, it must be established that the physician had the right to control and direct the nurse at the time of the negligent act. If the physician is found to be in exclusive control and if the nurse is deemed to be the physician's temporary special employee, the hospital is not generally liable for the nurse's negligent acts.

In the context of the operating room, the application of the borrowed servant doctrine generally is referred to as the captain of the ship doctrine. Under this doctrine, the surgeon is viewed as being the one in command in the operating room. The rationale for this concept was provided in the Minnesota case of *St. Paul-Mercury Indemnity Co. v. St. Joseph Hospital,* 4 N.W.2d 637 (Minn. 1942), when the court stated this:

> The desirability of the rule is obvious. The patient is completely at the mercy of the surgeon and relies upon him to see that all the acts relative to the operation are performed in a careful manner. It is the surgeon's duty to guard against any and all avoidable acts that may result in injury to his patient. In the operating room, the surgeon must be master. He cannot tolerate any other voice in the control of his assistants. In the case at bar, the evidence is clear that the doctor had exclusive control over the acts in question, and therefore the hospital cannot be said to have been a "joint master" or "comaster," even though the nurses were in its general employ and paid by it.

Id. at 638, 639.

In *Krane v. Saint Anthony Hospital Systems,* 738 P.2d 75 (Colo. Ct. App. 1987), the Colorado Court of Appeals held that even if we assume that the surgical nurse was the employee of the hospital, that she was negligent, and that such negligence caused the death of the plaintiff's husband, the so-called captain of the ship doctrine still precludes recovery against the hospital. The factual question that must be determined is whether, at the time of the alleged negligent act, the operating surgeon had assumed such control. If so, the responsibility of the surgeon supersedes that of the hospital. Because it was uncontradicted that the alleged negligent act of the surgical nurse took place over two and one-half hours into surgery, there could be no factual dispute that the surgeon had assumed control over the nurse.

Several courts have developed a distinction between a nurse's clerical or administrative acts and those involving professional skill and judgment, which are considered medical acts. The courts use this distinction in allocating liability for the acts of a nurse as between the surgeon and the hospital. If the act is characterized as administrative or clerical, it is the hospital's responsibility; if the act is considered to be medical, it is the surgeon's responsibility. This rule was followed in the Minnesota case of *Swigerd v. City of Ortonville,* 75 N.W.2d 217 (Minn. 1956), in which the court found that the hospital is liable as an employer for the negligence of its nurses in performing acts that are basically administrative (e.g., clerical acts). Administrative acts, although constituting a component of a patient's prescribed medical treatment, do not require the application of specialized procedures and techniques or the understanding of a skilled physician or surgeon.

The distinction between administrative and other acts occasionally is stated by the courts to determine whether a hospital or a physician is liable for a nurse's negligent acts. However, it is regarded by some jurisdictions as lacking sound judgment. Although the courts have narrowed those situations where a nonemployee staff physician will be held liable for the negligent acts of hospital employees, there continue to be cases holding physicians responsible for the negligent acts of nurses. The court of appeals in *Schultz v. Mutch,* 211 Cal. Rptr. 455 (Ct. App. 1985), held that the jury was correctly instructed as to a physician's *respondeat superior* liability for the acts and omissions of nurses. A physician's reliance, no matter how reasonable, on hospital nursing procedures does not extinguish his liability for the negligence of nurses under the *respondeat superior* doctrine of captain of the ship, which is founded in the doctor's power and resulting duty to direct nurses under his or her supervision.

Comparative Negligence

A defense of comparative negligence provides that the degree of negligence or carelessness of each party to a lawsuit must be established by the finder of fact and that each party then is responsible for his or her proportional share of any damages awarded. For example, where a plaintiff suffers injuries of $10,000 from an accident and where the plaintiff is found 20 percent negligent and the defendant 80 percent negligent, the defendant would be required to pay $8,000 to the plaintiff. Thus, with comparative negligence, the plaintiff can collect for 80 percent of the injuries, whereas an application of contributory negligence would deprive the plaintiff of any money judgment. This doctrine relieves the plaintiff from the hardship of losing an entire claim when a defendant has been successful in establishing that the plaintiff has contributed to his or her own injuries. A defense that provides that the plaintiff will forfeit an entire claim if he or she has been contributorily negligent is considered too harsh a result in jurisdictions that recognize comparative negligence.

In most states today, contributory negligence will not defeat a plaintiff's claim but may reduce the amount of damages. A patient's negligence was permitted as a defense to lessen the damages and to reflect her personal contribution to her injury in *Heller v. Medine,* 377 N.Y.S.2d 100 (App. Div. 1975). The patient had brought a malpractice action against a physician, alleging improper treatment of a herpes infection after cataract surgery on the right eye. The physician alleged that the plaintiff contributed to her own injury by failing to make two follow-up visits. The trial court entered a verdict in favor of the physician. On appeal, the appellate court held that the patient's failure to follow the physician's instructions did not defeat the action where the alleged improper professional treatment occurred before the patient's own negligence. Damages were reduced to the degree that the plaintiff's negligence increased the extent of the injury.

The plaintiff in *Quinones v. Public Administrator,* 373 N.Y.S.2d 224 (App. Div. 1975), sought to recover damages for the alleged negligence of the defendant's physicians for their failure to treat a fractured ankle. The plaintiff claimed that there was a nonunion of the fracture and that he was advised to put weight on his leg. As a result of this advice, the plaintiff claimed that there was an exacerbation of the original injury requiring two operative procedures, which resulted in the fusion of his left ankle. The defendant claimed that if there was any subsequent injury, it was the failure of the plaintiff to return for care. The supreme court entered a judgment in favor of the defendant hospital, and the plaintiff appealed. The supreme court, appellate division, held that a patient's failure to follow instructions does not defeat an action for malpractice where the alleged improper professional treatment occurred before the patient's own negligence. Damages would be reduced to the degree that the plaintiff's negligence increased the extent of the injury.

There are a variety of comparative negligence systems adopted by different states (e.g., the "pure" system, the "50 percent" system, and several modified systems). In a "pure" system, the plaintiff is permitted to recover an amount for damages reduced by the percentage of his or her fault, even if the plaintiff's share of negligence exceeds 50 percent. Under the "50 percent" system, the plaintiff is permitted to recover an amount for damages reduced by his or her fault, provided the plaintiff's share of negligence (depending on the exact wording of the statute) does not exceed 50 percent. Under the modified systems, most states provide that the plaintiff may not recover damages if the plaintiff's percentage of negligence is equal to that of the defendant. In other states, the plaintiff may not recover damages if his or her percentage of negligence exceeds that of the defendant.[8]

Contributory Negligence

Contributory negligence may be defined as any lack of ordinary care on the part of the person injured that, combined with the negligent act of another, caused the injury and without which the injury would not have occurred. When the issue of contributory negligence is raised, the defendant claims that the conduct of the injured person is below the standard of care reasonably prudent persons would exercise for their own safety. A person is contributorily negligent when that person does not exercise reasonable care for his or her own safety. As a general proposition, if a person has knowledge of a dangerous situation and disregards the danger, the person is contributorily negligent. Actual knowledge of the danger of injury is not necessary for a person to be contributorily negligent. It is sufficient if a reasonable person should have been aware of the possibility of the danger.

In some jurisdictions, contributory negligence, no matter how slight, is sufficient to defeat a plaintiff's claim. The two elements necessary to establish contributory negligence are (1) that the plaintiff's conduct fell below the required standard of personal care, and (2) that there is a causal connection between the plaintiff's careless conduct and the plaintiff's injury. Thus, the defendant contends that some, if not all, liability is attributable to the plaintiff's own actions. To establish a defense of contributory negligence, the defendant must show that the plaintiff's negligence was an active and efficient contributing cause of the injury. This was not the case in *Bird v. Pritchard,* 33 Ohio App. 2d 31, 291 N.E.2d 769 (1973), in which the plaintiff on July 3, 1970, slipped and fell, cutting her right hand on a mayonnaise jar and thus injuring the ulnar nerve. She was taken to Hocking Valley Memorial Hospital where she requested the services of Dr. Najm, a board-certified general surgeon. However, he was not available. The defendant, an osteopathic surgeon, was available, and he treated the patient's wound. The patient had complained that the fourth and fifth fingers of her right hand were numb. The defendant cleaned the wound and advised the patient to see him on Monday, July 7. The patient did not return to the osteopathic surgeon but went to see Dr. Najm that same Monday. A suit was filed, the court of common pleas rendered a judgment for the defendant, and the plaintiff appealed. The court of appeals held that the patient could not be found to have been contributorily negligent or to have assumed the risk where by the time of her scheduled visit, it was impossible to perform primary or secondary repair of the injured nerves that had not been treated on the initial visit when she had first complained of numbness. "For contributory negligence to defeat the claim of the plaintiff, there must not only be negligent conduct by the plaintiff but also a direct and proximate causal relationship between the negligent act and the injury the plaintiff received." 291 N.E.2d at 771.

The Delaware Supreme Court affirmed a lower court's dismissal of a wrongful death action against a medical center's emergency department personnel in *Rochester v. Katalan,* 320 A.2d 704 (Del. 1974). The decedent, Mr. Rochester, and a friend had been brought to the emergency department at approximately 6:30 P.M. under the custody of two police officers. Mr. Rochester and his friend, claiming to be heroin addicts suffering withdrawal symptoms, requested some form of medication. Mr. Rochester stated that he had a habit requiring four to five bags of heroin a day. His actions denoted symptoms of withdrawal. He and his friend were loud, abusive, and uncooperative. Mr. Rochester complained of abdominal pains, his eyes appeared glassy, and his body was shaking, among other symptoms that he exhibited. The physician on duty in the emergency department asked whether Mr. Rochester had ever participated in a methadone clinic program. Mr. Rochester indicated that he had, but that he had dropped out of it because he found a new supply source for heroin. The physician then ordered the administration of 40 mg methadone. Mr. Rochester continued to put on an act by beating his head against a wall and claiming that he was still sick and needed more methadone. The plea was granted, and the physician ordered a second dose of 40 mg methadone. After eventually calming down, Mr. Rochester was taken to a cell by the police officers. The following morning it was impossible to awaken him, and he was later pronounced dead. It was discovered that he had never been an addict or on a methadone program. Rather, the previous night he had been drinking beer and taking Librium. He had not told this to hospital authorities.

His estate sued the physician, and the trial court dismissed the suit. The appellate court affirmed, saying that by his failure to give the physician accurate information, the deceased had contributed to his own death. On appeal, the plaintiff had argued that the physician and staff could have done more to determine the truth of Mr. Rochester's assertions that he was a drug addict. The Delaware Supreme Court held that it already had assumed negligence in that respect. Mr. Rochester contributed to his own death by failing to provide a true account of the facts to the emergency department staff. He was guilty of negligent conduct, more accurately "willful" or "intentional" conduct, which was the proximate cause of his death, resulting from multiple drug intoxication. His estate was barred from recovering any monetary damages.

"Generally a relaxed standard of care is required in the contributory negligence situation by persons who are subject to the infirmities of old age." *Garner v. Crawford,* 288 So.2d 886 , 888 (La. Ct. App. 1973). The court in *Powell v. Parkview Estate Nursing Home, Inc.,* 240 So.2d 53 (La. Ct. App. 1970), found that when a resident is unable to physically and mentally care for herself "it logically follows she could not be held to the same degree of accountability as a normally healthy person." *Id.* at 57. The 77-year-old resident, who had been bedridden for a year or more and weighed less than 100 lbs., fell from her bed at 10:30 P.M. The nurse who found her placed her back in bed and raised the side rails. The nurse noted on the resident's chart that the resident apparently did not sustain any serious injuries, although she did suffer from abrasions and cuts on her face. The nurse also noted that the resident "does not complain of pain— hard to determine." *Id.* at 55. The night nurse was asked to observe the resident and told that if anything came up to notify the administrator of the nursing facility. The following morning a registered nurse determined that the resident's left leg was broken above the ankle and summoned the physician. From the testimony presented from witnesses and the nursing facility records entered into evidence, the trial judge concluded that the side rails were down at the time of the accident. In addition, the night table, which was usually placed close to the resident's bed to prevent her from falling, was not in position. Judgment was rendered for the plaintiff. On appeal, the court held that the defendant's employees were aware that the resident was senile and almost helpless and that both rails should have been raised or the table placed against the bed on the side where the rail was down to prevent the very accident that did occur. The "evidence establishes defendant's employees failed to exercise the care required of them under the law in this instance, and this failure constitutes fault. . . ." *Id.* at 57. The defendant's argument that the resident was contributorily negligent required that the defendant prove that the resident conducted herself in such a way as to constitute negligence. The defendant failed to do that.

The patient, Mr. Cammatte, in *Jenkins v. Bogalusa Community Medical Center,* 340 So.2d 1065 (La. Ct. App. 1976), was admitted to Bogalusa Community Medical Center on September 11, 1970, for the treatment of a severe gouty arthritic condition. He had been advised not to get out of bed without first ringing for assistance. On the morning of September 16, 1970, he got out of bed without ringing for assistance and went to a bathroom across the hall. As he returned to his room, he fell and fractured his hip. Mr. Cammatte was transferred to Touro Infirmary in New Orleans where he underwent hip surgery and died on October 5, 1970, during recuperation, caused by an apparent pulmonary embolism. The trial court entered judgment for the defendants, and the plaintiffs appealed. The appeals court found that the patient was in full possession of his faculties at the time he fell and fractured his hip. The accident was the result of the patient's knowing failure to follow instructions not to get out of bed without ringing for assistance. The injury in this case was not the result of any breach of the institution's duty to exercise due care.

The rationale for contributory negligence is based on the principle that all persons must be both careful and responsible for their acts. A plaintiff is required to conform to the broad standard of conduct of the reasonable person.

The plaintiff's negligence will be determined and governed by the same tests and rules as the negligence of the defendant.

Doctrine of Charitable Immunity

The doctrine of charitable immunity is a legal doctrine that developed out of the English court system and held charitable institutions blameless for their negligent acts. Historically, there was little consistency in the application of the doctrine in the United States. Some states permitted judgment for paying patients, but others did not hold hospitals liable even if it was shown they were negligent. Patients who were treated in charitable hospitals were said to have implicitly waived their right of suit because of negligence. Patients paying a reasonable charge were not considered to be the recipients of charity.

Today, the doctrine of charitable immunity is essentially history. Most states have abolished charitable immunity exemptions. Suits now may be brought against charitable institutions, and such institutions are liable for their negligent acts and those of their agents.

Good Samaritan Laws

The states have enacted good samaritan laws, which relieve physicians, nurses, dentists, and other health professionals, and in some instances, laymen, from liability in certain emergency situations. Good samaritan legislation encourages health professionals to render assistance at the scene of emergencies. New Jersey's statute provides that

> [a]ny individual, including a person licensed to practice any method of treatment of human ailments, disease, pain, injury, deformity, mental or physical condition, or licensed to render services ancillary thereto, or any person who is a volunteer member of a duly incorporated first aid and emergency or rescue squad association, who in good faith renders emergency care at the scene of an accident or emergency to the victim or victims thereof, or while transporting the victim or victims thereof to a hospital or other facility where treatment is to be rendered, shall not be liable for any civil damages as a result of any acts or omissions by such person rendering the emergency care.[9]

Minnesota state law provides for fines of up to $100 for persons who fail to aid others in emergency situations. The law in this instance provides that "reasonable assistance" should be given (i.e., obtain or attempt to obtain aid from medical and/or law enforcement personnel). The law protects an individual from liability unless he or she is reckless or intentionally cruel when rendering aid. If an individual at the scene of an emergency would have to place him- or herself or another in danger by assisting, each would be exempt from providing assistance.

Good samaritan statutes provide a standard of care that delineates the scope of immunity for those persons eligible under the law. The standards vary widely from state to state and sometimes are ambiguous. In most states, the scope of immunity generally is qualified by the statement that the person giving aid must act "in good faith." Some statutes require that a physician or the person rendering care must act with "due care," without "gross negligence," or without "willful or wanton" misconduct.

Despite problems of interpretation, it is clear that the purpose of the statutes is to encourage volunteer medical assistance in emergency situations. The language that grants immunity also supports the conclusion that the physician, nurse, or layman who is covered by the act will be protected from liability for ordinary negligence in rendering assistance in an emergency.

Under most statutes, immunity is granted only during an emergency or when rendering emergency care. The concept of emergency usually refers to a combination of unforeseen circumstances that require spontaneous action to avoid impending danger. Some states have sought to be more precise regarding what constitutes an emergency or accident. According to the Alaska statute, the emergency circumstances must suggest that the giving of aid is the only alternative to death or serious bodily injury.

Most statutes require that emergency services be rendered without payment or expectation of payment. Apparently, this provision was inserted to emphasize that the actions of a good samaritan must be voluntary. To be legally immune under the good samaritan laws, a physician or nurse must render help voluntarily and without expectation of later pay.

Ignorance of Fact and Unintentional Wrongs

Ignorance of the law is not a defense; otherwise, the ignorant would be rewarded simply by pleading ignorance. Arguing that a negligent act is unintentional is no defense. If such a defense were acceptable, all defendants would use it.

> Ignorance of the law excuses no man; not that all men know the law, but because it is an excuse every man will plead, and no man can tell how to confute him.
>
> John Selden (1584–1654)

Independent Contractor

An independent contractor is an individual who agrees to undertake work without being under the direct control or direction of another and is personally responsible for his or her negligent acts. This doctrine has been used by health care facilities as a defense to avoid liability caused by a physician's negligence. The mere existence of an independent contractual relationship is not sufficient to remove a facility from liability for the acts of certain of its professional personnel where the independent contractor status is not readily known to the injured party.

The appellate division of the New York State Supreme Court in *Mduba v. Benedictine Hospital,* 384 N.Y.S.2d 527 (App. Div. 1976), held that the hospital was liable for the emergency department physician's negligence, whether or not the physician was an independent contractor, even if under contract the physician was considered to be an independent contractor. The court held that the patient had no way of knowing of the existence of a contract and relied on the relationship between the hospital and the physician in seeking treatment in the emergency department. The appellant hospital in *Garcia v. Tarrio,* 380 So.2d 1068 (Fla. Dist. Ct. App. 1980), claimed that the evidence presented did not establish that Dr. Garcia, a surgeon, was the hospital's agent and that the negligence established was attributable to Dr. Garcia alone. The district court of appeals held that the appellant surgeon was the hospital's agent in that he had an agreement with the hospital guaranteeing him at least 50 percent of the work at the hospital.

Whether a physician is an employee or an independent contractor is of primary importance in determining liability for damages. A health care facility generally is not liable for injuries resulting from negligent acts or omissions of independent physicians. There is no liability on the theory of respondeat superior where a physician is an independent contractor so long as the physician is not an employee of the facility, is not compensated, maintains a private practice, and is chosen directly by his or her patients.

Intervening Cause

Intervening cause refers to an act of an independent agency that destroys the causal connection between the negligent act of a defendant and the wrongful injury; if the independent act, not the original wrongful act, is the proximate cause of injury, damages are not recoverable.

In *Cohran v. Harper,* 154 S.E.2d 461 (Ga. Ct. App. 1967), the patient sued a physician, charging him with malpractice for an alleged Staphylococcus infection she received from a hypodermic needle used by the physician's nurse. The nurse gave the patient an injection that resulted in osteomyelitis. The grounds of negligence included an allegation that the physician failed to sterilize properly the hypodermic needle that was used to administer a certain dose of penicillin. The evidence showed, without dispute, that a prepackaged sterilized needle and syringe were used in accordance with proper and accepted medical practice. The physician was not liable. There was inadequate proof that either the physician or his nurse was negligent. The court said that even if there was evidence that the needle was contaminated and that the patient's ailment was caused thereby, there was no evidence that either the physician or his nurse or anyone in his office knew, or by the exercise of ordinary care could have discovered, that the prepackaged needle and syringe were so contaminated. The defense of intervening cause would have been an adequate defense against recovery of damages if it had been established that the needle was contaminated when packaged.

Statute of Limitations

The statute of limitations refers to legislatively imposed conditions that restrict the period of time after the occurrence of an injury during which a legal action must be commenced. Should a cause of action be initiated later than the period of time prescribed, the case cannot proceed. Whether a suit for personal injury can be brought against a defendant often depends on whether the suit was commenced within a time specified by the applicable statute of limitations. The statutory period begins when an injury occurs, although in some cases (usually involving foreign objects left in the body during surgery) the statutory period commences when the injured person discovers or should have discovered the injury.

Many technical rules are associated with statutes of limitations. Statutes in each state specify that malpractice suits and other personal injury suits must be brought within fixed periods of time. That an injured person is a minor or is otherwise under a legal disability may extend the period within which an action for injury may be brought under the laws of many states. Computation of the period when the statute begins in a particular state may be based on any of the following factors: (1) the date that the physician terminated treatment, (2) the time of the wrongful act, (3) the time when the patient should have reasonably discovered the injury, (4) the date that the injury is discovered, and (5) the date when the contract between the patient and the physician ended.

The running of the statute will not begin if fraud (the deliberate concealment from a patient of facts that might present a cause of action for damages) is involved. The cause of action begins at the time fraud is discovered.

The Supreme Court has ruled that a five-year limitation on bringing certain medical malpractice cases is unconstitutional. The ruling stemmed in part from cases dealing with a serial killer, Donald Harvey. The Court struck down a protection long claimed by medical professionals and hospitals against negligence suits. Mr. Harvey was linked to deaths that occurred 20 years ago while he was working at a local hospital.[10]

In a 1949 Michigan case, *Buchanan v. Kull,* 35 N.W.2d 351 (Mich. 1949), a patient who had undergone a thyroidectomy suffered paralyzed vocal cords. The patient had been told that the injury was due to a lack of calcium. The patient later learned that the vocal cords had been cut. The statute of limitations normally would have run out in this case; however, the presence of fraud did not permit the statute to commence until the patient became aware of the fraud.

A New Hampshire patient in *Shillady v. Elliot Community Hospital,* 320 A.2d 637 (N.H. 1974), sued the hospital for negligence in treatment that was administered 31 years earlier. A needle had been left in the patient's spine after a spinal tap in 1940. In 1970, an x-ray showed the needle. The patient had suffered severe pain immediately after the spinal tap, which had decreased over the intervening years to about three "spells" a year. The court held that the six-year statute of limitations does not begin "until the patient learns or in the exercise of reasonable care and diligence should have learned of its presence." *Id.* Therefore, the defendant's motion to dismiss the case on the grounds that the statute of limitations had run out was not granted.

In *Whack v. Seminole Memorial Hospital,* 456 So.2d 561 (Fla. Dist. Ct. App. 1984), summary dismissal of a suit on the basis that the statute of limitations had tolled was ordered improperly in an action for wrongful death during the performance of a cesarean section. It was found that the cause of death could not have been determined until receipt of an autopsy report.

Sovereign Immunity

Sovereign immunity refers to the common-law doctrine by which federal and state governments historically have been immune from liability for harm suffered from the tortious conduct of employees. For the most part, sovereign immunity has been abolished by both federal and state governments.

Congress enacted the Federal Tort Claims Act (FTCA), which provides redress for those who have been negligently injured by employees of the federal government acting within their scope of employment. The *Feres* doctrine, which prohibits a serviceman from bringing an action against the United States under the FTCA, was first enunciated in *Feres v. United States,* 340 U.S. 135 (1950). In *Wooten v. United States,* 574 F. Supp. 200 (W.D. Tenn. 1982), the Veterans Administration Hospital of Memphis, Tennessee, was held negligent for injuries sustained by an 83-year-old heart patient who was found lying outside his room in a hallway of the hospital. This action was brought under the FTCA. The patient had suffered severe head injuries that required surgery.

Damages in the amount of $80,000 were awarded the plaintiff. The court held that the evidence was sufficient to raise a duty on the part of hospital personnel attending the patient to use reasonable care to protect him from getting out of bed and injuring himself. This duty was breached, and the patient was injured. The proximate cause of the patient's injuries was related to the hospital's failure to put up the patient's bed rails and its failure to remind him to call a nurse if he needed help. Evidence offered in this case indicated that the Veterans Administration hospital did not meet the standards of care rendered in other large Memphis hospitals.

Claims made are governed by the law of the state in which negligence is asserted. Action was brought on behalf of a minor in *Steele v. United States,* 463 F. Supp. 321 (D. Alaska 1978), who received treatment at a U.S. Army hospital and suffered injury because of the optometrist's failure to refer the child to an ophthalmologist for examination. The U.S. district court held that it was probable that an ophthalmologist would have diagnosed the child's problem and prevented the loss of his right eye. Recovery was permitted against the United States under the FTCA, 28 U.S.C.A. §1346 (b) 2671 *et seq.*

Immunity from intentional torts, claims arising from combat, etc., are exceptions to the FTCA. A serviceman brought a claim for medical malpractice against the United States in *Luce v. United States,* 538 F. Supp. 637 (E.D. Wis. 1982), under the FTCA. The district court held that the claim was barred under a doctrine prohibiting actions for injuries to a serviceman arising out of or in the course of activity incident to service. The holding was granted even though the operation was elective and the serviceman was absent from regular duty at the time of surgery. The state of Missouri was protected from liability by the doctrine of sovereign immunity in *Sherrill v. Wilson,* 653 S.W.2d 661 (Mo. 1983) (*en banc*). Action had been brought for the wrongful death of the plaintiff's son at the hands of an involuntary patient at a state mental hospital who failed to return to the institution from a two-day pass.

CLOSING STATEMENTS

After completion of the plaintiff's case and the defendant's defense, the judge calls for closing statements. The defense proceeds first and then the plaintiff. Closing statements provide attorneys an opportunity to summarize for the jury and the court what they have proven. They may point out faults in their opponent's case and emphasize points they wish the jury to remember.

If there appears to be only a question of law at the end of a case, a motion can be made for a directed verdict. A motion of this nature must be decided by the court. The court will grant the motion if there is no question of fact to be decided by the jury. The directed verdict also may be made on the grounds that the plaintiff has failed to present sufficient facts to prove his or her case or that the evidence fails to establish a legal basis for a verdict in the plaintiff's favor.

After the attorneys' summations, the court charges the jury before the jurors recess to deliberate. Because the jury determines issues of fact, it is necessary for the court to instruct the jury with regard to the applicable law. This is done by means of a charge. The charge defines the responsibility of the jury, describes the applicable law, and advises the jury of the alternatives available to it.

When a charge given by the court is not clear enough on a particular point or when it does not cover different issues in the case, it is the obligation of the attorneys for both sides to request clarification of the charge. When the jury retires to deliberate, the members are reminded not to discuss the case except among themselves.

If a verdict is against the weight of the evidence, a judge may dismiss the case, order a new trial, or set his or her own verdict. At the time judgment is rendered, the losing party has an opportunity to motion for a new trial. If the new trial is granted, the entire process is repeated; if not, the judgment becomes final, subject to a review of the trial record by an appellate court.

JUDGE'S CHARGE TO THE JURY

On completion of the closing statements by the plaintiff(s) and the defendant(s), the judge charges the jury as to the applicable law to be applied in the case. As an example, statements from the trial judge's oral charge to the jurors in *Estes Health Care Centers v. Bannerman,* 411 So.2d 109 (Ala. 1982), in which a nursing facility resident died after transfer to a hospital after suffering burns in a bath, included

> The complaint alleges the defendant Jackson Hospital, that the defendant undertook to provide hospital and nursing care to the deceased, and that the defendant negligently failed to provide proper hospital and nursing care to the plaintiff's intestate.
>
> • • • •
>
> The defendants in response to these allegations . . . have each separately entered pleas of the general issue or general denial. Under the law, a plea of the general issue has the effect of placing the burden of proof on the plaintiffs to reasonably satisfy you from the evidence, the truth of those things claimed by them in the bill of the complaint. The defendants carry no burden of proof.
>
> • • • •
>
> As to the defendant Jackson Hospital, the duty arises in that in rendering services to a patient, a hospital must use that degree of care, skill,

and diligence used by hospitals generally in the community under similar circumstances.

. . . .

Negligence is not actionable unless the negligence is the proximate cause of the injury. The law defines proximate cause as that cause which is the natural and probable sequence of events and without the intervention of any new or independent cause, produces the injury, and without which such injury would not have occurred. For an act to constitute actionable negligence, there must not only be some causal connection between the negligent act complained of and the injury suffered, but connection must be by natural and unbroken sequence, without intervening sufficient causes, so that but for the negligence of the defendant, the injury would not have occurred.

. . . .

If one is guilty of negligence which concurs or combines with the negligence of another, and the two combine to produce injury, each negligent person is liable for the resulting injury. And the negligence of each will be deemed the proximate cause of the injury. Concurrent causes may be defined as two or more causes which run together and act contemporaneously to produce a given result or to inflict an injury. This does not mean that the causes of the acts producing the injury must necessarily occur simultaneously, but they must be active simultaneously to efficiently and proximately produce a result.

. . . .

In an action against two or more defendants for injury allegedly caused by combined or concurring negligence of the defendants, it is not necessary to show negligence of all the defendants in order for recovery to be had against one or more to be negligent. If you are reasonably satisfied from the evidence in this case that all the defendants are negligent and that their negligence concurred and combined to proximately cause the injury complained by the plaintiffs, then each defendant is liable to the plaintiffs.

Id. at 114, 115.

JURY DELIBERATION AND DETERMINATION

After the judge's charge, the jury retires to the jury room and deliberates as to the guilt or innocence of the defendant(s). The jury returns to the courtroom upon reaching a verdict and their determinations are presented to the court.

DAMAGES

Monetary damages generally are awarded to individuals in cases of personal injury and wrongful death. Damages generally are fixed by the jury and are either nominal, compensatory, hedonic, or punitive.

Nominal damages are awarded as a mere token in recognition that wrong has been committed when the actual amount of compensation is insignificant.

Compensatory damages are estimated reparation in money for detriment or injury sustained (including loss of earnings, medical costs, and loss of financial support).

Hedonic damages are those damages awarded to compensate an individual for the loss of enjoyment of life. Such damages are awarded because of the failure of compensatory damages to compensate an individual adequately for the pain and suffering he or she has endured as a result of a negligent wrong. The first case to recognize hedonic damages was *Sherrod v. Berry,* 629 F. Supp. 159 (N.D. Ill. 1985), *aff'd,* 827 F.2d 195 (7th Cir. 1987), *vacated and remanded on other grounds,* 835 F.2d 1222 (7th Cir. 1988). An individual is more than a money-making machine. Not only was the youth's earning power destroyed in this case, but he was robbed of what all the wealth in the world could never purchase—the pleasure and enjoyment of living.

Punitive damages are additional money awards authorized when an injury is caused by gross carelessness or disregard for the safety of others.

Plaintiff's Schedule of Damages

Plaintiffs seek recovery from a great variety of damages:

- personal injuries sustained by the plaintiff
- permanent physical disabilities sustained by the plaintiff
- permanent mental disabilities sustained by the plaintiff
- past and future physical and mental pain and suffering sustained and to be sustained by the plaintiff
- loss of enjoyment of life by the plaintiff
- loss of consortium where spouse is injured in the accident
- loss of child's services where minor child is injured in the accident
- medical and hospital expenses reasonably paid or incurred or reasonably certain to be incurred in the future by plaintiff
- past and future loss of earnings sustained and to be sustained by plaintiff
- permanent diminution in the plaintiff's earning capacity[11]

A plethora of negligence cases have been litigated throughout the nation. The following cases illustrate the types of damages sought by plaintiffs.

Personal Injuries of Plaintiff

The plaintiff in *Burge v. Parker,* 510 So.2d 538 (Ala. 1987), suffered a laceration of his right foot on April 2 and was taken to St. Margaret's Hospital. A physician in the emergency department cleaned and stitched the laceration and released the patient with instructions to keep the foot elevated. Even though reports prepared by the fire medic who arrived on the scene of the accident and by ambulance personnel had indicated the chief complaint as being a fracture of the foot, no x-rays were ordered in the emergency department. The admitting clerk had typed a statement on the admission form indicating possible fracture of the right foot. However, a handwritten note stated the chief complaint as being a laceration of the right foot. The patient returned to the hospital later in the day with his mother, complaining of pain in the right foot. His mother asked if x-rays had been taken. The physician said that it was not necessary. The wound was redressed, and the patient was sent home again with instructions to keep the foot elevated. The pain continued to get worse, and the patient was taken to see another physician on April 5. X-rays were ordered, and an orthopedic surgeon called for a consultation diagnosed three fractures and a compartment syndrome, a swelling of tissue in the muscle compartments. The swelling increased pressure on the blood vessels, thus decreasing circulation, which tends to cause muscles to die. Approximately one-half pint of clotted blood had been removed from the wound. By April 11, the big toe had to be surgically removed. It was alleged that the physician had failed to obtain a full medical history, to order the necessary x-rays, and to diagnose and treat the fractures of the foot. As a result, the patient ultimately suffered loss of his great toe. The Circuit Court of Macon County awarded damages totaling $450,000 for loss of a big toe, and the physician appealed. The Supreme Court of Alabama found the damages not to have been excessive.

Punitive Damages

Punitive damages are awarded over and above that which is intended to compensate the plaintiff for economic losses resulting from the injury. Punitive damages cover such items as physical disability, mental anguish, loss of a spouse's services, physical suffering, injury to one's reputation, and loss of companionship. Punitive damages were referred to as "that mighty engine of deterrence" in *Johnson v. Terry,* No. 537-907 (Wis. Cir. Ct. Mar. 18, 1983).

The court in *Henry v. Deen,* 310 S.E.2d 326 (N.C. 1984), held that allegations of gross and wanton negligence incidental to wrongful death in the plaintiff's complaint gave sufficient notice of a claim against the treating physician and physician's assistant for punitive damages. The original complaint, which alleged that the treating physician, the physician's assistant, and the consulting physician agreed to create and did create false and misleading entries in the patient's medical record, was sufficient to allege a civil conspiracy. The decision of the lower court was reversed, and the case was remanded for further proceedings.

In *Estes Health Care Centers,* discussed above, the court stated,

> While human life is incapable of translation into a compensatory measurement, the amount of an award of punitive damages may be measured by the gravity of the wrong done, the punishment called for by the act of the wrongdoer, and the need to deter similar wrongs in order to preserve human life.

411 So.2d at 113.

At least 28 states have limited awards through legislation. Florida, for example, adopted a clear and convincing evidence standard of proof for punitive damage awards greater than three times the compensatory award.[12]

Surviving Spouse and Children

Damages may be awarded given evidence of a patient's pain and the mental anguish of the surviving husband and children. Damages in the amount of $180,000 in *Jefferson Hospital Association v. Garrett,* 804 S.W.2d 711 (Ark. 1991), were found not to be excessive given evidence of the patient's pain and the mental suffering of the surviving spouse and children.

In a California case, *Garcia v. Kantor,* 54 Cal. App. 3d 1025, 127 Cal. Rptr. 164 (1976), the court refused to allow recovery of money damages by married children in a case in which their father suffered injury because of a negligent defendant. The children had claimed that they lost the companionship of their father.

Emotional Distress

The court of appeals in *Haught v. Maceluch,* 681 F.2d 291 (5th Cir. 1982), held that under Texas law the mother was entitled to recover for her emotional distress, even though she was not conscious at the time her child was born. The mother had brought a medical malpractice action, alleging that the physician was negligent in the delivery of her child, causing her daughter to suffer permanent brain injury. The district court entered judgment of $1,160,000 for the child's medical expenses and $175,000 for her lost future earnings. The court deleted a jury award of $118,000 for the mother's mental suffering over her daughter's impaired condition. On appeal, the court of appeals permitted recovery, under Texas law, for mental suffering. The mother was conscious for more than 11 hours of labor and was aware of the physician's negligent acts, his absence in a near-emergency situation, and the overadministration of the labor-inducing drug Pitocin.

The supreme court, appellate division, in *Quijije v. Lutheran Medical Center,* 460 N.Y.S.2d 601 (App. Div. 1983), held that the plaintiff's mother may not recover for emotional injury rising solely from having to observe her baby suffer and die because of alleged denial of timely medical treatment. The plaintiff could not succeed by invoking a section of the Public Health Law that requires general hospitals to admit and provide emergency medical treatment to all in immediate need thereof without advance payment or questioning as to payment. Section 2805-b provided no basis for an action to recover money damages.

Excessive Damages

A jury verdict totaling $12,393,130 was considered an excessive award in *Merrill v. Albany Medical Center,* 512 N.Y.S.2d 519 (App. Div. 1987), in which damages were sought with respect to the severe brain damage sustained by a 22-month-old infant as the result of oxygen deprivation. This occurred when the infant went into cardiac arrest during surgery for removal of a suspected malignant tumor from her right lung. Reduction of the amount to $6,143,130 was considered appropriate.

The plaintiffs in *Campbell v. Pitt County Memorial Hospital,* 321 N.C. 260, 362 S.E.2d 273 (1987), brought an action to recover damages for personal injury suffered by an infant. The infant's mother had been admitted to the defendant hospital for delivery of her baby. The defendant physician, Dr. Deyton, determined that the baby was in a footing breech, feet first position. At 1:30 P.M. on the date of delivery, Dr. Deyton proceeded with a vaginal delivery despite the position of the baby. For several hours before delivery, the hospital nurses monitoring the baby observed complications that they believed were affecting adversely the condition of the fetus. One of the nurses expressed her concerns to Dr. Deyton; however, she did not contact her immediate supervisor or anyone else when Dr. Deyton failed to address her concerns. The infant's umbilical cord became wrapped around her legs. The infant sustained brain damage caused by severe asphyxia from the entangled cord. Today, the child suffers from cerebral palsy and requires constant care and supervision. Damages were sought for medical expenses, mental anguish, and trauma. The plaintiffs settled with the defendant physician and his professional association in the amount of $1,500,000, leaving Pitt County Memorial Hospital as the sole defendant. The trial court was found not to have abused its discretion when, after the jury awarded the infant damages in the amount of $4,850,000, it ordered a new trial, finding the damages awarded excessive. The jury award appeared to the court to have been made under the influence of passion and prejudice and was unsupported by the evidence. The defendant's motion for a new trial on this issue was granted. This decision was upheld on appeal to both the court of appeals and the Supreme Court of North Carolina.

Joint and Several Liability

The doctrine of joint and several liability permits the plaintiff to bring suit against all persons who share responsibility for his or her injury. The doctrine allows the plaintiff to recover monetary damages from any one of or all the defendants. Any one defendant, even though partially responsible for the plaintiff's injury, can be required to pay the full judgment awarded by the jury. Awards tend to fall in greater amounts on defendants with the better insurance. This is the "deep pockets" concept: Whoever has the most pays the greater percentage of the award.

APPEALS

An appellate court reviews a case on the basis of the trial record as well as written briefs and, if requested, concise oral arguments by the attorneys. A brief summarizes the facts of a case, testimony of the witnesses, laws affecting the case, and arguments of counsel. The party making the appeal is the appellant. The party answering the appeal is the appellee. After hearing the oral arguments, the court takes the case under advisement until such time as the judges consider it and agree on a decision. An opinion then is prepared explaining the reasons for a decision.

Grounds for appeal may result from one or more of the following: (1) The verdict was excessive or inadequate in the lower court, (2) evidence was rejected that should have been accepted, (3) inadmissible evidence was permitted, (4) testimony was excluded that should have been admissible, (5) the verdict was contrary to the weight of the evidence, or (6) the court improperly charged the jury. Notice of appeal must be filed with the trial court, the appellate court, and the adverse party. A "stay of execution" also should be filed by the party wishing to prevent execution of an adverse judgment until such time as the case has been heard and decided by an appellate court.

The appellate court may modify, affirm, or reverse the judgment or reorder a new trial on an appeal. The majority ruling of the judges in the appellate court is binding on the parties of a lawsuit. If the appellate court's decision is not unanimous, the minority may render a dissenting opinion. Further appeal may be made, as set by statute, to the highest court of appeals. If an appeal involves a constitutional question, it eventually may be appealed to the U.S. Supreme Court.

When a case is decided by the highest appellate court in a state, a final judgment results, and the matter is ended. The instances when one may appeal the ruling of a state court to the U.S. Supreme Court are rare. A federal question must be involved, and even then the Supreme Court must decide whether it will hear the case. A federal question is one involving the U.S. Constitution or a statute enacted by Congress, so it is unlikely that a negligence case arising in a state court would be reviewed and decided by the Supreme Court.

EXECUTION OF JUDGMENTS

Once the amount of damages has been established and all the appeals have been heard, the defendant must comply with the judgment. If he fails to do so, a court order may be executed requiring the sheriff or other judicial officer to sell as much of the defendant's property as necessary, within statutory limitations, to satisfy the plaintiff's judgment.

NOTES

1. Kern v. Gulf Coast Nursing Home of Moss Point, Inc., 502 So.2d 1198 (Miss. 1987) at 1202.

2. Pierce v. Ortho Pharmaceutical Corp., 417 A.2d 505, 509 (N.J. 1980).

3. Steve Cohen, *Malpractice,* NEW YORK MAGAZINE, October 1, 1990, at 43, 47.

4. James W. McElhaney, *Taking Sides*, 78 A.B.A. J., 82 (1992).

5. *Id.*

6. Roberts v. Ray, 45 Tenn. App. 280, 322 S.W.2d 435 (1958).

7. Spirito v. Temple Corp., 466 N.E.2d 491 (Ind. Ct. App. 1984).

8. S. EMANUEL, TORTS 184, 185 (1988).

9. N.J. STAT. ANN. §2A:62A-1.

10. *Kentucky: Malpractice Limit Struck*, 13 NAT'L L. J. 6 (1990).

11. 57A Am. Jur. 2d §342 (1989).

12. FLA. STAT. §768.73(1)(a)(b) (Supp. 1991).

Chapter **5**
Corporate Liability

OUTLINE

- Authority of Health Care Corporations
  - Express Corporate Authority
  - Implied Corporate Authority
  - *Ultra Vires* Acts
- Corporate Committees
  - Executive Committee
  - Bylaws Committee
  - Finance Committee
  - Joint Conference Committee
  - Long-Range Planning Committee
  - Patient Care Committee
  - Audit Committee
- Doctrine of *Respondeat Superior*
- Corporate Negligence
- Duties of Health Care Corporations
  - Duties Specified by Corporate Law
  - Duty To Appoint an Administrator
  - Duty To Comply with Statutes, Rules, and Regulations
  - Joint Commission on Accreditation of Healthcare Organizations
  - Duty To Provide Propitious Treatment
  - Duty To Avoid Self-Dealing and Conflict-of-Interest Situations
  - Duty To Provide Adequate Staff
  - Duty To Provide Adequate Facilities and Equipment
  - Duty To Provide Adequate Insurance
  - Duty To Provide Satisfactory Patient Care

The typical health care facility is incorporated under state law as a free-standing for-profit or not-for-profit corporation. The corporation has a governing body, which is generally referred to as a board of directors or board of trustees. The existence of this authority creates certain duties and liabilities for governing boards and their individual members. The governing body has ultimate responsibility for the operation and management of the institution with a necessary delegation of appropriate responsibility to administrative employees and the medical staff. The governing board or designated persons functioning as the governing body is legally responsible for establishing and implementing policies regarding the management and operation of the institution.

Not-for-profit health care facilities are usually exempt from federal taxation under section 501(c)(3) of the Internal Revenue Code of 1986, as amended. Such federal exemption usually entitles the organization to an automatic exemption from state taxes as well. Such tax exemption not only relieves the institution from the payment of income taxes, sales taxes, and the like, but also permits the institution to receive contributions from donors who then may obtain charitable deductions on their personal tax returns.

Although health care facilities may operate as sole proprietorships or partnerships, most function as corporations. Thus, an important source of law applicable to governing boards and to the duties and responsibilities of their members is found in state corporation laws. An incorporated health care facility is a legal person with recognized rights, duties, powers, and responsibilities. Because the legal "person" is in reality a "fictitious person," there is a requirement that certain humans be designated to exercise the corporate powers and that they be held accountable for corporate decision-making. These natural persons comprise the governing board. In an unincorporated institution, the powers and duties are held by one or more natural persons. There is no recognized fictitious person. This chapter discusses some of the main responsibilities as well as legal risks of health care facilities and their boards.

AUTHORITY OF HEALTH CARE CORPORATIONS

Health care corporations—governmental, charitable, or proprietary—have certain powers expressly or implicitly granted to them by state statutes. Generally, the authority of a corporation is expressed in the law under which the corporation was chartered and in the corporation's articles of incorporation. The existence of this authority creates certain duties and liabilities for governing boards and their individual members. Members of the board of directors of an institution have both express and implied corporate authority.

The governing board is organized to oversee and control all the activities of the corporation. It is therefore essential that the governing board have an appropriate degree of authority. In this way, there will be a rational and practical transition from formulating policy to implementing practice and procedure. Authority is conferred by corporation laws, regulations, and corporate charters.

The governing body is legally responsible for establishing and implementing policies regarding the management and operation of a health care facility. The general responsibilities of a facility include

- policy formation
- oversight of the management and operation of the institution
- assurance of the financial viability of the institution
- appointment of a qualified administrator
- provision of a safe physical plant equipped and staffed to maintain services in accordance with any applicable local and state regulations that may apply to federal programs in which the institution participates
- adoption of written policies assuring the protection of patients' rights
- determination of the frequency of meetings of the governing body and documentation of such meetings
- adoption of a written policy concerning potential conflict of interest on the part of members of the governing body, the administration, the medical and nursing staff, and other employees who might influence corporate decisions.

Express Corporate Authority

Express corporate authority is the authority specifically delegated by statute. A health care corporation derives its authority to act from the laws of the state in which it is incorporated. The articles of incorporation set forth the purpose(s) of the corporation's existence and the powers the corporation is authorized to exercise in order to carry out its purposes.

Implied Corporate Authority

Implied corporate authority is the authority to perform any and all acts necessary to exercise a corporation's expressly conferred authority and to accomplish the purpose(s) for which it was created. Generally, implied corporate authority arises from situations in which such authority is required or suggested as a result of a need for corporate powers not specifically granted in the articles of incorporation. A board of directors, at its own discretion, may enact new bylaws, rules, and regulations; purchase or mortgage property; borrow money; purchase equipment; select personnel; adopt corporate resolutions that delineate decision-making responsibilities; etc. These powers can be enumerated in the articles of incorporation and, in such cases, would be categorized as express rather than implied corporate authority.

Much of the litigation concerning excesses of corporate authority involve questions of whether a corporation has the implied authority, incidental to its express authority, to perform a questioned act. A hospital was permitted to construct a medical office building on land that had been donated for maintaining and carrying on a general hospital even though its certificate of incorporation did not authorize such an act specifically. The court, in recognizing a trend to encourage charitable hospitals to provide private offices for rental to staff members, held that such an act was within the implied powers of the hospital and that such offices aid in the work of a general hospital even though it went beyond the hospital corporation's express powers. *Hungerford Hospital v. Mulvey,* 225 A.2d 495 (Conn. 1966).

Ultra Vires Acts

A board can be held liable for acting beyond its scope of authority, which is either expressed (e.g., in its articles of incorporation) or implied in law. Acts of this nature are referred to as *ultra vires* acts. The governing body acts in and on behalf of the corporation. If any action is in violation of a statute or regulation, it is illegal. An example of an illegal act would be the employment of an unlicensed person in a position which by law requires a license. The state, through its attorney general, has the power to prevent the performance of an *ultra vires* act by injunction. Governing boards should have their corporate charters reviewed periodically by legal counsel to make certain that their express powers are consistent with the activities in which they presently engage or plan to undertake in the future.

In certain circumstances, members of an institution's governing board, as well as its corporate officers, may be individually responsible for *ultra vires* acts. This might be true, for example, if a member of a governing board or corporate officer exceeded the powers of the corporation for individual benefit.

The court of appeals in *Queen of Angels Hospital v. Younger,* 66 Cal. App. 3d 359, 136 Cal. Rptr. 36 (1977), held that the primary purpose of the corporation was the operation of a hospital and that the corporation could not abandon its operation in favor of neighborhood clinics. The hospital's board intended to use a substantial portion of funds it received from leasing the hospital to establish and operate additional medical clinics. Services provided by the Franciscan Sisters from the inception of the hospital were considered donated with the exception of certain compensated services, and no future remuneration was expected. The sisters' mother house had requested funds for a retirement plan. The court of appeals held that the retirement plan was not a proper exercise of either sound business judgment or the fiduciary duties of the Queen of Angels Hospital board. It is clear in this case that a board is acting beyond its scope of authority if it diverts funds to support activities not provided for in the hospital's articles of incorporation.

CORPORATE COMMITTEES

There are various committees through which a board conducts its business. A description of some of those committees is presented below.

Executive Committee

The executive committee is a smaller committee of the board that is delegated authority to act on behalf of the full board. It must act within the scope and authority assigned by the board. The duties and responsibilities of the executive committee should be delineated in the corporate bylaws. The executive committee may serve as a liaison between management and the full board; review and recommend on management proposals; and perform special assignments as may be delegated by the full board from time to time. Actions taken by the executive committee should be reported at regular sessions of the board and ratified.

Bylaws Committee

The bylaws committee reviews and recommends bylaws changes to the board.

Finance Committee

The finance committee is responsible for reviewing and overseeing the financial affairs of the organization. The committee reviews financial statements, operating budgets, major capital requests, etc. Actions of the committee must be approved by the board. Representation on the committee should include the chief executive officer and the chief financial officer.

Joint Conference Committee

The joint conference committee is often an informal committee consisting of an equal number of representatives from both the executive committees of the board and medical staff, along with representation from administration. This committee reviews issues that generally affect all three groups (e.g., planning for new equipment, expansion programs, and medical staff issues). The committee generally meets quarterly and reports back to the board.

Long-Range Planning Committee

The long-range planning committee is responsible for overseeing the preparation of capital budgets for future years, expansion programs, acquisition of major equipment, etc. The committee should have representation from the administration, board, and medical staff.

Patient Care Committee

The patient care committee reviews the quality of patient care rendered in the institution and makes recommendations for the improvement of such care. An effective committee should contain membership from the board, medical staff, administration, and appropriate ancillary departments. Actions and/or recommendations are reported to the board.

DOUGLAS A. EDEMA, M.D.
PRESIDENT/CEO

ADVANTAGE HEALTH

AN INTEGRATED APPROACH
TO HEALTH CARE

220 CHERRY ST., SE   SUITE 810   GRAND RAPIDS, MI 49503

PH 616-774-6557   FX 616-774-6586

Audit Committee

Health care facilities must be vigilant in conducting the financial affairs of the organization. As the boards of several investment institutions have experienced in recent years, failure to do so can result in major lawsuits, both civil and criminal. An effective audit committee can be extremely helpful in uncovering and thwarting bad or inept financial decision making. The corporate board can help to protect itself by establishing an audit committee. The committee should include members from the board and internal auditing staff. Responsibilities of the corporate audit committee include

- developing corporate auditing policies and procedures
- recommendation of independent auditors to the corporate board
- setting, overseeing, reviewing, and acting on the recommendations of the internal audit staff
- review of the internal accounting practices of the corporation, including policies and procedures
- reviewing with independent auditors the proposed scope and general extent of their auditing duties and responsibilities
- reviewing and evaluating financial statements (e.g., income statements, balance sheets, cash flow reports, investment accounts)

"Failure on the part of an audit committee to question management's representations may be the basis for audit committee malfeasance, since the audit committee and the board may be held liable for their failure to know what they were responsible for recognizing."[1]

DOCTRINE OF *RESPONDEAT SUPERIOR*

Respondeat superior (let the master respond) is the legal doctrine holding employers liable, in certain cases, for the wrongful acts of their employees. This doctrine also has been referred to as *vicarious liability,* whereby an employer is answerable for the torts committed by employees. In the health care setting, a hospital, for example, is liable for the negligent acts of its employees, even though there has been no wrongful conduct on the part of the institution. For liability to be imputed to the employer, (1) a master–servant relationship must exist between the employer and the employee; and (2) the wrongful act of the employee must have occurred within the scope of his or her employment.

The question of liability frequently rests on whether persons treating a patient are independent agents (responsible for their own acts) or employees of the institution. The answer to this depends on whether the institution can exercise control over the particular act that was the proximate cause of the injury.

The basic rationale for imposing liability on an employer developed because the employer possesses the right to control the physical acts of its employees. It is not necessary that the employer actually exercise control, but only that it possesses the right, power, or authority to do so.

Generally, the plaintiff's attorney will file suit against both employer and employee. This is done out of practical considerations, because the employer is generally in a better financial condition and also very likely will have insurance to cover the judgment.

The employer is not without remedy if liability has been imposed against it under *respondeat superior* for an employee's negligent act. Because the law holds negligent persons responsible for their negligent acts, employees are not absolved from liability when a health care facility is held liable through the application of *respondeat superior*. Not only may the injured party sue the employee directly, but also the employer, if sued, may seek indemnification (i.e., compensation for the financial loss occasioned by the employee's act) from the employee.

The plaintiff has the burden for establishing an employee–employer relationship. This can be difficult, especially in the case of independent physicians.

In the instance of wrongful conduct by an independent contractor, the doctrine of *respondeat superior* does not apply. An independent contractor relationship is established when the principal has no right of control over the manner in which the agent's work is to be performed. The independent contractor therefore is responsible for his or her own negligent acts. However, some cases indicate a hospital may be held liable for an independent contractor's negligence. For example, in *Mehlman v. Powell*, 46 U.S.L.W. 2227 (Md. Ct. App. 1977), the court held that a hospital may be found vicariously liable for the negligence of an emergency department physician who was not a hospital employee but who worked in the emergency department in the capacity of an independent contractor. The court reasoned that the hospital maintained control over billing procedures, maintained an emergency department in the main hospital, and represented to the patient that the members of the emergency department staff were its employees, which may have caused the patient to rely on the skill and competence of the staff.

The doctrine of *respondeat superior* may impose liability on a hospital for a nurse's acts or omissions that result in injury to a hospital patient. Whether such liability attaches depends on whether the conduct of the nurse was wrongful and whether the nurse was subject to the control of the hospital at the time the act in question was performed. Determination of whether the nurse's conduct was wrongful in a given situation depends on the standard of conduct to which the nurse is expected to adhere. In liability deliberations, the nurse who is subject to the control of the hospital at the time of the negligent conduct is considered a hospital employee and is not the borrowed servant of a staff physician or surgeon.

An officer or director of a corporation is not, merely as a result of his or her position, personally liable for the torts of corporate employees. To incur liability, the director or officer ordinarily must be shown to have in some way participated in or directed the tortious act. *Hunt v. Rabon,* 272 S.E.2d 643 (S.C. 1980).

CORPORATE NEGLIGENCE

> Corporate negligence is a doctrine under which the hospital is liable if it fails to uphold the proper standard of care owed the patient, which is to ensure the patient's safety and well-being while at the hospital. This theory of liability creates a nondelegable duty which the hospital owes directly to a patient. Therefore, an injured party does not have to rely on and establish the negligence of a third party.

Thompson v. Nason Hospital, 591 A.2d 703, 707 (Pa. 1991).

Corporate negligence occurs when a health care corporation fails to perform those duties it owes directly to a patient or to anyone else to whom a duty may extend. If such a duty is breached and a patient is injured as a result of that breach, the institution can be held culpable under the theory of corporate negligence.

A corporation owes certain duties to the general public and to its patients. These duties arise from statutes, regulations, principles of law developed by the courts, and the internal operating rules of the institution. A corporation is treated no differently than an individual. If a corporation has a duty to fulfill and fails to do so, it has the same liability to the injured party as an individual would have.

The benchmark case in the health care field, which has had a major impact on the liability of hospitals and physicians, was decided in 1965 when the U.S. Supreme Court denied review of the Illinois case of *Darling v. Charleston Community Memorial Hospital,* 33 Ill. 2d 326, 211 N.E.2d 253 (1965), *cert. denied,* 383 U.S. 946 (1966). The *Darling* case involved an 18-year-old college football player who was preparing for a career as a teacher and coach. The patient, a defensive halfback for his college football team, was injured during a play. He was rushed to the emergency department of a small, accredited community hospital where the only physician on emergency duty that day was Dr. Alexander, a general practitioner. Dr. Alexander had not treated a major leg fracture for three years.

The physician examined the patient and ordered an x-ray that revealed that the tibia and the fibula of the right leg had been fractured. The physician reduced the fracture and applied a plaster cast from a point three or four inches below the groin to the toes. Shortly after the cast had been applied, the patient began to complain continually of pain. The physician split the cast and continued to visit the patient frequently while the patient remained in the hospital. The physician did not call in any specialist for consultation because he did not think it was necessary.

After two weeks, the student was transferred to a larger hospital and placed under the care of an orthopedic surgeon. The specialist found a considerable amount of dead tissue in the fractured leg. During a period of two months, the specialist removed increasing amounts of tissue in a futile attempt to save the leg until it became necessary to amputate the leg eight inches below the knee. The student's father did not agree to a settlement and filed suit against the physician and the hospital. Although the physician later settled out of court for $40,000, the case continued against the hospital.

The documentary evidence that was relied on to establish the standard of care included

- rules and regulations of the Illinois Department of Public Health under the Hospital Licensing Act
- standards for hospital accreditation of the Joint Commission on Accreditation of Hospitals
- bylaws, rules, and regulations of Charleston Hospital

These documents were admitted into evidence without objection. No specific evidence was offered that the hospital had failed to conform to the usual and customary practices of hospitals in the community.

The trial court instructed the jury to consider those documents, along with all other evidence, in determining the hospital's liability. Under the circumstances in which the case reached the Illinois Supreme Court, it was held that the verdict against the hospital should be sustained if the evidence supported the verdict on any one or more of the 20 allegations of negligence. The two allegations specified asserted that the hospital was negligent in its failure to provide a sufficient number of trained nurses for bedside care of all patients at all times—in this case, capable of recognizing the progressive gangrenous condition of the plaintiff's right leg—and in the failure of its nurses to bring the condition to the attention of the hospital administration and staff so that adequate consultation could be secured and the condition rectified.

Although these generalities provided the jury with no practical guidance for determining what constitutes reasonable care, they were considered relevant to aid the jury in deciding what was feasible and what the hospital knew or should have known concerning hospital responsibilities for the proper care of a patient. There was no expert testimony characterizing when the professional care rendered by the attending physician should have been reviewed, who should have reviewed it, or whether the case required consultation.

Evidence relating to the hospital's failure to review Dr. Alexander's work, to require consultation or examination by specialists, and to require proper nursing care was found to be sufficient to support a verdict for the patient. Judgment was eventually returned against the hospital in the amount of $100,000.

The Illinois Supreme Court held that the hospital could not limit its liability as a charitable corporation to the amount of its liability insurance.

> [T]he doctrine of charitable immunity can no longer stand . . . a doctrine which limits the liability of charitable corporations to the amount of liability insurance that they see fit to carry permits them to determine whether or not they will be liable for their torts and the amount of that liability, if any.

211 N.E.2d at 260.

In effect, the hospital was liable as a corporate entity for the negligent acts of its employees and physicians. Among other things, the *Darling* case indicates the importance of instituting effective credentialing and continuing medical evaluation and review programs for all members of a professional staff.

Traditionally, hospitals were institutions that provided the tools and a place where physicians could practice their trade. Hospitals are no longer responsible for providing room and board only, but have a duty and responsibility to properly select and monitor physicians. The Supreme Court of Arizona in *Fridena v. Evans,* 127 Ariz. 516, 622 P.2d 463 (1980), affirmed that the hospital could be held liable for the negligent supervision of a physician where it has actual or constructive knowledge of the procedures carried on within the hospital. The patient in this case was involved in a motorcycle–automobile accident when she was 15 years old. She suffered a serious injury to her right leg, which required surgery. After surgery by Dr. Fridena, it was noted that the patient's right leg was 1 1/2 inches shorter than her left leg. The surgeon later attempted to lengthen the leg, which resulted in its being three inches shorter than before. The second operation gave rise to the malpractice suit, resulting in a $300,000 jury award to the patient.

The court of appeals in *Elam v. College Park Hospital,* 183 Cal. Rptr. 156 (Ct. App. 1982), held that a hospital is liable to a patient under the doctrine of corporate negligence for the negligent conduct of independent physicians and surgeons who are neither employees nor agents of the hospital. The hospital generally owes a duty to ensure the competency of its medical staff and to evaluate the quality of medical treatment rendered on its premises.

A hospital cannot be held liable under the doctrine of corporate negligence for granting privileges to a nonemployee doctor who commits malpractice while in his or her private office off hospital premises. A hospital's independent duty to select and maintain a competent medical staff does not require a hospital, to fulfill its duty of reasonable care, to supervise a physician's office practice. *Pedroza v. Bryant,* 101 Wash. 2d 226, 677 P.2d 166 (1984).

A hospital is responsible for failing to meet the standard of care required within the hospital. An action was brought against Morton Canton (who was masquerading as a physician, Dr. LaBella), a hospital, and others in *Insinga v. LaBella,* 543 So.2d 209 (Fla. 1989), for the wrongful death of a 68-year-old woman Mr. Canton had admitted. The patient died while she was in the hospital. Mr. Canton was found to be a fugitive from justice in Canada where he was under indictment for the manufacture and sale of illegal drugs. He fraudulently obtained a medical license from the state of Florida and staff privileges at the hospital by using the name of Dr. LaBella, a deceased Italian physician. Mr. Canton was extradited to Canada without being served process. The U.S. District Court for the Southern District of Florida directed a verdict in favor of the hospital. On appeal, the U.S. Court of Appeals for the Eleventh Circuit certified a question to the Florida Supreme Court, asking whether Florida law recognizes the corporate negligence doctrine and whether it would apply under the facts of this case. The Florida Supreme Court held that the corporate negligence doctrine imposes on hospitals an implied duty to patients to select and retain competent physicians who, although they are independent practitioners, would be providing in-hospital care to their patients through their hospital staff privileges. Hospitals are in the best position to protect their patients and consequently have an independent duty to select and retain competent independent physicians seeking staff privileges.

An officer or a director of a corporation is not, merely as a result of his or her position, personally liable for the torts of corporate employees. To incur liability, the director or the officer ordinarily must be shown to have in some way authorized, directed, or participated in a tortious act. The administrator of the estate of the deceased in *Hunt v. Rabon,* 272 S.E. 2d 643 (S.C. 1980), brought a malpractice action against hospital trustees and others for the wrongful death of the deceased during an operation at the hospital. A contractor had incorrectly crossed the oxygen and nitrous oxide lines of a newly installed medical gas system leading to the operating room. The trustees demurred to the complaint on the grounds that it failed to present facts sufficient for an action against them individually as trustees. The lower court sustained the demurrer, and the plaintiff appealed. On appeal, the Supreme Court of South Carolina held that the allegations presented were insufficient to hold the trustees liable for the wrongs alleged.

DUTIES OF HEALTH CARE CORPORATIONS

Along with the corporate authority that is granted to the governing board, duties are attached to its individual members. These responsibilities we call duties because they are imposed by law and they can be enforced in legal proceedings. Membership on a governing board should not be considered merely a recognition of social or community standing or financial well-being. Governing board members are considered by law to have the highest measure of accountability. They have a fiduciary duty that requires acting primarily for the benefit of the corporation. The general duties of a governing board are both implied and express. Failure of a board to function may constitute mismanagement of such a degree that the appointment of a receiver to manage the affairs of the corporation may be warranted.

The duty to supervise and manage is applicable to the trustees as it is to the managers of any other business corporation. In both instances, there is a duty to act as a reasonably prudent person would act under similar circumstances. The board must act prudently in administering the affairs of the institution and exercise its powers in good faith.

The basic management functions of the governing board include

- selection of corporate officers and agents
- general control over the compensation of such agents
- delegation of authority to the CEO/administrator and the administrator's subordinates for administrative actions
- selection and monitoring of the medical staff members and the delineation of clinical privileges
- establishment of institutional goals, policies, and procedures
- supervision and vigilance over the welfare and assets of the corporation

Specific management duties peculiar to hospitals include (1) determining the policies of the hospital in connection with community health needs, (2) maintaining proper professional standards in the hospital, (3) assuming a general responsibility for adequate patient care throughout the institution, and (4) providing adequate financing of patient care and assuming business-like control of expenditures.

Duties Specified by Corporate Law

A corporation has certain duties that are specified by the state's corporation laws. These include

- duty to hold meetings
- duty to establish policy

- financial duties
- duty to provide adequate insurance
- duty to pay taxes

The general duty to use due care in the management of the property and assets of an institution and the specific duty to manage its financial aspects includes maintenance of the physical plant and appropriating funds for such purpose as necessary. The governing board has a duty to protect the institution from the risk of loss because of fire, other destruction, or liability for the negligence of its employees. The governing board has a duty to pay all taxes that become due on any property so that no penalties are incurred.

Duty To Appoint an Administrator

Members of the governing board are responsible for appointing an administrator to act as their agent in the management of the institution. The administrator is responsible for the day-to-day operations of the institution. The individual selected as administrator must possess the competence and the character necessary to maintain satisfactory standards of patient care within the institution.

Minimum qualifications for administrators generally are contained in a state's hospital licensing statutes as well as in the rules and regulations promulgated under them. Where minimum qualifications exist, the governing board must at least satisfy these requirements in the appointment of an administrator. If the circumstances of a particular hospital necessitate employing an administrator of a higher level of qualification and competency, the governing board, at its discretion, may select an administrator that meets that need.

The responsibilities and authority of the administrator should be expressed in an appropriate job description, as well as in any formal agreement or contract that the institution has with the administrator. State health codes describe the responsibilities of administrators in broad terms. They generally provide that the administrator shall be responsible for

- overall management of the institution
- enforcement of any applicable federal, state, and local regulations, as well as the institution's bylaws, policies, and procedures
- appointment of, with the approval of the governing body, a qualified medical director
- liaison between the governing body and the medical and institution staff

• appointment of an administrative person to act during the administrator's absence from the institution.

The failure to remove an incompetent administrator or any other incapable agent of the hospital is as much a breach of a board's duty as is its failure to appoint competent employees. Termination of an administrator because of incompetence must be in accordance with hospital bylaws, which should set forth the administrator's due process rights. These rights should be included in an appropriately written contract for the administrator.

The general duty of a governing board is to exercise due care and diligence in supervising and managing the institution. This duty does not cease with the selection of a competent administrator. A governing board can be liable if the level of patient care becomes inadequate because of the board's failure to supervise properly the management of the institution. Administrators, as is the case with board members, can be personally liable for their own acts of negligence that injure others.

In some health care facilities, the administrator fills a dual role by serving as a member of the governing board in addition to his or her position as the institution's chief executive officer. When the administrator is a board member, he or she frequently serves in the capacity as secretary of the board.

Duty To Comply with Statutes, Rules, and Regulations

The governing board in general and its agents (assigned representatives) in particular are responsible for compliance with federal, state, and local rules and regulations regarding the operation of the institution. Depending on the scope of the wrong committed and the intent of the board, failure to comply could subject the board members and/or their agents to civil liability and even, in rare instances, to criminal prosecution.

Failure to comply with applicable statutory regulations can be costly. This was the case in *People v. Casa Blanca Convalescent Homes,* 206 Cal. Rptr. 164 (1984), in which there was evidence of numerous and prolonged deficiencies in resident care. The nursing home's practice of providing insufficient personnel constituted not only illegal practice but also unfair business practice in violation of Section 17200 of the Business and Professions Code. The trial court was found to have properly assessed a fine of $2,500 for each of 67 violations, totaling $167,500, where the evidence showed that the operator of the nursing home had the financial ability to pay that amount.

Joint Commission on Accreditation of Healthcare Organizations

The governing board through its agents is responsible for compliance with the standards of the Joint Commission on Accreditation of Healthcare Organizations. Noncompliance could cause a hospital to lose accreditation, which in turn would provide grounds for third-party reimbursement agencies (e.g., Medicare) to refuse payment for treatment rendered to patients.

Duty To Provide Propitious Treatment

Hospitals can be held liable for delays in treatment that result in injuries to their patients. For example, the patient in *Heddinger v. Ashford Memorial Community Hospital,* 734 F.2d 81 (1st Cir. 1984), filed a malpractice action against a hospital and its insurer, alleging that a delay in treating her left hand resulted in the loss of her little finger. Medical testimony presented at trial indicated that if proper and timely treatment had been rendered, the finger would have been saved. The U.S. District Court entered judgment on a jury verdict for the plaintiff in the amount of $175,000. The hospital appealed, and the U.S. Court of Appeals held that even if the physicians who attended the patient were not employees of the hospital but were independent contractors, the risk of negligent treatment was clearly foreseeable by the hospital. The court also held that although the award of damages was high, it was not so excessive as to require appellate reversal.

Duty To Avoid Self-Dealing and Conflict-of-Interest Situations

There should be full disclosure of each board member's dealings with the institution. Transactions between board members and the institution must be just and reasonable. Board members must refrain from self-dealing and avoid conflict-of-interest situations. Membership on the board or its committees should not be used for private gain. Board members are expected to disclose potential conflict-of-interest situations and withdraw from the board room at the time of voting. Board members who suspect a conflict-of-interest situation have a right and a duty to raise pertinent questions regarding any potential conflict. Conflict of interest is presumed to exist when a board member or a firm with which he or she is associated may benefit or lose from the passage of a proposed action.

Membership on the board of a nonprofit institution is deemed a public service. Neither the court nor the community expects or desires such public service to be turned to private gain. Thus, the standards imposed on board members regarding the investment of trust funds, self-dealing transactions, or personal compensation may be stricter than are those for directors of business corporations. The essential rules regarding self-dealing are clear. Generally, a contract between the institution and a trustee financially interested in the transaction is voidable by the institution in the event that the interested trustee spoke or voted in favor of the arrangement or did not disclose fully the material facts regarding his or her interest. This resolution of the self-dealing problem is based on the belief that if an interested board member does not participate in the board's action and does make full disclosure of his or her interest, the disinterested remaining members of the board are able to protect the institution's interests. If the fairness of the transaction is questioned, the burden of establishing fairness falls on the trustee involved.

Underlying the controversy of self-dealing is the knowledge that sometimes the most advantageous contract for an institution would be with one of its trustees or with a company in which the director is interested. These considerations are of great importance when dealings between a charitable corporation and a member of the board are involved. A rule denying this opportunity to the corporation would be too severe. However, statutory provisions in some states specifically forbid self-dealing transactions altogether, irrespective of disclosure or the fairness of the deal. The California Court of Appeals, interpreting a state conflict-of-interest statute in *Franzblau v. Monardo,* 166 Cal. Rptr. 610 (Ct. App. 1980), ruled that a president of a private nonprofit hospital was ineligible to hold office as a director of a public hospital district serving the same area.

Under sections 1877(b) and 1909(b) of the Social Security Act, it is considered a felony for anyone to knowingly and willfully offer, pay, solicit, or receive any payment in return for referring an individual to another for the furnishing, or the arranging for the furnishing, of any item or service that may be paid for by the Medicare or Medicaid programs. Persons convicted under these provisions are subject to fines of up to $25,000 and/or imprisonment of up to five years.

Duty To Provide Adequate Staff

Health care facilities must provide for adequate staffing. The court of appeal in *Leavitt v. St. Tammany Parish Hospital,* 396 So.2d 406 (La. Ct. App. 1981), held that the hospital owed a duty to respond promptly to patient calls for help. The hospital breached its duty by having less than adequate staff on hand and by failing to at least verbally answer an assistance light to inquire what the patient needed.

The patient in *Czubinsky v. Doctors Hospital,* 188 Cal. Rptr. 685 (Ct. App. 1983), appealed a judgment of the superior court that granted the hospital's motion for judgment notwithstanding the verdict after the jury had returned a verdict in favor of the patient. The patient recovering from anesthesia went into cardiac arrest, which resulted in permanent damages to the patient. The court of appeals held that the injuries sustained by the patient were the direct result of the hospital personnel's failure to properly monitor and render aid when needed in the immediate postoperative period. The registered nurse assigned to the patient had a duty to remain with her until the patient was transferred to the recovery room. The nurse's absence was the patent proximate cause of the patient's injuries. Failure of the hospital to provide adequate staff to assist the patient in the immediate postoperative period was an act in dereliction of duty—a failure that resulted in permanent damages, a readily foreseeable result.

Failure to comply with regulations relating to the professional staff can have serious consequences. Institutions that fail to meet federal standards can lose certification as a provider of health services. This then could lead to the denial of reimbursement under the different federal entitlement programs. Three nurses in *Montgomery Health Care Facility v. Ballard,* 565 So.2d 221, 224 (Ala. 1990), testified that the facility was understaffed. "One nurse testified that she asked her supervisor for more help but that she did not get it." The evidence in this case established that the care rendered to the deceased was deficient. A report by the Alabama Department of Health concerning the lack of patient care in the facility was admissible as evidence.

Duty To Provide Adequate Facilities and Equipment

Health care facilities are under a duty to exercise reasonable care to furnish adequate equipment, appliances, and supplies for use in the diagnosis or treatment of patients. The general rule seems to be that equipment furnished by a hospital should be fit for the purposes and uses intended.

Within its duty to provide adequate facilities and equipment, the board must exercise reasonable care and skill in supervising and managing facility property. This obligation includes protecting property from destruction and loss.

Health care facilities must be designed, constructed, equipped, and maintained to provide a safe, healthy, functional, sanitary, and comfortable environment for patients, employees, and the public. Buildings and equipment should be maintained and operated to prevent fire and other hazards to personal safety. Fires should be investigated promptly, and a written report of the investigation containing all pertinent information regarding the fire should be maintained on file.

Patient rooms should be designed and equipped for adequate nursing care, comfort, and privacy. Mechanical, electric, and patient care equipment should be maintained in a safe operating condition.

The nursing facility, Driftwood Convalescent Hospital, operated by Western Medical Enterprises, Inc., in *Beach v. Western Medical Enterprises, Inc.,* 171

Cal. Rptr. 846 (Ct. App. 1981), was fined $2,500 in civil penalties because of nonfunctioning hallway lights and the facility's failure to provide the required type and amount of decubitus preventive equipment necessary for resident care as required by Health and Safety Code regulations. The regulations require that equipment "necessary for care to patients, as ordered or indicated" be provided.

> Though no evidence was introduced to show that the decubitus equipment had been ordered by a physician, the phrase "as indicated" supports an inference that when a patient's condition requires certain equipment, the fact that no physician has ordered that equipment does not relieve the hospital (nursing facility) of the responsibility for providing equipment necessary for patient care.

Id. at 852.

Duty To Provide Adequate Insurance

One basic protection for tangible property is adequate insurance against fire and other risks. This duty extends to keeping the physical plant of the corporation in good repair and appropriating funds for such purpose when necessary.

The duty of the board is to purchase insurance against different risks. Institutions face as much risk of losing their tangible and intangible assets through judgments for negligence as they do through fires or other disasters. Where this is true, the duty to insure against the risks of negligence is as great as the duty to insure against fire, and the amount of insurance must be adequate for the circumstances.

Duty To Provide Satisfactory Patient Care

The most important aspect of a governing board's duty to the health care corporation is to operate it with due care and diligence in its responsibility to provide satisfactory patient care. It is only through the fulfillment of this duty that the basic purpose of the institution will be accomplished; this duty includes the maintenance of a satisfactory standard of medical care through supervision of the medical, nursing, and ancillary staffs of the institution.

A staff member or employee has a duty to recognize and report abnormalities in the treatment and condition of patients. If an attending physician fails to act after being informed of such abnormalities, it is incumbent on the institution's staff to so advise management so that appropriate corrective action can be taken.

Although the provision of satisfactory patient care clearly fulfills the purpose of nonprofit institutions, it might be asked whether this duty applies equally to proprietary institutions where the corporation's additional purpose is to provide a return on investment. The duty does apply equally, and the proprietary institution's liability for failure to provide satisfactory care is clear. State licensing laws and regulations impose the same standards on both proprietary and non-profit institutions, despite the fact that proprietary institutions are permitted to retain a profit.

Duty To Require Competitive Bidding

Many states have developed regulations requiring competitive bidding for work or services commissioned by public institutions. The fundamental purpose of this requirement is to eliminate or at least reduce the possibility that such abuses as fraud, favoritism, improvidence, or extravagance will intrude into an institution's business practices. Contracts made in violation of a statute are considered illegal and could result in personal liability for board members, especially if the members become aware of a fraudulent activity and allow it to continue. The mere appearance of favoritism toward one contractor over another could give rise to an unlawful action. For example, a board member's pressing the administrator to favor one ambulance transporter over others because of his or her social acquaintance with the owner is suspect and would likely ring a bad note in the ears of the courts. A board should avoid even the appearance of wrongdoing by requiring competitive bidding.

Duty To Provide a Safe Environment for Patients and Employees

It is essential that employers provide a safe environment for both employees and patients. Although one cannot guard against the unforeseeable, a health care facility is liable for injuries resulting from dangers that it knowingly failed to guard against or those that it should have known about and failed to guard against. A hospital, for example, is not generally liable for the shooting of an employee in its parking lot unless it knew or in the course of ordinary care should have known of or could reasonably have foreseen the danger to the employee. In *Mauter v. Toledo Hosp., Inc.,* 571 N.E.2d 470 (Ohio Ct. App. 1989), a man shot and killed his estranged wife, a nurse who was an employee of the hospital. The court of appeals held that the hospital had no duty to protect the nurse from that danger.

A hospital can be subject to corporate liability if it fails to ensure a patient's safety and well-being. *Thompson v. Nason Hospital,* 591 A.2d 703 (Pa. 1991). Health care corporations are liable for injuries to both employees and patients arising from environmental hazards.

Infection Control

Health care facilities are required to establish and maintain infection control programs that are designed to provide a safe, sanitary, and comfortable environment in which patients reside and to help prevent the development and transmission of disease and infection.

Chemical Hazards

Employees should be warned of any unusual hazards related to their jobs. For example, pregnant employees may abort because of exposure to anesthetic gases in the operating or delivery room; the fetus of a pregnant employee may suffer cell damage because of exposure to radiation in the radiology, nuclear medicine, or cobalt therapy department. No warnings are usually necessary where the danger is obvious.

A maintenance man's skin condition was found to be compensable in *Albertville Nursing Home v. Upton,* 383 So.2d 544 (Ala. Civ. App. 1980). The maintenance man had developed a severe skin condition on his hands and feet as a result of daily exposure to various caustic cleaning solutions that he used while performing his duties in the nursing facility. The court held that the claimant was entitled to disability benefits for a period of 26 weeks.

The proper test to determine whether a claimant's job caused his or her injury is set out in *Newman Brothers, Inc. v. McDowell,* 354 So.2d 1138 (Ala. Civ. App. 1987). That test is

> [i]f in the performance of his job he has to exert or strain himself or is exposed to conditions of risk or hazard and he would not have strained or exerted himself or been exposed to such conditions had he not been performing his job and the exertion or strain or the exposure to the conditions was, in fact, a contributing cause to his injury or death, the test whether the job caused the injury or death is satisfied.

Id. at 1140.

Construction Hazards

Health care facilities must provide a safe environment for patients, as well as employees. Failure to do so resulted in revocation of a nursing facility's operating certificate in *Slocum v. Berman,* 439 N.Y.S.2d 967 (App. Div. 1981), for violations of nursing home regulations relating to construction and safety standards. The most critical issues related to the structure, which was neither "protected wood frame" nor "fire resistive" as required by regulation, amounting to a violation that adversely affected the "health, safety and welfare of the occupants." *Id.* at 968. It was determined that the nursing home "could not be made reasonably safe or functionally adequate for nursing home occupancy." *Id.*

Floors

Floors are often a major source of lawsuits. To reduce liability caused by falls, floors should be maintained properly. Falls by patients usually involve mixed allegations of a failure to restrain, supervise, assist, or attend the patient and a variety of environmental hazards such as slippery floors. To reduce patient falls,

- Floors should not contain a dangerous amount of wax
- Caution signs (e.g., slippery floors) should be used where appropriate
- Floors should be cared for and maintained properly on rainy and/or snowy days
- Broken floor tiles should be repaired promptly
- Foreign matter should be quickly and completely wiped from the floor
- Signs, ropes, and lights should be used where appropriate
- Appropriate precautions should be taken for outdoor walkways, to guard against dangers such as icy conditions and construction hazards

Windows

Health care facilities are required to exercise reasonable care and diligence in safeguarding a patient, measured by the capacity of the patient to provide for his or her own safety. The plaintiffs in *Horton v. Niagara Falls Memorial Medical Center,* 51 App. Div. 2d 152, 380 N.Y.S.2d 116 (1976), sought recovery against the hospital for injuries sustained by the plaintiff/patient's fall from a second-story hospital window. The patient had been admitted to the hospital with a fever of unknown origin and was noted to be lacking in coordination and to have blurred vision. The patient had been placed in a private room with a single window that opened to a small balcony encircled by a 2- to 3-foot-high railing. Before the patient's fall, construction workers had notified hospital personnel that the patient was standing on his balcony calling for a ladder. The patient had been confused and disoriented. The attending physician on learning of the incident advised a nurse to keep the patient under restraint and to keep an eye on him. The patient's wife was called, and she indicated that her mother would come to the hospital in 10 to 15 minutes to watch her husband. The patient's fall occurred shortly before the mother's arrival. The Niagara Supreme Court had entered judgment for the plaintiffs and the hospital appealed. The supreme court, appellate division, held that the hospital had a duty to supervise the patient and prevent him from injuring himself.

Beds

Falls from beds are frequent occurrences in health care facilities. Maintaining beds in good repair so that side rails and bed adjustment controls function properly should be part of an ongoing preventative maintenance program.

Duty To Safeguard Patient Valuables

Appropriate procedures should be developed for handling the personal property of patients. A health care facility can be held liable for the negligent handling of a patient's valuables. The following points should be remembered and followed when handling the personal belongings and valuables of patients:

- send the belongings home when feasible
- deposit jewelry, wallets, and other appropriate items in the facility's safe
- select one department to handle valuables
- provide proper communication between the department handling lost and found articles and the department holding patient valuables for safekeeping
- encourage patients to keep with them as little money, jewelry, and other valuables as possible
- establish a valuables procedure for deceased patients, patients entering the emergency department, and patients scheduled to go to the operating room and/or other departments of the institution for treatment or diagnostic procedure
- provide prenumbered envelopes that lists those items placed in each valuables envelope. Verification of the contents should be made between the employee delivering an envelope and the employee accepting the envelope for safekeeping. A receipt should be given to the patient making a deposit. Strikeouts or corrections should not be permitted on the envelope; this will help prevent claims of mishandling

CEO/ADMINISTRATOR'S ROLE AND RESPONSIBILITY

The administrator is responsible for the supervision of the administrative staff and department heads, who assist in the daily operations of the health care facility. The administrator derives authority from the owner or board. The administrator of an institution owned and operated by a governmental agency may be an appointed public official.

Administrators, as is the case with board members, can be personally liable for their own acts of negligence that injure others. When an administrator exceeds the limits of his or her authority, the question of whether the institution will be responsible for the administrator's acts may arise. Questions of this nature most often occur when the administrator purports to enter into agreements on behalf of the institution with third parties. If the actions of the governing board give rise to a third party's reasonable belief that the administrator acts with the authority of the institution and such belief causes the third party to enter into an agreement with the administrator, expecting that the institution will be obligated under the contract, the institution generally is responsible under the concept of *apparent authority*. However, if a third party deals with the administrator in the absence of indications of the administrator's authority created by the board and thereby unreasonably assumes that the administrator possesses the authority to bind the institution to a contract, such third party deals with the administrator in an individual capacity and not as an agent of the health care facility. The administrator, not the institution, will be personally responsible. There are times when an administrator clearly may exceed the limitations of his or her authority, but the governing board subsequently may approve such actions through ratification—by accepting any resulting responsibility as though it had been authorized previously.

The administrator must implement the policies of the board, as well as interpret policies to the staff. Appropriate action must be taken where noncompliance with rules occurs. The administrator is responsible for making periodic reports to the board regarding policy implementation in institution operations.

There may be occasions when the administrator believes that following a direction of the board may create a danger to the patients or others. If the administrator knows or should have known, as a reasonably prudent administrator, of a danger or unreasonable risk or harm that will be created by certain directed activity but nevertheless proceeds as directed, he or she could become personally liable for any resulting injury. The administrator, therefore, must take appropriate steps to notify the board of any danger in carrying out policies that create dangers or unreasonable risks. Good communications with board members and suggestions for resolving policy issues will go a long way toward maintaining harmony with the board.

Although the administrator cannot assume the functions of the professional staff, he or she must ensure that proper admission and discharge policies and procedures are formulated and carried out. He or she must cooperate with the professional staff in maintaining satisfactory standards of medical care. The administrator must keep abreast of regulatory changes that affect institutional operations. Periodic meetings should be conducted to inform the staff of regulatory changes affecting their duties and responsibilities. The administrator should designate a representative for administrative coverage during those hours he or she is absent from the institution. This individual should be capable of dealing with administrative matters and be able to contact the administrator when major problems arise.

Health care administrators are subject to state laws and administrative regulations that control to some degree the scope of their activities. Nursing facility administrators historically have been subject to greater regulation than hospital administrators because of federal requirements that states enact licensing laws for nursing home administrators.

Tort Liability of Administrator

The wrongful injury to another by the administrator in the performance of his or her duties makes the administrator liable to the one injured. Because the administrator is subject to the control of the institution, it also may be liable for the torts of the administrator that occur within the scope of his or her employment. When performing the duties he or she was hired to do, the administrator is working for the benefit of the institution and not as an individual. Because the institution gains from the work performed by its employees, the law renders the institution legally responsible for the acts of employees while performing the work of the institution.

Administrator's Liability for the Acts of Others

The administrator is not liable for the negligent acts of other employees, so long as he or she personally took no part in the commission of the negligent act and was not negligent in selecting or directing the person committing the injury. Under the doctrine of *respondeat superior*, a health care facility can be liable for the employee's negligent acts.

Contract Liability of Administrator

The administrator is not personally liable on contracts entered into by him or her on behalf of the institution. However, if the administrator exceeds his or her authority, the institution generally cannot be bound by the contract. The administrator may be liable for damages occurring to the contracting party. The administrator generally possesses the authority to enter into a contract for a needed piece of equipment, such as medication cabinets. The contract of sale by the administrator as the agent of the home becomes the obligation of the institution. However, if the board had imposed a limitation on purchases that could be made without specific prior approval of the board, the price of the medication cabinets would determine whether the board was bound under the contract. If the cabinets were $7,000 and the limitation on purchases without specific board approval was $5,000, the administrator would have no authority to bind the institution for the purchase of the cabinets. The administrator generally would be liable to the supplier of the medication cabinets. As previously discussed, the two legal concepts of apparent authority and ratification may operate to alter the personal liability of the administrator.

MEDICAL STAFF

The role of the board in setting policy and supervision of the medical staff is extremely important. The board should ensure that the medical staff bylaws provide for the following:

- application requirements for clinical privileges and admission to the medical staff
- emergency procedures to be followed in medical emergencies
- procedures for arranging medical consultations
- procedures for the review and appraisal of the quality and appropriateness of medical care rendered by each physician
- procedures and responsibility for maintaining adequate medical records
- procedures for dealing with disruptive physicians and substance abuse (e.g., alcohol and drugs)
- procedures for corrective action (Disciplinary actions can take the form of a letter of reprimand, suspension, or termination of privileges.)

The commissioner of health was authorized by New York's Public Health Law to summarily suspend a petitioner ophthalmologist for a period of 60 days pending disciplinary hearings and determination of charges against him. The physician had been suspended on the grounds that he posed an imminent danger to the public. Proceedings against the ophthalmologist had been delayed since 1977; meanwhile, he had continued to practice, and 11 new charges had been filed against him. *John P. v. Axelrod,* 97 A.D.2d 950, 468 N.Y.S.2d 951, 462 N.E.2d 1192 (1984).

A physician whose privileges are either suspended or terminated must exhaust all remedies provided in a hospital's bylaws, rules, and regulations before commencing a court action. The physician in *Eidelson v. Archer,* 645 P.2d 171 (Alaska 1982), failed to pursue the hospital's internal appeal procedure before bringing suit. As a result, the Supreme Court of Alaska reversed a superior court's judgment for the physician in his action for compensatory and punitive damages.

CONCLUSION

There is a need for a new legal definition of the duties and responsibilities of hospital board members. A board meeting is not a social function, and board members must not delegate all decision making to the CEO or make decisions too slowly or hastily. *Smith v. Van Gorkum,* 488 A.2d 858 (Del. 1985), involved a board of directors that authorized the sale of its company through a cash-out merger for a tendered price per share nearly 50 percent over the market price. Although that might sound like a good deal, the board did not make any inquiry to determine if it was the best deal available. In fact, it made no decision during a hastily arranged, brief meeting in which it relied solely on the CEO's report regarding the desirability of the move. The Supreme Court of Delaware held that the board's decision to approve a proposed cash-out merger was not a product of informed business judgment and that it acted in a grossly negligent manner in approving amendments to the merger proposal.

The traditional business judgment doctrine is too vague in the light of the goals and missions of today's modern health care institutions. Attending a monthly meeting of the board and serving on several committees are not sufficient commitment in the light of the complexities and difficulties in operating multimillion dollar health care systems. Perhaps it is time to compensate board members for the time commitment they are required to make and the legal risks to which they are exposed. "[B]y examining the functions of corporate boards and their members, it is possible to create a new, more practical legal standard based upon the flow of responsibility, rather than on any single decision or action."[2]

NOTES

1. Louis Braiotta , *Auditing for Honesty,* 78 A.B.A. J., 79 (1992).
2. Manning, *The Director's Duty of Attention,* Corp. Board, Sept.–Oct. 1984, at 1(21).

Medical Staff

OUTLINE

Failure To Read X-Rays
Failure To Notify of X-Ray Results
Physician–Patient Relationship
• Conclusion

This chapter provides an overview of the responsibilities and the medical and legal risks of physicians. The practice of medicine includes three basic functions: diagnosis, treatment, and prescription. A physician's license demonstrates that the state, as the representative of the public, is satisfied that the physician has the basic training and ability to make diagnostic judgments and to prescribe courses of treatment that will alleviate or cure a patient's ailment.

The role of an attending physician in a health care facility is to integrate a comprehensive approach to patient care. This includes caring for acute illnesses and monitoring chronic diseases, as well as coordinating with staff for the provision of educational and psychological support for the patient and family. Health care facilities must ensure that

- the medical care of each patient is supervised by a physician
- a covering physician supervises the medical care of patients when their attending physician is unavailable
- the physician reviews each patient's total program of care including medications and treatments during each visit
- progress notes are current, signed, and dated
- all orders are signed
- patients are seen by a physician on a regular basis as described in the facility's bylaws and in accordance with any applicable federal and state statutes or regulations

The wide range of authority in treating patients has brought with it a broad range of lawsuits. The single most sued group of professionals is physicians. Malpractice suits have become part of the practice of medicine. Unfortunately, it is rare for the best of physicians to say they have not been involved in some kind of litigation. Medical acts, which often transpire over a few minutes' time span, are examined closely by the court years after the occurrence. This chapter discusses many of those areas in which physicians tend to be most vulnerable to lawsuits.

MEDICAL STAFF PRIVILEGES

The duty to select members of the medical staff is legally vested in the governing board as the body charged with managing the health care facility and maintaining a satisfactory standard of patient care. While cognizant of the importance of medical staff membership to physicians, the governing board must meet its obligation to maintain standards of good medical practice in dealing with matters of staff appointment, credentialing, and the disciplining of physicians for such things as disruptive behavior, incompetence, psychological problems, criminal actions, and abuse of alcohol or drugs.

Appointment to the hospital medical staff and the granting of medical staff privileges should be given only after the appropriate committees of the hospital's medical staff have made an effective and thorough investigation of the applicant. The delineation of privileges should be hospital-specific, based on appropriate predetermined criteria that adhere to a national standard.

Most state laws, as well as the standards set forth by the Joint Commission on Accreditation of Healthcare Organizations, clearly state that the governing board is ultimately responsible for the selection of medical staff members and the delineation of clinical privileges. Trustees have a duty and obligation to protect patients from physicians they know, or should know, are unqualified to practice medicine at their facilities. The courts will not permit any organization or institution to hide behind the cloak of ignorance in this responsibility.

MEDICAL STAFF APPOINTMENTS—THE SCREENING PROCESS

Because the board of directors or trustees has ultimate responsibility for the screening of medical staff applicants and appointments to the medical staff, it must assure that appropriate procedures have been implemented for processing applicants applying for medical staff privileges. The purpose of the appointment process is to evaluate the competency of the applicant to determine if he or she is qualified to be appointed to the medical staff.

The medical staff must be required to adhere to the written bylaws governing the medical staff and care of patients. The bylaws should be approved by the medical board and the governing body. Each member of the facility's medical staff should be required to sign a statement attesting that the medical staff bylaws have been read and understood and that the physician agrees to abide by the bylaws and other policies and procedures that may be adopted from time to time by the facility. The quality of care can be improved greatly and the incidence of malpractice suits kept to a minimum by following established guidelines for providing medical care.

Application

The board of trustees should establish a policy of nondiscrimination on the basis of race, color, sex, religion, national origin, age, and physical disability. The medical staff application should provide information regarding the applicant's

- residence
- office location (Geographic requirements should not be unreasonably restrictive. If the applicant does not meet the hospital's geographic requirements for residence and office location, provision should be available in the bylaws for exceptions that might be necessary to attract a distinguished consulting staff.)
- medical school
- internship
- residency
- board certification
- fellowship
- medical society membership (Board certification, fellowship, and medical society membership are not legally acceptable criteria for determining eligibility for medical staff appointment.[1])
- state license to practice medicine
- malpractice coverage
- special skills and talents
- privileges requested and specialty
- availability to provide on-call emergency department coverage where applicable
- availability to serve on medical staff and/or hospital committees
- other medical staff appointments
- previous disciplinary actions against applicant

The medical staff application should contain a signed statement by the applicant indicating his or her agreement to abide by all hospital and medical staff rules and regulations.

Physical and Mental Status

Inquiry should be made as to the physical and mental status of the applicant.

Consent for Release of Information

Consent for release of information from third parties should be obtained from the applicant.

Certificate of Insurance

The applicant should provide evidence of professional liability insurance. The insurance policy should provide minimum levels of insurance coverage—generally $1 million to $3 million.

License

The applicant must have a state license to practice medicine.

National Practitioner Data Bank

The National Practitioner Data Bank should be queried as to information in its files for all new applicants.

References

References should be checked thoroughly. Failure to do so can lead to corporate liability for a physician's negligent acts if a hospital fails to review a physician's credentials properly and such failure leads to injury of a patient. Both written and oral references should be obtained from previous institutions with which the applicant has been affiliated.

Interview Process

The interview process can become ineffective if there are too many layers. Too many interview levels can lead to a rubber-stamp mentality, each layer believing that prior interviewers have performed a more thorough interview or thinking that what pertinent information one committee or person fails to discover, the next layer will discover. Potential interviewers include

- section chief (e.g., director of gastroenterology)
- department chairman (e.g., director of medicine)
- credentials committee (including CEO/administrator and director of nurses)
- medical board
- joint conference committee

A committee should include representatives from both the medical board and the board of directors/trustees.

The Interview

- Be sure all documents have been received before the interview.
- Check to see if there is any unaccounted-for hiatus (break or gap) in education or employment.
- Is the applicant available for emergency coverage?
- Does the applicant have back-up and cross coverage?
- Does the applicant have any special skills or talents?
- Has the applicant reviewed medical staff bylaws, rules, and regulations; and where applicable, departmental rules and regulations?
- Does the applicant agree to abide by all hospital and medical staff bylaws, rules, and regulations?
- Has the applicant ever had his or her medical staff privileges suspended and/or revoked?
- Is the applicant familiar with diagnosis-related groups (DRGs) and their importance to the hospital?
- What is the applicant's ability to work with others?

The Board and Final Action

Appointments to the medical staff are made on recommendation to the board of directors by the medical staff and reviewing committees. The board has ultimate authority for granting medical staff privileges—this responsibility cannot be delegated. The *1992 Joint Commission Accreditation Manual for Hospitals* provides: "Medical staff membership and delineated clinical privileges are granted by the governing body, based on medical staff recommendations, in accordance with the bylaws, rules and regulations, and policies of the medical staff and hospital." Standard MS.2.1 at 55.

The board can grant privileges, grant limited privileges, or deny privileges.

STATE LICENSURE

The individual states have enacted medical practice acts that regulate the practice of medicine. The different states have a legitimate interest in regulating the practice of medicine. This interest includes assuring the health and welfare of individuals through the regulation and supervision of the practice of medicine. A state may set reasonable standards for determining the qualifications of those who hold themselves out as practitioners of the healing arts, and they also grant the authority to enforce standards to the administrative body. (*Reisinger v. Commonwealth of Pennsylvania State Board of Medical Education and Licensure, et. al.,* 399 A.2d 1160 (Pa. Cmwlth. Ct. 1979).

A physician's right to practice medicine is subject to the licensing laws contained in the statutes within the state in which the physician resides. The right to practice medicine is not a vested right but is a condition of a right subordinate to the police power of the state to protect and preserve the public health. Although the state has the power to regulate the practice of medicine, for the benefit of the public health and welfare, this power is not unrestricted, and regulations imposed must be reasonably related to the public health and welfare and must not amount to arbitrary or unreasonable interference with the right to practice one's profession. (*State Board of Medical Examiners of Florida v. Rogers,* 387 So.2d 8 (Fla. 1980). Health professions commonly requiring licensure include chiropractors, dentists, nurses, optometrists, osteopaths, physicians, and podiatrists.

Grounds for Revocation

Grounds for the revocation of a license to practice medicine include the following:

- a clear demonstration of the lack of good moral character
- deliberate falsification of a patient's medical record (This is particularly true when the motive for falsification is to protect the physician's own interests at the expense of the patient's. This can be viewed as gross malpractice endangering the life or health of a patient.)
- intentional fraudulent advertising
- gross incompetence
- sexual misconduct
- drug or alcohol abuse during working hours
- performance of unnecessary medical procedures
- billing for services not performed
- forged operative record

A physician whose license is revoked may have a right to a new hearing if he or she is denied the right to cross-examine key witnesses. *Dragan v. Connecticut Medical Examining Board,* 591 A.2d 150 (Conn. Ct. App. 1991).

DELINEATION OF CLINICAL PRIVILEGES

The delineation of clinical privileges is the process by which the medical staff determines precisely what procedures a physician is authorized to perform. This determination is based on predetermined criteria as to what credentials are necessary to competently perform the privileges requested.

The governing board bears ultimate responsibility for ensuring that applicants to the hospital's medical staff are qualified to perform the clinical procedures set forth in the delineation of privileges. Otherwise, a hospital may be liable for the negligent acts of its physicians. If a hospital is to be responsible for each physician's conduct, it must be permitted to determine the nature and extent of the privileges granted physicians to practice in the institution. However, in the light of the importance of staff appointments to physicians, the courts have prohibited hospital governing boards from acting unreasonably or capriciously in rejecting physicians for staff appointments or in limiting their privileges.

The surgeon in *Purcell & Tucson General Hospital v. Zimbelman,* 500 P.2d 335 (Ariz. Ct. App. 1972), performed inappropriate surgery because of his misdiagnosis of the patient's ailment. Prior malpractice suits against the surgeon revealed that the hospital had reason to know or should have known that the surgeon apparently lacked the skill to treat the patient's condition. The court held that the hospital had a clear duty to select competent physicians; to regulate the privileges granted to staff physicians; to ensure that privileges are conferred only for those procedures for which the physician is trained and qualified; and to restrict, suspend, or require supervision when a physician has demonstrated an inability to handle a certain type of problem. The hospital had assumed the duty of supervising the competence of its physicians. The Department of Surgery was acting for and on behalf of the hospital in fulfilling this duty. If the department was negligent in not taking action against the surgeon or recommending to the board of trustees that action be taken, the hospital would be negligent. The court noted that it is reasonable to conclude that had the hospital taken some action against the surgeon, the patient would not have been injured.

APPEAL PROCESS

The board should reserve the right to hear any appeals regarding a decision to deny privileges.

Challenging Requirements for Medical Staff Membership

Physicians have attempted to use state and federal antitrust laws to challenge determinations denying or limiting medical staff privileges. Generally, these actions claim that the facility conspired with other physicians to ensure that the complaining physician would not be granted privileges so that competition among the physicians would be reduced. To date, physicians generally have been unsuccessful in pursuing these antitrust claims.

Osteopaths

Osteopaths were properly denied privileges in *Silverstein v. Gwinnett Hospital Authority,* 672 F. Supp. 1444 (D. Ga. 1987), in which principles of due process and equal protection were not violated by the bylaws of a county hospital. These bylaws effectively excluded osteopathic physicians from medical staff membership by limiting staff privileges to physicians who had completed allopathic training requirements for certification by the appropriate American specialty board and who had completed a postgraduate training program approved by the Accreditation Council for Graduate Medical Education. The differences between the two schools and their approaches to medical treatment provided a rational basis for a public hospital to deny staff privileges to those who do not meet the hospital's bylaw requirements for obtaining medical staff privileges.

Doctors of osteopathy in *Hull v. Board of Commissioners of Halifax Hospital Medical Center,* 453 So.2d 519 (Fla. Dist. Ct. App. 1984), filed a complaint against members of the hospital's board, alleging that the eligibility requirements for medical staff membership were discriminatory against osteopaths. The Fifth District Court of Appeals of Florida held that the hospital's refusal to allow noneligible and noncertified medical board applicants positions on its staff was not an abuse of its discretion and was not done arbitrarily or unreasonably. The court also held that the fact that the hospital did not make a detailed evaluation of every applicant who failed to meet basic minimum bylaw requirements did not violate any statute.

Hospitals have responded to lawsuits in this area by demonstrating that they have followed pre-established policies and procedures. The board may exercise its authority to fix these policies for the hospital through the promulgation of rules and regulations for the conduct of the hospital, or like other responsibilities of the board, policy making may be delegated. This delegation may be broad or narrow as determined by the board. It may take the form of permission for the administrator, the administrator's subordinates, or committees in the hospital to make policies or formulate rules and regulations, subject to the review of the board. Policies made in this way (which do not contravene statute, charter, or bylaws) bind the hospital; they will be effective in determining the rights of beneficiaries of the hospital, its employees, and its professional staff.

NEGLIGENT GRANTING OF PRIVILEGES

Failure to screen a medical staff applicant's credentials properly can lead to liability for injuries suffered by patients as a result of that omission. The patient in *Johnson v. Misericordia Community Hospital,* 294 N.W.2d 501, 301 N.W.2d 156 (Wis. 1981), brought a malpractice action against the hospital and its liability insurer for alleged negligence in granting orthopedic privileges to a physician who performed an operation to remove a pin fragment from the patient's hip. The Wisconsin Court of Appeals found the hospital negligent for failing to scrutinize the physician's credentials before approving his application for orthopedic privileges. The hospital failed to adhere to procedures established under both its own bylaws and state statute. The measure of quality and the degree of quality control exercised in a hospital are the direct responsibilities of the medical staff. Hospital supervision of the manner of appointment of physicians to its staff is mandatory, not optional. On appeal by the hospital, the Wisconsin Supreme Court affirmed the appellate court's decision, finding that if the hospital had exercised ordinary care, it would not have appointed the physician to the medical staff.

An action was brought against a hospital in *Rule v. Lutheran Hospitals & Homes Society of America,* 835 F.2d 1250 (8th Cir. 1987), for birth injuries sustained during an infant's breech delivery. The action was based on allegations that the hospital had negligently failed to investigate the qualifications of the attending physician before granting him privileges. The jury's verdict of $650,000 was supported by evidence that the hospital administrator failed to check with other hospitals where the physician had practiced. The physician's privileges at one hospital had been limited in that breech deliveries had to be performed under supervision. A finding of causation likewise was permissible on the basis of evidence that there was sufficient time to summon a qualified physician once discovering that the infant was in a breech position.

PHYSICIAN SUPERVISION AND MONITORING

The hospital board has a duty to supervise the competence of its physicians. If a hospital has reason to know or should know that a physician lacks the necessary skill to care for patients, the facility has a clear duty to restrict, suspend, or require supervision of a physician who has demonstrated an inability to handle a certain type of procedure.

The medical staff is responsible to the board for the quality of care rendered by members of the medical staff. The landmark decision in this area occurred in *Darling v. Charleston Community Memorial Hospital,* 33 Ill. 2d 326, 211 N.E.2d 253 (1965), *cert. denied,* 383 U.S. 946 (1966), in which it was decided that the hospital governing board had a duty to establish mechanisms for the medical staff to evaluate, counsel, and when necessary, take action against an unreasonable risk of harm to a patient arising from the patient's treatment by a personal physician. Because the hospital has a responsibility for the quality of medical care afforded the patient in the institution, appropriate mechanisms for evaluating the competency of candidates for staff appointments and the privileges given physicians must exist.

Physician monitoring is best accomplished through a system of peer review. It involves the periodic evaluation of the competence of physicians by other physicians. Most states provide statutory protection from liability for peer review activities when they are conducted in a reasonable manner and without malice.

Responsibility To Know of a Physician's Incompetence

A hospital cannot defend itself against a lawsuit on the grounds that the medical staff is independent and self-governing. The governing board is under no obligation to delegate any of its management or its policy-making functions. Those delegated are subject to revocation by the governing board at any time. In other words, there is no obligation to delegate any part of a board's function, and there is no obligation to continue such delegation once it is made.

In *Gonzales v. Nork and Mercy Hospital,* No. 228566, (Cal., Sacramento Co. Super. Ct. 1973), *rev'd on other grounds,* 60 Cal. App. 3d 835, 131 Cal. Rptr. 717 (1976), the hospital was found negligent for failing to protect the patient, a 27-year-old man, from acts of malpractice by an independent, privately retained physician. The patient had been injured in an automobile accident and was operated on by Dr. Nork, an orthopedic surgeon. The plaintiff's life expectancy was reduced as a result of an unsuccessful and allegedly unnecessary laminectomy. It was found that the hospital knew or should have known of the surgeon's incompetence because the surgeon previously had performed many operations either unnecessarily or negligently. Evidence was presented showing that the surgeon had performed more than three dozen similar operations unnecessarily or in a negligent manner. Even if the hospital was not aware of the surgeon's acts of negligence, an effective monitoring system should have been in place for monitoring his abilities.

The hospital that employs a physician who commits malpractice will not escape liability in a negligence action naming the physician. A hospital owes its patients a duty of care, and this duty includes the obligation to protect them from negligent and fraudulent acts of those physicians with a propensity to commit malpractice. The courts will not permit hospitals to hide behind the cloak of ignorance in this responsibility.

For example, an orthopedic surgeon in California performed fraudulent, negligent, and/or unnecessary surgery on 38 patients. The defendant produced false and inadequate findings as well as false-positive myelograms. He deceived his patients with this information and caused them to undergo surgery. The court held the surgeon and the hospital jointly liable for damages suffered by the plaintiffs. *Gonzales v. Nork and Mercy Hospital,* No. 228566 (Cal., Sacramento Co. Super. Ct. Nov. 27, 1973).

Disruptive Physicians

Criteria other than academic credentials (e.g., a physician's ability to work with others) should be considered before granting medical staff privileges. That factor was considered by the court in *Ladenheim v. Union County Hospital District,* 76 Ill. App. 3d 90, 394 N.E.2d 770 (1979), which held that the physician's inability to work with other members of the staff was in itself sufficient grounds to deny him staff privileges. The physician's record was replete with evidence of his inability to work effectively with other members of the hospital staff. As stated in *Huffaker v. Bailey,* 273 Or. 273, 278, 279, 540 P.2d 1398, 1400 (1975), most other courts have found that the ability to work smoothly with others is reasonably related to the objective of ensuring patient welfare. The conclusion seems justified because health care professionals frequently are required to work together or in teams. A staff member who, because of personality characteristics or other problems, is incapable of getting along with others could severely hinder the effective treatment of patients.

The court in *Pick v. Santa Ana-Tustin Community Hospital,* 130 Cal. App. 3d 970 (1982), held that the petitioner's demonstrated lack of ability to work with others in the hospital setting was sufficient to support the denial of his application for admission to the medical staff. There was evidence that the petitioner presented a real and substantial danger to patients treated by him and that they might receive other than a high quality of medical care.

SUSPENSION AND TERMINATION OF PRIVILEGES

A physician whose privileges are either suspended or terminated must exhaust all remedies provided in a facility's bylaws, rules, and regulations before commencing a court action.

A hospital that denies a physician due process as provided in its medical staff bylaws could find itself involved in a lawsuit. The U.S. Court of Appeals in *Northeast Georgia Radiological Associates v. Tidwell,* 670 F.2d 507 (5th Cir. 1982), held that a contract with the hospital's radiologists, which incorporated the medical staff bylaws, sustained the plaintiffs' claim to a protected property interest entitling them to a hearing before the medical staff and the hospital authority.

REAPPOINTMENTS AND PEER REVIEW

Each physician's credentials and departmental evaluations should be reviewed at least every two years. The medical staff must provide effective mechanisms for monitoring and evaluating the quality of patient care and the clinical performance of physicians. For problematic physicians, consideration should be given to privileges with supervision, a reduction in privileges, suspension of privileges with purpose (e.g., suspension pending further training), or termination of privileges.

MEDICAL DIRECTOR

The appointment of a medical director is crucial to the provision of efficient and effective medical care. The medical director generally is responsible for taking corrective action in those instances in which attending physicians fail to provide patients with care and services that meet generally accepted standards of practice. The responsibilities of the medical director are generally to enforce bylaws governing medical care, assure that quality medical care is provided, serve as a liaison between the medical staff and the administration, and assure that each patient has an assigned personal physician.

The position of medical director must not be viewed as a "figurehead" appointment.

When a Texas nursing home was indicted by a grand jury in 1981 for the deaths of several residents, the medical director was also indicted. His plea that he merely signed papers and attended meetings did not absolve him of the responsibility 'to ensure the adequacy and the appropriateness of medical services. . . .'[2]

MEDICAL STAFF COMMITTEES

There is a cadre of medical staff committees with a wide variety of duties and responsibilities. Some of those committees are described below.

Executive Committee

The executive committee of the medical staff oversees the activities of the medical staff. It reviews and acts on the reports of the different department chairpersons and medical staff committees. Actions requiring approval of the governing board are forwarded directly to the board or through designated board committees. Membership on the executive committee should include the chief executive officer.

Credentials Committee

The credentials committee oversees the application process for new medical staff applicants, requests for specific clinical privileges, and reappointments to the medical staff. The committee makes its recommendations to the medical executive committee.

Infection Control Committee

The infection control committee is generally responsible for the development of policies and procedures for investigating, controlling, and preventing infections in the institution. Membership on infection control committees often includes representation from administration, medical staff, nursing, pharmacy, dietary, and housekeeping.

Medical Records Committee

The medical records committee is responsible for reviewing medical records for timeliness, accuracy, legibility, completeness, etc. The committee should make recommendations for disciplinary action as necessary. The committee should include representatives from administration, medical records, and nursing.

Pharmacy and Therapeutics Committee

The pharmacy and therapeutics committee is responsible for developing and/ or approving policies and procedures relating to the selection, distribution, handling, use, and administration of drugs and diagnostic testing materials. The committee is responsible for developing and maintaining a drug formulary, approving the use of investigational drugs, reviewing untoward drug reactions, and such other activities that may be delegated to it by the medical staff executive committee. Representation on this committee should include participation from administration and appropriate departments (e.g., nursing and pharmacy).

Patient Care Evaluation or Quality Assurance Committee

The patient care evaluation or quality assurance committee generally is charged with the responsibility for monitoring the quality of patient care and making appropriate recommendations to management for improving the quality of care being provided in the facility. Historically, quality assurance committees have not been as effective as they could be. "Too often quality assurance systems have been dutifully collecting reports from various departments and services, casually reviewing a few random charts, and referring to an executive committee conflicts regarding credentials. Quality assurance committees have not critically questioned the performance of colleagues or been critical of their own function."[3] Improvement in quality assurance programs can be

> ensured by ongoing assessment of the work of the staff, systematic collection of clinically relevant data, and appropriate appraisal and analysis of care and outcome. Quality committees must be willing to evaluate the process of physician decision and to identify need for consultation and education. A medical staff with day-to-day information on the principal medical conditions and surgical procedures in its repertoire can anticipate problems, rationally designate privileges, and be prepared to counsel, advise, and prescribe educational intervention when needed.[4]

Tissue Committee

The tissue committee reviews all surgical procedures conducted in the institution. Representation on the committee should include administration, the director of surgery, and the pathologist as chairperson.

PHYSICIAN LIABILITY

A New Jersey study of a major malpractice insurance carrier involved analysis of insurance claims filed against high-risk physicians (anesthesiology, obstetrics/gynecology, general surgery, and radiology). The study revealed that between 1977 and 1989

> patient management errors were cited most frequently as associated with claims of negligence. Technical performance problems like surgical "slips" accounted for one-third to one-half of injuries in all specialties except radiology. Only 6% to 11% of negligence claims were the result of medical and nursing staff coordination problems. Less than 15% of negligence claims were associated with failure to order diagnostic tests or employ monitoring techniques.[5]

The following cases illustrate some of the acts or omissions constituting negligence or malpractice. They are by no means exhaustive and are merely representative of the wide range of potential legal pitfalls in which physicians might find themselves.

Abandonment

The professional relationship that exists between physician and patient continues, for the most part, until it is terminated with the consent of both parties. However, a relationship can be discontinued through dismissal of the physician by the patient, or through physician withdrawal from the case, or at such time when the physician's services are no longer required. Failure to follow up after the acute stage of illness has subsided or neglect to provide a patient with necessary instructions could involve the physician in serious legal difficulties. Premature termination of treatment is often the subject of a legal action for abandonment, defined as the unilateral termination of a physician–patient relationship by the physician without notice to the patient. Closely related to this type of problem is one that occurs when the physician, although not intending to end the relationship with the patient, fails to ensure the patient's understanding that further treatment of the complaint is necessary.

All the following elements must be established in order for a patient to recover damages for abandonment:

- Medical care was unreasonably discontinued
- The discontinuance of medical care was against the patient's will (Termination of the physician–patient relationship must have been brought about by a unilateral act of the physician. There can be no abandonment if the relationship is terminated by mutual consent or by dismissal of the physician by the patient.)
- The physician failed to arrange for care by another physician (Refusal by a physician to enter into a physician–patient relationship by failing to respond to a call or render treatment is not considered a case of abandonment. A plaintiff will not recover for damages unless he or she can prove that a physician–patient relationship had been established.)
- Foresight indicated that discontinuance might result in physical harm to the patient
- Actual harm was suffered by the patient

The relationship between a physician and a patient, once established, continues until it is ended by the mutual consent of the parties, the patient's dismissal of the physician, the physician's withdrawal from the case, or the fact that the physician's services are no longer needed. A physician who decides to withdraw his or her services must provide the patient with reasonable notice so that the services of another physician can be obtained.

Aggravation of a Pre-Existing Condition

Aggravation of a pre-existing condition through negligence may cause a physician to be liable for malpractice. If the original injury is aggravated, liability will be imposed only for the aggravation, rather than for both the original injury and its aggravation.

In *Nguyen v. County of Los Angeles,* C538628 (Super. Ct. L.A. Co.), an eight-month-old girl went to the hospital for tests on her hip. She had been injected with air for a hip study and suffered a respiratory arrest. She later went into cardiac arrest and was resuscitated but suffered brain damage that was aggravated by further poor treatment. The Los Angeles Superior Court jury found evidence of medical malpractice, ordering payments for past and future pain and suffering as well as medical and total care costs that projected to the child's normal life expectancy.

Patient Falls

Patient falls are major causes of lawsuits for health care facilities. Physicians are not exempt from this area of risk. For example, the plaintiff in *Favalora v. Aetna Casualty & Surety Co.,* 144 So.2d 544 (La. Ct. App. 1962), sued the hospital and the radiologist for injuries she sustained when she fell while undergoing an x-ray examination. The patient had been admitted to the hospital by her personal physician for a general checkup and a gastrointestinal (GI) series. She had complained about stomach pains, general fatigue, and fainting. The morning after her admission to the hospital, she was taken from her room in a wheelchair to the radiology department. When preparations for the GI series were complete, two technicians brought the patient to the x-ray room. She then waited for the arrival of the radiologist. When he arrived, she was instructed to walk to the x-ray table and stand on the footboard. The technician instructed her to drink a glass of barium. A second cup of barium was handed to her by the technician who then took the exposed film to a nearby pass box leading to the adjacent darkroom, obtained a new film, and repeated the x-ray process. While the technician was depositing the second set of exposed film in the pass box, the patient suddenly fainted and fell to the floor. The radiologist did not see the plaintiff fall, nor did he detect any evidence of distress. The technician heard a noise, immediately turned on the lights, and found her lying on the floor. The radiologist instantly began administering to the patient while the technician summoned additional assistance. The patient was placed on the x-ray table, and x-rays were taken of those portions of her anatomy that indicated the possibility of injury. The x-rays revealed a fracture of the neck and of the right femur that subsequently required open reduction and the insertion of a metal pin by an orthopedic surgeon. As a result, a pre-existing vascular condition was aggravated, causing a pulmonary embolism, which, in turn, necessitated additional surgery. The failure of the radiologist to secure the patient's medical history before the x-ray examination was considered negligence constituting the proximate cause of the patient's injuries.

A defendant generally is required only to compensate a patient for the amount of aggravation caused. However, it is often difficult to determine what monetary damages should be awarded to a plaintiff. In many instances, aggravation is a matter of conjecture.

Wrongful Death

Death resulting from a negligent injury by a defendant gives rise to an action for wrongful death by the survivors. Most states have enacted wrongful death statutes allowing recovery by a defined group of persons for damages suffered through the loss of the decedent.

Damages were awarded in *Argus v. Scheppegrell,* 489 So.2d 392 (La. Ct. App. 1986), for the wrongful death of a teenage patient with a pre-existing drug addiction. It was determined that the physician had wrongfully supplied the patient with prescriptions for controlled substances in excessive amounts, with the result that the patient's pre-existing drug addiction had worsened, causing her death from a drug overdose. The Louisiana Court of Appeals held that the suffering of the daughter caused by drug addiction and deterioration of her mental and physical condition warranted an award of $175,000. Damages of $120,000 were to be awarded for the wrongful death claims of the parents, who not only suffered during their daughter's drug addiction caused by the physician in wrongfully supplying the prescription but also were forced to endure the torment of their daughter's slow death in the hospital.

Anesthesiology

Anesthesiology claims according to the New Jersey malpractice study revealed that most claims in this area "stemmed from performance errors rather than improper monitoring."[6]

Administration of Anesthetics

A physician's medical license was suspended for one year in *Kearl v. Division of Medical Quality,* 236 Cal. Rptr. 526 (Ct. App. 1986), because of gross negligence in the manner in which he administered anesthesia to a patient during spinal surgery. The finding was based on evidence that the physician failed to record the patient's vital signs at five-minute intervals, as required by prevailing community standards. The record further supported the conclusion that he was negligent and demonstrated a lack of knowledge and ability when in administering a spinal block to another patient who was undergoing a cesarean section, he selected an isobaric, rather than a hyperbaric, solution of anesthetic, permitted surgery to begin before the anesthetic was fixated, and allowed the patient to be placed in a head-down position, with the result that the patient suffered oxygen deprivation secondary to a "high spinal."

Captain of the Ship

Summary dismissal was properly ordered for those portions of a patient's medical malpractice action that sought to hold a surgeon vicariously liable for throat injuries suffered by his patient because of the negligent manner in which an endotracheal tube was inserted during the administration of anesthesia. *Thomas v. Raleigh,* 358 S.E.2d 222 (W. Va. 1987). The patient's allegations that the surgeon had exercised control over the administration of anesthesia were rebutted by evidence to the contrary. Liability of the surgeon could not be premised on the captain of the ship doctrine because that doctrine would not be recognized in West Virginia. The trend in medicine has created situations in which surgeons do not always have the right to control all persons within the operating room. An assignment of liability based on the theory of actual control more realistically reflects the actual relationship that exists in a modern operating room.

Failure To Maintain an Airway

On appeal by the defendant anesthesiologist in *Ward v. Epting,* 351 S.E.2d 867 (S.C. Ct. App. 1987), the issues of deviation from the standard of care and proximate cause were found to have been submitted properly to the jury. The anesthesiologist had failed to establish and maintain an adequate airway and resuscitate properly a postsurgical 22-year-old female patient, which resulted in her death from lack of oxygen. Expert testimony based on autopsy and blood gas tests showed that the endotracheal tube had been removed too soon after surgery and that the anesthesiologist, in an attempt to revive the patient, reinserted the tube into the esophagus. The record contained ample evidence that the anesthesiologist failed to conform to the standard of care and that such deviation was the proximate cause of the patient's death. The plaintiff was awarded $400,000 in damages.

Alternative Procedures

The potential for liability affects the choice of treatment a physician will follow in treating his or her patient. Use of unprecedented procedures that create an untoward result may cause a physician to be found negligent even though due care was followed. A physician will not be held liable for exercising his or her judgment in applying a course of treatment supported by a reputable and respected body of medical experts even if another body of expert medical opinion would favor a different course of treatment. The "two schools of thought" doctrine is only applicable in medical malpractice cases in which there is more than one method of accepted treatment for a patient's disease or injury. *Sinclair v. Block,* 594 A.2d 750 (Pa. Super. Ct. 1991). Under this doctrine, a physician will not be liable for medical malpractice if he or she follows a course of treatment supported by reputable, respected, and reasonable medical experts. *Levine v. Rosen,* 584 A.2d 319 (Pa. Super. Ct. 1990).

A physician's efforts do not constitute negligence simply because they were unsuccessful in a particular case. *Gielski v. State,* 216 N.Y.S.2d 85 (Ct. App. 1961). The trial court in *Bagherzadeh v. Roeser,* 825 F.2d 1000 (6th Cir. 1987), instructed the jury that a physician could not be "required to guarantee the results" of his or her treatment and that "the mere fact that an adverse result may occur following orthopedic treatment is not in and of itself any evidence of professional negligence." *Id.* at 1001. Innovation in the treatment for minor ailments would be questioned more likely than would innovation in the treatment of a major disease. A doctor treating a patient with a new procedure for an ordinary cold runs a greater risk of liability than does a doctor treating a patient with a new procedure for an acute and painful disease.

It is assumed by law that medicine has not become so standardized that it is unreasonable for two physicians to have differing opinions on the proper method of treating injuries or illnesses. If there is reason for the difference, the courts have held that neither side can be proven erroneous by the "proof" of the other. In *Coon v. Shields,* 39 P.2d 348 (1934), the plaintiff sustained a fracture of both bones of the leg immediately above the ankle. Gas gangrene set in, and it became necessary to amputate the leg. The plaintiff claimed that the surgeon was careless and negligent.

> [T]he real controversy between the parties arises over expert testimony offered by the plaintiff to the effect that iodine is not a disinfectant; that cultures should have been taken as an initial step to the treatment; that scrubbing with a stiff scrub brush was injurious and not beneficial to the wound; that the leg should have been exposed to the air in order to kill the gas bacilli; and that, in the opinion of the expert offered by the plaintiff, Dr. Shields, treatment was improper. This evidence was rejected by the court. In a case such as this confusion often arises over a failure to distinguish between the expert's opinion as to the proper method of treatment and his opinion as to whether or not the treatment applied conforms to what is generally accepted to be the proper

method. The practice of medicine or surgery has not become so stand-ardized that it is unreasonable for the two doctors to have different opinions as to the proper method of treating injuries.

Id. at 349.

Battery

A patient who consents to surgery and is operated on by another has an action for malpractice against the former and battery against the latter, even when the physicians are engaged in a group practice. *Perna v. Pirozzi,* 457 A.2d 431 (N.J. 1983).

Confidential Communications

Physician–patient privilege imposes on a physician an obligation to maintain the confidentiality of each patient's communications. This obligation applies to all health care professionals. An exception to the rule of confidentiality of patient communications is the implied right to make available to others involved in the patient's care the information necessary to that care. Information received by a physician in a confidential capacity relating to a patient's health should not be disclosed without the patient's consent. Disclosure may be made under com-pelling circumstances (e.g., suspected child abuse) to a person with a legitimate interest in the patient's health.

Delay in Treatment

A physician may not be liable for failing to respond promptly if it cannot be established that such inaction caused a patient's death. *John v. Jarrard,* 927 F.2d 551 (C.A. 11, Ga. 1991). A patient afflicted with lung cancer was awarded dam-ages in *Blackmon v. Langley,* 737 S.W.2d 455 (Ark. 1987), because of the failure of the examining physician to inform the patient in a timely manner that a chest x-ray showed a lesion in his lung. The lesion eventually was diagnosed as cancer-ous. The physician contended that because the evidence showed the patient had less than a 50 percent chance of survival at the time of the alleged negligence, he could not be the proximate cause of injury. The Arkansas Supreme Court found that the jury was properly entitled to determine that the patient suffered and lost more than would have been the case had he been notified promptly of the lesion.

Failure To Respond To an Emergency Department Call

Physicians on call for a specific service in a hospital's emergency department are expected to respond to requests for emergency assistance when such is considered necessary by designated hospital staff. Failure to respond is grounds for negligence should a patient suffer injury as a result of a physician's failure to respond.

Issues of fact in *Dillon v. Silver,* 520 N.Y.S.2d 751 (App. Div. 1987), precluded summary dismissal of an action charging that a woman's death from complications of an ectopic pregnancy occurred because of a gynecologist's refusal to treat her despite a request for aid by a hospital emergency department physician. Although the gynecologist contended that no physician–patient relationship had ever arisen, the hospital bylaws not only mandated that he accept all patients referred to him, but also stated that the emergency department physician had authority to decide which service physician should be called and required the service physician to respond to such a call.

Failure To Follow Up

Failure to follow up can result in a lawsuit if such failure results in injury to a patient. The Tennessee Supreme Court in *Truan v. Smith,* 578 S.W.2d 73 (Tenn. 1979), entered judgment in favor of the plaintiffs, who had brought action against a treating physician for damages alleged to have been the result of malpractice by the physician in the examination, diagnosis, and treatment of breast cancer. In January or February 1974, the patient noticed a change in the size and firmness of her left breast, which she attributed to an implant. She later noticed discoloration and pain on pressure. While being examined by the defendant on March 25, 1974, for another ailment, the patient brought her symptoms to the physician's attention but received no significant response, and no examination of the breast was made by the physician at that time. The patient brought her symptoms to the attention of her physician for the second time on May 6, 1974. She had been advised by the defendant to observe her left breast for 30 days for a change in symptoms, which at the time of the examination included discomfort, discoloration, numbness, and sharp pain. She was given an appointment for one month later. The patient, on the morning of her appointment, June 3, 1974, called the physician's office and informed the nurse that her symptoms had not changed and that she would like to know if she should keep her appointment. The nurse indicated that she would pass on her message to the physician. The patient assumed she would be called back if it was necessary to see the physician. By late June the symptoms became more acute, and the patient made an appointment to see the defendant physician on July 8, 1974. The patient also was scheduled to see a specialist on July 10, 1974, at which time she was admitted to the hospital and was diagnosed as having a malignant mass. A radical mastectomy was performed. Expert witnesses expressed the opinion that the mass had been palpable seven months before the removal, when the defendant undertook to give the plaintiff a complete physical examination, and that having embarked on a "wait and see" program as an aid in diagnosis, the physician should have followed his patient, who died before the conclusion of the trial. The supreme court held that the evidence was sufficient to support a finding that the defendant was guilty of malpractice in failing to inform his patient that cancer was a possible cause of her complaints and in failing to make any effort to see his patient at the expiration of the observation period instituted by him.

Hospitals, as well as physicians, are subject to legal action for failure to follow up. As an example, patients presenting themselves to emergency departments for care often are prescribed x-rays. The emergency department physician on duty will make a preliminary reading if there is no radiologist available. A second reading generally is made the following day when a radiologist is on duty. Periodically, the two findings conflict in that the emergency department physician reads the x-ray as negative and the radiologist actually finds a fracture. The failure generally occurs when the hospital staff does not inform the patient of the conflicting diagnosis. Failure to notify the patient can result in aggravation of a patient's initial injury if it is not treated in a timely fashion. A system of checks and balances must be in place to prevent such events from occurring.

Failure To Disclose/Informed Consent

The doctrine of informed consent is a theory of professional liability independent from malpractice. A physician's duty to disclose known and existing dangers associated with a proposed course of treatment is imposed by law. The patient in *Leggett v. Kumar,* 570 N.E.2d 1249 (Ill. App. Ct. 1991), was awarded $675,000 for pain and disfigurement resulting from a mastectomy procedure. The physician in this case failed to advise the patient of treatment alternatives. He also failed to perform the surgery properly.

It is the physician's role to provide the necessary medical facts and the patient's role to make the subjective decision concerning treatment based on his or her understanding of those facts. Before subjecting a patient to a course of treatment, the physician has a duty to disclose to each patient information that will enable the patient to evaluate options available and the risks attendant to a specific procedure. A failure to disclose any of a known and existing risk of proposed treatment when such risks might affect a patient's decision to forgo treatment constitutes a *prima facie* violation of a physician's duty to disclose. If a patient can establish that a physician withheld information concerning the inherent and potential hazards of a proposed treatment, consent is abrogated. Consent for a medical procedure may be withdrawn at any time before the act consented to is accomplished.

A lawsuit was brought against Dr. Hargiss, an ophthalmologist, and others in *Gates v. Jensen,* 595 P.2d 919 (Wash. 1979), for his failure to disclose to a patient that her test results for glaucoma were borderline and that her risk of glaucoma was increased considerably by her high blood pressure and myopia. Dr. Hargiss failed to perform a field vision test and to dilate and examine the eye. He wrote off the patient's problem of difficulty in focusing and gaps in vision as being related to difficulties with her contact lenses. Mrs. Gates visited the clinic 12 times during the following two years with complaints of blurriness, gaps in her vision, and loss of visual acuity. Mrs. Gates eventually was diagnosed as having open-angle glaucoma. By the time Mrs. Gates was properly treated, her vision had deteriorated from almost 20/20 to 20/200. The Supreme Court of Washington held that a duty of disclosure to a patient arises whenever a physician becomes aware of an abnormality that may indicate risk or danger. The facts that must be disclosed are those facts the physician knows or should know that a patient needs to be aware of to make an informed decision on the course that future medical care will take.

Failure To Order Diagnostic Tests

As medical technology becomes more advanced, it is likely that patients will claim that physicians should have ordered certain diagnostic procedures as opposed to the ones actually ordered by the physician. So long as the physician can demonstrate that the diagnostic procedure selected was consistent with the medical practice in the community, these claims will be difficult to sustain.

Ruptured Appendix

Failure to order diagnostic tests resulted in the misdiagnosis of appendicitis in *Steeves v. United States,* 294 F. Supp. 466 (D.S.C. 1968). In this case, physicians failed to order the appropriate diagnostic tests for a child who was referred to a Navy hospital with a diagnosis of possible appendicitis. Judgment in this case was entered against the United States, on behalf of the U.S. Navy, for medical expenses and for pain and suffering. The child had been referred by an Air Force dispensary where a test indicated a high white blood cell count. A consultation sheet had been given to the mother, indicating the possible diagnosis. The physician who examined the child at the Navy hospital performed no tests, failed to diagnose the patient's condition, and sent him home at 5:02 P.M., some 32 minutes after his arrival on July 21. The child was returned to the emergency department on July 22 at about 2:30 A.M., only to be sent home again by an intern who diagnosed the boy's condition as gastroenteritis. Once again, no diagnostic tests were ordered. The boy was returned to the Navy hospital on July 23, at which time diagnostic tests were performed. The patient was subsequently operated on and found to have a ruptured appendix. Holding the Navy hospital liable for the negligence of the physicians who acted as its agents, the court pointed out that a wrong diagnosis will not in and of itself support a verdict of liability in a lawsuit. However, a physician must use ordinary care in making a diagnosis. Only where a patient is examined adequately is there no liability for an erroneous diagnosis. In this instance, the physicians' failure to perform further laboratory tests the first two times the child was brought to the emergency department was found to be a breach of good medical practice.

Diagnostic Testing—An Acceptable Standard

Once a physician concludes that a particular test is indicated, it should be performed and evaluated as soon as practicable. Delay may constitute negligence. The law imposes on a physician the same degree of responsibility in making a diagnosis as it does in prescribing and administering treatment.

Physicians must conform to accepted standards. A plaintiff who claims that a physician has failed to order proper tests must show the following:

- It is a standard practice to use a certain diagnostic test under the circumstances of the case
- The physician failed to use the test and therefore failed to diagnose the patient's illness
- The patient suffered injury as a result

No damages can be awarded unless it can be shown that an incorrect therapeutic act or omission either caused injury to the patient or deprived the patient of a substantial chance for a cure.

Failure To Seek Consultation

A physician has a duty to consult and/or refer a patient whom he or she knows or should know needs referral to a physician familiar with and clinically capable to treat the patient's particular ailments. Whether the failure to refer constitutes negligence depends on whether referral is demanded by accepted standards of practice. To recover damages, the patient must show that the physician deviated from the standard of care and that the failure to refer resulted in injury.

The medical ethics statement of the American Medical Association indicates that physicians should seek consultations on a patient's request, when the physician is in doubt, in difficult cases, or when it appears that the quality of medical service thereby may be enhanced.[7] Violation or failure to abide by medical ethics does not in and of itself constitute malpractice.

A California Court of Appeals found that expert testimony is not necessary where good medical practice would require a general physician to suggest a specialist's consultation. The court ruled that because specialists were called in after the patient's condition grew worse, it is reasonable to assume that they could have been called in sooner. The jury was instructed by the court that a general practitioner has a duty to suggest calling in a specialist if a reasonably prudent general practitioner would do so under similar circumstances. *Valentine v. Kaiser Foundation Hospitals,* 194 Cal. App. 2d 282, 15 Cal. Rptr. 26 (1961) (*dictum*).

A physician is in a position of trust, and it is his or her duty to act in good faith. If a preferred treatment in a given situation is outside a physician's field of expertise, it is his or her duty to advise the patient. Failure to do so could constitute a breach of duty. Today, with the rapid methods of transportation and easy means of communication, the duty of a physician is not fulfilled merely by using the means at hand in a particular area of practice.

In *Doan v. Griffith,* 402 S.W.2d 855 (Ky. Ct. App. 1966), an accident victim was admitted to the hospital with serious injuries, including multiple fractures of his facial bones. The patient contended that the physician was negligent in not advising him at the time of discharge that his facial bones needed to be realigned by a specialist before the bones became fused. As a result, his face became disfigured. Expert testimony demonstrated that the customary medical treatment of the patient's injuries would have been to realign his fractured bones surgically as soon as the swelling subsided and that such treatment would have restored the normal contour of his face. The appellate court held that the jury reasonably could have found that the physician failed to provide timely advice to the patient on his need for further medical treatment and that such failure was the proximate cause of the patient's condition.

When a physician feels that medication, further office visits, or diet restrictions are indicated, the sufficiency of such instructions to the patient is a subjective, and not an objective, matter. Physicians cannot assume that instructions are adequate just because a reasonably prudent person would understand them. They must make orders clear for each patient, given his or her experience, education, and general knowledge and the nature of the disease. *Everts v. Worrell,* 58 Utah 238, 197 P. 1043 (1921). In general, instructions to children must be given to parents as well. *Sharpe v. Pugh,* 270 N.C. 598, 155 S.E.2d 108 (1967). If a patient is incompetent, instructions must be given to an appropriate member of the family or other responsible person (e.g., a guardian or committee).

If a consulting physician has suggested a diagnosis with which the treating physician does not agree, it would be prudent to consider obtaining the opinion of a second consultant who could either confirm or disprove the first consultant's theory.

Failure of an attending physician to recognize recommendations by consulting physicians, who determine a different diagnosis and recommend a different course of treatment in a particular case, can result in liability for damages suffered by the patient. This was the case in *Martin v. East Jefferson Gen. Hosp.,* 582 So.2d 1272 (La. 1991), in which the attending physician had continued to treat the patient for a viral infection despite three other physicians' diagnoses of lupus and their recommendations that the attending physician treat the patient for collagen vascular disease. The trial court found that lupus had been more probably than not the cause of the patient's death and that her chances of recovery had been destroyed by the physician's failure to rule out that diagnosis. Damages totaling $150,000 were awarded the plaintiff.

Fraud

The following elements must be established for a plaintiff to recover damages in an action for fraud:

- a representation to the plaintiff with the intent that he or she rely on it
- knowledge on the part of the defendant that the representation is false
- belief by the plaintiff that the representation is true
- reliance on such representation
- injury

Infections

The mere fact that a patient contracted an infection after an operation will not, in and of itself, cause a surgeon to be liable for negligence. The reason for this, according to the Nebraska Supreme Court in *McCall v. St. Joseph's Hospital,* 165 N.W.2d 85, 89 (Neb. 1969), is as follows:

> Neither authority nor reason will sustain any proposition that negligence can reasonably be inferred from the fact that an infection originated at the site of a surgical wound. To permit a jury to infer negligence would be to expose every doctor and dentist to the charge of negligence every time an infection originated at the site of a wound. We note the complete absence of any expert testimony or any offer of proof in this record to the effect that a staphylococcus infection would

automatically lead to an inference of negligence by the people in control of the operation or the treatment of the patient.

The district court of appeal held in *Gill v. Hartford Accident & Indemnity Co.,* 337 So.2d 420 (Fla. Dist. Ct. App. 1976), that the physician who performed surgery on a patient in the same room as the plaintiff should have known that the infection the patient had was highly contagious. The failure of the physician to undertake steps to prevent the spread of the infection to the plaintiff and his failure to warn the plaintiff led the court to find that hospital authorities and the plaintiff's physician caused an unreasonable increase in the risk of injury to the plaintiff. As a result, the plaintiff suffered injuries causally related to the negligence of the defendant.

A jury verdict in the amount of $300,000 was awarded in *Langley v. Michael,* 710 S.W.2d 373 (Mo. Ct. App. 1986), for damages arising from the amputation of the plaintiff's infected thumb. Evidence that the orthopedic surgeon failed to deeply cleanse, irrigate, and debride the injured area of the patient's thumb constituted proof of a departure from that degree of skill and learning ordinarily used by members of the medical profession, and that failure directly contributed to the patient's loss of the distal portion of his thumb.

Lack of Documentation

The importance of maintaining records of treatment rendered to a patient must not be underestimated. It may be many years after a patient has been treated before litigation is initiated; therefore, it is imperative that records of treatment in the physician's office, as well as in the hospital, be maintained. A jury may consider lack of documentation as sufficient evidence for finding a physician guilty of negligence.

In *Foley v. Bishop Clarkson Memorial Hospital,* 185 Neb. 89, 173 N.W.2d 881 (1970), a man sued the hospital for the death of his wife. During her pregnancy, the patient was under the care of a private physician. She gave birth in the hospital on August 20, 1964, and died the following day. She had been treated by her physician for a sore throat during July and August. Several days after her death, one of her children was treated in the hospital for a strep throat. There was no evidence in the hospital record that the patient had complained about a sore throat while in the hospital. The hospital rules required a history and physical examination to be written promptly (within 24 hours of admission). No history had been taken, although the patient had been examined several times in regard to the progress of her labor. The trial judge directed a verdict in favor of the hospital. On appeal, the appellate court held that the case should have been submitted to the jury for determination. A jury might reasonably have inferred that if the patient's condition had been treated properly, the infection could have been combated successfully and her life saved. It also might have been reasonably inferred that if a history had been taken promptly when she was admitted to the hospital, the cold and throat condition would have been discovered and the hospital personnel alerted to watch for possible complications of the nature that later developed. Quite possibly, this attention also would have helped in diagnosing the patient's condition, especially if it had been apparent that she was exposed at home to a strep throat condition. The court held that a hospital must guard not only against known physical and mental conditions of patients, but also against conditions that reasonable care should have uncovered.

Liability for the Acts of Others

The concept of holding a physician liable for the acts of nurses or other hospital employees is referred to commonly as the borrowed servant or captain of the ship doctrine. However, many authorities are rejecting this doctrine as the role of nurses and other health care professionals and paraprofessionals becomes more specialized and independent. The physician in *Karas v. Jackson,* 582 F. Supp. 43 (1983), was not held vicariously liable under either the captain of the ship doctrine or the general theory of *respondeat superior*. Dr. Jackson, who was the director of medical genetics at Thomas Jefferson University Hospital, did not at any time exercise or possess the right of control over an alleged negligent amniocentesis procedure conducted by another physician, which resulted in the death of the patient. Dr. Jackson did not perform the amniocentesis, nor was he present at any time during the procedure.

Medications and Prescriptions

Physicians should encourage the limited and judicious use of all medications and document periodically the reason for their continuation. Physicians periodically should review all drugs taken by patients and be alert to any contradictions and incompatibilities between drugs.

Lawsuits caused by medication errors are a risk for both physicians and nurses. Expert testimony in *Leal v. Simon,* 542 N.Y.S.2d 328 (App. Div. 1989), a medical malpractice action, supported the jury's determination that the physician had been negligent when he reduced the dosage of a resident's psychotropic medication, Haldol. The resident, a 36-year-old retarded individual who had been institutionalized his entire life, was a resident in an intermediate care facility. The drug had been used for controlling the resident's self-abusive behavior. Expert medical testimony showed that the physician failed to familiarize himself with the resident's history. He failed to secure the resident's complete medical records, and he failed to wean the resident slowly off the medication.

The Board of Registration in *Keigan v. Board of Registration,* 506 N.E.2d 866 (Mass. 1987), was found not to have acted arbitrarily or capriciously when it suspended a physician's license for one year and placed the physician on probation for four years. The physician was found to have prescribed controlled substances improperly for 13 drug-dependent individuals and to have failed to report their names and addresses and to maintain proper medical records with respect to such patients. The physician's arguments that such a sanction was overly severe because of his advanced age, that his actions had been well motivated, and that there was a lack of medical services for his indigent patients had no merit.

The Board of Regents in *Moyo v. Ambach,* 523 N.Y.S. 645 (App. Div. 1988), determined that a physician had prescribed methaqualone fraudulently and with gross negligence to 20 patients. The Board of Regents found that the physician did not prescribe methaqualone in good faith or for sound medical reasons. His abuse in prescribing controlled substances constituted the fraudulent practice of medicine. Expert testimony established that it was common knowledge in the medical community that methaqualone was a widely abused and addictive drug. Methaqualone should not have been used for insomnia without first trying other means of treatment. On appeal, the court found that there was sufficient evidence to support the board's finding.

Misdiagnosis

Misdiagnosis is the most frequently cited injury event in malpractice suits against physicians. Although diagnosis is a medical art and not an exact science, early detection can be critical to a patient's recovery and well-being. Misdiagnosis may involve the diagnosis and treatment of a disease different from that which the patient actually suffers or the diagnosis and treatment of a disease that the patient does not have. Misdiagnosis in and of itself will not necessarily impose liability on a physician, unless deviation from the accepted standard of care and injury can be established.

Not every treatment of a patient that falls short of complete success is malpractice because the attending physician has failed to consult a specialist. Before malpractice may be imputed to physicians, it must be shown that they knew or should have known that a condition to be treated was beyond their ability, knowledge, and/or capacity to treat. *Manion v. Tweedy,* 257 Minn. 59, 100 N.W.2d 124 (1959).

Although a physician is not an insurer or guarantor of good results, a physician is required to have and to exercise, in diagnosis and treatment, the skill ordinarily exercised in his or her profession. Medicine is not an exact science, and there is no implied warranty of cure or relief. Every patient should be aware that an unfavorable consequence can arise from a treatment. A physician who does fail to exercise the degree of care, skill, and knowledge ordinarily possessed and exercised in similar situations by the average member of a profession can be found liable for malpractice if such failure is the proximate cause of a patient's injuries. A physician who holds him- or herself out as a specialist must use not merely the skill of a general practitioner but also that special degree of skill normally possessed by the average physician who devotes special study and attention to a particular organ or disease or injury involved, having regard to the present state of scientific knowledge. *Lewis v. Read,* 193 A.2d 255 (N.J. 1963).

Appendicitis

Misdiagnosis does not always end in a verdict for the plaintiff. Summary judgment was properly entered in dismissing an action alleging that a physician had been negligent in failing to diagnose a pregnant patient's appendicitis in *Fiedler v. Steger,* 713 P.2d 773 (Wyo. 1986). The testimony of expert witnesses for both parties established that diagnosis of appendicitis during pregnancy is difficult, that it probably would not have been diagnosed on the dates in question, and that the appendix had probably ruptured postpartum.

Breast Cancer

The patient in *DeBurkarte v. Louvar,* 393 N.W.2d 131 (Iowa 1986), brought a medical malpractice action against her family physician, an osteopathic general practitioner, for his failure to diagnose in a timely manner a patient's breast lump as cancerous. The district court had entered a verdict in favor of the patient, and the physician appealed. The supreme court held that the findings of negligence and proximate cause were supported adequately by the evidence presented at trial. The patient's husband was entitled to recover for loss of consortium, and the award of $405,000 in damages to the patient was not excessive.

Diabetic Acidosis

A case in the Mississippi Supreme Court, *Hill v. Stewart,* 209 So.2d 809 (Miss. 1968), involved a patient who became ill and was admitted to the hospital. The physician was advised of the patient's recent weight loss, frequent urination, thirst, loss of vision, nausea, and vomiting. Routine laboratory tests were ordered, including a urinalysis, but not including a blood glucose test. On the following day, a consultant diagnosed the patient's condition as severe diabetic acidosis. Treatment was given, but the patient failed to respond to therapy and died. The attending physician was sued for failing to test for diabetes and for failing to diagnose and treat the patient on the first day in the hospital. The attending physician said in court that he had suspected diabetes and admitted that when diabetes is suspected, a urinalysis and a blood sugar test should be performed. An expert medical witness testified that failure to do so would be a departure from the skill and care required of a general practitioner. The witness also stated that the patient in this case probably would have had a good chance of survival if properly treated. The state supreme court reversed the directed verdict for the physician by a lower court and remanded the case for retrial. There was sufficient evidence presented to permit the case to go to the jury for decision.

Once a physician concludes that a particular test is indicated, it should be performed and evaluated as soon as practicable. Delay may constitute negligence. The law imposes on a physician the same degree of responsibility in making a diagnosis as it does in prescribing and administering treatment.

Heart Problem

The federal government in *Lauderdale v. United States,* 666 F. Supp. 1511 (Ala. 1987), was held liable under the Federal Tort Claims Act for the death of a patient whose mitral valve malfunction was misdiagnosed at a military medical clinic. Under the applicable Alabama law, the physician failed to conduct the necessary tests to determine the cause of a suspected heart problem. The physician never indicated to the patient that the problem was severe, that the treatment with digoxin was tentative, and that his well-being mandated that he return in a week. The patient subsequently died. He was found not to have been contributorily negligent by failing to return to the clinic. The patient had not been told sufficiently of the urgency of a return visit. This failure was considered the proximate cause of the patient's death because his illness might have been treated successfully.

Hyperparathyroidism

The jury found in *Koster v. Greenberg,* 502 N.Y.S.2d 395 (App. Div. 1986), that a physician was responsible for a patient's death because of his failure to diagnose her condition of hyperparathyroidism, which was supported by the record. Expert testimony demonstrated that death occurred because of a number of causes, including renal failure secondary to hyperparathyroidism.

Perforated Bowel

A clinic was found liable in *Gegan v. Backwinkel,* 417 N.W.2d 44 (Wis. Ct. App. 1987), for failing to diagnose a patient's perforated bowel. It was determined that the patient's chance of survival would have been better than 90 percent if the patient's condition had been properly diagnosed and treated by the clinic's physicians. The plaintiff was awarded $150,000 for the patient's mental anguish and suffering, which occurred during hospitalization as a result of unnecessary surgeries, and $250,000 was awarded to cover potential pecuniary losses for the financial support, college funds, and inheritance of the patient's children.

Pregnancy

A physician's license was suspended for 30 days in *Livingston v. Arkansas State Medical Board,* 701 S.W.2d 361 (Ark. 1986), for repeatedly diagnosing a patient as being pregnant over a period of four months when in reality she was not pregnant.

Skull Fracture

In *Ramberg v. Morgan,* 218 N.W. 492 (Iowa 1928), a police department physician, at the scene of an accident, examined an unconscious man who had been struck by an automobile. The physician concluded that the patient's insensibility was a result of alcohol intoxication, not the accident, and ordered the police to remove him to jail instead of the hospital. The man, to the physician's knowledge, remained semiconscious for several days and finally was taken from the cell to the hospital at the insistence of his family. The patient subsequently died, and the autopsy revealed massive skull fractures. The court said that any physician should reasonably anticipate the presence of head injuries when a person is struck by a car; failure to refer an accident victim to another physician or a hospital is actionable neglect of the physician's duty. Although a physician does not ensure the correctness of the diagnosis or treatment, a patient is entitled to such thorough and careful examination as his or her condition and attending circumstances permit, with such diligence and methods of diagnosis as usually are approved and practiced by medical people of ordinary or average learning, judgment, and skill in the community or similar localities.

Testicular Cancer

The hospital in *Brickner v. Osteopathic Hospital,* 746 S.W.2d 108 (Mo. Ct. App. 1988), was held vicariously liable for a surgical resident's failure to diagnose testicular cancer during exploratory surgery performed under the supervision of a staff physician. The hospital was not insulated from liability under the borrowed servant doctrine even though the supervising surgeon had authority over the resident during the operation. The hospital never relinquished control over the resident, who was required under the hospital's training program to assist in diagnosis and who could have taken a biopsy without express instructions of the operating surgeon. Liability was not precluded because of the hospital's lack of actual control over the resident's medical decision not to perform a biopsy. The resident was performing a service for which he had been employed.

Mistaken Identity

In *Southwestern Kentucky Baptist Hospital v. Bruce,* 539 S.W.2d 286 (Ky. 1976), a patient admitted for conization of the cervix was taken mistakenly to the operating room for a thyroidectomy. The physician was notified early during surgery that he had the wrong patient on the operating room table. The operation was terminated immediately. The thyroidectomy was not completed, and the incision was sutured. The patient filed an action for malpractice and recovered $10,000 from the physician and $90,000 from the hospital. That the patient mistakenly answered to the name of another patient who had been scheduled for a thyroidectomy did not excuse the failure of the surgeon, the anesthesiologist, and the surgical technician to determine the identity of the patient by examining her identification bracelet. The supreme court held that the verdict was not excessive in view of the injuries, which consisted of a four-inch incision along the patient's neck, which became infected and would require cosmetic surgery.

Obstetrics/Gynecology

One of the most vulnerable medical specialties with tremendous risk exposure to malpractice suits is obstetrics/gynecology. The New Jersey malpractice study revealed that "[o]bstetrical negligence claims most often stemmed from errors in physician judgment, whereas gynecologic claims were more likely the result of inadequate technical performance."[8] The following cases illustrate why the risks are high.

Failure To Perform a Cesarean Section

A medical malpractice action was brought against two obstetricians, a pediatrician, and the hospital in *Ledogar v. Giordano,* 505 N.Y.S.2d 899 (App. Div. 1986), due to a newborn infant's prenatal and postnatal hypoxia, which allegedly caused brain damage resulting in autism. The record contained sufficient proof of causation to support a verdict in favor of the plaintiff when an expert obstetrician testified that both obstetricians were negligent in failing to perform a cesarean section at an earlier time, that the hospital staff departed from proper medical standards of care by not monitoring the fetal heartbeat at least every 15 minutes, and that, with a reasonable degree of medical certainty, it was probable that the fetus had suffered hypoxia during labor.

Failure To Attend

The plaintiff in *Lucchesi v. Stimmell,* 149 Ariz. 76, 716 P.2d 1013 (1986), brought an action against a physician for intentional infliction of emotional distress, claiming that the physician had failed to be present during unsuccessful attempts to deliver her premature fetus and that he thereafter had failed to disclose to her that the fetus was decapitated during attempts to achieve delivery by pulling on the hip area to free the head. The judge instructed the jury that it could conclude that the physician had been guilty of extreme and outrageous conduct for staying at home and leaving delivery in the hands of a first-year intern and a third-year resident, neither of whom was experienced in breech deliveries.

Injury to the Brachial Plexus Nerves

The attending physician in *Jackson v. Huang,* 514 So.2d 727 (La. Ct. App. 1987), was negligent in failing to perform a timely cesarean section. The attending physician had applied too much traction when he was faced with shoulder dyscotia, a situation in which a baby's shoulder hangs under the pubic bone, arresting the progress of the infant through the birth canal. As a result, the infant suffered permanent injury to the brachial plexus nerves of his right shoulder and arm. On appeal of this case, there was no error found in the trial court's finding of fact when such finding was supported by testimony of the plaintiff's expert witness. The trial judge accepted the testimony of Dr. Forte, the expert witness, who testified that the defendant did possess the necessary skill and knowledge relevant to the practice of obstetrics and gynecology. The defendant, because of prolonged labor and weight of the baby, should have anticipated the possibility of shoulder dyscotia and performed a timely cesarean section. *Id.*

Joint Liability

An obstetrician and a pediatrician were held jointly liable in *Ravo by Ravo v. Rogatnick,* 514 N.E.2d 1104 (N.Y. 1987), for injuries suffered by a newborn child that resulted in mental retardation. Expert witnesses were unable to segregate the effects of the trauma and hypoxia allegedly caused by the obstetrician's negligence from the hyperbilirubinemia and an excessively high hematocrit level, which had been addressed inadequately by the pediatrician. Damages in the amount of $2,750,000 were awarded the plaintiff. The jury apportioned the fault by assigning 80 percent to the obstetrician and 20 percent to the pediatrician. This judgment did not affect the plaintiff's right to collect the entire amount from either defendant. The 80/20 percent apportionment between the obstetrician and the pediatrician defined the contribution that the defendants might claim from each other.

Emergency Assistance

An obstetrician who responds to an emergency call by a surgeon to assist in the completion of a tubal ligation most likely will entitle the obstetrician immunity from a negligence claim under the state's Good Samaritan law if he had a good-faith belief that the patient was in a life-threatening situation. Such was the case in *Pemberton v. Dharmani,* 469 N.W.2d 74 (Mich. Ct. App. 1991), where the court of appeals held that the Michigan Good Samaritan statute

> merely requires a good-faith belief by health-care personnel that they are attending a life-threatening emergency in order to be cloaked with the immunity provided by the statute, regardless of whether a life-threatening emergency actually exists. To construe the statute otherwise would controvert the purpose of the statute and render it meaningless. Healthcare personnel would be discouraged from giving treatment in emergency situations if an actual life-threatening situation were required to exist before they would be cloaked with immunity. Treatment may be even delayed in a given case, worsening the condition of the patient by waiting until the patient is in an obviously life-threatening situation before rendering treatment.

Id. at 76.

Nurse Assessment

The defendant physicians in *Cignetti v. Camel,* 692 S.W.2d 329 (Mo. Ct. App. 1985), ignored a nurse's assessment of a patient's diagnosis, which contributed to a delay in treatment and injury to the patient. The nurse had testified that she told the physician that the patient's signs and symptoms were not those associated with indigestion. The defendant physician objected to this testimony, indicating that such a statement constituted a medical diagnosis by a nurse. The trial court permitted the testimony to be entered into evidence. Section 335.016(8) of the Missouri Revised Statutes (as revised in 1975) authorizes a registered nurse to make an assessment of persons who are ill and to render a "nursing diagnosis." On appeal, the Missouri Court of Appeals affirmed the lower court's ruling, holding that evidence of negligence presented by a hospital employee, for which an obstetrician was not responsible, was admissible to show the events that occurred during the patient's hospital stay.

Wrongful Death of a Viable Unborn Fetus

Summary dismissal was found to have been ordered improperly in *Lobdell v. Tarrant County Hospital District,* 710 S.W.2d 811 (Tex. Ct. App. 1986), in an action by the parents of a stillborn child against the physician and hospital on the theory that no cause of action lay for the wrongful death of a viable unborn fetus. A child capable of independent life outside the mother's womb had an independent existence as a person apart from its mother, and damages were recoverable for the wrongful death. Under the Texas Wrongful Death Act, the parents had a right to recover for the negligent conduct proximately causing the intrauterine death of a viable fetus.

A medical malpractice action was filed against the physician in *Modaber v. Kelley,* 348 S.E.2d 233 (Va. 1986), for personal injuries and mental anguish caused by the stillbirth of a child. The circuit court entered judgment on a jury verdict against the obstetrician, and an appeal was taken. The supreme court held that the evidence was sufficient to support a finding that the obstetrician's conduct during the patient's pregnancy caused direct injury to the patient. Evidence at trial showed that the physician failed to treat the mother's known condition of toxemia, including the development of high blood pressure and the premature separation of the placenta from the uterine wall, and that the physician thereafter had failed to respond in a timely fashion when the mother went into premature labor. The supreme court also held that injury to the unborn child constituted injury to the mother and that she could recover for the physical injury and mental anguish associated with the stillbirth. The court found that the award of $750,000 in compensatory damages was not excessive.

Premature Dismissal of a Case

Physicians and hospitals run the risk of liability for the premature dismissal of a patient. It is better to be cautious than to regret prematurely dismissing a patient's complaint. One cannot be too circumspect even if a patient is well known by the treating physician.

Psychiatry

The main risk areas of psychiatry include commitment, electroshock, duty to warn, and suicide. Matters relating to admission, consent, and discharge are governed by statute in most states.

Commitment

One of the more difficult issues for physicians is how to handle the different situations that might arise with individuals requiring involuntary commitment for psychiatric care and evaluation. The recent emphasis on patient rights has had a major impact on the necessity to evaluate an individual effectively before commitment. The various state statutes often provide requirements granting an individual's rights to legal counsel and other procedural safeguards (e.g., patient hotline) governing the admission, retention, and discharge of psychiatric patients.

Most states have enacted administrative procedures that must be followed. The various statutes often require that two physicians certify the need for commitment. Physicians who participate in the commitment of a patient should do so only after first examining the patient and reaching his or her own conclusions. Reliance on another's examination and recommendation for commitment could give rise to a claim of malpractice. Commitment is generally necessary in those situations in which a person may be in substantial danger of injuring another person or property.

Involuntary. Proof of dangerousness in *In re Detention of Meistrell,* 733 P.2d 1004 (Wash. Ct. App. 1987), was found adequate to support an order of involuntary commitment. There was testimony that on two occasions the patient had jumped off a teeter-totter, causing his two small children to fall to the ground. A substantial risk of physical harm to others also was demonstrated by testimony that the patient had threatened his wife's ex-husband.

The likelihood of future harm was found sufficient in *In re Burmeister,* 391 N.W.2d 89 (Minn. Ct. App. 1986), to commit a patient suffering from paranoid schizophrenia. The record indicated that the patient, while living with his mother, had stuffed the family fireplace with a large amount of paper, lighted the fire, scorched the front of the fireplace, and then closed the damper while the fire continued to burn.

A psychiatrist filed a petition for additional detention of a person previously ordered admitted to a state hospital for pretrial psychiatric examination. The circuit court, after hearing testimony from the appellant's son, a social worker at the hospital, and the psychiatrist, ordered detention, and the detainee appealed. The court of appeals in *In re Todd,* 767 S.W.2d 589 (Mo. Ct. App. 1988), held that the testimony of the psychiatrist established clear and convincing evidence to meet a required standard that the detainee's actions presented risk of serious harm to herself or others. The episode giving rise to the involuntary commitment occurred when the appellant threw eggs at a house and various businesses and broke some windows at a house with a tire iron. She lightly bumped a police car and was charged with second-degree property damage. During her involuntary detention, she refused to take her medications, which were necessary because of her illness. The psychiatrist indicated his concern that she might harm her invalid husband on release. Additional detention was considered necessary until such time as the detainee's illness could be controlled by drugs.

A New York supreme court found a patient to be mentally ill and authorized his involuntary retention. On appeal, the supreme court, appellate division, held in *In re Carl C.,* 511 N.Y.S.2d 144 (App. Div. 1987), that the state had not shown by clear and convincing evidence that the patient's instability caused him to pose a substantial threat of physical injury to himself or others. The examining physician's testimony indicated that the patient did not pose a direct threat of physical harm to himself or others but that it was questionable whether he would be able to provide for the essentials of life. The patient had testified that he was aware of food needs, of where to get food, and how he would pay for it. He indicated that he would not sleep outside and that he had a bed in a rooming house where he had been paying rent for two years.

By Spouse. In *Bencomo v. Morgan,* 210 So.2d 236 (Fla. Dist. Ct. App. 1968), the plaintiff's husband filed a petition to have his wife declared incompetent. In a letter supporting the petition, the defendant physician, who had treated the wife ten years previously, stated that she was badly in need of a psychiatric examination. The plaintiff-wife attempted to sue the physician for libel and slander. The court held that the plaintiff had no cause for action because it was her husband who initiated the commitment procedures.

By Parent. The U.S. Supreme Court, in *Parham v. J.R., 442 U.S.* 584 (1979), held that the risk of error inherent in a parental decision to have a child institutionalized for mental health care is sufficiently great that an inquiry should be made by a neutral fact-finder to determine whether statutory requirements for admission are satisfied. Although a formal or quasi-formal hearing is not required and an inquiry need not be conducted by a law-trained judicial or administrative officer, such inquiry must probe a child's background carefully, using all available sources. It is necessary that a decision maker have the authority to refuse to admit a child who does not satisfy medical standards for admission. A child's continuing need for commitment also must be reviewed periodically by a similarly independent procedure.

Patient Due Process Rights. The principles of due process were violated in *Birl v. Wallis,* 619 F. Supp. 481 (D. Ala. 1985), when an involuntarily committed patient was conditionally released and reconfined without notice and opportunity for a hearing. Remand was required to permit the drafting of reconfinement procedures that would protect the patient's due process rights adequately.

Electroshock

Most states have laws and regulations governing the use of electroshock and other drastic treatments for psychiatric patients. Failure to abide by these statutory and regulatory guidelines may result in liability both to the hospital and to the treating physician.

Appropriate precautions should be taken to reduce the risks of fractures or other potential harm that might occur to patients. If appropriate precautions are taken, the likelihood of successful malpractice suits in this area will be limited. In *Collins v. Hand,* 431 Pa. 378, 246 A.2d 398 (1968), the court pointed out that fractures are a recognized risk of electroshock therapy and that negligence would have to be established by expert testimony.

Duty To Warn

In *Tarasoff v. Regents of the University of California,* 17 Cal. 3d 425, 551 P.2d 334, 131 Cal. Rptr. 14 (1976), a former patient allegedly killed a third party after revealing his homicidal plans to his therapist. His therapist made no effort to inform the victim of the patient's intentions. The California Supreme Court held that when a therapist determines or reasonably should determine that a patient poses a serious danger of violence to others, there is a duty to exercise reasonable care to protect the foreseeable victims and to warn them of any impending danger. Discharge of this duty also may include notifying the police or taking whatever steps are reasonably necessary under the circumstances.

Under Nebraska law, the relationship between a psychotherapist and a patient gives rise to an affirmative duty to initiate whatever precautions are reasonably necessary to protect the potential victims of a patient. This duty develops when a therapist knows or should know that a patient's dangerous propensities present an unreasonable risk of harm to others [see, e.g., *Lipari v. Sears, Roebuck & Co.,* 497 F. Supp. 185 (D. Neb. 1980)].

Exceptions to the Duty To Warn. The Maryland Court of Special Appeals, in *Shaw v. Glickman,* 415 A.2d 625 (Md. Ct. Spec. App. 1980), held that a plaintiff could not recover against a psychiatric team on the theory that they were negligent in failing to warn the plaintiff of the patient's unstable and violent condition. The court held that making such a disclosure would have violated statutes pertaining to privilege against disclosure of communications relating to treatment of mental or emotional disorders. The court found that a psychiatrist may have a duty to warn the potential victim of a dangerous mental patient's intent to harm; however, the duty could be imposed only if the psychiatrist knew the identity of the prospective victim. *Furr v. Spring Grove State Hospital,* 454 A.2d 414 (Md. Ct. App. 1983).

The psychiatrist in *Currie v. United States,* 836 F.2d 209 (4th Cir. 1987), was found not to have had a duty to seek the involuntary commitment of a patient who evidenced homicidal tendencies. Absent control over the patient, the federal government could not be held liable for a murder that the patient committed at his former place of employment. The psychiatrist had warned the patient's former employer and law enforcement officials about his dangerousness.

There was no duty on the part of the hospital or treating psychiatrists in *Sharpe v. South Carolina Department of Mental Health,* 354 S.E.2d 778 (S.C. Ct. App. 1987), to warn the general public of the potential danger that might result from a psychiatric patient's release from a state hospital. There was no identifiable threat to a decedent who was shot by the patient approximately two months after the patient's release from voluntary commitment under a plan of outpatient care. In addition, there was nothing in the record that indicated that the former patient and the decedent had known each other before the patient's release.

Suicide

The attendant in *Fernandez v. State,* 15 A.D.2d 125, 356 N.Y.S.2d 708 (1974), left the room for five minutes when the patient appeared to be asleep. During the attendant's absence, the patient injured herself in a repeated suicide attempt. The court found that even if the hospital had assumed a duty to observe the patient continually, such a five-minute absence would not constitute negligence. Therefore, the hospital could not be held liable for the patient's injuries.

A patient with a 14-year history of mental problems escaped from a hospital and committed suicide by jumping off a roof. Notations had been made in the record that the patient was to be checked every 15 minutes. There was no evidence that such checks had been made. The appellate court ruled that the facts showed a *prima facie* case of negligence. *Fatuck v. Hillside Hospital,* 45 A.D.2d 708, 356 N.Y.S.2d 105 (1974), *aff'd,* 36 N.Y.2d 736, 328 N.E.2d 791, 368 N.Y.S.2d 161 (1975) (no opinion).

The supreme court, appellate division, in *Eady v. Alter,* 380 N.Y.S.2d 737 (App. Div. 1976), held that an intern's notation on the hospital record that the patient tried to jump out the window was sufficient to establish a *prima facie* case against the hospital. The patient succeeded in committing suicide by jumping out the window approximately ten minutes after having been seen by the intern. Testimony had been given that the patient was restrained inadequately after the reported attempted suicide.

Surgery

Insurance carriers consider surgeons a high-risk group, especially in certain sub-specialties such as orthopedics and neurosurgery. The New Jersey study on medical malpractice, reviewed above, revealed that "general surgery claims were roughly evenly divided between patient management and technical performance errors."[9]

Assistants at Surgery

Physicians referred by another physician and who are not associates, employers, or employees—and who lend casual assistance at an operation—are not jointly liable for the negligence of the operating surgeon. In G*raddy v. New York Medical College,* 19 A.D.2d 426, 243 N.Y.S.2d 40 (1963), the court ruled that referral of a patient to another physician—absent partnership, employment, or agency—does not impose liability on the referring physician.

Foreign Objects

A physician who leaves a foreign object in a patient's body during surgery has a duty to disclose such information to the patient. Failure to do so can result in a successful lawsuit for damages suffered by the patient. Physicians who change hospital administraive procedures governing surgical operations—during surgery—can be liable for those acts, even if they are performed by hospital personnel.

In *Martin v. Perth Amboy General Hospital,* 104 N.J. Super. 335, 250 A.2d 40 (N.J. Super. Ct. App. Div. 1969), a patient sued the hospital, cardiovascular surgeon, and nurses for leaving a laparotomy pad in his stomach. The surgeon, Dr. Lev, who performed the operation, was assisted by two other physicians as well as by a scrub nurse and a circulating nurse. Before the laparotomy pads were brought into the operating room, a strip of radiopaque material was embedded between the folds of the laparotomy pads which would show on an x-ray if a pad was left in the abdomen. Rings were attached to the laparotomy pads to prevent errors in counts made by the nurses; however, before the pads were used, the rings were removed by the nurses at the direction of the operating surgeon. For some unknown reason, the sponge count at the end of the operation indicated that no sponges were missing.

Dr. Lev contended that the charge against him adopted the captain of the ship doctrine, which is not a doctrine recognized by the state of New Jersey. If Dr. Lev had not ordered the rings to be removed by the nurses, the court would have agreed that the charge was contrary to state judicial decisions. By exercising control over the nurses to the extent of directing them to remove the rings and thus eliminating the safeguards provided by the hospital to ensure a proper count by its employees, the surgeon became the nurses' "temporary or special employer" with regard to their duties involving the laparotomy pads used during the operation. Thus, the surgeon was equally liable with the hospital for the nurses' subsequent negligence in counting the pads.

The most common methods of preventing operating room objects from being left in the surgical wound are

(1) sponge or instrument counts,
(2) attachments on laparotomy pads and on drains and tubings, and
(3) X-rays taken at the time of the operation, sometimes made more effective by the use of radiopaque threads in sponges and pads. X-rays are also one of the postoperative methods of detecting foreign objects left in an operative wound.

Id. at 46, 10 A.L.R. 3d 9 (1966), at 16.

Hospital Liability for Negligent Surgery

Although a hospital is generally not liable for unsuccessful surgery, it could share in liability if it has reason to believe that the surgeon would commit malpractice. *Zajac v. St. Mary of Nazareth Hospital Center,* 571 N.E.2d 840 (Ill. App. Ct. 1991).

Timely Diagnosis

A physician can be liable for reducing a patient's chances for survival. The timely diagnosis of a patient's condition is as important as the need to diagnose a patient's injury or disease properly. Failure to do so can constitute malpractice if a patient suffers injury as a result of such failure.

Treatment Outside the Field of Competence

A physician should practice discretion when treating a patient outside his or her field of expertise or competence. The standard of care required in a malpractice case will be that of the specialty in which a physician is treating, whether or not he or she has appropriate credentials in that specialty.

In a California case, *Carrasco v. Bankoff,* 220 Cal. App. 2d 230, 33 Cal. Rptr. 673 (1963), a small boy suffering third-degree burns over 18 percent of his body was admitted to a hospital. During his initial confinement, there was little done except to occasionally dress and redress the burned area. At the end of a 53-day confinement, the patient was suffering hypergranulation of the burned area and muscular–skeletal dysfunction. The surgeon treating him was not a board-certified plastic surgeon and apparently not properly trained in the management of burn cases.

At trial, the patient's medical expert, a plastic surgeon who had assumed responsibility for care after the first hospitalization, outlined the accepted medical practice in cases of this nature. The first surgeon acknowledged this accepted practice. The court held that there was substantial evidence to permit a finding of professional negligence because of the defendant surgeon's failure to perform to the accepted standard of care and that such failure resulted in the patient's injury.

Radiology

According to the New Jersey study, diagnostic errors account for most radiology claims.[10] Several cases involving x-rays are discussed below.

Judicial Notice and X-Rays

The use of x-rays as a diagnostic aid in cases of fracture can be considered a matter of common knowledge to which a court, in the absence of expert testimony, could take judicial notice. Should a patient have a serious fall and a fracture is indicated, under the foregoing rule it is a matter of common knowledge that the ordinary physician in good standing, in the exercise of ordinary care and diligence, would have ordered x-rays.

Inadequate X-Ray Examination

The failure to order a proper set of x-rays is as legally risky as the failure to order any x-rays. In *Betenbaugh v. Princeton Hospital,* 50 N.J. 390, 235 A.2d 889 (1967) (*per curiam*), the plaintiff had been taken to a hospital when she injured the lower part of her back. One of the defendant physicians directed that an x-ray be taken of her sacrum. No evidence of a fracture was found. This finding was confirmed by the head of the hospital's radiology department. When the patient's pain did not subside, the family physician was consulted. He found that the films taken at the hospital did not include the entire lower portion of the spine and sent her to a radiologist for further study. On the basis of additional x-rays, a diagnosis of a fracture was made, and the patient was advised to wear a lumbosacral support. Two months later, the fracture was healed. The radiologist who had taken x-ray films on the second occasion testified that it was customary to take both an anterior–posterior and a lateral view when making an x-ray examination of the sacrum. In his opinion, the failure at the hospital to include the lower area of the sacrum was a failure to meet the standard required. The family physician testified that if the patient's fracture had been diagnosed at the hospital, appropriate treatment could have been instituted earlier, the patient would have suffered less pain, and recovery time would have been reduced. The evidence was sufficient to support findings that the physicians and the hospital were negligent by not having taken adequate x-rays and that such negligence was the proximate cause of the patient's additional pain and delay in recovery.

Failure To Consult with Radiologist

The internist in *Lanzet v. Greenberg,* 594 A.2d 1309 (N.J. 1991), failed to consult with the radiologist after his conclusion that the patient suffered from congestive heart failure. This factor most likely contributed to the death of the patient while on the operating table.

Failure To Read X-Rays

The patient in *Tams v. Lotz,* 530 A.2d 1217 (D.C. 1987), had to undergo a second surgical procedure to remove a laparotomy pad that had been left negligently in the patient during a previous surgical procedure. The trial court was found to have properly directed a verdict with respect to the patient's assertion that the surgeon who performed the first operation had failed to read a postoperative x-ray report, which allegedly would have put him on notice both that the pad was present and that there was a need for emergency surgery to remove the pad, therefore averting the need to remove a portion of his intestine.

The plaintiffs in *Killebrew v. Johnson,* 404 N.E.2d 1194 (Ind. Ct. App. 1980), had filed a complaint to recover damages from the physician, alleging that he was negligent by failing to inform himself of the results of x-rays he ordered to determine the possible location of an intrauterine contraceptive device. The superior court granted the physician's motion for judgment. The court of appeals held that the testimony of the plaintiff's medical witness and the treating physician's admission that he did not inform himself of the contents of the x-rays or the x-ray reports were sufficient to place before the jury the applicable standard of care.

The failure of a radiologist to read an x-ray properly does not necessarily constitute negligence. This is especially true in those cases in which the treatment rendered to the patient would have been the same regardless of the radiologist's findings.

Failure To Notify of X-Ray Results

The court of appeals in *Washington Healthcare Corp. v. Barrow,* 531 A.2d 226 (D.C. 1987), held that evidence was sufficient to sustain a finding that the hospital was negligent in failing to provide a radiology report demonstrating pathology on a patient's lung in a timely manner. An x-ray of the patient taken on April 4, 1982, disclosed a small nodular density in her right lung. Within a year, the cancerous nodule had grown to the size of a softball. The most significant testimony at trial was that of Theresa James, a medical student who worked for Dr. Oweiss until and including April 23, 1982. Ms. James testified that her job entailed combing through Dr. Oweiss's mail and locating abnormal x-ray reports, which she then would bring to his attention. Emphasizing that she had come to know the patient personally, Ms. James said that she would have been upset if she had come across an abnormal report on her. Ms. James claimed that she received no such report while working for the physician, thus accounting for 19 days after the x-ray was taken. Ms. James stated that the x-ray reports were usually received within four or five days after being taken. There was testimony to corroborate her testimony by Dr. Odenwald, who dictated the patient's report on April 4, 1982. Dr. Odenwald of Groover, Christie and Merritt, PC (GCM), which operated the radiology department at the Washington Hospital Center (WHC), stated that the x-ray reports usually were typed and mailed the same day they were dictated. The jury could have determined that if the report did not reach Dr. Oweiss by April 23, 1982, it did not reach him by May 3, 1982. The patient's record eventually was found; however, it was not in the patient's regular folder. One could infer that the record therefore was negligently filed. Questions also arise as to why Dr. Oweiss did nothing to follow up on the matter in ensuing months. Dr. Oweiss testified that he did receive the report by May 3, 1982, and that he informed Mrs. Barrow of its contents. Mrs. Barrow stated that although her folder was on the physician's desk at the time of her visit, he did not relay to her any information regarding an abnormal x-ray. Dr. Oweiss, however, was severely impeached at trial, and the jury chose not to believe him. Considering the entire record, there was reasonable probability that WHC was negligent and that Dr. Oweiss had not received the report. The plaintiff had settled with Dr. Oweiss, the patient's personal physician, in the amount of $200,000 during pendency in the district court, and the action against him was dismissed with prejudice. The record did not support WHC's request of indemnification from Dr. Oweiss. The trial court had directed a verdict in favor of GCM, leaving WHC as the sole defendant. The court of appeals remanded WHC's cross-claim for indemnification from GCM for further findings of fact and conclusions by the trial court.

Physician–Patient Relationship

The suggestions below, if followed, will help to decrease the probability of malpractice suits.

- Do not guarantee treatment outcome
- Provide for cross-coverage during days off
- Maintain timely, complete, and accurate records. Do not make erasures
- Personalize your treatment. A patient is more inclined to sue an impersonal physician than one with whom he or she has developed a good relationship
- Do not overextend your practice
- Provide sufficient time and care to each patient. Take the time to explain treatment plans and follow-up care to the patient, his or her family, and other professionals caring for your patient
- Prescribing over the telephone generally is not advisable
- Do not become careless because you know the patient
- Request consultations when indicated and refer if necessary
- Seek the advice of counsel should you suspect the possibility of a malpractice claim
- Ensure that female patient examinations, conducted by a member of the opposite sex, be performed in the presence of a third person, preferably another woman

CONCLUSION

The Oath of Hippocrates has been passed on as a living and workable statement of ideals to be cherished by the physician. This oath protects rights of the patient and appeals to the finer instincts of the physician without imposing sanctions or penalties. Other civilizations have developed written principles, but the Oath of Hippocrates has remained in Western civilization as an expression of ideal conduct for the physician. Adherence to professional medical ethics will go a long way in the prevention of lawsuits and the development of good physician–patient relationships.

NOTES

1. 42 C.F.R. §482.12(a)(7).

2. J.J. Patee, *Update on the Medical Director*, 28 FAM. PHYSICIAN 130 (1983).

3. *Standards for Peer Evaluation: The Hospital Quality Assurance Committee*, 82 AM. J. PUB. HEALTH 525 (1992).

4. *Id.* at 526.

5. The Robert Wood Johnson Foundation, *New Research, New Ideas*, 5 ADVANCES 5 (1992).

6. *Id.* at 6.

7. AMERICAN MEDICAL ASSOCIATION, OPINIONS AND REPORTS OF THE JUDICIAL COUNCIL (1966).

8. *New Research, New Ideas*, *supra* note 5, at 6.

9. *Id.* at 5.

10. *Id.* at 6.

Chapter **7**

Nursing and the Law

OUTLINE

    Failure To Note an Order Change
    Failure To Administer Medication
    Failure To Discontinue Medication
    Unsterile Needle
    Wrong Patient
    Allergic Reactions
- Burns
- Duty To Follow Established Nursing Procedures
    Isolation Techniques
    Decubitus Ulcers
- Duty To Follow Instructions
    Supervisor's Instructions
    Physician's Orders
- Duty To Report Physician Negligence
- Duty To Question Patient Discharge
- Failure To "Note" Changes in a Patient's Condition
- Failure To "Report" Changes in a Patient's Condition
- Failure To Report Defective Equipment
- Failure To Take Correct Telephone Orders
- Nursery
    Switching of Infants
- Patient Falls
    Bedside Rails
    Examination Tables
    Suicidal Patients
- Sponge and/or Instrument Miscounts in the Operating Room

This chapter describes many of the legal risks that nurses have encountered in different health care settings. Although a professional nurse is personally liable for her negligent acts and omissions, under the doctrine of *respondeat superior*, a health care facility, as the employer, is also liable for the nurse's negligent actions.

HISTORICAL PERSPECTIVE

Health care facilities of the nineteenth century were filled with discharging wounds. The atmosphere was so offensive that the use of perfume often was required to temper the odors. Nurses of that period are said to have used snuff to make working conditions tolerable. Physicians would wear their coats for months without washing them. The same bed linen served several patients. Pain, hemorrhage, gangrene, and infection were rife on the wards. Mortality from operations was as high as 90 percent.

Florence Nightingale's service in caring for the sick and injured was faithfully industrious. To appreciate her work, it must be remembered that for more than a century before her organization of nursing service, health care facilities resembled the worst type of prisons. The ill were at the mercy of attendants who were both heartless and unsympathetic. By 1854, during the Crimean War, her opportunity came. The English government, disturbed by reports of conditions among the sick and wounded soldiers, selected Florence Nightingale as the one person capable of improving the nursing service. On her arrival at the military hospital in Crimea, she found that the sick were lying on canvas sheets in the midst of dirt and vermin. There was no laundry, and beds were made of straw. With boundless energy and a small band of nurses she had assembled, she proceeded to establish order and cleanliness. She organized diet kitchens, a laundry service, and departments of supplies, often using her own funds to finance her projects. Ten days after her arrival, the newly established kitchens were feeding 1,000 soldiers. Within three months, 10,000 were receiving clothing, food, and medicine. It is said that as a result of her work, the death rate was reduced from 40 percent to 2 percent.[1] Ms. Nightingale has been credited with writing,

> A good nursing staff will perform their duties more or less satisfactorily under every disadvantage. But while doing so, their head will always try to improve their surroundings, in such a way as to liberate them from subsidiary work, and enable them to devote their time more exclusively to the care of the sick.[2]

As a result of her tremendous organizational skills, Florence Nightingale is considered by many to be the first true health care administrator. The culmination of her work came in 1860, after her return to England. There she founded the Nightingale School of Nursing at the St. Thomas Hospital. From this school, a group of 15 nurses graduated in 1863. They later became the pioneer heads of training schools throughout the world.

In 1886, the Royal British Nurses' Association (RBNA) was formed. The RBNA worked toward the establishment of a standard of technical excellence in nursing. A charter granted to the RBNA in 1893 denied nurses a register, although it did agree to the maintenance of a list of persons who could apply to have their name entered thereon as nurses.[3]

A unique opportunity presented itself to the nurse leaders of the 1890's. Mrs. Bedford Fenwick, a nurse leader in the English nurse registration movement, came to Chicago in 1893 to arrange the English nursing exhibit to be displayed in the Women's building at the Worlds Fair. As part of the Congress on Hospitals and Dispensaries, a nursing section included papers on establishing standards in hospital training schools, the establishment of a nurses' association, and nurse registration.

• • • •

The development of the hospital economics course at Teachers College, Columbia University, ushered in a new era in preparation of nurse leaders in America. This one-year certificate course was extended to a two-year post basic training program in 1905. The commitment of key nursing leaders to advancing educational preparation for nurse faculty fostered the subsequent development of baccalaureate education in nursing during the first quarter of the 20th century.

• • • •

Despite the opposition, the movement for legislation to protect the public from the untrained nurse spread across the country. Although New York nurses began to organize for passage of legislation in 1901, the first state to pass a nurse practice bill was North Carolina in 1903.[4]

Nursing today is significantly different than it was in the days of Florence Nightingale. It requires a wider variety of skills and specialized knowledge. As advances in medicine continue to develop, the duties and responsibilities of the nurse continue to expand as well. As nursing tasks become more complex, the element of risk to the patient increases, as well as the nurse's potential exposure to malpractice. This chapter provides an overview of some of the more common risks encountered by nurses.

THE PRACTICE OF NURSING

While nurses traditionally have followed the instructions of attendant physicians, doctors realistically have long relied on nurses to exercise independent judgment in many situations.[5]

Each state has its own Nurse Practice Act that defines the practice of nursing. Although most states have similar definitions of nursing, differences generally revolve around the scope of practice permitted. New York defines the practice of nursing as follows:

[R]egistered professional nurse is defined as diagnosing and treating human responses to actual or potential health problems through such services as casefinding, health teaching, health counseling, and provision of care supportive to or restorative of life and well-being, and executing medical regimens prescribed by a licensed physician, dentist or other licensed health care provider legally authorized under this title and in accordance with the commissioner's regulations. A nursing regimen shall be consistent with and shall not vary any existing medical regimen.

[A] licensed practical nurse is defined as performing tasks and responsibilities within the framework of casefinding, health teaching, health counseling, and provision of supportive and restorative care under the direction of a registered professional nurse or a licensed physician, dentist, or other care provider legally authorized under this title and in accordance with the commissioner's regulations.

The practice of registered professional nursing by a nurse practitioner . . . may include the diagnosis of illness and physical conditions and the performance of therapeutic and corrective measures within a specialty area of practice, in collaboration with a licensed physician qualified to collaborate in the specialty involved, provided such services are performed in accordance with a written practice agreement and written practice protocols. The written practice agreement shall include explicit provisions for the resolution of any disagreement between the collaborating physician and the nurse practitioner regarding a matter of diagnosis or treatment that is within the scope of practice of both. To the extent the practice agreement does not so provide, then the collaborating physician's diagnosis or treatment shall prevail.[6]

"Professional nursing . . . is in a period of rapid and progressive change in response to the growth of biomedical knowledge, changes in patterns of demand for health services, and the evolution of professional relationships among nurses, physicians and other health professions."[7] Although the actual authority of nurses to act varies considerably from state to state, the expanding scopes of nursing functions and licensure are illustrated clearly in the following examples:

- 1903—North Carolina enacted the first nurse registration act[8]
- 1938—New York enacted the first exclusive practice act. This act required mandatory licensure of everyone who performed nursing functions as a matter of employment

- 1957—The California Nurses' Association met with representatives of medical and hospital associations to draw up a statement supporting nurses in performing venipunctures
- 1966—The Michigan Heart Association favored the use of defibrillators by coronary care nurses
- 1968—The Hawaii nursing, medical, and hospital associations approved nurses performing cardiopulmonary resuscitation
- 1971—Idaho revised its nurse practice act by allowing diagnosis and treatment if such is promulgated jointly by the Idaho State Board of Medicine and the Idaho Board of Nursing
- 1972—New York expanded its nurse practice act and adopted a broad definition of nursing
- 1973—The first American Nurses' Association Guidelines for nurse practitioners were written for geriatric nurse practitioners. These were later modified and adapted to apply to other practitioners[9]
- 1975—Section 335.016(8) of the Missouri Revised Statutes (as revised in 1975) authorized a nurse to make an assessment of persons who are ill and to render a "nursing diagnosis." "The 1975 Act not only describes a much broader spectrum of nursing functions, it qualifies this description with the phrase 'including, but not limited to.' We believe this phrase evidences an intent to avoid statutory constraints on the evolution of new functions for nurses delivering health services." *Sermchief v. Gonzales,* 660 S.W.2d 683, 689 (Mo. 1983)
- 1985—New York revised its definition of nursing by providing that a registered professional nurse who has the appropriate training and experience may provide primary health care services as defined under the statutory authority of the Public Health Law and as approved by the hospital's governing authority. The term *primary health care services* means taking histories and performing physical examinations, selecting clinical laboratory tests and diagnostic radiology procedures, and choosing regimens of treatment. A physician's responsibility for the medical care of his or her patient is not altered by these provisions. New York Public Health Law, ch. 5, A, art. 1, p. 400.10 (1985)
- 1989—New York allowed nurse practitioners to diagnose, treat, and write prescriptions within their area of specialty with minimum physician supervision

The role of the nurse continues to expand because of a shortage of nurses as well as primary physicians in certain rural and inner-city areas, ever-increasing specialization, improved technology, public demand, and expectations within the profession itself. Although there is a nursing shortage, enrollment in nursing schools was up 14 percent in 1990, according to preliminary findings of a study conducted by the National League for Nursing.[10] However, because it will take several years before any gains in nursing personnel are realized from this increased enrollment, the crisis is far from over.

A matter of concern to professional nurses is whether certain patient care activities infringe on an area of practice reserved by state licensing legislation for physicians. The question can arise in almost any patient care setting, although it would appear to be an issue raised more frequently in emergency departments and special care units. A nurse who engages in activities beyond the legally recognized scope of practice runs the risk of violating a state's medical practice act, and the health care facility that employs the nurse also could be held responsible under criminal law for aiding and abetting the illegal practice of medicine.

THE EVER-BROADENING SCOPE OF PRACTICE

A nurse who exceeds her scope of practice as defined by state nurse practice acts can be found to have violated licensure provisions or to have performed tasks that are reserved by statute for another health professional. Because of increasingly complex nursing and medical procedures, it is sometimes difficult to distinguish the tasks that are clearly reserved for the physician from those that may be performed by the professional nurse.

> The broadening of the field of practice of the nursing profession . . . carries with it the profession's responsibility for continuing high educational standards and the individual nurse's responsibility to conduct herself or himself in a professional manner. The hallmark of the professional is knowing the limits of one's professional knowledge. The nurse, either upon reaching the limit of her or his knowledge or upon reaching the limits prescribed for the nurse by the physician's standing orders and protocols, should refer the patient to the physician. *Sermchief v. Gonzales,* 660 S.W.2d at 690.

The shortage of nursing staff and the resulting expansion of nurses' scope of responsibility can lead to overextension and ultimately result in increased exposure to malpractice suits. The law in some states would allow a jury to infer that a nurse was negligent if the nurse performed functions restricted by law to physicians and if harm was suffered by a patient. The burden then shifts to the nurse who must establish that his or her performance was not of a negligent character. Even where such an inference is not recognized, a plaintiff's attorney has the opportunity to put a nurse's performance in an unfavorable light if the facts suggest an intrusion into medical practice. Nurses, however, generally have not encountered lawsuits for exceeding their scope of practice unless negligence is an issue.

NURSE LICENSURE

The common organizational pattern of nurse licensing authority in each state is to establish a separate board, organized and operated within the guidelines of specific legislation, to license all professional and practical nurses. Each board is in turn responsible for the determination of eligibility for initial licensing and relicensing; for the enforcement of licensing statutes, including suspension, revocation, and restoration of licenses; and for the approval and supervision of training institutions.

According to the Supreme Court of Idaho, a licensing board has the authority to suspend a license; however, it must do so within existing rules and regulations. In *Tuma v. Board of Nursing,* 593 P.2d 711 (Idaho 1979), a statute allowing the suspension of a professional nursing license for unprofessional conduct could not be invoked to suspend the license of a nurse who allegedly interfered with the physician–patient relationship by discussing alternative treatment with the patient without some board of nursing rules or regulations to warn her adequately that such actions were prohibited.

Requirements for Licensure

Formal professional training is necessary for nurse licensure in all states. The course requirements vary, but all courses must be completed at board-approved schools or institutions.

Each state requires that an applicant pass a written examination, which generally is administered twice annually. The examinations may be drafted by the licensing board, or they may be prepared by professional examination services or national examining boards. Some states waive their written examination for applicants who present a certificate from a national nursing examination board. Graduate nurses are generally able to practice nursing under supervision while waiting for the results of their examination.

The four basic methods by which boards license out-of-state nurses are reciprocity, endorsement, waiver, or examination.

Reciprocity may be a formal or informal agreement between states whereby a nurse licensing board in one state recognizes licensees of another state if the board of that state extends reciprocal recognition to licensees from the first state. To have reciprocity, the initial licensing requirements of the two states must be essentially equivalent.

Although some nurse licensing boards use the term *endorsement* interchangeably with reciprocity, the two words have different meanings. In licensing by endorsement, boards determine whether the out-of-state nurse's qualifications were equivalent to their own state requirements at the time of initial licensure. Many states make it a condition for endorsement that the qualifying examination taken in the other state be comparable with their own. As with reciprocity, endorsement becomes much easier when uniform qualification standards are applied by the different states.

Licensing out-of-state nurses also can be accomplished by waiver and examination. When applicants do not meet all the requirements for licensure but have equivalent qualifications, the specific prerequisite of education, experience, or examination may be waived. Some states will not recognize out-of-state licensed nurses and make it mandatory that all applicants pass a licensing examination.

Most states grant temporary licenses for nurses. These licenses may be issued pending a decision by a licensing board on permanent licensure or may be issued to out-of-state nurses who intend to be in a jurisdiction for a limited time.

Nurse licensing boards are cautious in licensing persons educated in foreign countries. Graduates of schools in other countries are required to meet the same qualifications as are nurses trained in the United States. Many state boards have established special training, citizenship, and experience requirements for students educated abroad, and others insist on additional training in the United States.

Nurses who have completed their studies in a foreign country are required to pass an English proficiency examination and/or a licensing examination administered in English. A few states have reciprocity or endorsement agreements with some foreign countries.

Suspension and Revocation

All nurse licensing boards have the authority to suspend or revoke the license of a nurse who is found to have violated specified norms of conduct. Such violations may include procurement of a license by fraud; unprofessional, dishonorable, immoral, or illegal conduct; performance of specific actions prohibited by statute; and malpractice.

Suspension and revocation procedures are most commonly contained in the licensing act; in some jurisdictions, however, the procedure is left to the discretion of the board or is contained in the general administrative procedure acts. For the most part, suspension and revocation proceedings are administrative, rather than judicial, and do not carry criminal sanctions.

Liability for Practicing Without a License

Insofar as a health care facility's liability is concerned, the general considerations of the doctrine of *respondeat superior* apply. The mere fact that an unlicensed practitioner was hired and used by a facility would not impose additional liability unless a patient suffered harm as a result of an unlicensed nurse's negligence.

AMERICAN NURSES' ASSOCIATION

The American Nurses' Association (ANA) is the national professional organization of graduate registered nurses in the United States and its territories. ANA membership is available to all graduate nurses who are licensed in any jurisdiction of the United States. The purpose of the ANA is to

> foster high standards of nursing practice and to promote the professional and educational advancement of nurses and the welfare of nurses to the end that all people may have better nursing care. The association helps provide health protection for the American people, aids nurses to become more effective members of their profession, and promotes better health care for the people of the world.[11]

The standards of practice as developed by the ANA are as follows:

Standard I

The collection of data about the health status of clients/patients is systematic and continuous, the data are accessible, communicated, and recorded.

Standard II

Nursing diagnoses are derived from health status data.

Standard III

The plan of nursing care includes goals derived from the nursing diagnoses.

Standard IV

The plan of nursing care includes priorities and the prescribed nursing approaches or measures to achieve the goals derived from the nursing diagnoses.

Standard V

Nursing actions provide for client/patient participation in health promotion, maintenance and restoration.

Standard VI

Nursing actions assist the client/patient to maximize his health capabilities.

Standard VII

The client's/patient's progress or lack of progress toward goal achievement is determined by the client/patient and the nurse.

Standard VIII

The client's/patient's progress or lack of progress toward goal achievement directs reassessment, recording of priorities, new goal setting and revision of the plan of nursing care.[12]

NATIONAL LEAGUE FOR NURSING

The National League for Nursing (NLN) is a membership organization of individuals and agencies organized for the purpose of fostering development and improvement of hospital, public health, and other organized nursing service and nursing education through the coordinated action of nurses, allied professional groups, citizens, agencies, and schools so that the nursing needs of the people will be met.[13] The philosophy of the NLN is to bring together professional and paraprofessional health care workers and consumers to work toward improving nursing services and nursing education. The NLN is involved in nursing research, recruitment of students, testing services, workshops, conferences, seminars, consultation services, accreditation of nursing schools, fellowship aid, publications, and films. The NLN is funded through membership dues and grantors such as the American Hospital Association, the W.K. Kellogg Foundation, and the Rockefeller Fund.[14]

DIRECTOR OF NURSES AND NURSING SUPERVISORS

The director of nursing services is a qualified registered nurse employed full time who has, in writing, administrative authority, responsibility, and accountability for the function, activities, and training of the nursing services staff. If the director of nursing services has other institutional responsibilities, a qualified registered nurse serves as her assistant so that there is the equivalent of a full-time director of nursing services responsible for the development and maintenance of nursing service objectives, standards of nursing practice, nursing policy and procedure manuals, written job descriptions for each level of nursing personnel, scheduling of daily rounds to see all patients, methods for coordination of nursing services with other patient services, recommendations for the number and levels of nursing personnel to be employed, and nursing staff development.

The health codes of many states describe the minimum qualifications and responsibilities for the director of nurses. Although the duties of the director of nurses vary from state to state, directors are generally responsible for the supervision, provision, and quality of nursing care; coordination and integration of nursing services with other patient care services; development of job descriptions for nurses and nurses' aides; development of nursing service procedures; selection of nursing staff members; and development of orientation and training programs.

Although a nursing supervisor is liable for his or her own negligent acts, the employer is liable for the negligent acts of all employees, including supervisors (e.g., directors of nursing, assistant directors of nursing, and head nurses). Supervisors are not liable under the doctrine of *respondeat superior* for the negligent acts of those being supervised. They have the right to direct the nurses who are being supervised. In a health care facility, the supervisor's powers are derived directly from the facility's right of control.

A supervisor who knowingly fails to supervise an employee's performance or assigns a task to an individual he or she knows, or should know, is not competent to perform can be held personally liable if injury occurs. The employer will be liable under the doctrine of *respondeat superior* as the employer of both the supervisor and the individual who performed the task in a negligent manner. The supervisor is not relieved of personal liability even though the employer is liable under *respondeat superior*.

In determining whether a nurse with supervisory responsibilities has been negligent, the nurse is measured against the standard of care of a competent and prudent nurse in the performance of supervisory duties. Those duties include the setting of policies and procedures for the prevention of accidents in the care of patients. The director of nursing in *Moon Lake Convalescent Center v. Margolis,* 535 N.E.2d 956, 966–967 (Ill. App. Ct. 1989), was found to have violated her duty to maintain standards of nursing practice by not following the center's own bath policy and in failing to develop standards to prevent accidents from excessive temperatures. The nursing facility was fined $618 because the director of nurses failed to maintain the nursing standards of the facility.

A supervisor ordinarily may rely on the fact that a subordinate is licensed or certified as an indication of the subordinate's capabilities in performing tasks within the ambit of the license or certificate. Nonetheless, where the individual's past actions have led the supervisor to believe that the person is likely to perform a task in an unsatisfactory manner, assigning the task to that person can lead to liability for negligence on the part of the supervisor because the risk of harm to the patient is knowingly increased. If charting a patient's fluid intake was assigned to a nurse's aide not instructed in performing this task and if such an assignment normally was not made until the supervisor personally ascertained the aide's ability to chart fluids satisfactorily, the departure from the standard of care that causes a patient harm would justify imposing liability for negligence.

NURSE PRACTITIONER

A relatively new and exciting role for nurses is that of the nurse practitioner. The nurse practitioner is a registered nurse who has completed the necessary education to engage in primary health care decision making. According to the ANA, as of October 1989 there were 12,117 certified nurse practitioners, of which 1,149 were graduate nurse practitioners.[15]

The nurse practitioner is trained in the delivery of primary health care and the assessment of psychosocial and physical health problems such as the performance of routine examinations and the ordering of routine diagnostic tests. A physician may not delegate a task when regulations specify that the physician must perform it personally or when the delegation is prohibited under state law or by the facility's own policies.[16] Unfortunately,

> [f]or registered nurses who complete advanced training in geriatrics or gerontology, Federal reimbursement policy may actually restrict employment opportunities. The services of geriatric nurse practitioners are directly reimbursable by Medicare, but only when the geriatric nurse practitioner is supervised onsite by a licensed physician. In hospitals this requirement is easily met. In most nursing homes, however, this requirement makes reimbursement difficult to obtain. As a result, highly trained geriatric nurse practitioners are too expensive for most nursing homes to hire. Similarly, Medicaid's restricted payments for skilled nursing personnel appear to leave most nursing homes with a choice of paying high salaries to a few highly trained nurses or paying low salaries to a large number of unskilled aides.[17]

The potential risks of liability for the nurse practitioner are as real as the risks for any other nurse. The standard of care required most likely will be set by statute. If not, the courts will determine the standard based on the reasonable person doctrine (i.e., what would a reasonably prudent nurse practitioner do under the given circumstances?). The standard would be established through the use of expert testimony of other nurse practitioners in the field. Although case law in this area is practically nonexistent, nurse practitioners are required to meet the standards recognized in the field as reflecting the current status of the art. Because of potential liability problems and pressure from physicians, hospitals have been reluctant to use nurse practitioners to the full extent of their training.

A Veterans Administration hospital did use nurse practitioners in a program introduced for delivering health services to nursing home patients. Geriatric nurse practitioners were used by the hospital as primary resources in its associated nursing home unit. Results of the study revealed fewer transfers to acute care hospitals and significant improvements in functional status, patients' satisfaction, and morale.[18]

CLINICAL NURSE SPECIALIST

A clinical nurse specialist is a professional nurse with an advanced academic degree and a major in a specific clinical specialty such as pediatrics or psychiatry. The clinical nurse specialist concentrates her practice of nursing in one specialized clinical setting by applying advanced nursing procedures and techniques. The standard of care expected of the clinical nurse specialist is determined in a manner similar to that of the nurse practitioner. Hospitals do not seem to be as reluctant to use clinical nurse specialists as they are the nurse practitioners.

NURSE–ANESTHETIST

The negligent administration of anesthetics by a nurse–anesthetist can lead to liability on the part of a physician, as well as a hospital. In *McKinney v. Tromly,* 386 S.W.2d 564 (Tex. Civ. App. 1964), a suit was instituted against a physician for the negligence of a nurse in the administration of an anesthetic to the plaintiff's nine-year-old son who was undergoing a tonsillectomy. The Texas Court of Civil Appeals held that the nurse, an employee of the hospital, was an employee of the physician while in the operating room and under his control (applying the borrowed servant doctrine). Therefore, the physician was held liable for the death caused by the nurse in administering the anesthetic to the patient. Administration of an anesthetic is not an administrative function of the hospital but constitutes the practice of medicine.

The physician in *Weinstein v. Prostkoff,* 23 Misc. 2d 376, 191 N.Y.S.2d 310 (Sup. Ct. 1959), *rev'd,* 213 N.Y.S.2d 571 (Sup. Ct., App. Div. 1961), testified that an examination revealed that the unborn child was suffering from fetal distress. The patient was prepared immediately for delivery, taken into the delivery room, and administered an anesthetic. The nurse who responded to the delivery room call was told that the baby was in distress and that 100 percent oxygen was to be administered immediately to the mother. Although it was customary and exceedingly important to ascertain whether a patient had eaten any food within a reasonably short time before administration of the anesthesia, no such inquiries had been made. Approximately two minutes after the baby was born, the patient gave several gasps and died. The physician testified that he immediately saw large amounts of vomit coming from the patient's mouth. The immediate impression of those in attendance indicated the patient had suffocated as a result of aspirating gastric matter into the lungs.

The jury's verdict was in favor of the hospital and the nurse but against the physician. On the basis of contradictory evidence, the court set aside the jury verdict and held that if the physician could be found responsible for having failed to prepare for, direct, or supervise the anesthetic part of the delivery, then certainly the nurse, or the physician and the hospital, were equally, if not more, responsible. On retrial, verdicts in favor of the hospital and the nurse were set aside again. However, on appeal, these verdicts were reinstated.

NURSE MIDWIFE

A certified nurse midwife in *Sweeney v. Athens Regional Medical Center (ARMC),* 705 F. Supp. 1556 (M.D. Ga. 1989), brought an action against a public hospital and certain physicians, alleging violations of the Sherman Antitrust Act and First Amendment rights and intentional infliction of emotional distress arising out of a hospital's denying her access to a patient in the hospital. The hospital motioned for summary judgment. The district court held that a public hospital was a local governmental unit within the meaning of the Local Government Antitrust Act and thus was immune from the damage claim brought under the Sherman Act. The district court further held, even assuming that the hospital's decision to deny the nurse midwife access to certain patients, the hospital's interests in providing effective and safe medical care outweighed the nurse midwife's interests in exercising her right to speak out freely on matters of natural childbirth. The nurse did not state a claim for intentional infliction of emotional distress.

> ARMC found itself unavoidably involved in a dispute between those holding different philosophical beliefs on the subject of childbirth. When faced with a difficult decision it was forced to make because of no fault of its own, ARMC responded in a way that it felt would best

serve its primary concern, the safety and care of its patients. This court has found no basis in the law for requiring the Hospital to go to trial to defend that decision.

Id. at 1571.

NURSING ASSISTANTS

A nursing assistant is an aide who has been certified and trained to assist licensed and/or registered nursing personnel in the care of patients. Several cases involving nursing assistants are presented below.

Failure To Follow Procedures

A resident died in *Moon Lake Convalescent Center v. Margolis,* 535 N.E.2d 956 (Ill. App. Ct. 1989), after immersion in a tub of hot water. After an administrative hearing, the director of the Department of Public Health affirmed a hearing officer's decision to impose penalties and revoke Moon Lake's license. On administrative review, the trial court reversed the director's decision and the department appealed. On November 13, 1983, a nursing assistant prepared a tub bath for one of the center's residents, Benjamin Ovitz, a 73-year-old man who had suffered a stroke. He had paralysis of his left side and could only articulate the words *yes* and *no*. The nursing assistant checked the water with his hand and bathed the resident. Later in the day, a nurse noticed that the resident's leg was bleeding and his skin was sloughing off. The paramedics were contacted, and they transferred the resident to the Evanston Hospital after determining that the patient had suffered a third-degree burn. Dr. Drueck,

> the surgeon in charge at Evanston Hospital, observed that Ovitz had suffered third degree burns over 40% of his body, primarily on his back, buttocks, both sides, genitals and lower legs. Ovitz's knees were not burned, nor were there splatter burns. The burns were consistent with immersion in a discrete body of water.

Id. at 959.

Mr. Ovitz developed pneumonia during his hospitalization and died on January 15, 1984. There was testimony from Dr. Drueck that the cause of death was due to complications following the burns.

> Moon Lake's bathing policy, 'Prevent accidents—do not make water too hot (95 degrees to 100 degrees F.),' indicates it recognized the

importance of safe water temperatures with elderly residents who are susceptible to burns. Moon Lake's daily temperature logs for November 1983 also indicate that it knew that the water temperature in the system at times fluctuated above its bathing policy, at times exceeding 110 degrees. Yet, Moon Lake failed to take adequate measures to protect elderly residents from accidents from excessive water temperatures.

Id. at 966.

Written procedure was not followed when the nursing assistant left the resident unattended in his bath. This was a violation of written policy. *Id.* at 967. The appellate court held that revocation of the facility's license was warranted in this case.

Patient Fall

A nursing assistant in *Kern v. Gulf Coast Nursing Home of Moss Point, Inc.,* 502 So.2d 1198 (Miss. 1987), was attempting to give a resident a whirlpool bath. The resident had been placed in a special rolling seat and was being lifted by a hydraulic lifting device that was used to place residents in the whirlpool. In the process of lifting the resident, the seat, which had been connected to the lift, became disconnected. The resident fell to the floor, hitting her head and breaking her hip. The seat apparently had been connected improperly to the lift. The trial court entered a verdict in the amount of $20,000 for the plaintiff and the plaintiff appealed, stating that the award was "inadequate." The Supreme Court of Mississippi held that the "verdict was not so low as to shock the conscience of the court." *Id.*

SPECIAL DUTY NURSE

A special duty nurse is a nurse hired by the patient or the patient's family to perform nursing care for the patient. A hospital is generally not liable for the negligence of a special duty nurse unless a master–servant relationship can be determined to exist between the hospital and the special duty nurse. If a master–servant relationship exists between the hospital and the special duty nurse, the doctrine of *respondeat superior* may be applied to impose liability on the hospital for the nurse's negligent conduct.

Like a staff physician, a special duty nurse may be required to observe certain rules and regulations as a precondition to working in the hospital. The observance of hospital rules is insufficient, however, to raise a master–servant relationship between the hospital and the nurse. Under ordinary circumstances a special duty nurse is employed by the patient, and the hospital has no authority to hire or fire the nurse. The hospital does have the responsibility, however, to protect the patient from incompetent or unqualified special duty nurses.

STUDENT NURSES

Student nurses are entrusted with the responsibility of providing nursing care to patients. When liability is being assessed, a student nurse serving at a hospital is considered an agent of the hospital. This is true even if the student is at the hospital on an affiliation basis. Student nurses are personally liable for their own negligent acts, and the hospital is liable for their acts on the basis of *respondeat superior*. Students must be supervised by a registered professional nurse who is either the direct agent of the student's nursing school or one who has been designated by the school to serve in that capacity.

A student nurse is held to the standard of a competent professional nurse when performing nursing duties. The courts, in several decisions, have taken the position that anyone who performs duties customarily performed by professional nurses is held to the standards of professional nurses. Each and every patient has the right to expect competent nursing services even if the care is provided by students as part of their clinical training. It would be unfair to deprive the patient of compensation for an injury merely because a student was responsible for the negligent act. Until it is demonstrated clearly that student nurses are competent to render nursing services without increasing the risks of injury to patients, they must be supervised more closely than graduated nurses.

ADMINISTRATION OF DRUGS

Nurses are required to handle and administer a vast variety of drugs that are prescribed by physicians and dispensed by hospital pharmacies. Medications may range from aspirin to esoteric drugs that are administered through intravenous solutions. These medications must be administered in the prescribed manner and dose to prevent serious harm to patients.

The practice of pharmacy essentially includes preparing, compounding, dispensing, and retailing medications. These activities may be carried out only by a pharmacist with a state license or by a person exempted from the provisions of a state's pharmacy statutes.

Nurses are exempted from the various pharmacy statutes when administering a medication on the oral or written order of a physician. The improper administration of medications can lead to malpractice suits. The more common complaints involve

- administration without prescription
- the wrong medication
- the wrong dosage
- negligent injection
- the wrong route
- failure to note an order change
- failure to administer medication
- failure to discontinue medication
- using an unsterile needle
- the wrong patient
- allergic reactions

Administration Without Prescription

A director of nursing and a charge nurse were charged with second-degree assault, and individual defendants were charged with conspiracy to commit second-degree assault in *People v. Nygren,* 696 P.2d 270 (Colo. 1985). Evidence was considered sufficient to establish probable cause for charging the nurses with second-degree assault and conspiracy charges in the administration of unprescribed doses of Thorazine to a resident at a time when he was incapable of providing consent. The trial court was found to have erred in dismissing the information before the prosecution's first witness had completed his testimony. There was probable cause to believe that the defendants had committed the offense charged and that it would have been established if the prosecution had been permitted to present its witnesses, two of which would have testified that the nurses administered the unprescribed doses of the drug. The case was reversed and remanded for trial. The treating physician had told the special investigator from the attorney general's office that Thorazine never had been prescribed for the resident while he was in the nursing facility. The resident was mentally retarded and incapable of consenting to administration of the drug. Medical evidence of the amount of Thorazine in the resident's blood was consistent with stupor and impairment of physical and mental functions.

Wrong Medication

The injection of the wrong medication into a patient can lead to a malpractice suit. In *Abercrombie v. Roof,* 28 N.E.2d 772 (Ohio 1940), a solution was prepared by an employee and injected into the patient by a physician. The physician made no examination of the fluid, and the patient suffered permanent injuries as a result of the injection. An action was brought against the physician for malpractice. The patient claimed that the fluid injected was alcohol and that the physician should have recognized its distinctive odor. The court in finding for the physician stated that he was not responsible for the misuse of drugs prepared by an employee, unless the ordinarily prudent use of his faculties would have prevented injury to the patient.

Wrong Dosage

A nurse is responsible for making an inquiry if there is uncertainty about the accuracy of a physician's medication order in a patient's record. In the Louisiana case of *Norton v. Argonaut Insurance Co.,* 144 So.2d 249 (La. Ct. App. 1962), the court focused attention on the responsibility of a nurse to obtain clarification of an apparently erroneous order from the patient's physician. The medication order of the attending physician, as entered in the chart, was incomplete and subject to misinterpretation. Believing the order to be incorrect because of the dosage, the nurse asked two physicians present in the ward whether the medication should be given as ordered. The two physicians did not interpret the order as the nurse did and therefore did not share the same concern. They advised the nurse that the attending physician's instructions did not appear out of line. The nurse did not contact the attending physician but instead administered the misinterpreted dosage of medication. As a result, the patient died from a fatal overdose of the medication.

The court upheld the jury's finding that the nurse had been negligent in failing to get in contact with the attending physician before administering the medication. The nurse was held liable, as was the physician who wrote the ambiguous order that led to the fatal dose. In discussing the standard of care expected of a nurse who encounters an apparently erroneous order, the court stated that not only was the nurse unfamiliar with the medication in question, but also she violated the rule generally followed by the members of the nursing profession in the community, which requires that the prescribing physician be called when there is doubt about an order for medication. The court noted that it is the duty of a nurse, in such instances, to make absolutely certain what the doctor intended, regarding both dosage and route. The evidence leaves no doubt that while nurses do at times consult any available physician when unsure of another physician's orders, the nurses who testified agreed that the better practice is to consult the prescribing physician about doubtful orders for medication. This clarification was not sought from the physician who wrote the order, and the departure from the standard of competent nursing practice provided the basis for holding the nurse liable for negligence.

Negligent Injection

In *Bernardi v. Community Hospital Association,* 166 Colo. 280, 443 P.2d 708 (1968), a seven-year-old patient was in the hospital after surgery for the drainage of an abscessed appendix. The attending physician had left a written postoperative order at the hospital that the patient was to be given an injection of tetracycline every 12 hours. During the evening of the first day after surgery, the nurse, employed by the hospital and acting under this order, injected the prescribed dosage of tetracycline in the patient's right gluteal region. It was claimed that the nurse negligently injected the tetracycline into or adjacent to the sciatic nerve, causing the patient to permanently lose the normal use of the right foot. The court did not hold the physician responsible. It concluded that if the plaintiff could prove the nurse's negligence, the hospital would be responsible for the nurse's act under the doctrine of *respondeat superior.* The physician did not know which nurse administered the injection because he was not present when the injection was given, and he had no opportunity to control its administration. The hospital was found liable under *respondeat superior.* The appellate court said: "The hospital was the employer of the nurse. Only it had the right to hire and fire her. Only it could assign the nurse to certain hours, designated areas and specific patients."

Wrong Route

The nurse in *Fleming v. Baptist General Convention,* 742 P.2d 1087 (Okla. 1987), negligently injected the patient with a solution of Talwin and Atarax subcutaneously, rather than intramuscularly. The patient suffered tissue necrosis as a result of the improper injection. The suit against the hospital was successful. On appeal, the court held that the jury's verdict for the plaintiff found adequate support in the testimony of the plaintiff's expert witness on the issues of negligence and causation.

Failure To Note an Order Change

Failure to review a patient's record before administering a medication to ascertain whether an order has been modified may render a nurse liable for negligence. The case of *Larrimore v. Homeopathic Hospital Association,* 54 Del. 449, 181 A.2d 573 (1962), concerned a female patient who had been receiving a drug by injection over a period of time. There came a time when the physician wrote an instruction on the patient's order sheet changing the method of administration from injection to oral medication. When a nurse on the patient unit who had been off duty for several days was preparing to medicate the patient by injection, the patient objected and referred the nurse to the physician's new order. The nurse, however, told the patient she was mistaken and gave the medication by injection. Perhaps the nurse had not reviewed the order sheet after being told by the patient that the medication was to be given orally; perhaps the nurse did not notice the physician's entry. Either way, the nurse's conduct was held to be negligent. The court went on to say that the jury could find the nurse negligent by applying ordinary common sense to establish the applicable standard of care.

Failure To Administer Medication

In *Kallenberg v. Beth Israel Hospital,* 45 A.D.2d 1977, 357 N.Y.S.2d 508 (1974), a patient died after her third cerebral hemorrhage because of the failure of the physicians and staff to administer necessary medications. When the patient was admitted to the hospital, her physician determined that she should be given a specific drug to reduce her blood pressure and make her condition operable. For an unexplained reason, the drug was not administered. The patient's blood pressure rose, and after the final hemorrhage, she died. The jury found the hospital and physicians negligent in failing to administer the drug and ruled that the negligence had caused the patient's death. The appellate court found that the jury had sufficient evidence to decide that the negligent treatment had been the cause of the patient's death.

Failure To Discontinue Medication

A hospital will be held liable if a nurse continues to inject a solution after noticing its ill effects. In the Florida case of *Parrish v. Clark,* 107 Fla. 598, 145 So. 848 (1933), the court held that a nurse's continued injection of saline solution into an unconscious patient's breast after the nurse noticed ill effects constituted negligence. Thus, once something was observed to be wrong with the administration of the solution, the nurse had a duty to discontinue its use.

Unsterile Needle

The blood donor in *Brown v. Shannon West Texas Memorial Hospital,* 222 S.W.2d 248 (Tex. 1949), sought to recover from a serious injury allegedly caused by the use of an unsterile needle. The court held that the burden of proof was on the plaintiff to show, by competent evidence, that the needle was contaminated when used and that it was the proximate cause of the alleged injury. The mere proof, said the court, that infection followed the use of the needle or that the infection possibly could be attributed to the use of an unsterile needle was insufficient.

Wrong Patient

It is of utmost importance to check each patient's name bracelet before administering any medication. To ensure that the patient's identity corresponds to the name on the patient's bracelet, the nurse should address the patient by name when approaching the patient's bedside to administer any medication. Should a patient unwittingly be administered another patient's medication, the attending physician should be notified and appropriate documentation placed on the patient's chart.

Allergic Reactions

Any adverse reactions to a medication should be charted on the patient's medical record. The attending physician and hospital pharmacy should be advised as to the patient's allergic reaction.

BURNS

Burns by hot-water bottles, sitz baths, heating pads, etc., are main causes of liability suits against hospitals. The plaintiff in *Quinby v. Morrow,* 340 F.2d 584 (2d Cir. 1965), sought damages against the hospital, the instrument nurse, and the surgeon for third-degree burns sustained by her ward during a tonsillectomy. A hot metal gag had been placed in the patient's mouth, causing the severe burn. There was testimony that it was the duty of the circulating nurse, a hospital employee not named in the suit, to have a basin of water available to cool sterilized surgical instruments before their use. The surgeon testified that the basin was missing or at least not in its usual place and that this was a serious omission. The jury returned a verdict holding the hospital liable for $30,000 but found the surgeon and the instrument nurse not liable. These verdicts were affirmed by the appellate court, which held that evidence was sufficient to allow the jury to affix responsibility to the hospital, based on the acts of the circulating nurse, and to exonerate the surgeon and the instrument nurse.

The negligent use of a Bovie plate led to liability in *Monk v. Doctors Hospital,* 403 F.2d 580 (D.C. Cir. 1968), in which a nurse had been instructed by the physician to set up a Bovie machine. The nurse placed the contact plate of the Bovie machine under the patient's right calf in a negligent manner and the patient suffered burns. The patient introduced instruction manuals, issued by the manufacturer, supporting a claim that the plate was placed improperly. These manuals had been available to the hospital. The trial court directed a verdict in favor of the hospital and the doctor. The appellate court found that there was sufficient evidence from which the jury could conclude that the Bovie plate was applied in a negligent manner. There was also sufficient evidence, including the manufacturer's manual and expert testimony, from which the jury could find that the physician was independently negligent. Appropriate safety precautions can prevent incidents such as this.

DUTY TO FOLLOW ESTABLISHED NURSING PROCEDURES

The following cases present potential hazards to nurses who fail to follow established nursing procedures.

Isolation Techniques

Failure to follow proper infection control procedures (e.g., proper hand-washing techniques) can result in cross-contamination between patients. Staff members who administer to patients, moving from one patient to another without washing their hands after changing dressings, giving back rubs, and carrying out routine procedures, can open up a health care facility to major lawsuits.

The patient in *Helmann v. Sacred Heart Hospital*, 62 Wash.2d 136, 381 P.2d 605 (1963), had sustained chest injuries, a left hip dislocation, and multiple fractures in the area of the left hip socket and was paralyzed from the waist down. The patient was returned to his room after hip surgery. The patient's roommate complained of a boil under his right arm. Eight days later, a culture was taken of drainage from the wound. Three days later, the laboratory identified the infection as *Staphylococcus aureus*. The infected roommate was transferred immediately to an isolation room. Until this time, ward nurses and hospital attendants administered to both patients regularly, moving from one patient to another without washing their hands as they changed dressings, gave back rubs, and carried out routine procedures. On the day the roommate was placed in isolation, the plaintiff's wound erupted, discharging a large amount of purulent drainage. A culture of the drainage showed it to have been caused by the presence of *Staphylococcus aureus*. The infection penetrated into the patient's hip socket, destroying tissue and requiring a second operation. In the second operation, the patient's hip was fused in a nearly immovable position. The

Supreme Court of Washington affirmed a judgment for the patient. The court ruled that there was sufficient circumstantial evidence from which the jury could have found that the patients were infected with the same *Staphylococcus aureus* strain and that the infection was caused by the hospital's negligence in that its personnel failed to follow sterile techniques in ministering to its two patients.

In *Staphylococcus* infection cases, one must demonstrate negligence of the defendant and injury resulting from that negligence. The burden of proof is on the plaintiff to establish a causal relationship between the injury and the hospital's deviation from the accepted standard of care. Negligence on the nurse's part can arise from failure to follow appropriate isolation procedures. Sterile technique must be followed when a patient is suspected to have a *Staphylococcus* infection, even though it has not been confirmed. Negligence often arises from failure to make a proper diagnosis and/or to treat properly.

A practical nurse's license was revoked in *Homes v. Department of Professional Regulation Board of Nursing,* 504 So.2d 1338 (Fla. Dist. Ct. App. 1987), because of the nurse's failure to use proper aseptic techniques in inserting a catheter in a female patient who was observed to be in distress. The nurse had failed to properly assess and report a broken area on the patient's coccyx. The nurse's conduct constituted unprofessional conduct in violation of Florida statutes and was considered justification for revocation of her license. The revocation order by the board of nursing stated that the nurse was prohibited permanently from petitioning the board for reinstatement of her license. This was held to be improper because it conflicted with Florida statutes and with the rules of the Department of Professional Regulation.

Staphylococcus infections can often be prevented by (1) requiring the staff to have periodic physicals, including cultures, (2) maintaining an active infections committee, (3) following predetermined isolation procedures (which should be maintained in writing), and (4) taking other reasonable precautions.

Decubitus Ulcers

The failure of nurses to follow adequate nursing procedures in treating decubitus ulcers was found to be a factor leading to the death of a nursing facility resident in *Montgomery Health Care v. Ballard,* 565 So.2d 221 (Ala. 1990). "Two nurses testified that they did not know that decubitus ulcers could be life threatening. One nurse testified that she did not know that the patient's doctor should be called if there were symptoms of infection in the sore." *Id.* at 224. Such allegations would indicate that there was a lack of training and supervision of the nurses treating the patient. The seriousness of such failure was driven home when the court allowed $2 million in punitive damages.

DUTY TO FOLLOW INSTRUCTIONS

Supervisor's Instructions

Failure of a nurse to follow the instructions of a supervising nurse to wait for her assistance before performing a procedure can result in the revocation of the nurse's license. The nurse in *Cafiero v. North Carolina Board of Nursing,* 403 S.E.2d 582 (N.C. Ct. App. 1991), failed to heed the head nurse's instructions to wait for assistance before connecting a heart monitor to an infant. The incorrect connection of the heart monitor resulted in an electrical shock to the infant. The board of nursing, under the Nursing Practice Act, revoked the nurse's license for engaging in conduct endangering the public. The board had the authority to revoke the nurse's license even though her work before and after the incident had been exemplary. The dangers of electric cords are within the realm of common knowledge. The record showed that the nurse failed to exercise "ordinary care" in connecting the infant to the monitor.

Physician's Orders

A hospital can be held liable for the negligence of its nurses who fail to follow a physician's orders properly. In *Toth v. Community Hospital at Glen Cove,* 239 N.E.2d 368, 292 N.Y.S.2d 635 (Ct. App. 1968), twin girls were administered oxygen. One became completely blind, and the other suffered severe damage to one eye. It was established that the attending pediatrician, who was sued along with the hospital, had ordered administration of 6L oxygen per minute for the first 12 hours and 4L per minute thereafter. The nurses in the nursery, however, had given 6L per minute continuously over a period of several weeks. The jury found that the defendant physician was not negligent in ordering the oxygen and that he was not negligent for failure to reduce the level of oxygen himself. However, the hospital was liable for the negligence of its employees—the nurses in charge of the nursery—who failed to follow the physician's orders. The court of appeals, emphasizing that it is the duty of the nurse to follow the physician's orders, held it was an error for the case against the hospital to have been dismissed. It was wrong to preclude a jury from determining if there had been a deviation from normal practice that was the proximate cause of the patients' injuries. This question was to be considered in a new trial.

DUTY TO REPORT PHYSICIAN NEGLIGENCE

A hospital can be liable for the failure of nursing personnel to take appropriate action when a patient's personal physician is clearly unwilling or unable to cope with a situation that threatens the life or health of the patient. In a California case, *Goff v. Doctors General Hospital,* 166 Cal. App. 2d 314, 333 P.2d 29 (1958), a patient was bleeding seriously after childbirth because the physician failed to suture her properly. The nurses testified that they were aware of the patient's dangerous condition and that the physician was not present in the hospital. Both nurses knew the patient would die if nothing was done, but neither contacted anyone except the physician. The hospital was liable for the nurses' negligence in failing to notify their supervisors of the serious condition that caused the patient's death. Evidence was sufficient to sustain the finding that the nurses who attended the patient and who were aware of the excessive bleeding were negligent and that their negligence was a contributing cause of the patient's death. The measure of duty of the hospital toward its patients is the exercise of that degree of care used by hospitals generally. The court held that nurses who knew that a woman they were attending was bleeding excessively were negligent in failing to report the circumstances so that prompt and adequate measures could be taken to safeguard her life.

DUTY TO QUESTION PATIENT DISCHARGE

A nurse has a duty to question the discharge of a patient if he or she has reason to believe that such discharge could be injurious to the health of the patient. Jury issues were raised in *Koeniguer v. Eckrich,* 422 N.W.2d 600 (S.D. 1988), by expert testimony that the nurses had a duty to attempt to delay the patient's discharge if her condition warranted continued hospitalization and by permissible inferences from the evidence that the delay in treatment that resulted from the premature discharge contributed to the patient's death. Summary dismissal of this case against the hospital by a trial court was found to have been improper.

FAILURE TO "NOTE" CHANGES IN A PATIENT'S CONDITION

Failure to note changes in a patient's condition can lead to liability on the part of the nurse and the hospital. The recovery room nurse in *Eyoma v. Falco,* 589 A.2d 653 (N.J. Super. A.D. 1991), who had been assigned to monitor a post-surgical patient, (1) left the patient and (2) failed to recognize that the patient had stopped breathing. The nurse had been assigned to monitor the patient in the recovery room. She delegated that duty to another nurse and failed to verify that the other nurse accepted that responsibility.

Nurse Falco admitted she never got a verbal response from the other nurse, and that when she returned there was no one near the decedent. She acknowledged that Dr. Brotherton told her to watch the decedent's breathing, but claimed she was not told that decedent had been given narcotics. She maintained that upon her return she checked the decedent and observed his respirations to be eight per minute.

Thereafter, Dr. Brotherton returned and inquired about the decedent's condition. Nurse Falco informed the doctor that the patient was fine. However, upon his personal observation, Dr. Brotherton realized that decedent had stopped breathing.

• • • •

Decedent because of oxygen deprivation, entered a comatose state and remained unconscious for over a year until his death. . . .

Id. at 655.

The jury held the nurse to be 100 percent liable for the patient's injuries. The superior court, appellate division, held that there was sufficient evidence to support the verdict.

FAILURE TO "REPORT" CHANGES IN A PATIENT'S CONDITION

Nurses have the responsibility to observe the conditions of patients under their care and report any significant findings that may affect adversely a patient's well-being to the attending physician. If a physician should fail to respond to a call for assistance and such failure is likely to jeopardize a patient's health, the matter must be brought to the attention of the nursing supervisor, chief of the appropriate service, or administration. Failure to exercise this duty can lead to liability for the nurse, as well as the hospital, under the doctrine of *respondeat superior.*

A health care facility's policies and procedures should prescribe the guidelines for staff members to follow when confronted with a physician or other health professional whose action or inaction jeopardizes the well-being of a patient. Guidelines in place, but not followed, are of no value, as the following case illustrates. The plaintiff in *Utter v. United Hospital Center, Inc.,* 236 S.E.2d 213 (W. Va. 1977), suffered an amputation that the jury determined resulted from the failure of the nursing staff to properly report the patient's deteriorating condition. The nursing staff, according to written procedures in the nursing manual, was responsible for reporting such changes. It was determined that deviation from hospital policy constituted negligence. In *Goff v. Doctors General Hospital,* 166 Cal. App. 2d 314, 333 P.2d 29 (1958), the court held that nurses who knew that a woman they were attending was bleeding excessively were negligent in failing to report the circumstances so that prompt and adequate measures could be taken to safeguard her life.

In *Citizens Hospital Association v. Schoulin,* 48 Ala. 101, 262 So.2d 303 (1972), an accident victim sued the hospital and the attending physician for their negligence in failing to discover and properly treat his injuries. The court held that there was sufficient evidence to sustain a jury verdict that the hospital's nurse was negligent in failing to inform the doctor of all the patient's symptoms, in failing to conduct a proper examination of the plaintiff, and in failing to follow the directions of the physician. Thus, as the nurse was the employee of the hospital, the hospital was liable under the doctrine of *respondeat superior.*

On appeal by the hospital and the nurse, the Supreme Court of Kansas in *Hiatt v. Grace,* 215 Kan. 14, 523 P.2d 320 (1974), held that there was sufficient evidence to authorize the jury to find that the nurse was negligent in failing to notify the physician timely that delivery of the plaintiff's child was imminent. This delay resulted in an unattended childbirth with consequent injuries. The plaintiff had been awarded $15,000 by the trial court.

FAILURE TO REPORT DEFECTIVE EQUIPMENT

Failure to report defective equipment can cause a nurse to be held liable for negligence if the failure to report is the proximate cause of a patient's injuries. The defect must be known and not hidden from sight.

FAILURE TO TAKE CORRECT TELEPHONE ORDERS

Failure to take correct telephone orders can be just as serious as failure to follow, understand, and/or interpret correctly a physician's orders. Telephone orders are necessary because of the nature of a physician's practice. Nurses must be alert in transcribing orders because there are periodic contradictions between what physicians claim they ordered and what nurses allege they ordered. Orders should be repeated, once transcribed, for verification purposes. Verification of an order by another nurse on a second telephone is helpful, especially if an order is questionable. Any questionable orders must always be verified with the physician initiating the order. Physicians must countersign all orders—this should be a firm rule of the hospital. Nurses who disagree with a physician's order should not carry out an obviously erroneous order. In addition, they should confirm the order with the prescribing physician and report to the supervisor any difficulty in resolving a difference of opinion with the physician.

NURSERY

Switching of Infants

The inadvertent or negligent switching of babies born at the same time can lead to liability for damages. Damages in the amount of $110,000 were awarded for the inadvertent switching of two babies born at the same time in *De Leon Lopez v. Corporacion Insular de Seguros,* 931 F.2d 116 (C.A. 1, 1991).

PATIENT FALLS

Patients are highly susceptible to falling and the consequences of falling are generally more serious with older age groups. Among senior citizens, falls represent the fifth leading cause of death, and the mortality rate from falls increases significantly with age. For those aged 75 years and older, the mortality rate from falls is five times higher than for those in the 65- to 74-year age group, and the rate increases so that persons older than 80 years have eight times the chance of experiencing a fatal fall.[19]

Bedside Rails

The plaintiff in *Polonsky v. Union Hospital,* 418 N.E.2d 620 (Mass. App. 1981), suffered a fall and fractured her hip after the administration of a sleeping medication, commonly known by the trade name Dalmane. The superior court awarded damages in the amount of the statutory limit of $20,000, and the hospital appealed. The appeals court held that from the Dalmane warning provided by the drug manufacturer and the hospital's own regulation regarding bedside rails, without additional medical testimony, the jury could draw an inference that the hospital's nurse had failed to exercise due care when she failed to raise the bed rails after administering Dalmane.

The fall of a patient is not always attributable to negligence. The Court of Appeals of New York held that the evidence in *Stoker v. Tarentino,* 478 N.E.2d 184 (N.Y. 1985), did not support discipline of a nurse on a charge that a wheelchair resident was improperly left alone in the bathroom. The negligence charge against the petitioner was predicated on a wheelchair resident having been left alone in the bathroom after the petitioner assisted another nurse in moving the resident from the bed to the wheelchair to the bathroom. All the nurses who testified agreed that there was no order, written or verbal, requiring the nurse to remain with the resident while she was in the bathroom. Policies and procedures of the nursing facility and the health department contained no instructions concerning toilet procedures with respect to wheelchair residents. The court held that disciplinary action against the nurse should be annulled and expunged from the petitioner's personnel file.

Examination Tables

A judgment for the plaintiff was affirmed in *Petry v. Nassau Hospital,* 267 A.D. 996, 48 N.Y.S.2d 227 (1944), which was an action to recover damages for personal injuries suffered by the plaintiff's wife. The patient had been placed on a narrow examination table in the emergency department of the defendant hospital and fell from the table. The table had no sides, and the patient had been left unattended by the nurse in charge.

Suicidal Patients

A hospital and its staff have a duty to exercise reasonable care to protect suicidal patients against foreseeable harm to themselves. This duty exists whether the patient is voluntarily admitted or involuntarily committed. In *Abille v. United States,* 482 F. Supp. 703 (N.D. Cal. 1980), the district court held that evidence supported a finding that the attending physician had not authorized a change in status of a patient who had been admitted to a U.S. Air Force hospital in Alaska and diagnosed as being suicidal to permit him to leave the ward without an escort. The nursing staff allowed him to leave the ward, and he found a window from which he jumped. This constituted a breach of the standard of due care under Alaska law, where the act or omission occurred.

SPONGE AND/OR INSTRUMENT MISCOUNTS IN THE OPERATING ROOM

There is a plethora of cases involving foreign objects left in patients during surgery. The hospital in *Ross v. Chatham County Hospital Authority,* 367 S.E.2d 793 (Ga. 1988), was properly denied summary dismissal of an action in which a patient sought to recover damages for injuries suffered when a surgical instrument was left in the patient's abdomen during surgery. This incident occurred as a result of the failure of the operating room personnel to conduct an instrument and sponge count after surgery. The borrowed servant doctrine did not insulate the hospital from the negligence of its nurses because the doctrine only applies to acts involving professional skill and judgment. Foreign objects negligently left in a patient's body constitute an administrative act. A standard nursing checkoff procedure should be used to account for all sponges and/or instruments used in the operating room. Preventative measures of this nature will reduce a hospital's risk of liability.

NOTES

1. M.T. MacEachern, Hospital Organization and Management 17 (1962).

2. Byrnes, *Non-Nursing Functions: The Nurses State Their Case*, 82 Am. J. Nursing 1089 (1982).

3. C. Howse, *Registration: A Minor Victory*, Nursing Times, 85(49), Dec. 6, 1989, at 32.

4. D.J. Mason & S.W. Talbott, Political Action Handbook for Nurses 11–12 (1985).

5. Fraijo v. Hartland Hosp., 160 Cal. Rptr. 252 (1979).

6. N.Y. Nursing Laws §6902 (McKinney 1991).

7. Department of Health, Education and Welfare, Extending the Scope of Nursing Practice: A Report of the Secretary's Committee To Study Extended Roles for Nurses 8, Pub. No. (HSM) 73-2037 (1971).

8. Mason & Talbott, *supra* note 4.

9. American Nurses' Association, Guidelines for Short Term Continuing Education Programs Preparing the Geriatric Nurse Practitioner (1974).

10. *Enrollment in Nursing Schools Up 14% in 1990*, A.H.A. News, 27(1), Jan. 7, 1991, at 3.

11. E. Spalding, Professional Nursing: Trends/Responsibilities/Relationships 351 (1959).

12. American Nurses' Association, Standards of Nursing Practice 2–5 (1973).

13. Spalding, *supra* note 11, at 363.

14. *Id.* at 371.

15. American Nurses' Association, 1990 Certification Catalog (1990).

16. 42 C.F.R. §483.40 (1989).

17. *Id.* at 365.

18. D. Weiland, et. al., *Organizing an Academic Nursing Home, Impacts on Institutionalized Elderly*, 255 J. Am. Med. A. 2622–2627 (1986).

19. B. Hill & R. Johnson, *Reducing the Incidence of Falls in High Risk Patients*, 18 J. Nursing Admin. 24 (1988).

Chapter **8**

Liability of Health Professionals and Related Topics

OUTLINE

Assumption of a Risk by the Patient

Expert Testimony

• Respiratory Therapist

Failure To Report

Improper Procedure

• Security Guard

• X-Ray Technician

• Sexual Improprieties

Dentist

Nurse

Psychologist

Physician

• Certification of Health Professionals

• Licensing of Health Professionals

• Helpful Advice to All Health Professionals

There is a vast array of caregivers who provide different health services to patients. The combined services of physicians, nurses, social workers, physical therapists, physician assistants, nutritionists, activity therapists, etc., are all necessary and equally important in meeting the needs of patients.

All health professionals are liable for harm that results from their negligent acts. Each professional is held to the standard of care expected of others practicing in the same profession.

This chapter describes several relevant cases regarding the risks for selected health professions. Many of the cases presented in this chapter could have been discussed under one or more topics. However, they were placed here to illustrate that no health professional is exempt from the long arm of the legal system.

Cases presented in this chapter are by no means exhaustive for a specific profession. All professionals can learn from the experiences of others.

CHIROPRACTOR

Standard of Care Required

A chiropractor is required to exercise the same degree of care, judgment, and skill exercised by other reasonable chiropractors under like or similar circumstances. He or she has a duty to determine whether a patient is treatable through chiropractic means and to refrain from chiropractic treatment when a reasonable chiropractor would be or should be aware that a patient's condition will not respond to chiropractic treatment. Failure to conform to the standard of care can result in liability for any injuries suffered. *Kerkman v. Hintz*, 418 N.W.2d 795 (Wis. 1988).

Inflating Insurance Claims

The Court of Appeals of North Carolina held that a chiropractor's license was properly suspended for six months in *Farlow v. North Carolina State Board of Chiropractic Examiners*, 332 S.E.2d 696 (N.C. Ct. App. 1985), for inflating the insurance claims of victims of an automobile accident. Dr. Farlow had prescribed a course of treatment for several patients that was not justified by the injuries they had received. The treatment had been prescribed to inflate insurance claims.

Deceptive Advertising

A chiropractor's license was suspended in *Langlitz v. Board of Registration of Chiropractors*, 486 N.E.2d 48 (Mass. 1985), for deceptive advertising in the Yellow Pages of a telephone directory. The Board of Registration of Chiropractors determined that the chiropractor had advertised treatment that was beyond his scope of expertise and the statutory definition of "chiropractic" in that it included the offering of therapeutic nutrition, acupuncture, weight control, etc.

DENTAL ASSISTANT

The plaintiff in *Hickman v. Sexton Dental Clinic*, 367 S.E.2d 453 (S.C. 1988), brought a malpractice action against a dental clinic for a serious cut under her tongue. The dental assistant, without being supervised by a dentist, rammed a sharp object into the patient's mouth, cutting her tongue while taking impressions for dentures. The court of common pleas entered a judgment on a jury verdict in favor of the plaintiff, and the clinic appealed. The court of appeals held that the evidence presented was sufficient to infer without the aid of expert testimony that there was a breach of duty to the patient. The testimony of Dr. Tepper, the clinic dentist, was found pertinent to the issue of the common knowledge exception in which the evidence permits the jury to recognize breach of duty without the aid of expert testimony. Dr. Tepper testified regarding denture impressions:

Q. You also stated that you have taken I believe thousands?
A. Probably more than that.
Q. Of impressions?
A. Yes, sir.
Q. This never happened before?
A. No, sir, not a laceration.
Q. Would it be safe and accurate to say that if someone's mouth were to be cut during the impression process, someone did something wrong?
A. Yes, sir.

Id. at 455–456.

DENTIST

As with all health professionals, a dentist is held to the prevailing standard of care required in his or her profession, which includes proper examination, diagnosis, treatment, and follow-up care.

Anesthesia

The supreme court in *Everett v. State,* 99 Wash.2d 264, 661 P.2d 588 (1983), held that despite a license to practice dentistry and considerable expertise in the field of anesthesiology, the licensee's dental license did not authorize the administration of anesthesia for nondental purposes under the then-existing law. Dr. Everett had served a 33-month general anesthesia residency program administered through the Washington University Medical School. After his residency, Dr. Everett had been appointed an assistant professor in the Department of Anesthesiology at the Washington University Medical School. In his capacity as assistant professor and later as associate professor, Dr. Everett had taught general anesthesiology to both medical and dental students and had administered all types of anesthesia to both dental and nondental patients.

Unauthorized Treatment

Unauthorized treatment can result in successful suits. The plaintiff in *Gaskin v. Goldwasser,* 520 N.E.2d 1085 (Ill. App. Ct. 1988), brought a suit against an oral surgeon, alleging dental malpractice. The oral surgeon had removed 19 of the teeth remaining in the plaintiff's mouth. The defendant admitted that five of the 19 teeth were removed without the consent of the patient. The circuit court entered a judgment for the plaintiff on a jury verdict for damages resulting from the extraction of the five lower teeth. Count VI, willful and wanton misconduct, was dismissed. On appeal, the appellate court held that the patient was entitled to have the allegation of willful and wanton misconduct and battery for unauthorized removal of the five lower teeth submitted to the jury. The case was remanded for a new trial.

LABORATORY TECHNICIAN

A hospital must provide for clinical laboratory services to meet the needs of its patients. The hospital is responsible for the quality and timeliness of the services provided. Because it is often necessary to contract out certain tests, the hospital should make sure that it is contracting for services with a reputable licensed laboratory.

Mismatched Blood

A laboratory technician in *Barnes Hospital v. Missouri Commission on Human Rights,* 661 S.W.2d 534 (Mo. 1983), had been discharged because of inferior work performance. On three occasions, the employee allegedly had mismatched blood. The employee filed a complaint with the Commission on Human Rights, alleging racial discrimination as a reason for his discharge by the hospital. The hospital appealed, and the circuit court reversed the commission's order. The technician appealed to the Supreme Court of Missouri, which held that the evidence did not support the ruling of racial discrimination by the Missouri Commission on Human Rights.

Refusal To Work with Certain Blood Specimens

A laboratory technician was found to have been properly dismissed from her job for refusing to perform chemical examinations on vials with AIDS warnings attached in *Stepp v. Review Board of the Indiana Employment Security Division,* 521 N.E.2d 350 (Ind. Ct. App. 1988). The court of appeals held that the employee was dismissed for just cause and that the laboratory did not waive its right to compel employees to perform assigned tasks.

NURSE'S AIDE

Inappropriate Behavior

A nurse's aide was terminated for inappropriate behavior in the hospital dining room in *Eli v. Griggs County Hospital and Nursing Home,* 385 N.W.2d 99 (N.D. 1986). In the presence of patients and visitors, she cursed her supervisor and complained that personnel were working short-staffed. Given the nature of her employment and the high standard of care that persons reasonably expected from a nursing care facility, such behavior justified her termination on a charge of reported breach of patient-specific and facility-specific information. No defamation resulted from the entry of such charges in the aide's personnel file because the record established that the charges were true.

Patient Neglect

The record in *Jones v. Axelrod,* 519 N.Y.S.2d 738 (App. Div. 1987), indicated that a nurse's aide, while transferring a "total care" nursing home patient to her bed from a wheelchair, left the patient sitting on the edge of the bed. The patient subsequently fell to the floor. The aide acknowledged that the patient required restraints. The supervisor testified that the act of leaving the patient unrestrained and unattended on the edge of the bed was improper and inconsistent with safe procedure. Sufficient evidence supported a determination by the commissioner of health that the conduct of the nurse's aide constituted patient neglect.

OPTOMETRIST

Optometrists brought an action challenging a medical assistance plan that reimbursed ophthalmologists, but not optometrists, for eye care services. The Supreme Court of Louisiana held in *Sandefur v. Cherry,* 455 So.2d 1350 (La. 1984), that state officials could not discriminate between optometrists and ophthalmologists in reimbursement for Medicaid patients. Louisiana statutes prohibited limiting or restricting the freedom of patients in choosing a particular health professional for care.

PARAMEDIC

Many states have enacted legislation that provides civil immunity to paramedics who render emergency lifesaving services. The plaintiff in *Malone v.*

City of Seattle, 600 P.2d 647 (Wash. Ct. App. 1979), alleged the defendant was negligent in providing care to the plaintiff after an automobile accident. The plaintiff, on appeal, contended that the trial court wrongfully instructed the jury regarding a 1971 civil immunity statute. The following is an excerpt from the relevant Washington statute:

> No act or omission of any physician's trained mobile intensive care paramedic . . . done or omitted in good faith while rendering emergency lifesaving service . . . to a person who is in immediate danger of loss of life shall impose any liability upon the trained mobile intensive care paramedic . . . or upon a . . . city or other local governmental unit. . . .

1971 Wash. Laws §1783.

One of the issues raised was whether the legislature intended the 1971 statute to apply only to the rendition of cardiopulmonary emergency treatment by a paramedic. The court of appeals indicated that although the definition contained in the statute places special emphasis on the paramedic's training in all aspects of cardiopulmonary resuscitation, the act does not limit the paramedic to cardiopulmonary resuscitation. The act implicitly recognizes that paramedics may encounter different emergencies.

The Supreme Court of Pennsylvania in *Morena v. South Hills Health Systems,* 462 A.2d 680 (Pa. 1983), held that paramedics were not negligent in transporting a victim of a shooting to the nearest available hospital, rather than to another hospital located five or six miles farther away where a thoracic surgeon was present. The paramedics were not capable, in a medical sense, of accurately diagnosing the extent of the decedent's injury. Except for the children's center and the burn center, there were no emergency trauma centers specifically designated for the treatment of particular injuries.

PHARMACIST

A pharmacist can be subject to liability for the mishandling or misuse of drugs. Failure to meet and maintain required standards in the handling of drugs can lead to criminal or civil liability and even to the revocation of a pharmacist's license.

Medicaid Fraud

The court of appeals in the *State v. Beatty,* 308 S.E.2d 65 (N.C. Ct. App. 1983), upheld a lower court's finding that the evidence submitted against the defendant pharmacist was sufficient to sustain a conviction for Medicaid fraud. The state was billed for medications that were never dispensed, was billed for more medications than some patients received, and in some instances, was billed for the more expensive trade name drugs when cheaper generic drugs were dispensed.

The pharmacists in *People v. Kendzia,* 103 A.D.2d 999, 478 N.Y.S.2d 209 (1984), were convicted of mishandling drugs, and they appealed. The supreme court, appellate division, held that the evidence supported a finding that the pharmacists sold generic drugs in vials with brand name labels and was sufficient to support a conviction. Investigators, working undercover, were provided with Medicaid cards and fictitious prescriptions requiring brand name drugs to be dispensed as written. Between April and October 1979, the investigators had taken the prescriptions to the pharmacy where they were filled with generic substitutions in vials with the brand name labels.

Revocation of License

The supreme court, appellate division, held in *Heller v. Amback,* 78 A.D.2d 951, 433 N.Y.S.2d 281 (1980), that violation of statutes relating to the sale of controlled substances by a pharmacist amounted to unprofessional conduct and that the revocation of the defendant's license was justified for the protection of the public.

Inaccurate Records

The operator of a pharmacy, in a disciplinary proceeding before the California Board of Pharmacy, was found negligent because of inaccurate record keeping. The pharmacist had failed to keep accurate records of dangerous drugs, report thefts by employees, and report a burglary of pharmacy drugs. Such reporting was required by state statute. *Banks v. Board of Pharmacy,* 207 Cal. Rptr. 835 (Ct. App. 1984).

PHYSICAL THERAPIST

Physical therapy is the art and science of preventing and treating neuromuscular or musculoskeletal disabilities through the evaluation of an individual's disability and rehabilitation potential; the use of physical agents: heat, cold, electricity, water, and light; and neuromuscular procedures that, through their physiologic effect, improve or maintain the patient's optimum functional level.

Because of different physical disabilities brought on by various injuries and medical problems, physical therapy is an extremely important component of a patient's total health care.

Contracted Services

The physical therapist in *Armintor v. Community Hospital of Brazosport,* 659 S.W.2d 86 (Tex. Civ. App. 1983), was properly enjoined from entering the hospital's premises after termination of an oral contract to furnish services to hospital patients in need of physical therapy. Substantial evidence supported the court's finding that the hospital's attempt to establish a hospital-based physical therapy program would have been disrupted if the independent therapist had been permitted to continue treating patients. The court considered the exclusion of a therapist an administrative matter within the board's discretion. The therapist's entering the hospital without the permission of a staff physician would constitute trespass and would be in violation of hospital policy.

Neglect

A disciplinary proceeding was brought against a licensed physical therapist employed by a nursing facility for resident neglect. The therapist brought an Article 78 proceeding for judicial review. The proceeding was transferred to the appellate division by order of the supreme court, in *Zucker v. Axelrod,* 527 N.Y.S.2d 937 (App. Div. 1988). The physical therapist in this case had been charged with resident neglect for refusing to allow an 82-year-old nursing facility resident to go to the bathroom before starting his therapy treatment session. Undisputed evidence at a hearing showed that the petitioner refused to allow the resident to be excused to go to the bathroom. The petitioner claimed that her refusal was because she assumed that the resident had gone to the bathroom before going to therapy and that the resident was undergoing a bladder training program. The petitioner had not mentioned when she was interviewed after the incident or during her hearing testimony that she considered bladder training a basis for refusing to allow the resident to go to the bathroom. It is uncontroverted that the nursing facility had a policy of allowing residents to go to the bathroom whenever they wished to do so. The court held that the finding of resident neglect was supported sufficiently by the evidence.

PHYSICIAN'S ASSISTANT

One of the solutions to the shortage of physicians in certain rural and inner-city areas has been to train allied health professionals such as physician's assistants to perform the more routine and repetitive medical functions. A physician may delegate to a physician's assistant such tasks as suturing minor wounds, administering injections, and performing routine history and physical examinations. A physician may not delegate a task when regulations specify that the physician must perform it personally or when the delegation is prohibited under state law or by the facility's own policies.

Physician's assistants are responsible for their own negligent acts. If a physician's assistant is a hospital employee, the hospital can be held liable for the physician's assistant's negligent acts on the basis of *respondeat superior*. A physician, as an employer of a physician's assistant, also can be held liable on the basis of *respondeat superior*.

To limit the potential risk of liability to a physician's assistant, the physician should monitor and supervise the assistant's work closely. Guidelines and procedures also should be established to provide a standard mechanism for reviewing an assistant's performance.

In *Washington State Nurses Association v. Board of Medical Examiners,* 605 P.2d 1269 (Wash. 1980), the nurses' association brought an action challenging a regulation that authorized physician's assistants to issue prescriptions for medication and write medical orders for patient care. The superior court enjoined the board from effectuating the regulation, and the board appealed. The supreme court held that the regulation did not exceed the statutory authority of the board because statutes and regulations placed physician's assistants in the position of agent for their supervising physician, rather than of independent contractor, and thus nurses would not be exposed to statutory liability for executing prescriptions issued by physician's assistants.

PODIATRIST

Negligent Surgery

The podiatrist in *Strauss v. Biggs,* 525 A.2d 992 (Del. 1987), was found to have failed to meet the standard of care required of a podiatrist, and that failure resulted in injury to the patient. The podiatrist, by his own admission, stated that his initial incision in the patient's foot had been misplaced. The trial court was found not to have erred in permitting the jury to consider additional claims that the podiatrist had acted improperly by failing to refer the patient, stop the procedure after the first incision, inform the patient of possible nerve injury, and provide proper postoperative treatment. Testimony of the patient's experts was adequate to show that such alleged omissions had violated the standard of care.

Assumption of a Risk by the Patient

The patient in *Faile v. Bycura,* 346 S.E.2d 528 (S.C. 1986), was awarded $75,000 in damages by a jury on her allegations that a podiatrist had used inappropriate techniques during an unsuccessful attempt to treat her heel spurs. On appeal, it was held that the trial court erred in striking the podiatrist's defense of assumption of the risk. Evidence established that the patient had signed consent forms that indicated the risks of treatment as well as alternative treatment modalities.

Expert Testimony

A podiatrist in *Bethea v. Smith,* 336 S.E.2d 295 (Ga. Ct. App. 1985), was shown not competent to testify as to the standard of care required of an orthopedic surgeon in the treatment of an ankle fracture. Experts testifying regarding the defendant's specialty generally must have appropriate qualifications in the same specialty as the defendant does.

RESPIRATORY THERAPIST

Failure To Report

The court in *Poor Sisters of St. Francis v. Catron,* 435 N.E.2d 305 (Ind. Ct. App. 1982), held that the failure of nurses and an inhalation therapist to report to the supervisor that an endotracheal tube had been left in the plaintiff longer than the customary period of three or four days was sufficient to allow the jury to reach a finding of negligence. The patient experienced difficulty speaking and underwent several operations to remove scar tissue and open her voice box. At the time of trial, she could not speak above a whisper and breathed partially through a hole in her throat created by a tracheotomy. The hospital was found liable for the negligent acts of its employees and the resulting injuries to the plaintiff.

Improper Procedure

The respiratory therapist in *State University v. Young,* 566 N.Y.S.2d 79 (App. Div. 1991), was suspended for using the same syringe for drawing blood from a number of critically ill patients. The therapist had been warned several times of the dangers of that practice and that it violated the state's policy of providing high-quality care.

SECURITY GUARD

Celestine v. United States, 841 F.2d 851 (8th Cir. 1988), involved an individual who sought inpatient psychiatric care at a Veterans Administration (VA) hospital and became physically violent while waiting to be seen by a physician. The VA security guards were found to be justified in placing the individual in restraints and observing him for a short time until he could be examined by a psychiatrist. Under Missouri law, no false imprisonment or battery occurred in view of the common-law principle that a person believed to be mentally ill could be lawfully restrained if such was considered necessary to prevent immediate injury to that person or others.

X-RAY TECHNICIAN

The hospital is responsible for the quality and timeliness of radiology services. Services must meet applicable regulatory standards.

The x-ray technician in *Hayes v. Shelby Memorial Hospital,* 726 F.2d 1543 (11th Cir. 1984), brought an employment discrimination action against the hospital. The technician was fired by the hospital when it learned that she was pregnant. The U.S. District Court for the Northern District of Alabama found that the hospital had violated the Pregnancy Discrimination Act. On appeal by the hospital, the U.S. Court of Appeals, in affirming the lower court's decision, held that the hospital failed to consider less discriminatory alternatives to firing the technician.

The chief x-ray technician in *Paros v. Hoemako Hospital,* 681 P.2d 918 (Ariz. Ct. App. 1984), was dismissed because of a chronic argumentative and hostile attitude inconsistent with the performance of supervisory duties. The superior court entered a summary judgment in favor of the hospital and the administrator. On appeal, the appeals court held that the discharge was properly based on good cause and precluded recovery for breach of contract and wrongful discharge.

SEXUAL IMPROPRIETIES

A significant number of cases address health professionals who have been involved in sexual relationships with their patients. Such cases are being litigated, in many instances, in both civil and criminal arenas. Health professionals finding themselves in such unprofessional relationships must seek help for themselves as well as refer their patients to other appropriate professionals. Besides being subject to civil and criminal litigation, health professionals also are subject to having their licenses revoked.

Dentist

Revocation of a dentist's license on charges of professional misconduct was properly ordered in *Melone v. State Education Department,* 495 N.Y.S.2d 808 (App. Div. 1985), on the basis of substantial evidence that while acting in a professional capacity, the dentist had engaged in physical and sexual contact with five different male patients within a three-year period. Considering the dentist's responsible position, the extended time period during which the sexual contacts occurred, the young and impressionable nature of the victims (7 to 15 years of age), and the possibility of lasting effects on the victims, the penalty was not shocking to the court's sense of fairness.

Nurse

A nurse's sexual relations with a patient can give rise to disciplinary action resulting in the nurse's loss of license. In *Heineche v. Department of Commerce,* 810 P.2d 459 (Utah App. 1991), a male nurse lost his license after having a sexual relationship with a patient, even though she was no longer a patient at the hospital where he had met her and had the sexual relationship. The fact that the nurse resigned from the hospital and was living with the patient was not a defense sufficient to support such behavior.

Psychologist

A defense that sexual improprieties with clients did not take place during treatment sessions generally will not be upheld by the courts. The license of a psychologist was revoked by the Board of Psychologist Examiners in *Gilmore v. Board of Psychologist Examiners,* 725 P.2d 400 (Or. Ct. App. 1986), for sexual improprieties with clients. The psychologist petitioned for judicial review. She argued that therapy had terminated before the sexual relationships began. The court of appeals held that evidence supported the board's conclusion that the psychologist had violated an ethical standard in caring for her patients. When a psychologist's personal interests intrude into the practitioner–client relationship, the practitioner is obliged to re-create objectivity through a third party. The board's findings and conclusions indicated that the petitioner failed to maintain that objectivity.

Physician

A hospital technologist in *Copithorne v. Framingham Union Hospital,* 520 N.E.2d 139 (Mass. 1988), alleged that she had been raped by a staff physician during the course of a house call. The technologist's claim against the hospital had been summarily dismissed for lack of proximate causation. On appeal, the dismissal was found to be improper when the record indicated that the hospital had received notice of allegations that the physician had assaulted patients on and off the hospital's premises. The hospital had instructed the physician to have another individual present when visiting female patients and had instructed nurses "to keep an eye on him." The physician's sexual assault was foreseeable. There was evidentiary support for the proposition that failure to withdraw the physician's privileges had caused the rape when the technologist asserted that it was the physician's good reputation in the hospital that had led her to seek his services.

The physician in *Goomar v. Ambach,* 523 N.Y.S.2d 238 (App. Div. 1988), had his license revoked for professional misconduct and the fraudulent and incompetent practice of medicine. The decision was supported by evidence when four female patients testified as to the sexual improprieties of the physician. The surgeon in *Haley v. State Department of Health, Medicine Disciplinary Board,* 818 P.2d 1062 (Wash. 1991), was found guilty of unprofessional conduct for having a sexual relationship with a patient.

The sexual relationship a psychiatrist had with the spouse of a patient was found to be improper in *Richard v. Larry,* 243 Cal. Rptr. 807 (Ct. App. 1988). California Civil Code 43.5, abolishing causes of action for alienation of affection, criminal conversation, and seduction of a patient over the age of consent, did not bar damages for emotional distress caused by the alleged professional negligence of the psychiatrist who had sexual relations with the plaintiff's wife. The psychiatrist owed a special duty to use due care for his patient's health. The statute was not intended to lower the standard of care that psychiatrists owed their patients. Besides an action against the psychiatrist, allegations that the psychiatrist was an agent of the hospital stated a cause of action against the hospital.

CERTIFICATION OF HEALTH PROFESSIONALS

The certification of health professionals is the recognition by a governmental or professional association that an individual's expertise meets the stand-ards of that group. The standards established by professional associations generally exceed those required by government agencies. Some professional groups establish their own minimum standards for certification in those professions that are not licensed by a particular state. Certification by an association or group is a self-regulation credentialing process.

LICENSING OF HEALTH PROFESSIONALS

Licensure can be defined as the process by which some competent authority grants permission to a qualified individual or entity to perform certain specified activities that would be illegal without a license. As it applies to health personnel, licensure refers to the process by which licensing boards, agencies, or departments of the several states grant to individuals who meet certain predetermined standards the legal right to practice in a health profession and to use a specified health practitioner's title.

The commonly stated objectives of licensing laws are to limit and control admission to the different health occupations and to protect the public from unqualified practitioners by promulgating and enforcing standards of practice within the professions.

The authority of states to license health care practitioners is found in their regulating power. Implicit in the power to license is the authority to collect license fees, establish standards of practice, require certain minimum qualifications and competency levels of applicants, and impose on applicants other requirements necessary to protect the general public welfare. This authority, which is vested in the legislature, may be delegated to political subdivisions or to state boards, agencies, and departments. In some instances, the scope of the delegated power is made specific in the legislation; in others, the licensing authority may have wide discretion in performing its functions. In either case, however, the authority granted by the legislature may not be exceeded.

HELPFUL ADVICE TO ALL HEALTH PROFESSIONALS

- Do not criticize the professional skill of another publicly. Use appropriate, available reporting mechanisms when the skill of another is to be challenged
- Maintain complete and adequate medical records
- Provide each patient with good medical care comparable with national standards
- Seek the aid of consultants when indicated
- Obtain consent for diagnostic and therapeutic procedures
- Do not be afraid or too proud to ask questions
- Do not prescribe medications, blood, diagnostic tests, treatments, etc., indiscriminately
- Inform the patient, relatives, or parents of surgical procedures and the complications that may arise

- Practice in the fields in which you have been trained
- Participate in continuing education programs
- Maintain all confidential communication without violation
- Report equipment failures promptly. All patient equipment should be checked frequently for safety
- In terminating a physician–patient relationship, give adequate written notice to the patient. It is preferable to send a notice by registered mail return receipt
- Confirm all telephone prescriptions in writing
- Obtain a qualified substitute when you will be absent from your practice
- Do not be rigid or impersonal. Develop a relationship with the patient in which, for example, the patient begins to say, "That's my nurse," or "That's my doctor." Likewise, the nurse or doctor should say, "That's my patient"
- Be confident and professional in the presence of patients. A professional who is not self-confident and constantly complains about coworkers, physicians, and the institution will only serve to make patients more insecure and suit prone
- Investigate patient incidents promptly
- Maintain incident reports separately from patients' records. Incident reports prepared by a health professional, placed in a patient's record, and given to the administration are not protected by attorney–client privilege. If incident reports are prepared only for the attorney to provide legal services, they could be regarded as privileged communications
- Be a good listener and allow each patient sufficient time to express fears and anxieties
- Above all—be compassionate and understanding to each patient and one another as individuals

Hospital Departments

OUTLINE

This chapter presents a review of selected departments that provide either professional or institutional support services. Although it describes several health law cases, there is no intensive review of any specific department.

DIETARY

Health care facilities must provide each patient with a nourishing, palatable, well-balanced diet that meets the daily nutritional and special dietary needs of each patient. The dietitian has general responsibility for this function. Failure to do so can lead to negligence suits. The daughter of the deceased in *Lambert v. Beverly Enterprises, Inc.,* 753 F. Supp. 267 (W.D. Ark. 1990), filed an action claiming that her father had been mistreated. The notice of intent to sue indicated that the deceased "suffered various injuries and from malnutrition as a direct result of the acts or omissions of personnel" and that the plaintiff's father "suffered actual damages which included substantial medical expenses and mental anguish due to the injuries he sustained." *Id.* at 268. A motion to dismiss the case was denied.

ENGINEERING

The engineering department, among other duties, is responsible for the provision of heat, electricity, refrigeration, and maintenance of the institution's equipment and physical plant. The duties of the department often vary from one institution to the next—depending on the size of a particular institution.

Waste Disposal

One of the main responsibilities of the engineering department is to oversee the handling and disposal of the institution's waste products. The wash-up of medical wastes on East Coast beaches placed the seriousness of waste disposal in the public spotlight. Judges, lawyers, and regulators are continuing to grapple with the problem. There are an "estimated 20,000 hazardous-waste dump sites in the country, with ever-widening chemical contamination, and . . . no end in sight of the constant parade of state and federal rules in this area. . . ."[1] The fear of AIDS has only served to exacerbate the problem and has led to costly legislation and government scrutiny.

The regulation and cleanup of hazardous waste, along with tort liability arising from exposure to toxic substances, are major environmental problems facing the health care industry. Pollution issues have generated costly legislative and regulatory responses on the federal level [e.g., by the Environmental Protection Agency (EPA), the Occupational Safety and Health Administration (OSHA), and the Centers for Disease Control (CDC)] and on the state and local levels, and they have resulted in many lawsuits nationwide in the areas of enforcement, toxic torts, and products liability. Health care facilities—through their representative councils and their state and national associations—and physicians—through their medical societies and associations—should become more involved in the regulatory process to identify what wastes should be regulated and the methods most appropriate for their disposal.

The federal "Medical Waste Tracking Act" passed in late 1988 established a pilot program to be administered by EPA for tracking medical waste in three states—New York, New Jersey and Connecticut—and made the program optional for other states. The federal legislation and the increasing state regulation are multiplying restrictions on generators of wastes, haulers and landfills and causing confusion as to which of the regulators is the final authority.[2]

EPA reporting requirements are mandated by title III of the Superfund Amendment and Reauthorization Act of 1986 (SARA), which imposes significant penalties for noncompliance.

> Hospitals in North Carolina are being forced to change the way they dispose of waste under the state's new waste-disposal regulations. On Nov. 21 [1989], the state began regulating a new category of waste, called "mixed waste," which is both hazardous and radioactive. . . . The new rules will necessitate finding larger storage facilities to hold the additional waste until the radioactivity decays and then securing contracts to have it hauled away. . . . Just obtaining the permits to transport, store and dispose of mixed waste could easily cost $250,000.[3]

OSHA, under new standards, requires the labeling of containers of regulated wastes and the identifying of restricted areas containing hazardous wastes.[4]

Refuse generated by health care facilities can be divided into five separate categories:

- infectious
- biohazardous
- hazardous
- radioactive
- general (solid) waste

Each category poses its own particular problems—with no easy solutions available for any or all forms of waste.[5] However, potential polluters must keep in mind that "existing fines are stiff. One Minnesota hospital recently paid a $35,000 fine for improper incineration, and violators in states implementing the tracking systems face fines of up to $25,000 per day for each violation and criminal penalties of up to $50,000 a day per violation."[6]

Compliance

Health care facilities and physicians must be aware of what regulations apply to them. Health care facilities should develop a plan of action and organize an effective program by working through an appropriate committee, such as the safety committee, to review the needs of both the institution and the physicians. Membership should include the facility's director of environmental services and representation from finance, administration, medical staff, housekeeping, nursing (infection control nurse), and engineering. The committee should

- identify infectious wastes (e.g., cultures, blood and blood by-products, needles, and pathological wastes)
- review and develop appropriate protocols for disposal of wastes
- review the various methods of disposal (e.g., carting, incineration, recycling) from a cost point of view
- review recycling options (disposal methods vary depending on the kind of waste)
- identify waste-handling costs when purchasing
- develop employee safety programs to determine what handling, storage, and disposal procedures should be implemented for both employee and patient safety
- develop a monitoring system to assure that the different classifications of wastes are disposed of properly and that the hospital complies with the ever-expanding body of law regulating the disposal of medical waste

Insurance

Both health care facilities and physicians should review their insurance policies to determine if they have

- liability coverage for cleanup and disposal of hazardous wastes, environmental impairment, property damage claims, future injury claims, and demands for medical monitoring by claimants
- comprehensive general liability
- pollution exclusion clauses
- provisions covering the number of occurrences

Health care providers without such coverage should evaluate the need for its inclusion in their policies.

EMERGENCY DEPARTMENT

Emergency departments are high-risk areas that tend to be a main source of lawsuits for hospitals. A summary of claims reported by St. Paul insured hospitals (1989–1990) showed that nearly 19 percent of claims involving hospitals occur in "emergency departments." Of the 6,402 claims filed by St. Paul insured hospitals, 1,214 involved emergency departments.[7] Results of the Harvard Medical Practice Study revealed that the hospital emergency department is "a real 'hot spot' for negligence. In this study, 70 percent of adverse events in the emergency room were due to negligence. Hospital emergency rooms heavily used by patients as primary care clinics are a major source of adverse events because of poor follow-up."[8]

Both federal and state regulations as well as the standards set by the Joint Commission on Accreditation of Healthcare Organizations, may be considered by the courts as showing a duty of hospital emergency departments to provide emergency care to those who present themselves with the need for such care.

Emergency Medical Treatment and Active Labor Act

In 1986, Congress passed the Emergency Medical Treatment and Active Labor Act (EMTALA), which forbids "Medicare" participating hospitals from "dumping" patients out of emergency departments. The act provides that

> [i]n the case of a hospital that has a hospital emergency department, if any individual (whether or not eligible for benefits under this subchapter) comes to the emergency department and a request is made on the individual's behalf for examination or treatment for a medical condition, the hospital must provide for an appropriate medical screening examination within the capability of the hospital emergency department, including ancillary services routinely available to the emergency department, to determine whether or not an emergency medical condition . . . exists.[9]

Emergency Medical Condition Defined

The term *emergency medical condition* has been defined under the EMTALA as

> (A) a medical condition manifesting itself by acute symptoms of sufficient severity (including severe pain) such that the absence of immediate medical attention could reasonably be expected to result in—
>
> > (i) placing the health of the individual (or, with respect to a pregnant woman, the health of the woman or her unborn child) in serious jeopardy,
> > (ii) serious impairment to bodily functions, or
> > (iii) serious dysfunction of any bodily organ or part; or
>
> (B) with respect to a pregnant woman who is having contractions—
>
> > (i) that there is inadequate time to effect a safe transfer to another facility before delivery, or

(ii) that transfer may pose a threat to the health or safety of the woman or the unborn child.[10]

Stabilizing the Patient

Patients can be transferred only after they have been medically screened by a physician, stabilized, and cleared for transfer by the receiving institution. Stabilize "means, with respect to an emergency medical condition . . . to provide such medical treatment of the condition as may be necessary to assure, within reasonable medical probability, that no material deterioration of the condition is likely to result from or to occur during the transfer of the individual from a facility."[11] A patient should not be transferred from the emergency department to another health care facility unless

(A)(i) the individual (or a legally responsible person acting on the individual's behalf) after being informed of the hospital's obligations . . . and of the risk of transfer, in writing requests a transfer to another medical facility,

(ii) a physician . . . has signed a certification that based on the information available at the time of transfer, the medical benefits reasonably expected from the provision of appropriate medical treatment at another medical facility outweigh the increased risks to the individual and, in the case of labor, to the unborn child from effecting the transfer, or

(iii) if a physician is not physically present in the emergency department at the time an individual is transferred, a qualified medical person . . . has signed a certification . . . after a physician . . . in consultation with the person, has made the determination . . . and subsequently countersigns the certification; and

(B) the transfer is an appropriate transfer . . . to that facility.[12]

Refusal To Consent to Treatment

Patients have a right to refuse treatment. If a patient rejects treatment, he or she should be asked to sign a release. A hospital is deemed to meet the requirements of the EMTALA to provide emergency care if the hospital offers medical examination and treatment and an individual refuses to consent to examination and treatment. The hospital should take all reasonable steps to (1) inform the individual of the benefits and risks of treatment and (2) secure the individual's written informed consent to refuse examination and treatment.[13] If the individual refuses to sign such a consent, documentation of the refusal should be maintained by the hospital.

Enforcement

Failure to follow the EMTALA can result in civil penalties of up to $50,000 per occurrence (or not more than $25,000 in the case of a hospital with less than 100 beds).[14] In addition,

> Any individual who suffers personal harm as a direct result of a participating hospital's violation of a requirement . . . may, in a civil action against the participating hospital, obtain those damages available for personal injury under the law of the State in which the hospital is located, and such equitable relief as is appropriate.[15]

The EMTALA was violated in *Burditt v. U.S. Department of Health and Human Services*, 934 F.2d 1362 (C.A. 5, Tex. 1991), by a physician when he ordered a woman, with dangerously high blood pressure (210/130) and in active labor with ruptured membranes, transferred from the emergency department of one hospital to another hospital 170 miles away. The physician was assessed a penalty of $20,000. Dr. Louis Sullivan, secretary of Health and Human Services at that time, issued a statement: "This decision sends a message to physicians everywhere that they need to provide quality care to everyone in need of emergency treatment who comes to a hospital. This is a significant opinion and we are pleased with the result."[16] The American Public Health Association in filing an *amicus curie* advised the appeals court that "if Burditt wants to ensure that he will never be asked to treat a patient not of his choosing, then he ought to vote with his feet by affiliating only with hospitals that do not accept Medicare funds or do not have an emergency department."[17]

State Regulations

Legislation in many states imposes a duty on hospitals to provide emergency care. The statutes implicitly, and sometimes explicitly, require hospitals to provide some degree of emergency service.

If the public is aware that a hospital furnishes emergency services and relies on that knowledge, the hospital has a duty to provide those services to the public. Two Mexican children, burned in a fire at home, were refused admission or first aid by a local hospital. A lawsuit was filed, claiming that additional injury occurred as a result of the failure to render care. The suit was dismissed by the trial court. The Arizona Court of Appeals found the defendants liable, claiming that it was the custom of the hospital to render aid in such a case. On appeal, the Arizona Supreme Court also held the defendants liable. It reasoned that state statutes and licensing regulations mandate that a hospital may not deny a patient emergency care. *Guerrero v. Copper Queen Hospital,* 112 Ariz. 104, 537 P.2d 1329 (1975).

The New York State Emergency Medical Services Act of 1983 provides that every general hospital shall admit any person who is in need of immediate hospitalization. Any licensed medical practitioner who refuses to treat a person arriving at a general hospital for emergency medical treatment will be guilty of a misdemeanor and subject to up to one year in prison and a fine not to exceed $1,000. Emergency medical technicians, paramedics, and ambulance drivers are expected to report any refusals by general hospitals to treat emergency patients. Patients may be transferred after they have been stabilized if it is deemed by the attending physician to be in the best interest of the patient.

Case Law

The courts recognize a general duty to care for all patients presenting themselves to hospital emergency departments. Not only must hospitals accept, treat, and transfer emergency department patients if such is necessary for the patients' well-being, but they must adhere to the standards of care they have set for themselves, as well as to national standards.

Scope of Care

The objectives of emergency care are the same regardless of severity. No matter how trivial the complaint, each patient must be examined. Treatment must begin as rapidly as possible, function is to be maintained or restored, scarring and deformity are to be minimized, etc.

Every patient must be treated regardless of ability to pay.

> As the Sixth Circuit points out, there are many reasons other than indigence that might lead a hospital to give less than standard attention to a person who arrives at the emergency room. These might include: prejudice against the race, sex or ethnic group of the patient; distaste for the patient's condition (e.g., AIDS patients); personal dislike or antagonism between the medical personnel and the patient; disapproval of the patient's occupation; or political or cultural opposition. If a hospital refused treatment to persons for any of these reasons, or gave cursory treatment, the evil inflicted would be quite akin to that discussed by Congress in the legislative history, and the patient would fall squarely in the statutory language.

Cleland v. Bronson Health Care Group, 917 F.2d at 272 (6th Cir. 1990).

Emergency Department Call Rosters

Hospitals are expected to notify specialty on-call physicians when their particular skills are required in the emergency department. A physician who is on-call and fails to respond to a request to attend a patient can be liable for injuries suffered by the patient because of his or her failure to respond. In *Thomas v. Corso,* 265 Md. 84, 288 A.2d 379 (1972), a Maryland court sustained a verdict against a hospital and a physician. The patient had been brought to the hospital emergency department after he was struck by a car. He was not personally attended to by a physician although he was in shock, as indicated by dangerously low blood pressure. There was some telephone contact between the nurse in the emergency department and the physician who was providing on-call coverage. The physician failed to come to the hospital until the patient was close to death. The court reasoned that expert testimony was not even necessary to establish what common sense made evident: that a patient who had been struck by a car may have suffered internal injuries and should have been evaluated and treated by a physician. Lack of attention in such cases is not reasonable care by any standard. The concurrent negligence of the nurse, who failed to contact the on-call physician after the patient's condition had worsened, did not relieve the physician of liability for his failure to come to the emergency department at once. Rather, under the doctrine of *respondeat superior,* the nurse's negligence was a basis for holding the hospital liable as well.

Treatment rendered by hospitals is expected to be commensurate with that available in the same or similar communities or in hospitals generally. The Supreme Court of South Dakota in *Fjerstad v. Knutson,* 271 N.W.2d 8 (S.D. 1978), found that a hospital could be held liable for the failure of an on-call physician to respond to a call from the emergency department. An intern who attempted to contact the on-call physician and was unable to do so for three and one-half hours treated and discharged the patient. The hospital was responsible for assigning on-call physicians and assuring that they would be available when called. The patient died during the night in a motel room as a result of asphyxia resulting from a swelling of the larynx, tonsils, and epiglottis that blocked the trachea. Testimony from the medical director of laboratories indicated that the emergency department on-call physician was to be available for consultation and was assigned that duty by the hospital. Expert testimony also was offered that someone with the decedent's symptoms should have been hospitalized and that such care could have saved the decedent's life. The jury could have believed that an experienced physician would have taken the necessary steps to save the decedent's life.

Not only are hospitals required to care for emergency patients, but also they are to do so in a timely fashion. A Florida trial court in *Marks v. Mandel,* 477 So.2d 1036 (Fla. Dist. Ct. App. 1985), was found to have erred in directing a verdict against the plaintiff. It was decided that the relevant inquiry in this case was whether the hospital and the supervisor should bear ultimate responsibility for failure of the specialty on-call system to function properly. Jury issues had been raised by evidence that the standard for on-call systems was to have a specialist attending the patient within 30 minutes of being called.

Prevention of Lawsuits in the Emergency Department

The number of lawsuits originating in emergency departments can be reduced significantly by implementing and enforcing some very fundamental common-sense emergency department procedures and programs:

- Develop and implement appropriate emergency department policies and procedures, including

  1. the necessity to treat each patient courteously and promptly
  2. a requirement that all patients are to be treated—regardless of ability to pay
  3. established treatment priorities—emergency cases to be treated first, followed by urgent and less serious cases
  4. on-call roster procedures
  5. consultation requirements for specialists
  6. consent procedures for both adults and minors
  7. disaster procedures
  8. transfer procedures

- Communicate with the patient and the patient's family to ensure that a complete and accurate picture of the patient's symptoms and complaints are obtained
- Communicate among health professionals. This is imperative. Each professional gains a certain amount of information from a patient's history and that information must be communicated to the attending physician. Both the nurse and the physician must assume that each has certain pieces of information necessary to the proper treatment of the patient. A poor listener and a poor communicator have no place in the care of emergency department patients
- Provide for continuing education programs for all staff members
- Institute a preventative maintenance program for emergency department equipment

- Do not take lightly any patient's complaint. This may well be the single most fatal mistake of emergency departments
- Those professionals who cannot accept the concept that all patients regardless of ailment must be treated need to search for placement outside the emergency department

HEALTH CARE RECORDS

Many kinds of records are required to be maintained by health care facilities (e.g., financial, personnel, and purchasing records). The primary emphasis in this section lies with medical records—documentation of the facts of a patient's illness, symptoms, diagnosis, and treatment. Health care facilities are required to maintain a medical record for each patient in accordance with accepted professional standards and practices. Records must be complete, accurate, current, readily accessible, and systematically organized.

Medical records requirements generally are provided for in the public health laws of the different states. They generally have provisions requiring that each facility maintain a complete medical record for each patient that contains all pertinent information regarding the daily care and treatment of patients. Because medical records are the principal means of communication between health care professionals in matters relating to patient care, documentation of the facts of a patient's illness, symptoms, diagnosis, and treatment is an extremely important tool in furnishing modern health care.

The main purposes of the medical record are to provide a planning tool for patient care; to record the course of a patient's treatment and the changes in a patient's condition; to document the communications between the practitioner responsible for the patient and any other health professional who contributes to the patient's care; to assist in protecting the legal interests of the patient, the hospital, and the practitioner; to provide a data base for use in statistical reporting, continuing education, and research; and to provide information necessary for third-party billing and regulatory agencies.

The nurse is generally the one medical professional the patient sees more than any other. Consequently, the nurse is in a position to keep constant watch over the patient's illness, response to medication, display of pain and discomfort, and general condition. The patient's care, as well as the nurse's observations, should be recorded fully, factually, and promptly. The nurse should comply promptly and accurately with the orders the physician writes in the record and should check, in case of doubt, to make certain that the order is correct and that it has not been completed already.

Contents of the Medical Record

The medical record must be a complete, accurate, up-to-date report of the medical history, condition, and treatment of each patient. It is composed of at least two distinct parts, each of which is made up of several types of forms. The first part is compiled on admission and includes

- the admission record, which describes pertinent data regarding the patient's age, address, reason for admission, social security number, marital status, religion, addresses, and any other information necessary to meet both federal and state requirements
- the general consent and authorization-for-treatment forms allowing the health care facility to perform routine diagnostic testing, etc.

The second part, the clinical record, contains

- operative reports
- delivery records
- anesthesia records
- the medical history and physical examination, including provisional or working diagnosis, and plan for definitive diagnosis and/or treatment
- diagnostic and therapeutic orders, including all medications, treatments, diet, and restorative and special medical procedures required for the safety and well-being of the patient
- progress records describing significant changes in a patient's condition, written at the time of each visit
- nurse's notes containing observations made by nursing personnel
- medication and treatment record
- vital signs charts
- consultation notes and reports
- dental reports
- social service notes and reports
- occupational and activity therapy notes and reports
- physical therapy notes and reports
- dietary notes and reports
- laboratory, x-ray, and other diagnostic reports
- fluid intake and output charts
- discharge summary, etc.

Licensure rules and regulations contained in state statutes generally describe the requirements and standards for the maintenance, handling, signing, filing, and retention of medical records.

The failure of the physician or hospital to maintain a complete and accurate medical record reflecting the treatment rendered may affect the ability of the hospital and/or physician to obtain third-party reimbursement (e.g., from Medicare, Medicaid, or Blue Cross). Under federal and state laws, the medical record must reflect accurately the treatment for which the hospital or physician seeks payment. Thus, the medical record is important to the hospital for medical, legal, and financial reasons.

Legal Requirements

The scope and detail of record requirements vary from state to state. In addition to state regulations, minimum standards for record keeping have been established by the federal government for health care facilities receiving federal funding. To participate in federal programs, these minimum requirements must be met.

The medical records of all discharged patients must be completed promptly, filed, and retained in accordance with regulatory requirements. Policies should provide for the retention and safekeeping of each patient's records. If a patient is transferred to another health care facility, a copy of his or her record or an abstract thereof must accompany the patient. This is necessary so that the receiving institution will be aware of any and all conditions that affect the delivery of health care to the patient.

Ideally, the individual in charge of medical records should be a "Health Information Management Administrator" (HIMA), who is licensed by the American Health Information Association (AHIMA) as a Registered Record Administrator (RRA). The HIMA is responsible for assuring that the facility complies with all regulations and amendments affecting medical records. If a health care facility does not have a full- or part-time HIMA, an employee of the facility (e.g. Accredited Records Technician - "ART" - certified by AHIMA) must be assigned the responsibility for assuring that records are maintained, completed, and preserved. The designated individual must receive regular consultation from a Registered Record Administrator.

Medical Records and Diagnostic Related Groups

Diagnostic related groups (DRGs) refer to a methodology developed by professors at Yale University for classifying patients in categories according to age, diagnosis, and treatment resource requirements. It is the basis for the Department of Health and Human Services' prospective payment system, contained in the 1983 Social Security Amendments for reimbursing inpatient hospital costs for Medicare beneficiaries. The key source of information for determining the course of treatment of each hospital patient and the proper DRG assignment is the medical record. Reimbursement is based on pre-established average prices for each DRG. As a result of this reimbursement methodology, poor record keeping can precipitate financial disaster for a hospital. The main purpose of the amendments is to hold down the rise in Medicare expenditures before the Social Security system experiences serious deficits. The potential financial savings for Medicare are substantial. Under this system of payment, if hospitals can provide quality patient care at a cost under the price established for a DRG, they may keep the excess dollars paid. This is an incentive for hospitals to keep costs under control. There is, however, a fear that patients may, to their detriment, be discharged too early, for financial reasons. This in turn could lead to costly malpractice suits.

Incomplete Records/Grounds for Suspension of Medical Staff Privileges

Various licensing regulations require prompt completion of records after the discharge of patients. Persistent failure to conform to a medical staff rule requiring the physician to complete records promptly was held in *Board of Trustees Memorial Hospital v. Pratt,* 72 Wyo. 120, 262 P.2d 682 (1953), to provide a basis for suspension of a staff member.

Legal Proceedings and the Medical Record

The ever-increasing frequency of personal injury suits mandates that health care facilities maintain complete, accurate, and timely medical records. Their importance as an evidentiary tool in legal proceedings cannot be overemphasized. The integrity and completeness of the medical record is extremely important in reconstructing the events surrounding any alleged negligence in the care of the patient. Medical records provide information for determining the cause of death and indicate the extent of injury in workers' compensation or personal injury proceedings.

When health professionals are called as witnesses in a proceeding, they are permitted to refresh their recollections of the facts and circumstances of a particular case by referring to the medical record. Courts recognize that it is impossible for a medical witness to remember the details of every patient's treatment. The record therefore may be used as an aid in relating the facts of a patient's course of treatment.

The medical record itself may be admitted into evidence in legal proceedings. For medical record information to be admitted into evidence, the court must be assured that the information is accurate, that it was recorded at the time the event took place, and that it was not recorded in anticipation of a specific legal proceeding. Although it is recognized that witnesses may refresh their memories and that records may be admitted into evidence, there is nevertheless a need for assurance that the information is trustworthy.

When a medical record is introduced into evidence, its custodian, usually the health information management administrator, must testify as to the manner in which the record was produced and the way in which it is protected from unauthorized handling and change. Whether such records and other documents are admitted or excluded is governed by the facts and circumstances of the particular case, as well as by the applicable rules of evidence. Admission of a business record requires "the testimony of the custodian or other qualified witness." Federal Rules of Evidence 803(6).

> [A] writing is not admissible . . . merely because it may appear upon its face to be a writing made by a physician in the regular course of his practice. It must first be shown that the writing was actually made by or under the direction of the physician at or near the time of his examination of the individual in question and also that it was his custom in the regular course of his professional practice to make such a record.

Masterson v. Pennsylvania Railroad, 182 F.2d 793, 797 (3d Cir. 1950).

The records purportedly relating to a patient's treatment in *Belber v. Lipson,* 905 F.2d 549 (1st Cir. 1990), were not admissible as business records because the witness who had possession of them had no personal knowledge of the circumstances under which the records were prepared.

Whatever the situation, the record must be complete, accurate, and timely. If it can be shown that the record is inaccurate or incomplete or that it was made long after the event it purports to record, it will not be accepted into evidence.

Confidential Communications

The information on a patient's chart is confidential and should not be disclosed without the patient's permission. Those who come into possession of the most intimate personal information about patients have both a legal and an ethical duty not to reveal confidential communications. The legal duty arises because the law recognizes a right to privacy. To protect this right, there is a corresponding duty to obey. The ethical duty is broader and applies at all times.

All health care professionals who have access to medical records have a legal, ethical, and moral obligation to protect the confidentiality of the information in the records. The communications between a physician and his or her patient and the information generated during the course of the patient's illness are generally accorded the protection of confidentiality. However, "[p]atient confidentiality seems to have lost its meaning in the current health care environment, some experts say. Yet the dearth of litigation stemming from medical record disclosures clearly indicates that patients are not likely to sue over their loss of confidentiality."[18] Health professionals have a clear legal and moral obligation to maintain this confidentiality. As noted above, medical records, with proper authorization, may be used for the purposes of research, statistical evaluation, and education. The information obtained from medical records must be dealt with in a confidential manner; otherwise, a hospital could incur liability.

There are occasions when there is a legal obligation or duty to disclose information. The reporting of communicable diseases, gunshot wounds, child abuse, and other matters is required by law.

Privileged Communications

The Federal Health Care Quality Improvement Act of 1986, 42 U.S.C.A. §§11101–11152, insulates certain medical peer-review activities affecting medical staff privileges from antitrust liability. Peer review is protected so long as it is taken in the reasonable belief that it is conducted in the furtherance of quality health care. In enacting this legislation, Congress recognized that without such antitrust immunity, effective peer review may not be possible.

Many states have enacted different privilege and nondiscovery statutes protecting from discovery the recorded minutes and proceedings of such committees as risk management, quality assurance, and peer review. The California Court of Appeals in *Mt. Diablo Hospital District v. Superior Court,* 227 Cal. Rptr. 790 (Ct. App. 1986), held that the trial court erred in requiring the hospital to produce minutes of five medical staff committees that had been charged with establishing standards for granting physicians authority to use a procedure known as chemonucleolysis. The patient, in an action involving the hospital, allegedly suffered injuries as a result of this procedure for lower back pain in which a drug substance known as chymopapain or chymodiactin was injected into the patient. The court held that the documents in question so clearly fell within statutory privilege that there was no occasion to order *in camera* review to determine whether they should be produced.

Privileged communications statutes do not protect from discovery the records maintained in the ordinary course of doing business and rendering inpatient care. Such documents, however, often can be subpoenaed after showing good cause due to extraordinary circumstances. In *Sanderson v. Bryan,* 522 A.2d 1138 (Pa. Super. Ct. 1987), the superior court held that the Peer Review Protection Act of 1974, Pub. L. 564, No. 193, *as amended* October 5, 1978, Pub. L. 1121, No. 262, was violated by an order giving a plaintiff access through the discovery process to peer review information that was not directly related to his case. The act, however, does not prevent the plaintiffs from gaining access to their own medical records or other relevant business records of the hospital or from compelling persons with firsthand knowledge of the incident to testify.

Attorney–client privilege generally will preclude discovery of memorandums written to a hospital's general counsel by the hospital's coordinator of risk management. In *Mlynarski v. Rush Presbyterian-St. Luke's Medical Center,* 572 N.E.2d 1025 (Ill. App. Ct. 1991), a memorandum written by the risk management coordinator to the hospital's general counsel was barred from discovery. There was undisputed evidence that the risk management coordinator had consulted with and assisted counsel in determining the legal action to pursue and the advisability of settling a claim that she had been assigned to investigate. Information contained in the memorandum was available from witnesses whose names and addresses were made available to the plaintiff. If the hospital later at trial decided to attempt to impeach those witnesses based on the coordinator's testimony, privilege would be waived and the hospital would be required to produce the relevant reports.

Peer Review Documents/Confidentiality Exceptions

Peer review privilege will not necessarily preclude interrogatories requesting the identity of peer review committee members and individuals who may have given information to such committees. A state, for example, is entitled to access peer review reports relating to a physician suspected of criminal negligence. *People v. Superior Court,* 286 Cal. Rptr. 478 (Ct. App. 1991). In a civil action, a hospital may be required to identify all persons who have knowledge of an underlying event that is the basis of a malpractice action, whether or not they were members of a peer review committee. *Moretti v. Lowe,* 592 A.2d 855 (R.I. 1991).

The physician in *Dorsten v. Lapeer County General Hospital,* 88 F.R.D. 583 (E.D. Mich. 1980), had brought an action against a hospital and certain physicians on the medical board, alleging wrongful denial of her application for medical staff privileges. The plaintiff asserted claims under 42 U.S.C. §1983 for sex discrimination, violations of the Sherman Antitrust Act, and pendent claims for defamation and interference with advantageous business relations. The plaintiff had filed a motion to compel discovery of peer review reports to support her case. The U.S. district court granted the motion, holding that the plaintiff was entitled to discovery of peer review reports despite a state law, section 333.21515 of Michigan Compiled Laws Annotated, purporting to establish an absolute privilege for peer review reports conducted by hospital review boards.

The surgeon in *Robinson v. Magovern,* 83 F.R.D. 79, 521 F. Supp. 842 (W.D. Pa. 1981), brought an action under the Sherman Antitrust Act, as well as under state law, seeking recovery because he had been denied hospital privileges. The plaintiff moved in the U.S. District Court for an order compelling the defendants and certain third-party witnesses to respond to discovery requests and deposition questions. The defendants had objected, claiming the information sought was privileged and that the Pennsylvania Peer Review Protection Act seeks to foster candor and discussion at medical review committee meetings through grants of immunity and confidentiality. The court held that although there was a powerful interest in confidentiality embodied in the Pennsylvania Peer Review Protection Act, the act would not be applied to shield from discovery events surrounding the denial of staff privileges, including what occurred at meetings of the hospital's credentials committee and executive committee. The need for evidence was greater than the need for confidentiality in this case. The defendants' objections were overruled, and the motion to compel was granted.

The physician in *Ott v. St. Luke Hospital of Campbell County, Inc.,* 522 F. Supp. 706 (E.D. Ky. 1981), had brought a civil rights suit because his application for medical staff privileges was denied. The physician contended that he was not invited to several peer review committee meetings or given an opportunity to be heard. The hospital filed for a protective order that would bar discovery of the proceedings of the peer review committee. The hospital argued that such committees would become ineffective if their deliberations were discoverable and that the privilege claimed by the hospital is recognized in section 311.377 of the Kentucky Revised Statutes. The U.S. district court held that where there was no real showing that the peer review committee's functions would be impaired substantially, and where the benefit gained for correct disposal of the litigation by denying privilege was overwhelming, the hospital would not be permitted to assert privilege. The hospital's motion was therefore denied. The court reasoned that the efficiency of such committees may be fostered by an atmosphere of openness, and there may be less likelihood of reliance on bias, hearsay, and prejudice. A potential Louis Pasteur (French chemist and microbiologist), Joseph Lister (British surgeon), or Philipp Semmelweis (Hungarian physician) who advocates salutary changes in procedures may be excluded simply because he or she makes waves. The court, in concluding, indicated that it cannot permit the discharge of its responsibility to conduct a search for the truth to be thwarted by rules of privilege in the absence of strong countervailing public policies.

Ownership and Release of Medical Records

Ownership of medical records resides with the health care facility or professional rendering treatment. They are retained for the benefit of health care professionals in treating patients. Although medical records generally have been protected from public scrutiny by a general practice of nondisclosure, this practice has been waived under a limited number of specifically controlled situations.

Several jurisdictions recognize the principle that an individual has a right to privacy and to be protected from the mass dissemination of information pertaining to his or her personal or private affairs. The right of privacy generally is the right to be kept out of the public spotlight.

Requests by Patients

Health professionals and health care facilities, as a rule, have not released medical records to patients. The courts, however, have taken the view that patients have a legally enforceable interest in the information contained in their medical records and, therefore, have a right to access their records.

Some states have enacted legislation permitting patients access to their medical records. The New York Public Health Law was amended on January 1, 1989, by adding section 18, which provides that patients may have access to review and/or obtain copies of their medical records, x-rays, and laboratory and diagnostic tests. Access to information includes that maintained or possessed by a health care facility and/or a health practitioner who has treated or is treating a patient. Hospitals and physicians can withhold records if it is determined that the information could reasonably be expected to cause substantial and identifiable harm to the patient.

In cases of the mentally disabled, the legal guardian has the right to access the records of patients in psychiatric hospitals, institutions for the mentally disabled, and alcohol and drug treatment facilities. Qualified persons who are denied access to their medical records have appeal rights first to a medical record access review committee as appointed by the commissioner of health and ultimately to judicial review.

Failure to release a patient's record can lead to a legal action. The patient in *Pierce v. Penman,* 515 A.2d 948 (Pa. Super. Ct. 1986), brought a lawsuit seeking damages for severe emotional distress when physicians repeatedly refused to turn over her medical records. The defendants had rendered different professional services to the plaintiff for approximately 11 years. The patient moved and found a new physician, Dr. Hochman. She signed a release authorizing Dr. Hochman to obtain her records from the defendant physicians. Dr. Hochman wrote a letter for her records but never received a response. The defendants claimed they never received the request. The patient changed physicians again and continued in her efforts to obtain a copy of the records. There came a time when the defendants' offices were burglarized, and the plaintiff's records were allegedly taken. The detective in charge of investigating the burglary stated that he never was notified that any records were taken. The court of common pleas awarded the patient $2,500 in compensatory damages and $10,000 in punitive damages. On appeal, the superior court upheld the award. The physicians' contention that they relied on the advice of legal counsel did not insulate them from liability for punitive damages.

Requests by Third Parties

The medical record is a peculiar type of property because there is a wide variety of third party interests in the information contained in medical records. Health care facilities may not generally disclose information without patient consent. Policies regarding the release of information to third parties should be formulated to address the rights of patients, insurance carriers processing claims, physicians, medical researchers and educators, governmental agencies, etc.

Psychiatric Records

The psychotherapist–patient privilege that exists under the Federal Rules of Evidence (501) can be overcome if the evidentiary need for a psychiatric history outweighs a privacy interest. This was the case in *United States v. Diamond (In re Doe),* CA 2, No. 91-1467 (June 1, 1992), in which the privacy interests regarding the mental illness history of the person who initiated a criminal investigation against another individual were outweighed by the interests of the accused. Because the credibility of the witness will be the central issue at trial, his psychiatric history will be relevant to his credibility.

Criminal Investigations

There are several exceptions to the restriction on disclosing information obtained in a confidential relationship. For example, disclosure may be required when a patient is the victim of a crime. The hospital in *In re Brink,* 42 Ohio Misc. 2d 5, 536 N.E.2d 1202 (Ohio Com. Pl. 1988), sought to quash a grand jury request for the medical records pertaining to the blood tests administered to a person under investigation. The court of common pleas held that the physician–patient privilege did not extend to medical records subpoenaed pursuant to a grand jury investigation. A proceeding before a grand jury is considered secret in nature; therefore, a patient's interests in preserving the confidentiality of his or her records are protected.

Patient records are generally obtainable when investigating criminal actions such as Medicaid fraud. The grand jury in *People v. Ekong,* 582 N.E.2d 233 (Ill. App. Ct. 1991), was permitted to obtain certain patient files and records that were in the possession of the physician—who was under investigation for Medicaid fraud. The physician had contended that he could not release the files because of patient–physician privilege.

Drug and Alcohol Abuse Records

The federal Drug Abuse and Treatment Act of 1972, 21 U.S.C. §1175, and the federal regulations promulgated thereunder provide that patient records relating to drug and alcohol abuse treatment must be held confidential and not disclosed except as provided in these laws. Unlike other medical records, drug and alcohol abuse records cannot be released until the court has determined whether a claimed need for the records outweighs the potential injury to the patient, to the patient–physician relationship, and to the treatment services being rendered. Because of these strict requirements, the courts have been reluctant to order the release of records unless absolutely necessary.

Privacy Act of 1974

The Privacy Act of 1974, codified at 5 U.S.C. §552a, *et. seq.*, was enacted to safeguard individual privacy from the misuse of federal records, give individuals access to records concerning themselves that are maintained by federal agencies, and establish a Privacy Protection Safety Commission. A portion of the Privacy Act reads as follows:

> Sec. 2[a] The Congress finds that (1) the privacy of an individual is directly affected by the collection, maintenance, use, and dissemination of personal information by Federal agencies; (2) the increasing use of computers and sophisticated information technology, while essential to the efficient operations of the Government, has greatly magnified the harm to individual privacy that can occur from any collection, maintenance, use, or dissemination of personal information; (3) the opportunities for an individual to secure employment, insurance, and credit, and his right to due process, and other legal protections are endangered by the misuse of certain information systems; (4) the right to privacy is a personal and fundamental right protected by the Constitution of the United States; and (5) in order to protect the privacy of individuals identified in information systems maintained by Federal agencies, it is necessary and proper for the Congress to regulate the collection, maintenance, use, and dissemination of information by such agencies. [b] The purpose of this Act is to provide certain safeguards for an individual against an invasion of personal

privacy by requiring Federal agencies, except as otherwise provided by law, to—(1) permit an individual to determine what records pertaining to him are collected, maintained, used, or disseminated by such agencies; (2) permit an individual to prevent records pertaining to him obtained by such agencies for a particular purpose from being used or made available for another purpose without his consent; (3) permit an individual to gain access to information pertaining to him in Federal agency records, to have a copy made of all or any portion thereof, and to correct or amend such records; (4) collect, maintain, use, or disseminate any record of identifiable personal information in a manner that assures that such action is for a necessary and lawful purpose, that the information is current and accurate for its intended use, and that adequate safeguards are provided to prevent misuse of such information; (5) permit exemptions from the requirements with respect to records provided in this Act only in those cases where there is an important public policy need for such exemption as has been determined by the specific statutory authority; and (6) be subject to civil suit for any damages which occur as a result of willful or intentional action which violates any individual's rights under this Act.

Computerized Medical Records

Computers have invaded the health care industry. They are found in the admitting office, the business office, and even the operating room. They are in the laboratory, pharmacy, x-ray, and medical records departments. They are fast and accurate and have an almost endless capacity to store data. From research to treatment, they are here to stay.

Because of the tremendous amount of paperwork required under different regulations in caring for patients, computers have become an economic necessity. Problems associated with computerization include confidentiality, equipment failure, and questionable accuracy of input data by computer operators.

Health care facilities undergoing computerization must determine user needs, design an effective system, select appropriate equipment, develop user training programs, develop a disaster recovery plan (e.g., provisions for backup files and electrical shutdowns), provide for data security, etc. Experienced computer consulting firms can save health care facilities thousands of dollars with their expertise. Computers are not difficult to understand, but minor mistakes can cost major dollars.

Although computers are an economic necessity in the modern hospital, they are not faultless. Problems associated with computerization include the loss of confidentiality and the unauthorized disclosure of information, thus requiring the development of sophisticated security systems, equipment reliability, and the accuracy of input by computer operators.

Another potential shortcoming of computerized medical records is the lack of system responsiveness. A system must respond quickly to any request for information. Most forms of human–computer communication, such as computer keyboards and monitors, respond too slowly for effectiveness and patient safety. The need for a written patient care record will be with us for a long time.

Few cases, if any, have been litigated to date involving computer negligence in the health care field. As computers become more widely used in the health care industry, the potential for computer-related liability will increase.

In *Whalen v. Roe,* 423 U.S. 1313 (1975), an application had been made for a stay of judgment of a three-judge court sitting in the Southern District of New York. The applicant, the commissioner of health of the state of New York, had been enjoined by a three-judge court from enforcing certain provisions of the New York State Public Health Law that required the name and address of each patient receiving a schedule II controlled substance to be reported to the applicant. Schedule II drugs are those considered to have a high potential for abuse but also have an accepted medical use. Under the law, a physician prescribing a schedule II drug does so on a special serially numbered prescription form, one copy of which goes to the commissioner of health of New York, who transfers the data, including the name and address of the user, from the prescription form to a "centralized computer file." The respondent claimed that mandatory disclosure of the name of a patient receiving schedule II drugs violated the patient's right of privacy and interfered with the physician's right to prescribe treatment for his patient solely on the basis of medical considerations.

The court held that the patient identification requirement had been the product of an orderly and rational legislative decision about the state's broad police powers. The statute does not impair any private interest on its face and does not impair the right of physicians to practice medicine free from unwarranted state interference.

Retention of Records

The length of time medical records must be retained varies from state to state. Administration, with the advice of an attorney, should determine how long records should be maintained, taking into account patient needs, statutory requirements, future need for such records, and the legal considerations of having the records available in the event of a lawsuit.

The Medical Record Battleground

The medical record must not be used as a battleground against another professional or the health care facility. The medical record is a document that cannot be erased once a recording has been made. It should not be used as an instrument for registering a complaint against another health care professional or the institution. The health care professional who uses a patient's medical record unwisely may have vented his or her emotions for the moment but at the same time may have provided the basis for having to justify his or her actions to another professional, to the institution, or to a jury. It should be remembered that comments written during a time of anger may have been based on inaccurate information, which, in turn, could be damaging to one's credibility and future statements.

Falsification of Records

All professionals should be aware that falsification of medical and/or business records is grounds for criminal indictment, as well as for civil liability for damages suffered. In *People v. Smithtown General Hospital,* 402 N.Y.S.2d 318 (Sup. Ct. 1978), a motion to dismiss indictments against a physician and a nurse charged with falsifying business records in the first degree was denied. In each indictment, it was charged that the defendant was in violation of a duty imposed on him or her by law or by the nature of his or her position. The surgeon was charged because he omitted to make a true entry in his operative report; the nurse was charged because she failed to make a true entry in the operating room log.

Reproduction Charges

A reasonable charge for copies of medical records may be made. Because of the abuse by some providers in sitting fees for the reproduction of medical records, some states have set by statute the amount that a provider may charge for the reproduction of medical records. New York State, for example, provides for a maximum charge of seventy-five cents ($.75) per page for patients or their representatives (e.g. legal guardians, authorized insurance carriers, and attorneys). This fee includes any search or retrieval charges. (New York State Public Health Law Sects. 17 & 18 as amended 1992).

Charting—Some Helpful Advice

The medical record is the most important document in a negligence action. Both plaintiff and defendant use it as a basis for their action and defense. The following advice on documentation should prove to be helpful in charting:

- The medical record describes the care rendered to each patient. It should be sufficiently complete to allow those not treating a patient to review the record and assume continuing care when necessary

- Medical records entries should be legible, clear, and meaningful to each patient's course of treatment. Handwriting has long been a major problem in interpreting the events surrounding the care of patients. Illegible medical records not only damage one's ability to defend him- or herself but also can have an adverse effect on the credibility of other health professionals who read the record and act on what they read

- The medical record should be complete. This is often a problem with progress notes when there is little new information to report. Progress notes should describe the symptoms or condition being addressed, treatment rendered, patient response, and the patient's status at the time treatment is discontinued

- Do not write long, defensive, or derogatory notes. Stick to the facts. Criticism, complaints, emotional comments, and extraneous remarks have no place in the medical record. Such remarks can in and of themselves precipitate a malpractice suit

- Do not make erasures or use correction fluid to cover up entries, or tamper with the chart in any form. Draw a single line through a mistaken entry and write "error," enter the correct information, and then sign and date it. Tampering with records sends the wrong signal to jurors and can shatter one's credibility. Altered records can create a presumption of negligence. The court in *Matter of Jascalevich,* 442 A.2D 635, 182 N.J. Super. 455 (1982), held "that a deliberate falsification by a physician of his patient's medical record, particularly when the reason therefore is to protect his own interests at the expense of his patient's, must be regarded both as a gross malpractice endangering the health or life of his patient"

- Charts related to pending legal action should be placed in a separate file under lock and key. Legal counsel should be notified immediately of any potential lawsuit

- A medical record has many authors. Do not ignore the entries made by others. Good patient care is a team effort and entries made by other health professionals provide valuable information in treating the patient

PHARMACY

Among non-operative adverse events, drug-related problems are the leading cause of medical injury. Antibiotics, oncologic drugs, and anti-coagulants are the three categories of drugs responsible for the majority of drug-related adverse events.[19]

The practice of pharmacy essentially includes preparing, compounding, dispensing, and retailing medications. These activities may be carried out only by a pharmacist with a state license or by a person exempted from the provisions of a state's pharmacy statutes. The entire stock of drugs in a pharmacy (including the pharmacies of hospitals and other health care facilities) is subject to strict government regulation and control. The pharmacist is responsible for developing, coordinating, and supervising all pharmaceutic activities, and reviewing the drug regimens of each patient.

Government Control of Drugs

All drugs are subject to government regulation at the federal, state, and local levels. It is important that the administrator, pharmacist, nursing and medical staffs, and other personnel authorized to handle drugs understand the manner in which they are controlled.

The power and authority to regulate drugs, their products, packaging, and distribution rests (as a general rule) with both the federal and state governments. Consequently, there are often two sets of regulations and standards governing the same activity. In general, states have attempted to conform their laws to the federal laws. For example, most states have adopted the Uniform Controlled Substances Act (UCSA). This uniform law is based on and is in conformity with the federal Controlled Substances Act. Several states have modified the UCSA in various ways, frequently setting more stringent standards than are required under the federal law.

Federal Controls

Federal laws and regulations applicable to drugs include the Controlled Substances Act and the Federal Food, Drug and Cosmetic Act.

Controlled Substances Act

The Comprehensive Drug Abuse Prevention and Control Act of 1970, commonly known as the Controlled Substances Act, was signed into law on October 27, 1970, as Public Law No. 91-513. Virtually all pre-existing federal laws dealing with narcotics, depressants, stimulants, and hallucinogenics were replaced by this law.

Federal Food, Drug and Cosmetic Act

The Federal Food, Drug and Cosmetic Act (FDCA) applies to drugs and devices carried in interstate commerce and to goods produced and distributed in federal territory. The act's requirements apply to almost every drug that would be dispensed from a pharmacy, because nearly all drugs and devices, or their components, are eventually carried in interstate commerce.

Section 502 of the act sets forth the information that must appear on the labels or the labeling of drugs and devices. The label must contain, among other special information (1) the name and place of business of the manufacturer, packer, or distributor; (2) the quantity of contents; (3) the name and quantity of any ingredient found to be habit-forming, along with the statement "Warning— May be habit-forming"; (4) the established name of the drug or its ingredients; (5) adequate directions for use; (6) adequate warnings and cautions concerning conditions of use; and (7) special precautions for packaging.

The regulations (21 C.F.R. § 1.106) implementing the labeling requirements of section 502 exempt prescription drugs from the requirement that the label bear "adequate directions for use for laymen" if the drug is in the possession of a pharmacy or under the custody of a practitioner licensed by law to administer or prescribe legend drugs. This particular exemption applies only to prescription drugs meeting the other requirements. Ordinary household remedies in the custody or possession of a practitioner or pharmacist would not fall under the labeling exemption.

If the drug container is too small to bear a label with all the required information, the label may contain only the quantity or proportion of each active ingredient and the lot or control number. The prescription legend may appear on the outer container of such drug units. The lot or control number may appear on the crimp of a dispensing tube, and the remainder of the required label information may appear on other labeling within the package.

Besides the label itself, each legend drug must be accompanied by labeling, on or within the sealed package from which the drug is to be dispensed, bearing full prescribing information including indications; dosage; routes, methods, and frequency of administration; contraindications; side effects; precautions; and any other information concerning the intended use of the drug necessary for the prescriber to use the drug safely. This information usually is contained in what is known in the trade as the "package insert."

State Regulations

Besides federal laws affecting the manufacture, use, and handling of drugs, the different states have controlling legislation. All states regulate the practice of pharmacy, as well as the operation of pharmacies. State regulations generally provide that (1) each hospital must assure the availability of pharmaceutic services to meet the needs of patients; (2) pharmaceutic services must be provided in accordance with all applicable federal and state laws and regulations; (3) pharmaceutic services must be provided under the supervision of a pharmacist; (4) space and equipment must be provided within the hospital for the proper storage, safeguarding, preparation, dispensing, and administration of drugs; (5) each hospital must develop and implement written policies and procedures regarding accountability, distribution, and assurance of quality of all drugs; and (6) each hospital must develop and follow current written procedures for the safe prescription and administration of drugs.

Most state laws require that pharmacies be licensed and that they be under the supervision of a person licensed to practice pharmacy. The pharmacist usually can be either an employee of the hospital or a consultant pharmacist. The authority of a hospital to operate a pharmacy is conditioned on compliance with licensing requirements affecting the pharmacy premises and its personnel. The statutes applying to pharmacies usually empower regulatory agencies, such as the state pharmacy board, to issue rules and regulations as necessary.

The hospital is subject to liability for the negligent acts of its professional and nonprofessional employees in the handling of drugs and medications within the facility. Both the pharmacist and the hospital are subject to criminal liability, as well as civil liability, for the violation of statutory directives. Most states have regulations that dictate in detail the dispensing, distribution, administration, storage, control, and disposal of drugs within the health care facility.

Distribution, Dispensing, and Administration of Drugs

"Distribution" is the movement of a legend drug from a community pharmacy or institutional pharmacy to a nursing service area, while in the originally labeled manufacturer's container, labeled according to federal and state statutes and regulations.

The "dispensing" of medications is the processing of a drug for delivery or for administration to a patient pursuant to the order of a practitioner. It consists of checking the directions on the label with the directions on the prescription or order to determine accuracy; selecting the drug from stock to fill the order; counting, measuring, compounding, or preparing the drug; placing the drug in the proper container; and adding to a written prescription any required notations.

The "administration" of medications is an act in which a single dose of a prescribed drug is given to a patient by an authorized person in accordance with federal and state laws and regulations governing such act. The complete act of administration includes removing an individual dose from a previously dispensed, properly labeled container (including a unit dose container), verifying it with the physician's order, giving the individual dose to the proper patient, and recording the time and dose given.

Medications may be administered by licensed medical or nursing personnel in accordance with state regulations. Each dose of drug administered must be recorded on the patient's clinical records. A separate record of narcotic drugs must be maintained. The record must contain a separate sheet for each narcotic of different strength or type administered to the patient. The narcotic record must contain the following information: date and time administered, physician's name, signature of person administering the dose, and the balance of the narcotic drug on hand.

In the event that an emergency arises that requires the immediate administration of a particular drug, the patient's record should be documented properly, showing the necessity for administration of the drug on an emergency basis. Procedures should be in place for handling emergency situations.

Storage of Drugs

Drugs must be stored in their original containers and must be labeled properly. The label should indicate the patient's full name, physician, prescription number, strength of the drug, expiration date of all time-dated drugs, and the address and telephone number of the pharmacy dispensing the drug. The medication containers must be stored in a locked cabinet at the nurse's station. Medications containing narcotics or other dangerous drugs must be stored under double lock (e.g., a locked box within the medicine cabinet). The keys to the medicine cabinet and narcotics box must be in the possession of authorized personnel. Medications for "external use only" must be marked clearly and kept separate from medications for internal use. Medications that are to be taken out of use must be disposed of according to federal and state laws and regulations.

Drug Substitution

Drug substitution may be defined as the dispensing of a different drug or brand in place of the drug or brand ordered. Several states prohibit this and penal sanctions, including loss of license, are imposed for violation of the law.

Hospitals use a "formulary system," whereby physicians and pharmacists create a formulary listing drugs used in the institution. The formulary contains the brand names and generic names of drugs. Under the formulary system, a physician agrees that his or her prescription, which calls for a brand name drug, may be filled with the generic equivalent of that drug (i.e., a drug that contains the same active ingredients in the same proportions).

Authorization for using a generic equivalent should be given by the physician at the time he or she prescribes a formulary drug and should be evidenced by a written consent on the face of the prescription. When a formulary system is in use, the prescribing physician can require the use of a particular brand name drug, when he or she deems it necessary or desirable, by expressly prohibiting the use of the formulary system.

NOTES

1. M. LAUCHHEIMER, HAZARDOUS WASTE AND TOXIC TORTS 1 (1989).

2. Fields, *Containing Waste Disposal Costs*, FED'N AM. HEALTH SYS. REV., May–June 1989, at 53.

3. *Waste Disposal Rules*, A.H.A. NEWS, Dec. 11, 1989, at 7.

4. 56 Fed. Reg. 64,004 (1991).

5. Charlton, *Medical Hazardous Waste Issues Demand Attention*, FED'N AM. HEALTH SYS. REV., July–Aug. 1989, at 46.

6. Fields, *supra* note 2, at 55.

7. *St. Paul Hospital-Liability Premiums to Average 3.9% Increase*, A.H.A. NEWS, 27(37), Sept. 16, 1991, at 3.

8. The Robert Wood Johnson Foundation, *Negligent Medical Care: What Is It, Where Is It, and How Widespread Is It?*, ABRIDGE, Spring 1991, at 7.

9. 42 U.S.C.A. §1395dd(a) (1992).

10. 42 U.S.C.A. §1395dd(e)(1) (1992).

11. 42 U.S.C.A. §1395dd(e)(3)(A) (1992).

12. 42 U.S.C.A. §1395dd(c)(1) (1992).

13. 42 U.S.C.A. §1395dd(b)(2) (1992).

14. 42 U.S.C.A. §1395dd(d) (1992).

15. 42 U.S.C.A. §1395dd(d)(2)(A) (1992).

16. *Courts Uphold Law, Regulations Against Patient Dumping*, NATION'S HEALTH, Aug. 1991, at 1.

17. *Id.* at 17.

18. Ellen Weisman, *Liability for Medical Record Disclosure Is Real But Rare*, HOSPITALS, Aug. 20, 1990, at 32.

19. The Robert Wood Johnson Foundation, *supra* note 8.

Patient Consent

OUTLINE

Consent is the voluntary agreement by a person in the possession and exercise of sufficient mentality to make an intelligent choice to allow something proposed by another (e.g., administration of medication, performance of a procedure) to be performed on him- or herself. Consent changes a touching that otherwise would be nonconsensual to one that is consensual. It can be either express or implied consent.

"Express consent" can take the form of a verbal agreement to undergo a medical procedure, or it can be accomplished through the execution of a signed consent form. In modern health care, written consent is the preferred method of obtaining consent.

"Implied consent" is that which is manifested by some action or inaction of silence, which raises a presumption that consent has been authorized. For example, consent by a parent to the performance of a lumbar puncture to test for suspected meningitis could be implied from the life-threatening nature of a child's condition. In *Plutshack v. University of Minnesota Hospitals,* 316 N.W.2d 1 (Minn. 1982), the physician had been unable to contact the infant's mother. The child's grandmother had agreed to the performance of a lumbar puncture.

Consent must first be obtained from a patient, or from a person authorized to consent on a patient's behalf, before any medical procedure can be performed. Every individual has a right to refuse to authorize a touching. A touching of another without authorization to do so could be considered a battery.

Not every touching results in a battery. When a person voluntarily enters a situation in which a reasonably prudent person would anticipate a touching (e.g., riding in an elevator or rushing through a crowded subway), consent is implied. Consent is not required for the normal, routine, everyday touching and bumping that occurs in life.

In the process of caring for patients, it is inevitable that they will be touched and handled. Most touchings in the hospital are considered routine. Typical touchings might include bathing, administering medications, dressing changes, taking vital signs, etc.

A competent patient's refusal to consent to a medical or surgical procedure must be adhered to, whether the refusal is grounded on lack of confidence in the physician, fear of the procedure, doubt as to the value of a particular procedure, or mere whim. If a patient asserts that a touching was unauthorized, it will be necessary to prove that a consent was obtained in order to avoid liability for the unwanted touching.

The question of liability for performing a medical or surgical procedure without the consent is separate and distinct from any question of negligence or malpractice in performing a procedure. Liability may be imposed for a nonconsensual touching of a patient, even if the procedure improved the patient's health. The eminent Justice Cardozo, in *Schloendorff v. Society of New York Hospital,* 211 N.Y. 125, 129, 105 N.E. 92, 93 (1914), stated:

> Every human being of adult years and sound mind has a right to determine what shall be done with his own body and a surgeon who per-

forms an operation without his patient's consent commits an assault, for which he is liable in damages, except in cases of emergency where the patient is unconscious and where it is necessary to operate before consent can be obtained.

211 N.Y. at 129, 105 N.E. at 93.

PATIENT SELF-DETERMINATION ACT

The Patient Self-Determination Act of 1990 protects the rights of patients to make decisions regarding their own health care. The act provides that each individual has a right under state law (whether statutory or as recognized by the courts of the state) to make decisions concerning his or her medical care, including the right to accept or refuse medical or surgical treatment.[1]

INFORMED CONSENT

"Informed consent" is a legal concept predicated on the duty of the physician to disclose to the patient information necessary to enable the patient to evaluate a proposed medical or surgical procedure before submitting to it. Informed consent requires that a patient have a full understanding of that to which he or she has consented. An authorization from a patient—without an understanding of what he or she is consenting to—is not effective consent.

Patients must be given sufficient information to allow them to make intelligent choices from among the alternative courses of available treatment for their specific ailments. They have a right to refuse a specific course of treatment even if the medical procedure is advisable. Informed consent must be given despite a patient's anxiety or indecisiveness. Patients have a right to be secure in their persons from any touching, and they are free to reject recommended treatment.

Some courts have recognized that the condition of the patient may be taken into account to determine whether the patient has received sufficient information to give consent. The person seeking consent, usually the attending physician, must weigh the importance of giving full disclosure to the patient against the likelihood that such disclosure will seriously and adversely affect the condition of the patient.

A patient suffering from hypertension could very well receive a modified disclosure if the attending physician has reason to believe that a full explanation of a contemplated treatment could aggravate the hypertension, which, in turn, could have a detrimental effect on the body systems already impaired by age or illness. A modified disclosure consistent with the patient's condition may be adequate if it can be shown that other physicians in the community also would have made a modified disclosure.

A physician should provide as much information about treatment options as is necessary based on a patient's personal understanding of the physician's explanation of the risks of treatment and the probable consequences of the treatment. The needs of each patient can vary depending on age, maturity, and mental status. A patient instituting a lawsuit would have to show that he or she was provided information insufficient for informed consent. Physicians are reminded that patients are concerned with the risks of death and bodily harm. Taking the time to sit at a patient's bedside and explain a patient treatment plan will produce a first-rate physician–patient relationship and most likely result in fewer lawsuits.

When questions do arise as to whether adequate consent has been given, some courts take into consideration the information that is ordinarily provided by other physicians. A plaintiff suing under the theory of informed consent must prove that

- the defendant physician failed to adequately inform the plaintiff of a material risk before securing his or her consent to a proposed treatment
- if the plaintiff had been informed of the risk, he or she would not have consented to the treatment
- the adverse consequences that were not made known did in fact occur
- the plaintiff was injured as a result of submitting to treatment

The plaintiff in *Ramos v. Pyati*, 534 N.E.2d 472 (Ill. App. Ct. 1989), brought a medical malpractice action, alleging that the doctor performed surgery on his hand outside the scope of surgery to which he consented. The plaintiff had injured his thumb while at work. He was referred to the defendant after seeing three other doctors. The plaintiff was diagnosed as having a ruptured thumb tendon. The plaintiff consented to a surgical repair of the thumb. During surgery, the defendant discovered that scar tissue had formed, causing the ends of the tendons in the thumb to retract. As a result, the surgeon decided to use a donor tendon to make the necessary repairs to the thumb. He chose a tendon from the ring finger. The plaintiff on discovering additional disability from the surgery filed a suit alleging that his hand was rendered unusable for his employment as a mechanic and that the defendant had breached his duty by not advising him of the serious nature of the operation, by not exercising the proper degree of care in performing the operation, and by failing to discontinue surgery when he knew or should have known that the required surgery would most likely cause a greater disability than the already injured condition of the thumb. The plaintiff testified that although he signed a written consent form authorizing the surgery on his thumb, he did not consent to a graft of his ring finger tendon or any other tendon. The plaintiff's expert witness testified that the ring finger is the last choice of four other tendons that could have been selected for the surgery. The circuit court entered a judgment for the plaintiff, and the defendant appealed. The appellate court upheld the judgment for the plaintiff, finding that the plaintiff had not consented to use of the ring finger tendon for repair of the thumb tendon.

The scope of a physician's duty to disclose, as noted in *Wooley v. Henderson,* 418 A.2d 1123 (Me. 1980), is to be measured by those communications that a reasonable medical practitioner in that branch of medicine would make under the same or similar circumstances. The plaintiff ordinarily must establish this standard by expert medical evidence. The court held that causation should be judged by an objective standard. The plaintiff would have to show that a reasonable person in the position of the plaintiff would have declined the treatment after being informed of a risk that could result in harm.

An action was brought for injuries sustained when the patient's heart was punctured during the performance of a pulmonary arteriogram in *Fain v. Smith,* 479 So.2d 1150 (Ala. 1985). The trial court was found to have properly required an objective and not a subjective test of causation in its jury charge. No error resulted when it cautioned that the patient's own testimony on the issue was not determinative because it was hindsight and self-serving. The issue of proximate causation was to include the jury's assessment of whether a reasonable person in the patient's position would have withheld consent. The Supreme Court of Alabama held that the objective standard is to be applied in actions for medical malpractice in which the physician fails to obtain the informed consent of the patient.

The Supreme Court of Oklahoma in *Scott v. Bradford,* 606 P.2d 554 (Okla. 1979), determined that a patient suing under the theory of informed consent must prove that the defendant physician failed to inform him adequately of a material risk before securing his consent to the proposed treatment; that if he had been informed of the risk, he would not have consented to surgery; that the adverse consequences that were not made known did occur; and that he was injured as a result of submitting to treatment. With regard to material risk, the court noted that

> [t]here is no bright line separating the material from the immaterial, it is a question of fact. A risk is material if it would be likely to affect a patient's decision. When non-disclosure of a particular risk is open to debate, the issue is for the finder of the facts.

Id. at 558.

Because this decision imposed a new duty on physicians with respect to disclosure of the risk of treatment, the opinion was ordered to apply prospectively, affecting those causes of action arising after the date this opinion was promulgated.

PROOF OF CONSENT

Oral Consent

Oral consent, if proved, is as binding as written consent, for there is, in general, no legal requirement that a patient's consent be in writing. However, an oral consent is generally more difficult to corroborate.

Written Consent

Written consent is the preferred form of consent. It provides visible proof of a patient's wishes. Physicians have a legal duty to inform their patients of any procedures they are ordering. This duty should not be delegated to another. Because the function of a written consent form is to preserve evidence of informed consent, the nature of the treatment and the risks and consequences involved should be incorporated into the form. States have taken the view that consent, to be effective, must be "informed consent." An informed consent form should include the following elements:

- the nature of the patient's illness or injury
- the procedure or treatment consented to
- the nature and purpose of the proposed treatment
- the risks and probable consequences of the proposed treatment
- the probability that the proposed treatment will be successful
- any alternative methods of treatment and their associated risks and benefits
- the risks and prognosis if no treatment is rendered
- an indication that the patient understands the nature of any proposed treatment, the alternatives, the risks involved, and the probable consequences of the proposed treatment
- the signatures of the patient, physician, and witnesses
- the date the consent is signed

Hospital personnel and physicians should be alert to any changes in a patient's decision or attitude to undergo a specified procedure or treatment after a consent is signed.

The nurse and other health professionals have an important role in the realm of informed consent. They can be instrumental in averting major lawsuits by being observant as to doubts, changes of mind, confusion, or misunderstandings expressed by a patient regarding any proposed procedures he or she is about to undergo.

General Consent

Many physicians and hospitals have relied on consent forms worded in such general terms that they permit the physician to perform almost any medical or surgical procedure believed to be in the patient's best interests. This kind of form usually is signed by the patient at the time of admission, but it does not constitute valid consent. There is little difference between a surgical patient who signs no authorization and one who signs a form consenting to whatever procedure the physician deems advisable.

A general written consent form should be executed properly at the time of a patient's admission to the hospital. The general consent form records the patient's consent to routine services, general diagnostic procedures, medical treatment, and the everyday routine touchings of the patient. The admitting office should explain to the patient or his or her guardian the need for the consent form. The danger from its use arises from the potential of unwarranted reliance on it for specific, potentially high-risk procedures or treatments.

General emergency care consent forms provided by school officials, teachers, or camp counselors when they bring injured students or campers to the emergency department for treatment provide limited protection in the care of a particular child. This consent indicates a parent's desire and intent to have the school official, teacher, or counselor seek emergency treatment when necessary. Such consent allows the hospital to initiate treatment while an attempt is being made to reach the family for consent. Such a consent is no panacea and certainly does not provide a hospital or physician with a right to render *carte blanche* care. However, it does provide the hospital with some protection against frivolous malpractice suits.

Special Consent

A special consent form should be executed when a proposed treatment program may involve some unusual risk(s) to the patient. A list of procedures and treatments requiring special written consent should be maintained and appropriate consent forms used by the nursing and medical staff. The special consent form should be signed, dated, and witnessed at the time the physician explains to the patient the procedure he or she plans to perform. For special consents to be effective, they should be signed within a reasonable time before a scheduled procedure or treatment.

HOSPITAL LIABILITY

A hospital can be held liable if a medical or surgical procedure is performed without a patient's consent. It is the hospital's duty to protect a patient when it knows or should know of a patient's objections to a medical or surgical procedure. Treatment without consent is clearly a battery, and if performed by facility personnel, the facility would be liable.

Under the doctrine of *respondeat superior,* a hospital is liable for any wrongs of its employees while they are performing their duties. The patient's wife in *Krane v. Saint Anthony Hospital Systems,* 738 P.2d 75 (Colo. Ct. App. 1987), brought a wrongful death action against the hospital and the physicians. The patient had died during an elective surgical procedure. The district court entered a judgment in favor of the hospital. The plaintiff appealed, arguing, on one of three issues, that the hospital failed to advise the husband of the risks of his surgery. The court of appeals held that the hospital was not liable for any failure of the physician to sufficiently advise the patient of the risks of surgery. It is the surgeon who should obtain the informed consent of a patient about to undergo surgery. The surgeon, and not the hospital, has the technical knowledge and training necessary to advise the patient of the risks of surgery.

Hospitals generally do not have a duty to inform patients regarding surgical risks unless it knows or should know of a physician's propensity to fail to obtain informed consent before surgery. The reason for imposing such a duty on hospitals is to protect a patient's right to be informed of the risks of surgery before his or her giving consent. There were no allegations in the *Krane* case that the surgeon regularly failed to obtain the informed consent of his or her patients before surgery.

The parents of an injured patient in *Kesyer v. St. Mary's Hospital, Inc.,* 662 F. Supp. 191 (D. Idaho 1987), brought a medical malpractice action against a physician and the hospital. The hospital moved to dismiss certain claims regarding informed consent, and the district court held on one of the claims that the hospital had no duty to obtain informed consent. The responsibility for informed consent in Idaho is placed statutorily on the physician.

A physician in *Mele v. Sherman Hospital,* 838 F.2d 923 (7th Cir. 1988), had nicked a membrane in the patient's abdomen during performance of a tubal ligation by laparoscopy. The physician then performed a laparotomy to correct the bleeding that developed. The patient brought action against the hospital on the grounds that she had never consented to a laparotomy. The trial court directed a verdict in favor of the hospital. On appeal, the appeals court upheld the trial court's finding. The evidence presented at trial, which established that the consent form in question warned of the possibility of blood loss and authorized additional procedures to remedy unforeseen conditions, was considered adequate. The plaintiff argued that the bylaws of Sherman Hospital provided that "a surgical operation will be performed only on consent of the patient . . . except in emergencies and that the hospital negligently failed to obtain her informed consent." *Id.* at 923, 924. The U.S. district court was found to have correctly stated,

The bylaw does not say that the hospital has a duty to inform patients about risks. It says nothing of that sort. It is hard for me to believe that a reasonable jury could even find that the bylaws imposes, self imposes on the hospital a duty to disclose risks or conditions of every particular surgery.

Id. at 925.

WHO MAY CONSENT

Consent of the patient ordinarily is required before treatment. However, when the patient is either physically unable or legally incompetent to consent and no emergency exists, consent must be obtained from a person who is empowered to consent on the patient's behalf. The person who authorizes for the treatment of another must have sufficient information to make an intelligent judgment on behalf of the patient.

Competent Patients

A competent adult patient's wishes concerning his or her person may not be disregarded. The court in *Erickson v. Dilgard,* 44 Misc. 2d 27, 252 N.Y.S.2d 705 (Sup. Ct. 1962), was confronted with a request by the hospital to authorize a blood transfusion over the patient's objection. The court recognized that the patient's refusal might cause his death, but it would not authorize the blood transfusion, holding that a competent individual has the right to make this decision even though it may seem unreasonable to medical experts.

The court in *In re Melideo,* 88 Misc. 2d 974, 390 N.Y.S.2d 523 (Sup. Ct. 1976), held that every human being of adult years has a right to determine what shall be done with his or her own body and cannot be subjected to medical treatment without his or her consent. When there is no compelling state interest that justifies overriding an adult patient's decision, that decision should be respected.

In the Illinois case of *In re Estate of Brooks,* 32 Ill. 2d 361, 205 N.E.2d 435 (1965), the court held that competent adult patients without minor children cannot be compelled to accept blood transfusions that they steadfastly have refused because of religious beliefs. In this case, the patient had made her beliefs known to her physician and the hospital before consenting to any medical treatment. She was aware at all times of the meaning of her decision and had signed a statement releasing the hospital and her attending physician from liability for any consequences of her refusal to accept a blood transfusion.

Only a compelling state interest will justify interference with an individual's free exercise of religious beliefs. Application of this principle in *Application of President & Directors of Georgetown College, Inc.,* 331 F.2d 1100, (D.C. Cir.), *cert. denied,* 337 U.S. 978 (1964), involved a pregnant patient at the Georgetown Hospital. The hospital was granted a court order authorizing blood transfusions because the patient's physicians said they were necessary to save her life. The patient and her husband had refused authorization because of their religious beliefs. To learn whether the woman was in a mental condition to make a decision, the judge asked her what the effect would be, in terms of her religious beliefs, if the blood transfusions were authorized. Her response was that the transfusions would no longer be her responsibility. In its decision, the court stressed that the woman had come to the hospital seeking medical attention and that it was convinced she wanted to live. Furthermore, according to the woman's statement, if the court undertook to authorize the transfusions without her consent, she would not be acting contrary to her religious beliefs. The effect of the court order preserved for Mrs. Jones the life she wanted without sacrificing her religious beliefs.

> The final, and compelling reason, for granting the emergency writ was that a life hung in the balance. There was no time for research and reflection. Death could have mooted the cause in a matter of minutes, if action were not taken to preserve the status quo. To refuse to act, only to find later that the law required action, was a risk I was unwilling to accept. I determined to act on the side of life.

Id. at 1009–1010.

The Court of Appeals of the District of Columbia noted in *In re Osborne,* 294 A.2d 372 (D.C. 1972), that the state's concern for the welfare of the children could override a patient's decision to refuse treatment for religious reasons. However, the court found in this case that the patient had made sufficient financial provisions for the future well-being of his two young children, so they would not become wards of the state if he should die. Under the circumstances, the court held that there was no compelling state interest to justify overriding the patient's intelligent and knowing refusal to consent to a transfusion because of his religious beliefs.

The New Jersey Supreme Court took the position in *John F. Kennedy Memorial Hospital v. Heston,* 58 N.J. 576, 279 A.2d 670 (1971), that the state's power to authorize a blood transfusion does not rest on the fact of the patient's condition or competence; it rests on the fact of the state's compelling interest in protecting the lives of its citizens, which in this case was sufficient to justify overriding the patient's determination to refuse vital aid.

The Supreme Court, Suffolk County, in *Fosmire v. Nicoleau,* 536 N.Y.S.2d 492 (App. Div. 1989), issued an order authorizing blood transfusions for a patient who had refused them. The plaintiff applied for an order vacating the supreme court's order. The supreme court, appellate division, held that the patient's constitutional rights of due process were violated by the supreme court's issuing an order authorizing blood transfusions in the absence of notice or opportunity for the patient or her representatives to be heard. The rights of a competent patient to refuse medical treatment, even if premised on fervently held religious beliefs, is not unqualified and may be overridden by compelling state interests. However, a state's interest in preserving a patient's life is not inviolate and in and of itself may not, under certain circumstances, be sufficient to overcome the patient's express desire to exercise her religious belief and forgo blood transfusion. The appellate division held in part that the state's interest would be satisfied if the other parent survived.

The court of appeals went further by stating that "[t]he citizens of the state have long had the right to make their own medical care choices without regard to their medical condition or status as parents." *Matter of Fosmire v. Nicoleau,* No. 267, January 18, 1990. The court of appeals held that a competent adult has both a common-law and statutory right under sections 2504 and 2805-d of the Public Health Law to refuse life-saving treatment. Citing the state's authority to compel vaccination to protect the public from the spread of disease, to order treatment for persons who are incapable of making medical decisions, and to prohibit medical procedures that pose a substantial risk to the patient alone, the court of appeals did note that the right to choose was not absolute.

In the final analysis, if there is no compelling state interest to justify overriding a patient's intelligent and knowing refusal to consent to a medical procedure because of his or her religious beliefs, states are reluctant to override such a decision.

Guardian

A guardian is an individual who by law is invested with the power and charged with the duty of taking care of a patient by protecting the patient's rights and managing the patient's estate. Guardianship is often necessary in those instances in which a patient is incapable of managing or administering his or her private affairs because of physical and/or mental disabilities or because he or she is under the age of majority.

Temporary Guardianship

Temporary guardianship can be granted by the courts if it is determined that such is necessary for the well-being of the patient. Temporary guardianship was granted by the court in *In re Estate of Dorone,* 534 A.2d 452 (Pa. 1987). In this case, the physician and administrator petitioned the court on two occasions for authority to administer blood. A 22-year-old male patient brought to the Lehigh Valley Hospital Center by helicopter after an automobile accident was diagnosed as suffering from an acute subdural hematoma with a brain contusion. It was determined that the patient would die unless he underwent a cranial operation. The operation required the administration of blood to which the parents would not consent because of their religious beliefs. After a hearing by telephone, the court of common pleas appointed the hospital's administrator as temporary guardian, authorizing him to consent to the performance of blood transfusions during emergency surgery. A more formal hearing did not take place because of the emergency situation that existed. Surgery was required a second time to remove a blood clot, and the court once again granted the administrator authority to authorize administration of blood. The superior court affirmed the orders, and the parents appealed. The Supreme Court of Pennsylvania held that the judge's failure to obtain direct testimony from the patient's parents and others concerning the patient's religious beliefs was not in error when death was likely to result from withholding blood. The judge's decisions granting guardianship and the authority to consent to the administration of blood were considered absolutely necessary in the light of the facts of this case. Nothing less than a fully conscious contemporary decision by the patient himself would have been sufficient to override the evidence of medical necessity.

Consent for Minors

When a medical or surgical procedure is to be performed on a minor, the question arises whether the minor's consent alone is sufficient and, if not, from whom consent should be obtained. The courts have held, as a general proposition, that the consent of a minor to medical or surgical treatment is ineffective and that the physician must secure the consent of the minor's parent or someone standing in *loco parentis*; otherwise, he or she will risk liability. Although parental consent should be obtained before treating a minor, treatment should not be delayed to the detriment of the child.

Parental consent is not necessary when the minor is married or otherwise emancipated. Most states have enacted statutes making it valid for married and emancipated minors to provide effective consent. Several courts have held the consent of a minor to be sufficient authorization for treatment in certain situations. In any specific case, a court's determination that the consent of a minor is effective and that parental consent is unnecessary will depend on such factors as the minor's age, maturity, mental status, and emancipation and the procedure involved, as well as public policy considerations.

The Massachusetts Supreme Judicial Court took into consideration a some-what unusual factor in determining whether a minor's consent would be effective. In *Masden v. Harrison,* No.68651 Eq. (Mass. June 12, 1957), the court decided that a healthy twin, 19 years old, could give an effective consent to an operation in which one of his kidneys would be removed and implanted in his sick twin. After hearing a psychiatrist's report, the court found that the operation was to the healthy twin's psychological benefit even though it might not have been to his physical benefit. The court ruled that the healthy twin had sufficient capacity to understand the planned procedure and consent.

The court of appeals in *Carter v. Cangello,* 164 Cal. Rptr. 361 (Ct. App. 1980), held that a 17-year-old girl who was living away from home, in the home of a woman who gave her free room and board in exchange for household chores, and who made her own financial decisions, legally could consent to medical procedures performed on her. The court made this decision knowing that the girl's parents provided part of her income by paying for her private schooling and certain medical care. The physician was privileged under statute to act on the minor's consent to surgery, and such privilege insulated him from liability to the parents for treating their daughter without their consent.

Many states have recognized by legislation that treatment for such conditions as pregnancy, venereal disease, and drug dependency does not require parental consent. State legislatures have reasoned that a minor is not likely to seek medical assistance when parental consent is demanded. Insisting on parental consent for the treatment of these conditions would increase the likelihood that a minor would delay or do without treatment to avoid explanation to the parents.

Parental Refusal for Treatment

A court ruling should be sought in those cases in which refusal of treatment poses a serious threat to a patient's health, especially in the case of minors.

Consent of the Mentally Ill

A person who is mentally incompetent cannot legally consent to medical or surgical treatment. Therefore, consent of the patient's legal guardian must be obtained. When no legal guardian is available, a court that handles such matters must be petitioned to permit treatment.

Subject to applicable statutory provisions, when a physician doubts a patient's capacity to consent, even though the patient has not been judged legally incompetent, the consent of the nearest relative should be obtained. If a patient is conscious and mentally capable of giving consent for treatment, the consent of a relative without the consent of the competent patient would not protect the physician from liability.

Implied Consent

Although the law requires consent for the intentional touching that involves medical or surgical procedures to be performed on a patient, exceptions do exist with respect to emergency situations. Implied consent generally exists when immediate action is required to save a patient's life or to prevent permanent impairment of a patient's health. If it is impossible in an emergency to obtain the consent of the patient or someone legally authorized to give consent, the required procedure may be undertaken without any liability for failure to procure consent. An emergency situation removes the need for consent. This rule also applies when conditions discovered during an operation must be corrected immediately and the consent of the patient or someone authorized to give consent is not obtainable. This privilege to proceed in emergencies without consent is accorded physicians because inaction at such times may cause greater injury to the patient and would be contrary to good medical practice.

Unconscious patients are presumed under law to approve treatment that appears to be necessary. It is assumed that such patients would have consented if they were conscious and competent. However, if a patient expressly refuses to consent to certain treatment, such treatment may not be used after the patient becomes unconscious. Similarly, conscious patients suffering from emergency conditions retain the right to refuse consent.

If a procedure is necessary to protect one's life or health, every effort must be made to document the medical necessity for proceeding with medical treatment without consent. It must be shown that the emergency situation constituted an immediate threat to life or health.

In *Collins v. Davis,* 44 Misc. 2d 622, 254 N.Y.S.2d 666 (Sup. Ct. 1964), a hospital administrator sought a court order to permit a surgical operation on an irrational adult patient whose life was in jeopardy. The consent of the patient's wife had been sought, but she refused to grant authorization for the procedure for reasons that she thought were justified, although they were medically unsound. The court authorized the surgery for the reason that the patient himself had sought medical attention. The court ruled that the hospital was trying to provide the necessary medical treatment in conformity with sound medical judgment and that the spouse was interfering.

If a procedure is necessary to protect the life or health of a patient, documentation justifying the need to treat before obtaining informed consent should be maintained. In *Luka v. Lowrie,* 171 Mich. 122, 136 N.W. 1106 (1912), involving a 15-year-old boy whose left foot had been run over and crushed by a train, consultation by the treating physician with other doctors was an important factor in determining the outcome of the case. On the boy's arrival at the hospital, the defending physician and four house surgeons decided it was necessary to amputate the foot. The court said it was inconceivable that, had the parents been present, they would have refused consent in the face of a determination by five physicians that amputation would save the boy's life. Thus, despite testimony at the trial that the amputation may not have been necessary, professional consultation before the operation supported the assertion that a genuine emergency existed and could be implied consent. In the case of an emergency in which a physician fails to proceed because of lack of parental consent, the physician could be held liable if the patient suffers injury because of a failure to act.

The hospital and the physician should be able to establish that, under circumstances in which the patient is unconscious, obtaining the consent of the patient or someone legally authorized to give consent could mean a delay likely to increase unnecessary risk to the patient.

Consent also can be implied in nonemergency situations. For example, a patient may voluntarily submit to a procedure, implying consent, without any explicitly spoken or written expression of consent. In the Massachusetts case of *O'Brien v. Cunard Steam Ship Co.,* 154 Mass. 272, 28 N.E. 266 (1891), a ship's passenger who joined a line of people receiving injections was held to have implied his consent to a vaccination. The rationale for this decision is that individuals who observe a line of people and who notice that injections are being administered to those at the head of the line should expect that if they join and remain in the line, they will receive an injection. Therefore, the voluntary act of entering the line and the plaintiff's opportunity to see what was taking place at the head of the line were accepted by the jury as manifestations of consent to the injection. The *O'Brien* case contains all the elements necessary to imply consent from a voluntary act: the procedure was a simple vaccination, the proceedings were at all times visible, and the plaintiff was free to withdraw up to the instant of the injection.

Whether a patient's consent can be implied is frequently asked when the condition of a patient requires some deviation from an agreed-on procedure. If a patient expressly prohibits a specific medical or surgical procedure, consent to the procedure cannot be implied. The same consent rule applies if a patient expressly prohibits a particular extension of a procedure even though the patient voluntarily submitted to the original procedure.

Incompetent Patients

The definition of legal incompetence varies from state to state. In most jurisdictions, the test used by the court to determine incompetence and the need for guardianship is either (1) the ability to make or communicate responsible decisions or (2) the ability to manage one's own property and/or care for oneself. The most frequently cited conditions indicative of incompetence are mental illness, mental retardation, senility, physical incapacity, and chronic alcohol or drug abuse. Several states also include a spendthrift provision defining certain practices that waste the assets of the estate as evidence of incompetence. A handful of states permit the appointment of a guardian to protect mental incompetents. A patient who is not competent to manage his or her property may very well be competent to refuse medical care.

The ability to consent to treatment is a question of fact. The attending physician, who is in the best position to make the determination, should become familiar with his or her state's definition of legal incompetence. In any case in which the physician doubts a patient's capacity to consent, the consent of the nearest relative should be obtained. If there are no relatives to consult, application should be made for a court order that would allow the procedure. It may be the duty of the court to assume responsibility of guardianship for a patient who is *non compos mentis*.

A patient who is mentally incompetent cannot legally consent to medical care. The consent of the patient's legal guardian must, therefore, be obtained. When the legal guardian is unavailable to authorize necessary treatment, a court may be requested to authorize the procedure.

It may be the duty of the court to assume responsibility of guardianship for a patient who is *non compos mentis* to the extent of authorizing treatment if necessary to save his or her life even though the medical treatment authorized may be contrary to the patient's religious beliefs. A hospital was entitled to a court order authorizing medical personnel to provide necessary treatment, including the administering of blood and plasma, in *University of Cincinnati Hospital v. Edmund,* 506 N.E.2d 299 (Ohio Com. Pl. 1986). The administration of blood had been determined to be medically necessary to preserve the life of a Jehovah's Witness who was unable to express her own specific wishes with respect to her treatment because of the ingestion of excessive amounts of alcohol and the effects of a gunshot to her liver. Although the patient's children and members of her church testified that her religious beliefs precluded the administering of blood and plasma, there was a compelling state interest that permitted the hospital without prior consent to administer blood and provide other necessary treatment until such time as she personally might express her wishes concerning future treatment.

CONSENT AND CHANGE OF MIND

Patients are permitted to change their minds and give or withdraw consent to a procedure. The husband in *Randolph v. City of New York,* 69 N.Y.2d 844, 507 N.E.2d 298 (1987), brought a wrongful death action against the city, the city health and hospital corporation, and doctors arising out of the death of his wife, a Jehovah's Witness. Although the patient initially had refused a blood transfusion because of her religious beliefs during a cesarean section, witnesses had testified that the patient had been alive when authorization for a transfusion was later received and that her life could still have been saved if she had been transfused properly. The jury returned a verdict finding a physician and the New York City Health and Hospital Corporation 50 percent liable for the death of the patient. On appeal by the defendants, the supreme court, appellate division, dismissed the complaint on the grounds that the verdict had been based on insufficient evidence. On appeal by the plaintiff, the court of appeals held that there was evidence supporting the jury verdict for the plaintiff. Action against the city was found to have been properly dismissed.

REFUSAL OF TREATMENT

Adult patients who are conscious and mentally competent have the right to refuse medical care to the extent permitted by law even when the best medical opinion deems it essential to life. Such a refusal must be honored whether it is grounded in religious belief or mere whim. Every person has the legal right to refuse to permit a touching of his or her body. Failure to respect this right can result in a legal action for assault and battery. If a patient refuses consent, every effort should be made to explain the importance of the procedure. Coercion through threat, duress, or intimidation must be avoided.

Release Form

A patient's refusal to consent to treatment, for any reason, religious or otherwise, should be noted in the medical record, and a release form should be executed. The completed release form provides documented evidence of a patient's refusal to consent to a recommended treatment. A release form will help protect the hospital and physicians from liability should a suit arise as a result of a failure to treat. The best possible care must be rendered to the patient at all times within the limits imposed by the patient's refusal.

Should a patient refuse to sign the release form, this should be noted in the patient's medical record. Advice of legal counsel should be sought in those cases in which refusal of treatment poses a serious threat to a patient's health.

With the advice of legal counsel, the hospital should formulate a policy regarding treatment when consent has been refused. An administrative procedure should be developed to facilitate application for a court order when one is necessary and there is sufficient time to obtain one. Even though a signed consent form may not unequivocally constitute proof that informed consent was obtained from a patient, it does create a presumption that it was, thereby shifting the burden of responsibility to the patient to prove that it was not.

STATUTORY CONSENT

Many states have adopted legislation concerning emergency care that deals with consent. An emergency situation in most states eliminates the need for consent. When a patient's life is in jeopardy and he or she is clinically unable to give consent to a lifesaving emergency treatment, the law implies consent on the presumption that a reasonable person would consent to lifesaving emergency treatment.

When an emergency situation does arise, there may be little opportunity to contact the attending physician, much less a consultant. The patient's records, therefore, must be complete with respect to the description of his or her illness and condition, the attempts made to contact the physician as well as relatives, and the emergency measures taken and procedures performed. If a relative refuses to consent, it may be necessary to seek a court order. If time does not permit a court order to be obtained, a second medical opinion, when practicable, is advisable.

The motor vehicle laws in some states provide that accepting the privilege of driving on the highways implies a person's consent to furnishing a sample of blood or urine for chemical analysis when charged with driving while intoxicated. Generally, these statutes imply authorization of a test, and an action for assault and battery would not be upheld. A New York statute, for example, protects physicians, hospitals, and their employees from any liability for obtaining a blood sample from a nonconsenting individual when a police officer has requested the sample. Section 1194(3) of the New York Vehicle and Traffic Law (McKinney 1970) states the following in regard to chemical tests:

> b. No physician, registered nurse . . . or hospital employing such physician, registered professional nurse . . . and no other employer of such physician, registered professional nurse . . . shall be sued or held liable for any act done or omitted in the course of withdrawing blood at the request of a police officer pursuant to this section.

LACK OF CONSENT

In the absence of statutory protection, a procedure performed despite an individual's refusal to consent would constitute a battery. However, recovery most likely would be limited to nominal damages unless physical harm resulted from negligent performance.

Lack of informed consent in New York State is the failure of the person providing the professional treatment or diagnosis to disclose alternatives to the patient and to cite the reasonably foreseeable risks and benefits involved; this disclosure must parallel what a reasonable medical practitioner under similar circumstances would have disclosed, in a manner permitting the patient to make a knowledgeable evaluation. The plaintiff in *Gonzales v. Moscarella,* 530 N.Y.S.2d 218 (App. Div. 1988), failed to present expert medical testimony in support of his claim concerning the adequacy of information provided to him before performance of a surgical procedure. On appeal, the supreme court, appellate division, held that the trial court properly dismissed the plaintiff's action, which was based on the lack of informed consent. Although the plaintiff's expert witness did outline the risks inherent in the operative procedure performed and expressed a medical opinion that it would have been good medical practice to advise the patient of the risks and alternatives, the physician never once expressed an opinion as to the adequacy of the information provided to the patient.

DEFENSE AND FAILURE TO INFORM

The burden of establishing proof—on a complaint of lack of informed consent—is on the plaintiff. The plaintiff must establish that (1) a reasonably prudent person in the patient's position would not have undergone the treatment or diagnosis if fully informed and (2) the lack of informed consent is a proximate cause of the injury or condition for which recovery is sought.

In a lawsuit, testimony would be necessary to establish the extent of the patient's actual knowledge and understanding of the treatment rendered. It is possible for a patient, after treatment, to claim a lack of advance knowledge about the nature of a physician's treatment. And it is possible that a jury will believe the patient and impose liability on the physician and/or the hospital.

Several defenses are available to defendants who have been sued on the basis of failure to provide their patients with sufficient information to make an informed decision. Some of the defenses are included in state statutes. New York, for example, provides the following as defenses against recovery for lack of informed consent:

(a) the risk not disclosed is too commonly known to warrant disclosure; or

(b) the patient assured the medical practitioner he would undergo the treatment, procedure, or diagnosis regardless of the risk involved, or the patient assured the medical practitioner that he did not want to be informed of the matters to which he would be entitled to be informed; or

(c) consent by or on behalf of a patient was not reasonably possible; or
(d) the medical practitioner, after considering all of the attendant facts and circumstances, used reasonable discretion as to the manner and extent to which such alternatives or risks were disclosed to the patient because the practitioner reasonably believed that the manner and extent of such disclosure could reasonably be expected to adversely and substantially affect the patient's condition.[2]

A patient's condition during surgery may be recognized as different from that which had been expected and explained to the patient, requiring a different procedure than the one to which the patient initially had consented. The surgeon may proceed to treat the new condition; however, the patient must have been aware of the possibility of extending the procedure. The patient in *Winfrey v. Citizens & Southern National Bank,* 254 S.E.2d 725 (Ga. Ct. App. 1979), brought a suit against the deceased surgeon's estate, alleging that the surgeon during exploratory surgery had performed a complete hysterectomy without her consent. The superior court granted summary judgment for the surgeon's estate, and the patient appealed. The court of appeals held that even though the patient may not have read the consent document, when no legally sufficient excuse appeared, she was bound by the terms of the consent document that she voluntarily executed. The plain wording of the binding consent authorized the surgeon to perform additional or different operations or procedures that he might consider necessary or advisable in the course of the operation. Relevant sections of the consent signed by the patient included the following:

1. I authorize the performance on (patient's name) of the following operation—laparoscopy, possible laparotomy. . . .
2. I consent to the performance of operations and procedures in addition to or different from those now contemplated, which the above named doctor or his associates or assistants may consider necessary or advisable in the course of the operation. . . .

• • • •

7. I acknowledge that the nature and purpose of the operation, possible alternative methods of treatment, the risks involved, and the possibility of complications have been fully explained to me.

Id. at 727.

NOTES

1. 42 U.S.C.S. §1395cc (1992).
2. N.Y. PUB. HEALTH LAW §2805-d (McKinney 1985).

Legal Reporting Obligations

OUTLINE

A society wishes the best possible environment for its members. It works through government to protect its people by health regulations and statutes. Only through reliable observations and reports can proper measures be instituted to safeguard the environment of society.

Of prime importance to the health professional are health statutes requiring that certain information be transmitted to appropriate administrative bodies. Although most statutory reporting requirements do not contain an express immunity from suit for disclosure without the permission of the person affected, as a general rule a person making a report in good faith and under statutory command is protected.

DISEASES IN NEWBORNS

Most states have legislative reporting requirements for diseases in newborns. Hospitals are required to report instances of diarrhea, staphylococcal disease, and other infections. Most states provide penalties for violation of these laws.

Phenylketonuria

Phenylketonuria (PKU) is a reportable condition. The chief concern in reporting PKU is to encourage the testing and treatment of infants for PKU.

A state's regulations do not exempt the state automatically from liability if it fails in its responsibility in the diagnosis of PKU. The state of Louisiana was held liable for damages in *Marcel v. Louisiana State Department of Health & Human Resources,* 492 So.2d 103 (La. Ct. App. 1986), for the mental retardation and physical disabilities that a child suffered as a result of a state laboratory's failure to diagnose PKU. An initial Guthrie test was positive for PKU. The state was directly liable because of its institution of a substandard PKU program, when expert evidence established that a urine test was unreliable when compared with the more accurate blood tests and that a third Guthrie test should have been performed when the second screening test showed a negative. The state also was held vicariously liable for the negligence of laboratory personnel who received samples of the newborn's blood, ran a second Guthrie test, improperly found a negative test result, and closed her file.

CHILD ABUSE

The physically abused or neglected child is a medical, social, and legal problem. What constitutes an abused child is difficult to determine because it is often impossible to ascertain whether a child was injured intentionally or accidentally.

There was a time when health practitioners were somewhat reluctant to report cases of possible child abuse. Given the significant level of uncertainty as to the true cause of a child's condition and the tremendous amount of social reprobation associated with such a charge or claim, physicians hesitated to act as self-appointed police. Additionally, a person who made a report of suspected child abuse to the proper authorities could have been sued by the child's parents on the claim that the report was a defamation of the parents' character or an invasion of their privacy.

Today, however, all states and the District of Columbia have enacted laws to protect abused children. Furthermore, almost all states protect the persons required to report cases of child abuse.

The laws differ in their definition of an abused child. Generally, an abused child is one who has had serious physical injury inflicted by other than accidental means. The injuries may have been inflicted by a parent or any other person responsible for the child's care. Some states extend the definition to include a child suffering from starvation. Other states include moral neglect in the definition of abuse. For example, Arizona mentions immoral associations; Idaho includes endangering a child's morals; Mississippi incorporates location of a child in a disreputable place or association with vagrant, vicious, or immoral persons. Sexual abuse also is enumerated as an element of neglect in the statutes of some states.

Most state laws require certain people to report suspected cases of abuse. In a few states, certain identified individuals who are not required to report instances of child abuse, but who do so, are protected. The child abuse laws may or may not provide penalties for failure to report. The individuals covered by the various statutes range from physicians to "any person." Many of the statutes specifically include hospital administrators.

Any report of suspected child abuse must be made with a good-faith belief that the facts reported are true. The definition of good faith as used in a child abuse statute may vary from state to state. However, when a health practitioner's medical evaluation indicates reasonable cause to believe a child's injuries were not accidental and when the health practitioner is not acting from his or her desire to harass, injure, or embarrass the child's parents, making the report will not result in liability.

Reporting laws specify the nature of what constitutes child abuse. Statutes generally require that when a person covered by statute is attending a child as a staff member of a hospital or similar institution and suspects child abuse, the staff member must notify the person in charge of the institution, who in turn makes the necessary report. Typical statutes provide that an oral report be made immediately, followed by a written report. Most states require the report to contain the following information:

- the name and address of the child
- the persons responsible for the child's care
- the child's age
- the nature and extent of the child's injuries (including any evidence of previous injuries)
- any other information that might be helpful in establishing the cause of the injuries, such as photographs of the injured child and the identity of the perpetrator

An action for damages was brought by a minor child and his mother against physicians for failing to diagnose disease and filing erroneous child abuse reports in *Awkerman v. Tri-County Orthopedic Group,* 143 Mich. App. 722, 373 N.W.2d 204 (1985). The Wayne County Circuit Court granted the physicians' motions for partial summary judgment, and the plaintiffs appealed. The Court of Appeals of Michigan held that the child abuse reporting statute, section 722.625 of Michigan Compiled Laws Annotated, provides immunity to persons who file child abuse reports in good faith even if the reports were filed because of negligent diagnosis of the cause of the child's frequent bone fractures, which eventually was diagnosed as osteogenesis imperfecta. The court of appeals also held that damages for shame and humiliation were not recoverable pursuant to Michigan statute. Immunity from liability did not extend to damages for malpractice that may have resulted from the failure to diagnose the child's disease as long as all the elements of negligence were present.

PATIENT ABUSE

Forty-three states including the District of Columbia have enacted statutes or adult protective services laws to require the mandatory reporting of elder abuse. A report by the Senate Subcommittee on Elder abuse indicated that abuse of the elderly is less likely to be reported than child abuse. Although one of three child abuse cases is reported, only one of every eight elder abuse cases is reported. Some states, such as Louisiana, have stopped providing elder abuse protective services because of financial constraints.[1]

A major study on resident abuse in nursing homes conducted by the Office of Evaluations and Inspections, one of three major offices within the Office of Inspector General, revealed that nearly all respondents indicate abuse is a problem in nursing homes.

> Physical neglect, verbal and emotional neglect, and verbal or emotional abuse are perceived as the most prevalent forms of abuse. Nursing home staff, medical personnel, other patients, and family or visitors all contribute to abuse. However, aides and orderlies are the primary abusers for all categories of abuse except medical neglect.[2]

Nursing home residents often fail to report incidents of abuse because they fear both retaliation and not being believed, as well as because of the difficulty in proving such charges.

> Hospital patients are not dependent upon the facility operator in the same manner as a resident in a nursing home. Persons are usually hospitalized for only brief periods of time, whereas nursing home residents may be dependent upon the facility operator for a period of

years. Thus, the potential for long-term abuse and neglect is far greater for nursing home residents than it is for hospital patients.[3]

Even the courts have recognized that "all is not well in the nation's nursing homes." *Estate of Smith v. O'Halloran,* 557 F. Supp. 289 (D. Colo. 1983).

> The evidentiary record also supports a general finding that . . . the enormous expenditures of public funds and the earnest efforts of public officials and public employees have not produced an equivalent return in benefits. That failure of expectations has produced frustration and anger among those who are aware of the realities of life in some nursing homes which provide so little service that they could be characterized as orphanages for the aged.

Id. at 293.

COMMUNICABLE DISEASES

Most states have enacted laws that require the reporting of actual or suspected cases of communicable diseases. The need for statutes requiring the reporting of communicable diseases is clear. If a state is to protect its citizens' health through its power to quarantine, it must ensure the prompt reporting of infection or disease.

BIRTHS AND DEATHS

All births and deaths are reportable by statute. Births occurring outside of hospitals should be reported by the legally qualified physician in attendance at a delivery or, in the event of the absence of a physician, by the registered nurse or other attendant. Death certificates must be signed by the physician pronouncing a death. Statutes requiring the reporting of births and deaths are necessary to maintain accurate census records. Census reports are of great importance to states seeking funding of federally sponsored programs, which often grant funds based on population statistics.

SUSPICIOUS DEATHS

Greater than a state's interest in the recording of all births and deaths is the state's desire to review unnatural deaths that may be the result of some form of criminal activity. Unnatural deaths must be referred to the medical examiner for review. Such cases may include violent deaths, deaths caused by unlawful acts or criminal neglect, and/or deaths that may be considered suspicious or unusual. The medical examiner may make an investigation of such cases and issue an autopsy report. The purpose of a medical examiner's investigation is to determine the actual cause of death and thereby provide assistance for any further criminal investigation that may be considered necessary.

CRIMINAL ACTS

Besides reporting the subjects specified by statute, there may be a legal duty to report to the police such acts as attempted suicide, assault, rape, child molestation, or the unlawful dispensing or taking of narcotic drugs. Much of this information may be learned while caring for patients and therefore may be privileged communication. Without a patient's express consent to disclose such information or a statutory mandate that a report be made, it may be a violation of the patient's rights to report a suspected criminal act.

REPORTING PROFESSIONAL MISCONDUCT/NATIONAL PRACTITIONER DATA BANK

The Health Care Quality Improvement Act of 1986 (title IV of Pub. L. 99-660), signed by President Reagan on November 14, 1986, was enacted to encourage greater efforts in professional peer review and to restrict the ability of incompetent practitioners who move from state to state attempting to avoid discovery of previous substandard performance or unprofessional conduct. The law established the National Practitioner Data Bank, to be operated under the authority of the secretary of Health and Human Services. Responsibility for data bank implementation resides in the Bureau of Health Professions, Health Resources and Services Administration of Health and Human Services. The act authorizes the data bank to be used to collect and release information on the professional competence and conduct of physicians, dentists, and other health care practitioners. Reporting and disclosure requirements for the National Practitioner Data Bank also are set out in regulations.[4]

After several delays and changes since it was mandated by Congress in 1986, the National Practitioner Data Bank became operational September 1, 1990. The regulations are intended to encourage good-faith professional review activities. The data bank was established because

(1) The increasing occurrence of medical malpractice and the need to improve the quality of medical care have become nation-

wide problems that warrant greater efforts than those that can be undertaken by any individual State.

(2) There is a national need to restrict the ability of incompetent physicians to move from State to State without disclosure or discovery of the physician's previous damaging or incompetent performance.

(3) This nationwide problem can be remedied through effective professional peer review.

(4) The threat of private money damage liability under Federal laws, including treble damage liability under Federal antitrust law, unreasonably discourages physicians from participating in effective professional peer review.

(5) There is an overriding national need to provide incentive and protection for physicians engaging in effective professional peer review.[5]

The National Practitioner Data Bank presents a number of challenges to health care institutions. A major one will be to educate the medical staff so that the data bank will not erode medical staff participation in risk management.[6] The purpose of the data bank is not punishment but prevention and deterrence.

Reporting Requirements

The regulations establish reporting requirements applicable to hospitals; health care entities; boards of medical examiners; professional societies of physicians, dentists, or other health care practitioners that take adverse licensure or professional review actions (e.g., reduction, restriction, suspension, revocation, or denial of clinical privileges or membership in a health care entity of 30 days or longer); and individuals and entities (including insurance companies) making payments as a result of medical malpractice actions or claims. A medical malpractice action or claim has been defined as a written complaint or claim demanding payment based on a health care practitioner's provision of or failure to provide health care services, including the filing of a cause of action based on tort law, brought in any state or federal court or other adjudicative body.[7]

Reports must be submitted on an "Adverse Action Report" form. An "Additional Information" form must be used in conjunction with an Adverse Action Report when the forms do not provide sufficient space for recording the information requested. Information gathered by the data bank will be maintained in computer format.

Required Queries and Medical Staff Privileges

Health care facilities must query the data bank every two years on the renewal of staff privileges of physicians and dentists. The data bank will serve as a "flagging system" whose principal purpose is to facilitate a more comprehensive review of professional credentials. As a nationwide flagging system, it provides another resource to assist state licensing boards, hospitals, and other health care entities in conducting extensive independent reviews of the qualifications of health care practitioners they seek to license or hire or to whom they wish to grant clinical privileges. Data bank information also can be used for reviewing current medical staff members.

Who Should Report?

For those health care providers who question whether they are covered under this law, the Department of Health and Human Services prefers to define the term *entity* broadly, rather than to attempt to focus on the myriad of health care organizations, practice arrangements, and professional societies, to ensure that the regulations include all entities within the scope of the statute.[8] The definition of health care entity is as follows:

(a) A hospital;
(b) An entity that provides health care services, and engages in professional review activity through a formal peer review process for the purpose of furthering quality health care, or a committee of that entity;. . . .[9]

Health care practitioners include all health care practitioners authorized by a state to provide health care services by whatever formal mechanism the state uses (e.g., certification, registration, and licensure).[10] Examples of "other" health care practitioners include nurses, chiropractors, pharmacists, dietitians, and physical therapists.

Data Bank Queries

Data bank queries can be made by state licensing boards, hospitals, other health care entities, and professional societies, which have entered or may be entering employment or affiliation relationships with a physician, dentist, or other health care practitioner who has applied for clinical privileges or appointment to a medical staff. A plaintiff's attorney is permitted to obtain information from the data bank when a malpractice action has been filed and the practitioner on whom information has been sought is named in the suit. A request for data bank information must be submitted on a "Request for Information Disclosure" form. When information is requested from the data bank on more than one practitioner, the requesting body may use one or more "Request for Information Disclosure—Supplement" forms along with the Request for Information Disclosure form. The use of the supplement form will save time in that the need to repeat certain information has been eliminated.

Data Bank Query Fees

Under data bank rules, there is a nominal fee for data bank queries each time a physician and dentist apply for medical staff privileges at their facilities. Health and Human Service's Health Resources and Services Administration, which administers the data bank, hopes to keep the user fee to a minimum.[11]

Penalties for Failing To Report

Hospitals or other health care entities that fail to report adverse professional review actions limiting the clinical privileges of physicians or dentists lasting more than 30 days can lose immunity protection provided by title IV for a three-year period. Insurance carriers will be subject to a $10,000 penalty for each medical malpractice payment they make and fail to report on behalf of a physician, dentist, or other health practitioner.

Confidentiality of Data Bank Information

Information reported to the data bank is considered strictly confidential. Individuals and entities who knowingly and willfully report to or query the data bank under false pretenses or fraudulently access the data bank computer directly will be subject to civil penalties.

> (a) Limitations on disclosure. Information reported to the Data Bank is considered confidential and shall not be disclosed outside the Department of Health and Human Services, except as specified in Sec. 60.10, Sec. 60.11 and Sec. 60.14. Persons and entities which receive information from the Data Bank either directly or from another party must use it solely with respect to the purpose for which it was provided. Nothing in this paragraph

shall prevent the disclosure of information by a party which is authorized under applicable State law to make such disclosure.

(b) Penalty for violations. Any person who violates paragraph (a) shall be subject to a civil money penalty of up to $10,000 for each violation. . . .[12]

INCIDENT REPORTING

Incident reports contain statements made by employees and physicians regarding a noteworthy deviation from what is considered acceptable patient care. Some state health codes provide that hospitals and nursing facilities must investigate incidents regarding patient care and require that certain incidents must be reported in a manner prescribed by regulation. Reportable incidents often include such things as those incidents that have resulted in a serious injury or patient's death, an event such as fire or loss of emergency electric generator power, certain infection outbreaks, and strikes by personnel.

Incident reports should not be placed in the medical record. They should be directed to counsel for legal advice. This will help prevent discovery on the basis of client–attorney privilege. There is conflicting case law in that some courts will not permit incident reports to be discovered whereas others will allow discovery. A Florida appeals court ruled that incident reports prepared in anticipation of litigation are not discoverable, even though the information contained in the report was not available by any other means. *Dade County Public Health Trust v. Parker,* 551 So.2d 532 (Fla. Ct. App. 1990). In *Berg v. Des Moines General Hospital Co.,* 456 N.W.2d 173 (Iowa 1990), the Iowa Supreme Court ruled that, because of the time lapse between the actual incident and the inability of the nurses to recall the incident, discovery of the written incident report was allowed.

The New York State Public Health Law requires hospitals to investigate incidents regarding patient care and report them to the department of health.

> Any incident required to be reported . . . shall be reported to the department's Office of Health Systems Management on a telephone number maintained for such purpose. Hospitals shall report such incidents within 24 hours of when the incident occurred or when the hospital has reasonable cause to believe that such an incident has occurred and shall take no more than seven calendar days to determine whether an incident defined . . . is reportable and subject to the requirements of this section. The hospital shall give written notification within seven calendar days of the initial notification. This notification shall be submitted in a format specified by the department and

shall record the nature, classification and location of the incident; medical record numbers of all patients directly affected by the incident; the full name and title of physicians and hospital staff directly involved in the incident as well as their license, permit, certification or registration numbers; the effect of the incident on the patient; follow-up treatments and evaluations planned; the expected completion date for the hospital's investigation and identification information required by the department.

Official Compilation of Codes, Rules & Regulations of the State of New York, tit. 10(c), ch. V, pt. 400, sect. 405.8, 12/31/88.

Section 405.8 requires the reporting of the following incidents within 24 hours of occurrence to the Office of Health Systems Management:

* patients' deaths in circumstances other than those related to the natural course of illness
* fires or internal disasters in the facility
* equipment malfunction or equipment user error during treatment or diagnosis of a patient that did or could have adversely affected a patient or personnel
* poisoning occurring within the facility
* reportable infection outbreaks
* patient elopements and kidnapings
* strikes by personnel
* disasters or other emergency situations external to the hospital environment that affect facility operations
* unscheduled termination of any services vital to the continued safe operation of the facility

Although there are but a few cases dealing with incident reporting, hospital staff designated to report incidents must do so if required by a state's statute. The director of nursing at a nursing facility in *Choe v. Axelrod,* 534 N.Y.S.2d 739 (App. Div. 1988), was fined $150 for failure to report an instance of patient neglect. An anonymous telephone call had been placed with the department of health regarding two incidents of alleged patient neglect. In one incident, a patient had been left unattended in a shower by an orderly, and the patient sprayed himself with hot water, which resulted in second-degree burns on his forehead. On a second occasion, a similar incident occurred but no one was injured. On investigation by the department of health, a determination was made that both incidents constituted patient neglect and that failure to report these incidents was a violation of section 2803-d of the Public Health Law and title 10, section 81 of the Official Compilation of Codes, Rules & Regulations of the State of New York. After a hearing by an administrative law judge, the charge in the first incident was sustained and the second incident was dismissed. The director of nurses petitioned to annul the administrative determination. She contended that the department of health failed to establish a *prima facie* case of patient neglect and that the incident was an unavoidable accident and that the department of health's proof is based on hearsay evidence. *Id.* at 741. The court held that evidence supported a finding that the director of nurses had failed to report an incident of patient neglect as required by statute. On the question of hearsay evidence:

> "It is now well established that an agency can prove its case through hearsay evidence. . . ." In the final analysis, the evidence showed that the patient was left unattended, albeit momentarily, O'Brien (the orderly) was disciplined for that act, and petitioner did not report the incident. The finding is thus supported by the "kind of evidence on which reasonable persons are accustomed to rely in serious affairs."

Id. at 741.

Although it may not always be clear as to when an incident report should be filed, appropriate procedures should be in place addressing how questionable events should be handled.

NOTES

1. SENATE SUBCOMMITTEE ON HEALTH AND LONG-TERM CARE, ELDER ABUSE: A DECADE OF SHAME AND INACTION, Comm. Pub. No. 752 (1990), at x–xiv.

2. OFFICE OF INSPECTOR GENERAL, OFFICE OF INSPECTIONS AND EVALUATIONS, RESIDENT ABUSE IN NURSING HOMES, Pub. No.OEI-06-88-00360 (1990), at ii–iii.

3. Harris v. Manor Healthcare Corp., 49 N.E.2d 1374 (Ill. 1986).

4. 45 C.F.R. §60.1 (1991).

5. 42 U.S.C. §11101 (1991).

6. Teresa Hudson, *Risk Managers See New Regulations as Boon and Burden*, HOSPITALS, Sept. 20, 1990, at 48.

7. 45 C.F.R. §60.3 (1991).

8. 45 C.F.R. §60 (1991).

9. *Supra* note 8.

10. *Id.*

11. The guidebook is meant to serve as a resource for the users of the National Practitioner Data Bank. It is one of a number of efforts to inform the U.S. health care community about the Data Bank and what is required to comply with the requirements established by title IV of Public Health Law

99-660, the Health Care Quality Improvement Act of 1986. The Data Bank Help Line (1-800-767-6732) is a toll-free telephone service that provides health care entities and health care practitioners with information about the data bank.

12. 45 C.F.R. §60.13 (1991).

Chapter 12
Issues of Procreation

OUTLINE

- Abortion
  - Supreme Court Decisions
    - 1973—*Roe v. Wade*
      - First Trimester
      - Second Trimester
      - Third Trimester
    - 1973—*Doe v. Bolton*
    - 1976—*Danforth v. Planned Parenthood*
    - 1977—*Maher v. Roe*
    - 1979—*Colautti v. Franklin*
    - 1979—*Bellotti v. Baird*—Parental Consent
    - 1980—*Harris v. McRae*
    - 1981—*H.L. v. Matheson*
    - 1983—*City of Akron v. Akron Center for Reproductive Health*
    - 1989—*Webster v. Reproductive Health Services*
    - 1991—*Rust v. Sullivan*
    - 1992—*Planned Parenthood v. Casey*
  - State Regulation
  - Consent
    - Spouse
    - Parental Consent
    - Incompetent Persons
  - Employee Refusal To Participate in Abortions
  - Funding
  - Limiting Services

335

ABORTION

Abortion is the premature termination of pregnancy. It can be classified as spontaneous or induced. It may occur as an incidental result of a medical procedure, or it may be an elective decision on the part of the patient. As of 1985, there were 1.588 million abortions annually in the United States,[1] up from 0.586 million in 1972. Abortion, besides having substantial ethical, moral, and religious implications, has proven to be a major political issue in the 1980s and will continue as such well into the 1990s and beyond.

By the end of the decade, the right to an abortion was battered but still standing. The Supreme Court had agreed to hear new abortion challenges, but there were no credible predictions on what would happen to abortion in the 1990s. The only certainties were that more laws would be proposed, more laws would be passed, and more lawsuits would wend their way up to the Supreme Court.[2]

Supreme Court Decisions

1973—Roe v. Wade

Roe v. Wade, 410 U.S. 113, 164 (1973), gave strength to a woman's right to privacy in the context of matters relating to her own body, including how a pregnancy would end. However, the Supreme Court also has recognized the interest of the states in protecting potential life and has attempted to spell out the extent to which the states may regulate and even prohibit abortions.

In *Roe v. Wade,* the U.S. Supreme Court held the Texas penal abortion law unconstitutional, stating: "State criminal abortion statutes . . . that except from criminality only a lifesaving procedure on behalf of the mother, without regard to the stage of her pregnancy and other interests involved, is violating the Due Process Clause of the Fourteenth Amendment."

First Trimester. During the first trimester of pregnancy, the decision to undergo an abortion procedure is between the woman and her physician. A state may require that abortions be performed by a physician licensed pursuant to its laws. However, a woman's right to an abortion is not unqualified because the decision to perform the procedure must be left to the medical judgment of her attending physician. "For the stage prior to approximately the end of the first trimester, the abortion decision and its effectuation must be left to the medical judgment of the pregnant woman's attending physician." *Id.* at 164.

Second Trimester. In *Roe v. Wade* at 164, the Supreme Court stated, "For the stage subsequent to approximately the end of the first trimester, the State, in promoting its interest in the health of the mother, may, if it chooses, regulate the abortion procedure in ways that are reasonably related to maternal health."

Thus, during approximately the fourth to sixth months of pregnancy, the state may regulate the medical conditions under which the procedure is performed. The constitutional test of any legislation concerning abortion during this period would be its relevance to the objective of protecting maternal health.

Third Trimester. The Supreme Court reasoned that by the time the final stage of pregnancy has been reached, the state has acquired a compelling interest in the product of conception, which would override the woman's right to privacy and justify stringent regulation even to the extent of prohibiting abortions. In the *Roe* case, the Court formulated its ruling as to the last trimester in the following words: "For the stage subsequent to viability, the State in promoting its interest in the potentiality of human life, may, if it chooses, regulate, and even proscribe, abortion except where it is necessary, in appropriate medical judgment for the preservation of the life or health of the mother." *Id.* at 164.

Thus, during the final stage of pregnancy, a state may prohibit all abortions except those deemed necessary to protect maternal life or health. The state's legislative powers over the performance of abortions increase as the pregnancy progresses toward term.

1973—Doe v. Bolton

The Court then went on to delineate what regulatory measures a state lawfully may enact during the three stages of pregnancy. In the companion decision, *Doe v. Bolton*, 410 U.S. 179, 93 S. Ct. 739 (1973), where the Court considered a constitutional attack on the Georgia abortion statute, further restrictions were placed on state regulation of the procedure. The provisions of the Georgia statute establishing residency requirements for women seeking abortions and requiring that the procedure be performed in a hospital accredited by the Joint Commission on Accreditation of Hospitals were declared constitutionally invalid. In considering legislative provisions establishing medical staff approval as a prerequisite to the abortion procedure, the Court decided that "[i]nterposition of the hospital abortion committee is unduly restrictive of the patient's rights and needs that . . . have already been medically delineated and substantiated by her personal physician. To ask more serves neither the hospital nor the State." *Id.* at 198.

The Court was unable to find any constitutionally justifiable rationale for a statutory requirement of advance approval by the abortion committee of the hospital's medical staff. Insofar as statutory consultation requirements are concerned, the Court reasoned that the acquiescence of two copractitioners has no rational connection with a patient's needs and, furthermore, unduly infringes on the physician's right to practice.

Thus, by using a test related to patient needs, the Court in *Doe v. Bolton* struck down four preabortion procedural requirements commonly imposed by state statutes: (1) residency, (2) performance of the abortion in a hospital accredited by the Joint Commission, (3) approval by an appropriate committee of the medical staff, and (4) consultations.

1976—Danforth v. Planned Parenthood

The U.S. Supreme Court ruled in *Danforth v. Planned Parenthood*, 428 U.S. 52 (1976), that it is unconstitutional to require all women younger than the age of 18 years to obtain parental consent in writing before obtaining an abortion; however, the Court failed to provide any definitive guidelines as to when and how parental consent may be required if the minor is too immature to fully comprehend the nature of the procedure.

1977—Maher v. Roe

In *Maher v. Roe*, 432 U.S. 464 (1977), the Supreme Court considered the Connecticut statute that denied Medicaid benefits for first-trimester abortions that were not medically necessary. The Court rejected the argument that the state's subsidy of medical expenses incident to pregnancy and childbirth created an obligation on the part of the state to subsidize the expenses incident to non-therapeutic abortions. The Supreme Court voted 6–3 that the states may refuse to spend public funds to provide nontherapeutic abortions for women.

1979—Colautti v. Franklin

The Supreme Court voted 6–3 that the states may seek to protect a fetus that a physician has determined could survive outside the womb.

1979—Bellotti v. Baird—Parental Consent

The Supreme Court in *Bellotti v. Baird*, 443 U.S. 622 (1979), ruled 8–1 that a Massachusetts statute requiring parental consent before an abortion could be performed on an unmarried woman younger than the age of 18 years was held to be unconstitutional. Justice Stevens, joined by Justices Brennan, Marshall, and Blackmun, concluded that the Massachusetts statute was unconstitutional, because under that statute as written and construed by the Massachusetts Supreme Judicial Court, no minor, no matter how mature and capable of informed decision making, could receive an abortion without the consent of either both parents or a superior court judge, thus making the minor's abortion subject in every instance to an absolute third-party veto.

1980—Harris v. McRae

The Supreme Court in *Harris v. McRae*, 448 U.S. 297 (1980), upheld 5–4 the Hyde Amendment, which restricts the use of federal funds for Medicaid abortions. Under this case, the different states are not compelled to fund Medicaid recipients' medically necessary abortions for which federal reimbursement is unavailable, but may choose to do so.

1981—H.L. v. Matheson

The Supreme Court in *H.L. v. Matheson*, 49 U.S.L.W. 4255 (U.S. Mar. 1981), in a 6–3 vote upheld a Utah statute that required a physician to "notify, if possible" the parents or guardian of a minor on whom an abortion is to be performed. In this case, the physician advised the patient that an abortion would be in her best medical interest but, because of the statute, refused to perform the abortion without notifying her parents. The Supreme Court ruled that although a state may not constitutionally legislate a blanket, unreviewable power of parents to veto their daughter's abortion, a statute setting out a mere requirement of parental notice when possible does not violate the constitutional rights of an immature, dependent minor.

1983—City of Akron v. Akron Center for Reproductive Health

The Supreme Court voted 6–3 that the different states cannot mandate what physicians tell abortion patients or require that abortions for women more than three months pregnant be performed in a hospital.

1989—Webster v. Reproductive Health Services

Webster v. Reproductive Health Services, 492 U.S. 490, 109 S. Ct. 3040 (1989), began the Court's narrowing abortion rights by upholding a Missouri statute providing that no public facilities or employees should be used to perform abortions and that physicians should conduct viability tests before performing abortions.

1991—Rust v. Sullivan

Federal regulations that prohibit abortion counseling and referral by family planning clinics that receive funds under title X of the Public Health Service Act were found not to violate the constitutional rights of pregnant women or title X grantees in a 5–4 decision by the Supreme Court in *Rust v. Sullivan,* 111 S. Ct. 1759, (U.S. 1991). Proponents of abortion counseling argue that the regulations impermissibly burden a woman's privacy right to abortion. Prohibiting the delivery of abortion information, even as to where such information could be obtained, the regulations deny a woman her constitutionally protected right to choose under the First Amendment. The question arises: How can a woman make an informed choice between two options when she cannot obtain information as to one of them? In *Sullivan,* however, the Supreme Court found that there was no violation of a woman's or provider's First Amendment rights. The court has extended the doctrine that government need not subsidize the exercise of the fundamental rights to free speech. The plaintiff argued that the government may not condition receipt of a benefit on the relinquishment of constitutional rights.

The White House directed the Department of Health and Human Services to make an exception to the "gag rule," which bars abortion counseling at federally funded clinics, by revising the rule to allow physicians to discuss and provide medical information regarding abortions to their patients. The U.S. Circuit Court of Appeals held that the revised gag rule, making an exception for physicians in abortion counseling, was adopted illegally. The court held that the White House must provide opportunity for public comment prior to ordering an exception to the rule. As anticipated,[3] the gag rule was rescinded during the first week of the Clinton administration.

1992—Planned Parenthood v. Casey

The Supreme Court affirmed Pennsylvania law restricting a woman's right to abortion. *Planned Parenthood v. Casey,* 91-744 (1992). The Court was one vote shy of overturning *Roe v. Wade.* The Supreme Court ruling, as enunciated in *Roe v. Wade,* reaffirmed

- the constitutional right of women to have an abortion before viability of the fetus, as first enunciated in *Roe v. Wade*
- the state's power to restrict abortions after fetal viability, so long as the law contains exceptions for pregnancies that endanger a woman's life or health
- the principle that the state has legitimate interests from the outset of the pregnancy in protecting the health of the woman and the life of the fetus

The Supreme Court rejected the trimester approach in *Roe v. Wade*, which limited the regulations states could issue on abortion depending on the development stage of the fetus. In place of the trimester approach, the Court will evaluate the permissibility of state abortion rules based on whether they unduly burden a woman's ability to obtain an abortion. (A rule is an undue burden if its purpose or effect is to place a substantial obstacle in the path of a woman seeking an abortion before the fetus attains viability.) The Supreme Court ruled that it is "not an undue burden" to require

- a woman be informed of the nature of the abortion procedure and the risks involved
- a woman be offered information on the fetus and on the alternatives to abortion
- a woman give her informed consent before the abortion procedure
- parental consent for a minor seeking an abortion, providing for a judicial bypass option if the minor does not wish or cannot obtain parental consent
- a 24-hour waiting period before any abortion can be performed

and that it is an undue burden to require spousal consent.

State Regulation

The effect of the Supreme Court's 1973 decisions in *Roe* and *Doe* was to invalidate all or part of almost every state abortion statute then in force. The responses of state legislatures to these decisions were varied, but it is clear that many state laws had been enacted to restrict the performance of abortions as much as possible. Although *Planned Parenthood v. Casey* was expected to clear up some issues, it is clear that the states have been given more power to regulate the performance of abortions.

Consent

Spouse

A Florida statute had required written consent of the husband before a wife could be permitted to obtain an abortion. The husband's interest in the baby was held to be insufficient to force his wife to face the mental and physical risks of pregnancy and childbirth. *Poe v. Gerstein,* 517 F.2d 787 (5th Cir. 1975).

In *Doe v. Zimmerman,* 405 F. Supp. 534 (M.D. Pa. 1975), the court declared unconstitutional the provisions of the Pennsylvania Abortion Control Act, which required that the written consent of the husband of a married woman be secured before the performance of an abortion. The court found that these provisions impermissibly permitted the husband to withhold his consent either because of his interest in the potential life of the fetus or for capricious reasons. The natural father of an unborn fetus in *Doe v. Smith,* 486 U.S. 1308 (1988), was found not to be entitled to an injunction to prevent the mother from submitting to an abortion. Although the father's interest in the fetus was legitimate, it did not outweigh the mother's constitutionally protected right to an abortion, particularly in the light of the evidence that the mother and father had never married. The father had demonstrated substantial instability in his marital and romantic life. The father was able to beget other children and, in fact, did produce other children.

In the 1992 decision of *Planned Parenthood v. Casey,* the Supreme Court ruled that spousal consent would be an undue burden on the woman.

Parental Consent

The trial court *In re Anonymous,* 515 So.2d 1254 (Ala. Civ. App. 1987), was found to have abused its discretion when it refused a minor's request for waiver of parental consent to obtain an abortion. The record indicated that the minor lived alone, was within one month of her eighteenth birthday, lived by herself most of the time, and held down a full-time job.

Incompetent Persons

An abortion was found to have been authorized properly by a family court in *In re Doe,* 533 A.2d 523 (R.I. 1987), for a profoundly retarded woman. She had become pregnant during her residence in a group home as a result of a sexual attack by an unknown person. The record had supported a finding that if the woman had been able to do so, she would have requested the abortion. The court properly chose welfare agencies and the woman's guardian *ad litem* (a guardian appointed to prosecute or defend a suit on behalf of a party incapacitated by infancy, mental incompetence, etc.) as the surrogate decision makers, rather than the woman's mother. The mother apparently had had little contact with her daughter over the years.

Employee Refusal To Participate in Abortions

Hospital personnel have a right to refuse to participate in abortions and can abstain from involvement in abortions as a matter of conscience or religious or moral conviction. In a Missouri case, *Doe v. Poelker,* 515 F.2d 541 (8th Cir. 1975), the city was ordered to obtain the services of physicians and personnel who had no moral objections to participating in abortions. The city also was required to pay the plaintiff's attorney's fees because of the wanton disregard of the indigent woman's rights and the continuation of a policy to disregard and/or circumvent the U.S. Supreme Court's rulings on abortion.

Funding

Several states have placed an indirect restriction on abortion through the elimination of funding. Under the Hyde Amendment, the U.S. Congress, through appropriations legislation, has limited the types of medically necessary abortions for which federal funds may be spent under the Medicaid program. Although the Hyde Amendment does not prohibit states from funding nontherapeutic abortions, this action by the federal government opened the door to state statutory provisions limiting the funding of abortions.

In *Beal v. Doe,* 432 U.S. 438 (1977), the Pennsylvania Medicaid plan was challenged on the basis of denial of financial assistance for nontherapeutic abortions. The Supreme Court held that title XIX of the Social Security Act (the Medicaid program) does not require the funding of nontherapeutic abortions as a condition of state participation in the program. The state has a strong interest in encouraging normal childbirth, and nothing in title XIX suggests that it is unreasonable for the state to further that interest. The Court ruled that it is not inconsistent with the Medicaid portion of the Social Security Act to refuse to fund unnecessary (although perhaps desirable) medical services.

A Michigan statute, section 400.109a of the Mich. Comp. Laws, which prohibited the use of Medicaid funds to pay for an abortion for a minor who became pregnant as a result of a rape, was held to be unconstitutional. The statute violated the state's equal protection clause under the state's constitution. *Doe v. Director of Department of Social Services,* 468 N.W.2d 862 (Mich. Ct. App. 1991).

The West Virginia Supreme Court of Appeals held that the state may fund abortions for Medicaid recipients who do not qualify for reimbursement under the Hyde Amendment. *Boley v. Miller,* W. Va., No. 20158 (5/15/92). In contrast, the Michigan Supreme Court held that a Michigan statute barring funds to pay for an abortion unless it is necessary to save the woman's life does not violate the state constitution's equal protection clause. *Doe v. Director of the Michigan Department of Social Services,* Mich., No. 91092 (6/9/92).

Limiting Services

In Nebraska, a teaching hospital was permitted to limit the number of abortions to be performed at the hospital so long as the limitation was in the interest of education. *Orr v. Koefoot,* 377 F. Supp. 673 (1974).

Continuing Controversy

While "pro choice" advocates are arguing the rights of women to choose, they are also pointing out the fact that legalized abortions are safer. "In 1972, for example, the year before *Roe v. Wade* was upheld, the number of deaths from abortions in the U.S. is estimated by experts to have reached the thousands. By 1985 (the latest figures available) the figure was six."[4] In addition, "pro choice" advocates argue that women who have a right to an abortion when pregnancy threatens the life of the mother also have the right to an abortion when pregnancy is the result of incest or rape. "Right-to-Life" advocates argue that life comes from God and that no one has a right to deny the right to life.

There will most likely be a continuing stream of court decisions, as well as political and legislative battles, in the decade of the 1990s. Given the emotional, religious, and ethical concerns, as well as those of women's rights groups, it is unlikely that this matter will be resolved anytime soon.

Physicians are feeling the heat and are concerned about the ongoing abortion controversy. The physician, for example, whose picture was published in an abortion calendar without the physician's consent in *Beverley v. Choices Women's Medical Center,* 565 N.Y.S. 833 (App. Div. 1991), brought a civil rights action against the for-profit medical center for publication of her picture. The calendar was disseminated to the public by the center. The center, among other things, performs abortions from which it derives approximately 50 percent of its income. The plaintiff was awarded $50,000 in compensatory damages and $25,000 in punitive damages. The physician testified that the publication of her picture caused her to suffer physical and mental injury. She also testified as to the effect of the publication on her lifestyle and career decisions.

STERILIZATION

Sterilization is the termination of the ability to produce offspring. Sterilization often is accomplished by either a vasectomy for the man or a tubal ligation for the woman. A vasectomy is a surgical procedure in which the vas deferens is severed and tied to prevent the flow of the seminal fluid into the urinary canal. A tubal ligation is a surgical procedure in which the fallopian tubes are cut and tied, preventing passage of the ovum from the ovary to the uterus. Sterilizations are often sought because of

- economic necessity—to avoid the additional expense of raising a child
- therapeutic purposes—to prevent harm to a woman's health (e.g., to remove a diseased reproductive organ)
- genetic reasons—to prevent the birth of a defective child

Elective Sterilization

Voluntary or elective sterilizations on competent individuals present few legal problems, so long as proper consent has been obtained from the patient and the procedure is performed properly. Civil liability for performing a sterilization of convenience may be imposed if the procedure is performed in a negligent manner. The physician in *McLaughlin v. Cooke,* 774 P.2d 1171 (Wash. 1989), was found negligent for mistakenly cutting a blood vessel in the patient's scrotum while he was performing a vasectomy. Excessive bleeding at the site of the incision was found to have occurred because of the physician's negligent postsurgical care. On appeal, the jury's finding of negligence was held to have been supported properly by testimony that the physician's failure to intervene sooner and to remove a hematoma had been the proximate cause of tissue necrosis, which later required the removal of the patient's testicle.

The parents in *Goforth v. Porter Medical Associates, Inc.,* 755 P.2d 678 (Okla. 1988), brought a medical malpractice action for expenses resulting from the negligence of the physician in performing a sterilization on August 2, 1980. The physician assured the plaintiff that she was sterile. The patient subsequently became pregnant and delivered a child on October 9, 1981. The plaintiff argued that as a result of the physician's negligence, she incurred $2,000 in medical bills and will incur $200,000 for the future care of the child. The district court dismissed the case. On appeal, the Supreme Court of Oklahoma held that the parents could not recover the expenses of raising a healthy child; however, they could maintain an action for expenses resulting from the negligent performance of a sterilization and the unplanned pregnancy.

Regulation of Sterilization of Convenience

Like abortion, voluntary sterilization is the subject of much debate over its moral and ethical propriety. Some health care institutions have adopted policies restricting the performance of such operations at their facilities. The U.S. Court of Appeals for the First Circuit has ruled in *Hathaway v. Worcester City Hospital,* 475 F.2d 701 (1st Cir. 1973), that a governmental hospital may not impose greater restrictions on sterilization procedures than on other procedures that are medically indistinguishable from sterilization with regard to the risk to the patient or the demand on staff or facilities. The court relied on the Supreme Court decisions in *Roe v. Wade,* 410 U.S. 113 (1973), and *Doe v. Bolton,* 410 U.S. 179 (1973), which accorded considerable recognition to the patient's right to privacy in the context of obtaining medical services. The extent to which hospitals may prohibit or substantially limit sterilization procedures is not clear, but it appears likely that such hospitals will be allowed considerable discretion in this matter.

At least one state, Kansas, has enacted legislation declaring that hospitals are not required to permit the performance of sterilization procedures and that physicians and hospital personnel may not be required to participate in such procedures or be discriminated against for refusal to participate. Such legislation, which more frequently is enacted in relation to abortion procedures, often is referred to by the term *conscience clause* and was not found objectionable in Supreme Court decisions striking down most state abortion laws.

Therapeutic Sterilization

If the life or health of a woman may be jeopardized by pregnancy, the danger may be avoided by terminating her ability to conceive or her husband's ability to impregnate. Such an operation is a therapeutic sterilization—one performed to preserve life or health. The medical necessity for sterilization renders the procedure therapeutic. Sometimes a diseased reproductive organ has to be removed to preserve the life or health of the individual. The operation results in sterility, although this was not the primary reason for the procedure. Such an operation technically should not be classified as a sterilization because the sterilization is incidental to the medical purpose.

Involuntary/Eugenic Sterilization

The term *eugenic sterilization* refers to the involuntary sterilization of certain categories of persons described in statutes, without the need for consent by, or on behalf of, those subject to the procedures. Persons classified as insane, mentally deficient, feeble-minded, and in some instances epileptic, are included within the scope of the statutes. Several states also have included certain sexual deviates and persons classified as habitual criminals. Such statutes ordinarily are said to be designed to prevent the transmission of hereditary defects to succeeding generations, but several statutes also have recognized the purpose of preventing procreation by individuals who would not be able to care for their offspring.

Although there have been many judicial decisions to the contrary, the U.S. Supreme Court in *Buck v. Bell,* 224 U.S. 200 (1927), specifically upheld the validity of such eugenic sterilization statutes, provided that certain procedural safeguards are observed.

Several states have laws authorizing eugenic sterilization. The decision in *Wade v. Bethesda Hospital,* 337 F. Supp. 671 (E.D. Ohio 1971), strongly suggests that in the absence of statutory authority, the state cannot order sterilization for eugenic purposes.

At the minimum, eugenic sterilization statutes provide the following:

- a grant of authority to public officials supervising state institutions for the mentally ill or prisons and to certain public health officials to conduct sterilizations
- a requirement of personal notice to the person subject to sterilization and, if that person is unable to comprehend what is involved, notice to the person's legal representative, guardian, or nearest relative
- a hearing by the board designated in the particular statute to determine the propriety of the prospective sterilization; at the hearing, evidence may be presented, and the patient must be present or represented by counsel or the nearest relative or guardian
- an opportunity to appeal the board's ruling to a court

The procedural safeguards of notice, hearing, and the right to appeal must be present in sterilization statutes to fulfill the minimum constitutional requirements of due process. An Arkansas statute was found to be unconstitutional in that it did not provide for notice to the incompetent patient and opportunity to be heard, as well as the patient's entitlement to legal counsel. *McKinney v. McKinney,* 805 S.W.2d 66 (Ark. 1991).

Current statutes do not authorize castration—many laws specifically prohibit it—and most eugenic sterilization statutes provide for vasectomy or salpingectomy. This prohibition against castration, along with provisions granting immunity only to persons performing or assisting in a sterilization that conforms to the law, is an added safeguard for persons subject to sterilization. Civil or criminal liability for assault and battery may be imposed on one who castrates or sterilizes another without following the procedure required by law.

ARTIFICIAL INSEMINATION

Generally, artificial insemination is the injection of seminal fluid into a woman to induce pregnancy. The term also may include insemination that takes place outside of the woman's body, as with so-called test-tube babies. If the semen of the woman's husband is used to impregnate her, the technique is called homologous artificial insemination (AIH), but if the semen comes from a donor other than the husband, the procedure is called heterologous artificial insemination (AID).

AID raises several problems with which legislation has begun to deal. The first state to pass a comprehensive statute dealing with the problems attendant to AID was Oklahoma. This statute provides guidelines for the physician and the hospital and resolves some of the questions arising from AID that have been litigated. Subsequent to the Oklahoma legislation, a few other states have passed laws dealing generally with the same issues.

The absence of answers to many questions concerning AID may have discouraged couples from seeking to use the procedure and physicians from performing it. Some of the questions concern the procedure itself; others concern the status of the offspring and the effect of the procedure on the marital relationship.

Consent

The Oklahoma AID statute resolves the issue of whose consent should be obtained by specifying that husband and wife must consent to the procedure. It is obvious that the wife's consent must be obtained because, without it, the touching involved in the artificial insemination would constitute a battery. Besides the wife's consent, it is important to obtain the husband's consent to ensure against liability accruing if a court adopted the view that without the consent of the husband, AID was a wrong to the husband's interest for which he could sustain a suit for damages. Because AID involves the impregnation of the woman with the semen of a person other than her husband, failure to obtain the husband's consent may raise the issue of whether the woman has committed adultery.

The Oklahoma statute also deals with establishing proof of consent; it requires the consent to be in writing and to be executed and acknowledged by the physician performing the procedure and by the local judge who has jurisdiction over the adoption of children, as well as by the husband and wife.

In states without specific statutory requirements, medical personnel should attempt to avoid such potential liability by establishing the practice of obtaining the written consent of the couple requesting the AID procedure.

Legal Status of Offspring

The Oklahoma AID statute resolves the questions that have arisen with respect to the legitimacy of a child conceived by means of AID, the duty of support owed an AID child by the nondonor husband, the effect of AID birth on the child's right of intestate succession, and the right to custody of such a child. The law declares that any child born as a result of AID performed in accordance with the statute's requirements is to be considered in all respects the same as a naturally conceived, legitimate child.

Several states have enacted legislation declaring that children conceived by artificial insemination with the consent of the parents are to be considered legitimate and natural children. California has declared by statute that the husband of a woman who bears a child as a result of artificial insemination shall be liable for support of the child as though he were the natural father if he consented in writing to the artificial insemination.

Confidentiality of the Procedure

Another problem that directly concerns medical personnel involved in AID birth is preserving confidentiality. This problem is met in the Oklahoma AID statute, which requires that the original copy of the consent be filed pursuant to the rules for the filing of adoption papers and is not to be made a matter of public record.

Ethical and Moral Implications

There are many religious and ethical views as to the propriety of artificial insemination. However, the present state of the law does not appear to forbid AIH or AID, and a hospital would not be liable for permitting artificial insemination to take place on its premises, provided appropriate consents are obtained from both husband and wife and statutory requirements are complied with.

WRONGFUL BIRTH, WRONGFUL LIFE, AND WRONGFUL CONCEPTION

There is substantial legal debate regarding the impact of an improperly performed sterilization. Suits have been brought on such theories as wrongful birth, wrongful life, and wrongful conception. Wrongful life suits are generally unsuccessful, primarily because of the court's unwillingness, for public policy reasons, to permit financial recovery for the "injury" of being born into the world.

However, some success has been achieved in litigation by the patient (and his or her spouse) who allegedly was sterilized and subsequently proved fertile. Damages have been awarded for the cost of the unsuccessful procedure, pain and suffering as a result of the pregnancy, the medical expense of the pregnancy, and the loss of comfort, companionship services, and consortium of the spouse. Again, as a matter of public policy, the courts have indicated that the joys and benefits of having the child outweigh the cost incurred in the rearing process.

There have been many cases in recent years involving actions for wrongful birth, wrongful life, and wrongful conception. Such litigation originated with a California case, *Curlender v. Bio-Science Laboratories,* 106 Cal. App. 3d 811, 165 Cal. Rptr. 477 (1980), in which a court found that a genetic testing laboratory can be held liable for damages from incorrectly reporting genetic tests, leading to the birth of a child with defects. Injury caused by birth had not been previously actionable by law. The court of appeals held that medical laboratories engaged in genetic testing owe a duty to parents and their as yet unborn child to use ordinary care in administering available tests for the purpose of providing information concerning potential genetic defects in the unborn. Damages in this case were awarded on the basis of the child's shortened life span.

Wrongful Birth

In a "wrongful birth" action, the plaintiff(s) claim that but for a breach of duty by the defendant(s) (e.g., improper sterilization), the child would not have been born. A wrongful birth claim can be brought by the parent(s) of a child born with genetic defects against a physician who or a laboratory that negligently fails to inform them, in a timely fashion, of an increased possibility that the mother will give birth to such a child, therefore precluding an informed decision as to whether to have the child.

Recovery for damages was permitted for wrongful birth but not wrongful life in *Smith v. Cote,* 513 A.2d 341 (N.H. 1986). The physician in this case was negligent in that he failed to test in a timely fashion for the mother's exposure to rubella and to advise her of the potential for birth defects. She therefore was entitled to maintain a cause of action for wrongful birth. However, for compelling reasons of public policy, the mother would not be permitted to assert on the child's behalf a claim for damages on the basis of wrongful life.

The parents of a handicapped child stated a cause of action for wrongful birth in *Proffitt v. Bartolo,* 412 N.W.2d 232 (Mich. Ct. App. 1987), against a physician who allegedly failed to properly interpret a rubella test performed during the mother's first trimester of pregnancy, thereby precluding the option of abortion. The physician had a duty to advise the parents so that they would have an opportunity to exercise the option of an abortion. If it could be established that the physician breached such a duty and that the parents would have terminated the pregnancy, the necessary causal connection would be demonstrated, and the parents would be entitled to recover for their extraordinary costs of raising the handicapped child and for any emotional harm they might have suffered as a result of their child's handicap.

Wrongful Life

A "wrongful life" claim is brought by the parent(s) or child who claims to have suffered harm as a result of being born. The plaintiffs generally contend that the physician or laboratory negligently failed to inform the child's parents of the risk of bearing a genetically defective infant and hence prevented the parents' right to choose to avoid the birth. *Smith v. Cote,* at 344. Because there is no recognized legal right "not" to be born, wrongful life cases are generally not successful.

> [L]egal recognition that a disabled life is an injury would harm the interests of those most directly concerned, the handicapped. Disabled persons face obvious physical difficulties in conducting their lives. They also face subtle yet equally devastating handicaps in the attitudes and behavior of society, the law, and their own families and friends. Furthermore, society often views disabled persons as burdensome misfits. Recent legislation concerning employment, education, and building access reflects a slow change in these attitudes. This change evidences a growing public awareness that the handicapped can be valuable and productive members of society. To characterize the life of a disabled person as an injury would denigrate both this new awareness and the handicapped themselves.

Smith v. Cote, at 353.

A cause of action for wrongful life was not cognizable under Kansas law in *Bruggeman v. Schimke,* 239 Kan. 245, 718 P.2d 635 (1986). A child born with congenital birth defects was not entitled to recover damages on the theory that physicians had been negligent when, after a prior sibling was born with congenital anomalies, they mistakenly advised the parents that the first child's condition was not due to a known chromosomal or measurable biochemical disorder. In view of the fundamental principle of law that human life is valuable, precious, and worthy of protection, a legal right not to be born—to be dead, rather than to be alive with deformities—could not be recognized. The Supreme Court of Kansas held that there was no recognized cause for wrongful life.

A wrongful life action was brought against the physicians in *Speck v. Finegold,* 408 A.2d 496 (Pa. Super. Ct. 1979), on behalf of an infant born with defects. The court held that regardless of whether the claim was based on wrongful life or otherwise, no legally cognizable cause of action was stated on behalf of the infant even though the defendants' actions of negligence were the proximate cause of her defective birth. The parents could recover pecuniary expenses that they had borne and would bear for care and treatment of their child and that resulted in the natural course of things from the commission of the tort. The tort in this case was the failure of the urologist to perform a vasectomy properly and the failure of the obstetrician/gynecologist to perform an abortion properly. Recovery for negligence was allowed because the plaintiff parents did set forth a duty owed to them by the physicians and breached by the physicians with resulting injuries to the plaintiffs. Claims for emotional disturbance and mental distress were denied.

The California Supreme Court in *Turpin v. Sortini,* 643 P.2d 954 (Cal. 1982), denied a child born with total deafness the right to seek damages from a physician and hospital for wrongful life. However, the court did hold that either the parents or the child could recover for the extraordinary medical and other expenses incurred because of the hearing impairment.

In *Pitre v. Opelousas General Hospital,* 530 So.2d 1151 (La. 1988), the parents of a child born with a congenital defect filed a malpractice suit seeking damages for themselves and their child, alleging that the surgeon had been negligent in performing a tubal ligation. The suit also claimed that the hospital and the physician failed to inform Mrs. Pitre that the operation was unsuccessful. A pathology report had revealed that the physician had severed fibromuscular tissue, rather than fallopian tissue, during the surgical procedure. The parents were not informed of this finding. The mother became pregnant and gave birth to an albino child. The court of appeals dismissed the child's claim for wrongful life and struck all the parents' individual claims with the exception of expenses associated with the pregnancy and the husband's loss of consortium. On a writ of *certiorari* to review the ruling, the Supreme Court of Louisiana held that the physician owed a duty to warn the parents regarding the failure of the tubal ligation, the physician did not have a duty to protect the child from the risk of albinism, and the parents were entitled to damages relating to the pregnancy and the husband's consortium. Special damages relating to the child's deformity were denied.

Wrongful Conception/Wrongful Pregnancy

"Wrongful conception" or "wrongful pregnancy" refer to a claim for damages sustained by the parents of an unexpected child based on an allegation that conception of the child resulted from negligent sterilization procedures or a defective contraceptive device. *Cowe v. Forum Group, Inc.,* 575 N.E.2d 630, 631 (Ind. 1991). Damages sought for a negligently performed sterilization might include:

- pain and suffering associated with pregnancy and birth
- expenses of delivery
- lost wages

- father's loss of consortium
- damages for emotional or psychological pain
- suffering resulting from the presence of an additional family member in the household
- the cost and pain and suffering of a subsequent sterilization
- damages suffered by a child born with genetic defects

The most controversial item of damages claimed is that of raising a normal healthy child to adulthood. The mother in *Hartke v. McKelway,* 707 F.2d 1544 (D.C. Cir. 1983), had undergone a sterilization for therapeutic reasons to avoid endangering her health from pregnancy. The woman became pregnant as a result of a failed sterilization. She delivered a healthy child without injury to herself. It was determined that "the jury could not rationally have found that the birth of this child was an injury to this plaintiff. Awarding child rearing expense would only give Hartke a windfall." *Id.* at 1557.

The costs of raising a normal healthy child in *Jones v. Malinowski,* 473 A.2d 429 (Md. 1984), were recoverable. The plaintiff had three previous pregnancies. The first pregnancy resulted in a breech birth; the second child suffered brain damage; and the third child suffered from heart disease. For economic reasons, the plaintiff had undergone a bipolar tubal laparoscopy, which is a procedure that blocks both fallopian tubes by cauterization. The operating physician misidentified the left tube and cauterized the wrong structure, leaving the left tube intact. As a result of the negligent sterilization, Mrs. Malinowski became pregnant. The court of appeals held the costs of raising a healthy child are recoverable and that the jury could offset these costs by the benefits derived by the parents from the child's aid, comfort, and society during the parents' life expectancy. The jury was instructed not to consider that the plaintiffs "might have aborted the child or placed the child out for adoption [since] . . . as a matter of personal conscience and choice parents may wish to keep an unplanned child." *Id.* at 431.

The cost of raising a healthy newborn child to adulthood was recoverable by the parents of the child conceived as a result of an unsuccessful sterilization by a physician employee at Lovelace Medical Center. The physician in *Lovelace Medical Center v. Mendez,* 805 P.2d 603 (N.M. 1991) found and ligated only one of the patient's two fallopian tubes and then failed to inform the patient of the unsuccessful operation. The court held that

the Mendezes' interest in the financial security of their family was a legally protected interest which was invaded by Lovelace's negligent failure properly to perform Maria's sterilization operation (if proved at trial), and that this invasion was an injury entitling them to recover damages in the form of the reasonable expenses to raise Joseph to majority."

Id. at 612.

Some states bar damage claims for emotional distress and the costs associated with the raising of healthy children but will permit recovery for damages related to negligent sterilizations. In *Butler v. Rolling Hills Hospital,* 582 A.2d 1384 (Pa. Super. Ct. 1990), the Superior Court of Pennsylvania held that the patient stated a cause of action for the negligent performance of a laparoscopic tubal ligation. The patient was not, however, entitled to compensation for the costs of raising a normal healthy child.

> In light of this Commonwealth's public policy, which recognizes the paramount importance of the family to society, we conclude that the benefits of joy, companionship, and affection which a normal, healthy child can provide must be deemed as a matter of law to outweigh the costs of raising that child.

Id. at 1385.

As the Court of Common Pleas of Lycoming County, Pennsylvania, in *Shaheen v. Knight,* 11 Pa. D. & C.2d 41, 46 (1957) stated:

> Many people would be willing to support this child were they given the right of custody and adoption, but according to plaintiff's statement, plaintiff does not want such. He wants to have the child and wants the doctor to support it. In our opinion, to allow such damages would be against public policy.

Prevention of Wrongful Birth, Wrongful Life, and Wrongful Conception Lawsuits

The occurrence of a pregnancy is not necessarily the result of negligence. Although slight, there is known to be a given failure rate. Physicians can prevent lawsuits by informing each patient in writing as to the likelihood of an unsuccessful sterilization, as well as the inherent risks in the procedure.

NOTES

1. U.S. DEPARTMENT OF COMMERCE, BUREAU OF THE CENSUS, STATISTICAL ABSTRACT OF THE UNITED STATES, 1989 (109th ed., 1989).

2. Andrew Blum, et. al., *The 80's: The Year in Review*, NAT'L L.J., 12 (16 and 17), Dec. 25, 1989–Jan.1, 1990, at S15.

3. The Associated Press, *U.S. Court Blocks Abortion 'Gag Rule,'* NEWSDAY, 54(63), November 4, 1992, at 13.

4. *Abortion: A World View*, SELF, November 1992, at 54.

Patient Rights and Responsibilities

OUTLINE

Every individual possesses certain rights guaranteed by the Constitution of the United States and its amendments, including freedom of speech, religion, and association and the right not to be discriminated against on the grounds of race, color, creed, or national origin. The Supreme Court has interpreted the Constitution as also guaranteeing certain other rights not expressly mentioned, such as the right to privacy and the right to self-determination. An individual's rights are not automatically waived on entering a health care facility. Besides rights, individuals have responsibilities, such as the duty to obey the law and the duty to refrain from injuring others. Specific responsibilities of patients in health care facilities are discussed later in this chapter.

PATIENT RIGHTS

The continuing trend of consumer awareness, coupled with increased governmental regulations, makes it advisable for every administrator and staff member to understand the scope of patient rights and how to ensure them. The Patient Self-Determination Act of 1990 (PSDA), for example, made a significant advance in the protection of the rights of patients to make decisions regarding their own health care. Health care facilities may no longer merely passively permit patients to exercise their rights but must "protect and promote" such rights. The PSDA provides that each individual has a right under state law (whether statutory or as recognized by the courts of the state) to make decisions concerning his or her medical care, including the right to accept or refuse medical or surgical treatment and the right to formulate advance directives.[1]

Persons entering a health care facility continue to have the same civil and property rights they had before entering the facility. Health care facilities participating in the Medicare and Medicaid programs must have established patient rights policies. Informational brochures describing patient rights should be available to both patients and visitors.

Patient rights may be classified as either legal—those emanating from law—or human—statements of desirable principles, such as the right to health care or the right to be treated with human dignity. Both staff and patients should be aware and understand not only their own rights and responsibilities but also the rights and responsibilities of the other.

ADMISSION

At the time of admission, the patient should be informed fully, in writing, of his or her rights and responsibilities. If necessary, each patient has a right to have those rights explained.

Health care facilities must not discriminate by reason of race, creed, color, sex, religion, or national origin. Those that do discriminate violate constitutionally guaranteed rights. They also may be in violation of federal, state, and local laws. Discrimination in some states can be considered a misdemeanor and also may carry a civil penalty. Federal and state funds may be withheld from those institutions that practice discrimination.

Most federal, state, and local programs specifically require, as a condition for receiving funds under such programs, an affirmative statement on the part of the hospital that it will not discriminate. For example, the Medicare program and the Medicaid program specifically require affirmative assurances by the hospitals and other health care institutions that no discrimination will be practiced.

Federal and State Regulations

Civil rights are rights assured by the U.S. Constitution and by the acts of Congress and the state legislatures. Generally, the term includes all the rights of each individual in a free society.

Discriminatory practices in hospitals and other health facilities have been dealt with by Congress and the federal courts. Discrimination in the admission of patients and segregation of patients on racial grounds are prohibited in any hospital receiving federal financial assistance. Pursuant to title VI of the Civil Rights Act of 1964, the guidelines of the Department of Health and Human Services (DHHS) prohibit the practice of racial discrimination by any hospital or agency receiving money under any program supported by DHHS. This includes all "providers of service" receiving federal funds under Medicare legislation.

According to the Fourteenth Amendment to the Constitution, a state cannot act to deny any person equal protection of the laws. If a state or a political subdivision of a state, whether through its executive, judicial, or legislative branch, acts in such a way as to deny unfairly to any person the rights accorded to another, the amendment has been violated.

Civil rights are rights assured by the U.S. Constitution and by the acts of Congress and the state legislatures. Generally, the term includes all the rights of each individual in a free society. Some of these statutes declare that life, liberty, and the pursuit of happiness should not be denied; others adhere closely to the language of federal civil rights legislation.

Government Facilities

Whether a person is entitled to admission to a particular governmental institution depends on the statute establishing that institution. Governmental hospitals, for example, are by definition creatures of some unit of government; their primary concern is service to the population within the jurisdiction of that unit. In all cases, connection with the unit operating the hospital is necessary to entitle one to use the hospital facilities. Some of the statutes cover all inhabitants of the geographic area and, in addition, are broad enough to apply to any person within the area who falls ill or suffers traumatic injury and requires hospital care. However, many of the statutes limit use of the hospital facilities to patients of the governmental unit operating the hospital.

Although persons who are not within the statutory classes have no right of admission, hospitals and their employees owe a duty to extend reasonable care to those who present themselves for assistance and are in need of immediate attention. With respect to such persons, governmental hospitals are subject to the same rules that apply to private hospitals.

The patient in *Stoick v. Caro Community Hospital,* 421 N.W.2d 611 (Mich. Ct. App. 1988), brought a medical malpractice action against a government physician in which she alleged the following facts. The physician determined that the patient was having a stroke and required hospitalization but refused to hospitalize her. The plaintiff's daughter-in-law called the defendant, Caro

Family Physicians, P.C., where the patient had a 1:30 appointment. She was told to take the patient to Caro Community Hospital. On arriving at the hospital, there was no physician available to see the patient, and she was directed by a nurse to Dr. Loo's clinic in the hospital. On examination, Dr. Loo found right-side facial paralysis, weakness, dizziness, and an inability to talk. He told the patient that she was having a stroke and that immediate hospitalization was necessary. Dr. Loo refused to admit her because of a hospital policy that only the patient's family physician or treating physician could admit a patient. The plaintiff went to her physician, Dr. Quines, who instructed her to go to the hospital immediately. He did not accompany her to the hospital. At the hospital she waited approximately one hour before another doctor from Caro Family Physicians arrived and admitted her. Dr. Loo claimed that he did not diagnose the patient as having a stroke and that there was no bad faith on his part. The circuit court granted the physician's motion for summary judgment on the grounds of governmental immunity. The court of appeals reversed, holding that the plaintiff did plead sufficient facts constituting bad faith on the part of Dr. Loo. His failure to admit or otherwise treat the patient is a ministerial act for which governmental immunity does not apply and may be found by a jury to be negligence.

Placement of Patients in Rooms

The individual needs of each patient should be taken into consideration when placing him or her within the facility. When possible, an alert patient should not be placed with a confused and noisy patient. A patient who is seriously ill should be placed near the nursing station. Patients who do not share compatible lifestyles and habits would not be a healthy match. For example, a chainsmoker and a nonsmoker would not be considered compatible roommates.

DISCHARGE

A patient may not be detained in a health care facility for inability to pay. An unauthorized detention of this nature could subject a facility to charges of false imprisonment.

The release of a minor should be made only to a parent or authorized guardian. An incompetent should be released in the care of an appropriate family member or guardian. At times, patients will refuse discharge if they have no place to go. These cases should be handled on an individual basis and in consultation with hospital counsel if necessary.

Discharge Orders

When discharging a patient, a physician should issue and sign all discharge orders. Patients in critical condition should never be discharged. If there is no need for immediate attention, the patient should be advised to seek follow-up care. The plaintiff in *Palmer v. Forney,* 429 N.W.2d 712 (Neb. 1988), brought a negligence action against the physicians and the hospital, charging that her deceased spouse was discharged negligently from the hospital at a time when his condition was worse than when he had entered the hospital. Mr. Palmer had suffered chest injuries (at least one fractured rib and a partial collapse of the lower lungs) and abdominal injuries in a car accident and was admitted to the hospital on October 29. He was discharged on November 8 and was provided follow-up care in the physician's office on November 10. Although the patient was continuing to experience some pain in his chest, Dr. Meyers, his physician, claimed that he was doing "quite well." On November 12, Mrs. Palmer called Dr. Meyers, indicating to him that Mr. Palmer was "profoundly short of breath" and was experiencing chest pains, a condition that existed the evening before. He died en route to the hospital as the result of a pulmonary embolism. The district court entered a judgment for the defendants. On appeal, the Supreme Court of Nebraska affirmed the district court's judgment for the defendants.

Delaying Discharge

Patients with communicable diseases can be held by a health officer to prevent the spread of infection. Psychiatric patients can be detained if they are considered to be dangerous to themselves or others. The decision to hold a patient must be done in accordance with federal and state laws.

TRANSFER

Placement of patients outside a health care facility is just as important as placement within the facility. The health needs of a community are best served when it has at its disposal facilities that are capable of handling the health problems of its citizens, not only those acutely ill, but also those requiring recuperative and follow-up care. For this reason, a complete health care program will include transfer agreements with both hospitals and extended care facilities.

Health care facilities should have in effect a written transfer agreement with one or more other facilities to help assure the smooth transfer of patients from one institution to another when such is determined appropriate by the attending physician(s). Generally speaking, a transfer agreement is a written document that sets forth the terms and conditions under which a patient may be transferred to a facility that more appropriately provides the type of care required by the patient. It also establishes procedures to admit patients of one facility to another when their condition warrants a transfer.

It is important that a transfer agreement be written in compliance with and reflect the provisions of the many federal and state laws, regulations, and standards affecting health care institutions. The parties to a transfer agreement should be particularly aware of applicable federal and state regulations.

Transfer agreements need not be limited to a single health care facility. Every effort should be made to establish such agreements between different health care facilities which will aid in bringing about maximum use of the services of each facility and in assuring the best possible care for patients.

The basic elements of a transfer agreement include

- identification of each party to the agreement, including the name and location of each institution to the agreement
- purpose of the agreement
- policies and procedures for transfer of patients: Language in this section of the agreement should make it clear that the patient's physician makes the determination as to the patient's need for the facilities and services of the receiving institution. The receiving institution should agree that, subject to its admission requirements and availability of space, it will admit the patient from the transferring institution as promptly as possible
- institutional responsibilities in arranging and making the transfer: The transferring institution is generally responsible for making transfer arrangements. The agreement should specify who will bear the costs involved in the transfer
- exchange of information: The agreement must provide a mechanism for the interchange of medical and other information relevant to the patient
- retention of autonomy: The agreement should make clear that each institution retains its autonomy and that the governing boards of each facility will continue to exercise exclusive legal responsibility and control over the management, assets, and affairs of the respective facilities. It should also be stipulated that neither institution assumes any liability by virtue of the agreement for any debts or obligations of a financial or legal nature incurred by the other
- procedure for settling disputes: The agreement should include a method of settling disputes that might arise over some aspect of the patient transfer relationship
- procedure for modification or termination of the agreement: The agreement should provide that it can be modified or amended by mutual consent of the

parties. It also should provide for termination by either institution on notice within a specified time period

- sharing of services: Depending on the situation, cooperative use of facilities and services on an outpatient basis (e.g., laboratory and x-ray testing) may be an important element of the relationship between institutions. The method of payment for services rendered should be carefully described in the agreement

- publicity: The agreement should provide that neither institution will use the name of the other in any promotional or advertising material without prior approval of the other

- exclusive vs. nonexclusive agreement: In this age of patient rights, it is advisable for institutions, when and where possible, to have transfer agreements with more than one institution. The agreement may include language to the effect that either party has the right to enter into transfer agreements with other institutions

Besides the actual agreement between the transferring and receiving facilities, there should be a written consent from the patient indicating his or her agreement to the transfer. The right to choose a receiving facility must be honored when and where possible.

The Medicaid patient in *Macleod v. Miller,* 612 P.2d 1158 (Colo. Ct. App. 1980), was found to be entitled to an injunction preventing his involuntary transfer from the nursing home. The patient had not been accorded a pretransfer hearing as was required by applicable regulations. In addition, it was determined that the suffering from "transfer trauma" might result in irreparable harm to the patient. The appeals court remanded the case to the trial court with directions to enter an order enjoining the defendants from transferring the plaintiff pending exhaustion of his administrative remedies.

PATIENT'S BILL OF RIGHTS

A large number of documents have been prepared on the national and state levels regarding patient rights. The following is an excerpt from the Joint Commission's *1992 Accreditation Manual for Hospitals*:

The organization respects the rights of the patient, recognizes that each patient is an individual with unique health care needs, and, because of the importance of respecting each patient's personal dignity, provides considerate, respectful care focused upon the patient's individual needs.

The organization affirms the patient's right to make decisions regarding his/her medical care, including the decision to discontinue treatment, to the extent permitted by law.

The organization assists the patient in the exercise of his/her rights and informs the patient of any responsibilities incumbent upon him/her in the exercise of those rights. [2]

The Joint Commission's manual should be viewed as a document with legal significance whether or not the state in question has adopted a similar code. It would most likely be admissible in evidence in a case where the rights of the patient were concerned.

The following excerpt from the Rules and Regulations of New York State at 10 NYCRR 405.7(c), January 1, 1989, is generally consistent with documents regarding patients' rights in other states.

As a patient in a hospital in New York State, you have the right, consistent with law, to:
1. Understand and use these rights. If for any reason you do not understand or you need help, the hospital must provide assistance, including an interpreter.
2. Receive treatment without discrimination as to race, color, religion, sex, national origin, disability, sexual orientation, or source of payment.
3. Receive considerate and respectful care in a clean and safe environment free of unnecessary restraints.
4. Receive emergency care if you need it.
5. Be informed of the name and position of the doctor who will be in charge of your care in the hospital.
6. Know the names, positions, and functions of any hospital staff involved in your care and refuse their treatment, examination, or observation.
7. A no smoking room.
8. Receive complete information about your diagnosis, treatment and prognosis.
9. Receive all the information that you need to give informed consent for any proposed procedure or treatment. This information shall include the possible risks and benefits of the procedure or treatment.
10. Receive all the information you need to give informed consent for an order not to resuscitate. You also have the right to designate an individual to give this consent for you if you are too ill to do so. If you would like additional information, please ask for a copy of the pamphlet, Do Not Resuscitate—A Guide for Patients and Families.
11. Refuse treatment and be told what effect this may have on your health.

12. Refuse to take part in research. In deciding whether or not to participate, you have a right to a full explanation.
13. Privacy while in the hospital and confidentiality of all information and records regarding your care.
14. Participate in all decisions about your treatment and discharge from the hospital. The hospital must provide you with a written discharge plan and written description of how you can appeal your discharge.
15. Review your medical record without charge and obtain a copy of your medical record for which the hospital can charge a reasonable fee. You cannot be denied a copy solely because you cannot afford to pay.
16. Receive an itemized bill and explanation of all charges.
17. Complain without fear of reprisal about the care and services you are receiving and to have the hospital respond to you and if you request it, a written response. If you are not satisfied with the hospital's response, you can complain to the New York State Health Department. The hospital must provide you with the Health Department phone number. [3]

PATIENT RESPONSIBILITIES

Patients have responsibilities as well as rights. The court of appeals in *Fall v. White,* 449 N.E.2d 628 (Ind. Ct. App. 1983), affirmed the superior court's ruling that the patient had a duty to provide the physician with accurate and complete information and to follow the physician's instructions for further care or tests. Patients are expected to abide by the rules and regulations of the hospital and treat others with the respect and dignity they themselves would expect. The patient has the responsibility to report unexpected changes in his or her condition to the responsible practitioner. A patient is responsible for making it known whether he or she clearly comprehends a contemplated course of action and what is expected of him or her.

No constitutional right is absolute. Even the First Amendment rights to free speech will not protect a person who shouts "Fire" in a crowded room and causes injury to others. By analogy, the patient exercising his or her right to free speech might disturb fellow patients. The right to speak then is conflicting with the right to privacy, which includes the right to peace and quiet.

The following is an excerpt from Cornwall General Hospital's "Rules for Patients," which were posted in that hospital in 1897:

1. Patients on admission to the Hospital must have a bath, unless orders to the contrary are given by the Attending Medical Attendant.

• • • •

6. Patients must be quiet and exemplary in their behaviour and conform strictly to the rules and regulations of the Hospital, and carry out all orders and prescriptions of the various officers of the establishment.

• • • •

8. No male patient shall, under any pretense whatever, enter the apartments or wards for the females, nor shall a female patient enter the apartments or wards for males, without express orders from the Medical Attendant or Lady Superintendent.

• • • •

10. Every patient shall retire to bed at 9 p.m. from First May to First November, and at 8 p.m. from November to May; and those who are able shall rise at 6 a.m. in the Summer and 7 a.m. in the Winter.

11. Such patients as are able, in the opinion of the physicians and surgeons, shall assist in nursing others, or in such services as the Lady Superintendent may require.

• • • •

13. Patients must not take away bottles, labels or appliances when leaving the Hospital.

14. No patients shall enter into the basement story, operating theatre, or any of the officers' or attendants' rooms, except by permission of an officer of the Hospital.

• • • •

17. Any patient bringing spirituous liquors into the Hospital or the grounds, or found intoxicated, will be discharged.

18. Whenever patients misbehave or violate any of the standing rules of the Hospital, the Attending Physician may remove or discharge them, as provided by clauses 91 and 93 of Rules for Medical Staff.

Today, patient responsibilities are stated somewhat differently than they were in 1897. Patient responsibilities include the responsibility for:

• providing accurate and complete information regarding complaints, past illnesses, hospitalizations, medications, etc.
• reporting unexpected changes in condition to the treating practitioner
• making it known whether he or she clearly understands the contemplated course of action and what is expected of him or her
• following the treatment plan recommended by the practitioner. This may include following the instructions of nurses and allied health personnel

- following the institution's rules and regulations
- keeping appointments and, when unable to do so, notifying the responsible practitioner or health care facility
- consequences if he or she refuses treatment or does not follow the practitioner's instructions
- being considerate of the rights of others, including health care personnel
- assisting in the control of noise, smoking, and the number of visitors in the room
- being respectful of the property of other persons and of the health care facility

---

NOTES

1. 42 U.S.C.S. §1395cc (1992).

2. JOINT COMMISSION ON ACCREDITATION OF HEALTHCARE ORGANIZATIONS, 1992 ACCREDITATION MANUAL FOR HOSPITALS, 103 (1992).

3. Title 10 NYCRR 405.7(c), Jan. 1, 1989, *as amended*.

Chapter 14
Acquired Immunodeficiency Syndrome

OUTLINE

- Reporting Requirements
- AIDS Emergency Act
- Occupational Safety and Health Act
- AIDS Education
- Some Progress

Acquired immunodeficiency syndrome (AIDS) generally is accepted as a syndrome—a collection of specific, life-threatening, opportunistic infections and manifestations that are the result of an underlying immune deficiency. It is caused by a virus designated as the human immunodeficiency virus (HIV) and is the most severe form of the HIV infection. HIV is considered to be a highly contagious blood-borne virus.

AIDS is a fatal disease that destroys the body's capacity to ward off bacteria and viruses that ordinarily would be fought off by a properly functioning immune system. Although there is no effective long-term treatment of the disease, indications are that proper management of the disease can improve the quality of life and delay progression of the disease.

AIDS IN THE WORLD

Internationally, AIDS is posing serious social, ethical, economic, and health problems throughout the world. AIDS has been reported in more than 140 countries.[1] A release by the World Health Organization (WHO) states, "It is very unlikely that the global prevalence of HIV infections will stabilize or level off for at least several decades."[2]

> Estimates from the World Health Organization show that AIDS cases in the world will increase tenfold over the next eight years, from 1.5 million today to an estimated 12–18 million by the year 2000.
>
> During the same period the number of those infected with the HIV is estimated to triple or quadruple, rising from 9–11 million today to 30–40 million by the turn of the century, WHO estimates.[3]

The Harvard Global AIDS Policy Commission estimated that from 1981 to 1992, the number of people infected with HIV increased from 100,000 to 12.9 million worldwide. "Alarming projections to the year 2000 anticipate that between 38 million and 110 million adults and more than 10 million children will be infected."[4]

There has been a global response to prevention, education, and treatment of persons with AIDS. According to Jonathan Mann, Director of the World Health

Organization's Global Program on AIDS, by the end of 1988 virtually every nation in the world had established an education program to educate its population about AIDS.[5]

AIDS IN THE UNITED STATES

AIDS has already killed more young Americans than the Korean and Viet Nam wars combined, and it has now become the leading cause of death for U.S. women between the ages of 25 and 40 years.[6]

The first case of AIDS appeared in the literature in 1981.[7] Since that time, many reports have followed, describing patients with unusual immune defects later identified as being caused by the AIDS virus. Since identification of the first AIDS case in 1981, more than 120,000 cases have been reported to the Centers for Disease Control (CDC) through January 1990.[8]

To date, about 54 percent of all reported cases have resulted in death. An estimated 1.5 million Americans are afflicted with the virus that causes AIDS, with a large percentage of them expected to develop the full symptoms of the disease. As of January 1990, 72,578 adults and children had died from AIDS.[9] The Centers for Disease Control recently reported that the AIDS epidemic has killed 100,777 people since it was first recognized almost ten years ago. It has been estimated that another 165,000 to 215,000 patients may die within the next three years. Of the deaths that have occurred so far, 31,196 were reported in 1990 alone.[10] The costs associated with treating persons with AIDS are certain to rise. It has been estimated that life and health insurance claims related to the AIDS syndrome totaled $1 billion in 1989.[11] As with other parts of the world, HIV infection is appearing with increasing frequency in the nonintravenous drug-using heterosexual population. In addition, it is no longer confined to major urban areas.[12]

SPREAD OF AIDS

AIDS is spread by direct contact with infected blood or body fluids, such as vaginal secretions, semen, and breast milk. At the present time, there is no evidence that the virus can be transmitted through food, water, or casual body contact. HIV does not survive well outside the body. Although there is presently no cure for AIDS, early diagnosis and treatment with new medications can help HIV-infected persons remain healthy for longer periods. High-risk groups include homosexual men, intravenous drug users, Haitian immigrants, and those who require transfusions of blood and blood products, such as hemophiliacs.

Blood Transfusions

The administration of blood is considered to be a medical procedure. It results from the exercise of professional medical judgment that is composed of two parts: (1) diagnosis, deciding the need for blood; and (2) therapy, the actual administration of blood.

Suits often arise as a result of a person with AIDS claiming that he or she contracted the disease as a result of a transfusion of contaminated blood or blood products. In blood transfusion cases, the standards most commonly identified as having been violated concern blood testing and donor screening. An injured party generally must prove that a standard of care existed, that the defendant's conduct fell below the standard, and that this conduct was the proximate cause of the plaintiff's injury.

The most common occurrences that lead to lawsuits in the administration of blood involve

- transfusion of mismatched blood
- improper screening and transfusion of contaminated blood
- unnecessary administration of blood
- improper handling procedures (i.e., inadequate refrigeration and storage procedures)

The Maryland Court of Special Appeals held in *Roberts v. Suburban Hospital Ass'n*, 532 A.2d 1081 (Md. Ct. Spec. App. 1987), that a blood transfusion constituted provision of a service (i.e., the rendering of health care rather than the sale of a product) and was subject to the exhaustion of Maryland's Health Claims Arbitration Act. It followed then that the complaint should have been dismissed for failure to follow the required administrative remedy. The *Roberts* case involved the contraction of AIDS by a hemophiliac through the transfusion of contaminated blood. The court stated: "A transfusion is not just a sale of blood which the patient takes home in a package. The transfusion of the blood —the injecting of it into the patient's bloodstream, is what he really needs and pays for, and that involves the application of medical skill." *Id.* at 1088.

The risk of HIV infection and AIDS through a blood transfusion has been reduced significantly through health history screening and blood donations testing. All blood donated in the United States has been tested for HIV antibodies since May 1985. Blood units that do test positive for HIV are removed from the blood transfusion pool.

A summary dismissal against a hospital and the American Red Cross was ordered properly in *Kozup v. Georgetown University*, 663 F. Supp. 1048 (D. D.C. 1987), in which it was alleged that the death of a premature infant was due to causes related to AIDS contracted through a blood transfusion given in January 1983 without the parent's informed consent. The case was dismissed on the basis that no reasonable jury would have found that the possibility of contracting AIDS from a blood transfusion in 1983 was a material risk. Dismissal also was justified on the basis that the transfusion was the only method of treating the child for a life-threatening condition.

The hemophiliac patient in *McKee v. Miles Laboratories,* 675 F. Supp. 1060 (D.C. Ky. 1987), had contracted AIDS from a coagulation protein (factor VIII), which was provided by the defendants, and subsequently died. The defendants moved for summary judgment as to the merits of the case, contending that at the time the plaintiff's decedent contracted AIDS, there were no tests that would have revealed the presence of the AIDS virus. The plaintiff argued that there was a genuine issue of material fact as to whether an alternative testing method was available when the decedent contracted AIDS in 1983. The district court held that the provision of blood and blood by-products was a service and not a sale and that the lack of any test to purify or screen blood or blood by-products for the AIDS virus demonstrated that the supplier did not violate industry standards.

The methods available for testing for AIDS during the early 1980s were analyzed carefully in the *Kozup* case, in which the court determined that it was not until 1984 that the medical community reached a consensus as to the proposition that AIDS was transmitted by blood. The district court in *McKee* held that there was no need to rehash the same chronologic medical history of AIDS that the *Kozup* case so methodically composed.

The plaintiff in *McKee* appealed the district court's decision to the U.S. Court of Appeals for the Sixth Circuit, *McKee v. Cutter Laboratories,* 866 F.2d 219 (6th Cir. 1989). The court of appeals upheld the district court's decision that the manufacturer was not negligent.

Sexual Transmission

Heterosexual relations is becoming a main conduit for the spread of AIDS. The World Health Organization reports that "currently 60 percent of HIV transmission is heterosexual and by the turn of the century 75 to 80 percent will result from heterosexual intercourse. Heterosexual transmission is the predominant mode of infection in developing countries now, and is increasing slowly but steadily in developed countries."[13] In Kinshasa, the capital city of Zaire, where homosexuality is rare, it is estimated that 6 percent to 8 percent of the population are seropositive with 80 percent to 90 percent of AIDS being transmitted through sexual contact.[14]

AIDS AND HEALTH CARE WORKERS

The number of AIDS cases cared for in health care facilities is on the rise, as are the costs associated with treatment.[15] A national breakdown by profession of reported AIDS cases among health care workers since the early 1980s revealed the following[16]:

Nurses	1,358
Health Aides	1,101
Technicians	941
Therapists	319
Dentists and Hygienists	171
Paramedics	116
Surgeons	47
Others	1,680

Centers for Disease Control, 3/31/91.

"An estimated 50,000 health workers are thought to be infected with HIV; nearly all are believed to be still working."[17] The American Medical Association and the American Dental Association, in a somewhat unpopular fashion, are recommending that physicians and dentists inform their patients if they are carrying the AIDS virus.

All doctors and dentists who have the AIDS virus should either inform their patients they are infected or cease practicing surgery, other forms of invasive medicine and most dentistry, the American Medical Association and American Dental Association said yesterday in a controversial reversal of their previous positions.[18]

The ever-increasing likelihood that health care workers will come into contact with persons carrying the AIDS virus demands the development of and compliance with approved safety procedures. This is especially important for those who come into contact with blood and body fluids of HIV-infected persons.

The federal Centers for Disease Control is following over 1,000 health care workers who have experienced blood-to-blood or blood-to-mucous membrane exposure to the body fluids of AIDS patients; many of these workers have had needlestick injuries while treating AIDS patients. To date, about 25 health care workers who experienced punctures or other exposures to blood have become infected.

These cases demonstrate the need for health care workers to strictly follow safety guidelines to prevent direct exposure to blood and body fluids in the care of patients.[19]

Suspension of Surgical Privileges

An AIDS-infected surgeon in New Jersey was unable to recover on a discrimination claim when the hospital restricted his surgical privileges. The Superior Court of New Jersey in *Estate of Behringer v. Medical Center at Princeton,* 592 A.2d 1251 (N.J. Super. L. 1991), held that the hospital acted properly in initially suspending a surgeon's surgical privileges, thereafter imposing a requirement of informed consent and ultimately barring the surgeon from performing surgery. The court held that in the context of informed consent, the risk of a surgical accident involving an AIDS-positive surgeon and implications thereof would be a legitimate concern to a surgical patient that would warrant disclosure of the risk. "The 'risk of harm' to the patient includes not only the actual transmission of HIV from the surgeon to patient but the risk of a surgical accident, i.e., a scalpel cut or needle stick, which may subject the patient to post-surgery HIV testing." *Id.* at 1255.

CONFIDENTIALITY

A formidable and troublesome ethical question continues to go unanswered—Should a physician with HIV notify his or her patients that he or she has tested positive for the AIDS virus? Guidelines drafted by the CDC call on health care workers who perform "exposure-prone" procedures to undergo tests voluntarily to determine whether they are infected. The guidelines also recommend that patients be informed.[20]

Both health care workers and patients claim mandatory HIV testing violates their Fourth Amendment right to privacy. The dilemma is how to balance these rights against the rights of the public in general to be protected from a deadly disease.[21]

State laws have been developed that protect the confidentiality of HIV-related information. Also, some states have developed informational brochures, consent, release, and partner notification forms. The unauthorized disclosure of confidential HIV-related information can subject an individual to civil and/or criminal penalties.[22]

Information regarding a patient's diagnosis as being HIV-positive must be kept confidential and should be shared with other health professionals only on a need-to-know basis. Each person has a right to privacy as to his or her personal affairs. The plaintiff surgeon in the *Estate of Behringer v. Medical Center at*

Princeton, was entitled to recover damages from the hospital and its laboratory director for the unauthorized disclosure of the patient's condition during his stay at the hospital. The hospital and the director had breached their duty to maintain confidentiality of the surgeon's medical records by allowing placement of the patient's test results in his medical chart without limiting access to the chart, which they knew was available to the entire hospital community. "The medical center breached its duty of confidentiality to plaintiff, as a patient, when it failed to take reasonable precautions regarding plaintiff's medical records to prevent patient's AIDS diagnosis from becoming a matter of public knowledge." *Id.* at 1255.

The hospital in *Tarrant County Hospital District v. Hughes,* 734 S.W.2d 675 (Tex. Ct. App. 1987), was found to have properly disclosed the names and addresses of blood donors in a wrongful death action alleging that a patient contracted AIDS from a blood transfusion administered in the hospital. The physician–patient privilege expressed in section 509 of the Texas Rules of Evidence did not apply to preclude such disclosure because the record did not reflect that any such relationship had been established. The disclosure was not an impermissible violation of the donors' right of privacy. The societal interest in maintaining an effective blood donor program did not override the plaintiff's right to receive such information. The order prohibited disclosure of the donors' names to third parties.

A patient who was infected with HIV-contaminated blood during surgery in *Doe v. University of Cincinnati,* 538 N.E.2d 419 (Ohio Ct. App. 1988), brought an action against a hospital and a blood bank. The trial court granted the patient's request to discover the identity of the blood donor, and the defendants appealed. The court of appeals held that the potential injury to a donor in revealing his identity outweighed the plaintiff's modest interest in learning of the donor's identity. A blood donor has a constitutional right to privacy not to be identified as a donor of blood that contains HIV. At the time of the plaintiff's blood transfusion in July 1984, no test had been developed to determine the existence of AIDS antibodies. By May 27, 1986, all donors donating blood through the defendant blood bank were tested for the presence of HIV antibodies. Patients who received blood from donors that tested positive were to be notified through their physicians. The plaintiff's family in this case was notified because of the plaintiff's age and other disability.

Any new HIV-related regulations must address the rights and responsibilities of both patients and health care workers. Although this will require a delicate balancing act, it must not be handled as a back burner issue by legislators.

Medical Records

Health care institutions must be sure to adopt appropriate and effective policies and procedures for protecting the rights of patients with HIV. As with mental health records, a higher degree of confidentiality generally is expected of the treating institution because of the negative impact on persons who have contracted HIV.

AIDS AND THE RIGHT TO KNOW

Health Professionals

Health professionals and others working with AIDS patients have a right to know when they are caring for patients with highly contagious diseases. There are times when the duty to disclose outweighs the rights of confidentiality. The U.S. Court of Appeals for the Tenth Circuit in *Dunn v. White,* No. 88-2194 (10th Cir. Aug. 1, 1989), declared that there is no Fourth Amendment impediment to a state prison's policy of blood testing all inmates for HIV. Under the U.S. Supreme Court's drug-testing decisions, the proper analysis is to balance the prisoner's interest in being free from bodily intrusion inherent in a blood test against the prison's institutional rights in combating the disease. The U.S. court of appeals held that in or out of prison a person has only a limited privacy interest in not having his or her blood tested. The court cited *Schmerber v. California,* 384 U.S. 757 (1966), which rejected a Fourth Amendment challenge to the blood testing of a suspected drunken driver. Against the prisoner's minimal interest, prison authorities have a strong interest in controlling the spread of HIV.

Sexual Partner

A person has a right to know when his or her partner has tested positive for HIV.

Under the HIV confidentiality law (New York), doctors must strongly counsel an HIV positive patient to notify his/her sexual or needle-sharing partners or to seek help in doing so from public health officials. If a patient refuses to do so, a physician may, without the patient's consent, notify a sexual partner known to be at risk of HIV infection.[23]

Patients

An AIDS notification bill in Illinois, if approved by the governor, would require notifying more than 67,000 patients that they may be at risk of being infected with the AIDS virus. The patients were exposed when they underwent invasive procedures performed by 204 health care workers who tested positive for the virus.[24]

MANDATORY TESTING

The U.S. district court found that routine testing of firefighters and paramedics for the AIDS virus does not violate an individual's Fourth Amendment or constitutional privacy rights. *Anonymous Fireman v. Willoughby, Ohio,* D.C. N. Ohio, No. C88-1182, (Dec. 31, 1991). Because the tested employees are a high-risk group for contracting and transmitting HIV to the public, the city has a compelling interest and legal duty to protect the public from contracting the virus. Firefighters and paramedics are in a higher-risk category than hospital personnel because they work in a noncontrolled setting. *Skinner v. Railway Executives Ass'n,* 489 U.S. 602, 57 U.S.L.W. 4324 (1989), confirmed "society's judgment that blood tests do not constitute an unduly extensive imposition on an individual's privacy and bodily integrity." However,

> [m]andatory testing by a governmental agency for the sole purpose of obtaining a baseline to determine whether an employee contracted AIDS on the job, and thereby to determine the validity of any future worker's compensation claim, is not valid. Mandatory AIDS testing of employees can be valid only if the group of employees involved is at risk of contracting or transmitting AIDS to the public.[25]

NEWS MEDIA

The superior court in *Stenger v. Lehigh Valley Hospital Center, Appeal of The Morning Call, Inc.,* 554 A.2d 954 (Pa. Super. Ct. 1989), upheld the court of common pleas' order denying the petition of The Morning Call, Inc., which challenged a court order closing judicial proceedings to the press and public in a civil action against a hospital and physicians. A patient and her family had all contracted AIDS after the patient received a blood transfusion. The access of the media to pretrial discovery proceedings in a civil action is subject to reasonable control by the court in which the action is pending. The protective order limiting public access to pretrial discovery material did not violate the newspaper's First Amendment rights. The discovery documents were not judicial records to which the newspaper had a common-law right of access. Good cause existed for nondisclosure of information about the intimate personal details of the plaintiffs' lives, disclosure of which would cause undue humiliation.

DISCRIMINATION

Discrimination against persons who have contracted the AIDS virus often is found to be in violation of their constitutional rights. The sufferings and hardships of those who have contracted the disease extend to family as well as "best friends." The infringements of those infected with HIV include discrimination in access to health care, education, employment, housing, insurance benefits, and military service. Those who believe that they have been discriminated against can contact their state's human rights commission.

Access to Health Care

The American Civil Liberties Union in New York City charged in a recent report that nursing homes discriminate against AIDS patients. "The report is based on a study of 13,000 AIDS discrimination incidents that occurred between 1983 and 1988. The report shows that 'public accommodations'—including nursing homes—accounted for 16 percent of the incidents."[26] A Long Island man stricken with AIDS spent the final three years of his life searching for a nursing home. He died in Nassau County Medical Center after he had been rejected by 22 different homes. The Health Systems Agency, along with the efforts of some state and local officials, were able to "persuade nursing homes in Nassau and Suffolk counties to open their doors to people with AIDS."[27]

The need for nursing home care for AIDS patients is growing, particularly for those who are homeless or have no family support system. An AIDS survey conducted by mail in Oregon revealed that 79 percent of those hospitals responding had adequate resources to care for AIDS patients, 26 percent of skilled nursing facilities, and 69 percent of home health agencies.[28] In response to the need for nursing home care, some health departments (e.g., New York) are encouraging the development of specialized HIV/AIDS nursing homes that will combine medical services and drug treatment for AIDS patients who have become infected through drug abuse.[29]

Education

A school's refusal to admit students with the AIDS virus generally is considered an unnecessary restriction on an individual's liberty. *Board of Education v. Cooperman,* 209 N.J. Super. 174, 507 A.2d 253 (Super. Ct. App. Div. 1986); *District Community School Board v. Board of Education,* 130 Misc. 2d 398, 502 N.Y.S.2d 325 (Sup. Ct. 1986). However, there are circumstances where it "would be unreasonable to infer that Congress intended to force institutions to accept or readmit persons who pose a significant risk of harm to themselves or others." *Doe v. New York University,* 666 F.2d 761 (2d Cir. 1981). For example, in *Doe v. Washington University,* 780 F. Supp. 628 (E.D. Mo. 1991), the university disenrolled a dental student based on his positive HIV status—"the circumstance surrounding plaintiff's HIV status presented little alternative to those charged with evaluating plaintiff's ability to qualify as a dental student." *Id.* at 634.

Employment

AIDS-related employment issues involve a two-sided coin, with employment discrimination on one side and the refusal of employees to care for AIDS patients on the flip side. The growing consensus of case law indicates that employment-related discrimination is unlawful. The California Court of Appeals, Second District, in *Raytheon v. Fair Employment & Housing Commission,* No. BO35809 (Cal. Ct. App. Aug. 7, 1989), determined that an employee with AIDS who was admitted to and treated in a hospital was unlawfully denied his right to return to work after treatment in the hospital. The court held that AIDS is a protected physical handicap under California's Fair Employment and Housing Act and that the employer failed to prove its defense of protecting the health and safety of its other workers. The employer had ignored the advice of county health officials and communicable disease authorities that there was no risk to other employees at the plant.

Employees who have contracted the AIDS virus and whose symptoms warrant should not be placed in positions that threaten the health and safety of patients and employees. The court in *School Board of Nassau County v. Airline,* 107 S. Ct. 1131 (1987), noted that "a person who poses a significant risk of communicating an infectious disease will not be otherwise qualified for his or her job if reasonable accommodations will not eliminate the risk." In severe cases, it may be necessary to place the employee on a medical leave of absence.

Situations may arise from time to time in which employees may refuse to treat AIDS patients. There are two basic approaches that can be taken in dealing with such problems. The most beneficial course of action for the employee and the institution would be to embark on a thorough program of educating the staff. The alternative and less desirable response to the problem may require that disciplinary steps be initiated against the employee. Such action could be justified on the basis that the health care facility has a right to manage its work force by assigning staff in a responsible manner to carry out its mission of caring for the sick.

In the final analysis, many competing issues (e.g., humanitarian, legal, moral, ethical, and religious) pertain to the rights of patients and caregivers who have contracted the AIDS virus, as well as those who have not, and employers. As the search for answers continues, the debates and controversies will be heated.

Hopefully, solutions will be forthcoming that will meet the needs of those who have been infected with the AIDS virus and those who are involved with providing health care to them.

Housing

Discrimination in housing generally is prohibited. Several municipalities have ordinances prohibiting discrimination against those who have or are perceived to have AIDS or related conditions. Several cities have such ordinances: Berkeley, California; Los Angeles, California; San Francisco, California; and Austin, Texas[30], among others.

Case law is developing in housing. For example, in *People v. 49 West 12 Tenants Corp.*, No. 43604183 (Sup. Ct. of New York County 1983), a cooperative building in New York City sought to evict a physician who treated several persons with AIDS. The trial court held that the physician's office was a public accommodation under the New York Human Rights Law, that the physician and the patients had standing to pursue the claim, and that AIDS is a disability under applicable state law. The court granted a temporary injunction, and the litigation subsequently was settled before trial.

Insurance Benefits

Discrimination in the provision of insurance benefits has made it difficult for those persons diagnosed as carrying HIV to obtain health insurance coverage. Private health insurance companies in New York State were found to be able to use the results of HIV testing in determining a potential enrollee's coverage eligibility, according to a ruling of a state appellate court.[31]

Medicaid recipients who were denied benefits for AZT treatments, in *Weaver v. Reagan*, 886 F.2d 194 (8th Cir. 1989), were found to be entitled to summary judgment in their class action suit to require Missouri's authorities to provide Medicaid coverage for the cost of AZT treatments. The U.S. Court of Appeals for the Eighth Circuit decided that states must provide Medicaid coverage for the drug AZT to HIV-infected individuals who are eligible for Medicaid and whose physicians had certified that AZT was a medically necessary treatment. The state had argued that its reliance on the Food and Drug Administration's approval statement in limiting coverage for AZT treatments was a reasonable exercise of its discretion. The Eighth Circuit disagreed.

> In denying coverage for AZT to the plaintiff class, the defendants have done nothing to overcome that presumption except to rely on the FDA approval process in a manner expressly rejected by the FDA. In

the face of widespread recognition by the medical community and the scientific and medical literature that AZT is the only available treatment for most persons with AIDS, we find that Missouri Medicaid's approach to its coverage of the drug AZT is unreasonable and inconsistent with the objectives of the Medicaid Act.

Id. at 200.

NEGLIGENCE

Negligent Record Keeping

A service member brought an action under the Federal Tort Claims Act in *Johnson v. United States,* 735 F. Supp. 1 (D.D.C. 1990), alleging that Army physicians and medical personnel negligently, on or about October 8, 1986, wrongly advised her that she had AIDS after she donated blood to a public blood drive sponsored by the Army hospital, which resulted in her having an unnecessary and unwanted abortion. It was not until February 3, 1987, nearly four months later, that she was told by a Walter Reed physician that there had been an error in the paperwork, and she did not have AIDS.

> In November 1986, prior to being notified of this error, plaintiff discovered that she was pregnant. On November 21, 1986, doctors at Army Reed advised plaintiff that her child would most certainly be born with AIDS and would not live beyond five years. The doctor indicated that under these circumstances it would be better for plaintiff to have an abortion than to carry the child to term. As a result of this counseling, and for no other reason, plaintiff had an abortion on December 4, 1986.

Id. at 2.

The United States had moved to have the case dismissed on the grounds that the action was barred by the *Feres* doctrine. Under this doctrine, the United States is not liable under the Federal Tort Claims Act for injuries that arise out of or are in the course of activity incident to service. The district court held that the donation of blood was not "incident to service," and therefore, the *Feres* doctrine did not bar the action.

Surgery

The *Feres* doctrine did not bar a serviceman's claim that he had been infected with the AIDS virus during surgery performed on him while he was on active duty and who allegedly spread the virus both to his wife and daughter, *C.R.S. v. United States,* 761 F. Supp. 665 (D.C. Minn. 1991). The policy rationale for the *Feres* doctrine was not appropriate for barring the claims made in this case. *Id.* at 670.

CRIMINAL ACTIONS

On June 24, 1987, the defendant, an inmate at the Federal Medical Center in Rochester, was convicted by a jury of assault and battery with a deadly or dangerous weapon. The indictment indicated that he had tested positive for the HIV antibody and later had assaulted two federal correctional officers with his mouth and teeth. *United States v. Moore,* No. Crim. 4-87-44 (D. Minn. Sept. 3, 1987). The defendant motioned the U.S. district court for a judgment of acquittal and for a new trial. Evidence at trial showed that AIDS can be transmitted through body fluids such as blood and semen. The defendant had been informed that he had both the AIDS virus and the hepatitis antibody and that he potentially could transmit the diseases to other persons. He bit one officer on the leg twice, leaving a 4-in. saliva stain. He bit the second officer, leaving a mark that was visible five months later at trial. Expert testimony at trial indicated that any human bite can cause a serious infection and that blood is sometimes present in the mouth, particularly if an individual has ill-fitting teeth or gum problems. In the defendant's motion for a new trial, he claimed that the court erred in denying his requested Jury Instruction 12, which would have prohibited the officers' testimony as to medical instructions they were given to avoid infecting their families from being entered into evidence. The evidence was considered probative of the dangerousness of the bites inflicted by the defendant, and the probative value outweighed any prejudicial effect. The defendant's motions for a judgment of acquittal and a new trial were denied.

REPORTING REQUIREMENTS

Because of the social stigma associated with AIDS, there is a worldwide tendency to under-report the incidence of the disease. This is particularly true in developing countries, where the problem is compounded by the lack of efficient reporting systems. For example, in Africa, for every person with AIDS, between 50 and 100 more are estimated to be infected with HIV. Most cases are not reported, and some governments are unwilling to admit to the problem. Few

African countries possess the medical resources to deal with this epidemic. Whole sectors of African economies face ruin. The social stigma is not endemic to African countries. In the United States, health information is merely more readily available because of sophisticated reporting systems.[32]

> AIDS is now a reportable communicable disease in every state. . . . Physicians and hospitals must report every case of AIDS—with the patient's name—to government public health authorities. New York State does not require reports of ARC or of positive blood test for HIV antibodies, but some states do. . . . Cases reported to local health authorities are also reported to the federal Centers for Disease Control (CDC), with the patients' names encoded by a system known as Soundex. CDC records come under the general confidentiality protections of the federal Privacy Act of 1974. However, the statute permits disclosures to other federal agencies, under certain circumstances.[33]

AIDS EMERGENCY ACT

AIDS has been reported in all 50 states. Approximately 22 percent of all AIDS cases have been reported in New York and 20 percent in California. Because the incidence of HIV affects different localities of the United States disproportionately, the Senate and House of Representatives enacted the Ryan White Comprehensive AIDS Resources Emergency Act of 1990. The purpose of the act is to

> provide emergency assistance to localities that are disproportionately affected by the Human Immunodeficiency Virus epidemic and to make financial assistance available to States and other public or private nonprofit entities to provide for the development, organization, coordination and operation of more effective and cost efficient systems for the delivery of essential services to individuals and families with the HIV disease.[34]

Under the HIV Care Grants section of the act, a state may use grant funds

> (1) to establish and operate HIV care consortia within areas most affected by HIV disease that shall be designated to provide a comprehensive continuum of care to individuals and families with HIV disease . . .
> (2) to provide home- and community-based care services for individuals with HIV disease . . .

(3) to provide assistance to assure the continuity of health insurance coverage for individuals with HIV disease . . .

(4) to provide treatments, that have been determined to prolong life or prevent serious deterioration of health to individuals with HIV disease . . .[35]

OCCUPATIONAL SAFETY AND HEALTH ACT

The Occupational Safety and Health Act (OSHA) requires that health care facilities implement strict procedures to protect employees against the AIDS virus. OSHA requires strict adherence to guidelines developed by the Centers for Disease Control. Complaints investigated by OSHA can result in the issuance of fines for failure to comply with regulatory requirements.

AIDS EDUCATION

The number of AIDS cases cared for in health care facilities is on the rise, as well as the costs associated with treatment.[36] The ever-increasing likelihood that health care workers will come into contact with persons carrying HIV demands the development of and compliance with approved safety procedures. This is especially important for those who come into contact with blood and body fluids of HIV-infected persons. The Centers for Disease Control expanded its infection control guidelines and has urged hospitals to adopt "universal precautions" to protect their workers from exposure to patients' blood and other body fluids. Hospitals are following universal precautions in the handling of body fluids. Universal precaution is the accepted standard for employee protection.

Health care institutions have a responsibility for protecting their workers from occupational exposure to HIV. American Health Association Senior Counsel Margaret Hardy, after a $1.35 million out-of-court settlement in the case of Veronica Prego, M.D., said, "This just adds another reminder, from a different sector, that hospitals have to be serious about [protecting their workers]."[37]

Because of the fear of contracting HIV from an infected individual, health care workers, in some instances, have refused to care for AIDS patients. In New York, such refusal can lead to firing and even disciplinary action by the state.

Hospitals and ambulance services have a responsibility to care for the sick, and to assemble a staff capable of carrying out that mission. There is a need for greater educational efforts to ensure that all health care workers understand the potential routes of transmission of HIV and follow recommended safety precautions.[38]

A wide variety of AIDS-related educational materials is available on the market. One of the most important sources of AIDS information is the Centers for Disease Control in Atlanta, Georgia. The process of staff education in preparing to care for patients with AIDS is extremely important and must include a training program on prevention and transmission in the work setting. Educational requirements specified by OSHA for health care employees include epidemiology, modes of transmission, preventive practices, and universal precautions.

SOME PROGRESS

Although the statistics appear to be insurmountable, there has been some progress.

> We know quite precisely how the virus is transmitted and how it is not and what it does to human cells and immune mechanisms, and we know enough about its structure and life-cycle to have identified multiple potential points to get at it. Thus, prospects for designing better therapeutic agents or even vaccines that can prevent or modify infection seem much better than heretofore.[39]

The AIDS hysteria is far more contagious than the disease. It exists in every corner of our society and affects attorneys, judges, court clerks, physicians, nurses, aides, orderlies, families, and friends. The answers are not simple and will be difficult to find; however, through compassion, research, and education, we can all be winners in our fight against this dreaded disease.

NOTES

1. N.Y. STATE DEPARTMENT OF HEALTH, 100 QUESTIONS AND ANSWERS, AIDS 7 (May 1990).

2. *WHO Predicts Up to 30 Million World AIDS Cases by the Year 2000,* NATION'S HEALTH, XXI(1), Jan. 1991, at 1.

3. *WHO Predicts 10-Fold Rise in AIDS Cases,* NATION'S HEALTH, Apr. 1992, at 15.

4. Anke A. Ehrhardt, *Trends in Sexual Behavior and The HIV Pandemic,* AM. J. PUB. HEALTH, 82(11), Nov. 1992, at 1459.

5. Wagner, *The World's Struggle against AIDS,* FUTURIST, May/June 1989, at 17–20.

6. *Report Card on Our National Response to the AIDS Epidemic—Some A's, Too Many D's,* 82(4), AM. J. PUB. HEALTH, 522 (1992); and J. Curran, CDC testimony before the National Commission on Acquired Immune Deficiency Syndrome, Washington, D.C. (Dec. 15, 1991).

7. Cantwell, *AIDS: The Mystery and the Solutions,* L.A. (1986), at 54.

8. N.Y. STATE DEPARTMENT OF HEALTH, *supra* note 1, at 6.

9. *Id.* at 7.

10. *A Possible 215,000 AIDS Deaths in Next 3 Years,* NATION'S HEALTH, XXI(2), Feb. 1991, at 1.

11. *AIDS Insurance Claims Totaled $1 Billion in 1989,* A.H.A. NEWS, 26(45), Nov. 12, 1990, at 2.

12. Roberts, *Introduction*, CHANGING ISSUES IN THE MANAGEMENT OF HIV INFECTION, SYMPOSIUM 2 (Sept. 1990).

13. *WHO Predicts Up to 30 Million World AIDS Cases by the Year 2000, supra* note 2, at 8.

14. Bernard, *AIDS-Related Knowledge, Sexual Behavior, and Condom Use among Men and Women in Kinshasa, Zaire*, 81 (1), AM. J. PUB. HEALTH, 53 (1991).

15. *Public Hospitals Squeezed by AIDS Patients' Costs*, NATION'S HEALTH, XXX(1), Jan. 1991, at 4.

16. Rick Bland and B.D. Cohen, *LI Dentist Was HIV-Positive*, NEWSDAY, 51(314), July 14, 1991, at 40.

17. Garrett, *Doctors with Aids Asked To Inform Patients or Quit*, NEWSDAY, 51(137), Jan. 18, 1991, at 13.

18. *Id.*

19. N.Y. STATE DEPARTMENT OF HEALTH, *supra* note 1, at 6.

20. *CDC's HIV-Testing Guidelines Get Mixed Reviews*, A.H.A. NEWS, 27(29), July 22, 1991, at 1.

21. Editorial, *AIDS: Balancing Patient, Health Care Worker Rights*, Sunday News-J., (Daytona Beach, Fla.), Dec. 16, 1990, at B1.

22. N.Y. STATE DEPARTMENT OF HEALTH, *supra* note 1, at 17.

23. *Id.*

24. *AIDS-Notification Bill Passes*, A.H.A. NEWS, 27(30), July 29, 1991, at 7.

25. Anonymous Fireman v. Willoughby, 60 LW 2412 (1/7/92).

26. *Long-Term Care*, HOSPITALS, 64, Nov. 20, 1990, at 20.

27. *The High Cost of the State's "Little Cuts,"* NEWSDAY, 51(209), Mar. 31, 1991, at 7.

28. White & Berger, *Response of Hospitals, Skilled Nursing Facilities, and Home Health Agencies in Oregon to AIDS: Reports of Nursing Executives*, 81(4) AM. J. PUB. HEALTH, 495 (1991).

29. N.Y. STATE DEPARTMENT OF HEALTH, *supra* note 1, at 11.

30. LAMBDA LEGAL DEFENSE AND EDUCATION FUND, INC., AIDS LEGAL GUIDE 8-1 (1987).

31. *Briefs*, A.H.A. NEWS, 26(50), Dec. 24, 1990, at 1.

32. *Incalculable Cost of AIDS*, ECONOMIST (U.K.), Mar. 12, 1988, at 44.

33. LAMBDA LEGAL DEFENSE AND EDUCATION FUND, INC., LIVING WITH AIDS 7 (1987).

34. Pub. L. No. 101-381, 1990 U.S. CODE CONG. & AD. NEWS (104 Stat.) 576.

35. *Id.* at 586.

36. *Public Hospitals Squeezed by AIDS Patients' Costs*, NATION'S HEALTH, XXX(1), Jan. 1991, at 4.

37. Green, *Prego AIDS Case: Settlement Leaves Few Answers for Hospitals*, A.H.A. NEWS 26(11), Mar. 19, 1990, at 8.

38. *Id.* at 18.

39. *Report Card on our National Response to the AIDS Epidemic—Some A's, Too Many D's, supra* note 5.

Chapter 15

Euthanasia, Death, and Dying

OUTLINE

The human struggle to survive and dreams of immortality have been instrumental in pushing humankind to develop means to prevent and cure illness.

Advances in medicine and related technologies that have resulted from human creativity and ingenuity have given society the power to prolong life. However, the process of dying also can be prolonged. Those victims of long-term pain and suffering, as well as patients in vegetative states and irreversible comas, are the most directly affected. Today, rather than watching hopelessly as a disease destroys a person or as a body part malfunctions, causing death to a patient, physicians can implant artificial body organs. Also, exotic machines and antibiotics are new weapons in a physician's arsenal to help extend a patient's life. Such situations have generated vigorous debate. There seems to be an absence of controversy only when a patient who is kept alive by modern technology is still able to appreciate and maintain control over his or her life. However, when patients and their families perceive a deterioration of the quality of life and no end to unbearable pain, it is then that conflict arises between health care professionals who are trained to save lives and patients and their families who wish to end the suffering. This conflict centers around the concept of euthanasia and its place in the modern world.

From its inception, euthanasia has evolved into an issue with competing legal, medical, and moral implications, which continue to generate debate, confusion, and conflict. Currently, there is a strong movement advocating death with dignity, which excludes machines, monitors, and tubes.

DEFINING EUTHANASIA

Even the connotation of the word *euthanasia* has changed with time and with those persons attempting to define it. Originating from the Greek word *euthanatos*, euthanasia, meaning "good death" or "easy death," was accepted in situations in which people had what were considered to be incurable diseases. Euthanasia is defined broadly as "the mercy killing of the hopelessly ill, injured or incapacitated."[1]

In the religions of Confucianism and Buddhism, suicide was an acceptable answer to unendurable pain and incurable disease. The Celtic people went a step farther, believing that those who chose to die of disease or senility, rather than committing suicide, would be condemned to hell.[2] Such acceptance began to change during the nineteenth century when Western physicians refused to lessen suffering by shortening a dying patient's life. Napoleon's physician, for example, rejected Napoleon's plea to kill plague-stricken soldiers, insisting that his obligation was to cure rather than to kill people.[3]

In the late 1870s, writings on euthanasia began to appear, mainly in England and the United States. Although such works were written, for the most part, by lay authors, the public and the medical community began to consider the issues raised by euthanasia. Then defined as "the act or practice of painlessly putting to death persons suffering from incurable conditions or diseases,"[4] it was considered to be a merciful release from incurable suffering. By the beginning of the twentieth century, however, there were still no clear answers or guidelines regarding the use of euthanasia. Unlike in prior centuries when society as a whole supported or rejected euthanasia, different segments of today's society apply distinct connotations to the word, generating further confusion. Some believe euthanasia is meant to allow a painless death when one suffers from an incurable disease, yet is not dying. Others, who remain in the majority, perceive euthanasia as an instrument to aid only dying people in ending their lives with as little suffering as possible.

It has been estimated that of the "two million Americans who die each year, 80 percent die in hospitals or nursing homes, and 70 percent of those die after a decision to forego life-sustaining treatment has been made."[5] Although such decisions are personal in nature and based on individual moral values, they must comply with the laws applicable to the prolonging of the dying process. Courts have outlined the ways in which the government is allowed to participate in the decision-making process. The misconceptions and confusion regarding the topic have led to wide disparity among jurisdictions, both in legislation and in judicial decisions. As a result, the American Medical Association, the American Bar Association, legislators, and judges are actively attempting to formulate and legislate clear guidelines in this sensitive, profound, and as yet not fully understood area. To ensure compliance with the law, while serving the needs of their patients, it is incumbent on health care providers to keep themselves informed of the legislation enacted in this ever-changing field.

CLASSIFYING EUTHANASIA

To address the topic of euthanasia properly, it is necessary to understand the precise meaning of the recognized forms. Rhetorical phrases such as "right to die," "right to life," and "death with dignity" have obfuscated, rather than clarified, the public's understanding of euthanasia.

Active or Passive

The labeling of euthanasia as active or passive is, for many, the most controversial distinction. Active euthanasia is commonly understood to be the commission of an act, such as giving a patient a lethal drug that results in death. The act, if committed by the patient, is thought of as suicide. Moreover, if the patient cannot take his or her own life, any person who assists in the causing of the death could be subject to criminal sanction for aiding and abetting suicide.

Passive euthanasia occurs when life-saving treatment (such as a respirator) is withdrawn or withheld, allowing the patient diagnosed as terminal to die a natural death. Passive euthanasia generally is allowed by legislative acts and judicial decisions. *In re Estate of Brooks,* 32 Ill. 2d 361, 205 N.E.2d 435 (1965); *Superintendent of Belchertown State School v. Saikewicz,* 373 Mass. 728, 370 N.E.2d 417 (1977); *In re Quinlan,* 81 N.J. 10, 355 A.2d 647 (1976). These decisions, however, generally are limited to the facts of the particular case. The distinction between active and passive euthanasia is minor at best. The end result in both scenarios is the same.

The distinctions are important when considering the duty and the liability of a physician who must decide whether to continue or initiate treatment of a comatose or terminally ill patient. Physicians are bound to use reasonable care to preserve health and to save lives, so unless fully protected by the law, they will be reluctant to abide by a patient's or family's wishes to terminate life-support devices.

Although there may be a duty to provide life-sustaining machinery in the immediate aftermath of cardiopulmonary arrest, there is no duty to continue its use once it has become futile and ineffective to do so in the opinion of qualified medical personnel. Two physicians in *Barber v. Superior Court,* 147 Cal. App. 3d 1006, 195 Cal. Rptr. 484 (1983), were charged with the crimes of murder and conspiracy to commit murder. The charges were based on their acceding to requests of the patient's family to discontinue life-support equipment and intravenous tubes. The patient had suffered a cardiopulmonary arrest in the recovery room after surgery. A team of physicians and nurses revived the patient and placed him on life-support equipment. The patient had suffered severe brain damage that placed him in a comatose and vegetative state, from which, according to tests and examinations by other specialists, he was unlikely to recover. The patient, on the written request of the family, was taken off life-support equipment. The patient's family (his wife and eight children) made the decision together after consultation with the physicians. Evidence had been presented that the patient, before his incapacitation, had expressed to his wife that he would not want to be kept alive by machine or "become another Karen Ann Quinlan." There was no evidence indicating that the family was motivated in their decision by anything other than love and concern for the dignity of their loved one. The patient continued to breathe on his own. Showing no signs of improvement, the physicians again discussed the patient's poor prognosis with the family. The intravenous lines were removed, and the patient died sometime thereafter.

A complaint then was filed against the two physicians. The magistrate who heard the evidence determined that the physicians did not kill the deceased, because their conduct was not the proximate cause of the patient's death. The superior court determined as a matter of law that the evidence required the magistrate to hold the physicians to answer and ordered the complaint reinstated. The court of appeals held that the physicians' omission to continue treatment, although intentional and with knowledge that the patient would die, was not an unlawful failure to perform a legal duty. The evidence amply supported the magistrate's decision. The superior court erred in determining that as a matter of law the evidence required the magistrate to hold the physicians to answer. The peremptory writ of prohibition to restrain the Superior Court of Los Angeles from taking any further action in this matter, other than to vacate its order reinstating the complaint and to enter a new and different order denying the people's motion, was granted.

Recently, however, other states have been confronted increasingly with the question of whether it is ever right for a physician to provide a patient with aid in dying. On July 26, 1991, a Monroe County, New York, grand jury answered yes when it failed to indict Dr. Timothy Quill for giving a leukemia patient sleeping pills to enable her to take her own life. Dr. Quill, an associate chief of medicine at a hospital in Rochester, New York, wrote an article in the *New England Journal of Medicine* focusing on the suffering of terminal patients. Moreover, he discussed how doctors could relieve an individual's suffering. He is not alone in his support of physician-assisted suicide. In the best-selling book, *The Final Exit*, Derek Humphry, executive director of the Hemlock Society (a nationally known organization advocating the right to die), describes methods of self-assisted suicide for terminally ill people.

In the state of Washington, "voters in November 1991 rejected a euthanasia initiative. The measure, which lost by a margin of 54 percent to 46 percent, would have amended Washington's Natural Death Act to permit terminally ill adults to request and receive 'aid-in-dying' from physicians."[6]

Voluntary or Involuntary

Both active and passive euthanasia may be either voluntary or involuntary. Voluntary euthanasia occurs when the suffering incurable makes the decision to die. To be considered voluntary, the request or consent must be made by a legally competent adult and be based on material information concerning the possible ramifications and alternatives available. The term *legally competent* was addressed in a right-to-refuse-treatment case, *Lane v. Candura*, 6 Mass. App. Ct. 377, 376 N.E.2d 1232 (1979). The case involved a patient who twice refused to permit surgeons to amputate her leg to prevent gangrene from spreading. The patient's daughter sought to be appointed as a legal guardian to enable her to consent to her mother's surgery. The appellate court, finding no evidence indicating that Mrs. Lane was incapable of appreciating the nature and consequence of her decision, overturned the trial court's holding of incompetence.

Therefore, even though Mrs. Lane's decision ultimately would lead to her death, she was found to be competent, and thus she was allowed to reject medical treatment.

The *Lane* court and others have defined legal competence as the mental ability to make a rational decision. A patient must exhibit perception and appreciation of all relevant facts and then make decisions based on those facts. In the active euthanasia context, the patient would be demonstrating that by voluntarily requesting euthanasia, he or she would be selecting death over life. *State Department of Human Services v. Northern*, 563 S.W.2d 197, 209 (Tenn. Ct. App.), *appeal dismissed as moot*, 436 U.S. 923 (1978).

In the case of *In re Lydia Hall Hospital*, 455 N.Y.S.2d 266 (Sup. Ct. 1981), the patient, who was terminally ill and requiring dialysis, was taken off all medication to ensure that his mind would be clear when psychiatrists examined him to determine whether he was competent. Recent case law asserts that the standard of proof required for a finding of an incurable's incompetence is that of clear and convincing evidence. *In re Lydia E. Hall Hospital*, 455 N.Y.S.2d 706, 712 (N.Y. 1982) [quoting *In re Storar*, 438 N.Y.S.2d 266, 274 (N.Y. 1981)]. This is a higher standard than the normal fair preponderance of the credible evidence required in civil proceedings.

Involuntary euthanasia, however, occurs when a person other than the incurable makes the decision to terminate an incompetent or an unconsenting competent person's life.[7]

The patient's lack of consent could be due to mental impairment or comatose unconsciousness. Important value questions face courts dealing with involuntary euthanasia: Who should decide to withhold or withdraw treatment? On what factors should the decision be based? Are there viable standards to guide the courts? Should criminal sanctions be imposed on a person assisting in ending a life? When does death occur?

CONSTITUTIONAL CONSIDERATIONS

To analyze the important questions regarding whether life-support treatment can be withheld or withdrawn from an incompetent patient, it is necessary to consider first what rights a competent patient possesses. Both statutory law and case law have presented a diversity of policies and points of view. Some courts point to common law and the early case of *Schloendorff v. Society of New York Hospital*, 105 N.E. 92 (N.Y. 1914), to support their belief in a patient's right to self-determination. The *Schloendorff* court stated: "Every human being of adult years has a right to determine what shall be done with his own body; and the surgeon who performs an operation without his patient's consent commits an assault for which he is liable for damages." *Id.* at 93. This right of self-determination was emphasized in *In re Storar,* 438 N.Y.S.2d 266 (N.Y. 1981), when the court announced that every human being of adult years and sound mind has the right to determine what shall be done with his own body. *Id.* at 272.

The *Storar* case was a departure from the New Jersey Supreme Court's rationale in the case of *In re Quinlan,* 81 N.J. 10, 355 A.2d 647 (1976). The *Quinlan* case was the first to significantly address the issue of whether euthanasia should be permitted when a patient is terminally ill.[8] The *Quinlan* court, relying on *Roe v. Wade,* 410 U.S. 113 (1973), announced that a patient's right to self-determination is protected by the constitutional right to privacy. The court noted that the right to privacy "is broad enough to encompass a patient's decision to decline medical treatment under certain circumstances, in much the same way as it is broad enough to encompass a woman's decision to terminate pregnancy under certain conditions." 81 N.J. at 40, 355 A.2d at 663.

Most cases today follow the right to privacy argument. The court, in reaching its decision, applied a test balancing the state's interest in preserving and maintaining the sanctity of human life against Karen Quinlan's privacy interest. It decided that, especially in light of the prognosis (physicians determined that Karen was in an irreversible coma), the state's interest did not justify interference with Karen's right to refuse treatment. Thus, Karen's father was appointed her legal guardian, and the respirator was shut off. Opponents of euthanasia argue that before the *Quinlan* decision, any form of euthanasia was defined as murder by our legal system. Although acts of euthanasia did take place, the law was applied selectively, and the possibility of criminal sanction against active participants in euthanasia was enough to deter physicians from assisting a patient in committing self-euthanasia.

Despite intense criticism by legal and religious scholars, the *Quinlan* decision paved the way for courts to consider extending the right to decline treatment to incompetents as well. The U.S. Supreme Court has not yet addressed this issue, but state courts have; even though the state courts recognize the right, they differ on how this right is to be exercised.

In the same year as the *Quinlan* decision, the case of *Superintendent of Belchertown State School v. Saikewicz,* 373 Mass. 728, 370 N.E.2d 417 (1977), was decided. There, the court, using the balancing test enunciated in *Quinlan,* approved the recommendation of a court-appointed guardian *ad litem* that it would be in Mr. Saikewicz's best interests to end chemotherapy treatment. Mr. Saikewicz was a mentally retarded, 67-year-old patient, suffering from leukemia. The court found from the evidence that the prognosis was dim, and even though a "normal person" would probably have chosen chemotherapy, it allowed Mr. Saikewicz to die without the treatment to spare him the suffering.

Although the court also followed the reasoning of the *Quinlan* opinion in giving the right to an incompetent to refuse treatment, based on either the objective "best interests" test or the subjective "substituted judgment" test, which it favored because Mr. Saikewicz always had been incompetent, the court departed from *Quinlan* in a major way. It rejected the *Quinlan* approach of entrusting a decision concerning the continuance of artificial life support to the patient's guardian, family, attending physicians, and a hospital "ethics committee." The *Saikewicz* court asserted that even though a judge might find the opinions of physicians, medical experts, or hospital ethics committees helpful in reaching a decision, there should be no requirement to seek out the advice. The court decided that questions of life and death with regard to an incompetent should be the responsibility of the courts, which would conduct detached but passionate investigations. The court took a "dim view of any attempt to shift the ultimate decision-making responsibility away from duly established courts of proper jurisdiction to any committee, panel, or group, ad hoc or permanent." *Id.* at 758, 370 N.E.2d at 434.

This main point of difference between the *Saikewicz* and *Quinlan* cases marked the emergence of two different policies on the incompetent's right to refuse treatment. One line of cases has followed *Saikewicz* and supports court approval before physicians withhold or withdraw life support. Advocates of this view argue that it makes more sense to leave the decision to an objective tribunal than to extend the right of a patient's privacy to a number of interested parties, as was done in *Quinlan*. They also attack the *Quinlan* method as being a privacy decision effectuated by popular vote.[9]

Six months after *Saikewicz*, the Massachusetts Appeals Court narrowed the need for court intervention in *In re Dinnerstein,* 6 Mass. App. Ct. 466, 380 N.E.2d 134 (1978), in finding that "no code" orders are valid to prevent the use of artificial resuscitative measures on incompetent terminally ill patients. The court was faced with the case of a 67-year-old woman who was suffering from Alzheimer's disease. It was determined that she was permanently comatose at the time of trial. Further, the court decided that *Saikewicz*-type judicial proceedings should take place only when medical treatment could offer "a reasonable expectation of effecting a permanent or temporary cure of or relief from the illness." 380 N.E.2d at 138.

The Massachusetts Supreme Judicial Court attempted to clarify its *Saikewicz* opinion with regard to court orders in *In re Spring,* 405 N.E.2d 115 (Mass. 1980). It held that such different factors as the patient's mental impairment and his or her medical prognosis with or without treatment must be considered before judicial approval is necessary to withdraw or withhold treatment from an incompetent patient. The problem in all three cases is that there is still no clear guidance as to exactly when the court's approval of the removal of life-support systems would be necessary. *Saikewicz* seemed to demand judicial approval in every case. *Spring*, however, in partially retreating from that view, stated that it did not have to articulate what combination of the factors it discussed, thus making prior court approval necessary. A Maine court ruled that it was within the scope of a guardian's powers and rights to request and instruct the treating physicians and hospital to stop all life support including food, water, and antibiotics—without prior court approval. *In re Hallock* (Kennebec County Prob. Ct. Sept. 26, 1988).

The inconsistencies presented by the Massachusetts cases have led most courts since 1977 to follow the lead set by *Quinlan*, requiring judicial intervention. In cases in which the irreversible nature of the patient's loss of consciousness has been certified by physicians, an ethics committee (actually a neurologic team) could certify the patient's hopeless neurologic condition. Then a guardian would be free to take the legal steps necessary to remove life-support systems. The main reason for the appointment of a guardian is to ensure that incompetents, like all other patients, maintain their right to refuse treatment. Most holdings indicate that because a patient has the constitutional right of self-determination, those acting on the patient's behalf can exercise that right when rendering their best judgment concerning how the patient would assert the right. This substituted judgment doctrine could be argued on standing grounds, whereby a second party has the right to assert the constitutional rights of another when that second party's intervention is necessary to protect the other's constitutional rights. The guardian's decision is more sound if based on the known desires of a patient who was competent immediately before becoming comatose.

Courts adhering to the *Quinlan* rationale have recognized that fact, and in 1984 the highest state court of Florida took the lead and accepted the living will as persuasive evidence of an incompetent's wishes. The Supreme Court of Florida, in *John F. Kennedy Memorial Hospital v. Bludworth,* 452 So.2d 925 (Fla. 1984), allowed an incompetent patient's wife to act as his guardian, and in accordance with the terms of a living will he executed in 1975, she was told to substitute her judgment for that of her husband. She asked to have a respirator removed. The court declined the necessity of prior court approval, finding that the constitutional right to refuse treatment that had been decided for competents in *Satz v. Perlmutter,* 362 So.2d 160 (Fla. Dist. Ct. App. 1978), *aff'd,* 379 So.2d 359 (Fla. 1980), extends to incompetents. The court required the attending physician to certify that the patient was in a permanent vegetative state, with no reasonable chance for recovery, before a family member or guardian could request termination of extraordinary means of medical treatment.

In keeping with *Saikewicz*, the decision maker would attempt to ascertain the incompetent patient's actual interests and preferences. Court involvement would be mandated only to appoint a guardian or in one of the following cases: (1) if family members disagree as to the incompetent's wishes, (2) if physicians disagree on the prognosis, (3) if the patient's wishes cannot be known because he or she always has been incompetent, (4) if evidence exists of wrongful motives or malpractice, or (5) if no family member can serve as a guardian. *John F. Kennedy Memorial Hospital v. Bludworth,* 452 So.2d 925, 430 (Fla. 1984) (citing *In re Welfare of Colyer,* 99 Wash. 2d 114, 660 P.2d 738 (1983), in which the court found prior court approval to be "unresponsive and cumbersome").

DEFINING DEATH

The decision in *John F. Kennedy Memorial Hospital v. Bludworth* increased the desire of the public, courts, and religious groups to know when a patient is considered to be legally dead and what type of treatment can be withheld or withdrawn at that point. Most cases dealing with euthanasia speak of the necessity that a physician diagnose a patient as being either of the following:

- in a persistent vegetative state, *Severns v. Wilmington Medical Center*, 425 A.2d 156 (Del. Ch. 1980) (incompetent's right to refuse medical treatment may be expressed through a guardian when the patient is in a chronic vegetative state); *Leach v. Akron General Medical Center*, 68 Ohio Misc. 1, 426 N.E.2d 809 (Ohio Com. Pl. 1980) (right to privacy includes right of a terminally ill patient in a vegetative state to determine his or her own course of treatment)
- terminally ill, *Satz v. Perlmutter*, 379 So.2d 359 (Fla. 1980) (constitutional right to privacy supports decision of a competent adult suffering from a terminal illness to refuse extraordinary treatment); *Superintendent of Belchertown State School v. Saikewicz*, 373 Mass. 728, 370 N.E.2d 417 (1977) (right to refuse medical treatment for terminal illness extends to incompetent patients)

This diagnostic role of the physician acts as a limitation on the decision-making role of the family or the guardian. When death is actually present, the termination of mechanical or other similar devices would be a consistent and permissible act.

Traditionally, the definition of death adopted by the courts has been the *Black's Law Dictionary* definition: "cessation of respiration, heartbeat, and certain indications of central nervous system activity, such as respiration and pulsation." *Schmitt v. Pierce*, 344 S.W.2d 120, 133 (Mo. 1961). At present, however, modern science has the capacity to sustain vegetative functions of those in irreversible comas. Machinery can sustain heartbeat and respiration even in the face of brain death. "With 10,000 patients existing in the twilight state at this time,"[10] every appellate court that has ruled on the question has recognized that the irreversible cessation of brain function constitutes death.

Further, ethicists who advocate the prohibition on taking action to shorten life agree that "where death is imminent and inevitable, it is permissible to forego treatments that would only provide a precarious and painful prolongation of life, as long as the normal care due to the sick person in similar cases is not interrupted."[11]

Relying on the 1968 Harvard Criteria set forth by the Ad Hoc Committee of the Harvard Medical School To Examine the Definition of Brain Death, the American

Medical Association in 1974 accepted that death occurs when there is "irreversible cessation of all brain functions including the brain stem."[12] Most states now recognize brain death by statute or judicial decision. New York, for example, in *People v. Eulo*, 482 N.Y.S.2d 436 (1984), in rejecting the traditional cardiopulmonary definition of death, announced that the determination of brain death need be made only according to acceptable medical standards to be valid. The court also repeated its holding in *In re Storar*, 438 N.Y.S.2d 266 (1981), that clear and convincing evidence of a person's desire to decline extraordinary medical care may be honored and that a third person may not exercise this judgment on behalf of a person who has not or cannot express the desire to decline treatment. Following the *Bludworth* logic, the court noted that health professionals acting within the cases should not face liability. Nearly half the states, in response to cases since *Quinlan*, have enacted laws setting forth statutory guidelines for terminating life support.

The clear and convincing evidence standard recently was defined more succinctly by the New York Court of Appeals in *In re Westchester County Medical Center ex rel. O'Connor*, 72 N.Y.2d 517, 531 N.E.2d 607, 534 N.Y.S.2d 886 (1988). There the court determined that artificial nutrition could be withheld from Mary O'Connor, a stroke victim who was unable to converse or feed herself. The court held that "nothing less than unequivocal proof of a patient's wishes will suffice when the decision to terminate life support is at issue." 534 N.Y.S.2d at 891. The factors outlined by the court in determining the existence of clear and convincing evidence of a patient's intention to reject the prolongation of life by artificial means were

- the persistence of statements regarding an individual's beliefs
- the desirability of the commitment to those beliefs
- the seriousness with which such statements were made
- the inferences that may be drawn from the surrounding circumstances

The Missouri Supreme Court has followed the *Westchester* ruling and has held that the family of a woman who has been in a persistent vegetative state since 1983 cannot order physicians to remove artificial nutrition. In 1983 Nancy Cruzan sustained injuries in a car accident, in which her car overturned, after which she was found face down in a ditch without respiratory or cardiac function. Although unconscious, her breathing and heartbeat were restored at the site of the accident. On examination at the hospital to which she was taken, a neurosurgeon diagnosed her as having suffered cerebral contusions and anoxia. It was estimated that she had been deprived of oxygen for 12 to 14 minutes. After remaining in a coma for three weeks, Ms. Cruzan went into an unconscious state. At first she was able to ingest some food orally. Thereafter, surgeons implanted a gastrostomy feeding and hydration tube, with the consent of her husband, to make feeding her easier. She did not improve, and until December 1990, she lay in a Missouri state hospital in a persistent vegetative state that was determined to be "irreversible, permanent, progressive and ongoing." *Cruzan v. Harman,* 760 S.W.2d 408, 411 (Mo. 1988) (*en banc*). She was not dead, according to the accepted definition of death in Missouri, and physicians estimated that she could live in the vegetative state for an additional 30 years. Because of the prognosis, Ms. Cruzan's parents asked the hospital staff to cease all artificial nutrition and hydration procedures. The staff refused to comply with their wishes without court approval. The state trial court granted authorization for termination, finding that Nancy Cruzan had a fundamental right—grounded in both the state and federal constitutions—to refuse or direct the withdrawal of death-prolonging procedures. Testimony at trial from a former roommate of Nancy Cruzan indicated to the court that Ms. Cruzan had stated that if she were ever sick or injured, she would not want to live unless she could live halfway normally. The court interpreted that conversation, which had taken place when Ms. Cruzan was 25 years old, as meaning that she would not want to be forced to take nutrition and hydration while in a persistent vegetative state.

The case was appealed to the Missouri Supreme Court, which reversed the lower court decision. The court not only doubted that the doctrine of informed consent applied to the circumstances of the case, it moreover would not recognize a broad privacy right from the state constitution that would "support the right of a person to refuse medical treatment in every circumstance." *Id.* at 417, 418. Since Missouri recognizes living wills, the court held that Ms. Cruzan's parents were not entitled to order the termination of her treatment, because "no person can assume that choice for an incompetent in the absence of the formalities required under Missouri's Living Will statutes or the clear and convincing, inherently reliable evidence absent here." *Id.* at 425. The court found that Ms. Cruzan's statements to her roommate did not rise to the level of clear and convincing evidence of her desire to end nutrition and hydration.

The U.S. Supreme Court, in June 1990, heard oral arguments and held that

(1) the U.S. Constitution does not forbid Missouri from requiring that there be clear and convincing evidence of an incompetent's wishes as to the withdrawal of life sustaining treatment;

(2) the Missouri Supreme Court did not commit constitutional error in concluding that evidence adduced at trial did not amount to clear and convincing evidence of Cruzan's desire to cease hydration and nutrition;

(3) due process did not require the state to accept the substituted judgment of close family members, absent substantial proof that their views reflected those of the patient.

Cruzan v. Director, Missouri Department of Health, 110 S. Ct. 2841 (1990).

In delivering the opinion of the Court, Justice Rehnquist noted that although most state courts have applied the common-law right to informed consent or a combination of that right and a privacy right when allowing a right to refuse treatment, the Supreme Court analyzed the issues presented in the *Cruzan* case in terms of a Fourteenth Amendment liberty interest, finding that a competent person has a constitutionally protected right grounded in the due process clause to refuse life-saving hydration and nutrition. The Court, however, did not accept that an incompetent person has the same right, because he or she could not exercise the right based on any informed and voluntary choice. Missouri provided for the incompetent by allowing a surrogate to act for the patient in choosing to withdraw hydration and treatment. Moreover, it put into place procedures to ensure that the surrogate's action conforms to the wishes expressed by the patient when he or she was competent. While recognizing that Missouri had enacted a restrictive law, the Supreme Court held that right-to-die issues should be decided pursuant to state law, subject to a due process liberty interest, and in keeping with state constitutional law. After the Supreme Court rendered its decision, the Cruzans returned to Missouri probate court, where on November 14, 1990, Judge Charles Teel authorized physicians to remove the feeding tubes from Nancy Cruzan. The judge determined that testimony presented to him early in November demonstrated to him clear and convincing evidence that Ms. Cruzan would not have wanted to live in a persistent vegetative state. Several of her co-workers had testified that she told them before her accident that she would not want to live "like a vegetable." On December 26, 1990, two weeks after her feeding tubes were removed, Nancy Cruzan died.

THE LEGISLATIVE RESPONSE

After the *Cruzan* decision, states have begun to rethink existing legislation and draft new legislation in the areas of living wills, durable powers of attorney, health care proxies, and surrogate decision making. Pennsylvania, which has not handled many right-to-die cases, and Florida were two of the first states to react to the *Cruzan* decision. The new Pennsylvania law is applied to terminally ill or permanently unconscious patients. The statute, the Advance Directive for Health Care Act,[13] deals mainly with individuals who have prepared living wills. It includes in its definition of life-sustaining treatment the administration of hydration and nutrition by any means if it is stated in the individual's living will. The statute mandates that a copy of the living will be given to the physician to be effective. Further, the patient must be incompetent or permanently unconscious. If there is no evidence of the presence of a living will, the Pennsylvania probate codes allow an attorney-in-fact who was designated in a properly executed durable power of attorney document to give permission for "medical and surgical procedures to be utilized on an incompetent patient." 20 Pennsylvania Consolidated Statutes Annotated §5602(a)(9) (1988). The Supreme Court stated in *Cruzan* that only 15 percent of the population has signed any living wills or other types of medical directives. In the light of that, more states will have to address the problem of surrogate decision making for an incompetent. Legislation would not only have to include direction to consider evidence of an incompetent's wishes that had been expressed when he or she was competent, it also would have to include provisions for consideration and protection of an incompetent who never stated what he or she would want done if in a terminally ill or persistent vegetative state.

Unless there is some uniformity in the legislation nationally, patients and their families will shop for states that will allow them to have medical treatment terminated or withdrawn with as few legal hassles as possible. For example, on January 18, 1991, a Missouri probate court judge authorized a father to take his 20-year-old brain-damaged daughter, Christine Busalacchi, from the Missouri Rehabilitation Center to Minnesota for testing by a proeuthanasia physician, Dr. Ronald Cranford. Dr. Cranford, who practices at the Hennepin County Medical Center, has been at the center of controversy in Minnesota. In January 1991, Pro Life Action Ministries demanded Dr. Cranford's resignation, claiming that he "desires to make Minnesota the killing fields for the disabled."[14] He, however, views himself as an advocate of patients' rights. However the situation involving Dr. Cranford is resolved, it is clear that the main reason Mr. Busalacchi sought authorization to take his daughter to Minnesota is that he believed that he would have to deal with fewer legal impediments there to allow his daughter to die. Minnesota is the state in which the courts presently are grappling with a right-to-die case in which physicians and family members are on the sides opposite to their traditional positions on this issue. Helga Wanglie is an 87-year-old woman who is in a persistent vegetative state as a result of a heart attack that caused brain damage. Physicians have determined that she has no chance of recovery and that any further treatment would be meaningless to any recovery. They therefore have sought court permission to discontinue further life-sustaining care. Wanglie's husband of 53 years asserted that his wife would not have wanted anything to shorten her life, and thus he is fighting to maintain life-supporting treatment for her.[15]

Because of the continuing litigation concerning the right-to-die issue, it is clear that the public must be educated about the necessity of expressing their wishes concerning medical treatment while they are competent. Uniformity with regard to the legal instruments available for demonstrating what a patient wants should be a common goal of legislators, courts, and the medical profession. If living wills, surrogates, and durable powers of attorney were to be enacted pursuant to national rather than individual state guidelines, the result should be a greater ease in resolving the myriad of conflicting issues in this area. Several states have addressed the problem by statutorily providing for these instruments, thereby enabling individuals to have a say in the medical care they should receive if they become unable to speak for themselves.

Chief Justice Dore of the Supreme Court of Washington voiced his opinion that a legislative response to right-to-die issues could be better addressed by the legislature.

> The United States Supreme Court, in *Cruzan*, questioned whether a federally protected right to forgo nutrition and hydration existed. The *Cruzan* Court confronted the same philosophical issues that we face today and wisely recognized and deferred to the Legislature's superior policy-making abilities. As was the case in *Cruzan*, our legislature is far better equipped to evaluate this complex issue and should not have its power usurped by the court.

Farnam v. Crista Ministries, 807 P.2d 830, 849 (Wash. 1991).

The Patient Self-Determination Act of 1990

As a result of implementation of the Patient Self-Determination Act of 1990, health care facilities participating in the Medicare and Medicaid reimbursement programs must deal with patient rights regarding life-sustaining decisions and other advance directives. Health care facilities have a responsibility to explain to patients, staff, and families that patients do have a legal right to direct their own medical and nursing care as it corresponds to existing state law, including right-to-die directives. A person's right to refuse medical treatment is not lost when the person's mental or physical status changes; when a person is no longer competent to exercise his or her right of self-determination, the right still exists but the decision must be delegated to a surrogate decision maker. Those facilities that do not comply with a patient's directives or those of a legally authorized decision maker on treatment are exposing themselves to the risk of a lawsuit.[16]

Until recently, the family of an incompetent patient was relied on to assist the physician in making medical decisions for the patient. The courts were used many times to relieve a physician of any criminal or civil liability if the physician withdrew or withheld life-sustaining treatment. It became clear that the courts were not equipped to handle this type of medical–ethical conflict. Moreover, cases involving life-sustaining decisions by their very nature demand immediate action. The taking of a case to court is an expensive and time-consuming process.

The federal Council on the Aging, in its 1988 Annual Report to the President, stated that "[f]air and realistic guardianship, living wills, powers of attorney, and trust standards must be a priority of all state legislatures, as well as the public in general, as increased longevity makes mental and physical incapacity more commonplace among the U.S. senior population."[17] At least 38 states have addressed this problem by enacting natural death, living will, or death with dignity statutes that grant statutory recognition to advance directives, wherein a patient, while competent, expressed his or her wishes with respect to life-sustaining treatment. The currently recognized instruments are living wills, durable powers of attorney, and health care proxies.

The Patient Self-Determination Act of 1990 (PSDA),[18] which went into effect on December 1, 1991, provides that patients have a right to formulate advance directives and to make decisions regarding their health care. Self-determination includes the right to accept or refuse medical treatment. Health care providers (including hospitals, nursing homes, home health agencies, Health Maintenance Organizations, and hospices) receiving federal funds under Medicare are required to comply with the new regulations. Providers are not entitled to reimbursement under the Medicare program if they fail to meet PSDA requirements.

Each state is required under PSDA to provide providers with a description of the law in the state regarding advance directives, whether such directives are based on state statutes or judicial decisions. Providers must ensure that written policies and procedures with respect to all adult individuals regarding advance directives are established

    (A) to provide written information to each such individual concerning—
        (i) an individual's rights under State law (whether statutory or as recognized by the courts of the State) to make decisions concerning such medical care, including the right to accept or refuse medical or surgical treatment and the right to formulate advance directives . . . , and
        (ii) written policies of the provider organization respecting the implementation of such rights;
    (B) to document in the individual's medical record whether or not the individual has executed an advance directive;
    (C) not to condition the provision of care or otherwise discriminate against an individual based on whether or not the individual has executed an advance directive;
    (D) to ensure compliance with requirements of State law (whether statutory or recognized by the courts of the State) respecting advance directives at the facilities of the provider or organization; and
    (E) to provide (individually or with others) for education for staff and the community on issues concerning advance directives.[19]

Although the PSDA is being cheered as a major advancement in clarifying and nationally regulating this often hazy area of law and medicine, there will be continuing problems and new issues that must be ironed out.

Substituted Judgment/Guardianship

Guardianship or conservatorship is a legal mechanism by which the court declares a person incompetent and appoints a guardian. The court transfers the responsibility for managing financial affairs, living arrangements, and medical care decisions to the guardian.[20] A resolution by the federal Council on the Aging recommends the implementation of guardianship programs and laws for the benefit and protection of older Americans "as exemplified by the Statement of Recommended Judicial Practices adopted by the National Conference of the Judiciary on Guardianship Proceedings for the Elderly."[21] The Statement of Recommended Judicial Practices is available from the American Bar Association, 1800 M Street, N.W., Washington, D.C.

The right to refuse medical treatment on behalf of an incompetent person is not limited to legally appointed guardians but may be exercised by health care proxies or surrogates such as close family members or friends. When a patient has not expressed instructions concerning his or her future health care in the event of later incapacity but has merely delegated full responsibility to a proxy, designation of a proxy must have been made in writing.

Durable Power of Attorney

Power of attorney is a legal device that permits one individual known as the "principal" to give to another person called the "attorney-in-fact" the authority to act on his or her behalf. The attorney-in-fact is authorized to handle banking and real estate affairs, incur expenses, pay bills, and handle a wide variety of legal affairs for a specified period of time. The power of attorney may continue indefinitely during the lifetime of the principal so long as that person is competent and capable of granting power of attorney. If the principal becomes comatose or mentally incompetent, the power of attorney automatically expires, just as it would if the principal dies.[22]

Because a power of attorney is limited by the competency of the principal, some states have authorized a special legal device for the principal to express intent concerning the durability of the power of attorney, to allow it to survive disability or incompetency.[23] The "durable power of attorney" is more general in scope, and the patient does not have to be in imminent danger of death, as is necessary in a living will situation. Although it need not delineate desired medical treatment specifically, it must indicate the identity of the principal's attorney-in-fact and that the principal has communicated his or her health care wishes to the attorney-in-fact. Although the laws vary from state to state, all 50 states and the District of Columbia have durable power of attorney statutes. This legal device is an important alternative to guardianship, conservatorship, or trusteeship. Because a durable power of attorney places a considerable amount of power in the hands of the attorney-in-fact, it should be drawn up by an attorney in the state in which the client resides.

Health Care Proxy

A health care proxy allows a person to appoint a "health care agent" to make treatment decisions in the event he or she becomes incapacitated and unable to make decisions for him- or herself. Thirteen states authorize the appointment of health care proxies.[24] The agent must be made aware of the patient's wishes regarding nutrition and hydration in order to be allowed to make a decision concerning withholding or withdrawing them. In contrast to a living will, a health care proxy does not require a person to know about and consider in advance all situations and decisions that could arise. Rather, the appointed agent would know about and interpret the expressed wishes of the patient and then make decisions about the medical care and treatment to be administered or refused. The *Cruzan* decision indicates that the Supreme Court views advance directives as clear and convincing evidence of a patient's wishes regarding life-sustaining treatment.

Although most of the statutes fail to cover incompetents, cases such as *Quinlan* and *Saikewicz* created a constitutionally protected obligation to terminate the incurable incompetent's life when the doctrine of substituted judgment is used by guardians. Further, some states provide for proxy consent in the form of durable power of attorney statutes. Generally, these involve the designation of a proxy to speak on the incompetent incurable's behalf.[25] They represent a combination of the intimate wishes of the patient and the medical recommendations of the physicians.

Oral declarations are accepted only after the patient has been declared terminally ill. Moreover, the declarant bears the responsibility of informing the physician to ensure that the document becomes a part of the medical record. The California statute provides that the document be re-executed after five years. Other statutes differ in the length of time of effectiveness. Most states allow the document to be effective until revoked by the individual. To revoke, the patient must sign and date a new writing, destroy the first document him- or herself, direct another to destroy the first document in his or her presence, or orally state to the physician an intent to revoke.[26] The effect of the directive varies among the jurisdictions. However, there is unanimity in the promulgation of regulations that specifically authorize health care personnel to honor the directives without fear of incurring liability. The highest court of New York in *In re Eichner*, 52 N.Y.2d 363, 420 N.E.2d 64 (1981), complied with the request of a guardian to withdraw life-support systems from an 83-year-old brain-damaged priest. The court reached its result by finding the patient's previously expressed wishes to be determinative.

Before exercising an incompetent patient's right to forego medical treatment, the surrogate decision maker must satisfy the following conditions:

- The surrogate must be satisfied that the patient executed any document (e.g., Durable Power of Attorney for Health Care and Health Care Proxy) knowingly, willingly, and without undue influence, and that the evidence of patient's oral declaration is reliable
- The patient does not have reasonable probability of recovering competency so that the right could be exercised by the patient
- The surrogate must take care to ensure that any limitations or conditions expressed either orally or in written declarations have been considered carefully and satisfied

Determining Incapacity

Before declaring an individual incapacitated, the attending physician must find with a reasonable degree of medical certainty that the patient lacks capacity. A chart entry must be made describing the cause, nature, extent, and probable duration of incapacity. Before withholding or withdrawing life-sustaining treatment, a second physician must confirm the incapacity determination and make an appropriate entry on the patient's medical record. Once incapacity has been determined, a notification must be placed in the patient's medical record before honoring new decisions by the health care agent.

Agent Rights

A health care agent's rights are no greater than what those of a competent patient would be. However, the agent's rights are limited to any specific instructions included in the proxy document. An agent's decisions take priority over any other person except the patient. The agent has the right to consent or refuse to consent to any service or treatment, routine or otherwise; to refuse life-sustaining treatment; and to access "all" the patient's medical information to make informed decisions. The agent must make decisions based on the patient's moral and religious beliefs. If a patient's wishes are not known, decisions must be based on a good-faith judgment of what the patient would have wanted. In New York, the agent must consult with either a physician, a registered nurse, a licensed clinical psychologist, or a certified social worker before making health care decisions.

Living Will

A "living will," also referred to in many states as a "directive" or "declaration," is the instrument or legal document that describes those treatments an individual wishes or does not wish to receive should he or she become incapacitated and unable to make medical decisions for him- or herself. Typically, a living will allows a person, when competent, to inform caregivers in writing of his or her wishes with regard to withholding and withdrawing life-supporting treatment, including nutrition and hydration. The living will is helpful to health professionals in that it provides guidance about a patient's wishes for treatment, provides legally valid instructions about treatment, and protects patient rights and the provider that honors them.

The living will should be signed and dated by two witnesses who are not blood relatives or beneficiaries of property. A living will should be discussed with the patient's physician and a signed copy should be placed in the patient's medical record. A copy also should be given to the individual designated to make decisions in the event the patient is unable to do so. A person who executes a living will when healthy and mentally competent cannot predict how he or she will feel at the time of a terminal illness. Therefore, it should be updated regularly so that it accurately reflects a patient's wishes.[27] The written instructions become effective when a patient is either in a terminal condition, permanently unconscious, or suffering irreversible brain damage.

Forty-one states have enacted statutes that enable individuals to state their wishes in advance regarding the use of life-sustaining procedures during a terminal illness.[28] California was the first state to enact what has been called a Natural Death or Living Will Act in 1976. Cal. Health & Safety Code §7185-95 (West 1983). California's legislation is typical of similar laws existing in 38 other states that allow the creation of documents that provide a legally recognized way for competent adults to express in advance their desires regarding life-crucial medical decisions in the event they become terminally ill and death is imminent. Governor John D. Waihee of Hawaii has signed a bill that "would recognize the right to control a person's medical decisions as an 'unqualified right whose exercise requires no one else's approval, neither families, physicians, ethics committees, lawyers nor courts of law.'"[29]

Right-To-Die Tag

A Montana law allows the use of identification bracelets to alert health care providers, including ambulance crews, of the wearer's serious medical condition and his or her request not to be resuscitated. The ID bracelets will be made available through the Montana Health Department.[30]

FEEDING TUBES

Theologians and ethicists have long recognized a distinction between ordinary and extraordinary medical care. The theologic distinction is based on the belief that life is a gift from God that should not be destroyed deliberately by humans. Therefore, extraordinary therapies that extend life by imposing grave burdens on the patient and family are not required. A patient, however, has an ethical and moral obligation to accept ordinary or life-sustaining treatment.[31] Although the courts have accepted decisions to withhold or withdraw extraordinary care, especially the respirator, from those who are comatose or in a persistent vegetative state with no possibility of emerging, they have been unwilling until now to discontinue feeding, which they have considered ordinary care.

However, in 1985, the case of *In re Claire C. Conroy,* 486 A.2d 1209 (N.J. Sup. Ct. 1985), was heard by the New Jersey Supreme Court. The case involved an 84-year-old nursing home patient whose nephew petitioned the court for authority to remove the nasogastric tube that was feeding her. The court overturned the appellate division decision and held that life-sustaining treatment, including nasogastric feeding, could be withheld or withdrawn from incompetent nursing home patients who will, according to physicians, die within one year, in three specific circumstances:

- when it is clear that the particular patient would have refused the treatment under the circumstances involved (the subjective test)
- when there is some indication of the patient's wishes (but he or she has not "unequivocally expressed" his or her desires before becoming incompetent) and the treatment "would only prolong suffering" (the limited objective test)
- when there is no evidence at all of the patient's wishes, but the treatment "clearly and markedly outweighs the benefits the patient derives from life" (the pure objective test based on pain)

A procedure involving notification of the state Office of the Ombudsman is required before withdrawing or withholding treatment under any of the three tests. The ombudsman must make a separate recommendation. *Id.* at 1232.

The court also found tubal feeding to be a medical treatment, and as such, it is as intrusive as other life-sustaining measures. The court in its analysis emphasized duty, rather than causation, with the result that medical personnel acting in good faith will be protected from liability. If physicians follow the *Quinlan/Conroy* standards and decide to end medical treatment of a patient, the duty to continue treatment ceases; thus, the termination of treatment becomes a lawful act.

Although *Conroy* presents case-specific guidelines, there is concern that the opinion will have far-reaching repercussions. There is fear that decisions to discontinue treatment will not be based on the "balancing of interests" test, but rather that a "quality of life" test similar to that used by Hitler will be used to end the lives of severely senile, very old, decrepit, and burdensome people.[32]

Those quality of life judgments would be most dangerous for nursing home patients in which age would be a factor in the decision-making process. "Advocates of 'the right to life' fear that the 'right to die' for the elderly and handicapped will become a 'duty to die.'"[33] In both the *Saikewicz* and *Spring* cases, age was a determining factor weighing against life-sustaining treatment. Further, in *In re Hier*, 464 N.E.2d 959 (Mass. 1984), the court found that Mrs. Hier's age of 92 years made the "proposed gastrostomy substantially more onerous or burdensome . . . than it would be for a younger, healthier person." *Id.* at 964. Moreover, a New York Superior Court held that the burdens of an emergency amputation for an elderly patient outweighed the benefit of continued life. Finding that prolonging her life would be cruel, the court stated that life had no meaning for her. In *In re Beth Israel Medical Center*, 519 N.Y.S.2d 511, 517 (Sup. Ct. 1987), some courts are recognizing and other courts must address the difference between *Quinlan*-type patients and elderly, confined, and conscious patients who can interact but whose mental or physical functioning is impaired.

However, at least in one recent situation, the New Jersey ombudsman denied a request to remove feeding tubes from a comatose nursing home patient.[34] In applying the *Conroy* tests, the ombudsman decided that Hilda Peterson might live more than one year, the period that *Conroy* used as a criterion for determining whether life support can be removed.

To further complicate this issue, on March 17, 1986, the American Medical Association changed its Code of Ethics on comas. Now physicians may ethically withhold food, water, and medical treatment from patients in irreversible comas or persistent vegetative states with no hope of recovery—even if death is not imminent.[35] Although physicians can consider the wishes of the patient and family or the legal representatives, they cannot cause death intentionally. The wording is permissive, so those physicians who feel uncomfortable withdrawing food and water may refrain from doing so. The American Medical Association's decision does not comfort those who fear abuse or mistake in euthanasia decisions, nor does it have any legal value as such. There are physicians, nurses, and families who are unscrupulous and have their own, and not the patient's, interests in mind. Even with the *Conroy* decision and the American Medical Association's Code of Ethics change, the feeding tube issue is not settled.

On April 23, 1986, the New Jersey Superior Court ruled that the husband of severely brain-damaged Nancy Jobes could order the removal of her life-sustaining feeding tube, which would ultimately cause the 31-year-old comatose patient, who had been in a vegetative state in a hospice for the past six years, to starve to death. In *In re Jobes*, 108 N.J. 394, 403, 529 A.2d 434, 438 (1987), Dr. Fred Plum created and defined the term "persistent vegetative state" as one in which

the body functions entirely in terms of its internal controls. It maintains temperature. It maintains digestive activity. It maintains heart beat and pulmonary ventilation. It maintains reflex activity of muscles and nerves for low level conditioned responses. But there is no behavioral evidence of either self-awareness or awareness of the surroundings in a learned manner.

Medical experts testified that the patient could, under optimal conditions, live another 30 years. Relieving the nursing home officials from performing the act on one of its residents, the court ruled that the patient may be taken home to die (with the removal to be supervised by a physician and medical care to be provided to the patient at home).

The nursing home had petitioned the court for the appointment of a "life advocate" to fight for continuation of medical treatment for Mrs. Jobes, which, it argued, would save her life. The court disallowed the appointment of a life advocate, holding that case law does not support requiring the continuation of life-support systems in all circumstances. Such a requirement, according to the court, would contradict the patient's right of privacy.

The court's decision applied "the principles enunciated in *Quinlan* and . . . *Conroy*" and the "recent ruling by the American Medical Association's Council on Judicial Affairs that the provision of food and water is, under certain circumstances, a medical treatment like any other and may be discontinued when the physician and family of the patient feel it is no longer benefiting the patient."[36]

The Illinois Supreme Court in *In re Estate of Longeway,* 549 N.E2d 292 (1989), agreed with the logic of the *Jobes* decision and other sister state rulings regarding the characterization of artificial nutrition and hydration as medical treatment. The Illinois court found that the authorized guardian of a terminally ill patient in an irreversible coma or persistent vegetative state has a common-law right to refuse artificial nutrition and hydration. The court found that there must be clear and convincing evidence that the refusal is consistent with the patient's interest. The court also required the concurrence of the patient's attending physician and two other physicians. "Court intervention is also necessary to guard against the remote, yet real possibility that greed may taint the judgment of the surrogate decision maker." *Id.* at 790. Dissenting, Judge Ward said, "The right to refuse treatment is rooted in and dependent on the patient's capacity for informed decision, which an incompetent patient lacks." *Id.* at 793.

Also, Elizabeth Bouvia, a mentally competent cerebral palsy victim, won her struggle to have feeding tubes removed even though she was not terminally ill. *Bouvia v. Superior Court (Glenchur),* 225 Cal. Rptr. 297 (Ct. App. 1986). The California Court of Appeals announced on April 16, 1986, that she could go home to die. The court found that Ms. Bouvia's decision to "let nature take its course" did not amount to a choice to commit suicide with people aiding and abetting it. The court stated that it is not "illegal or immoral to prefer a natural, albeit sooner, death than a drugged life attached to a mechanical device." *Id.* at

306. The court's finding that it was a moral and philosophic question, not a legal or medical one, leaves one wondering if the courts are opening the door to permitting "legal starvation" to be used by those who are not terminally ill but who do wish to commit suicide.

ASSISTED SUICIDE

Unfortunately, there are those in the health care field who are using their knowledge to develop new instruments of death to assist those who are terminally ill and want to end their lives. Dr. Jack Kevorkian of Michigan announced in October 1989 that he had developed a device that would end one's life quickly, painlessly, and humanely.[37] He described his invention as a metal pole with bottles containing three solutions that feed into a common intravenous line. When the intravenous line is inserted into the patient's vein, a harmless saline solution will flow to clean the line of air. The patient then can flip a switch causing an anesthetic to render the patient unconscious. Sixty seconds later, a lethal dose of potassium chloride will flow into the patient, causing heart seizure and death. The news of this invention motivated the medical community and society at large to repeat their fear that individuals would abuse the practice of euthanasia despite any safeguards that are in place. Dr. Kevorkian assisted Janice Adkins, a 54-year-old Alzheimer's disease patient in committing suicide on June 4, 1990. In December, he was charged with first-degree murder, but the charge was dismissed because Michigan has no law against assisted suicide. He was ordered, however, not to help anyone else commit suicide or to give advice about it. On February 6, 1991, he violated the court order by giving advice about the preparation of the drug to a terminally ill cancer patient.[38] Additional murder charges were lodged against him in October 1991, when he instructed two Michigan women in the use of his "suicide machine." In dismissing the charges against him on July 21, 1992, Oakland County Circuit Court Judge David Breck stated that "some people with intractable pain cannot benefit from treatment." While emphasizing that Michigan has no law against assisting suicide, the judge also expressed his belief that physician-assisted suicide remains an alternative for patients experiencing "unmanageable pain."[39]

The Michigan House approved legislation placing a temporary ban on assisted suicide on November 24, 1992. The Senate approved the temporary ban after Dr. Kevorkian helped a sixth terminally ill patient kill herself. On December 15, 1992, Michigan Governor John Engler signed the law just hours after two more women committed suicide with Kevorkian's aid.

The new law, which will become effective on April 1, 1993, will make assisting suicide a felony punishable by up to four years in prison and a $2,000 fine. Under the new law, assisted suicide is banned for 15 months. During this time period a special commission will study assisted suicide and submit its recommendations to the Michigan legislature for review and action. The new law apparently raises constitutional questions and may be challenged by the Civil Liberties Union of Michigan because of the claim that it fails to recognize that "the terminally ill have the right to end their lives painlessly and with dignity."[40]

DO NOT RESUSCITATE ORDERS

Before the *Quinlan* decision, which began the focus on the withdrawal of life-sustaining machines, the life-sustaining treatment most discussed was cardiopulmonary resuscitation, in terms of whether to issue a Do Not Resuscitate (DNR) order.

DNR orders are those given by a physician, indicating that in the event of a cardiac or respiratory arrest, no resuscitative measures should be used to revive the patient. Such orders must be in writing, signed, and dated by the physician. Also, appropriate consents must be obtained from the resident/patient or his or her family or a patient advocate, as appropriate. Many states have acknowledged the validity of DNR orders in cases involving terminally ill patients where no objections to such orders are made by the patient's family. New York law allows out-of-hospital DNR orders only for those individuals enrolled in a hospice program.[41]

DNR orders must comply with statutory requirements, be of short duration, and be reviewed periodically to determine whether the patient's condition or other circumstances (e.g., change of mind by the patient or family) surrounding the "no code" orders have changed. Presently, it generally is accepted that if a patient is competent, the DNR order is considered to be the same as other medical decisions in which a patient may choose to reject life-sustaining treatment. In the case of an incompetent, absent any advance written directives, the best interests of the patient would be considered. A lower court decision in favor of a physician was overturned by the Indiana Court of Appeals in *Payne v. Marion General Hospital*, 549 N.E.2d 1043 (Ind. Ct. App. 1990). The physician had issued a no code status on Mr. Payne despite evidence given by a nurse that up to a few minutes before his death Mr. Payne could communicate. The physician had determined that Mr. Payne was incompetent, thereby rendering him unable to give informed consent to treatment. Because no written directives were left by Mr. Payne, the physician relied on one of Mr. Payne's relatives who asked for the DNR order. The court found that there was evidence that Mr. Payne was not incompetent and should have been consulted before a DNR order was given. Further, the court reviewed testimony that one year earlier Mr. Payne had suffered and recovered from the same type of symptoms, leading to the conclusion that there was a possibility he could have survived if resuscitation had continued. There was no DNR policy in place at the hospital to assist the physician in making his decision. To avoid this type of problem, health care providers should adopt policies with respect to the issuance of no code orders.

HEALTH CARE ETHICS

The tremendous advances in technology and the resulting capability to extend life beyond the point of what some may consider "a reasonable quality of life" have given rise to many ethical and moral as well as medical and legal issues for long-term care facilities and society in general. The issues of patient rights, when to transfer a patient to a health care facility providing a higher level of care, when to maintain a patient and provide those medications and treatments necessary to keep the patient as comfortable as possible, when to connect or disconnect life-support equipment, etc., are dilemmas for patients, their families, health care professionals, religious communities, and advocacy groups.

Public policy issues in the ethics arena include what percentage of the health care budget the nation should allocate to care for its aging population; who should have access to elder care; and whether insurance coverage should provide for unlimited care, which could affect other important health care programs negatively. These are difficult questions with no easy answers. Although there are no simple solutions to these dilemmas, a continuing effort must be made to search for the most acceptable solutions.

Ethics Committees

An alternative to court litigation that has been considered to ensure the safeguarding of a patient's interests is the institutional ethics committee. An ethics committee is a consultative committee whose role is to analyze ethical dilemmas and to advise and educate health care providers, patients, and families regarding difficult treatment decisions. Ethics committees have been formed in several health care settings to deal with difficult ethical issues. They had their origins with the 1976 landmark *Karen Ann Quinlan* case. "Since then, ethics committees have continued to become more popular, having had a significant burst of interest in the early 1980's largely as a result of a series of well-publicized cases involving decisions to forego or terminate life sustaining treatment."[42]

The *Quinlan* court looked to the prognosis committee to verify Karen Quinlan's medical condition. It then factored in the committee's opinion with all other evidence to reach the decision to allow the withdrawing of her life-support machine. To date, ethics committees, which are commonly comprised of religious leaders, health care professionals, attorneys, and ethicists, do not have sole surrogate decision-making authority. However, they play an ever-increasing role in developing policy and procedural guidelines to assist in resolving the ethical dilemmas inherent in a right-to-forego-treatment case.

Ethics committees must take special care in resolving any dispute that involves the treatment of incompetent patients, especially when no family or friends are involved. In those situations, the committee must not fall victim to arriving at a decision too quickly without considering all available information and alternatives. The best-interests-of-the-patient standard must be applied to determine what treatment should be or should not be rendered.

The elderly often are treated as though they are incapable of making their own treatment decisions. This faulty thinking must be corrected. They are very special people, and every effort must be made to treat them as the adults that they are. Their age must not diminish the recognition and respect they rightfully deserve.

> Thus, a decisionally capable elderly patient has the right to be informed of the diagnosis, prognosis, proposed intervention, risks of that intervention, availability of other options and their risk, and consequences of not intervening at all. After receiving this information, he or she is legally empowered to either consent to or refuse the intervention, even if that refusal should lead to serious harm or death for the patient.[43]

Committee Composition

Ethics committees are often composed of a multidisciplinary group of individuals and have included religious leaders, health professionals not associated with the facility, and legal counsel. Noting that physicians are the practitioners of medicine, not health care institutions, their representation on ethics committees is considered extremely important. A comment made by George Annas, a medical ethicist, is appropriately applicable to all health care facilities providing medical care: "Hospitals are corporations that have no natural personhood, and hence are incapable of having moral or ethical objections to action. . . . Hospitals don't practice medicine, physicians do."[44]

Committee Function

The functions of ethics committees can be multifaceted and include the development of policy and procedure guidelines to assist in resolving ethical dilemmas, staff and community education, conflict resolution, individual case review and support, and consultation on specific cases. The degree to which an ethics committee serves each of these functions varies in different health care facilities.

Policy and Procedure Development. Health care facilities need to adopt policy and procedure guidelines that health care workers can look to in making difficult ethical decisions on issues that arise in the health care setting. Ethics committees can play a major role in the development of such guidelines. The guidelines should be available for public review and constructive input.

Educational Role. The most common and agreed on role of ethics committees is staff education. There is a need to sensitize health care workers regarding the ethical issues and conflicts that arise in the health care setting.[45]

Support Role. Ethics committees can advise and provide support, when and where appropriate, with patients; their families, surrogates, or proxies; and those health care professionals responsible for their care.

> Most health care professionals are neither intellectually prepared to address all of the ethical issues that arise in the delivery of medical care, nor emotionally comfortable talking about them. Successful resolution of many of the ethical dilemmas arising in nursing facilities today demands calling on a wide range of perspectives. NFECs (Nursing Facility Ethics Committees) can bring a diversity of personal and community values, and moral and professional perspectives that lead to valuable insights and advice beyond the limits of individuals.[46]

Ethics committees weigh the different religious, ethical, and moral issues that pertain to a given situation. They strive to provide viable alternatives that will lead to the optimal resolution of the dilemmas confronting the continuing care of the patient. It is important to remember that an ethics committee functions in an advisory capacity and should not be considered a substitute proxy for the patient.

Consultation. The availability of consultation from ethics committees can be of tremendous value to health care workers faced with difficult ethical dilemmas. Ethics committees can serve as a forum for discussing and resolving ethical concerns regarding specific cases. Where ethics committees have been instituted, consultation services should be available to the staff, families, and patients to assist in making difficult treatment decisions.

There is a wealth of information available regarding the establishment of ethics committees. Health care facilities that are in the process of establishing such a committee should review the literature, as well as seek advice from those who have gone through the process of setting up their own committees.

Figures 15-1 and 15-2 illustrate and summarize the numerous ramifications of euthanasia, as discussed in this chapter.

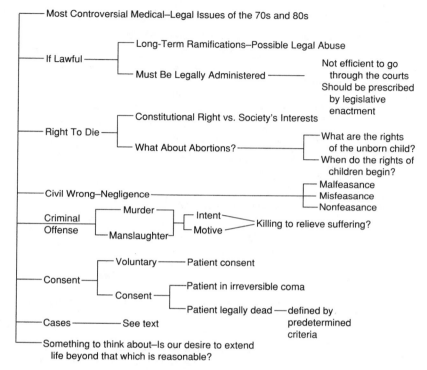

Figure 15-1 Legal Ramifications of Euthanasia

CONCLUSION

Any discussion of euthanasia obliges a person to confront a human's greatest fear—death. The courts and legislatures have faced it and have made advances in setting forth some guidelines to assist decision makers in this area. However, more must be accomplished. Society must be protected from the risks associated with permitting the removal of life-support systems. We cannot allow the complex issues associated with this topic to be simplified to the point where we accept that life can be terminated based on subjective quality-of-life considerations. The legal system must ensure that the constitutional rights of the patient will be maintained, while at the same time protecting society's interests in preserving life, preventing suicide, and maintaining the integrity of the medical profession. In the final analysis, "the edges of the boundaries of patient rights remain very uncertain."[47]

We have come a long way from a time when there were multiple patients in the same beds of rat-infested facilities where infections ran rampant without

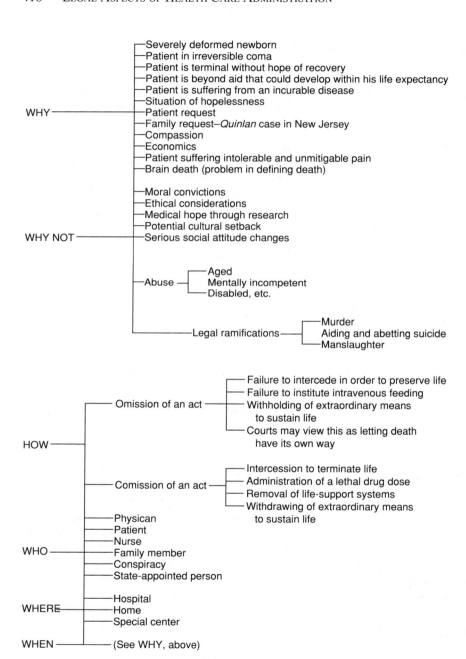

Figure 15-2 Considerations in Euthanasia

cures. We have come a long way from the scourges of malaria, yellow fever, smallpox, malnutrition, and the many other diseases afflicting underdeveloped countries. We have come to a new age with modern facilities and numerous medical advances capable of extending our lifespan by many years. As a result of major advances in nutrition, hygiene, and health care, modern medicine can often hold us captive in nonfunctioning bodies when it is time to let go. Because of the increasing number of individuals being maintained on life-support systems and their desire to let go, many legal, ethical, moral, and religious issues continue to concern us all.

NOTES

1. J. Podgers, *Matters of Life and Death*, A.B.A. J., 78, May 1992, at 60.

2. R. GILLON, SUICIDE AND VOLUNTARY EUTHANASIA: HISTORICAL PERSPECTIVE IN EUTHANASIA AND THE RIGHT TO DEATH, 182 (1969).

3. Reiser, *The Dilemma of Euthanasia in Modern Medical History: The English and American Experience,* in ETHICS IN MEDICINE PERSPECTIVES AND MEDICAL CONCERNS 20 (1977).

4. WEBSTER'S THIRD NEW INTERNATIONAL DICTIONARY OF THE ENGLISH LANGUAGE UNABRIDGED 786 (1976).

5. Cruzan v. Director, Mo. Dept. of Health, 110 S. Ct. 2841, 2864 (1990).

6. Podgers, *supra* note 1, at 61.

7. Sherlock, *For Everything There Is a Season: The Right To Die in the United States,* B.Y.U. L. REV. 545 (1982).

8. Karen Ann Quinlan, at age 22 years, was in a coma caused by an overdose of valium and alcohol. As a result, she was hooked up to a life-supporting respirator.

9. Gelford, *Euthanasia and the Terminally Ill Patient,* 63 NEB. L. Rev. 741, 747 (1984).

10. Coyle, *Fast Furious Questioning Marks Session on Coma Case,* NAT'L L. J., Dec. 18, 1989, at 8; Wallis, *To Feed or Not To Feed?,* TIME, Mar. 31, 1986, at 60.

11. Connery, *Prolonging Life: The Duty and Its Limits, Moral Responsibility in Prolonging Life's Decisions,* in TO TREAT OR NOT TO TREAT 25 (1984).

12. A.M.A HOUSE OF DELEGATES, RESOLUTION 77—STATEMENT OF MEDICAL OPINION RE: "BRAIN DEATH" (June 1974).

13. Pa. S.646, Amendment A3506, Printer's No. 689, Oct. 1, 1990.

14. *Hospital Wants To Let Wife Die,* NEWSDAY, Jan. 11, 1991, at 13.

15. *Id.*

16. *Advance Directives Linked to Residents' Rights Mandate,* PROVIDER FOR LONG TERM CARE PROFESSIONALS, 17(2), Feb. 1991, at 32–34.

17. FEDERAL COUNCIL ON THE AGING, ANNUAL REPORT TO THE PRESIDENT 18 (1988).

18. Patient Self-Determination Act, P.W.L. No. 101-508, 104 Stat. 291 (1990).

19. 42 U.S.C.S. §1395cc (1992).

20. U.S. DEPARTMENT OF HEALTH AND HUMAN SERVICES, OFFICE OF HUMAN DEVELOPMENT SERVICES, ADMINISTRATION ON AGING, WHERE TO TURN FOR HELP FOR OLDER PERSONS 27 (1987).

21. FEDERAL COUNCIL ON THE AGING, *supra* note 8, at 11.

22. *Id.* at 25.

23. *Id.* at 26.

24. *Cruzan,* 110 S. Ct. at 2858.

25. *The Physician's Responsibility toward Hopelessly Ill Patients*, NEW ENG. J. MED., Apr. 12, 1984 at 955.

26. Novak, *"Natural Death Acts": Let Patients Refuse Treatment*, HOSPITALS, Aug. 1, 1984, at 72.

27. U.S. DEPARTMENT OF HEALTH AND HUMAN SERVICES, *supra* note 20, at 26.

28. *Montana OKs Right-To-Die Tag*, NEWSDAY, Apr. 26, 1991, at 29.

29. *Hawaii: Living Will Legislation*, A.H.A. NEWS, 27(23), June 10, 1991, at 7.

30. *Montana OKs Right-To-Die Tag, supra* note 28, at 4, 29.

31. McCormick, *To Save or Let Die: The Dilemma of Modern Medicine,* 229 J.A.M.A. 172 (1974).

32. Wallis, *supra* note 10.

33. U.S. CONGRESS, OFFICE OF TECHNOLOGY ASSESSMENT, LIFE-SUSTAINING TECHNOLOGIES AND THE ELDERLY, Pub. No. OTA-BA-306 (1987), at 48.

34. Sullivan, *Ombudsman Bars Food Tube Removal,* N.Y. Times, Mar. 7, 1986, at 82.

35. *AMA Changes Code of Ethics on Comas*, NEWSDAY, Mar. 17, 1986, at 2.

36. *Man Wins Right To Let Wife Die*, NEWSDAY, Apr. 24, 1986, at 3.

37. Fireman, *MD Invents Mercy Death Device*, NEWSDAY, Oct. 27, 1989, at 6.

38. *Dr. Death at Work*, NEWSDAY, Feb. 7, 1991, at 12.

39. *Kevorkian Charges Dropped*, NEWSDAY, July 22, 1992, at 4.

40. *Opponents Attack Michigan Law that Bans Assisted Suicide*, THE NEWS JOURNAL, Dec. 17, 1992, at 6A.

41. *Montana OKs Right-To Die Tag, supra* note 28, at 29.

42. Miller, *A Look at Long Term Care Ethics: Dilemmas and Decisions*, 16 PROVIDER 12 (1990).

43. U.S. CONGRESS, OFFICE OF TECHNOLOGY ASSESSMENT, *supra* note 33, at 107.

44. Annas, *Transferring the Ethical Hot Potato*, 17 HASTINGS CENTER REP. 20, 21 (1987).

45. Miller, *supra* note 42, at 14.

46. *Id.* at 13.

47. Podgers, *supra* note 1, at 63.

Autopsy, Donation, and Experimentation

The rule uniformly recognized in different states provides that the person entitled to possession of a body for burial has certain legally protected interests. Generally, the primary right to custody of a dead body belongs to the surviving spouse. When there is no spouse, the right passes to the adult children of the decedent, if any, and then to the decedent's parents. Damages awarded in cases of liability through interference with the rights of a surviving spouse or near relative in the body of a decedent are based on the emotional and mental suffering that results from such interference. For damages to be awarded, the conduct of the alleged wrongdoer must be sufficiently disturbing to a person of ordinary sensibilities as to cause emotional harm. Cases involving the wrongful handling of dead bodies may be classified into four groups: mutilation of a body; unauthorized autopsy; wrongful detention; and unauthorized use or publication of photographs taken after death.

In many states, intentionally mutilating a dead body is a punishable crime as well as a basis for civil liability. Obviously, such acts could be said to cause substantial emotional suffering for those who loved and respected the decedent. Similarly, an unauthorized autopsy may disturb persons whose religious beliefs prohibit such a procedure as well as those persons who have a general aversion to the procedure. When autopsies have been performed without statutory authorization and without the consent of the decedent, the surviving spouse, or an appropriate relative, liability may be imposed.

To limit lawsuits regarding the disposition of dead bodies, appropriate handling and release procedures should be established. Such procedures should be reviewed by legal counsel. Interfering with rights to a body has resulted in liability. For example, in the case of *Lott v. State,* 32 Misc. 2d 296, 225 N.Y.S.2d 434 (Ct. Cl. 1962), two bodies in a hospital were mistagged. The body of a person of the Roman Catholic faith was prepared for Orthodox Jewish burial, and the person of the Orthodox Jewish faith was prepared for Roman Catholic burial. This negligent conduct interfered with burial plans and caused mental anguish, for which liability was imposed.

AUTOPSY

Autopsies, or postmortem examinations, are conducted to ascertain the cause of a person's death, which, in turn, may resolve several legal issues. An autopsy may reveal whether death was the result of criminal activity, whether the cause of death was one for which payment must be made in accordance with an insurance contract, whether the death is compensable under worker's compensation and occupational disease acts, or whether death was the result of a specific act or a culmination of several acts. Aside from providing answers to these specific questions, the information gained from autopsies adds to medical knowledge. As such, medical schools have an interest in autopsies for educational purposes.

Autopsy Consent Statutes

Recognizing both the need for information that can be secured only through the performance of a substantial volume of autopsies and the valid interests of relatives and friends of the decedent, most states have enacted statutes dealing with autopsy consent. Such legislation seems intended to have a twofold effect: first, to protect the rights of the decedent's relatives, and second, to guide those performing autopsies in establishing procedures for consent to autopsy. Most autopsy consent statutes establish an order for obtaining consent to autopsy based on the degree of family relationship.

Authorization by the Decedent

Most autopsy consent statutes provide that deceased persons may authorize an autopsy on their remains. Ordinarily such consent must be in writing. There may be legal as well as practical problems in obtaining authorization for an autopsy from a patient before death if the state does not provide by statute for such authorization.

In states where there is neither an autopsy consent statute nor a statute permitting donation that may be construed to include autopsy, it is unwise to rely exclusively on the authorization of a decedent to perform an autopsy. This is especially true when relatives of the deceased who assume custody of the body for burial object to an autopsy. Although the courts have upheld the wishes of the deceased with respect to the place of interment or the manner of disposition of the remains (i.e., by burial or cremation), it is possible that the courts will not afford the same weight to the decedent's wishes concerning an autopsy. In such instances, compelling reasons presented by certain next of kin of the decedent, especially the surviving spouse, may prevail over the wishes of the decedent.

It is possible that a patient might specifically request that no autopsy be performed on his or her body. This request may stem from religious convictions or personal preference. Some state legislatures have recognized specifically the right to refuse an autopsy. For example, in New York, it is provided:

> Except as required by law, no dissection or autopsy shall be performed on the body of any person who is carrying an identification card upon his person indicating his opposition to such dissection or autopsy. To be valid, this card must be signed and dated by the person opposed to the dissection or autopsy and must be notarized.
> New York Public Health Law §4209-a (1981).

Authorization by Person Other than Decedent

In the absence of statutes furnishing a preference order of responsibility for burial and consent for autopsy, the order usually followed is surviving spouse, adult children of the deceased, parents, adult brothers and sisters, grandparents, uncles and aunts, and finally cousins. A court may find that a surviving spouse's unwillingness to assume responsibility for burial is sufficient to permit the right to custody of the body to devolve on a relative who is willing to assume such responsibility.

Scope and Extent of Consent

Legal issues may arise as a result of an autopsy even if consent has been obtained from the person authorized by law to grant such consent. If autopsy procedures go beyond the limits imposed by the consent or if the consent to an autopsy is obtained by fraud or without the formal requisites, liability may be incurred. It is a fundamental principle that a person who has the right to refuse permission for the performance of an act also has the right to place limitations or conditions on consent.

It is especially important that the hospital and its personnel adhere to any limitations or conditions placed on the permission to autopsy; if such limitations are exceeded, the physician or the hospital has no defense on the ground of emergency or medical necessity. The principle involved in limiting the scope of an autopsy has been expressed as follows:

> One having the right to refuse to allow an autopsy has the right to place any limitations or restrictions on giving consent to such procedure, and one who violates such stipulations renders himself liable.[1]

While consent to autopsy also may encompass authorization for removal of body parts for examination, a separate question may arise concerning disposal of tissues and organs on completion of the examination: May the hospital and its personnel dispose of such material in a routine manner or use it for the hospital's own purposes, or must the hospital return the tissue and organs to the body before burial? In *Hendriksen v. Roosevelt Hospital,* 297 F. Supp. 1142 (1969), permission had been granted for a complete autopsy including an examination of the central nervous system by a scalp incision. Yet the court held that liability might be imposed on the hospital if the jury found that the hospital retained parts of the body. Pursuant to a New York statute requiring the authorization of the next of kin, consent was given for dissection; however, the court held that this statute should be construed narrowly and that separate consent would have to be obtained to retain the internal organs of the decedent.

Consent given with the understanding that organs and tissue could be removed and retained for examination would seem to authorize the hospital to dispose of such materials in a suitable manner or to use them after the autopsy. However, the *Hendriksen* decision raises doubts on this matter. Where the party giving consent expressly stipulates that parts severed from the body are to be returned to the body for burial, conduct deviating from this provision may result in liability. Also, it would appear that consent to autopsy does not include authorization to mutilate or disfigure the body. Therefore, when autopsy involves the removal of exterior body parts and the physical appearance of the body cannot be restored without return of such parts, the hospital may be subject to liability for exceeding the scope of the authorization if the removed parts are not returned.

Fraudulently Obtained Consent

It is a long-accepted principle that consent obtained through fraud or material misrepresentation is not binding and that the person whose consent is so obtained stands in the same position as if no consent had been given. This principle can apply to autopsies when facts are misrepresented to the person who has the right to consent to induce his or her consent. If a physician or a hospital employee states, as fact, something known to be untrue to gain consent, the autopsy would be unauthorized, and liability might follow.

ORGAN DONATIONS

Developments in medical science have enabled physicians to take tissue from persons immediately after death and use it for transplantation to replace or rehabilitate diseased or damaged organs or other parts of living persons. Progress in this field of medicine has created the problem of obtaining a sufficient supply of replacement body parts. Throughout the country, there are tissue banks and other facilities for the storage and preservation of organs and tissue that can be used for transplantation and for other therapeutic services.

Should body or organ donations be requested by a patient, the hospital must be aware of the patient's wishes. The ever-increasing success of organ transplants and demand for organ tissue require the close scrutiny of each case, making sure that established procedures have been followed in the care and disposal of all body parts.

Section 1138, title XI, of the Omnibus Budget Reconciliation Act of 1986 requires hospitals to establish organ procurement protocols or face a loss of Medicare and Medicaid funding. Physicians, nurses, and other paramedical personnel assigned with this responsibility often are confronted with several legal issues. Liability can be limited by complying with applicable regulations and adhering to hospital procedures implementing these regulations.

Organs and tissues to be stored and preserved for future use must be removed almost immediately after death. Therefore, it is imperative that an agreement or arrangement for obtaining organs and tissue from a body be completed before death, or very soon after death, to enable physicians to remove and store the tissue promptly.

Persons aware of the shortage of dead bodies needed for medical education and transplantation may wish to make arrangements during their lifetime for the use of their bodies after death for such purposes. A surviving spouse may, however, object to such disposition. In such cases, the interest of the surviving spouse or other family member could supersede that of the deceased.

A Uniform Anatomical Gift Act drafted by the Commission on Uniform State Laws has been endorsed by the American Bar Association. This statute has been enacted by many states and has many detailed provisions that apply to the wide variety of issues raised in connection with the making, acceptance, and use of anatomic gifts. State statutes regarding donation usually permit the donor to execute the gift during his or her lifetime.

The right to privacy of the donor and his family must be respected. Information should not be disseminated regarding transplant procedures that publish the names of the donor or donee without adequate consent.

States have enacted legislation to facilitate donation of bodies and body parts for medical uses. Virtually all the states have based their enactments on the Uniform Anatomical Gift Act, but it should be recognized that in some states there are deviations from this act or additional laws dealing with donation.

Summary of the Uniform Anatomical Gift Act

Individuals who are of sound mind and 18 years of age or older are permitted to dispose of their own bodies or body parts by will or other written instrument for medical or dental education, research, advancement of medical or dental science, therapy, or transplantation. Among those eligible to receive such donations are any licensed, accredited, or approved hospitals; accredited medical or dental schools; surgeons or physicians; tissue banks; or specified individuals who need the donation for therapy or transplantation. The statute provides that when only a part of the body is donated, custody of the remaining parts of the body shall be transferred to the next of kin promptly after removal of the donated part.

In cases of donation made by a written instrument other than a will, the instrument must be signed by the donor in the presence of two witnesses, who, in turn, must sign the instrument in the donor's presence. If the donor cannot sign the instrument, the document may be signed by a person authorized by the donor, at the donor's direction and in the presence of the donor and the two signing witnesses. Delivery of the document during the donor's lifetime is not necessary to make the donation valid. A donation by will becomes effective immediately on the death of the testator, without probate, and the gift is valid and effective to the extent that it has been acted on in good faith. This is true even if the will is not probated or is declared invalid for testimonial purposes.

A donation by a person other than the decedent may be made by written, telegraphic, recorded telephonic, or other recorded consent. In the absence of a contrary intent evidenced by the decedent or of actual notice of opposition by a member of the same class or a prior class in the preference order, the decedent's body or body parts may be donated by the following persons in the order specified:

• surviving spouse
• adult child

- parent
- adult brother or sister
- decedent's guardian
- any other person or agency authorized to dispose of the body

Although failure to obtain consent for removal of body tissue can give rise to a law suit, not all such claims are successful.

As in *Nicoletta v. Rochester Eye & Human Parts Bank,* 519 N.Y.S.2d 928 (Sup. Ct. 1987), where the father of a deceased patient brought an action against a hospital for alleged emotional injuries resulting from the removal of his son's eyes for donation after a fatal motorcycle accident. The hospital was immune from liability under the provisions of the Uniform Anatomical Gift Act because the hospital had neither actual nor constructive knowledge that the woman who had authorized the donation was not the decedent's wife. The hospital was entitled to the immunity afforded by the "good-faith" provisions of section 4306(3) of the act in which its agents had made reasonable inquiry as to the status of the purported wife, who had resided with the decedent for ten years and was the mother of their two children. The hospital had no reason to believe that any irregularity existed. The father, who was present at the time his son was brought to the emergency department, failed to object to any organ donation and failed to challenge the authority of the purported wife to sign the emergency department authorization.

There are several methods by which a donation may be revoked. If the document has been delivered to a named donee, it may be revoked by

- a written revocation signed by the donor and delivered to the donee
- an oral revocation witnessed by two persons and communicated to the donee
- a statement to the attending physician during a terminal illness that has been communicated to the donee
- a written statement that has been signed and on the donor's person or in the donor's immediate effects

If the written instrument of donation has not been delivered to the donee, it may be revoked by destruction, cancellation, or mutilation of the instrument. If the donation is made by a will, it may be revoked in the manner provided for revocation or amendment of wills. Any person acting in good-faith reliance on the terms of an instrument of donation will not be subject to civil or criminal liability unless there is actual notice of the revocation of the donation.

Determination of Death

The time of death must be determined by a physician in attendance at the donor's death, or a physician certifying death, who shall not be a member of the team of physicians engaged in the transplantation procedure.

Consideration of legal duties regarding the use, handling, and disposition of dead bodies cannot be divorced from the legal questions involved in determining when death occurs. In many contexts, such as deciding rights to the property of the deceased person, the determination of death does not involve the hospital or its personnel. However, when permission has been granted for use of a patient's body or organs for the benefit of another patient or science in general, determination of the point of death becomes critical. New technology, specifically medical advancement in artificially sustaining life and transplanting vital organs, raises both legal and moral questions regarding the viability of the traditional methods of determining death. (See section on Defining Death in Chapter 15—Euthanasia, Death, and Dying.)

UNCLAIMED DEAD BODIES

Persons entitled to possession of a dead body must arrange for release of the body for transfer to an undertaker for final disposal. The recognition by the courts of a quasi-property right in the body of a deceased person imposes a duty on a health care facility to make reasonable efforts to give notice to persons entitled to claim the body. When there are no known relatives or friends of the family who can be contacted by the facility to claim the body, the facility has a responsibility to dispose of the body in accordance with law. Most states have statutes providing for the disposal of such bodies.

Unclaimed bodies generally are buried at public expense; a public official, usually a county official, has the duty to bury or otherwise dispose of such bodies. Most states have statutes providing for the disposal of unclaimed bodies by delivery to institutions for educational and scientific purposes. The public official in charge of the body has a duty to notify the government agency of the presence of the body. The agency then arranges for the transfer of the body in accordance with the statute. If no such agency exists under the statute, the health care facility or a public official may be authorized to allow a medical school or other institution or person, designated by the statute as an eligible recipient of unclaimed dead bodies, to remove the body for scientific use.

Certain categories of persons usually are excluded from these provisions permitting the distribution of bodies for educational and scientific use. For public health reasons, the statutes usually do not permit distribution of the bodies of persons who have died from contagious diseases.

Although most of these statutes explicitly require notification of relatives and set time limits for holding the body to allow relatives an opportunity to claim the body, strict compliance with the statutory provisions is often impossible because of the very nature of the problems that arise in the handling of dead bodies and in the required procedures themselves. Noncompliance in such instances would not appear to cause liability. An example of such a provision is the requirement that relatives be notified immediately on death and that the body be held for 24 hours subject to claim by a relative or friend. The procedure of locating and notifying relatives may consume the greater part of the 24-hour period after death; if relatives who are willing to claim the body are located, the body should be held for a reasonable time to allow them to arrange custody for burial.

EXPERIMENTATION

The Nuremberg Code and the Declaration of Helsinki provided guidelines for the development of federal regulations for medical research and the protection of human subjects in the United States. Federal regulations control federal grants that apply to experiments involving new drugs, new medical devices, or new medical procedures. Generally, a combination of federal and state guidelines and regulations ensures proper supervision and control over experimentation that involves human subjects. For example, federal regulations require hospital-based researchers to obtain the approval of an institutional review board. This board functions to review proposed research studies and conduct follow-up reviews on a regular basis.

Federal and state regulations impose several other requirements on experiments involving human subjects. Institutions conducting medical research on human subjects must do the following:

- fully disclose the inherent risks to the patient
- make a proper determination that the patient is competent to consent
- identify treatment alternatives
- obtain written consent from the patient

California has enacted legislation that protects the rights of research subjects and provides for fines and imprisonment if proper consent procedures are not followed. California Health & Safety Code, §§24170–24179.5, 26668.4.

Failure to obtain consent for the administration of experimental drugs can give rise to a law suit. The district court in *Blanton v. United States,* 428 F. Supp. 360 (D.D.C. 1977), held that when a "new drug" of unknown effectiveness was administered to a patient at a Navy medical center, despite the availability of other drugs of known effectiveness, the hospital violated the accepted medical standards and its duty of due care, so that in the absence of the patient's consent to the experiment, the United States was liable for the resulting injury.

The Food and Drug Administration, under enormous criticism over the years because of the "red tape" involved in the approval of new drugs, issued new rules to fast track the approval process.[2] The new rules permit the use of experimental drugs outside a controlled clinical trial if the drugs are used to treat a life-threatening condition.

A written special consent form for the use of investigational drugs must be obtained from the patient. Federal regulations require that the nature of the drug and possible adverse consequences be explained.

Nursing Homes

The Health Care Financing Administration survey process includes a review of the rights of any nursing facility residents participating in experimental research. Surveyor(s) will review the records of residents identified as participating in a clinical research study. They will determine whether informed consent forms have been executed properly. The form will be reviewed to determine if all known risks have been identified. Appropriate questions may be directed to both the staff and residents or the residents' guardians.

Possible questions to ask staff include

- Is the facility participating in any experimental research?
- If yes, what residents are involved? (Interview a sample of these residents.)[3]

Residents or guardians may be asked questions such as

- Are you participating in the_____study?
- Was this explained to you well enough so that you understand what the study is about and any risks that might be involved?[4]

Residents participating in research studies should understand fully the implications of the study. A nursing facility will not be in compliance with the resident rights regulations if a resident participates in a clinical study without full knowledge of the study.[5]

NOTES

1. 22 AM. JUR. 2D *Dead Bodies* §64 (1988).

2. 52 Fed. Reg. 19,466 (1987), *rev.* 53 Fed. Reg. 41515 (Oct. 21, 1988).
3. 2 C.F.R. §488.115 (1989).
4. *Id.*
5. *Id.*

Chapter 17
Malpractice Insurance

I never was ruined but twice—once when I gained a lawsuit, and once when I lost one.

Francois Marie de Voltaire (1694–1778)

OUTLINE

Today, almost everyone has some form of insurance. We insure our automobiles against collision and theft and our homes against fire. We insure our personal property, ourselves, and members of our family. Professionals buy insurance to protect themselves from suit in the event that others are injured as a result of their professional services.

The cost of malpractice insurance continues to be a major concern for the health care industry because of the many malpractice claims and exorbitant jury awards. Malpractice became a major problem for the health care industry in the 1960s. The rise in the occurrences of malpractice claims has resulted in unwieldy malpractice insurance rates for both physicians and health care organizations.[1]

According to 1,100 physicians from New York and Long Island responding to a *Newsday* survey on "What Bothers Doctors," 17.4 percent of physicians consider insurance to be today's main health care problem.[2] A $3.1 million 1,100 page Harvard Medical Practice Study, commissioned by the state of New York because of sharply increasing malpractice rates, showed that "[t]he risk of sustaining an adverse event increased with age. Persons over 65 had twice the chance of being injured by health practitioners than patients between 16 and 44."[3]

Spencer C. Johnson, president of the Michigan Hospital Association, during an interview with *A.H.A. News* stated that Michigan has "the most significant medical-liability problem in the United States. Hospitals and physicians pay about $500 million a year for coverage. That's enough money to fund the Canadian health care system for two-and-a-half years."[4]

Health care facilities continue to be sued for malpractice on the grounds of poor or substandard care. For nursing facilities, the incidence of malpractice suits is likely to increase with the implementation of different cost containment strategies that has resulted in nursing facilities caring for sicker residents (e.g., diagnosis-related groups).[5]

The medical professional insurance marketplace is relatively small in comparison with other lines of insurance. Only a handful of insurance companies offer medical professional liability insurance, excluding statewide association programs.

Medical professional insurance, as all insurance, is subject to the cyclical nature of the insurance market. Further problems intrinsic in malpractice insurance include the uncertainty of our legal system, the effects of inflation on ultimate claim values, emerging technology treatments, and diseases.[6]

Health care facilities and professionals of the mid-1970s and mid-1980s experienced difficult times in obtaining medical liability insurance coverage. Competition between insurers was minimal, with high premiums and adequate umbrella coverage difficult to obtain. Between those hard markets was a soft market that brought steady premium reduction and greater availability of coverage.[7] Since 1986, there has been another softening of the market. In 1988, insurers of medical professional liability coverage provided increased flexibility of programs, premium reductions, and broadened coverage. The short-term outlook is good. Additional insurers and additional capacity are becoming available. Costs may not be reduced, but large increases were not seen in 1989 and 1990 premiums. On a long-term basis, the cyclic underwriting pattern of the insurance industry might very well result in a return once again to a crisis in the medical malpractice insurance market.[8] Those who are familiar with the insurance cycle can appreciate that a crisis can and probably will recur.[9]

Malpractice insurance rates have affected the availability as well as the cost of insurance significantly. Many commercial insurance carriers discontinued underwriting professional liability coverage since the middle to late 1970s. As a result, some states required insurance carriers to join a consortium of insurance companies to underwrite medical malpractice insurance. These consortiums were referred to as joint underwriting associations. According to one study, there were only 12 such consortiums in 1986.[10] Concern regarding insurance industry practices is strong on the federal level for some public officials. Senator Jay Rockefeller, in an interview by American Hospital Association staff regarding his health agenda for 1991, stated

> Insurance reform is right up there. Unless the private insurance industry can demonstrate that they are about the business of managing and controlling costs in health care and not just avoiding them, which is what they do now, I predict that they will not survive this decade.[11]

THE INSURANCE POLICY

Insurance is a contract that creates legal obligations on the part of both the insured and the insurer. It is a contract in which the insurer agrees to assume certain risks of the insured for consideration or payment of a premium. Under the terms of the contract, also known as the insurance policy, the insurer promises to pay a specific amount of money if a specified event takes place. An insurance policy contains three necessary elements: identification of the risk covered, the specific amount payable, and the specified occurrence.

Insurance companies are required by the laws of the different states to issue only policies that contain certain mandated provisions and to maintain certain financial reserves to guarantee to policyholders that their expectations will be met when coverage is needed. The basic underlying concept of insurance is the spreading of risk. By writing coverage for a large enough pool of individuals, the company has determined actuarially that a certain number of claims will arise within that pool, and if the premium structure has been established correctly and the prediction of claims made accurately, the company ought to be able to meet those claims and return a profit to its shareholders.

Risk Categories

A risk is the possibility that a loss will occur. The main function of insurance is to provide security against this loss. Insurance does not prevent or hinder the occurrence of the loss, but it does compensate for the damages.

An insured individual may be exposed to three categories of risk: risk of property loss or damage, risk of personal injury or loss of life, and risk of incurring legal liability. Property risk is the possibility that an insured's property may be damaged or destroyed by fire, flood, tornado, hurricane, or other catastrophe. Personal risk is the possibility that the insured may be injured in an accident or may become ill; the possibility of death is a personal risk covered in the typical life insurance plan. Legal liability risk is the possibility that the insured may become legally liable to pay money damages to another and includes accident and professional liability insurance.

Policy Types

The two basic kinds of malpractice policies are

- *occurrence policies*, which cover all incidents that arise during a policy year, regardless of when they are reported to the insurer
- *claims-made policies*, which cover only those claims made or reported during the policy year, regardless of when they occurred

LIABILITY OF THE PROFESSIONAL

A nurse or a physician who provides professional services to another person may be legally responsible for any harm the person suffers as a result of negligence and subject to a loss of money in the form of legally awarded damages. Many professionals protect themselves from their exposure to a legal loss by acquiring a professional liability insurance policy.

Do Nurses Need Insurance?

Should nurses carry malpractice insurance? From a legal standpoint, the answer is yes. Even though a hospital, as a nurse's employer, can be held responsible for the negligence of a nurse pursuant to the doctrine of *respondeat superior*, a nurse may be held liable for his or her own negligence. From a cost-benefit standpoint, the answer is also yes. Malpractice insurance premiums for nurses continue to be reasonable. Malpractice insurance coverage is especially important if a nurse is working

- as a volunteer at a clinic or health fair not sponsored by his or her employer
- as an independent contractor providing a service in a patient's home
- for an independent agency or nurse registry
- for a hospital that is covered by an insurance policy that has an exclusionary provision by which the insurance company disclaims liability for malpractice actions brought against the insured hospital

If a private agency has inadequate insurance coverage, there is always a possibility that recovery will be sought against a nurse's estate.

There are disadvantages to nurses obtaining malpractice insurance. First, acquisition of malpractice coverage by nurses could encourage naming nurses as defendants in malpractice suits. Second, an increase in complaints against nurses could cause a rise in insurance premiums— eventually placing the cost of malpractice insurance outside their financial means.

The court in *Jones v. Medox, Inc.,* 413 A.2d 1288, 430 A.2d 488 (D.C. 1981), held that only the nurse's insurance carrier, Globe Insurance, was liable for injuries sustained by the plaintiff while at Doctors Hospital; these injuries resulted from an injection administered by the nurse. Ms. Jones was employed by Medox, Inc., a corporation providing temporary medical personnel to Doctors Hospital. After settlement of the claim against the nurse, the hospital, and the nurse's employer, the nurse and her insurer brought an action against Doctors Hospital, Medox, Inc., and their insurers. The trial court granted summary judgment in favor of the hospital and its insurer and dismissed the claim against Medox, Inc. and its insurer.

A nurse's insurance policy was primary with respect to the first $100,000 of a settlement that resulted from a malpractice action against the nurse in *American Nurses' Ass'n v. Passaic General Hospital,* 98 N.J. 83, 484 A.2d 670 (1984). The National Fire Insurance Company had issued an insurance policy covering the contractual obligation of the American Nurses' Association to its members. The Supreme Court of New Jersey held that the judgment against the nurse in excess of $100,000 was properly apportioned equally between the hospital's liability insurer and the association's liability insurer.

Private Duty Nurse

A private duty nurse is not an employee of an institution but rather is engaged by the patient (or the patient's family) to provide services to that patient. As such, the nurse should obtain personal coverage. The patient engaging the nurse would be well advised to ask about the availability of such coverage, as would the institution in which the nurse is providing professional care for that patient.

Even though a special duty nurse is employed by a patient, a hospital can be liable for damages resulting from a nurse's negligent conduct. The existence of an employer–employee relationship, which determines the applicability of *respondeat superior*, is a matter to be determined by the jury.

A hospital also can be liable for damages awarded in a malpractice action if a nurse and his or her registry have inadequate insurance to cover a jury award. In such instances, a hospital then would have a right to seek recovery from the nurse and the registry.

Students

The potential for liability is not limited to licensed professionals. Students engaged in learning a profession and paraprofessionals such as therapists who engage in activities involving the care and treatment of others face potential liability for their acts. For this reason, these individuals often obtain personal insurance coverage or assure themselves of such coverage through the institution in which they are employed or the institution in which they are enrolled to obtain their education.

THE INSURANCE AGREEMENT

A health care facility, nurse, physician, and other health practitioners who are covered by an insurance policy must recognize the rights and duties inherent in the policy. The professional should be able to identify the risks that are covered, the amount of coverage, and the conditions of the contract.

Although the policies of different insurance companies may vary, the standard policy usually provides that the insurance company will "pay on behalf of the insured all sums which the insured shall become legally obligated to pay as damages because of injury arising out of malpractice error, or mistake in rendering or failing to render professional services."

A standard liability insurance policy has five distinct parts:

- the insurance agreement
- defense and settlement
- the policy period
- the amount payable
- conditions of the policy

The insurer, under the terms of the policy, has a legal obligation to pay any sum that has been agreed to or determined by a court, up to the policy limit, including legal fees. It will not pay or respond merely because the insured professional feels a moral obligation toward an injured party.

Under a professional liability policy, the professional is protected from damages arising from rendering or failing to render professional services. Thus, a professional who performs a negligent act resulting in legal liability or who fails to perform a necessary act (thereby incurring damages) is personally protected from paying an injured party. The actual payment of the legal money damages to the injured party is made by the insurer.

Defense and Settlement

In the defense and settlement portion of the insurance policy, the insured and the insurance company agree that the company will defend any lawsuit against the insured arising from performance or nonperformance of professional services and that the company is delegated the power to effect a settlement of any claims as it deems necessary. In a professional liability policy, the duty of the insurer under this clause is limited to the defense of lawsuits against the insured that are a consequence of professional services.

The insurance company fulfills its obligation to provide a defense by engaging the services of an attorney on behalf of the insured. The obligation of the attorney is to the insured directly, because the insured is the attorney's client. There is, to some extent, a divided loyalty because the attorney looks to the insurance company to obtain business. Nevertheless, the attorney–client relationship exists only between the attorney and the insured, and the insured has the right to expect the attorney to fulfill the requirements of such a relationship.

If an insurance company has established the right to obtain a settlement of any claim before trial, the company's only obligation is to act reasonably and not to the detriment of the insured.

Policy Period

The period of the policy always is stated in the insurance contract. Under the "occurrence" form of coverage, the contract provides protection only for claims that occur during the time frame within which the policy is stated to be in effect. Any incident that occurs before or after the policy period would not be covered under the insuring agreement. Occurrence policies provide coverage for all claims that may arise out of a policy period. The actual reporting time has no bearing on the validity of the claim, as long as it is filed before the applicable statute of limitations runs out. Although the reporting time has no bearing on the validity of the claim from the standpoint of coverage under the policy, the conditions of the policy will require notice within a specified time. Failure to provide such notice could void the insurer's obligation under the policy if it can be demonstrated that the carrier's position was compromised as a result of the late report or filing of a claim.

A "claims-made policy" provides coverage for only those claims instituted during the policy period. Notice of a claim is required during the policy period. Failure to give notice of a claim to the insurer in a claims-made policy until after the policy expires can result in denial by the insurance company to cover the claim. *St. Paul Fire & Marine Insurance Co.,* 811 P.2d 432 (Colo. Ct. App. 1991).

Coverage—The Amount Payable

The amount to be paid by the insurer is determined by the amount of damage incurred by the injured party. This determination may be made by a trial jury, or the insurance company and the injured party may reach a settlement before the lawsuit comes to trial or before the jury has determined the amount of damages.[12] In any event, the insurance company will pay the injured party no more than the maximum limit stated in the insurance policy. The insured professional must personally pay any damages that exceed the policy limit. For example, under a policy with a maximum coverage of $1 million for each claim and $3 million for aggregate claims (the total amount payable to all injured parties), the insured is protected on each individual claim up to $1 million and up to $3 million in a policy period.

Punitive Damages

A claim for punitive damages awarded in a malpractice suit was submitted to an insurance carrier for payment but was subsequently denied by the carrier. The insurance carrier cited Florida public policy, which prohibits coverage of punitive damage awards. *American Medical Nursing Centers—Greenbrook v. Heckler,* 592 F. Supp. 1311, 1312 (D. D.C. 1984).

Obligation To Defend

The insurer of a nursing facility in *Hartford Accident & Idemnity v. Regent Nursing Home,* 413 N.Y.S.2d 195 (App. Div. 1979), was found to have an obligation to defend the facility despite an exclusion for malpractice coverage in the policy. The "complaint in primary action gave sufficient notice that alleged breach of duty may have encompassed ordinary negligence as well as professional malpractice." *Id.*

Intentional Torts

An action was brought by a comprehensive liability insurer for declaratory judgment as to its duty to defend insureds in civil actions alleging slander, interference with business relations, and violations of the federal antitrust laws in *St. Paul Insurance Co. v. Talladega Nursing Home,* 606 F.2d 631 (5th Cir. 1979). The federal district court ruled for the insurer and the nursing facility appealed. The Fifth Circuit held that the insurer has no duty to defend or provide coverage for alleged intentional torts. Under Alabama law, all contracts insuring against loss from intentional wrongs are void as being against public policy.

Conditions of the Policy

Each insurance policy contains a number of important conditions. Failure to comply with these conditions may cause forfeiture of the policy and nonpayment of claims against it. Generally, insurance policies contain the following conditions:

- *notice of occurrence*—When the insured becomes aware that an injury has occurred as a result of acts covered under the contract, the insured must notify the insurance company promptly. The form of notice may be either oral or written, as specified in the policy
- *notice of claim*—Whenever the insured receives notice that a claim or suit is being instituted, prompt notice must be sent by the insured to the insurance company. This provides the insurance company with an opportunity to investigate the facts of a case. The policy will specify what papers are to be forwarded to the company. The mere failure to advise timely may be in and of itself a breach of the insurance contract, entitling the insurer to decline coverage. It may not matter that the insurer has in no way been prejudiced by the late notification. The mere fact that the insured has failed to carry out obligations under the policy may be sufficient to permit the insurer to avoid its obligations. When the insurer has refused to honor a claim because of late notice and the insured wishes to challenge such refusal, an action can be brought, asking a court to determine the reasonableness of the insurer's position
- *assistance of the insured*—The insured must cooperate with the insurance company and render any assistance necessary to reach a settlement

- *other insurance*—If the insured has pertinent insurance policies with other insurance companies, the insured must notify the insurance company so that each company may pay the appropriate amount of the claim
- *assignment*—The protections contracted for by the insured may not be transferred unless permission is granted by the insurance company. Because the insurance company was aware of the risks the insured would encounter before the policy was issued, the company will endeavor to avoid protecting persons other than the policyholder
- *subrogation*—This is the right of a person who pays another's debt to be substituted for all rights in relation to the debt. When an insurance company makes a payment for the insured under the terms of the policy, the company becomes the beneficiary of all the rights of recovery the insured has against any other persons who also may have been negligent. For example, if several nurses were found liable for negligence arising from the same occurrence and the insurance company for one nurse pays the entire claim, the company will be entitled to the rights of that nurse and may collect a proportionate share of the claim from the other nurses
- *changes*—The insured cannot make changes in the policy without the written consent of the insurance company. Thus, an agent of the insurance company ordinarily cannot modify or remove any condition of the liability contract. Only the insurance company, by written authorization, may permit a condition to be altered or removed
- *cancellation*—A cancellation clause spells out the conditions and procedures necessary for the insured or the insurer to cancel the liability policy. Written notice usually is required. The insured person's failure to comply with any terms of the policy can result in cancellation and possible nonpayment of a claim by the insurance company. As a legal contract, failure to meet the terms and conditions of an insurance policy can result in a breach of contract and voidance of coverage

MEDICAL LIABILITY INSURANCE

The fundamental tenets of insurance law and their application to the typical liability insurance policy are pertinent to the provisions of medical professional liability insurance as applied to individuals and institutions. Professional liability policies vary in the broadness, the exclusions from coverage, and the interpretations a company places on the language of the contract.

There are three medical professional liability classes:

- individuals including (but not limited to) physicians, surgeons, dentists, nurses, osteopaths, chiropractors, opticians, physiotherapists, optometrists, and different types of medical technicians. This category also may include medical laboratories, blood banks, and optical establishments.
- health care institutions, such as hospitals, extended care facilities, homes for the aged, institutions for the mentally ill, sanitariums, and other health institutions where bed and board are provided for patients or residents
- clinics, dispensaries, and infirmaries where there are no regular bed or board facilities. These institutions may be related to industrial or commercial enterprises; however, they are to be distinguished from facilities operated by dentists or physicians, which usually are covered under individual professional liability contracts

The insuring clause usually will provide for payment on behalf of the insured if an injury arises from either of the following:

- malpractice, error, or mistake in rendering or failing to render professional services in the practice of the insured's profession during the policy period
- acts or omissions on the part of the insured during the policy period as a member of a formal accreditation or similar professional board or committee of a health care facility or a professional society

Although injury is not limited to bodily injury or property damage, it must result from malpractice, error, mistake, or failure to perform acts that should have been performed.

The most common risks covered by medical professional liability insurance are

- negligence
- assault and battery as a result of failing to obtain consent to a medical or surgical procedure
- libel and slander
- invasion of privacy for betrayal of professional confidences

Coverage may vary from company to company, but standards of policy coverage generally are followed. The premium rates generally are approved by state insurance departments as filed by insurance companies. Rates will differ for individuals by profession and specialty and by type of health care facility (e.g., nursing facility and hospital).

MEDICAL MALPRACTICE INSURANCE ASSOCIATIONS

The difficulty that health care facilities and physicians had in obtaining malpractice insurance in many states during the early 1980s resulted in the formation of medical malpractice insurance associations. The purpose of these associations is to provide a market for institutions or physicians who are unable to obtain medical malpractice insurance in the open market at a reasonable price. Legislation was introduced requiring all insurance carriers engaged in writing personal liability insurance within a particular state to provide malpractice coverage through these associations (similar to "assigned risk" pools for problem automobile drivers).

> Most physician-owned liability insurance companies are not-for-profit enterprises. In general, their policies are set by physician boards of directors, but their business operations are managed by professional insurance executives. Most of these companies were established by and retain close ties to medical societies. Most physician-owned companies were established in order to maintain access to malpractice insurance when commercial insurers withdrew from the market in the late 1970's.[13]

SELF-INSURANCE

Exorbitant malpractice insurance premiums often have produced situations in which the premium cost of insurance has approached and, on occasion, reached the face amount of the policy. Because of the extremely high cost of maintaining such insurance, some institutions have sought alternatives to this conventional means of protecting against medical malpractice. One alternative is self-insurance. When a health care facility self-insures its malpractice risks, it no longer purchases a policy of malpractice insurance but instead periodically sets aside a certain amount of its own funds as a reserve against malpractice losses and expenses. An institution that self-insures generally retains the services of a self-insurance consulting firm and of an actuary to determine the proper level of funding that the institution should maintain.

A self-insurance program need not involve the elimination of insurance coverage in its entirety. A health care facility may find it prudent to purchase excess coverage whereby the institution self-insures the first agreed-on dollar amount of risk and the insurance carrier insures the balance. For example, in a typical program the facility may self-insure the first $1 million of professional liability risk per year. Since most claims will be disposed of within such limitation, the cost of excess insurance may be quite reasonable.

Before a corporation makes a decision to self-insure, not only must it determine the economic aspects of such a decision and the necessary funding levels to maintain an adequate reserve for future claims, but it also must determine whether there are any legal impediments to such a program. A corporation that has obtained funding from governmental sources or that has issued bonds or other obligations containing certain covenants may find itself unable to self-insure because of these prior commitments. Health care facilities should consult legal counsel to review appropriate and applicable documentation before making the self-insurance decision.

OTHER INSURANCE COVERAGES

Besides insurance coverage for liability risks, a health care facility typically is involved in several other insurance situations. For example, it provides fringe benefits to its employees that may include health insurance, disability insurance, life insurance, and a pension or other retirement plan also involving insurance. These programs require appropriate administration and create rights and obligations on the part of the facility and its personnel. Issues such as eligibility for coverage, coverage for particular circumstances, and termination of coverage can give rise to substantial legal problems and possibly even litigation.

Other insurance coverages include those for physical plant, motor vehicles, and where applicable, construction projects. In the course of a construction project, appropriate insurance coverages for liability risks, fire risks, and other similar hazards must be considered. Also, the requirement that contractors obtain a payment and performance bond to ensure the completion of their work and the payment of all subcontractors and material suppliers is important. Substantial litigation can arise during the course of or at the conclusion of a construction project involving large sums of money because of inappropriate construction; failure to complete construction; failure to follow plans or specifications; and/or to adhere to schedules.

TRUSTEE COVERAGE

Trustees should be covered by liability insurance just as physicians and other health professionals. Liability coverage for trustees should be provided by the institution. Such coverage is helpful in attracting qualified board members. In *Lynch v. Redfield Foundation,* 9 Cal. App. 3d 293, 88 Cal. Rptr. 86 (1970), a California bank refused to honor corporate drafts unless all trustees concurred. They could not agree, and funds in a noninterest-bearing account continued to grow in principal from $4,900 to $47,000 over a five-year period. Although two trustees did try to carry on corporate functions despite the dissident trustee, their good faith did not protect them from liability in this case. The money could have been transferred to at least an interest-bearing account without the third trustee's signature. The trustees were held jointly liable to pay to the corporation the statutory rate of simple interest.

Before an insurer writing a trustee policy (generally known as directors' and officers' liability insurance) will respond to defend or pay a claim on behalf of a trustee, it must be shown that the trustee acted in good faith and within the scope of his or her responsibilities. Ordinarily, coverage would not be afforded when a trustee is accused of acting improperly in his or her relationship with the corporation. Also, insurance coverage for officers' and directors' liability generally excludes as a covered event the failure to obtain other necessary insurance for the institution (e.g., fire insurance).

MANDATED MEDICAL STAFF INSURANCE COVERAGE

Physicians often are required by health care institutions to carry their own malpractice insurance. A federal district court in New Orleans has ruled that a hospital has the legal right to suspend a staff physician for failing to comply with its requirement that physicians carry medical malpractice insurance coverage. The decision resulted from a suit brought against Methodist Hospital in New Orleans by a physician whose staff privileges were suspended because he failed to comply with a newly adopted hospital requirement that all staff physicians provide proof of malpractice coverage of at least $1 million. The court rejected the physician's charges that the requirement violated his civil rights and antitrust laws in *Pollack v. Methodist Hospital,* 392 F. Supp. 393 (E.D. La. 1975).

A California court in *Wilkinson v. Madera Community Hospital,* 144 Cal. App. 3d 436, 192 Cal. Rptr. 593 (1983), held that a Health and Safety Code provision providing that a health facility may require every member of its medical staff to have professional liability insurance as a condition to being on staff was permissible. Dr. Wilkinson was refused reappointment because he failed to maintain malpractice insurance with a "recognized insurance company" as required by the hospital.

INVESTIGATION AND SETTLEMENT OF CLAIMS

An injured party may request settlement of a claim before instituting legal action. Most malpractice claims are settled before reaching the courtroom. A study by the U.S. General Accounting Office indicates that approximately 90 percent of malpractice claims are settled in this manner.[14]

As a first step toward settlement of a claim, the insurance carrier may send an investigator to interview a claimant regarding the details of the alleged occurrence that led to the injury. Itemization of damages (e.g., lost wages and medical expenses) and a request for a physical examination may be made by the insurance company. After an investigation, the insurance company may agree to a settlement if liability is questionable and the risks of proceeding to trial are too great. Should settlement negotiations fail, an attorney may be employed by the injured party to negotiate a settlement. If the attorney fails to obtain a settlement, either the claim is dropped or legal action may be commenced.

If a claim is settled, a general release is signed by the plaintiff, surrendering the right of action against the defendant. Should a claimant be married, a general release also should be obtained from the spouse, because there may be a cause of action because of loss of the injured spouse's services (e.g., companionship). A parent's release surrenders only a parental claim. Approval of a court may be necessary to release a child's claim. Release by a minor, in some instances, may be repudiated by the minor on reaching majority. A general release can be voided if the releasee

- is intoxicated, under the influence of drugs, in shock, or in extreme pain which prevents sufficient understanding of a general release and therefore prevents or voids its execution
- does not understand the language of the release
- has not had the opportunity to obtain appropriate legal consultation
- has been the victim of mental or physical duress
- has executed the release as a result of misrepresentation or fraud
- is mentally incompetent and cannot give a valid release—in this instance, a court-appointed guardian is required to execute a release on behalf of a mental incompetent, and a court must pass on the terms of any settlement

---

NOTES

1. U.S. DEPARTMENT OF HEALTH AND HUMAN SERVICES, TASK FORCE ON MEDICAL LIABILITY AND MALPRACTICE 3 (1987); AMERICAN MEDICAL ASSOCIATION, SOCIOECONOMIC MONITORING SYSTEM SURVEY (1986).

2. R.F. Clay, *What Bothers Doctors*, NEWSDAY, Jan. 13, 1991, at 15.

3. D. Zinman, *Study Finds Hospitals "Harm" Some*, NEWSDAY, 50(177), Mar. 1, 1990, at 17.

4. *Universal Coverage for Michigan Citizens High Priority:Johnson*, A.H.A. NEWS, 27(22), June 3, 1991, at 7.

5. M. Kapp, *Preventing Malpractice Suits in Long Term Care Facilities*, Q.R.M. MONTHLY, Mar. 1986, at 109.

6. AMERICAN SOCIETY FOR HEALTHCARE RISK MANAGEMENT PROCEEDINGS, RISK FINANCIAL MANAGEMENT MECHANISM, ORLANDO, FLA., 35 (1989).

7. *Id.*

8. The Robert Wood Johnson Foundation, *Profile: Walter Wadlington, LLB, Director, RWJF Medical Malpractice Program*, ADVANCES, Spring 1991, at 4.

9. The Robert Wood Johnson Foundation, *Medical Malpractice: The Push for Reform Is Still Strong*, ADVANCES, V(2), Spring 1992, at 5.

10. NATIONAL ASSOCIATION OF INDEPENDENT INSURERS, REPORT OF THE FINANCIAL SOLVENCY OF STATE MEDICAL MALPRACTICE JUAs TO THE NAII LAWS COMMITTEE (1986).

11. M. Burke, *Congressional Leaders Outline Their Health Agendas: Sen. Jay Rockefeller*, HOSPITALS, 65(1), Jan. 5, 1991, at 26.

12. Some states have provisions mandating that, before any settlement of a negligence claim, consent of the court or, in the alternative, a medical malpractice panel to any proposed resolution must be obtained to best protect the minor's interests.

13. U.S. DEPARTMENT OF HEALTH AND HUMAN SERVICES, *supra* note 1, at 147.

14. U.S. GENERAL ACCOUNTING OFFICE, MEDICAL MALPRACTICE, CHARACTERISTICS OF CLAIMS CLOSED IN 1984 (1987).

Chapter **18**

Labor Relations

OUTLINE

  Wage and Hour Laws
  Child Labor Acts
  Workers' Compensation
    Physical Injury
    Job Stress
    'Flu Shot Reaction
• Labor Rights
• Management Rights
  Right To Receive Strike Notice
  Right To Hire Replacement Workers
  Right To Restrict Union Activity to Prescribed Areas
  Right To Prohibit Union Activity During Working Hours
  Right To Prohibit Supervisors from Participating in Union Activity
• Equal Employment Opportunity—Affirmative Action Plan
• Patient Rights During Labor Disputes
• Injunctions
• Administering a Collective Bargaining Agreement

The relationship between employers and employees is regulated by both state and federal laws (and, to a lesser extent, local laws). Health care facilities are not exempt from the impact of these laws and therefore are required to take into account such matters as employment practices (wages, hours, and working conditions), union activity, workers' compensation laws, occupational safety and health laws, and employment discrimination laws.[1]

Federal or state regulation generally pervades all areas of employer–employee relationships. The most significant piece of federal legislation dealing with labor relations is the National Labor Relations Act (NLRA). Although federal laws generally take precedence over state laws when there is a conflict between the state and the federal laws, state laws are applicable and must be considered, especially when state standards are more stringent than those mandated by the federal government.

UNIONS AND HEALTH CARE FACILITIES

Through the mid-1930s, union organizational activity in the health care industry was minimal, and it continued that way with relatively slow growth until the late 1950s. Union activity has been successful most often in those geographic areas in which unions have been active in other industries. As a result, labor relations has become an important factor in the operation of health care facilities.

Many labor organizations now are involved heavily in attempts to become the recognized collective bargaining representatives in health care facilities. There are craft unions, which devote their primary organizing efforts to skilled employees such as carpenters and electricians, and industrial unions and unions of governmental employees, which seek to represent large groups of unskilled or semiskilled employees. Professional and occupational associations, such as state nurses' associations, historically known for their social and academic efforts, have involved themselves in collective bargaining for their profession. To the extent that the professional organizations seek goals directly concerned with wages, hours, and other employment conditions and engage in bargaining on behalf of employees, they perform the functions of labor unions.

FEDERAL LABOR ACTS

National Labor Relations Act of 1935

The NLRA[2] was enacted in 1935. It defines certain conduct of employers and employees as unfair labor practices and provides for hearings on complaints that such practices have occurred. This NLRA was modified by the Taft-Hartley amendments of 1947 and the Landrum-Griffin amendments of 1959.

Jurisdiction

Nearly all proprietary health care facilities, for some time, have been subject to the provisions of the NLRA. The National Labor Relations Board (NLRB), which is entrusted with enforcing and administering the act, has jurisdiction over matters involving proprietary and not-for-profit health care facilities with gross revenues of at least $250,000 per year and nurses' associations and health care-related facilities with gross revenues of more than $100,000 per year.[3] *Butte Medical Properties,* 168 N.L.R.B. Dec. (CCH) ¶ 226 (1967).

The NLRB's basic method of operation is to investigate claims or complaints of unfair practices submitted by the employer or employees, or both. The board reviews the claim, determining whether there have been unfair labor practices, and recommends a remedy.

Most questions submitted to the board involve claims by employees that their rights to self-organization or the choosing of their collective bargaining representative have been interfered with by the employer. Employers also may submit complaints to the NLRB (e.g., when two unions are seeking recognition and

one of them intimidates employees by making allegations that a sweetheart relationship exists between the employer and the competing union in an effort to
disrupt the certification process).

An exemption for governmental institutions was included in the 1935 enactment of the NLRA, and charitable health care institutions were exempted in
1947 by the Taft-Hartley Act amendments to the NLRA.[4] However, a July 1974
amendment to the NLRA extended coverage to employees of nonprofit health
care institutions that previously had been exempted from its provisions. In the
words of the amendment, a health care facility is "any hospital, convalescent
hospital, health maintenance organization, health clinic, nursing home, extended
care facility, or other institution devoted to the care of the sick, infirm or aged."[5]

The amendment also enacted unique, special provisions for employees of
health care facilities who oppose unionization on legitimate religious grounds.
These provisions allow a member of such an institution to make periodic contributions to one of three nonreligious charitable funds selected jointly by the
labor organization and the employing institution rather than paying periodic
union dues and initiation fees. If the collective bargaining agreement does not
specify an acceptable fund, the employee may select a tax-exempt charity.

Elections

The NLRA sets out the procedures by which employees may select a union as
their collective bargaining representative to negotiate with health care facilities
over employment and contract matters.[6] A health care facility may choose to
recognize and deal with the union without resorting to the formal NLRA procedure. If the formal process is adhered to, the employees vote on union representation in an election held under NLRB supervision.[7] If the union wins, it is certified by the NLRB as the employees' bargaining representative.

The NLRA provides that the representative, having been selected by a majority of employees in a bargaining unit, is the exclusive bargaining agent for all
employees in the unit. *Montgomery Ward & Co.,* 137 N.L.R.B. Dec. (CCH) ¶
346, 50 L.R.R.M. (BNA) 1137 (1962). The scope of the bargaining unit is often
the subject of dispute, for its boundaries may determine the outcome of the election, the employee representative's bargaining power, and the level of labor
relations stability.

When the parties cannot agree on the appropriate unit for bargaining, the
NLRB has broad discretion to decide the issue. But the NLRB's discretion is
limited to determining appropriate units for only those employees who are classified as professional, supervisory, clerical, technical, or service and maintenance employees when they are included in units outside their particular category. This is the case unless there has been a self-determination election in which
the members of a certain group vote, as a class, to be included within the larger

bargaining unit. For example, nurses and other professional employees can be excluded from a bargaining unit composed of service and maintenance employees unless the professionals are first given the opportunity to choose separate representation and reject it. Supervisory nurses also have been held to be entitled to a bargaining unit separate from the unit composed of general duty nurses.[8] *St. Francis Hospital,* 265 N.L.R.B. Dec. (CCH) ¶ 1025 (1982).

Although the NLRA does not require employee representatives to be selected by any particular procedure, the act provides for the NLRB to conduct representation elections by secret ballot. The NLRB may conduct such an election only when a petition for certification has been filed by an employee, a group of employees, an individual, a labor union acting on the employees' behalf, or an employer. When the petition is filed, the NLRB must investigate and direct an election if it has reasonable cause to believe a question of representation exists. After an election, if any party to it believes that certain conduct created an atmosphere that interfered with employee free choice, that party may file objections with the NLRB.[9]

The NLRB has held in *NLRB v. Woodview-Calabasas Hospital,* 112 L.R.R.M. (BNA) 3290 (9th Cir. 1983), that strikers are eligible to vote in a decertification election even though they may be employed elsewhere during the strike.

Unfair Labor Practices

The NLRA prohibits health care facilities from engaging in certain conduct classified as employer unfair labor practices.[10] For example, discriminating against an employee for holding union membership is not permitted. The NLRA stipulates that the employer must bargain in good faith with representatives of the employees; failure to do so constitutes an unfair labor practice. *NLRB v. Reed & Prince Manufacturing Co.,* 205 F.2d 131 (1st Cir.), *cert. denied,* 346 U.S. 887 (1953). The NLRB may order the employer to fulfill the duty to bargain.

If the employer dominates or controls the employees' union or interferes and supports one of two competing unions, the employer is committing an unfair labor practice. Such employer support of a competing union is illustrated clearly in a situation in which two unions are competing for members in the same facility, as well as for recognition as the employees' bargaining organization. If the facility permits one of the unions to use its facilities for its organizational activities but denies the use of the facilities to the other union, an unfair labor practice is committed. Financial assistance to one of the competing unions also constitutes an unfair labor practice.[11]

The NLRA also places duties on labor organizations and prohibits certain employee activities that are considered unfair labor practices. Coercion of employees by the union constitutes an unfair labor practice; such activities as mass picketing, assaulting nonstrikers, and following groups of nonstrikers away from the immediate area of the facility plainly constitute coercion and will be ordered stopped by the NLRB.[12] Breach of a collective bargaining contract by the labor union is another example of an unfair labor practice.

Norris–LaGuardia Act

Congress enacted the Norris–LaGuardia Act to limit the power of the federal courts to issue injunctions in cases involving or growing out of labor disputes. The act's strict standards must be met before such injunctions can be issued. Essentially, a federal court may not apply restraints in a labor dispute until after the case is heard in open court and the finding is that unlawful acts will be committed unless restrained and that substantial and irreparable injury to the complainant's property will follow. *United States v. Hutcheson,* 312 U.S. 219 (1941).

The Norris–LaGuardia Act is aimed at reducing the number of injunctions granted to restrain strikes and picketing. An additional piece of legislation designating procedures limiting strikes in health institutions is the 1974 amendment to the NLRA.[13]

This amendment sets out special procedures for handling labor disputes that develop from collective bargaining at the termination of an existing agreement or during negotiations for an initial contract between a health institution and its employees. The procedures were designed to ensure that the needs of patients would be met during any work stoppage (strike) or labor dispute in such an institution.

The amendment provides for creating a board of inquiry if a dispute threatens to interrupt health care in a particular community.[14] The board is appointed by the director of the Federal Mediation and Conciliation Service (FMCS) within 30 days after notification of either party's intention to terminate a labor contract. The board then has 15 days in which to investigate and report its findings and recommendations in writing. Once the report is filed with the FMCS, both parties are expected to maintain the status quo for an additional 15 days.

The board's findings provide a framework for arbitrators' decisions, while recognizing both the community's need for continuous health services and the good-faith intentions of labor organizations to avoid a work stoppage whenever possible and to accept arbitration when negotiations reach an impasse.

The amendment also mandates certain notice requirements by labor groups in health care institutions: (1) the institution must be given 90 days notice before a collective bargaining agreement expires, and (2) the FMCS is entitled to 60 days notice. Previously, only 60 days notice to the employer and 30 days notice to the FMCS were required. However, if the bargaining agreement is the initial contract between the parties, only 30 days notice need be given to the FMCS.

More significantly, ten days notice is required in advance of any strike, picketing, or other concerted refusal to work, regardless of the source of the dispute.[15] This allows the NLRB to determine the legality of a strike before it occurs and also gives health care institutions ample time to ensure the continuity of patient treatment. At the same time, any attempt to use this period to undermine the bargaining relationship is implicitly forbidden.

The ten-day notice may be concurrent with the final ten days of the expiration notice. Any employee violation of these provisions amounts to an unfair labor practice and automatically may result in the discharge of the employee. Also, injunctive relief may be available from the courts if circumstances warrant.

In summary, the amendment's provisions are designed to ensure that every possible approach to a peaceful settlement is explored fully before a strike is called.[16]

Labor–Management Reporting and Disclosure Act of 1959

The Labor–Management Reporting and Disclosure Act of 1959 places controls on labor unions and the relationships between unions and their members. Also, it requires that employers report payments and loans made to officials or other representatives of labor organizations or any promises to make such payments or loans. Expenditures made to influence or restrict the way employees exercise their rights to organize and bargain collectively are illegal unless they are disclosed by the employer. Agreements with labor relations consultants, under which such persons undertake to interfere with certain employee rights, also must be disclosed.

Reports required under the act must be filed with the secretary of labor and are then made public. Both charitable and proprietary health care facilities that make such payments or enter into such agreements must file reports. Penalties for failing to make the required reports or for making false reports include fines up to $10,000 and imprisonment for one year.

Fair Labor Standards Act

The Fair Labor Standards Act, 29 U.S.C. ch. 8, establishes minimum wages and maximum hours of employment. The employees of all governmental, charitable, and proprietary health care facilities are covered by this act. Employers must conform to the minimum wage and overtime pay provisions. However, bona fide executive, administrative, and professional employees are exempted from the wage and hour provisions.

The law permits employers to enter into agreements with employees, establishing a work period of 14 consecutive days as an alternative to the usual seven-day week. If the alternative period is chosen, the employer must pay the overtime rate only for hours worked in excess of 80 hours during the 14-day period. The alternate 14-day work period does not relieve a facility from paying overtime for hours worked in excess of eight in any one day even if no more than 80 hours are worked during the period.

Equal Pay Act of 1963

The Equal Pay Act (EPA) of 1963, 29 U.S.C. ch. 8, is essentially an amendment to the Fair Labor Standards Act and was passed to address wage disparities based on sex. The EPA prohibits sex discrimination in the payment of wages for women and men performing substantially equal work in the same establishment. Under the EPA, a lawsuit may be filed by the Equal Employment Opportunity Commission (EEOC) or by individuals on their own behalf. If a complainant is paid full back wages under EEOC supervision or if the EEOC takes legal action first, a private suit may not be filed.

The EPA is applicable everywhere that the minimum wage law is applicable and is enforced by the EEOC. The EPA, simply stated, requires that employees who perform equal work receive equal pay. There are situations in which wages may be unequal so long as they are based on factors other than sex, such as in the case of a formalized seniority system or a system that objectively measures earnings by the quantity or quality of production.

The EPA of 1963 and title VII of the Civil Rights Act of 1964 were violated when a female nurse's aide was paid less than male orderlies were paid for similar work in *Odomes v. Nucare, Inc.,* 653 F.2d 246 (6th Cir. 1981). The nursing facility had argued that the orderlies performed heavy lifting chores and provided a form of security for the mostly all-female shift. "[U]ncontradicted testimony of the orderlies who testified for Mrs. Odomes was that they did little or nothing that the nurse's aides didn't do." *Id.* at 250. The security aspects of an orderly's job was at best his presence on the shift and his periodic checking of the facility's premises. The facility argued that the orderlies were involved in a training program that justified higher pay. The court considered this an "illusory postevent justification for unequal pay for equal work." *Id.* at 247.

The Supreme Court stated in *Corning Glass Works v. Brennan,* 417 U.S. 188 (1974):

> Congress' purpose in enacting the Equal Pay Act was to remedy what was perceived to be a serious and endemic problem of employment discrimination in private industry—the fact that the wage structure of many segments of American industry has been based on an ancient

but outmoded belief that a man, because of his role in society, should be paid more than a woman even though his ideas are the same.

Id. at 195.

Equal Employment Opportunity Act of 1972

Title VII of the Civil Rights Act of 1964, as amended by the Equal Employment Opportunity Act of 1972, prohibits private employers and state and local governments from discriminating on the basis of age, race, color, religion, sex, or national origin. An exception to prohibited employment practices may be permitted when religion, sex, or national origin is a bona fide occupational qualification necessary to the operation of a particular business or enterprise. *Griggs v. Duke Power Co.,* 401 U.S. 424 (1971).

The act also exempts hospitals operated by religious corporations or societies, but only with respect to employees directly concerned with religious activities. Practically all employment in hospitals operated by religious bodies is unrelated to religious activity.

Many states have enacted protective laws with respect to the employment of women. The EEOC guidelines on sex discrimination make it clear that state laws limiting the employment of women in certain occupations are superseded by title VII and are no defense against a charge of sex discrimination.

Racial Discrimination

A complaint alleging racial discrimination was filed against a nursing facility by Ms. Lorraine Young, a black applicant for a nurse's aide position in *Buckley Nursing Home v. Massachusetts Commission Against Discrimination,* 478 N.E.2d 1292 (Mass. App. Ct. 1985). Ms. Young had responded to a newspaper advertisement for a nurse's aide position. She had filed an application on March 1, 1974, and was interviewed by the acting supervisor of nursing. The applicant called to inquire about the position on several occasions and eventually was told that the position had been filled. The advertisement ran again in the newspaper, and the applicant again called in response to the advertisement. Ms. Young was told that her application was on file and that she would be called as needed. The facility hired four full-time and one part-time nurse's aides for the evening shift between March 1, 1974, and July 1, 1974.

On the upper right hand corner of Young's application, there is a hand-written notation "no openings," even though during the relevant time periods there were openings and other persons were hired for the evening shift. That notation does not appear on any other application, and none of Buckley's witnesses could identify who wrote it or when it appeared.

• • • •

Despite testimony to the contrary, the commission found that there was discussion about Young's race and that Buckley decided not to hire her on that basis.

• • • •

The commission thus concluded that Buckley's reason for not hiring Young (that she was not the best qualified applicant for the job) was a pretext and that she would have been hired but for her race.

Id. at 1295.

The commission awarded Ms. Young $6,986 plus interest for lost wages and $2,000 for emotional distress. Besides the monetary award to Ms. Young, the nursing home had been instructed by the commission to develop a minority recruitment program. On appeal by the facility, the trial court upheld the commission's decision. On further appeal, the appeals court held that the evidence was sufficient to support a reasonable inference that the nursing facility's rejection of the applicant occurred after consideration of her race.

✓ **Age Discrimination in Employment Act of 1967**

Persons 40 years of age or older are protected by the the Age Discrimination in Employment Act (ADEA) of 1967, 29 U.S.C. ch. 14, as amended, which prohibits age-based employment discrimination. The purpose of this law is to promote employment of older persons on the basis of their ability without regard to their age. The law prohibits arbitrary age discrimination in hiring, discharge, pay, term, conditions, or privileges of employment. ADEA covers private employers with 20 or more employees, state and local governments, employment agencies, and most labor unions. The Age Discrimination and Claims Assistance Amendment of 1990 extends the suit filing period for ADEA charges meeting certain criteria. There are strict time frames in which charges of age discrimination must be filed.

Occupational Safety and Health Act of 1970

Congress enacted the Occupational Safety and Health Act of 1970, 29 U.S.C. §651, to establish administrative machinery for the development and enforcement of standards for occupational health and safety.[17] The legislation was enacted based on congressional findings that personal injuries and illnesses arising out of work situations impose a substantial burden on and are substantial hindrances to interstate commerce in terms of lost production, wage loss, medical expenses, and disability compensation payments. The Congress declared that its purpose and policy was to assure, so far as possible, every working man and woman in the nation safe and healthful working conditions and to preserve our human resources:

(1) by encouraging employers and employees in their efforts to reduce the number of occupational safety and health hazards at their places of employment, and stimulating employers and employees to institute new and to perfect existing programs for providing safe and healthful working conditions;

(2) by providing that employers and employees have separate but dependent responsibilities and rights with respect to achieving safe and healthful working conditions;

(3) by authorizing the Secretary of Labor to set mandatory occupational safety and health standards applicable to businesses affecting interstate commerce, and by creating an Occupational and Health Review Commission for carrying out adjudicatory functions under the Act;

(4) by building upon advances already made through employer and employee initiative for providing safe and healthful working conditions;

(5) by providing for research in the field of occupational safety and health, including the psychological factors involved, and by developing innovative methods, techniques, and approaches for dealing with occupational safety and health problems;

(6) by exploring ways to discover latent diseases, establishing causal connections between diseases and work in environmental conditions, and conducting other research relating to health problems, in recognition of the fact that occupational health standards present problems often different from those involved in occupational safety;

(7) by providing medical criteria that will assure, insofar as practicable, that no employee will suffer diminished health, functional capacity, or life expectancy as a result of his or her work experience;

(8) by providing for training programs to increase the number and competence of personnel engaged in the field of occupational safety and health;

(9) by providing for the development and promulgation of occupational safety and health standards;

(10) by providing an effective enforcement program which shall
include a prohibition against giving advance notice of any
inspection and sanctions for any individual violating this prohibition;

(11) by encouraging the States to assume the fullest responsibility
for the administration and enforcement of their occupational
safety and health laws by providing grants to the States to
assist in identifying their needs and responsibilities in the area
of occupational safety and health, to develop plans in accordance with the provisions of this Act, to improve the administration and enforcement of state occupational safety and health
laws, and conducting experimental and demonstration projects
in connection therewith;

(12) by providing for appropriate reporting procedures with respect
to occupational safety and health which procedures will help
achieve the objectives of this Act and accurately describe the
nature of the occupational safety and health problem;

(13) by encouraging joint labor–management efforts to reduce
injuries and disease arising out of employment.[18]

The employer must comply with the occupational and health standards under
the act and employees must follow the rules, regulations, and orders issued
under the act that are applicable to their actions and conduct on the job. The
duties of employers and employees under the act are as follows:

(a) Each employer—

(1) shall furnish to each of his employees employment and a place
of employment which is free from recognized hazards that are
causing or are likely to cause death or serious physical harm to
his employees;

(2) shall comply with occupational safety and health standards promulgated under this Act.

(b) Each employee shall comply with occupational safety and health
standards and all rules, regulations, and orders pursuant to this Act
which are applicable to his own actions and conduct[19]

Infectious Body Fluids

The Occupational Safety and Health Administration (OSHA) issued new
standards on December 2, 1991, that are to be followed by employers to protect

employees from blood-borne infections. Universal precautions are mandatory and employees who are likely to be exposed to body fluids must be provided with protective clothing (e.g., masks, gowns, and gloves). In addition, postexposure testing must be available to employees who have been exposed to body fluids.[20]

The OSHA Survey

OSHA is responsible for administering the act, issuing standards, and conducting on-site inspections to ensure compliance with the act. OSHA develops and promulgates occupational safety and health standards for the workplace. It develops and issues regulations, conducts investigations and inspections to determine the status of compliance, and issues citations and proposes penalties for noncompliance.

In recent developments, OSHA inspectors have called for stiffer penalties for health and safety violations to deter violations. "OSHA inspectors surveyed by Congress' General Accounting Office said further criminal enforcement authority was needed to enforce this nation's workplace health and safety standards."[21]

State Regulation

Employees or their representatives have the right to file their complaints with an OSHA office and request a survey when they believe that conditions in the workplace are unsafe or unhealthy. If a violation of the act is found at the time of a survey, the employer receives a citation stating a time frame within which a violation must be corrected.

The states also have statutes charging employers with the duty to furnish employees with a safe working environment. The city and county in which a health care facility is located also may prescribe rules regarding the health and safety of employees. Many communities have enacted sanitary and health codes that require certain facilities or standards.

Legal Liability

From a liability point of view, an employer can be held legally liable for damages suffered by employees through exposure to dangerous conditions that are in violation of OSHA standards. Proof of an employee's exposure to noncompliant conditions is generally necessary to find an employer liable.

Rehabilitation Act of 1973

The essential purpose of the Rehabilitation Act of 1973, 29 U.S.C. ch. 14, is to afford protection to handicapped employees. The law basically is adminis-

tered by the Department of Health and Human Services, which derives its jurisdiction from the fact that health care facilities participate in such federal programs as Medicare, Medicaid, and Hill-Burton. The law therefore is applied to
both public and private institutions, because both participate in these programs.

Section 503 of the act applies to government contractors whose contracts
exceed $2,500 in value. Section 504, which applies to employers who are
recipients of federal financial assistance, states, "No . . . qualified handicapped
individual in the United States . . . shall solely by reason of his handicap, be
excluded from participation in, be denied the benefits of, or be subjected to discrimination under any program as actively receiving Federal financial assistance." Section 504 applies to virtually every area of personnel administration,
including recruitment, advertising, processing of applications, promotions,
rates of pay, fringe benefits, and job assignments.

Since July 1977, all institutions receiving federal financial assistance from
the Department of Health and Human Services have been required to file assurances of compliance forms. Each employer must designate an individual to
coordinate compliance efforts. A grievance procedure should be in place to
address employee complaints alleging violation of the regulation. All employment decisions must be made without regard to physical or mental handicaps
that are not disqualifying (e.g., an employer is not obligated to employ a person
with a highly contagious disease that can be easily transmitted to others).

Employers receiving federal funds are required to perform a self-evaluation
as to their compliance with section 504 of the Rehabilitation Act of 1973. If discriminatory practices are identified through the self-evaluation process, remedi-
al steps are to be taken to eliminate the effects of any discrimination. Records of
the evaluation are to be maintained on file for at least three years after the
review for public inspection. 45 C.F.R. §4.6(c).

Limitations on Number of Bargaining Units/1989

A major area of concern for health care institutions is the number of bargaining units allowed in any one institution. New rules and regulations issued on
April 21, 1989, by the NLRB allow up to eight collective bargaining units in
health care facilities as opposed to the three normally allowed before the regulations. The American Hospital Association had brought an action to enjoin the
NLRB from enforcing the newly promulgated regulation recognizing up to
eight bargaining units. A federal district court enjoined enforcement of the rule.
The NLRB and intervening unions appealed. In *American Hospital Ass'n v.
NLRB*, 899 F.2d 651 (7th Cir. 1990), the Seventh Circuit held that the rule was
not arbitrary and was within the authority of the NLRB. No rule is necessary to
confer the rights already conferred by statute entitling guards and professional
employees to form separate bargaining units.

In making unit determinations the Board is thus required to strike a balance among the competing interests of unions, employees (whose interests are not always identical with those of unions), employers, and the broader public. The statute can be read to suggest that the tilt should be in favor of unions and toward relatively many, rather than relatively few, units.

Id. at 654.

This balancing act is not spelled out in the statute, thus requiring an NLRB decision. "The decision is particularly difficult and delicate in the health care industry because the work force of a hospital, nursing home, or rehabilitation center tends to be small and heterogeneous." *Id.* at 654–655.

On appeal, the U.S. Supreme Court, on April 23, 1991, on unanimous decision upheld an NLRB rule allowing hospital workers to form up to eight separate bargaining units, including those for

- physicians
- registered nurses
- other professionals
- technical employees
- clerical employees
- skilled maintenance employees
- other nonprofessional employees
- security guards[22]

It is anticipated that there will be increased union activity in health care facilities, thus increasing administrative costs. Management must strive to maintain open lines of communications with employees and strive to improve working conditions. An honest and open relationship with employees will go a long way toward maintaining a union-free environment.

> [O]fficials at one long term care facility effectively countered an organizing attempt by educating their employees about the union and what it realistically could do for them. In March, employees of St. Anthony Home, Crown Point, IN, voted against representation by a national steelworker's union.[23]

Americans with Disabilities Act of 1990

Findings of the U.S. Congress demonstrate that some 43 million Americans have one or more physical or mental disabilities. The number of disabled

Americans is increasing as the population grows older. Society has tended to isolate and segregate individuals with disabilities, and despite some improvements, discrimination against individuals with disabilities continues to be a serious and pervasive social problem. Discrimination continues in such crucial areas as employment, housing, public accommodations, education, transportation, and health services. Unlike individuals who have experienced discrimination on the basis of race, color, sex, national origin, religion, or age, those who have been disabled have had no legal recourse to redress such discrimination. Individuals with disabilities continually encounter different forms of discrimination, including outright intentional exclusion; the discriminatory effects of architectural, transportation, and communication barriers; the failure to make modifications to existing facilities and practices; exclusionary qualification standards and criteria; segregation; and relegation to lesser services, programs, activities, benefits, jobs, or other opportunities.

Census data, national polls, and other studies have documented that people with disabilities, as a group, occupy an inferior status in society. The nation's proper goals regarding individuals with disabilities are to ensure equality of opportunity, full participation, independent living, and economic self-sufficiency for such individuals.[24]

As a result of the continuing discrimination against the disabled, Congress enacted title 1 of the Americans with Disabilities Act (ADA) of 1990. The act prohibits job discrimination in hiring, promotion or other provisions of employment against qualified individuals with disabilities by private employers, state and local governments, employment agencies, and labor unions. On July 26, 1991, EEOC issued final regulations implementing title 1 of the ADA. All employers, including state and local government employers with 25 or more employees, must comply with title 1 as of July 26, 1992. All employers, including state and local government employers with 15 or more employees, must comply with title 1 after July 26, 1994. Charges of job discrimination may be filed after these dates. The EEOC has developed materials that are available to employers by calling (800) 669-EEOC.

It is the purpose of the ADA to

- provide a clear and comprehensive national mandate for the elimination of discrimination against individuals with disabilities
- provide clear, strong, consistent, enforceable standards addressing discrimination against individuals with disabilities
- ensure that the federal government plays a central role in enforcing the standards established in the act on behalf of individuals with disabilities
- invoke the sweep of congressional authority, including the power to enforce the Fourteenth Amendment and to regulate commerce to address the main areas of discrimination faced day-to-day by people with disabilities[25]

The general rule of discrimination under title I of the act provides that

> [n]o covered entity shall discriminate against a qualified individual
> with a disability because of the disability of such individual in regard
> to job application procedures, the hiring, advancement, or discharge
> of employees, employee compensation, job training, and other terms,
> conditions, and privileges of employment.[26]

A defense to a charge of discrimination under the act would require a showing that the screening out of a specific disability was job-related and consistent
with business necessity and that performance cannot be accomplished by "reasonable" accommodation.[27]

Tips for Employers

- Train management personnel as to the requirements of ADA (e.g., it is
  unlawful to ask an applicant whether he or she is disabled; however, it is OK
  to ask a prospective employee if he or she is able to perform job-related
  functions)
- Review and revise the employment application and job descriptions, as necessary, to bring them into compliance with ADA requirements
- Make the necessary construction and renovation changes necessary to bring
  the physical environment into compliance with ADA requirements
- Post a notice on the employee bulletin board(s) describing the purposes of
  the ADA

STATE LAWS

The federal labor enactments serve as a pattern for many state labor laws that
comprise the second labor regulation system touching health care facilities.
State labor acts vary from state to state. Therefore, it is important that each
institution familiarize itself not only with federal regulations but also with state
regulations affecting labor relations within the institution.

State Labor–Management Relations Act

Because the NLRA excludes from coverage health care institutions operated
by the state or its political subdivisions, regulation of labor–management relations in these institutions is left to state law.[28] However, most states do not have

labor relations statutes. Unless the constitution in such a state guarantees the right of employees to organize and imposes the duty of collective bargaining on the employer, health care facilities do not have to bargain collectively with their employees. However, in states that do have labor relations acts, the obligation of an institution to bargain collectively with its employees is determined by the applicable statute.

State laws vary considerably in their coverage, and often employees of state and local governmental institutions are covered by separate public employee legislation. Some of these statutes cover both state and local employees, whereas others cover only state or only local employees. Several states have statutes similar to the Norris–LaGuardia Act, restricting the granting of injunctions in labor disputes. There are anti-injunction acts in several other states that are different from this type, and decisions under them do not fall into an easily recognized pattern.

Some of the states that have labor relations acts granting employees the right to organize, join unions, and bargain collectively have specifically prohibited strikes and lockouts and have provided for compulsory arbitration whenever a collective bargaining contract cannot otherwise be executed amicably. Anti-injunction statutes would not forbid injunctions to restrain violations of these statutory provisions.

The doctrine of federal pre-emption, as applied to labor relations, displaces the states' jurisdiction to regulate an activity that is arguably an unfair labor practice within the meaning of the NLRA. Nonetheless, the U.S. Supreme Court has ruled that states can still regulate labor relations activity that also falls within the jurisdiction of the NLRB when deeply rooted local feelings and responsibility are affected. *Amalgamated Ass'n of Street, Electric Railway & Motor Coach Employees v. Lockridge,* 403 U.S. 274 (1971).

Union Security Contracts and Right-To-Work Laws

Labor organizations frequently seek to enter union security contracts with employers. Such contracts are of two types: the "closed shop" contract, which provides that only members of a particular union may be hired, and the "union shop" contract, which makes continued employment dependent on membership in the union, although the employee need not have been a union member when applying for the job.

More than one-third of all the states have made such contracts unlawful. Statutes forbidding such agreements generally are called "right-to-work" laws on the theory that they protect everyone's right to work even if a person refuses to join a union. Several other state statutes or decisions purport to restrict union security contracts or specify procedures to be completed before such agreements may be made.

Wage and Hour Laws

When state minimum wage standards are higher than federal standards, the state's standards are applicable.

Child Labor Acts

Many states prohibit the employment of minors younger than a specified certain age and restrict the employment of other minors. Child labor legislation commonly requires that working papers be secured before a child may be hired, forbids the employment of minors at night, and prohibits minors from operating certain types of dangerous machinery.

This kind of legislation rarely exempts charitable institutions, although some exceptions may be made with respect to the hours when student nurses may work.

Workers' Compensation

Workers' compensation is a program by which an employee can receive certain wage benefits because of work-related injuries. An employee who is injured while performing job-related duties is generally eligible for workers' compensation. Workers' compensation programs are administered by the states.

State legislatures have recognized that it is difficult and expensive for employees to recover from their employers and therefore have enacted workers' compensation laws.[29] Employers are required to provide worker compensation as a benefit. Worker's compensation laws give the employee a legal way to receive compensation for injuries on the job. The acts do not require the employee to prove that the injury was the result of the employer's negligence. Workers' compensation laws are based on the employer–employee relationship and not on the theory of negligence.

The scope of workers' compensation varies widely. Some states limit an employee's compensation to the amount recoverable by the workers' compensation law, and further lawsuits against the employer are barred. Other states permit employees to choose whether they accept the compensation provided by law or institute a lawsuit against the employer. Some acts go farther and provide a system of insurance that may be under the supervision of state or private insurers. Recovery by an employee begins with a hearing on the claim before a board of commissioners. The commissioners decide whether the injury is covered by the act,[30] and whether there is a connection between the employment and the injury. The commissioners then award compensation according to a predetermined schedule based on the nature of the injury. Generally, workers' compensation boards tend to be liberal in interpreting the law to provide compensation for employees.

Physical Injury

The courts have been somewhat liberal in allowing workers' compensation benefits to be paid to employees injured while on duty, even when challenged by the employer under seemingly justifiable circumstances. The employee, for example, in *Fondulac Nursing Home v. Industrial Commission,* 460 N.E.2d 751 (Ill. 1984), was found to be entitled to workers' compensation despite orders that she was not to lift patients because of a back injury. When a patient was being transferred from her wheelchair to her bed and began to fall, the nurse attempted to prevent the fall, injuring herself. The nurse acted within her scope of employment by attempting to prevent the fall—to her own detriment and her employer's best interests—by protecting the patient from injury.

Job Stress

Workers' compensation has been awarded for depression related to job stress. In *Elwood v. SAIF,* 676 P.2d 922 (Or. Ct. App. 1984), a registered nurse had filed a workers' compensation claim for an occupational disease based on depression. The referee and the Workers' Compensation Board affirmed the insurer's denial of the claim and the claimant sought judicial review. The questions that needed to be answered to determine job stress, as in *McGarrah v. SAIF,* 296 Or. 145, 675 P.2d 159 (1983), were

1. What were the "real" events and conditions of plaintiff's employment?
2. Were those real events and conditions capable of producing stress when viewed "objectively," even though an average worker might not have responded adversely to them?
3. Did plaintiff suffer a mental disorder?
4. Were the real stressful events and conditions the "major contributing cause" of plaintiff's mental disorder?

Elwood v. SAIF, 676 P.2d at 923.

The record established that many events and conditions of her employment, including her termination, were real and capable of producing stress when viewed objectively. The claimant's treating physician advised her that she was suffering from anxiety and depression and stress and advised her to seek a psychiatric evaluation. *Id.* at 924. The court held that the claimant established that her condition was compensable.

'Flu Shot Reaction

A hospital employee's reaction to a 'flu injection given by an emergency department employee while he or she is on duty will most likely be a compensable injury under workers' compensation. A housekeeping employee in *Monette v. Manatee Memorial Hospital,* 579 So.2d 195 (Fla. Dist. Ct. App. 1991), suffered a serious reaction to the influenza vaccination administered to her while on duty and was entitled to workers' compensation.

LABOR RIGHTS

Rights and responsibilities run concurrently. Employee rights include

- right to organize and bargain collectively
- right to solicit and distribute union information during nonworking hours (i.e., mealtimes and coffee breaks)
- right to picket. Picketing is the act of patrolling, by one or more persons, of a place related to a labor dispute. It varies in purpose and form; it may be conducted by employees or nonemployees and, like strikes, some picketing may be legislatively or judicially disapproved and subject to regulation
- right to strike. A strike may be defined as the collective quitting of work by employees as a means of inducing the employer to assent to employee demands. Employees possess the right to strike, although this right is not absolute and is subject to limited exercise. The 1974 amendments to the NLRA have added new requirements with respect to strikes and picketing in an attempt to reduce the interruption of health care services. The NLRB is urged to give top priority to settling labor–management disputes resulting in the loss of health care personnel or medical services

Employees granted the above rights have the concomitant responsibility to perform their work duties properly. A nursing home housekeeper, for example, was terminated properly after repeated oral and written reprimands concerning her improper cleaning of rooms in *Ford v. Patin,* 534 So.2d 1003 (La. Ct. App. 1988). Her substandard performance despite repeated warnings evidenced willful and wanton disregard of her employer's interest and constituted misconduct within purview of Louisiana Rev. Stat. 23:1601(2).

MANAGEMENT RIGHTS

As with labor, management also has certain rights and responsibilities. Specific management rights are reviewed below.

Right To Receive Strike Notice

Management has a right to a ten-day advance notice of a bargaining unit's intent to strike.[31]

Right To Hire Replacement Workers

Although management may not discharge employees in retaliation for union activity, concomitant with the employees' right to strike is management's right to hire replacement workers in the event of a strike. The nursing home in *Charlesgate Nursing Center v. State of Rhode Island,* 723 F. Supp. 859 (D. R.I. 1989), brought an action against the state, seeking a determination that a state statute prohibiting struck employers from using the services of a third party to recruit replacement workers during a strike was unconstitutional. Employees of the nursing home went on strike June 2, 1988, and Charlesgate hired temporary replacement workers to provide continued services for its patients. The employees were hired through employment agencies. The actions of Charlesgate and the agencies had violated the sections 28-10-10 and 28-10-12 of the General Laws of Rhode Island (1956) (1986 Re-enactment), which read:

> 28-10-10. Recruitment prohibited—It shall be unlawful for any person, partnership, agency, firm or corporation, or officer or agent thereof, to knowingly recruit, procure, supply or refer any person who offers him or herself for employment in the place of an employee involved in a labor strike or lockout in which such person, partnership, agency, firm, or corporation is not directly interested.
>
> 28-10-12. Agency for procurement—It shall be unlawful for any person, partnership, firm or corporation, or officer or agent thereof, involved in a labor strike or lockout to contract or arrange with any other person, partnership, agency, firm or corporation to recruit, procure, supply, or refer persons who offer themselves for employment in the place of employees involved in a labor strike or lockout for employment in place of employees involved in such labor strike or lockout.

Id. at 861.

Citing these statutes, the labor unions involved in the strike notified nursing pools throughout the state that it was unlawful to provide Charlesgate with replacement workers. At the same time, the unions urged the City of Providence and the Rhode Island Attorney General to prosecute Charlesgate, at which time

Charlesgate filed its suit claiming that the Rhode Island statutes were unconstitutional.

Although the strike was settled before any actions by the city and the Attorney General, the case was not required to be dismissed. The federal district court held that the statute was unconstitutional because it prohibited activity that Congress had intended to leave open to struck employers as a peaceful weapon of economic self-help.

Right To Restrict Union Activity to Prescribed Areas

Management has the right to reasonably restrict union organizers to certain locations in the health care facility and to certain time periods to avoid interference with facility operations.

Right To Prohibit Union Activity During Working Hours

Management has the right to prohibit union activities during employee working hours.

Right To Prohibit Supervisors from Participating in Union Activity

Management has the right to prohibit supervisors from engaging in union organizational activity. A nursing supervisor brought a lawsuit for wrongful discharge against a nursing facility and its director of nursing. She was dismissed for her activities in attempting to form an organization to represent the nurses. The circuit court granted summary judgment for the defendants and the appeals court affirmed. On review, the Supreme Court of Wisconsin held in *Arena v. Lincoln Lutheran of Racine,* 149 Wis. 2d 35, 437 N.W.2d 538 (1989), that after the NLRB had determined that the nurses in this case were "supervisors" rather than "employees" within the meaning of the NLRA, federal labor law pre-empted the state court from determining whether the nurse's discharge for engaging in concerted activities was wrongful under Wisconsin law.

Employees who are supervisors as defined in the NLRA are treated differently than professional employees. The definition of the term supervisor found in section 2(11) provides:

> The term "supervisor" means any individual having authority, in the interest of the employer, to hire, transfer, suspend, lay off, recall, promote, discharge, assign, reward, or discipline other employees, or

responsibly to direct them, or to adjust their grievances, or effectively to recommend such action, if in connection with the foregoing the exercise of such authority is not merely a routine or clerical nature, but requires the use of independent judgment.

29 U.S.C. §152(11) (1965).

The petitioner alleged in her complaint that she had become concerned with certain policies that included nurses being treated in an arbitrary manner. The petitioner had held a meeting outside of Racine with the nurses to discuss their concerns and the possibility of forming an association to represent the collective interests of the nurses. The NLRA did not protect the nursing supervisor because she was a supervisor rather than an employee. Congress excluded supervisors from protection afforded rank-and-file employees engaged in concerted activity for their mutual benefit to assure management of the undivided loyalty of its supervisory personnel by making sure that no employer would have to retain as its agent one who is obligated to a union.

Seven registered nurses at a small 72-bed nursing home were found not to function as supervisors and were, therefore, eligible for a separate bargaining unit in *NLRB v. Res-Care, Inc.,* 705 F.2d 1461 (7th Cir. 1983). Although the nurses had the authority to assign nurses' aides, their exercise of this authority was merely routine and did not require independent judgment. The nurses were not shown to have any authority to hire, discipline, and/or fire any of the nursing aides. Such authority, if present, would have indicated some sort of supervisory status. Allowing seven nurses to form their own collective bargaining unit rather than merging them into a unit consisting of nurses' aides and other workers was not found to be improper nor was it an undue proliferation of bargaining units at the facility.

Certification of 17 registered nurses as an employee bargaining unit in *NLRB v. American Medical Services,* 705 F.2d 1472 (7th Cir. 1983), was shown to be improper. The nursing home had contended that a very low ratio of supervisors to employees would occur if the NLRB's decision was upheld. Substantial evidence had been presented to the court showing that the nurses exercised substantial supervisory powers, including the authority to issue work assignments and discipline employees.

> Taft-Hartley applied some brakes, so that the balance of power between companies and unions would not shift wholly to the union side. The exclusion of supervisors is one of the breaks. If supervisors were free to join or form unions and enjoy the broad protection of the Act for concerted activity, see Sec. 7, 29 U.S.C. Sec. 157, the impact of a strike would be greatly amplified because the company would not

be able to use its supervisory personnel to replace strikers. More important, the company—with or without a strike—could lose control of its work force to the unions, since the very people in the company who controlled hiring, discipline, assignments, and other dimensions of the employment relationship might be subject to control by the same union as the employees they were supposed to be controlling on the employer's behalf.

NLRB v. Res-Care, Inc., 705 F.2d at 1465.

EQUAL EMPLOYMENT OPPORTUNITY—AFFIRMATIVE ACTION PLAN

Health care facilities are required to comply with all applicable Department of Health and Human Services regulations "including but not limited to those pertaining to non-discrimination on the basis of race, color, or national origin (45 C.F.R. part 80), non-discrimination on the basis of handicap (45 C.F.R. part 84), non-discrimination on the basis of age (45 C.F.R. part 91), protection of human subjects of research (45 C.F.R. part 46), and fraud and abuse (42 C.F.R. part 455). Although these regulations are not in themselves considered requirements under this part, their violation may result in the termination or suspension of or the refusal to grant or continue payment with federal funds."[32] To comply with the spirit of these regulations and Executive Order 11246, health care facilities should have an equal employment opportunity or affirmative action plan in place.

An affirmative action program includes such things as the collection and analysis of data on the race and sex of all applicants for employment and a statement in the personnel policy and procedure manuals and employee handbooks that would read, for example, "Health Care Facility, Inc., is an equal opportunity/affirmative action employer and does not discriminate on the basis of race, color, religion, sex, national origin, age, handicap, or veteran status."

PATIENT RIGHTS DURING LABOR DISPUTES

Just as labor and management have different rights and responsibilities, the same is true for patients. For example, patients' rights take precedence over employee and management rights when a patient's right to privacy or well-being is in jeopardy because of labor disputes.

INJUNCTIONS

An injunction is an order by a court directing that a certain act be performed or not performed. Persons who fail to comply with court orders are said to be in "contempt of court." The earliest uses of injunctions in labor relations was by employers to stop strikes or picketing by employees. Today, the general rule limits the availability of injunctive relief to halt work stoppages. The federal government and many states have enacted anti-injunction acts. These acts restrict the power of the courts to limit injunctions in labor disputes by setting strictly defined standards that must be met before injunctions can be granted to restrain activities such as strikes and picketing.

ADMINISTERING A COLLECTIVE BARGAINING AGREEMENT

Once a collective bargaining agreement has been negotiated "in good faith," it should be administered with care and good faith as well.

The first-line supervisors are responsible for administering the agreement at the grass roots level. They should familiarize themselves with the provisions of the agreement. Formal orientation programs can be provided by an institution's human resources department. Special emphasis should be placed on the use of corrective discipline, as provided under the contract, and on how to respond to grievances. The institution's management through its human relations department maintains the ultimate responsibility in the facility for the fair and effective administration of its union contract(s).

Maintaining propitious records of all grievances, grievance meetings, and grievance resolutions is the responsibility of supervisors and management alike. Regardless of whether a grievance is meritorious and settled by management or whether it is spurious and therefore denied, clear and complete records should be maintained. An ability to document resolutions of particular problems, as well as management's approach to grievances, is especially important if arbitration is required to settle a grievance.

Employers and unions often provide for arbitration because the procedure is generally quicker and less expensive than it would be if court adjudication were required, and because labor arbitrators have greater expertise in labor affairs than do most judges.

Arbitration procedures are set in motion when the union files a demand for arbitration either with the employer or with the arbitration agency named in the contract. The arbitration hearing is a relatively informal proceeding at which management frequently chooses to be represented by counsel. The arbitrator's decision is binding on both parties.

The arbitrator's decision can be upset by showing any of the following:

• The arbitrator has clearly exceeded his or her authority under the collective bargaining agreement

- The decision is the product of fraud or duress
- The arbitrator has been guilty of impropriety
- The award violates the law or requires a violation of the law

NOTES

1. 29 U.S.C. §151 *et seq.*

2. *Id.*

3. NLRA Amendments of 1974, Pub. L. No. 93-360.

4. NATIONAL LABOR RELATIONS BOARD, LEGISLATIVE HISTORY OF THE LABOR–MANAGEMENT RELATIONS ACT OF 1947, at 303, 359 (1949). There exists almost no debate regarding this exclusion, although Senator Tydings of Maryland did justify this approach on the rationale that nonprofit hospitals were charitable institutions subject to local governmental regulations and, at least in 1947, were in dire financial straits. NLRB, LEGISLATIVE HISTORY OF THE LABOR MANAGEMENT RELATIONS ACT OF 1947, at 1464-65 (1948).

5. NLRA §2 (14).

6. *Id.* §9.

7. *Id.*

8. *Id.* §9(b)(1) & (b)(3).

9. *Id.* §8.

10. *Id.* §§8, 9.

11. *Id.* §8(a)(1) & (a)(3).

12. *Id.* §8(b)(7); Landrum-Griffin Amendments of 1959, Pub. L. No. 86-257 (1959).

13. *Id.* §8(g).

14. *Id.*

15. *Id.* §8(d).

16. SUBCOMMITTEE ON LABOR OF THE SENATE COMMITTEE ON LABOR AND PUBLIC WELFARE, 93D CONG., 2D SESS., LEGISLATIVE HISTORY OF THE COVERAGE OF NON-PROFIT HOSPITALS UNDER THE NATIONAL LABOR RELATIONS ACT OF 1974, at 412–414 (1974).

17. 29 U.S.C. §651 *et seq.*

18. Pub. L. No. 91-596, Dec. 29, 1970, §2, 84 Stat. 1590; *see also* 29 U.S.C.A. §651 (1990).

19. Pub. L. No. 91-596, *supra* note 18, at §5, 84 Stat. 1593; 29 U.S.C.A., *supra* note 18, at §654.

20. 56 Fed. Reg. 64,004 (1991).

21. *OSHA's Inspectors Call for Stiffer Penalties for Violations,* NATION'S HEALTH, XXI (1), Jan. 1991, at 7.

22. *Supreme Court Upholds NLRB Bargaining-Unit Rule,* A.H.A. NEWS, 27(17), Apr. 29, 1991, at 1.

23. *Despite NLRB Ruling, Hospitals Can Counter Unions: Experts,* A.H.A. NEWS, 27(21), May 27, 1991, at 4.

24. Act of July 26, 1990, Pub. L. No. 101-336, 1990 U.S. CODE CONG. & AD. NEWS (104 Stat.) 327–329.

25. *Id.* at 329.

26. *Id.* at 331–332.

27. *Id.* at 333–334.

28. NLRA, §2(3); 29 U.S.C. §152(3), Pub. L. No. 93-360 (1974).

29. REPORT OF THE NATIONAL COMMISSION ON STATE WORKMEN'S COMPENSATION LAWS (1972). The statute that authorized the study and subsequent report was the Occupational Safety and Health Act of 1970.

30. This refers to the particular state statute in effect at the time of the injury.

31. 29 U.S.C. §158(g).

32. 42 C.F.R. §483.75 (1989).

Employment, Discipline, and Discharge

OUTLINE

According to a study for the Bureau of National Affairs, more than 25,000 wrongful discharge cases are pending in state and federal courts.[1] "The study estimates that wrongful discharge cases more than doubled between 1982 and 1987."[2] For the health care executive, an unexpected termination may mean a significant setback in career progression, financial hardship, and loss of self-esteem. For the institution and its community, a termination means a lack of stability in the management structure and possible disruption and realignment of services provided. A growing consensus is that the current high turnover rates are unhealthy and provide a disservice to an industry already suffering from cost constraints and other pressures.[3]

In 1989, the American College of Healthcare Executives published phase I results of its CEO turnover study. The report showed that overall turnover had increased from 16.9 percent in 1981–82 to 24.2 percent in 1986–87, and every indication was that rates would be a major concern in the near future. Although not all turnover reflects termination, there is evidence that a large proportion of CEOs leave involuntarily.[4]

Fairly balancing the rights of the employee and the needs of the organization is an extremely complex objective. This chapter provides some direction in this balancing act.

EMPLOYMENT AT WILL

The common-law "employment-at-will" doctrine provides that employment is at the will of either the employer or the employee and that employment may be terminated by the employer or the employee at any time for any or no reason, unless there is a contract in place that specifies the terms and duration of employment. Historically, termination of employees for any reason was widely accepted. However, contemporary thinking does not support this concept.

> In recent years the rule that employment for an indefinite term is terminable by the employer whenever and for whatever cause he chooses without incurring liability has been the subject of considerable scholarly debate, and judicial and legislative modification. Consequently, there has been a growing trend toward a restricted application of the at-will employment rule whereby the right of an

employer to discharge an at-will employee without cause is limited by either public policy considerations or an implied covenant of good faith and fair dealing.[5]

In *Sides v. Duke Hospital*, 328 S.E.2d 818 (N.C. Ct. App. 1985), the Court of Appeals of North Carolina found it to be an

> obvious and indisputable fact that in a civilized state where reciprocal legal rights and duties abound the words "at will" can never mean "without limit or qualification," as so much of the discussion and the briefs of the defendants imply; for in such a state the rights of each person are necessarily and inherently limited by the rights of others and the interests of the public. An at will prerogative without limits could be suffered only in an anarchy, and there not for long—it certainly cannot be suffered in a society such as ours without weakening the bond of counter balancing rights and obligations that holds such societies together.
>
> • • • •
>
> If we are to have law, those who so act against the public interest must be held accountable for the harm inflicted thereby; to accord them civil immunity would incongruously reward their lawlessness at the unjust expense of their innocent victims.

The concept of the employment-at-will doctrine is embroiled in a combination of legislative enactments and judicial decisions. Some states have a tendency to be more employer-oriented, such as New York, whereas others, such as California, emerge as being much more forward thinking and in harmony with the constitutional rights of the employee. A study of 120 wrongful discharge cases in California between 1980 and 1986, conducted by the Rand Corporation, revealed that plaintiffs won 67.5 percent of the time and were awarded an average of $646,855.[6]

> The employment at will common law doctrine is not truly applicable in today's society and many courts have recognized this fact. In the last century, the common law developed in a laissez-faire climate that encouraged industrial growth and improved the right of an employer to control his own business, including the right to fire without cause an employee at will. . . . The twentieth century has witnessed significant changes in socioeconomic values that have led to reassessment of the common law rule. Businesses have evolved from small and medium size firms to gigantic corporations in which ownership is separate from management. Formerly there was a clear delineation between

employers, who frequently were owners of their own businesses, and employees. The employer in the old sense has been replaced by a superior in the corporate hierarchy who is himself an employee.

Pierce v. Ortho Pharmaceutical Corp., 417 A.2d 505, 509 (N.J. 1980).

The employment-at-will doctrine provides employees with few employment rights. Employers who experience favorable court decisions in wrongful discharge claims are often the losers because of the bad press and the negative effects a discharge has on employee morale. "Wrongful discharge claims are difficult, time consuming and expensive lawsuits to defend and, when they reach the jury, employers are losing about 75% of the time."[7]

As discussed below, exceptions to the employment-at-will doctrine involve contractual relationships, public policy issues, defamation, retaliatory discharge, and fairness. Besides public policy issues in general, it would seem that the doctrine has little applicability in today's modern society.

CONTRACTUAL RELATIONSHIPS

Express Agreement

An employer's right to terminate an employee can be limited by express agreement with the employee or through a collective bargaining agreement to which the employee is a beneficiary. No such agreement was found to exist in *O'Connor v. Eastman Kodak Co.,* 492 N.Y.S.2d 9 (N.Y. 1985), in which the court held that an employer had a right to terminate an employee at will at any time and for any reason or no reason. The plaintiff did not rely on any specific representation made to him during the course of his employment interviews, nor did he rely on any documentation in the employee handbook, which would have limited the defendant's common-law right to discharge at will. The employee had relied on a popular perception of Kodak as a womb-to-tomb employer.

Implied Contracts

The rights of employees have been expanding through judicial decisions in the different states. Court decisions have been based on verbal promises, historical practices of the employer, and documents such as employee handbooks and administrative policy and procedure manuals that describe employee rights. The following are a few of the many cases that involve published personnel policies and procedures.

Employee Handbooks

An employee brought suit against his employer for wrongful termination in *Weiner v. McGraw-Hill*, 57 N.Y.2d 458, 443 N.E.2d 441, 457 N.Y.S.2d 193 (1982). The court held that although the plaintiff was not engaged by the defendant for a fixed term of employment, he pleaded a good cause of action for breach of contract. The plaintiff allegedly was discharged without the "just and sufficient cause" or the rehabilitative efforts specified in the defendant's handbook and allegedly promised at the time the plaintiff accepted employment. Furthermore, on several occasions when the plaintiff had recommended that certain of his subordinates be dismissed, he allegedly was instructed to proceed in strict compliance with the handbook and policy manuals. The employment application that the plaintiff had signed stated that his employment would be subject to the provisions of McGraw-Hill's "handbook on personnel policies and procedures."

An employee handbook or other policy statement may modify an at-will employment contract. The provisions of an employee handbook were held binding in *Duldulao v. St. Mary of Nazareth Hospital Center*, 505 N.E.2d 314 (Ill. 1985). The Supreme Court of Illinois held that (1) a presumption that an employee hired for an indefinite term was an employee at will could be rebutted by evidence that the parties contracted to the contrary; (2) language in the employee handbook to the effect that a nonprobationary employee could be discharged after written notice was sufficient to modify the at-will nature of the plaintiff's employment; and (3) the plaintiff qualified as a "nonprobationary employee," for purpose of the language in the handbook.

A nurse's aide was awarded $20,000 in *Watson v. Idaho Falls Consolidated Hospitals, Inc.*, 720 P.2d 632 (Idaho 1986), for damages when the hospital, as employer, violated the provisions of its employee handbook in the manner in which it terminated her employment. Evidence that the employee was making $1,000 a month at the time of her discharge and was not able to find suitable employment after her discharge supported the award of $20,000 in her favor for wrongful discharge. Although the nurse's aide had no formal written contract, the employee handbook and the hospital policies and procedures manual constituted a contract in view of evidence to the effect that these documents had been intended to be enforced and complied with by both employees and management. Employees read and relied on the handbook as creating terms of an employment contract and were required to sign for the handbook to establish receipt of a revised handbook explaining hospital policy, discipline, counseling, and termination. A policy and procedure manual placed on each floor of the hospital also outlined termination procedures.

The nurse in *Churchill v. Waters*, 731 F. Supp. 311 (C.D. Ill. 1990), brought a civil rights action against the hospital and hospital officials after her discharge. The federal district court held for the defendants on motion for summary judgment, finding that the hospital employee handbook did not give the nurse a protected property interest in continued employment. "Absent proof that the handbook contained clear promises which indicated the intent to bind the parties, no contract was created." *Id.* at 321–322. The handbook contained a disclaimer expressly disavowing any attempt to be bound by it and stated that its contents were not to be considered conditions of employment. The handbook was "presented as a matter of information only and the language contained herein [was] not intended to constitute a contract between McDonough District Hospital and . . . the employee." *Id.* at 315–316. Although an employee handbook may delineate specific disciplinary procedures, that fact does not in and of itself constitute an enforceable contract. *Chesnick v. Saint Mary of Nazareth Hospital,* 570 N.E.2d 545 (Ill. App. Ct. 1991).

The above cases point out the importance of drafting appropriate personnel guidelines and manuals.

> Employment guidelines and manuals are very helpful in obtaining employee good will and maintaining good employee relations. They can also be excellent tools in maintaining a union-free environment. Therefore, the use, drafting, and implementation of an employment manual should be taken seriously. When drafting such manuals, employers should keep in mind the legal consequences of each provision and take care to avoid restrictive or tightly worded language. An employee handbook can both be written in accordance with the stated guidelines and help to maintain good employee communication and effective employee relations.[8]

PUBLIC POLICY ISSUES

The public policy exception to the employment-at-will doctrine provides that employees may not be terminated for reasons that are contrary to public policy. Public policy originates with legislative enactments that prohibit, for example, the discharge of employees on the basis of handicap, age, race, color, religion, sex, national origin, pregnancy, filing of safety violation complaints with various agencies (e.g., the Occupational Safety and Health Administration), or union membership. Any attempt to limit, segregate, or classify employees in any way that would tend to deprive any individual of employment opportunities on these bases is contrary to public policy.

Public policy also can arise as a result of judicial decisions that address those issues not covered by statutes, rules, and regulations. "[I]t can be said that public policy concerns what is right and just and what affects the citizens of the state collectively. It is to be found in the state's constitution and statutes and, when they are silent, in its judicial decisions." *Palmateer v. International Harvester Co.,* 421 N.E.2d 876, 878 (Ill. 1981).

> Public policy favors the exposure of crime, and the cooperation of citizens possessing knowledge thereof is essential to effective implementation of that policy. Persons acting in good faith who have probable cause to believe crimes have been committed should not be deterred from reporting them by the fear of unfounded suits by those accused.

Joiner v. Benton Community Bank, 411 N.E.2d 229, 231 (Ill. 1980).

In those instances in which state and federal laws are silent, not all courts concur with the use of judicial decisions as a means for determining public policy. A California court has determined that a public policy exception to the at-will employment doctrine must be based on constitutional or statutory provisions rather than judicial policymaking. *Gantt v. Sentry Insurance,* Cal. Sup. Ct. No. SO14212, (Feb. 27, 1992). "A public policy exception carefully tethered to fundamental policies that are delineated in constitutional or statutory provisions strikes the proper balance among the interests of employers, employees, and the public."[9]

Sex Discrimination

Title VII of the Civil Rights Act of 1964 "requires the elimination of artificial, arbitrary, and unnecessary barriers to employment that operate invidiously to discriminate on the basis of race." *Griggs v. Duke Power Co.,* 401 U.S. 424 (1971). In *Jones v. Hinds General Hospital,* 666 F. Supp. 933 (D. Miss. 1987), a *prima facie* case of sex discrimination was established by evidence showing that a hospital laid off female nursing assistants while retaining male orderlies who performed the necessary functions. The court held that title VII of the Civil Rights Act was not violated by the hospital's use of gender as a basis for laying off its employees. Gender was a bona fide occupational qualification for orderlies because a substantial number of male patients objected to the performance of catheterizations and surgical preparation by female assistants.

Pregnancy Discrimination

An employer may not discriminate against an employee because of pregnancy. The x-ray technician in *Hayes v. Shelby Memorial Hospital,* 726 F.2d 1543

(11th Cir. 1984), brought an employment discrimination action against the hospital. The technician was fired by the hospital when it learned that she was pregnant. The federal district court found that the hospital had violated the Pregnancy Discrimination Act. In affirming the lower court's decision, the appellate court held that the hospital failed to consider less discriminatory alternatives to firing the technician.

Racial Discrimination

Discharge of an employee on the basis of racial bias is actionable under state and federal laws. An at-will employee's claim of racially motivated retaliatory discharge for filing a discrimination complaint can be actionable in tort as a violation of public policy.

Reporting of Patient Abuse

An employer may not discharge an employee for fulfilling societal obligations or in those instances in which the employer acts with a socially undesirable motive.[10] A tort claim for wrongful discharge was stated in *McQuary v. Air Convalescent Home,* 684 P.2d 21 (Or. Ct. App. 1984), by allegations that the plaintiff was discharged wrongfully from her position at the nursing facility as in-service director of nurses training and education in retaliation for threatening to report to state authorities instances of alleged patient mistreatment. Such mistreatment purportedly involved violation of a patient's rights under the Nursing Home Patient's Bill of Rights. To prevail, the discharged employee was not required to prove that patient abuse actually had occurred but only that she acted in good faith.

> This conclusion is consistent with established Oregon law. Statutes which protect employees against retaliation do not require that the alleged violation which the employee claims be ultimately proved. *See, e.g.,* ORS 652.355 (protects an employee who merely consults an attorney or agency about a wage claim); ORS 654.062(5) (protects any employee who makes a complaint under the Oregon Safe Employment Act); ORS 659.030(1)(f) (prohibits discrimination against an employee who filed a civil rights complaint); ORS 633.120(3) (prohibits discrimination against an employee for filing an unfair labor practices complaint). We have, in fact, upheld awards for retaliation despite holding that the original complaint did not show discrimination.

• • • •

Similar considerations of public policy lead to our conclusion that an employee who reports a violation of a nursing home patient's statutory rights in good faith should be protected from discharge for that action.

Id. at 24.

This case, which had been dismissed in the lower court, was reversed and remanded for trial.

Whistleblowing

Whistleblowing has been defined as an act of someone "who, believing that the public interest overrides the interest of the organization he serves, publicly 'blows the whistle' if the organization is involved in corrupt, illegal, fraudulent, or harmful activity."[11]

[A]ccording to the public policy exception, an employer may not rely on the at-will doctrine as a basis for escaping liability for discharging an employee because of the doing of, or the refusing to do, such an act. Moreover, statutes in several jurisdictions protect an employee from an employer's retaliation for engaging in certain types of protected activities, such as whistleblowing.

99 A.L.R. Fed. 775.

DEFAMATION ACTIONS

Employers across the country are facing a new kind of potential liability with every employee they hire—a defamation action if the relationship does not work out. Observers say an increasing number of defamation claims is being brought by current and former workers, apparently because of a greater awareness by those employees—and a growing recognition by the courts—of new protections available to them.[12] According to the Bureau of National Affairs study of wrongful discharge cases between 1982 and 1987, "plaintiffs recovered damages in 78.9% of all defamation claims filed against former employers."[13]

Defamation actions are being attached to—or are taking the place of—wrongful discharge suits. "[P]laintiffs must overcome an employer's qualified privilege and show malice in order to recover."[14] In Indiana, an employee's defamation action against the employer does not constitute just cause for dismissal under Indiana law. *Tacket v. Delco Remy,* CA 7, No. 91-1307, (Mar. 27, 1992).

Dismissal was ordered properly for claims of wrongful termination and defamation in *Eli v. Griggs County Hospital & Nursing Home,* 385 N.W.2d 99 (N.D. 1986), in which a nurse's aide was terminated on the basis of an incident in the hospital dining room. In the presence of patients and visitors, she cursed her supervisor and complained that personnel were working short-staffed. Given the nature of her employment and the high standard of care that persons reasonably expected from a nursing care facility, such behavior justified her termination on a charge of reported breach of patient-specific and facility-specific information. No defamation resulted from the entry of such charges in the aide's personnel file, because the record established that the charges were true.

The nurse's aide in *Watson v. Idaho Falls Consolidated Hospitals,* 720 P.2d 632 (Idaho 1986), claimed that the head nurse intentionally interfered with her employment relationship with the hospital, that both the head nurse and the hospital had intentionally inflicted emotional distress, and that accusations before discharge constituted slander. The defendants made a motion for summary judgment, which was granted in part as to the nurse's aide's claim for slander. Although the nurse's aide did not appeal the issue of slander, it seems clear that actions for defamation will appear in an ever-increasing number of cases.

RETALIATORY DISCHARGE

There is a tendency for those in power to abuse that power through threats, abuse, intimidation, and retaliatory discharge, all of which are cause for legal action. Employees who become the targets of a vindictive supervisor often have difficulty in proving a bad-faith motive. In an effort to reduce the probability of wrongful discharge, some states, such as Connecticut,[15] Maine,[16] Montana,[17] and Michigan,[18] have enacted legislation that protects employees from terminations found to be arbitrary and capricious. The Montana Supreme Court upheld state legislation that protects workers against arbitrary discharge, while at the same time limiting the damages they can win.[19]

"Employees have . . . brought claims alleging abusive discharge in violation of public policy. This type of action is usually found to sound in tort, and thus in certain circumstances punitive damages have been awarded."[20] The burden of proof for establishing some hidden motive for discharge from employment rests on discharged employees.

> The National Labor Relations Act and other labor legislation illustrate the governmental policy of preventing employers from using the right of discharge as a means of oppression.

• • • •

Consistent with this policy, many states have recognized the need to protect employees who are not parties to a collective bargaining agreement or other contract from abusive practices by the employer.

• • • •

Recently those states have recognized a common law cause of action for employees at will who were discharged for reasons that were in some way "wrongful." The courts in those jurisdictions have taken various approaches: some recognizing the action in tort, some in contract.

Pierce v. Ortho Pharmaceutical Corp., 417 A.2d., at 509.

The court in *Khanna v. Microdata Corp.*, 215 Cal. Rptr. 860 (Ct. App. 1985), held that substantial evidence supported a finding that the employer fired the employee in bad-faith retaliation for bringing a lawsuit against the employer, thus violating an implied covenant of good faith and fair dealing. "Under the traditional common-law rule, codified in section 2922 of the Labor Code, an employment contract of indefinite duration is in general terminable at the will of either party. During the past several decades, however, judicial authorities in California and throughout the United States have established the rule that, under both common law and the statute, an employer does not enjoy an absolute or totally unfettered right to discharge even an at-will employee." 215 Cal. Rptr. at 865. A cause of action was stated for the employer's breach of an implied-in-fact covenant to terminate only for good cause.

In *Shores v. Senior Manor Nursing Center*, 518 N.E.2d 471 (Ill. App. Ct. 1988), a formerly employed nurse's assistant brought an action against the nursing facility on the basis of retaliatory discharge. The circuit court dismissed the complaint for failure to state a cause of action and the decision was appealed. The appellate court held that the allegation of the former nursing facility employee that she was discharged in retaliation for reporting to the nursing home administrator that the charge nurse was performing her functions as a nurse improperly, which allegedly violated the Nursing Home Care Reform Act, stated a cause of action for retaliatory discharge. The circuit court was reversed, and the case was remanded for further proceedings.

The former director of nursing administration brought an action against the hospital and others for breach of contract, violation of civil rights, and interference with contractual relations in *Hobson v. McClean Hospital Corp.*, 402 Mass. 413, 522 N.E.2d 975 (1988). The Supreme Judicial Court of Massachusetts held (1) the complaint stated a cause of action for breach of an employment contract and interference with the employment contract, (2) the complaint stated a cause of action for discharge in violation of public policy, but (3) the complaint did not state a cause of action under the Civil Rights Act. The director of nursing administration alleged that the hospital bylaws for professional staff conferred privileges on employees and that the hospital terminated her without good cause ("wrongfully terminated employee in retaliation for her enforcement of State municipal laws and regulations"). *Id.* at 976. There were no counselings and no warnings.

Dismissal of an employee shortly after a request for a grievance hearing regarding a salary discrepancy with another employee can raise an issue of liability for retaliatory discharge. The physician in *Jones v. Westside-Urban Health Center,* 760 F. Supp. 1575 (D.C. Ga. 1991), was found to have established a *prima facie* case of retaliatory discharge in which the record indicated that he had been fired from the hospital five days after his request for a grievance hearing on an alleged salary discrepancy.

FAIRNESS—THE ULTIMATE TEST

"Is it fair?" is the ultimate question that a supervisor must ask when considering a termination. In general, "bad-faith" and "inexplicable" terminations are subject to the scrutiny of the courts. Some courts and legislative enactments have overturned the view that employers have total discretion to terminate workers who are not otherwise protected by collective bargaining agreements or civil services regulations. Montana legislation grants every employee the right to sue the employer for wrongful discharge. The mere fact that an employment contract is terminable at will does not give the employer an absolute right to terminate it in all cases. The court in *Cleary v. American Airlines,* 199 Cal. Rptr. 722 (1980), held that the longevity of the employee's services, together with the express policy of the employer, operated as a form of estoppel, precluding any discharge of the employee by the employer without good cause, and thus, the employee stated a cause of action for wrongful discharge.

There is an implied covenant of good faith and fair dealing in every contract that neither party will do anything that will injure the right of the other to receive benefits from the agreement. The employee in *Pugh v. See's Candies,* 116 Cal. App. 3d 311, 171 Cal. Rptr. 917 (1981), was found to have shown a *prima facie* case of wrongful termination in violation of an implied promise that the employer would not act arbitrarily in dealing with the employee. The employer's right to terminate an employee is not absolute. It is limited by fundamental principles of public policy and by expressed or implied terms of agreement between the employer and the employee.

Procedural issues are as important as issues of discrimination. The Supreme Court of Michigan in *Renny v. Port Huron Hospital,* 398 N.W.2d 327 (Mich. 1986), found, as did the jury, that the employee's discharge hearing was not final and binding because it did not comport with elementary "fairness." The court found that there was sufficient evidence for the jury to find that the employee had not been discharged for just cause. The existence of a just-cause contract is a question of fact for the jury when the employer establishes written policies and procedures and does not expressly retain the right to terminate an employee at will. That the hospital followed the grievance procedure with the plaintiff is evidence that a just-cause contract existed on which the plaintiff relied.

The employee handbook provided for a grievance board as a fair way to resolve work-related complaints and problems. This was not a mandatory procedure to which the hospital's employees had to submit. The employee was not bound by the grievance board determination that her discharge was proper, in that evidence supported a finding that she was not given adequate notice of who the witnesses against her would be. She was not permitted to be present when the witnesses testified, and she was not given the right to present certain evidence.

There was sufficient evidence for the jury to conclude that the plaintiff had suffered damages in the amount of $100,000. Evidence presented indicated that her subsequent professional employment did not equal her earnings before discharge and that she had experienced increased expenses because of the loss of her health insurance as well as other financial losses that she suffered as a result of her discharge.

An employee, especially a supervisor, who believes he or she has been unfairly discharged will be most likely to seek access to the following information in defense of his or her claim:

- minutes of any meetings
- written reports, typed or handwritten
- personnel file
- tapes
- letters, cards, and handwritten notes written on the employee's behalf from the public
- personnel handbook
- personnel and departmental policies and procedures books
- oral testimony from fellow employees and supervisors

Employers must document carefully and fairly any disciplinary proceedings that might be subject to discovery by a disgruntled employee. Failure to do so could place a board or a supervisor at an uncomfortable disadvantage should a complaint reach the courts.

Unemployment Compensation

Fair dealing in termination also should include fair dealing with the terminated employee who files for unemployment benefits. The nursing facility in

Euclid Manor Nursing Home v. Board of Review, 501 N.E.2d 635 (Ohio Ct. App. 1985), appealed from a court decision affirming an order of the Bureau of Employment Services granting unemployment benefits to the claimant. The claimant had worked for the home only four weeks before being terminated. She knowingly had been hired for a supervisory position even though she was a recent graduate with one year of experience in a nonsupervisory position. The appeals court held that the nursing home's termination of the claimant was without "just cause," so that termination did not preclude claimant from receiving benefits.

In another case, *Mankato Lutheran Home v. Miller,* 358 N.W.2d 96 (Minn. Ct. App. 1984), a nursing assistant was found not to be disqualified from receiving unemployment benefits because of a single episode of profanity directed toward her supervisor while she was ill, frustrated, and in part, provoked by actions of her supervisor. The nursing assistant had no prior record of misconduct in five years of employment; however, her illness and frustration at having to work after she repeatedly had indicated that she was not feeling well increased over the course of several hours until she exploded emotionally. She had asked her supervisor, Ms. Darkow, if she could go home but was refused because of the probability of being unable to replace her in the middle of a shift.

> At about 5:30 a.m. Darkow entered a patient's room where Miller was helping a resident get dressed. When she asked how Miller was feeling, Miller became upset and said, "What the hell do you care, you don't think I'm sick anyway. I could drop over dead and still have to do these . . . (Bleep) people." Darkow retorted that Miller should not have come to work if she was so sick, and Miller yelled back "I never had this . . . (Bleep) pain until I came to this . . . (Bleep) hole.

Id. at 98.

Although the assistant's outburst was directed toward her supervisor, one of two residents in the room who heard the incident was upset by it. *Id.* The episode did not represent a disregard for the employer's interests or of the nursing assistant's duties and responsibilities.

Fair dealing does not always imply that every discharged employee should be entitled to unemployment benefits. For example, in *Forbis v. Wesleyan Nursing Home,* 325 S.E.2d 651 (1985), unemployment compensation was denied because of an employee's discharge resulting from theft of a patient's clock. The theft constituted willful and wanton disregard for the nursing home's interests. The Employment Security Commission on its investigation made the following findings of fact:

> 2. The claimant was discharged . . . for theft [of] patient property.
> 3. . . . [A] patient accused the claimant of taking the patient's clock.

4. Upon being confronted with the patient's accusation, the claimant produced the missing clock from her pocket and admitted taking it.

Id. at 652.

In another case, a nursing assistant was properly denied unemployment benefits as a result of being terminated for poor work attendance, even though her most recent absence had been excused. The employee's record indicated that the center had shown great tolerance in allowing the employee to continue employment for as long as it did. *Love v. Heritage House Convalescent Center,* 463 N.E.2d 478 (Ind. Ct. App. 1983).

Voluntary termination because of a change in working conditions will not necessarily make an employee eligible for unemployment benefits. In *Montclair Nursing Home v. Wills,* 371 N.W.2d 121 (Neb. 1985), a licensed practical nurse was found not to be eligible for unemployment benefits when she resigned after reassignment to a night shift. Voluntary termination because of a change in working hours was not considered sufficient good cause to grant unemployment benefits, absent an "improper" purpose or motive in the change in the employee's work hours.

TERMINATION

A decision to terminate an employee should be reviewed carefully by a member of management familiar with the issues of wrongful discharge. Oral counseling, written counseling, written counseling with suspension, and written counseling with termination are the textbook responses to disciplinary action and discharge. Textbook theories are fine in a black-and-white world, but then who lives in such a world? Whatever form of discipline is used, it should be designed to produce a more effective and productive employee. The following listing presents some alternatives to terminating employees.

- Use inter- and intradepartmental transfers when indicated. Transfers are generally more effective in larger corporations such as multisite health care systems where relocation is geographically possible
- Substitute suspension for termination when possible. Do not have the courts do it for you
- Provide an opportunity for early retirement
- Consider a redeployment of personnel, a hiring freeze, a reduction of overtime, etc., before personnel cutbacks are made because of financial difficulties

The employer's right to terminate an employee is not absolute. It is limited by fundamental principles of public policy and by express or implied terms of agreement between the employer and the employee.

Formulating a standard for substantive fairness in employee dismissal law requires accommodating a number of different interests already afforded legal recognition. The legal interest of employees to be protected against certain types of unfair and injurious action . . . are at the core of any employee dismissal proposal. Arrayed against these interests are employer and societal interests in effective management of organizations, which require that employees not be shielded from the consequences of their poor performance or misconduct, and that supervisors not be deterred from exercising their managerial responsibilities by the inconvenience of litigating employees' claims.[21]

Before termination of an employee, the employer should review the following questions:

- Was the termination
  1. a violation of any policy or procedure outlined in an administrative manual, the employee handbook, the personnel department's policies and procedures, or any other health care facility policies and procedures or regulations?
  2. arbitrary and capricious?
  3. discriminatory on the basis of age, disability, race, creed, color, religion, gender, national origin, or marital status?
  4. a violation of any contract—oral or written?
  5. a violation of any public policy—federal, state, or local?
  6. consistent with the reasons for discharge?
  7. discriminatory against the employee for filing a lawsuit?
  8. fixed before any appeal actions that might be available to the employee? If an appeal was granted, was the employee given an opportunity to be represented by counsel?
- Was there
  1. retaliatory action because of a refusal to perform an illegal act or a questioning of a management practice?
  2. defamation of character?
  3. a conspiracy?
  4. a personal vendetta?
  5. threat or intimidation?
  6. unlawful activity?
  7. an attempt to bribe?

8. a denial of constitutional rights to freedom of speech?

9. an interference with an employee's rights as secured by the laws or Constitution of the United States?

Employment Disclaimers

A disclaimer is the denial of a right that is imputed to a person or that is alleged to belong to him or her. Although a disclaimer is often a successful defense for employers in wrongful discharge cases, it should not be considered a license to discharge at will and at the whim of the supervisor in an arbitrary and capricious manner.

Employers can help prevent successful lawsuits for wrongful discharge that are based on the premise that an employee handbook or departmental policy and procedure manual is an implied contract by incorporating disclaimers in published manuals, such as that described in *Battaglia v. Sisters of Charity Hospital,* 508 N.Y.S.2d 802 (App. Div. 1986), in which a personnel manual could not be interpreted to limit the hospital's power to terminate an at-will employee. Language in the manual indicated that the personnel manual was not a contract; that it could be modified, amended, or supplemented; and that the hospital retained the right to make all necessary management decisions for the delivery of patient care services and the selection, direction, compensation, and retention of employees.

Handbooks that do not contain disclaimers can alter an employee's at-will status. An appeals court in *Trusty v. Big Sandy Health Care Center,* No. 89-CA-2272-MR, (Ky. Ct. App. March 22, 1991), noted that the handbook did not contain any disclaimer or any other language that employment was at will. The court held that there was sufficient evidence to establish that the handbook had altered the employee's at-will status and determined that the employee could bring a wrongful discharge suit.

Disclaimers must be clear to the employee. The court in *Harvet v. Unity Medical Center,* 428 N.W.2d 574 (Minn. Ct. App. 1988), held in a wrongful discharge suit that the hospital's employee handbook was sufficiently definite to form an employment contract.

> Unity's handbook contained detailed provisions on conduct and procedures for discipline. As the trial court observed, "there can be no question that [respondent's] handbook provisions are sufficiently definite to form a contract." The handbook represents much more than Unity's general statement of policy. Moreover, the terms of the handbook were sufficiently definite to allow a fact finder to determine whether there had been a breach.

• • • •

Respondent contends the handbook contained the following reservations on the part of the employer indicating it was not being offered as a contract: "Exceptions to any personnel policy or procedure may be permitted on a documented form showing of good and sufficient cause."

• • • •

In the present case the trial court correctly found, "the clause does not clearly tell employees that the handbook is not part of an employment contract."

Id. at 577.

The employer's disclaimers were considered clear in *Simonson v. Meader Distribution Co.,* 413 N.W.2d 146 (Minn. Ct. App. 1987), in which an employee filed a breach of contract suit alleging a dismissal was outside company-adopted disciplinary guidelines. The court held that the company could and did reserve the discretion to discipline employees outside adopted guidelines. The policy manual contained the following three specific reservations of management discretion:

Management reserves the right to make any changes at any time by adding to, deleting, or changing any existing policy.

The rules set out below are as complete as we can reasonably make them. However, they are not necessarily all-inclusive, because circumstances that we have not anticipated may arise. Some currently unanticipated circumstances may warrant the application of discipline, including discharge.

Management may vary from the above policies if, in its opinion, the circumstances require.

Id. at 147.

Health care facilities can be successful when confronted with wrongful discharge suits based on breach of contract by placing similar language in their personnel manuals.

Termination for Cause

A termination for cause only clause in an employment contract is binding. An employment contract in *Eales v. Tanana,* 663 P.2d 958 (Alaska 1983), that provided that an employee hired up to retirement age could be terminated only for cause was upheld by the court.

Violation of Published Policies

Unemployment compensation was properly denied a nursing assistant for breach of a no-smoking rule in *Selan v. Commonwealth Unemployment Compensation Board of Review,* 415 A.2d 139 (Pa. Commw. Ct. 1980). The nursing facility's personnel handbook clearly provided that smoking was allowed only in specified areas.

> Smoking can be very offensive. It also creates a health and fire problem.
>
> You must refrain from smoking in offices, resident areas, elevators, corridors, or any area where it might be hazardous. In fact, you should not smoke in the public view. All "no smoking signs" must be observed. Your Department Director will inform you of the areas in which you are permitted to smoke.
>
> Smoking is permitted during break times and at meal times in these designated smoking areas.
>
> Smoking is permitted in vehicles only if residents are not present.
>
> Use ashtrays to keep The Home clean and to prevent fires. Special care must be exercised when oxygen or other inflammable gases may be present.

Id. at 140.

The nursing home assistant admitted that she was smoking but argued that she did not break the facility's smoking rules. The court disagreed. Evidence was sufficient to show that the employee knowingly violated Methodist Home's rule by smoking in a patient's bathroom. "Deliberate violation of a reasonable employer rule, without due cause, constitutes willful misconduct warranting disqualification for unemployment compensation. 43 P.S. §802(e)." *Id.*

Termination Because of Financial Necessity

No breach of employment contract occurred in *Wilde v. Houlton Regional Hospital,* 537 A.2d 1137 (Me. 1987), when, because of financial difficulties and overstaffing, a hospital terminated the employment of two nurses, a ward clerk, and a dietary supervisor. Even if the employees were correct in contending that their indefinite contracts of employment had been modified by virtue of a "dismissal for cause" provision in the employee's handbook and by management's oral assurances that they were permanent, full-time employees whose jobs were secure so long as they performed satisfactorily, the employees' discharge for financial or other legitimate business reasons did not offend the employment contracts as thus modified. A private employer had an essential business prerogative to adjust its work force as market forces and business necessity required, and the layoffs in question violated no compelling public policy.

> [T]he appellants have failed to set forth specific facts showing that they were discharged for any reasons other than financial difficulties and overstaffing. The record does not suggest, for example, that financial difficulties were a pretext for discharges that were actually motivated by Houlton Regional's bad faith or retaliatory purpose.

Id. at 1138.

Termination for Failing Licensure Examinations

Although a nurse may be discharged for failing to pass licensing examinations, the nurse may be entitled to unemployment benefits. *Clarke v. North Detroit General Hospital,* 470 N.W.2d 393 (Mich. 1991).

Termination Because of Hostile Attitude

A county nursing facility employee's discharge was warranted in *Langford v. Lane,* 921 F.2d 677 (6th Cir. Tenn. 1991), in which the employee refused, in front of other employees and patients, to discuss with the administrator her hostile attitude toward management. The employee's refusal to speak with the administrator directly threatened the administrator's authority and constituted insubordination, which was sufficient independent justification for the employee's discharge. The employee's refusal was not constitutionally protected speech.

The chief x-ray technician in *Paros v. Hoemako Hospital,* 681 P.2d 918 (Ariz. Ct. App. 1984), was dismissed because of a chronic argumentative and hostile attitude inconsistent with the performance of supervisory duties. The trial court entered a summary judgment in favor of the hospital and the administrator. On appeal, the appeals court held that the discharge was properly based on good cause and precluded recovery for breach of contract and wrongful discharge.

Termination Because of Misconduct

A nurse's aide in *Daniels v. Hillcrest Homes,* 594 S.W.2d 64 (Ark. Ct. App. 1980), was terminated for the following alleged reasons: (1) the aide was uncooperative with other aides; (2) she did not report to work as scheduled; (3) she was abusive to residents; and (4) her boyfriend had on occasions interfered with her job by coming to her place of work. *Id.* at 65. The Arkansas Unemployment Compensation Board of Review determined, by the evidence presented (three unsworn handwritten statements), that the nurse's aide was not terminated because of misconduct and that she was eligible for unemployment benefits. The circuit court reversed the board's determination, and an appeal was taken. The Court of Appeals of Arkansas held that the Board's decision granting unemployment benefits was supported by substantial evidence.

> Credibility of witnesses and the weight to be accorded the testimony are matters to be resolved by the Administrative Agency. The trial judge could reverse if the findings of the Board of review were arbitrary, capricious, unreasonable and without substantial evidence to support them or in fraud or corruption. Moreover, a reviewing court may not substitute its findings for those of the Administrative Agency even though the court might reach a different conclusion if it had made the original determination upon the same evidence considered by the Agency. Even if the evidence is undisputed, the drawing of inferences is for the Agency, not the courts.

Id. at 65, 66.

It is important to recognize from this case the significance of well-documented employee counselings and disciplinary actions.

Termination Because of Improper Billing Practices

The hospital in *Jagust v. Brookhaven Memorial Ass'n,* 541 N.Y.S.2d 41 (App. Div. 1989), was found to have properly dismissed a staff physician from his administrative position as director of the hospital's family practice residency program without a hearing. The hospital learned that the physician had engaged in improper billing practices by submitting bills for services that he never rendered. The physician was an employee at will as far as his administrative position was concerned. Neither the hospital's administrative procedure manual nor the employee handbook stated that the employee was subject to discharge for cause. Procedural protection was provided in the medical staff bylaws; however, the bylaws pertained to medical staff privileges and not administrative positions.

Termination Because of Theft

A nurse's discharge in *Waara v. Mesabi Regional Medical Center,* 415 N.W.2d 362 (Minn. Ct. App. 1987), involved misconduct so gross as to deny unemployment compensation when it was based on charges that she had stolen supplies of Demerol for her own use and that she had falsified patient records to conceal such thefts.

Termination Because of Poor Work Performance

A nurse's aide had been terminated from the county infirmary for misconduct in that, among other things, she failed to timely report bumping and injuring a resident's leg, failed to properly feed a resident as ordered by the resident's physician, and on another occasion, fed a resident food that burned the resident's mouth. On review in *Yerry v. Ulster County,* 512 N.Y.2d 592 (Ct. App. Div. 1987), the court held that eyewitness testimony and believable hearsay was sufficient to sustain the findings of the hearings officer who recommended her termination.

> As to the imposition of discipline, when petitioner's serious performance deficiencies are considered in light of her experience and the grave responsibility her work demanded in caring for helpless and dependent patients, we find that the penalty imposed was not disproportionate to the offenses. She showed an insensitivity and a lack of ability that made her unsuitable for the work and constituted a danger to the well-being of the infirmary's elderly residents.

Id. at 593.

Unemployment compensation was properly denied to a nurse's aide in *Starks v. Director of the Division of Employment Section,* 462 N.E.2d 1360 (Mass. 1984), who had been discharged for leaving a resident unattended and unrestrained on a commode and for using the property (medicated cream) of another resident, both of which are violations of the employer's policies. The court held that the examiner's findings of fact were adequate to support a conclusion that the claimant was discharged solely for misconduct in willful disregard of the employer's interest. *Id.* The examiner had found that the employee had been trained adequately and was capable of accomplishing her work and that she already had been warned that her job was in jeopardy. *Id.* at 1361.

No cognizable claim was stated in *Hinson v. Cameron,* 742 P.2d 549 (Okla. 1987), by a nurse's aide whose at-will employment was terminated by a hospital on the basis of a supervisor's charge that the aide failed to administer an enema to a patient. The nurse's aide had not been ordered to perform an illegal act, and thus the tort of wrongful discharge could not be made out. In this case, the hospital's employee manual could not be read as conferring tenured employment or job security. The Supreme Court of Oklahoma held that although the employee manual listed examples of some grounds for termination, it was not an exclusive listing of all grounds for termination. Even though there might be an implied covenant of good faith and fair dealing in every at-will employment relationship, that covenant does not operate to forbid employment severance except for good cause.

The plaintiff in *Silinzy v. Visiting Nurse Ass'n,* 777 F. Supp. 1484 (E.D. Mo. 1991), brought an action claiming racial discrimination and retaliatory discharge. The court granted a motion for summary judgment by the defendant-employer. The district court held that the plaintiff failed to establish a *prima facie* case of racial discrimination and retaliatory discharge. The plaintiff's poor job performance was the reason for her discharge. "Defendant has produced ample evidence that plaintiff was not performing her job adequately. Numerous complaints regarding her negative attitude and poor job performance, from a variety of sources, are documented." *Id.* at 1487.

Termination Because of Alcoholism

Discharge of an employee because of alcoholism is not necessarily a discriminatory practice. The hospital's discharge of a staff physician for alcoholism in *Soentgen v. Quain & Ramstad Clinic,* 467 N.W.2d 73 (N.D. 1991), was found "not" to be a discriminatory practice. The physician had been discharged on a bona fide occupational qualification reasonably necessary for a physician within the meaning of NDCC 14-02.4-08.

Termination and Damages

An employee who is wrongly discharged may maintain a cause of action in contract or tort, or both. In a tort action for wrongful discharge, the court can award punitive damages. This remedy is not available under the law of contract.

> Recent headlines highlight that the damages awarded in employment related litigation may not be limited to back pay, fringe benefits and other forms of compensatory relief. In June 1988, a federal jury in the Eastern District of Kentucky awarded a total of $3 million in punitive damages to two former executives of Ashland Oil, Inc. who prevailed in a wrongful termination suit. . . . The plaintiffs alleged that they were dismissed for opposing and then failing to cover up illegal payments made to foreign government representatives. The jury assessed punitive damages against the corporation, its chairman, former chairman and a senior vice president.[22]

A California Supreme Court decision that prohibits plaintiffs from seeking punitive and emotional distress damages from former employers in wrongful dismissal cases applies retroactively to thousands of cases pending in that state's courts. In *Newman v. Emerson Radio Corp.,* 772 P.2d 1059 (Cal. 1989), the court, by a 4–3 vote, decided that its December 29 decision in *Foley v. Interactive Data Corp.,* 765 P.2d 373, 47 Cal. Rptr. 3d 211 (1988), applies to all wrongful dismissal cases pending as of January 30. The Supreme Court of California held in *Foley* that a wrongful discharge claim asserting a breach of an implied covenant of good faith and fair dealing may give rise to contract, but not tort, damages. As a result of this ruling, punitive damages will not ordinarily be available to successful wrongful discharge plaintiffs.

The Montana Supreme Court held that a Montana statute that limits the damages recoverable in wrongful discharge suits to four years wages and benefits does not violate the state constitution. *Meech v. Hillhaven West, Inc.,* 776 P.2d 488 (Mont. 1989). According to the court, the state constitution's guarantee of "full legal redress" affords the plaintiff, a former nursing home administrator, only a right to judicial access to obtain remedies, not a fundamental right to full redress. The statute abolishes common-law causes of action for discharge and creates a statutory action. It is the first of its kind in the nation. Punitive damages are available only on clear and convincing evidence that the employer acted with actual malice or committed actual fraud.

EFFECTIVE HIRING PRACTICES

Health care facilities can improve the quality of personnel in their institutions by implementing more effective screening practices. Because it is unlikely that an applicant will reveal any criminal convictions on his or her application, thorough background checks on prospective employees are mandatory. Many states recognize liability for negligent hiring when an employer knew or should have known that an employee posed a foreseeable risk of harm or danger to others.[23] Texas mandates background checks on individuals applying for nursing home positions.[24] Because employment laws do vary from state to state, it is important that background investigations be conducted within operative state law.

It is possible for employers to reduce their exposure to liability for wrongful discharge by developing appropriate guidelines. The best way for the human resources manager to prevent negligent-hiring litigation for the employer is to become familiar with the risks and avoid hiring workers who are likely to become problem employees.

- Take appropriate precautions to prevent the hiring of those who might be a hazard to others

- Develop clear policies and procedures on hiring, disciplining, and terminating employees
- Review each applicant's background and past work behavior
- Become familiar with any state laws that might be applicable when hiring an individual with a past criminal record
- Develop an application that realistically determines an applicant's qualifications before hiring
- Develop a two-tiered interview system for screening applicants (The interviews should be conducted first by an appropriately trained member of the personnel department and then by the department head of the service to which the applicant is applying.)
- Solicit references with the applicant's permission using a release form, and follow up with a telephone call for further information
- Clearly define personnel policies and procedures in the form of a personnel handbook and present a job description to each new employee. Signed documentation should be maintained in the employee's personnel folder indicating that the employee received, read, and understood the employee handbook and job description
- Develop constructive performance evaluations that reinforce good behavior and provide instruction in those areas needing improvement. The performance evaluation should include a written statement regarding the employee's performance
- Develop a progressive disciplinary action policy
- Provide in-service education programs for supervisors on such subjects as employee interviews, evaluations, and discipline (Various colleges, universities, and consultants provide in-service education programs for employers.)
- Be mindful of the importance of developing appropriate employment contract language, as well as administrative manuals and employee handbooks

Employers must communicate clearly to prospective employees that their employment is at will and can be terminated at any time by either the employer or the employee. During the course of employment, handbooks and personnel manuals must provide a fair and unambiguous standard for employee discipline and termination.

NOTES

1. M. Geyelin, *Fired Managers Winning More Lawsuits*, Wall St. J., Sept. 7, 1989, at B1.
2. *Id.*
3. *The Governing Board's Quest for "Supermanager,"* HEALTHCARE EXECUTIVE, 5, Sept./Oct. 1990, at 19.

4. *Id.* at 18.

5. 44 A.L.R. 4th 1136 (1986).

6. M. Geyelin, *supra* note 1.

7. OFFICE OF GENERAL COUNSEL OF AMERICAN HOSPITAL ASSOCIATION, THE WRONGFUL DISCHARGE OF EMPLOYEES IN THE HEALTH CARE INDUSTRY 1 (Legal Memorandum No. 10) (1987).

8. P.I. WEINER, S.H. BOMPEY, & M.G. BRITTAIN, JR., WRONGFUL DISCHARGE CLAIMS, N.Y.C.: PRACTICING LAW INSTITUTE 98 (1986).

9. Gantt v. Sentry Insurance, 60 U.S.L.W. 36 (2/27/92).

10. Delaney v. Taco Time Intl., 681 P.2d 114 (Or. 1984), involved an employer found liable by the Supreme Court of Oregon for the wrongful discharge of an at-will employee who was discharged for fulfilling a societal obligation in that he refused to sign a false and arguably tortious statement that cast aspersions on the work habits and moral behavior of a former employee.

11. WHISTLEBLOWING: THE REPORT OF THE CONFERENCE OF PROFESSIONAL RESPONSIBILITY 6 (R. Nader, P. Petkas, & K. Blackwell, eds., 1972). *See also* 99 A.L.R. FED. 778.

12. Martha Middleton, *Employers Face Upsurge in Suits Over Defamation*, NAT'L L. J., May 4, 1987, at 1.

13. Geyelin, *supra* note 1.

14. *Id.*

15. CONN. GEN. STAT. ANN. §31–51m(a) (West 1987).

16. ME. REV. STAT. ANN. tit. 26, §§ 831–840 (1987).

17. MONT. CODE ANN. §39-2-901 (1987).

18. MICH. COMP. LAWS ANN. §§15.361–369 (West 1981).

19. M. Geyelin, *supra* note 1.

20. Furfaro & Josephson, *Punitive Damages in Employment Cases*, N.Y.L.J., Apr. 7, 1989, at 4.

21. H.H. PERRITT, EMPLOYEE DISMISSAL LAW AND PRACTICE 354 (1984).

22. Furfaro & Josephson, *supra* note 20, at 3.

23. J. Green, *Programs Help Uncover Skeletons in Job Applicants' Closets*, A.H.A. NEWS, 25(19), May 14, 1990, at 6.

24. *Id.*

Chapter 20
Tort Reform

OUTLINE

The traditional negligence-based system for adverse medical outcomes has seriously broken down. Compensation as a deterrent to malpractice has failed to hold the number of claims to a reasonable level. Expensive jury awards and malpractice insurance premiums continue to have a negative impact on the nation's health care system, bringing it ever closer to a day of reckoning with financial disaster.

Although many states have made some progress in tort reform, a more aggressive approach on a national basis is necessary. "Tinkering with the nation's medical malpractice system apparently has helped to stabilize premiums. But health care and legal experts contend that the system will require a complete overhaul before it can function fairly for either patients or physicians."[1] Efforts are under way to generate malpractice reform on a national basis. Early in 1990, President Bush directed the Domestic Council to recommend federal reforms of the medical malpractice system.[2]

The Robert Wood Johnson Foundation in 1985 viewed medical malpractice as an issue that potentially threatened the accessibility, affordability, and quality of health care. As a result of this concern, it funded 19 research and demonstration grants for approximately $4.5 million over a two-year period. Findings from a variety of projects indicate that

- the tort and insurance liability systems, as they are now structured, provide neither an efficient nor an equitable means of compensation for injured parties nor adequate deterrence against medical negligence
- current systems of risk management and professional regulation, in general, do a poor job of identifying and correcting negligent behavior
- there is considerable potential to prevent injuries through the development of new, more formal professional standards and through the identification and correction of incident-prone situations and settings. There is also potential, albeit more limited, to reduce the frequency of maloccurrence by better addressing the problem of negligence-prone physicians
- several alternatives to the existing insurance/tort system may hold promise for more efficient and equitable compensation of injured claimants and for more effective injury prevention.[3]

The tort system as it is presently designed fosters the practice of defensive medicine. After four years of research involving more than 30,000 medical records, a Harvard Medical Practice Study team found that

physicians are three times more likely to believe they will be sued in a given year than actually are. Physicians who believe themselves at greater risk of being sued order more tests and procedures ("defensive medicine"). They also tend to reduce the scope of their practices, performing fewer risky procedures and treating fewer high-risk patients.[4]

Those physicians who wish to practice medicine and survive have accepted the concept of practicing "defensive medicine." Defensive medicine is believed to be one of the most harmful effects produced by the threat of malpractice litigation. Defensive medicine is practiced to forestall potential litigation and provide an advantageous legal defense should a lawsuit be instituted. Medical records are becoming more defensive and will become even more so with closer scrutiny by insurance carriers. Because of the risk and potential for liability in most diagnostic and therapeutic procedures, physicians are practicing defensive medicine.

The fear of malpractice litigation precipitates an ineffective use of scarce health care resources. Defensive medicine often results in either undertreatment, by avoiding high-risk tests and procedures, or overtreatment, such as the excessive use of diagnostic tests.

Because the federal government is a major payer of health care benefits, greater attention will be given to the costly effects of defensive medicine and the need for tort reform.

> Many of those involved in medical malpractice legal reforms say that it's easy to see why the players on the federal level have taken such an interest. "The government is paying for close to 50 percent of the nation's health care bill among Medicare, Medicaid, CHAMPUS, Veteran's Administration, and federal employee benefit health programs," says a staff member of Sen. Orrin G. Hatch (R-UT). The President and members of Congress are concerned that defensive medicine—in addition to other malpractice defense costs—is contributing to the high cost of health care.[5]

It has been estimated that defensive medicine cost the health care industry $19.3 billion in 1988.[6]

For tort reform to be successful, it probably will be necessary for the federal government to tie financial incentives to such reform. The Bush Administration, in a May 15, 1991 proposal sponsored at the request of the White House by Senator Orrin Hatch, would give the states until 1995 "to adopt recommended liability reforms or lose access to a federally sponsored pool of funds that would pay malpractice awards."[7] Specific reforms would include (1) placing caps on nonmedical payments (e.g., limiting malpractice awards for pain and suffering to $250,000); (2) settling disputes outside the courtroom through mediation and arbitration; (3) barring double recovery of damages; (4) eliminating joint and several liability; (5) providing for structured awards; and (6) establishing guidelines for clinical practice.[8]

The emotions regarding the President's plan run high. Some strongly believe that the President's plan for tort reform is misguided. Richard Carlson in a *Newsday* editorial comments:

Besides being wrong and ineffective in so many ways, the Bush bill is dangerous because it seeks to remove one of the few lights on what is a very private and dimly lit world: that of medical practice in the United States.

• • • •

Let patients sue for millions, let them be awarded millions, until people say, "Wait, this makes no sense, there is something corrupt and unhealthy here."

Then perhaps the creaking cottage industry of American medicine will be dismantled and constructed anew in an atmosphere of service, communication and trust, beneficial to care-user and care-giver alike.[9]

The following listing summarizes a wide variety of suggested programs for coping with the malpractice crisis:

- Strictly regulate insurance practices
- Require coordinated malpractice prevention programs that would identify and assist in preventing negligent acts
- Scrutinize health professionals more closely before granting hospital privileges
- Resolve patient complaints promptly
- Require precalendar conferences to encourage settlements before trial
- Establish and set guidelines for medical malpractice panels to facilitate professional malpractice actions
- Expedite the adjudication of malpractice cases by limiting the time allotted for discovery proceedings
- Legislate a statute of limitations that prescribes a time frame within which a lawsuit must be initiated that could begin to run when the injury is discovered and the physician–patient relationship has ended
- Require that a certificate of merit be filed by the plaintiff, before initiating a suit, indicating that the plaintiff consulted with an expert medical witness who established that a negligent act was committed (Legislation could be enacted that would impose a penalty against those filing frivolous claims.)
- Disclose qualifications of any expert witness, and mandate that only experts in an appropriate field be allowed to present admissible testimony in court
- Provide defendants with access to the medical records of the plaintiff
- Set a cap on the amount of awards for pain and suffering
- Limit contingency fees on a sliding scale basis with the percentage decreasing as the award to the plaintiff increases, and/or provide for a lesser fee if a claim is settled without going to trial

- Establish guidelines that juries must follow in setting punitive damage awards. Provide structured awards for the periodic payment of judgments by establishing a reversible trust fund for specified parts of awards due patients (This would provide compensation during a patient's lifetime and would eliminate an unwarranted windfall to the patient's beneficiaries in the event of death.)
- Limit liability awards. "More than 20 states have already enacted laws that limit malpractice awards"[10]
- Revise the doctrine of joint and several liability by limiting each defendant's responsibility, in a multidefendant action, for payment to the percentage of fault ascribed to each defendant
- Allow the defendant(s) to recover court costs and damage awards from both the plaintiff(s) and their attorneys for frivolous claims and counterclaims
- Reduce the award if the plaintiff(s) received compensation from other sources
- Generate malpractice reform, from a legislative viewpoint, on a national basis
- Introduce a no-fault system of compensating injured parties for economic losses without regard to fault
- Establish an effective quality assurance and risk management program
- Periodically review the credentials, physical and mental capacity, and competency of health professionals employed or associated with a hospital
- Institute continuing education programs for health professionals in their areas of responsibility
- Institute general education programs that include patient safety, fire prevention, etc.

Selected schemes for tort reform and suggested programs for coping with the malpractice crisis are reviewed in the following paragraphs.

MEDIATION AND ARBITRATION

Mediation is the process whereby a third party, the mediator, attempts to mediate a settlement between the parties of a complaint. The mediator cannot force a settlement.

Arbitration is the process by which parties to a dispute voluntarily agree to submit their differences to the judgment of an impartial mediation panel for resolution. It is used as a means to evaluate, screen, and resolve medical malpractice disputes before they reach the courts. Arbitration can be accomplished by mutual consent of the parties or statutory provisions. A decision made at arbitration may or may not be binding, depending on prior agreement between the parties or statutory requirements.

Among the many factors contributing to the malpractice crisis is the high cost of litigation. Trial by jury is lengthy and expensive. If case disputes can be handled out of court, the process and expense of a lawsuit can be reduced greatly. Arbitration is one means for simplifying and expediting the settlement of claims.

Medical malpractice arbitration panels can facilitate professional malpractice actions. A 1975 Alabama law provides that after a health care provider has rendered services to a patient out of which a claim has arisen, the parties may agree to settle the dispute by arbitration. Such agreement is binding and irrevocable.[11] A 1988 Florida statute provides that on completion of presuit investigation, with preliminary reasonable grounds for a medical negligence claim intact, the parties may elect to have damages determined by an arbitration panel. Arbitration is undertaken with the understanding that damages shall be limited as specified in the arbitration statute.[12] Michigan law provides that the health care provider may not revoke the agreement after its execution.[13]

On the federal level, Senator Pete V. Domenici (R-New Mexico) introduced a bill that would require mandatory arbitration. The bill would allow states or private agencies to resolve disputes.[14]

STRUCTURED AWARDS

Structured awards are set up for the periodic payment of judgments by establishing a reversible trust fund for specified parts of awards due patients. The purpose of a structured award is to provide compensation during a patient's lifetime. It would eliminate an unwarranted windfall to the patient's beneficiaries in the event of death. Some states have sought to deal with award limitations by mandating so-called structured recoveries when recoveries exceed a certain dollar amount. Arizona, for example, provides for mandatory periodic payment of future economic damages when there has been an effective election by a party.

Structured recoveries provide that money awarded to the plaintiff be placed in a trust fund and invested appropriately so that those funds will be available to the plaintiff over a long period. The rationale behind such legislation is that an immediate award of a large sum of money is not necessary for a plaintiff to be well taken care of after suffering injuries at the hands of the defendant. The prudent investment of a smaller amount of money can produce a recovery commensurate with the needs and the rights of the plaintiff. This, in turn, requires a smaller cash outlay by the defendant or the defendant's insurance company, thereby holding down the costs of malpractice insurance and the ultimate cost of medical care to the consumer.

PRETRIAL SCREENING PANELS

Pretrial screening panels are designed to evaluate the merits of medical injury claims to encourage the settlement of claims outside the courtroom. "Panels render an opinion on provider liability and, in some cases, on damages. In most states, the panel's decision on the merit of the claim is admissible in court."[15] Unlike binding arbitration, the decision of a screening panel is not binding and is imposed as a condition precedent to trial, whereas arbitration is conducted in lieu of a trial. Mandatory screenings of alleged negligence cases are useful in discouraging frivolous lawsuits from proceeding to trial.

In 1986, Maine passed a number of liability reform measures, which included pretrial screening of medical malpractice lawsuits. The Maine statute provides that medical injury claims must be submitted to a screening and mediation panel, unless all parties agree to bypass a panel hearing. Any panel findings that are unanimous and unfavorable to either the defendant or claimant are admissible as evidence at any subsequent trial.[16] The law appears to have helped to reduce the number of "frivolous" suits.[17]

The Supreme Court of Alaska in *Keyes v. Humana Hospital Alaska,* 750 P.2d 343 (Alaska 1988), held that a statute creating mandatory pretrial review of medical malpractice claims by an expert advisory panel did not impermissibly infringe on the plaintiff's constitutional right to a trial by jury. The statute was a reasonable legislative response to the medical malpractice insurance crisis. The constitutionality of a Virginia statute in *Speet v. Bacaj,* 377 S.E.2d 397 (Va. 1989), provided that admission of a medical review panel's opinion into evidence did not infringe on the plaintiff's right to a trial by jury as guaranteed by the Virginia Constitution.

COLLATERAL SOURCE RULE

The collateral source rule is a common-law principle that prohibits a court or jury from taking into account when setting an award that part, or even all, of the plaintiff's damages are covered by other sources of payment (e.g., health insurance, disability, and compensation). Several states have modified the collateral source rule so that evidence regarding other sources of payment to the plaintiff may be introduced for purposes of reducing the amount of the ultimate award to the plaintiff. The jury then would be permitted to assign the evidence such weight as it chooses. The award could be reduced to the extent the plaintiff received compensation from other sources.

Imposition of the collateral source rule often can result in recoveries to plaintiffs far in excess of their economic loss. Such excessive payments contribute significantly to the high cost of malpractice insurance and the high cost of medicine to the public. When evidence regarding collateral sources of payment can be introduced to mitigate the damages payable to a plaintiff, excessive recoveries may be discouraged.

A Tennessee statute provided that

> [i]n a malpractice action in which liability is admitted or established, the damages awarded may include (in addition to other elements of damages authorized by law) actual economic losses suffered by the claimant by reason of the personal injury, including but not limited to cost of reasonable and necessary medical care, rehabilitation services, and custodial care, loss of services and loss of earned income, but only to the extent that such costs are not paid or payable and such losses are not replaced, or indemnified in whole or in part, by insurance provided by an employer, either governmental or private, by social security benefits, service benefit programs, unemployment benefits, or any other source except the assets of the claimants or of the members of the claimants' immediate family and insurance purchased in whole or in part, privately and individually.[18]

The malpractice litigants in *Baker v. Vanderbilt University,* 616 F. Supp. 330 (D. Tenn. 1985), sought a court order declaring the provisions of the Tennessee statute abrogating the collateral source rule in medical malpractice cases to be unconstitutional. The district court held that the Tennessee statute did not deny the litigants equal protection as compared with victims of other torts.

CONTINGENCY FEE LIMITATIONS

A contingency fee is payment for services rendered by an attorney predicated on the favorable outcome of a case. Payment is based on a pre-established percentage of the total award. Some states set this percentage by statute or court rule. Under a contingency agreement, if there is no award to the plaintiff, the attorney receives no payment for services rendered.

Physicians argue that the contingency fee arrangement serves to encourage frivolous prosecution and an inordinate number of lawsuits. Attorneys reason that if they or their clients must bear the initial cost of a lawsuit, only those with obvious merit will be brought forward. The contingency fee structure also allows those unable to bear the cost of litigation to initiate a suit for damages.

Limiting contingency fees on a sliding scale basis, with the percentage decreasing as the award to the plaintiff increases, and/or providing for a lesser fee if a claim is settled without going to trial seems to have some merit.

A Connecticut law provides that in any contingency fee arrangement, the fee shall not exceed

- 33⅓ percent of the first $300,000
- 25 percent of the next $300,000
- 20 percent of the next $300,000
- 15 percent of the next $300,000
- 10 percent of any amount that exceeds $1.2 million.[19]

A Maine law provides for

- 33⅓ percent of the first $100,000 recovered
- 25 percent of the next $100,000 recovered
- 20 percent of any amount recovered more than $1 million.[20]

Some states provide for a maximum percentage of the amount recovered by the plaintiff. Florida, for example, provides that attorney fees may not exceed 15 percent when the claimant has agreed to binding arbitration. When a defendant has refused a claimant's offer to arbitrate, claimant's attorney fees may not exceed 25 percent.[21] Michigan provides a maximum allowable fee of 33⅓ percent,[22] and Oklahoma allows 50 percent of the net amount of a judgment.[23]

A third approach to limiting contingency fees occurs in those states where regulations provide for court review of attorney fees. Hawaii, for example, provides that in all tort actions in which a judgment is entered by a court of competent jurisdiction, attorney fees for both the plaintiff and the defendant shall be limited to a reasonable amount as approved by the court.[24] In New Hampshire, at the time of settlement or judgment of any action, all counsel of record are required to submit a complete review of all fees received for services for said action. All fees for actions resulting in settlement or judgment of $200,000 or more are subject to approval by the court.[25]

PRECALENDAR CONFERENCE

Precalendar conferences should be encouraged to settle disputes between the parties to a lawsuit. Trial proceedings are costly and should be avoided when a less costly course of action such as a precalendar conference is feasible.

DISCOVERY PROCEEDINGS

Discovery is a very costly aspect of pretrial proceedings. Adjudication of malpractice cases can be expedited by limiting the time allotted for such proceedings.

EXPERT WITNESSES

The qualifications of expert witnesses should be disclosed before trial. Only qualified experts should be permitted to present expert testimony in court.

STATUTES OF LIMITATIONS

Statutes of limitations should begin to run when an injury is discovered and the physician–patient relationship has ended. The time frame within which a lawsuit must be initiated must be reasonable.

FRIVOLOUS CLAIMS

Health providers, in some instances, are filing countersuits after being named in what they believe to be malicious, libelous, slanderous, frivolous, and non-meritorious medical malpractice suits. Remedies for such actions vary from one jurisdiction to the next. For a physician to prevail in a suit against a plaintiff or plaintiff's attorney, the physician must show that

• the suit was frivolous
• that the motivation of the plaintiff was not to recover for a legitimate injury
• that the physician has suffered damages as a result of the suit

The plaintiff's attorney has a legal and ethical responsibility to make sure that any suits filed are backed by sufficient and reasonable facts.

There have been arguments that defendants should be allowed to recover court costs and damage awards from both the plaintiff(s) and their attorneys for frivolous claims and counterclaims. The courts thus far have not looked favorably on countersuits for frivolous and unscrupulous negligence actions. Some state legislatures have taken limited action in this area. An Arkansas statute, for example, provides that in any civil action in which the court finds that there was a complete absence of a judicial issue of either law or fact raised by the losing party or his or her attorney, the court shall award, with certain stipulations, an attorney fee in an amount not to exceed $5,000 or 10 percent of the amount in controversy, whichever is less, to the prevailing party.[26]

In *Berlin v. Nathan,* 64 Ill. App. 3d 940, 381 N.E.2d 1367 (1978), a radiologist, a surgeon, and a hospital were sued for alleged malpractice by a patient who sought $250,000 because the defendants did not diagnose a fracture of her little finger properly. The radiologist missed the break, but he claimed that it was not evident on the x-ray taken at the hospital and that there was no error on his part. Furthermore, the finger was placed in a splint just as if it had been broken, so the treatment was correct regardless of the diagnosis. The radiologist countersued, so that the malpractice suit and countersuit were tried together. When the jury was selected, the patient withdrew the malpractice suit, but the radiologist persisted with his case. The jury awarded the radiologist $2,000 as compensation and $6,000 in punitive damages, presumably convinced that the patient and her attorneys acted improperly in bringing the lawsuit and that the lawyers were negligent in their investigation of the patient's case before filing suit.

When the case was taken to an appellate court, the decision of the lower court was reversed on the grounds that the physician had failed to plead special damages and (because the countersuit had been filed prematurely) had failed to plead a favorable result in the original suit. The appellate court went on to say that a showing of special damages is essential in a case of this type in order that the public's right to free access to the court system not be impeded by the threat of counterlitigation. The court reasoned that persons who believe they have legitimate claims should not be dissuaded from using the court system solely because of the fear of liability in the event their claim is unsuccessful.

The appellate court holding in the *Berlin* case represents the majority judicial view across the country regarding countersuits. Courts generally do not find in favor of the countersuing party because they fear that persons who otherwise would bring such suits will be discouraged simply because of a concern over the possibility of a countersuit.

Frivolous and unscrupulous malpractice actions have caused physicians to place limitations on their scope of practice. Many obstetricians/gynecologists, for example, have dropped the high-risk obstetrics portion of their practices to reduce their malpractice premiums. There is also an ever-increasing reluctance by physicians to perform heroic measures on accident victims because of the high risks of malpractice exposure. Neurosurgeons, for example, are reluctant to treat patients with spinal cord injuries and prefer to stabilize and transfer them to specialty care centers.

Given the difficulties in the present tort system, we often become victims of the failures of medicine as opposed to beneficiaries of its many successes. Physicians have lost in that they have changed, limited, or closed their practices after having spent the most energetic years of their lives training for such work. Patients have lost in that the physicians of their choice, with whom they have developed trusting relationships, are no longer available to care for them. It is certain that the malpractice problem and its effects are truly a societal problem.

The distress of physicians is illustrated in a $15 million malpractice award in West Virginia, where, "[s]even Charleston obstetricians stopped accepting new patients . . . and others say they may leave the state in reaction to a $15 million malpractice decision against another Charleston obstetrician. . . . 'The award may further worsen the increasing shortage of obstetricians in the state,' said Ben E. Lusk, associate director of the West Virginia State Medical Association. He explained that, largely because of the high cost of malpractice insurance, the number of obstetricians in West Virginia has dropped by about one-half during the last five years."[27]

JOINT AND SEVERAL LIABILITY

The doctrine of joint and several liability provides that a person causing an injury concurrently with another person can be held liable for the entire judgment awarded by a court. It is proposed by some that each defendant in a multidefendant action should be limited to payment for the percentage of fault ascribed to him or her. Some states have taken action to modify the doctrine. A 1986 Wyoming statute, for example, provides that each defendant to a lawsuit is only liable for that proportion of the total dollar amount of damages according to the percentage of the amount of fault attributed to him or her.[28] A Minnesota statute provides that a defendant whose fault is 15 percent or less may be jointly liable for a percentage of the whole award not greater than four times his or her percentage of fault.[29]

MALPRACTICE CAPS/AWARD LIMITATIONS

The impetus for malpractice caps is due, in part, because jury awards often vary substantially from one jurisdiction to the next within the same state. As a result, negligence attorneys often prefer to try personal injury cases in those jurisdictions in which a jury is likely to grant a higher award. Attorneys for the American Hospital Association, in an *amicus curiae* brief filed December 21, 1990, with the Oklahoma Supreme Court, argued that juries should receive guidance from the courts to ensure that the punitive damages they assess are rational and fair.[30]

Different states are attempting to stem the tide of rising malpractice costs by passing laws that impose restrictions on limiting the total dollar damages allowable in malpractice actions. A Kansas statute, for example, provides that in any personal injury action the total amount recoverable by each party from all defendants for noneconomic losses shall not exceed $250,000.[31] Maryland allows for up to $350,000 for noneconomic damages.[32]

Although there have been challenges to statutes limiting awards, it would appear that limitations on malpractice recoveries are not unconstitutional. The Supreme Court of Idaho in *Jones v. State Board of Medicine*, 97 Idaho 859, 555 P.2d 399 (1976), held that the state's limitation on malpractice recoveries ($150,000) need not necessarily be unconstitutional. The court held that there was no inherent right to an unlimited amount of damages and that the state had a legitimate interest in controlling excessive medical costs caused by large malpractice recoveries, and thus the statute could be held constitutional.

The Supreme Court of California in *Fein v. Permanente Medical Group,* 38 Cal. 3d 137, 695 P.2d 665, 211 Cal. Rptr. 368 (1985), found that provisions in the Medical Injury Compensation Reform Act of 1975, section 3333.2 of the Civil Code, that limit noneconomic damages for pain and suffering in medical malpractice cases to $250,000 are not unconstitutional. The legislature did not place limits on a plaintiff's right to recover for economic damages, such as medical expenses and lost earnings resulting from an injury.

A Virginia statute that places a cap of $750,000 on damages recoverable in a malpractice action was found not to violate the Seventh Amendment separation of powers principles or the Fourteenth Amendment due process or equal protection clauses. *Boyd v. Bulala,* 877 F.2d 1191 (4th Cir. 1989), *reversing* 56 U.S.L.W. 2285.

It is unlikely that setting a cap on awards for pain and suffering will do much to reduce the costs of malpractice insurance. "Placing limits on malpractice awards is no solution to the lack of coordinated planning that reflects this country's approach to health care. Capping awards would do nothing to help patients."[33] A study examining the impact of Indiana's 1975 tort reform laws on injured patients revealed that claimants are treated "quite generously," despite a seemingly strict system that caps damages at $750,000 and mandates pretrial screenings. The average claim in Indiana is about $430,000 compared with $290,000 in Michigan and $303,000 in Ohio.[34] The malpractice reforms in Indiana, which set upper limits on damage awards and a mandatory review of malpractice claims by a physician panel, did not deter people from filing malpractice claims.[35]

NO-FAULT SYSTEM

A no-fault system compensates injured parties for economic losses regardless of fault. It is intended to compensate more claimants with smaller awards. A no-fault system compensates victims of medical injury whether or not they can prove medical negligence. "Proponents of the no-fault approach cite as its advantages swifter and less expensive resolution of claims and more equitable compensation of patients."[36]

A no-fault system of compensation has its drawbacks. Opponents to the no-fault system "are largely concerned about the loss of whatever deterrence effect the present tort system exerts on health care providers."[37] The system's lower administrative costs can be an incentive to file lawsuits and, therefore, not produce the desired outcome of reducing the incidence of malpractice claims.

Estimates from a 1975 California study indicated that a no-fault system would cost California approximately $800 million annually. The traditional tort system of compensation was only costing $250 million at the time.[38]

PEER REVIEW ORGANIZATIONS

Public Law No. 92-603 of the Social Security Amendments of 1972 and Public Law No. 94-182 of the Social Security Act of 1975 created a nationwide review agency known as Professional Standard Review Organizations (PSROs) under title XI of the Social Security Act. Their purpose is to ensure that medical care provided to patients is of high quality and reflects the most appropriate and efficient use of institutional health care services.

PSRO norms, standards, and criteria were to be used as guidelines of acceptable medical care to measure the standard of care rendered to beneficiaries of Medicare, Medicaid, and maternal and child health programs. PSROs compiled and studied physician profiles of care to determine whether services rendered in a given area were consistent with the standards of learning and skill of the average reputable physician, either nationwide or in communities similar to those under examination.

In 1982 Congress repealed the PSRO program, replacing it with the Peer Review Improvement Act (title XI, section 143, part B). Under this act, Peer Review Organizations (PROs) perform functions similar to those of the PSROs. Hospitals must have agreements with PROs as a condition of receiving Medicare payments under the prospective payment system (PPS), as required by the Deficit Reduction Act of 1984 (Pub. L. No. 98-369). PROs can deny reimbursement for substandard care. They also can recommend that a practitioner be suspended from the Medicare and Medicaid programs, as well as be fined for a pattern of poor performance.

Peer review documents generally are protected from discovery so long as they are maintained in compliance with a formalized quality assurance program. The U.S. Supreme Court in *Patrick v. Burget,* 486 U.S. 94 (1988), by an 8-0 vote reversed the decision of the Ninth Circuit Court of Appeals, which had held that the peer review process was exempt from antitrust scrutiny under the so-called state action doctrine.

> Because we conclude that no state actor in Oregon actively supervises hospital peer-review decisions, we hold that the state action doctrine does not protect the peer-review activities challenged in this case from application of the federal antitrust laws. In so holding we are not unmindful of the policy argument that respondents and their amici have advanced for reaching the opposite conclusion. They contend that effective peer review is essential to the provision of quality med-

ical care and that any threat of antitrust liability will prevent physicians from participating openly and actively in peer-review proceedings. This argument, however, essentially challenges the wisdom of applying the antitrust laws to the sphere of medical care, and as such is properly directed to the legislative branch. To the extent that Congress has declined to exempt medical peer review from the reach of the antitrust laws, peer review is immune from antitrust scrutiny only if the state effectively has made this conduct its own. The State of Oregon has not done so.

Id. at 105.

Compliance with the Health Care Quality Improvement Act is the only way health care facilities and their medical staffs can hope to protect credentialing and peer review activities from antitrust liability. The Supreme Court endorsed the act in the *Patrick* opinion, holding that the Home Care Quality Improvement Act, "which was enacted well after the events at issue in this case and is not retroactive, essentially immunizes peer review action from liability if the action was taken in the reasonable belief that [it] was in the furtherance of quality health care." *Id.* at 105.

A physician who resigned after evaluation of his suspected alcohol, drug, or emotional problem filed a complaint against the hospital and the assistant administrator on the theories of slander, coercion, intentional infliction of emotional distress, and intentional interference with his employment contract as medical director of the hospital's department of perinatology. Alcohol had been detected on the physician's breath while he was performing certain medical procedures. Interviews were conducted by a chemical dependency specialist with members of the hospital's staff who had contact with the plaintiff. According to the witnesses, the plaintiff was subject to mood swings, became abrupt and tactless with patients, boasted of becoming intoxicated, and occasionally would leave work and return "wired." The plaintiff had been described as bizarre and paranoid. In conducting the interviews with the hospital staff, the witnesses believed that something was wrong with the plaintiff, but they were reluctant to speak because of their fondness for him.

Acting on the advice of the chemical dependency specialist, the vice president of medical staff affairs for the hospital formed a committee that met for the purpose of confronting the physician regarding the alleged behavior problem. The physician reluctantly agreed to an evaluation by a physician experienced in treating impaired physicians. The plaintiff was evaluated later that day at a nearby hospital. The record is silent as to the results of that evaluation, except to indicate that the plaintiff did not require hospitalization. The circuit court dismissed the complaint, and the physician appealed. On appeal, the appellate court held that the Hospital Licensing Act provided the defendants with absolute immunity from liability for the hospital peer review committee's investigation of the physician's conduct. *Cardwell v. Rockford Memorial Hospital Ass'n,* 183 Ill. App. 3d 1072, 132 Ill. Dec. 516, 539 N.E.2d 1322 (1989).

PROFESSIONAL MISCONDUCT

State boards of medical misconduct have been established in several states. New York has a panel within the state department of health to deal with issues of medical misconduct. The panel is appointed by the commissioner of health. Committees are appointed from among the members to investigate each complaint of professional misconduct received, regardless of the source.

Professional misconduct generally includes

- obtaining a license fraudulently
- practicing a profession fraudulently, beyond its authorized scope, with gross incompetence on a particular occasion, or with negligence or incompetence on more than one occasion
- practicing a profession while the ability to practice is impaired by alcohol, drugs, physical disability, or mental disability
- refusing to provide professional service to a person because of such person's race, creed, color, or national origin
- permitting, aiding, or abetting an unlicensed person to perform activities requiring a license
- being convicted of committing an act constituting a crime

The penalties that may be imposed on a licensee found guilty of professional misconduct include

- suspension of the license to practice
- revocation of the license to practice
- limitation on registration or issuance of any further licenses
- imposition of a fine

In New York, the chief executive officer, the chief of the medical staff, and the department chairpersons of every institution established pursuant to article 2803-e, as amended, of the New York State Public Health Law are required to report to the Board of Regents without malice any information that reasonably appears to show that a physician is guilty of professional misconduct. Section 2803-e of the law provides that hospitals must report within 60 days the termination or curtailment of privileges of physicians for alleged malpractice, incompetence, misconduct, or alleged mental or physical impairment; resignation or withdrawal of association or privileges from a facility to avoid disciplinary action; and the facility's receipt of information that indicates that a professional licensee has been convicted of a crime.

The physician in *Gunduy v. Commissioner of Education,* 460 N.Y.S.2d 664 (App. Div. 1983), appealed the commissioner of education's decision to revoke his license for being convicted under federal law on seven counts of an indictment. The physician was involved in the possession and distribution of large amounts of amphetamines and furnished false information in required reports and records. The court confirmed the commissioner's decision and noted that professionals have considerable responsibility not to abuse the trust that licensure places on them by violating the laws controlling dangerous drugs.

REGULATION OF INSURANCE PRACTICES

Many believe that the regulation of insurance practices is necessary to prevent windfall profits. Both the medical profession and the legal profession believe that insurance carriers have raised premiums disproportionately to their losses and that, despite their claims of substantial losses, they have reaped substantial profits.

SETTING STANDARDS OF MEDICAL CARE

Setting and following pre-established medical standards can help reduce the number of lawsuits in any given medical specialty.

> Many of the specialty societies either have drafted or are drafting practice guidelines for their medical area of expertise. For example, the American Society of Anesthesiologists developed guidelines for intraoperative monitoring in 1986. During the following year, no lawsuits were brought for hypoxic injuries; in previous years hypoxic injury suits averaged six per year.[39]

RISK MANAGEMENT

Risk management is "a systematic program designed to reduce preventable injuries and accidents and minimize the financial severity of claims."[40] It involves the identification of potential accidents with an emphasis on claims prevention. In risk management, steps are taken on a team effort basis to improve the quality of care and eliminate or minimize the number of accidents that become potential lawsuits. Liability insurers have been strong proponents of risk management; in many cases, insurers have cut premiums for physicians and health care facilities who adopt sanctioned risk management practices.

Risk management must include a heightened sensitivity to the emotional needs of patients. The input of the provider–patient relationship cannot be overemphasized when the provider–patient relationship is intense and inescapable. Individuals, not incidents, bring lawsuits.[41] Good relationships with patients are very important in preventing malpractice suits. Public relations for health care professionals is a challenge. It is not only good medical practice "but it is at the very core of the problem of medical malpractice."[42]

Increasing insurance costs and general financial constraints have pressured hospitals to assume leadership in the prevention of medically related injuries. Risk management programs should include the following components:

- an in-hospital grievance or complaint mechanism designed to process and resolve as promptly and effectively as possible grievances by patients or their representatives
- collection of data with respect to negative health care outcomes (whether or not they give rise to claims)
- medical care evaluation mechanisms, which shall include a tissue committee or medical audit committee to periodically assess the quality of medical care being provided
- education programs for hospital staff personnel engaged in patient care activities dealing with patient safety, medical injury prevention, the legal aspects of patient care, problems of communication and rapport with patients, and other relevant factors known to influence malpractice claims and suits

Elements of a Risk Management Program

Valuable components of a risk management program include

- early intervention and sympathetic care after accidental injury to a patient
- preparation of incident reports
- prompt identification and investigation of specific incidents of patient injuries and, when possible, intervention
- definition of the cause of each incident
- generation and maintenance of a risk data base from which hazardous trends and areas may be identified and corrected

- evaluation of the frequency and severity of incident exposure
- formulation and implementation of corrective actions to reduce risk and exposure to liability
- training and education of employees and clinicians to assist in reducing exposure
- continuing attention of a safety committee
- use of a suggestion box
- a public relations program (Employees should be trained in completing timely incident reports that document the facts and that are not used to cover up unfortunate incidents but to train personnel and identify problems.)

Risk Management Committee

A risk management committee with representation from a hospital's board, administration, and medical staff should be established. The committee should be chaired by a person trained in medical audits and the risk management process. The risk manager should be responsible for the development and coordination of strategic prevention programs. Information from all hospital committees (i.e., pharmacy, transfusion, infections, safety, audit, utilization, tissue, medical records, personnel, credentials, continuing education, product review, etc.) regarding potential liability hazards should be funneled into this committee for review, evaluation, and appropriate action. This committee serves to monitor all potential hazards. The hospital's attorney should be readily available for legal counsel.

Because the board has ultimate responsibility for adequate patient care, involvement in the risk management process is mandatory. The board must be just as concerned with reviewing the competence of the medical staff as it is with the financial aspects of institutional operations. Public expectations place a broad responsibility on hospitals to ensure quality care whether that care involves administrative, nursing, or physician activities.

CONCLUSION

The medical malpractice crisis continues to be a major dilemma for the health care industry. Although there have been many approaches to resolving the crisis, there appears to be no one magic formula. The solution most likely will require a variety of efforts, including tort reform.

The ever-increasing proliferation of regulations by policymakers, which have been designed to control costs and improve the quality of care, has alienated health care providers and added fuel to the practice of defensive medicine.

Physicians, who are on the front lines, have often been excluded from the decision-making processes that threaten their autonomy and financial security. A concerted effort must be made to include them in policy development and implementation. The present system of punishment for all because of the inadequacies of the few has proven to be costly and far from productive. The key to improving quality and controlling costs is cooperation, not alienation. Policymakers have failed in this arena and must return to a common-sense approach in policy development by including those who are on the front lines of medicine.

Greater efforts must be made to reduce the risks leading to injury. This is best accomplished at the bedside; after all is said and done, an ounce of prevention is better than a pound of cure.

NOTES

1. *Tinkering on Tort Reform Not Enough To Solve Problem: Experts,* A.H.A. NEWS, 27(11), Mar. 18, 1991, at 1.

2. *Experts Debate Reforming Medical-Malpractice System,* A.H.A. NEWS, 26(41), Oct. 15, 1990, at 2.

3. The Robert Wood Johnson Foundation, *The Medical Malpractice Program: Overview,* ABRIDGE, Spring 1991, at 1.

4. The Robert Wood Johnson Foundation, *Malpractice Research Points Toward Reform,* ADVANCES, III(4), Winter 1990, at 11.

5. Teresa Hudson, *Tort Reform Legislation: Can It Help Hospitals,* HOSPITALS, May 20, 1990, at 29.

6. *Malpractice on Agenda,* NATION'S HEALTH, XXI(3), Mar. 1991, at 5.

7. *White House Pro Incentives in Malpractice Reform,* A.H.A. NEWS, 27(20), May 20, 1991, at 1.

8. *Id.*

9. R. Carlson, *Bush's Malpractice Plan: Cap It!,* NEWSDAY, 51(289), June 19, 1991, at 49.

10. Congressman Robert J. Mrazek (3d District, New York), correspondence dated July 11, 1989, at 1.

11. ALA. CODE §6-5-485 (1975).

12. FLA. STAT. §§766.207–.212 (1988).

13. MICH. COMP. LAWS §§600.5040–.5065 (1975).

14. *Malpractice Plan Calls for Mandatory Arbitration,* A.H.A. NEWS, 27(23), June 10, 1991, at 2.

15. The Robert Wood Johnson Foundation, *Legal Reform,* ABRIDGE, Princeton, Spring 1991, at 3.

16. ME. REV. STAT. ANN. tit. 24, §§2851–2859 (1986).

17. *Maine: Malpractice Reform,* A.H.A. NEWS, 26(37), Sept. 17, 1990, at 7.

18. TENN. CODE ANN. §29-26-119 (1975).

19. CONN. GEN. STAT. §52-251c (1986).

20. ME. REV. STAT. ANN. tit. 24, §2961 (1986).

21. FLA. STAT. §§766.207, 766.209 (1988).

22. MCR 8.121(B).

23. OKLA. STAT. tit. 5, §7 (1953).

24. HAWAII REV. STAT. §607-15.5 (1986).

25. N.H. Rev. Stat. Ann. §508:4-e (1986).

26. Ark. Stat. Ann. §16-22-309 (1987).

27. *U.S. Wrap-up, West Virginia/$15 Million Malpractice Award,* A.H.A. News, 26(12), March 26, 1990, at 7.

28. Wyo. Stat. §1-1-109 (1986).

29. Minn. Stat. §604.02 (1988).

30. *Briefs,* A.H.A. News, 26(50), Dec. 24, 1990, at 1.

31. Kan. Stat. Ann. §60-19a02 (1988).

32. Md. Cts. & Jud. Proc. Code Ann. §11-108 (1986).

33. Carlson, *supra* note 9, at 89.

34. *Experts Debate Reforming Medical Malpractice System, supra* note 2.

35. The Robert Wood Johnson Foundation, *Malpractice Research Points Toward Tort Reform, supra* note 4.

36. The Robert Wood Johnson Foundation, *Insurance Reform,* Abridge, Spring 1991, at 5.

37. *Id.*

38. *Id.* at 4.

39. The Robert Wood Johnson Foundation, *Preventing Negligence,* Abridge, Spring 1991, at 8.

40. J. Showalter, *Quality Assurance and Risk Management: A Provider of Two Important Monuments,* J. Legal Med., 497, Sept. 1984.

41. I. Press, *The Predisposition To File Claims: The Patient Perspective,* Law, Med. & Health Care, 53, April 1984, at 53.

42. R.R. Sanderson, *Medical Practice and Malpractice,* Legal Asp. of Med. Prac., 45, June 1987.

Chapter **21**
Hospital Reorganization

OUTLINE

- Existing Structures
- Corporate Reorganization
  Taxation
  Third-Party Reimbursement
  Certificate of Need
  Financing
  Safe-Harbor Rules
- Restructuring Alternatives
  Parent Holding Company Model
  Controlled Foundation
  Independent Foundation
- General Considerations
- The Medical Staff and Restructuring
- Fund Raising
- Regulatory Authority Checklist
- Anticompetition

Traditionally, hospitals have functioned as independent, free-standing corporate entities or as units or divisions of multihospital systems. Until recently, a free-standing hospital functioned as a single corporate entity with most programs and activities carried out within such entity to meet increasing competition.

Dependence on government funding and related programs (e.g., Medicare, Medicaid, and Blue Cross) and the continuous shrinkage occurring in such revenues have forced hospitals to seek alternative sources of revenue. Greater competition from nonhospital sources also has contributed to this need to seek alternative revenue sources. It has become apparent that traditional corporate structures may no longer be appropriate to accommodate both normal hospital activities and those additional activities undertaken to provide alternative sources of revenue.

EXISTING STRUCTURES

The typical hospital is incorporated under state law as a free-standing for-profit or not-for-profit corporation. The corporation has a governing body (generally known as a board of directors, or board of trustees). Such governing body has overall responsibility for the operation and management of the hospital with a necessary delegation of appropriate responsibility to administrative employees and the medical staff.

Not-for-profit hospitals are usually exempt from federal taxation under section 501(c)(3) of the U.S. Internal Revenue Code of 1986 as amended. Such federal exemption usually entitles the organization to an automatic exemption from state taxes as well. Such tax exemption not only relieves the hospital from the payment of income taxes, sales taxes, and the like but also permits the hospital to receive contributions from donors who then may obtain charitable deductions on their personal tax returns.

CORPORATE REORGANIZATION

Given the need to obtain income and to meet competition, hospitals have begun to consider establishing business enterprises. They also may consider other nonbusiness operations, such as the establishment of additional non-exempt undertakings (e.g., hospices and long-term care facilities). Because hospitals have resources including the physical plant, administrative talent, and technical expertise in areas that are potentially profitable, the first option usually considered is direct participation by the hospital in health-related business enterprises. There are, however, regulatory and legal pressures that present substantial impediments.

Taxation

Income earned by tax-exempt organizations from nonexempt activities is subject to unrelated business income taxes under the Internal Revenue Code. These taxes are similar to those paid by profit-making organizations. In addition, tax-exempt status may be lost if a substantial portion of the corporation's activities are related to nonexempt activities and/or if the benefits of the tax-exempt status accrue to individuals who control the entity either directly or indirectly (private inurement). Care also must be taken to avoid use of facilities exempt from real estate taxation because this may lead to a partial or complete loss of such exemption.

Third-Party Reimbursement

Medicare, Medicaid, Blue Cross, and other third parties that reimburse hospitals directly for patient care require that no reimbursement be available for activities unrelated to the provision of such care. Thus, costs associated with unrelated activities must be deducted from costs submitted to third-party payers for reimbursement. The "carving out" of these costs can be detrimental to the hospital unless alternative revenues are found.

Certificate of Need

Generally, hospitals may not add additional programs or services nor may they expend monies for the acquisition of capital in excess of specified threshold limits without first obtaining approval from appropriate state regulatory agencies. The process by which this approval is granted generally is referred to as the certificate of need (CON) process.

The National Health Planning and Resources Development Act of 1974, Public Law No. 93-641, sought to encourage state review of all plans calling for the construction, expansion, or renovation of health facilities or services by conditioning receipt of certain federal funds on the establishment of an approved state CON program. Most states responded to this law by instituting state CON programs that complied with federal standards. Although the federal law is now history, CON programs remain in effect in many states. According to a survey by the American Hospital Association, CON programs remain in effect in some form in 39 states and the District of Columbia. The CON process has been eliminated in 11 states.[1] Many states continue to maintain control over Medicaid expenditures for hospital and nursing home care by controlling the number of beds through the CON process. This process can be lengthy and expensive. Further, it may not always result in approval of the request to offer the new program or service or to make the capital expenditure.

CON requirements have been criticized by health care providers because they require review of those expenditures "by or on behalf of a health care facility" but may allow groups of physicians or independent laboratories to make large expenditures for equipment or services without triggering the state review mechanism.

Disapprovals of CONs often occur because they do not comply with state health plans that are designed to limit programs and services and prevent overbedding in predefined geographic areas. Some CON applicants have attempted to seek revisions in state health plans to obtain approval of their project. *Nursing Home of Dothan v. Alabama State Health Planning & Development Agency,* 542 So.2d 935 (Ala. Civ. App. 1989), was one such case. The nursing home had filed a CON application with the State Health Planning Agency (SHPA) to construct a 110-bed nursing home. SHPA informed Dothan that the state health plan failed to indicate a need for additional beds and advised Dothan to seek an amendment to the state health plan before proceeding with the CON process. The defendant filed the proposed amendment with the State Health Coordinating Council, which approved the defendant's request for additional beds. The amendment, which required the governor's approval, was rejected by him. On appeal of the circuit court's finding for SHPA, denying Dothan's proposed amendment to the state health plan and subsequent denial of the CON application, the appeals court held that the governor properly disapproved the requested amendment.

Disapproval of a CON application also can be based on the financial feasibility of the project. A CON proposal to construct a long-term care nursing facility with 65 percent Medicaid beds was found to have been properly denied in *National Health Corp. v. South Carolina Department of Health & Environmental Control,* 380 S.E.2d 841 (S.C. App. 1989). The Department of Health and Environmental Control's decision was considered proper, reasonable, and consistent with applicable laws and regulations. The unsuccessful applicant had failed to establish its project's financial feasibility because of the unavailability of Medicaid funding. Discrepancies also existed between its budgets and its cost reports.

> The record contains clear evidence that Medicaid funds would not be available for the NHC beds. The Board also found that inconsistencies in four budgets submitted by NHC and the discrepancies between those budgets and the cost reports submitted by NHC to State Health and Human Services Finance Commission raised serious questions regarding the financial feasibility of the NHC project.

Id. at 845.

The agency's competitor had shown the financial feasibility of its project and was, therefore, granted a CON.

There can be disagreement among justices within the same court as to whether an applicant has established the criteria for need within a specific geographic area. The record in *Heritage of Yankton, Inc. v. South Dakota Department of Health,* 432 N.W.2d 68 (S.D. 1988), was found to have supported denial of a CON application for additional beds based on the argument that there was no need for additional beds in the service area. The department of health was found not to have acted arbitrarily and capriciously in denying the application. It provided valid reasons for rejecting new information submitted at a rehearing. The department of health rejected an argument that a bed shortage in the county demonstrated a need for more beds.

> The Department argues it has never considered county boundaries in determining bed need, and that the population of the facility's service area is the proper area for consideration. In view of its policy to maintain high occupancy rates in all facilities, the Department also rejected Heritage's claim that the Department's formula forces the elderly to be separated from their families and home communities.

Id. at 71.

Justice Henderson stated in a dissenting opinion

> This health care facility submitted three items of new evidence which had not been previously considered. This consisted of population projections for the area and an in-and-out migration data with information pertaining to the existence of alternative services. The Department, summarily, expressed that it refused to consider this new evidence. Instead of opening its mind and then opening the door of reconsideration with relevant evidence, the Department of Health chose to be unyielding with its grip on the single formula and methodology it employed. If this health facility's evidence had been reconsidered, an open mind would see that there was an extensive need for beds existing in the city of Yankton and Yankton county.
>
> • • • •
>
> I cannot in good conscience, join the majority opinion which prevents elderly citizens from having a bed, with medical care and treatment, administered compassionately, in a community where their children and grandchildren reside. I would elevate reality over a single methodology and accordingly dissent.
>
> "[T]herefore never send to know for whom the bell tolls; it tolls for thee." John Donne (1573–1631), *Devotions upon Emergent Occasions,* Meditation XVII. My mind drifts to Ernest Hemingway. And a clod of dirt. Chipped away at the shores of Europe by the sea. "If a clod be washed away by the sea, Europe is the less. . . ." *Supra.* All from whence Hemingway's great novel was born. And, yes, not a person is turned away from a bed of repose, in his older years, but

South Dakota is lesser—in spirit. A refrain also comes to my mind: "And crown thy good, with Brotherhood, from sea to shining sea."

Id. at 76, 77.

Financing

Even when a hospital has determined that it can and should add a program or service and when it is allowed to do so, it may lack the necessary capital financing. The hospital could join with private investors (who may, in fact, be members of the medical staff) to gain greater access to capital. Care must be taken, however, that no venture that includes physicians who refer to the hospital can be construed as providing an incentive or a reward for such referrals. Federal antifraud and abuse laws and regulations and similar state regulations impose severe penalties for such violations.

Recognizing the problems enumerated above and further recognizing the need to develop alternate sources of revenue, hospitals have determined that the establishment of an additional or a restructured organization is necessary. Besides the need to develop alternate sources of capital, some restructurings come about simply because of the evolution of a multi-institutional system. Thus, when hospitals merge or consolidate, restructuring is virtually automatic. Also, when several hospitals fall under common ownership or when additional health enterprises are undertaken, restructuring usually evolves as more institutions are added to the system. In these instances, general legal principles applicable to corporations, as well as proper management considerations, will control the development of the appropriate corporate structure.

Safe-Harbor Rules

Final regulations governing the proposed Department of Health and Human Services—Office of the Inspector General "safe-harbor rules" for hospitals and physicians issued on January 23, 1989,[2] were issued on July 29, 1991, in the *Federal Register*.[3] The rules describe 11 safe-harbor business arrangements that outline how health care providers must structure financial arrangements to be exempt from prosecution. The safe-harbor rules cover (1) investment interests; (2) space rentals; (3) equipment rentals; (4) personal services and mandatory contracts; (5) sales of practice; (6) referral services; (7) warranties; (8) discounts; (9) employees; (10) group purchasing organizations; and (11) waivers of beneficiary coinsurance and deductibles (for inpatient hospital services under PPS). "Under the final rules, providers must be under no obligation to refer business to the venture. In addition, providers' financial return must be in proportion to the amount of their investment and not tied to their business referrals."[4] Failure to comply with the regulations can result in civil or criminal sanctions, as well as exclusion from Medicare and Medicaid programs.

RESTRUCTURING ALTERNATIVES

Assuming the existence of a single not-for-profit tax-exempt hospital, any restructuring undertaken normally will involve the creation of at least one additional not-for-profit tax-exempt entity. This entity may be referred to as a parent or holding company or foundation. Its general function is to serve as the corporate vehicle to receive the ultimate benefits from the revenue-producing activities and to confer some of or all these benefits on the hospital. Under current rules regarding income taxation, income received directly (by providing goods or services) or indirectly (by means of dividends or other investment income) does not give rise to any tax obligation if the receiver of such benefit is exempt from taxation under any of several subsections of section 501(c) of the Internal Revenue Code, provided that exempt activities are the organization's main source of income and expense.

Parent Holding Company Model

Under this model, a new not-for-profit corporation is formed in conformity with the laws of the state in which the hospital is located. This corporation then can seek to obtain a tax exemption under the Internal Revenue Code. The overall purposes of the corporation are general in nature but involve a promotion of the health and welfare of the public and also may directly involve benefit to a named hospital or hospitals. In some states, when one organization exists to benefit a licensed hospital, such organization must itself be approved through a CON or similar process. The government of the parent holding company usually is derived from the governing body of the hospital. Qualifications for certain categories of exempt status under the Internal Revenue Code may require overlapping governing bodies between the hospital and the new entity. Section 509(a) of the Internal Revenue Code deals with the qualification of a tax-exempt entity as a "private and/or nonprivate" foundation. Nonprivate is the preferred status, and the qualification for such status may depend in part on the relationship between the entity seeking tax exemption and the already exempt entity (i.e., the hospital).

Because there is no stock involved in a not-for-profit corporation (the ownership of which would confer control by one corporation over another), control of the not-for-profit hospital by the not-for-profit parent holding company generally arises when the parent holding company is the sole "member" of the hospital corporation. Membership carries with it the right to elect directors and thus creates the necessary linkage for the "parent–subsidiary" relationship.

As a tax-exempt entity, the parent holding company also may own one or more for-profit subsidiaries. Although such ownership cannot represent most activities of the parent holding company, the ownership of such entities would not in and of itself disqualify the parent holding company from achieving and maintaining a tax-exempt status. It is through the subsidiaries that for-profit activities are carried on. The for-profit ventures (which may be independent corporations, joint ventures with other investors, etc.) are tax-paying entities. The net revenues (after payment of taxes) are paid out as dividends to the entity owning the stock or other ownership interest (the parent holding company), which, being tax exempt, pays no taxes on the receipt of such dividends. The parent holding company may then, as a donation, confer benefits directly on the hospital or any other entity intended to benefit from the parent holding company. Again, it is important to monitor closely the activities of this corporation so that its participation in or ownership of for-profit entities does not destroy its tax-exempt status. The Internal Revenue Service is becoming increasingly concerned about this issue and has stepped up its auditing activities dramatically.

Controlled Foundation

An alternative structure to the parent holding company model is one in which the new not-for-profit entity is controlled directly by the hospital. Instead of the parent holding company's being a member of the hospital corporation, the reverse is true. The hospital is the member of the new entity. The structure described above to carry out for-profit activities would then fall under the controlled foundation. In many states, the regulators would view such a controlled foundation as nothing more than the alter ego of the hospital and therefore impose on this entity all regulatory restrictions, reimbursement restrictions, and the like.

Independent Foundation

The establishment of a separate not-for-profit corporation and the substructure below it for carrying out for-profit activities may be accomplished independent of the hospital. Even though members of the hospital's governing body are involved in the creation of the new not-for-profit entity, the two corporations themselves may not necessarily be linked. This "brother–sister" relationship frequently is found to be desirable when the governing body of a hospital does not favor the creation of a parent organization to control the hospital but nevertheless seeks to create a viable structure within which for-profit activities may be carried on outside the hospital. A concern frequently expressed in this brother–sister relationship is that the new entity, not being controlled directly by the hospital or in the alternative not controlling the hospital, may "run away" and not necessarily ultimately benefit the hospital as was originally intended. Whether such a concern will materialize is naturally dependent on the degree to which the governing bodies of the two organizations overlap and the degree to which each organization remains responsive to the other. The use of this model also may have certain reimbursement advantages regarding earnings on donated monies. If reimbursement regulations ever change to offset charitable gifts from reimbursable activities, an "independent" organization also may prove useful. Although no such proposal is being entertained seriously at this time, this could change in the future.

GENERAL CONSIDERATIONS

None of the structures described above is intended to alter the way the hospital is managed or the way the hospital delivers care. The driving force behind the creation of alternative structures is the desire to develop alternate sources of revenue and/or to streamline management of multi-institutional systems. In many states, substantial changes in the governance of a hospital require regulatory approval. The establishment of the alternative structures previously described normally does not require such regulatory approval so long as the hospital continues to be governed by a governing body and so long as the hospital continues to carry out its functions in accordance with applicable laws, rules, and regulations.

Once restructuring has taken place, obviously many additional entities will require legal and accounting attention. These entities (normally corporations) must maintain minutes, books, and records; file tax returns; and make such other filings as are required by state laws and by federal and state income tax laws and regulations. It is important that the structures be viewed as running independently, one from the other. This includes the establishment of separate bank accounts, the holding of regular meetings among officers and directors, and the maintenance of appropriate minutes. Too often the activities and records of one entity are difficult to discern from those of another, and then the benefits of the separate organizations may be lost. The concept of "piercing the corporate veil" may come into play when each corporate entity is not maintained separate and apart from every other entity. The corporate veil will be pierced when a court determines that the activities of the corporation are indistinguishable from the activities of either another corporation or the corporation's directors, officers, or members.

The parent corporation in *Boafo v. Hospital Corp. of America,* 338 S.E.2d 477 (Ga. Ct. App. 1985), was held not liable for injuries sustained by a patient at a subsidiary hospital. Even though the parent corporation shared some officers with the subsidiary and furnished it with substantial administrative services, there was no basis for piercing the corporate veil of the parent absent some showing that the subsidiary was a sham formed for the purpose of promoting fraud, defeating justice, concealing crime, or evading contractual or tort responsibility. Although the hospital was a wholly owned subsidiary of a national management corporation, it was a fully capitalized corporate entity that was insured, owned the hospital property, autonomously managed and operated the hospital on a day-to-day basis, maintained its own payroll, and employed its own employees. There was therefore no basis for holding the parent corporation liable.

THE MEDICAL STAFF AND RESTRUCTURING

Any discussion of corporate reorganization undertaken by a hospital must necessarily involve the medical staff. Although a reorganization may have little or no direct impact on the medical staff, the perception of major change requires, at the very least, a full explanation and involvement in the process.

Many hospitals have come to realize that the medical staff presents a fertile area for developing relationships and projects leading to additional revenues. Projects such as imaging centers, laboratories, durable medical equipment businesses, and the like may be organized in conjunction with one or more members of the medical staff. Other likely candidates to participate in joint ventures include existing laboratories, home care companies, durable medical equipment companies, drug companies, surgical supply houses, and the like. As previously noted, ventures involving physicians are coming under significantly greater scrutiny and regulation. Laws and regulations have been designed to curb the practice of physicians and other health professionals of referring patients to facilities or enterprises in which they have a financial interest. *See, e.g.,* Social Security Act, 18 U.S.C. §6204 (amended 1989).

Joint ventures with physician groups are not without risk, as was shown in *Arango v. Reyka,* 507 So.2d 1211 (Fla. Dist. Ct. App. 1987), in which a hospital entered into a joint venture with an anesthesiology group and thus was vicariously liable for the malpractice of the members of that group. The hospital billed patients for anesthesiologic services, retained 12 percent of all collections, owned and furnished anesthesiology equipment and medications used by the group, scheduled patients, and referred to the group as the hospital's department of anesthesiology. As a result, there existed a common purpose to provide anesthesiologic services to hospital patients. Control was shared between the hospital and the group over the provision of anesthesia services, and there was a joint interest in the financial benefits and profits generated by the combination of their resources and services. That the physicians had an obligation to maintain control over their medical judgment did not prevent the creation of a joint venture contract.

Development of a business involving equity participation must be considered in the light of state and federal securities laws and other relevant laws, rules, and regulations to determine that there is full compliance. Shares of stock, shares in linked partnerships, and other similar equity participation interests may fall within the definition of a public offering of securities requiring filings and/or registrations under state and federal securities laws.

FUND RAISING

A not-for-profit hospital generally raises funds. Any new not-for-profit corporation formed as part of restructuring also may be able to engage in fund raising if such entity obtains a tax exemption under the Internal Revenue Code.

Also, as part of a reorganization and despite the creation of a new entity as indicated, hospitals frequently determine that it is desirable to create an additional foundation, the sole purpose of which is fund raising for the hospital. This therefore may lead to as many as three organizations with both the capability and the intent to engage in fund raising to benefit the hospital. Obvious confusion may arise in the minds of the public being asked to give to these organizations. A coordinated approach to fund raising is critical to avoid such confusion.

Any organization engaged in fund raising may have local filing requirements at the state or other governmental level. Care must be taken that the public is informed completely as to the ultimate beneficiary of such fund raising and the manner in which the monies raised will be spent. A donor to a charity may have a claim against that charity if the donor can show that he or she was misled as to the ultimate beneficiary of the gift or as to the purposes for which the gift would be used. Members of the public may be reluctant to donate when capital is to be used to fund for-profit enterprises. The overall charitable purposes of the entity must be carried out, and the activities may not be so concentrated on the operation or participation in for-profit ventures that either the tax exemption is jeopardized or it is determined (usually by the state attorney general) that the funds have been raised improperly from the public.

REGULATORY AUTHORITY CHECKLIST

In considering restructuring, the following regulatory authority checklist may be helpful:

- Not-for-profit corporations
  - not-for-profit corporation law
  - Internal Revenue Code (exemption and taxpayer identification number)
  - state and local tax laws on exemptions (including real property)
  - attorney general or similar charitable registration
  - requirements
  - bylaws, organization minutes, minutes of first governing board meeting
  - bank account
- For-profit corporations
  - business corporation law
  - taxpayer identification number
  - bylaws, organization minutes, minutes of first board meeting, issuance of stock
  - bank account
- Hospitals
  - reimbursement regulations
  - certificate of need regulations
  - governing board bylaws and relationship to additional corporations
  - fraud and abuse laws, rules, and regulations

ANTICOMPETITION

Because a hospital exerts a certain amount of influence and dominance over its patient population, the participation in for-profit enterprises to which hospital patients are referred may give rise to anticompetitive activities and antitrust claims. Patients must be permitted a free choice in connection with goods and services. For example, if the hospital (through its reorganized structure) participates in a durable medical equipment (DME) business and seeks to recommend such business to its patients on discharge, such patients must be allowed to choose an alternate supplier. Patients must be advised that they are not required to use the vendor recommended by the hospital. It also may be wise for the hospital to disclose its relationship to the DME company so that the patient knows the hospital's involvement in advance of making a choice.

Care must be taken that local vendors and merchants who have a traditional relationship with the hospital or with the patients are not so affected by the proposed for-profit activity that not only is ill will generated within the community but also a potential legal claim regarding anticompetitive activity may evolve.

Restructuring requires a multidisciplinary approach. The issues to be considered include legal, financial, accounting, tax, regulatory, and reimbursement concerns. These disciplines must provide input on an ongoing basis, not merely at inception. Changing requirements and interpretations, especially in the areas of taxation and Medicare/Medicaid fraud and abuse regulations, mandate a continuous process of review and modification so that desired goals are not subverted by legal and financial problems.

> Nonetheless, a word of caution. Today's ventures require additional planning for the possibility that some, or part of an enterprise might ultimately be found illegal. Therefore, potential buyers, and hopefully arrangements with them, as well as appropriate dissolution and unwinding provisions, now more than ever, need to be part of the fabric and documentation of any new joint venture. As well, the documentation of existing ventures must be reviewed in the light of current considerations and where necessary, needed revisions crafted.[5]

The Federal Trade Commission (FTC) determined that the Hospital Corporation of America (HCA), a proprietary hospital chain, violated section 7 of the Clayton Act, as amended, 15 U.S.C. §18 (1982), by acquiring two hospital corporations, Hospital Affiliates International, Inc., and Health Care Corporation, in the Chattanooga area for $700 million. HCA already owned one hospital in the area. Hospital Affiliates International held management contracts with two other area hospitals. This in effect gave HCA control over five of the 11 hospitals in the Chattanooga area. The management contract with one of the hospitals was canceled after the FTC began investigating HCA's acquisition of Hospital Affiliates. HCA sought judicial review by petitioning the court of appeals to set aside the decision of the FTC. The court of appeals held that there was substantial evidence to support the commission's determination that the acquisitions were likely to foster collusive practices harmful to consumers. *Hospital Corp. of America v. Federal Trade Commission,* 807 F.2d 1381 (7th Cir. 1986).

Restructuring is an undertaking that requires careful planning and legal and accounting advice and should be undertaken not because it is "fashionable" but rather because it will provide the hospital with opportunities not available under its current structure.

NOTES

1. *U.S. Wrap-Up,* A.H.A. News, 27(28), July 15, 1991, at 7.
2. 54 Fed. Reg. 3088 (1989).
3. 56 Fed. Reg. 35952 (1991).
4. *HHS's Final 'Safe-Harbor' Regulations Limit Referrals,* A.H.A. News, 27(30), July 29, 1991, at 1.
5. Weissburg, *Joint Ventures: To Be or Not To Be,* Fed'n of Am. Health Sys. Rev., May–June 1989, at 50.

Chapter 22
Restraint of Trade

OUTLINE

• Sherman Antitrust Act
• Exclusive Contracts
• Restricting Medical Staff Privileges
• Conclusion

Health care expenditures are a major segment of the nation's economy and are considered a significant cause of inflation. This has resulted in a demand from both the public and the private sectors for the development of more cost-effective approaches to the delivery of health care. This, in turn, has led to significant competition for the health care "dollar" and is changing the very nature of how health care delivery is viewed by the courts.

Probably the most dramatic example of this is in the area of antitrust. Antitrust litigation and enforcement in the health care field were nearly nonexistent before 1975; since then, it has become a major legal issue with health care providers.

The increasing number of health care professionals and alternative delivery systems and the resultant competition create the potential for illegal activities to restrain trade. The emphasis on free enterprise and a competitive marketplace have resulted in careful scrutiny by the Federal Trade Commission, the federal agency responsible for monitoring the marketplace and enforcing federal antitrust laws.

SHERMAN ANTITRUST ACT

The primary federal law that comes into play in the health care area is the Sherman Antitrust Act. The Sherman Act proscribes the following:

Section 1. Every contract, combination in the form of trust or otherwise, or conspiracy, in restraint of trade or commerce among the several states . . . is declared to be illegal.
Section 2. Every person who shall monopolize, or attempt to monopolize, or combine or conspire with any other person or persons, to
monopolize any part of the trade or commerce among the several
states . . . shall be deemed . . . guilty of a felony. . . .

15 U.S.C. §1 (1982).

Areas of concern for hospitals include mergers that reduce market competition,
price fixing, actions that bar or limit new entrants to the field, preferred provider
arrangements, and exclusive contracts.

For example, hospitals must be cognizant of the potential problems that may
exist in limiting the number of physicians that it will admit to its medical staff.
Because closed staff determinations can effectively limit competition from other
physicians, medical groups, health maintenance organizations, etc., the governing board must ensure that the decision-making process in granting hospital
privileges is based on legislative, objective criteria and is not dominated by
those who have the most to gain competitively by denying privileges.

Physicians have attempted to use state and federal antitrust laws to challenge
hospital determinations denying or limiting medical staff privileges. Generally,
these actions claim that the hospital conspired with other physicians to ensure
that the complaining physician would not get privileges so that competition
among the physicians would be reduced. To date, physicians generally have
been unsuccessful in pursuing these antitrust claims.

However, the U.S. Supreme Court in *Patrick v. Burget,* 108 S. Ct. 1658
(1988), upheld a $2 million jury verdict in favor of a surgeon, practicing in
Astoria, Oregon, who claimed that other physicians had conspired to terminate
his staff privileges at the only hospital in town and thus drove him out of practice. The defendant physicians argued that their conduct should be immune
from liability under the state action doctrine because Oregon, like many states,
has state agencies that generally regulate the procedures hospitals may use to
grant or deny staff privileges. This state action defense was rejected by the
Supreme Court in the light of the egregious facts of the case (the defendant
physicians were also participants in the state processes) and the fact that
Oregon's statutory scheme did not supervise medical staff determinations
actively. Significantly, the *Patrick* case was decided before the effective date
of the Federal Health Care Quality Improvement Act of 1986, 42 U.S.C.A.
§§11101–11152.

EXCLUSIVE CONTRACTS

Hospitals often enter into an exclusive contract with physicians and/or medical groups for the purpose of providing a specific service to the hospitals. Exclusive contracts generally occur within the hospital's ancillary services (i.e., radiology, anesthesiology, and pathology).

Physicians who seek to practice at hospitals in these ancillary areas but who are not part of the exclusive group have attempted to invoke the federal antitrust laws to challenge these exclusive contracts. These challenges generally have been unsuccessful.

In *Jefferson Parish Hospital v. Hyde,* 466 U.S. 2 (1984), the defendant hospital had a contract with a firm of anesthesiologists that required that all anesthesia services for the hospital's patients be performed by that firm. Because of this contract, the plaintiff anesthesiologist's application for admission to the hospital's medical staff was denied. Dr. Hyde commenced an action in the federal district court, claiming the exclusive contract violated section 1 of the Sherman Antitrust Act. The district court rejected the plaintiff's complaint, but the U.S. Court of Appeals for the Fifth Circuit reversed, finding the contract illegal *per se.* The Supreme Court reversed the Fifth Circuit, holding that the exclusive contract in question does not violate section 1 of the Sherman Antitrust Act. The Supreme Court's holding was based on the fact that the defendant hospital did not possess "market power" and therefore patients were free to enter a competing hospital and to use another anesthesiologist instead of the firm. Thus, the Court concluded that the evidence was insufficient to provide a basis for finding that the contract, as it actually operates in the market, had unreasonably restrained competition.

Similarly, the anesthesiologists in *Belmar v. Cipolla,* 96 N.J. 199, 475 A.2d 533 (1984), brought an action challenging a hospital's exclusive contract with a different group of anesthesiologists. The Supreme Court of New Jersey held that under state law the hospital's exclusive contract was reasonable and did not violate public policy.

RESTRICTING MEDICAL STAFF PRIVILEGES

Moratorium and closed medical staff, as used in the health care field, describe a hospital's policy of prohibiting further appointments to its medical staff. A *moratorium* is generally for a specified period of time. It is lifted at such time as the purpose for which it was instituted no longer exists. A *closed staff* is of a more permanent nature and relates to the mission of the institution, such as a commitment to teaching and research. Such institutions are very selective in their medical staff appointments. Physicians who are appointed generally have high academic interests and abilities as well as national recognition for expertise in their specialties.

Hospital boards have adopted a moratorium policy in certain instances because of a high inpatient census and the difficulties that would be encountered in accommodating new physicians. If left unchecked, the closing of hospital medical staffs eventually could have the effect of discouraging a competitive environment in the physician marketplace.

Hospital boards that adopt a closed staff policy must do so on a rational basis and take the following into consideration before closing the medical staff to new applicants:

- effect on the quality of patient care
- effect on the hospital census
- hospital and community needs for additional physicians in certain medical and surgical specialties and subspecialties
- strain that additional staff will put on the hospital's supporting departments (e.g., radiology and laboratory services)
- effect of denying medical staff privileges to applicants who presently are located within the geographic area of the hospital and serving community residents
- effect on any contracts the hospital may have with other health care delivery systems, such as health maintenance organizations
- effect a moratorium will have on physician groups that may desire to add a partner
- effect additional staff may have on the quality of care rendered at the hospital
- whether closing the staff will confine control of the hospital's beds to the existing medical staff, allowing them to enhance their economic interests at the expense of other qualified physicians and their patients
- effect of a limited moratorium by specialty as opposed to a comprehensive one involving all specialties (Closing a staff in all departments and sections indiscriminately without a review could be considered an action in restraint of trade.)
- existence of a mechanism for periodic review of the need to continue a moratorium
- effect that medical staff resignations during the moratorium may have on the hospital's census
- existence of a mechanism for notifying potential medical staff candidates at such time that the hospital determines there is a need for an expanded medical staff

- characteristics of the medical staff (i.e., is the staff aging and in need of new membership?)
- potential for restraint of trade legal action under the antitrust laws
- effect of increasing competition from free-standing surgicenters, emergency care centers, hospice programs, nursing homes, etc., on the hospital census
- long-term effects
- effect on physicians without staff privileges whose patients are admitted to a hospital's emergency department
- formation of a committee composed of representatives from the board of managers, medical staff, administration, and legal counsel to develop an appropriate moratorium policy
- selection of a consultant who would study the demographics marketplace, physician referral patterns, literature, and hospital use; conduct a medical staff opinion poll; develop patient–physician population ratios; determine population shifts; develop a formula to determine optimal staffing levels by department and section; and provide this information to the board for use in determining the appropriateness of closing the staff in selected departments

The continuing pressure of new technology, government, third-party payers, a host of regulations (e.g., utilization reviews, length of stay reviews, appropriateness of care reviews, alternate levels of care, diagnostic related groupings, and professional review organizations), and an increasing number of physicians demand that hospitals review the fast-changing health care delivery systems and seriously consider ways they can expand effectively and compete in the marketplace. In the light of this, the imposition of a moratorium or the closing of a hospital's medical staff may prove to be counterproductive to the long-term survival of an institution.

A moratorium must be applied with consistency and nondiscrimination. In *Walsky v. Pascack Valley Hospital,* 367 A.2d 1204 (N.J. 1976), the New Jersey Supreme Court held that the moratorium discriminated against newly admitted members of the staff who were required to agree not to seek staff privileges elsewhere, whereas those admitted to the staff before the moratorium were not subject to the same restriction, and that the moratorium represented an arbitrary and capricious exercise of discretion on the part of the board of trustees and defendant hospital.

Medical staff privileges in *Desai v. St. Barnabas Medical Center,* 510 A.2d 662 (N.J. 1986), were closed to new applicants with the exception of physicians who had become affiliated with current staff members. This was considered arbitrary and discriminatory against otherwise competent physicians. The hospital argued that the exception was necessary to help cover the practices of physicians who were already on the hospital's medical staff. It was decided that such arguments involved mere supposition.

The New Jersey Supreme Court in *Berman v. Valley Hospital,* 103 N.J. 100, 510 A.2d 673 (1986), held that a policy denying medical staff privileges to physicians who practiced in the hospital's service area for more than two years was arbitrary and not enforceable. The hospital had claimed that it was over-crowded and overused and that this was attributable to physicians from surrounding areas obtaining medical staff privileges. The hospital stated that its medical/surgical bed occupancy rate in 1977 had reached 89 percent and that the number of physicians increased from 172 in 1968 to 260 in 1977. The hospital conceded that it would have empty beds if it limited admissions to its primary service area.

The governing board must ensure that any proposed action to close a hospital's medical staff is based on objective criteria. In several states, state agencies monitor the actions of a hospital's governing board with respect to the granting or denial of clinical privileges. Unless the hospital can show that its actions are based on legitimate patient care concerns or concerns related to the objectives of the hospital, physicians may be successful in using antitrust and tort law to challenge the hospital's actions.

CONCLUSION

Hospital privileges are both professionally and economically important to health professionals in the practice of their chosen professions. Hospital trustees must be selective in the granting of hospital privileges to maintain quality standards. Every effort must be made to prevent anticompetitive abuses. As competition increases between podiatrists and orthopedic surgeons, psychologists and psychiatrists, nurse midwives and obstetricians, nurse anesthetists and anesthesiologists, chiropractors and orthopedic surgeons, nurse practitioners and family practice physicians, etc., it must be understood that there is a clear difference in denying hospital privileges to an individual on a quality basis and denying such privileges to an entire group of professionals; the latter will serve only to raise a red flag and increase the chances of scrutiny by the courts. The stage has been set for tough competition for a dwindling number of patients, which in turn increases the potential for denial of staff privileges to prevent competitors from effectively entering the marketplace and practicing their respective professions.

Glossary

Abandonment: Unilateral severance by the physician of the professional relationship between him- or herself and the patient without reasonable notice at a time when the patient still needs continuing attention.

Abortion: Premature termination of pregnancy at a time when the fetus is incapable of sustaining life independent of the mother.

Activities program: Planned schedule of recreational, social, and other purposeful activity for patients/residents, designed to make their life more meaningful, to stimulate and support their desire to use their physical and mental capabilities to the fullest extent, to enable them to maintain a sense of usefulness and self-respect, but not specifically designed to correct or remedy any disability.

Administration on Aging (AoA): Administration on Aging, an agency of the U.S. Department of Health and Human Services, is devoted exclusively to the concerns and potential of older people. The AoA develops federal programs and coordinates community services. For information, write: Office of Management and Policy, 330 Independence Avenue, S.W., Washington, DC 20201, or call (202) 245-0641.

Administrative agency: Government body charged with administering or implementing particular legislation.

Admissibility (of evidence): Refers to the issue of whether a court, applying the rules of evidence, is bound to receive or permit introduction of a particular piece of proof.

Adult day care centers: Places where senior citizens receive care one to five days a week. The care generally is provided on a full- or half-day basis and can involve meals, transportation, social activities (e.g., shopping and entertainment), and different therapies (e.g., art and music).

Adult homes: Facilities that provide a home for elderly persons who are basically healthy and able to care for themselves. They provide some sense of security and are an alternative to living alone. These facilities attempt to provide a home-like atmosphere.

Advance directives: Written instructions expressing an individual's health care wishes in the event that he or she becomes incapacitated and unable to make them for him- or herself.

Affidavit: A voluntary statement of facts, or a voluntary declaration in writing of facts, that a person swears to be true before an official authorized to administer an oath.

Agency: Relationship in which one person acts for or represents another with the latter's authority, for example, insurance agent and insurance company.

Allegation: Statement that a person expects to be able to prove.

American Association of Homes for the Aging (AAHA): National organization of more than 3,700 not-for-profit nursing homes, continuing care retirement communities, senior housing facilities, and community service organizations serving more than 600,000 older Americans each year. The AAHA provides services that include representation and advocacy before Congress and federal agencies on major issues, continuing education, public relations programs, publications, enhancement of financial strength through group purchasing, and long-term care insurance programs. For information, write: Suite 500, 901 E Street, N.W., Washington, DC 20004-2837, or call (202) 783-2242.

American Association of Retired Persons (AARP): Nation's leading organization for people aged 50 years and older. It serves their needs and interests through legislative advocacy, research, informative programs, and community services provided by a network of local chapters and experienced volunteers throughout the country. The AARP offers members a wide range of special membership benefits, including the magazine *Modern Maturity* and a monthly bulletin. For information, write: 1909 K Street, N.W., Washington, DC 20049, or call (202) 872-4700.

American Bar Association, Commission on the Legal Problems of the Elderly: Program of the American Bar Association that analyzes and responds to the legal needs of older people in the United States. For information, write: Second Floor, South Lobby, 1800 M Street, N.W., Washington, DC 20036, or call (202) 331-2297.

Americans with Disabilities Act: Federal act that bars employers from discriminating against disabled persons in hiring, promotion, or other provisions of employment. For information, call: (800) 669-EEOC.

Appellant: Party who appeals the decision of a lower court to a court of higher jurisdiction.

Appellee: Party against whom an appeal to a higher court is taken.

Area Agency on Aging: Local agencies designated by the governor of each state that are concerned with all matters that relate to the needs of the elderly in the community. Many services funded by the Older Americans Act are available through the Area Agency on Aging, such as information and referral, transportation, home delivered meals, homemaker/home health aides, and other supportive services.

Assault: Intentional act that is designed to make the victim fearful and produces reasonable apprehension of harm.

Assignment: Transfer of rights, responsibilities, or property from one party to another.

Attainder: Legislative act that is directed against a specified person finding him or her guilty of some offense and imposing a penalty on him or her.

Attestation: Act of witnessing a document in writing.

Audiology: Comprehensive diagnostic auditory assessment of an individual's hearing loss, rehabilitation services, and hearing aid orientation, instruction, advisement, and consultation.

Autonomy: Right of an individual to make his or her own independent decisions.

Battery: Intentional touching of one person by another without the consent of the person being touched.

Best evidence rule: Legal doctrine requiring that primary evidence of a fact (such as an original document) be introduced or that an acceptable explanation be given before a copy can be introduced or testimony given concerning the fact.

Bona fide: In good faith; openly, honestly, or innocently; without knowledge or intent of fraud.

Borrowed servant doctrine: Refers to a situation in which an employee is temporarily under the control of someone other than his or her primary employer. The traditional example is that of a nurse employed by a hospital who is "borrowed" and under the control of the attending surgeon during a procedure in the operating room. The temporary employer of the borrowed servant can be held responsible for the negligent acts of the borrowed servant under the doctrine of *respondeat superior*.

Caregiver: One who provides care to a resident/patient.

Case citation: Means of describing where the court's opinion in a particular case can be located. It identifies the parties in the case, the text in which the case can be found, the court writing the opinion, and the year in which the case was decided. For example, the citation *"Bouvia v. Superior Court (Glenchur)*, 225 Cal. Rptr. 297 (Ct. App. 1986)" is described as follows:

- *Bouvia v. Superior Court (Glenchur)*—Identifies the basic parties involved in the lawsuit.
- 225 Cal. Rptr. 297—Identifies the case as being reported in volume 225 of the California Reporter at page 297.
- Ct. App. 1986—Identifies the case as being in the California Court of Appeals in 1986.

Case law: Aggregate of reported cases on a particular legal subject as formed by the decisions of those cases.

Certiorari: Writ that commands a lower court to certify proceedings for review by a higher court. This is the common method of obtaining review by the U.S. Supreme Court.

Charitable immunity: Legal doctrine that developed out of the English court system and held charitable institutions blameless for their negligent acts.

Civil law: Body of law that describes the private rights and responsibilities of individuals. It is that part of law that does not deal with crimes. It involves actions filed by one individual against another (e.g., actions in tort and contract).

Clinical privileges: On qualification, the diagnostic and therapeutic procedures an institution allows a physician to perform on a specified patient population. Qualification includes a review of a physician's credentials, such as medical school diploma, state licensure, and residency training.

Closed shop contract: Labor–management agreement that provides that only members of a particular union may be hired.

Common law: Body of principles that has evolved and continues to evolve and expand from court decisions. Many of the legal principles and rules applied by courts in the United States had their origins in English common law.

Complaint: In a negligence action, the first pleading that is filed by the plaintiff's attorney. It is the first statement of a case by the plaintiff against the defendant and states a cause of action, notifying the defendant as to the basis for the suit.

Concurring opinion: *See* Opinion of the court.

Confidentiality: *See* Privileged communication.

Congressional Record: Document in which the proceedings of Congress are published. It is the first record of debate officially reported, printed, and published directly by the federal government. Publication of the record began March 4, 1873.

Consent: Simply stated, a voluntary act by which one person agrees to allow someone else to do something.

Coroner's jury: Special jury called by the coroner to determine whether evidence concerning the cause of death indicates that death was brought about by criminal means.

Counterclaim: Defendant's claim in opposition to a claim of the plaintiff.

Crime: Act against society in violation of the law. Crimes are prosecuted by and in the name of the state.

Criminal law: Division of the law dealing with crime and punishment. It involves a legal action filed by a state or by the United States against a particular individual or individuals.

Criminal negligence: Reckless disregard for the safety of others. It is the willful indifference to an injury that could follow an act.

Day care: Service in which a person receives care during the day only and does not remain overnight in the facility.

Decedent: Deceased person.

Decubitus ulcer: Lesion or cavity on the skin often caused by lying in one position for a prolonged period of time.

Defamation: Injury of a person's reputation or character caused by the false statements of another made to a third person. Defamation includes both libel and slander.

Defendant: In a criminal case, the person accused of committing a crime. In a civil suit, the party against whom the suit is brought, demanding that he or she pay the other party legal relief.

Dementia: Severe impairment of mental function and global cognitive abilities of long duration in an alert individual.

Demurrer: Formal objection by one of the parties to a lawsuit that the evidence presented by the other party is insufficient to sustain an issue or case.

Deposition: Sworn statement of fact, made out of court, that may be admitted into evidence if it is impossible for a witness to attend a trial in person.

Diagnostic related groups (DRGs): Prospective payment system for hospital care based on patient diagnosis.

Directed verdict: When a trial judge decides either that the evidence and/or law is clearly in favor of one party or that the plaintiff has failed to establish a case and that it is pointless for the trial to proceed further, the judge may direct the jury to return a verdict for the appropriate party. The conclusion of the judge must be so clear and obvious that reasonable minds could not arrive at a different conclusion.

Discharge summary: That part of a medical record that summarizes a patient's initial complaints, course of treatment, final diagnosis, and suggestions for follow-up care.

Discovery: To ascertain that which was previously unknown through a pretrial investigation; it includes testimony and documents that may be under the exclusive control of the other party. Discovery facilitates out-of-court settlements.

Dissenting opinion: *See* Opinion of the court.

Do-not-resuscitate (DNR): Directive of a physician to withhold cardiopulmonary resuscitation in the event a patient experiences cardiac or respiratory arrest.

Durable power of attorney: Legal instrument enabling an individual to act on another's behalf. In the health care setting, it includes the authority to make medical decisions for another.

Emergency: Sudden unexpected occurrence or event causing a threat to life or health. The legal responsibilities of those involved in an emergency situation are measured according to the occurrence.

Employee: One who works for another in return for pay.

Employer: Person or firm that selects employees, pays their salaries or wages, retains the power to dismiss them, and can control their conduct during working hours.

Euthanasia: Act conducted for the purpose of causing the merciful death of a person who is suffering from an incurable condition.

Evidence: Proof of a fact, which is legally presented in a manner prescribed by law, at trial.

Expert witness: Person who has special training, experience, skill, and knowledge in a relevant area and who is allowed to offer an opinion as testimony in court.

Facility: In the context of this text, a "facility," in most instances, is referring to health care facilities in general, unless within the context of its usage it is referring to a particular institution, such as acute care hospitals or nursing facilities/homes.

Federal Council on Aging (FCoA): Created in 1973, the functional successor to the earlier and smaller Advisory Council on Older Americans (authorized by the Older Americans Act of 1965). The functions of the FCoA include the continuing review and evaluation of federal policies and programs, serving as a spokesperson, and providing public forums for discussing and publicizing the needs of older Americans. For information, write: 330 Independence Avenue, S.W., Washington, DC 20201, or call (202) 619-2451.

Federal question: Legal question involving the U.S. Constitution or a statute enacted by Congress.

Felony: Serious crime usually punishable by imprisonment for a period of longer than one year or by death.

Gerontological Society of America: Professional organization that promotes the scientific study of aging in the biologic and social sciences. For information, write: Suite 350, 1275 K St., N.W., Washington, DC 20005-4006, or call (202) 842-1275.

Gerontology: Study of the process of aging.

Good Samaritan laws: Laws designed to protect those who stop to render aid in an emergency. These laws generally provide immunity for specified persons from any civil suit arising out of care rendered at the scene of an emergency, provided that the one rendering assistance has not done so in a grossly negligent manner.

Governing board: Official body of an institution vested with the legal responsibility for its operation.

Government facility: Facility operated under federal, state, or local government auspices.

Grand jury: Jury called to determine whether there is sufficient evidence that a crime has been committed to justify bringing a case to trial. It is not the jury before which the case is tried to determine guilt or innocence.

Grand larceny: Theft of property valued at more than a specified amount (usually $50), thus constituting a felony instead of a misdemeanor.

Guardian: Person appointed by a court to protect the interests of and make decisions for a person who is incapable of making his or her own decisions.

Habeas corpus: Writ to challenge the legality of imprisonment or detention.

Harvard Medical Malpractice Study: Study commissioned by New York State to determine the rate of medical injury in New York hospitals. The study, which cost $3.1 million and ran 1,200 pages, was funded primarily by New York State with a grant from the Robert Wood Johnson Foundation. The study involved four years of research and included the review of more than 30,000 medical records. The study revealed that 3.7 percent of patients entering New York Hospitals in 1984 were injured by the care provided, "but only a tenth of those who were treated negligently filed malpractice suits."[1]

Health: According to the World Health Organization, "[a] state of complete physical, mental, and social well-being and not merely the absence of disease or infirmity."

Health Care Financing Administration (HCFA): Federal agency that coordinates the federal government's participation in the Medicare and Medicaid programs. For information, write: 200 Independence Avenue, S.W., Washington, DC, or call (202) 245-6145.

Health care proxy: Document that delegates the authority to make one's own health care decisions to another adult, known as the health care agent, when one has become incapacitated or is unable to make his or her own decisions.

Hearsay rule: Rule of evidence that restricts the admissibility of evidence that is not the personal knowledge of the witness. Hearsay evidence is admissible only under strict rules.

Holographic will: Will handwritten by the testator.

Home health agency: Any public agency or private organization, or a subdivision of such an agency or organization, whether operated for profit or not, that provides home health services. Home health care involves an array of services provided to patients in their homes or foster homes because of acute illness, exacerbation of chronic illness, and disability. Such services are therapeutic and/or preventive.

Home health aide: Person who has completed a basic training program in personal care services to provide selected aspects of resident/patient care under nursing supervision, and other professional supervision when required by the type of care provided, to patients receiving home health agency services.

Hospice: Long-term care facility for terminally ill persons. It is provided in a setting more economical than that provided in a hospital or nursing home. Hospice care generally is sought after a decision has been made to discontinue aggressive efforts to prolong life. A hospice program includes such characteristics as support services by trained individuals, family involvement, and control of pain and discomfort.

Hydration: Intravenous addition of fluids to the circulatory system.

Impeachment: Legislative proceeding designed to remove an executive or judicial officer from office because of misconduct.

Incompetent: Individual determined by a court to be incapable of making rational decisions on his or her own behalf.

Independent contractor: One who agrees to undertake work without being under the direct control or direction of the employer.

Indictment: Formal written accusation, found and presented by a grand jury, charging a person therein named with criminal conduct.

Informed consent: Legal concept that provides that a patient has a right to know the potential risks and benefits of a proposed procedure before subjecting the patient to a course of treatment.

Injunction: Court order either requiring one to do a certain act or prohibiting one from doing a certain act.

***In loco parentis*:** Legal doctrine that permits the courts to assign a person to stand in the place of parents and possess their legal rights, duties, and responsibilities toward a child.

Interrogatories: List of questions sent from one party in a lawsuit to the other party to be answered under oath.

Judge: Officer who guides court proceedings to ensure impartiality and enforces the rules of evidence. The trial judge determines the applicable law and states it to the jury. The appellate judge hears appeals and renders decisions concerning the correctness of the actions of the trial judge, the law of the case, and the sufficiency of the evidence.

Judicial notice: Act by which a court, in conducting a trial or forming a decision, will of its own motion and without evidence recognize the existence and truth of certain facts bearing on the controversy at bar (e.g., serious falls require x-rays).

Jurisdiction: Right of a court to administer justice by hearing and deciding controversies.

Jurisprudence: Philosophy or science of law on which a particular legal system is built.

Jury: Certain number of persons selected and sworn to hear the evidence and determine the facts in a case.

Larceny: Taking of another person's property without consent with the intent to permanently deprive the owner of its use and ownership.

Legal wrong: Invasion of a protected right.

Liability: As it relates to damages, an obligation one has incurred or might incur through a negligent act.

Liability insurance: Contract to have someone else pay for any liability or loss thereby in return for the payment of premiums.

Libel: False or malicious writing that is intended to defame or dishonor another person and is published so that someone other than the one defamed will observe it.

License: Permit from the state allowing certain acts to be performed, usually for a specific period of time.

Life care community: Self-sufficient residential community that provides residential, social, medical, and nursing services to its members.

Litigation: Trial in court to determine legal issues, rights, and duties between the parties to the litigation.

Living will: Document in which an individual expresses in advance his or her wishes regarding the application of life-sustaining treatment in the event he or she is incapable of doing so at some future time.

Long-term care: Provision of different services (e.g., personal, medical, and social) to individuals who are unable to care for themselves. Such services generally are required by the elderly, as a result of diminishing health, or by others who might be disabled from some illness or other disability. Long-term care facilities used for providing services and programs include nursing facilities, adult day care centers, and home health agencies.

Malfeasance: Execution of an unlawful or improper act.

Malpractice: Professional misconduct, improper discharge of professional duties, or failure to meet the standard of care of a professional that resulted in harm to another. The negligence or carelessness of a professional person, such as a nurse, pharmacist, physician, or accountant.

Mandamus: Action brought in a court of competent jurisdiction to compel a lower court or administrative agency to perform or not to perform a specific act.

Mayhem: Crime of intentionally disfiguring or dismembering another.

Medicaid: Medical assistance provided in title XIX of the Social Security Act. Medicaid is a state administered program for the medically indigent.

Medical staff: All physicians and dentists appointed by the governing authority and responsible to such authority for the adequacy and quality of the medical care rendered to the residents/patients in a facility.

Medicare: Medical assistance provided in title XVIII of the Social Security Act. Medicare is a health insurance program administered by the Social Security Administration for persons aged 65 years and older and for disabled persons who are eligible for benefits. Medicare part A benefits provide coverage for inpatient hospital care, skilled nursing facility care, home health care, and hospice care. Medicare part B benefits provide coverage for physician services, outpatient hospital services, diagnostic tests, different therapies, durable medical equipment, medical supplies, and prosthetic devices.

Misdemeanor: Unlawful act of a less serious nature than a felony, usually punishable by a jail sentence for a term of less than one year and/or a fine.

Misfeasance: Improper performance of an act.

National Council on the Aging (NCA): Nonprofit membership organization for professionals and volunteers that serves as a national resource for information, technical assistance, training, and research relating to the field of aging.

For information, write: West Wing 100, 600 Maryland Avenue, S.W., Washington, DC 20024, or call (202) 479-1200.

National Foundation for Long-Term Health Care: Private nonprofit organization that works on behalf of professionals who provide long-term care to older persons and the chronically ill. For information, write: Suite 402, 1200 15th Street, N.W., Washington, DC 20005, or call (202) 659-3148.

National Geriatrics Society: Nonprofit educational scientific organization that works to advance the quality of care provided to older, chronically ill, disabled, or convalescent patients. For information, write: 212 West Wisconsin Avenue, Milwaukee, WI 53203.

National Institute on Aging (NIA): NIA is the principal federal agency for conducting and supporting biomedical, social, and behavioral research related to the aging process as well as the diseases and special problems of older persons. For information, write: Public Information Office, Federal Building, Room 6C12, 9000 Rockville Pike, Bethesda, MD 20892, or call (301) 496-1752.

Negligence: Omission or commission of an act that a reasonably prudent person would or would not do under given circumstances. It is a form of heedlessness or carelessness that constitutes a departure from the standard of care generally imposed on members of society.

Next of kin: Those persons who by the law of descent would be adjudged the closest blood relatives of the decedent.

Non compos mentis: "Not of sound mind"; suffering from some form of mental defect.

Nonfeasance: Failure to act, when there is a duty to act, as a reasonably prudent person would in similar circumstances.

Notary public: Public official who administers oaths and certifies the validity of documents.

Nuncupative will: Oral statement intended as a last will made in anticipation of death.

Nursing assistant/aide: Unlicensed worker employed and trained to assist licensed and/or registered nursing personnel in the personal care needs of patients/residents.

Nursing facility: *See* Nursing home.

Nursing home: Facility with three or more beds that provides nursing care or personal care to adults, such as help with bathing, correspondence, walking, eating, using the toilet, or dressing, and/or supervision over such activities as money management, ambulation, and shopping. A nursing facility may be either free-standing or a distinct unit of a larger facility.

Occupational therapy: Art and science of evaluation and treatment of physical and psychological dysfunctions through the use of such activities as creative, manual, industrial, educational, recreational, social, and self-help activities to enable the patient/resident to achieve his or her optimal level of self-care and productivity.

Older Americans Act: Act that established a National Network on Aging, which is comprised of the U.S. Administration on Aging, state and area Agencies on Aging, tribal organizations, and service providers. Through this network, older persons in each community have access to supportive and nutrition services. The type of services available in each community varies based on the needs of the people and resources of a given area.

Ombudsman: Person who is designated to speak and act on behalf of a patient/resident, especially in regard to his or her daily needs.

Opinion of the court: In an appellate court decision, the reasons for the decision. One judge writes the opinion for the majority of the court. Judges who agree with the result, but for different reasons, may write concurring opinions explaining their reasons. Judges who disagree with the majority may write dissenting opinions.

Ordinance: Law passed by a municipal legislative body.

Palliative care: Care that is intended to keep a person comfortable but not intended to prolong life.

Peer review organization (PRO): Organization that has a contract with the Health Care Financing Administration (HCFA) to review, under part B of title XI of the Social Security Act, the health care services or items furnished or proposed to be furnished to Medicare beneficiaries.

Perjury: Willful act of giving false testimony under oath.

Petit (petty) larceny: Theft of property valued below a set monetary amount. This offense usually is classified as a misdemeanor.

Physical therapy: Art and science of preventing and treating neuromuscular or musculoskeletal disabilities through evaluation of an individual's disability and rehabilitation potential; use of such physical agents as heat, cold, electricity, water, light; and neuromuscular procedures that, through their physiologic effect, improve or maintain the patient's optimum functional level.

Plaintiff: Party who brings a civil suit seeking damages or other legal relief.

Police power: Power of the state to protect the health, safety, morals, and general welfare of the people.

Preadmission screening: Assessment of the appropriateness of nursing facility placement before admission.

Privileged communication: Statement made to an attorney, physician, spouse, or anyone else in a position of trust. Because of the confidential nature of such information, the law protects it from being revealed even in court. The term is applied in two distinct situations. First, the communications between certain persons, such as physician and patient, cannot be divulged without consent of the patient. Second, in some situations the law provides an exemption from liability for disclosing information where there is a higher duty to speak, such as statutory reporting requirements.

Probate: Judicial proceeding that determines the existence and validity of a will.

Probate court: Court with jurisdiction over wills. Its powers range from deciding the validity of a will to distributing property.

Prognosis: Informed judgment regarding the likely course and probable outcome of a disease.

Proprietary nursing facility: Nursing facility operated under private commercial ownership.

Proximate: In immediate relation with something else. In negligence cases, the careless act must be the proximate cause of injury.

Real evidence: Evidence furnished by tangible things, such as weapons, bullets, and equipment.

Rebuttal: Giving of evidence to contradict the effect of evidence introduced by the opposing party.

Registered nurse: One who is qualified for the title of R.N. by meeting the educational and licensure requirements of the state in which he or she is licensed.

Regulatory agency: Arm of the government that enforces legislation regulating an act or activity in a particular area—for example, the federal Food and Drug Administration.

Rehabilitation therapy services: Therapy services that include, but are not limited to, occupational therapy, physical therapy, speech pathology, or audiology.

Release: Statement signed by one person relinquishing a right or claim against another.

Remand: Referral of a case by an appeals court back to the original court, out of which it came, for the purpose of having some action taken there.

Res gestae: "The thing done"; all the surrounding events that become part of an incident. If statements are made as part of the incident, they are admissible in court as *res gestae* despite the hearsay rule.

Res ipsa loquitur: "The thing speaks for itself"; a doctrine of law applicable to cases where the defendant had exclusive control of the thing that caused the harm and where the harm ordinarily could not have occurred without negligent conduct.

Res judicata: "The thing is decided"—that which has been acted on or decided by the courts.

Resident, nursing home: Individual who has been admitted to and resides in a nursing home and who is entitled to receive care, treatment, and services.

Resource utilization group: Prospective payment system of reimbursement for nursing facility care under Medicaid based on the characteristics and care needs of a facility's residents.

Respite care: Program of informal support for family members who are in need of relief from their own caregiving responsibilities. It can, for example, be given in the caregiver's home or a nursing facility.

Respondeat superior: "Let the master answer"; an aphorism meaning that the employer is responsible for the legal consequences of the acts of the servant or employee who is acting within the scope of his or her employment.

Restraint: Restraints can be either "physical" or "chemical." A physical restraint involves a device (e.g., safety belts, safety bars, geriatric chairs, and bed rails) that restricts or limits voluntary movement and that cannot be removed by the resident.

Slander: False oral statement, made in the presence of a third person, that injures the character or reputation of another.

Social Security Administration (SSA): SSA is the federal agency responsible for the Social Security retirement, survivors and disability insurance and supplemental security income programs. For information, write: Office of Public Inquiries, 402 Security Boulevard, Baltimore, MD 21235, or call (301) 594-1234.

Speech pathology: Nonmedical evaluation, diagnosis, and treatment of human language, voice, and speech disorders and their etiologies.

Standard of care: Description of the conduct that is expected of an individual in a given situation. It is a measure against which a defendant's conduct is compared.

Stare decisis: "Let the decision stand"; the legal doctrine that prescribes adherence to those precedents set forth in cases that have been decided.

Statute of limitations: Legal limit on the time allowed for filing suit in civil matters, usually measured from the time of the wrong or from the time when a reasonable person would have discovered the wrong.

Statutory law: Law that is prescribed by legislative enactments.

Stipulation: Agreement, usually in writing, by attorneys on opposite sides of an issue as to any matter pertaining to the proceedings. A stipulation is not binding unless agreed on by the parties involved in the issue.

Subpoena ad testificandum: Court order requiring one to appear in court to give testimony.

Subpoena duces tecum: Court order that commands a person to come to court and to produce whatever documents are named in the order.

Subrogation: Substitution of one person for another in reference to a lawful claim or right.

Suit: Court proceeding in which one person seeks damages or other legal remedies from another.

Summary judgment: Generally, an immediate decision by a judge, without jury deliberation.

Summons: Court order directed to the sheriff or other appropriate official to notify the defendant in a civil suit that a suit has been filed and when and where to appear.

Surrogate decision maker: Individual who has been designated to make decisions on behalf of an individual determined incapable of making his or her own decisions.

Tertiary care: Highly specialized care generally provided in a major medical center, often a teaching hospital.

Testimony: Oral statement of a witness given under oath at a trial.

Tort: Civil wrong committed by one individual against another. Torts may be classified as either intentional or unintentional. If a tort is classified as a criminal wrong (e.g., assault, battery, and false imprisonment), the wrongdoer could be held liable in a criminal action as well as a civil action.

Tort-feasor: Person who commits a tort.

Trial court: Court in which evidence is presented to a judge or jury for decision.

Union shop contract: Labor–management agreement making continued employment contingent on joining the union.

Venue: Geographic district in which an action is or may be brought.

Verdict: Formal declaration of a jury's findings of fact, signed by the jury foreman and presented to the court.

Voluntary nonprofit nursing facility: Nursing facility operated under voluntary or nonprofit auspices, including church-related facilities.

Waiver: Intentional giving up of a right, such as allowing another person to testify to information that ordinarily would be protected as a privileged communication.

Will: Legal declaration of the intentions a person wishes to have carried out after death concerning property, children, or estate. A will designates a person or persons to serve as the executor(s) responsible for carrying out the instructions of the will.

Witness: Person who is called to give testimony in a court of law.

Writ: Written order that is issued to a person or persons, requiring the performance of some specified act or giving authority to have it done.

Wrongful birth: Applies to the cause of action of the parents who claim that the negligent advice or treatment deprived them of the choice of aborting conception or of terminating the pregnancy.

Wrongful life: Refers to a cause of action brought by or on behalf of a defective child who claims that but for the defendant (e.g., a laboratory's negligent testing procedures or a physician's negligent advice or treatment of its parents), the child would not have been born.

NOTES

1. D. Zinman, *Study Finds Hospitals 'Harm' Some*, NEWSDAY, 50(177), Mar. 1, 1990 at 17.

Index of Cases

Index

About the Author

George D. Pozgar has had more than 20 years of experience as an administrator, author, teacher, and consultant in virtually every aspect of health care. He received his MBA in Health Care Administration from The George Washington University, Washington, D.C. Mr. Pozgar served as an administrative resident at the Baptist Memorial Hospital in Jacksonville, Florida; as an assistant administrator at Huntington Hospital, Huntington, New York; as administrator at St. John's Episcopal Hospital, Smithtown, New York; and as Vice President for Corporate Affairs for Episcopal Health Services, Inc., a multifacility health care system in Hempstead, New York.

Mr. Pozgar is presently President of his own consulting firm, GP Management Consulting, Int'l. He is also an instructor in a health care administration graduate program at the New School for Social Research in New York City, and an instructor in an undergraduate program in health care administration at St. Joseph's College in Brooklyn, New York. Mr. Pozgar has served as an on-site faculty member of The George Washington University, Washington, D.C.; as an instructor at St. Francis College of Brooklyn; and also as an instructor at various conferences on the legal aspects of health care administration, including conferences held at Molloy College and the C.W. Post College of Long Island University.

Mr. Pozgar is an active member of the American College of Health Care Executives, the American College of Health Care Administrators, and the American Public Health Association. He has served on the editorial staff of *The Health Care Supervisor*, as a member of the Nassau/Suffolk Hospital Council, as Vice President of the Nassau/Suffolk Health Care Associates, and as President of the Huntington Township Emergency Medical Services Committee. Mr. Pozgar is author of various articles and the recently published text, *Long-Term Care and the Law: A Legal Guide for Health Care Professionals*, an Aspen publication.